Case Histories in
International Politics

Case Histories in
International Politics

THIRD EDITION

Kendall W. Stiles

Loyola University of Chicago

PEARSON
Longman

New York • San Francisco • Boston
London • Toronto • Sydney • Tokyo • Singapore • Madrid
Mexico City • Munich • Paris • Cape Town • Hong Kong • Montreal

Vice President and Publisher: Priscilla McGeehon
Executive Editor: Eric Stano
Senior Marketing Manager: Megan Galvin-Fak
Supplements Editor: Kristi Olson
Media Editor: Patrick McCarthy
Production Manager: Joseph Vella
Project Coordination, Text Design, and Electronic Page Makeup: Thompson Steele Inc.
Cover Designer/Manager: John Callahan
Cover Photo: Courtesy of Getty Images
Manufacturing Buyer: Roy L. Pickering, Jr.
Printer and Binder: R. R. Donnelley & Sons
Cover Printer: Phoenix Color Corporation

For permission to use copyrighted material, grateful acknowledgment is made
to the copyright holders on pp. 433, which are hereby made part of this copyright page.

Library of Congress Cataloging-in-Publication Data

Stiles, Kendall W.
    Case histories in international politics / Kendall W. Stiles.—3rd ed.
        p. cm.
    Includes bibliographical references and index.
    ISBN 0-321-15970-5
        1. World politics—1945-—Case studies. 2. World politics—20th century—Case studies.
    I. Title.

D843 .S82 2003
327'.09'04—dc21   2003048263

Visit us at www.ablongman.com

ISBN 0-321-15970-5

1 2 3 4 5 6 7 8 9 10—DOH—06 05 04 03

Contents

Figures,
Maps, and Tables

Preface

It is easy to be overwhelmed by the pace of events and their importance. Each day seems to bring new announcements of impending war or heightened alert. It might even be tempting to simply refuse to deal with it all and retreat to a cocoon of ignorance. But the stakes are too high to settle for this. We owe it to ourselves to make some effort to understand what is happening, even if we may not always be able to predict it.

So—where do we start? To begin, we must reach some agreement on what it is we're talking about. Simply observing world affairs is not enough, because there is so much noise and commotion. After all, how do we know whether a group of men in uniform carrying guns is an army, a militia, a terrorist group, or a gun club? And if that group of uniformed individuals begins walking toward another town, killing people in their path, are we witnessing a revolution, a war, a terrorist incident, or a gang war? Most events in world affairs have little meaning in and of themselves. It is only after observers agree among themselves on the concepts they all will use to describe and categorize events that we can begin communicating with each other. Thus concepts and their definitions are fundamental to the study of world affairs.

Once we have begun to label world events, we can look at different events and make comparisons. If we have decided that a group of armed men attacking a village is an act of war because of certain mitigating circumstances, then we can look for other instances of armed attack to see how they differ and how they are the same. For example, are more troops involved in one incident? Are they better armed? Are they moving more swiftly and with greater efficiency? Is the number of victims higher? Are the troops more confident and cheerful? Can an observer determine what the goals of the armies are?

Once we can compare different events, we can begin the process of looking for patterns. In some cases, this can be done by simply taking a few examples and studying them in depth. One can also take a large number of cases and draft numerical or statistical summaries. By laying out these numbers or these cases, it might be possible to identify coincidences or sequences of events and/or conditions. For example, we may find that large numbers of troops go on the march immediately after a prolonged drought or famine. We may note that where the people vote to choose their leaders, few troops ever march. We may find that wars often occur in the same place for what appears to be the same purpose over time. And so forth.

Identifying coincidences and sequences of events is the beginning of many explanations. Theories are simply systematic forms of explanation linking various events and conditions in a logical way. We may begin with a general set of rules and principles ("humanity can learn from its mistakes," "the powerful force themselves on the weak," "freedom breeds peace" . . .) and from them derive our theories (wars will tend to diminish in number over time, powerful states tend to create empires, democracies will usually not fight each other . . .). Or we may simply observe patterns and begin to generalize—which is to say, develop general rules and theories that may apply to new situations. For example, some have noted that the city-states of the Greek peninsula in the days of Athens and Sparta bear interesting similarities to the Cold War era.[1,2]

At some point, these broad generalizations will need to be put to the test, either with detailed case-study work or with broader comparative studies. This can be done by deriving "testable hypotheses" from the theories and then returning to the facts and events to see whether our predictions are correct. For example, a liberal thinker may believe firmly that democracies are inherently more peaceful for a variety of reasons (some ideological). From this, she may derive a simple hypothesis that states with democratic governments (defined, let's say, as a state where the people vote for a national legislature in free and fair elections) will not go to war with each other. The next step would be to identify all the wars in history, or at least back to the Age of Enlightenment era, when modern democracy emerged, and then classify all the various types of governments of the warring parties. This done, it would be a rather simple thing to count how many democracies were at war with each other compared to nondemocracies. It may be useful to conduct a statistical test to make sure that a low number can't be explained by the fact that there are simply few democracies (if there are only two democracies and fifty nondemocracies, the fact that they didn't go to war may be a fluke). Once all this is done, the findings will either support or disconfirm the hypothesis, which in turn may cause us to have different opinions of the underlying theory.[3]

Note that, even at the most sophisticated level, the matter still comes back to defining concepts and studying history. This is why this text is structured as it is. I believe it is essential for students to have a basic understanding of some of the most fundamental concepts in the international relations literature. The chapters of this text present thumbnail definitions of

[1] Dingman, Robert V. "Theories of, and Approaches to, Alliance Politics" in Paul Gordon Lauren, ed. *Diplomacy: New Approaches in History, Theory, and Policy* (New York: Free Press, 1979), 245–266.

[2] Evangelista, Matthew. "Issue-Area and Foreign Policy Revisited." *International Organization* 43 #1 (Winter 1989): 147.

[3] Maoz, Zeev and Bruce Russett. "Normative and Structural Causes of Democratic Peace, 1946–1986." *American Political Science Review* 87 #3 (September 1993): 624–639.

two dozen essential concepts in the field. One could easily add another dozen or so, and there may be some who would take out a few. But the list is a good start. You will find short definitions of "state," the "nation," "power," the "balance of power," "public opinion," "international law," and so forth. Taken alone, these definitions will likely help you to understand more clearly some of the material you will find in other readings and your instructor's lectures. They are the building blocks of the literature.

But since the concepts are derived from observing history, and since history becomes understandable through the concepts, I felt the best way to understand the ideas is to present an illustration in the form of a historical case study. The case studies are mostly stories of important events or problems in the twentieth and twenty-first centuries. Most of the events I select took place after the end of the Second World War (1945), and several are quite recent. But in order to make sure the cases are significant and are likely to be meaningful for years to come, I have focused on material that has its roots in decades-old and even centuries-old antecedents. Thus, the case study on the situation in the former Yugoslavia begins with a description of the region in the Middle Ages. The chapter on sweatshops describes the dawn of the Industrial Revolution. The discussion of the "Great Debate" over the general direction of U.S. foreign policy harks back to previous "great debates" in the 1920s and 1930s.

By the time you finish reading this, you will not only have been exposed to some of the key concepts in the discipline, which should help you understand both history and current events, but you will also have studied the two World Wars, the Cold War, the post–Cold War era, the process of colonialism and decolonization, economic expansion and environmental decay, and human rights. While I urge you to take a conventional course on the history of world civilization and the twentieth century, this text provides a useful overview.

What will you do with this material? To be frank, that is up to you. The material you read, however, is more than a small encyclopedia. It offers you the ingredients to create your own theories and begin to test hypotheses. You will see enough different events and developments that you will be able to begin developing your own generalizations. For example, by seriously considering the cases found in the first section of the text (Great Power Relations), you can begin to answer the following questions: What priorities drive the decisions of great powers to accumulate weapons and use them in war? Does democracy make powerful states less inclined to start wars? What prompts countries to enter into alliances and other agreements not to fight? These are all weighty issues on which the future of the planet may hinge. By comparing the behavior of the Soviet Union under Leonid Brezhnev to Soviet policies under Mikhail Gorbachev, one can begin to ask about the place of one individual in history. It might be interesting to compare Gorbachev to Richard Nixon and Henry Kissinger or even Bill Clinton. Did these leaders act in particular ways that resembled each other, and, if so, was it because of or in spite of their governments and societal structures?

By looking across the cases and combining concepts, you are in a position to get the most from this text. You will be engaged in the most fundamental activity of the profession. You may even develop new theories and generalizations that will allow you to better understand some new event that no one has yet foreseen.

Another purpose of this text is to show that there is never just one view of history. It has been said that history keeps repeating itself because no one was listening the first time. I tend to think history repeats itself precisely because people were listening very carefully. The problem is that each listener hears a different tune.

Consider the end of the First World War, for example. After 16 million casualties, a continent in ruin, and major powers devastated, citizens and leaders of the warring states reached many conclusions: Woodrow Wilson and other idealists reached the conclusion that this type of war should never be allowed to happen again. They concluded that it had been no one's fault, except perhaps the balance of power system itself. And so, they set out to eliminate the balance of power and replace it with collective security (see The United Nations and the Use of Force). They wrote treaties, created institutions, and promised to eliminate weapons.

Others came to the end of the war and concluded that it was all Germany's fault. Only by forcing the Kaiser to abdicate, demilitarizing the country, declaring whole regions off-limits to future troop deployments, and forcing it to pay for the cost of the war could justice be served and things made right. This attitude animated much of the drafting of the Versailles Treaty in 1919. Still others concluded that the lesson of World War I was that Germany should never be unprepared for war, and that it could trust no other European power. Add to that a feeling that secret cabals and foreign races were conspiring to destroy Germany, and we find the seeds of fascism.

Three very different conclusions—all based on precisely the same experience. Such a diversity of interpretations is not unusual in world affairs—rather it is typical. As we see in chapter eight, Americans disagree on what should be the nation's overriding approach to international relations, mostly because they draw different interpretations of history based on different values. The same thing will likely happen in your reading of this text. I have tried to give the reader a great deal of latitude to interpret the stories in his own way, but sometimes I find cannot help but offer my own slant. I do not doubt that many readers will disagree with my observations and conclusions. In fact, I hope this will be the case. One of the most dangerous tendencies in the telling of history is for those who write the textbooks to set themselves up as authorities, when in fact they are providing at best only one of many possible interpretations. I urge the reader to look up the materials listed in the bibliography and on the websites given at the end of each chapter. It is best to think of these chapters as a "first cut" rather than the final word.

On a more practical level, I would like to give some suggestions to instructors who use this text. Students and instructors could use this text in several ways. One could organize the presentation of the cases based on the broad themes provided in the section headings ("Great Power Relations" and so forth). Alternatively, the cases could be presented chronologically as part of a world history course. I would suggest the following sequencing:

General 1950–2000: Cases 3, 10
Pre-1960: Cases 1, 2, 12
1960–1980: Cases 4, 6, 7, 13, 14, 18, 19
1980–2000: Cases 5, 8, 9, 11, 15, 16, 17, 20, 21, 22, 23, 24

It would also be possible to use this text in a course on comparative politics by focusing on particular regions. For example, the cases could be organized along the following lines (note that some chapters cover more than one region):

U.S. Foreign Policy: Cases 2, 3, 4, 5, 6, 7, 8, 9, 11, 18, 19, 20, 21, 23
European Affairs: Cases 1, 3, 10, 12, 15, 22, 24
Western Asia: Cases 9, 16, 17, 18
Other Developing Areas: Cases 3, 4, 13, 14, 19, 20, 21, 24

Finally, I hope that readers will find this text to be a useful reference work for purposes beyond the classroom, as many readers of the first edition have told me they have done. The background provided here to contemporary problems does not change, although naturally its interpretation does. As new problems emerge in new parts of the world, this background will give the reader an advantage in appreciating the sources of these problems.

New Materials

This third edition provides some revisions to the second edition. To begin, this edition includes two new cases 11 (Kyoto) and 17 (al Qaeda) as well as updates to most of the other cases. Although there will no doubt be disappointment that a few cases were deleted, I believe the current collection better reflects the priorities of international relations scholarship as well as issues that have become especially relevant since the first edition appeared. The third edition also adds a "key figures" section in most chapters, expanded chronologies, and a new "debate topic" to facilitate integrating the text in classroom discussion. As before, this text can be used in an introductory course in international relations, comparative politics, or U.S. foreign policy. The instructor is invited to consult the valuable pedagogical work on the use of case studies organized by Georgetown University's Pew Case Studies Project as well as the International Studies Association's Active Learning section. Also, this text can serve as a reference work for student and instructor alike. I hope that after reading this book, you will come away with a strong background in post–World War II international history, whatever your motivation.

Thanks

I would like to extend thanks to a number of individuals who helped bring about this third edition. Eric Stano, the staff at Longman, and Nancy Freihofer at Thompson Steele were supportive from the outset and provided valuable advice and direction. They also showed remarkable flexibility that allowed the text to be updated at the last minute. I would also like to thank the reviewers of this edition: Dan Reiter, Emory University; Larry Elowitz, Georgia College and State University; and John M. Cotter, University of Kentucky, for their sound advice. Finally, I thank my wife Rebecca and our children—Renee, Alexander, and Christina—who showed considerable patience for my preoccupation with preparing the manuscript.

KEN STILES

Great
Power
Relations

CASE

1

Germany—People and Territory
THE NATION-STATE

Introduction

The nation-state is broadly assumed to be the central actor of international affairs. The nation-state involves the conjunction of the legal unit known as the state and a societal grouping known as the nation. Where these come together in a coherent whole, one finds fulfilled the dream of self-determination. Creating a nation-state has therefore been the ambition of virtually every nationalist. In reality, less than one-fourth of the United Nations' members fit the description, which explains why so many ethnic and national groups are dissatisfied.

The nation-state is considered the central and most powerful unit in international affairs. No other actor can directly shape the rules that make up international law, and no other actor has a monopoly on the legitimate use of force, can wage war, mint currency, and so forth. Although many rivals to the nation-state have emerged over the years (including firms, guilds, and churches), by the late 1600s the dominance of states and their modern manifestation, the nation-state, has been largely unassailable.

Becoming a nation-state has therefore been a struggle worth fighting. Interestingly, very few of the nation-states that are familiar to us now are more than a hundred years old. Before them, groups of people who spoke the same language and/or belonged to the same racial, ethnic, religious, or historic category lived under many different political authorities. They often did not think of themselves as a unified group, although opportunistic politicians may have done so for their own ends. The process of creating a national "consciousness" and forging a unified political structure has dominated world politics since the French Revolution in 1789. One of the most dramatic stories, and one that has several times engulfed the world in brutal and protracted conflict, is the unification of Germans.

Since the beginning of the eighteenth century, much blood has been spilled and many words have been written on the question of the status of Germany. Two world wars, a Holocaust, and a forty-five-year Cold War grew from recent attempts to impose a solution to the so-called German Question. Germany's reunification in 1990 has left many observers wondering whether the issue has finally been resolved.

Germany exemplifies the problems inherent in the development of many nation-states. First, it is difficult to identify with any degree of exactness who is and who is not German. Over the years, language has been the most obvious common link. In reality, the German language is shared by many people with different national loyalties. German-speaking Swiss have not felt any yearning to join any German federations, and speakers of Dutch and Scandinavian languages—all Germanic in origin— certainly do not consider themselves "German." To a certain extent, a person who calls himself German is, by definition, German. Otto von Bismarck saw Germans in geostrategic terms, in that he sought to annex territory that would increase Prussia's power. Adolf Hitler attempted to define Germans in racial terms, with horrific consequences. More recently, Germans have been forced to decide whether forty years of division have given those living under communism in East Germany a new identity and culture that makes them inherently different from capitalist West Germans.

Second, Germany shows how difficult it can be to determine what form of political organization a nation can or should have. From the very loose federation of princes of the Holy Roman Empire to the sprawling totalitarian monstrosity of Hitler's Third Reich to the modern Federal Republic, Germans have experimented with the gamut of political structures. The record shows that the formation of a federal, democratic, united Germany in October 1990 was far from inevitable, and it may prove temporary.

Finally, Germany illustrates how national sovereignty is very much a problem that lies in other nations' hands. No nation has come into being without the consent of its international neighbors. Sovereignty is a privilege rather than an inherent right, and it must be granted by the existing community of states. This community's treatment of Germany over the years has been schizophrenic, to say the least. The same countries that hailed Germany's unification in 1871 and 1990 took part in its division in 1918 and 1945.

In this case study, we will first present an overview of the development of Germany in modern times. Then we will look at these three issues—national identity, government structure, and international reactions—in succession.

GERMANY—PEOPLE AND TERRITORY
KEY FIGURES

Otto von Bismarck—Prussian Premier, 1862–1871; Germany Chancellor, 1871–1890. He is generally credited with masterminding the unification of Germany under Prussian authority and the rise of the country as a major industrial power.

(continued)

William I (Wilhelm I)—King of Prussia, 1858–1871; Emperor of Germany, 1871–1888.

William II (Wilhelm II)—German Emperor, 1888–1919. For his role in World War I, he was forced to abdicate by the victors.

Adolf Hitler—Totalitarian leader of the German Reich, 1933–1945. He spearheaded German expansionism, fueled by an aggressive racial intolerance that led to World War II and the Holocaust.

Frederick the Great of Prussia—Powerful leader of Prussia, 1740–1786. He expanded Prussian influence across Europe, leading to what became known as a "golden age."

Konrad Adenauer—Chancellor of the Federal Republic of Germany (West Germany), 1949–1963. A pro-American conservative, he helped revitalize Germany's economy and brought the country into NATO and the European Community.

Helmut Kohl—German Chancellor, 1982–1998. He directed the country's reunification with East Germany in the early 1990s and strengthened Germany's role in European institutions.

Erich Honecker—Leader of East Germany's Communist Party, 1971–1989. He was instrumental in keeping East Germany squarely within the Soviet orbit. He was overthrown in 1989 and lived the rest of his life in exile, escaping conviction by a German court on account of his failing health.

Overview of German History

For centuries after the collapse of the Roman Empire, a large number of German-speaking princes and kings ruled domains in central Europe. They attempted to join into a federation at various junctures and were known collectively as the Holy Roman Empire. This "empire" lasted until the Renaissance period, when the nation-state emerged as an actor on the European stage. By the end of the eighteenth century, Prussia and Austria were the most powerful German-speaking kingdoms in central Europe (see Map 1.1).

Little thought had been given to a united, German-speaking nation until the invasion of Napoleon's armies (1796–1815) forced German states to reckon with their collective response. After periods of neutrality, subjugation, and even alliance, German states helped to defeat Napoleon. The Congress of Vienna awarded Austria and Prussia with new territory and created the Germanic Confederation—an international German organization complete with a parliamentary council of kings and princes (the Diet). Prussia stepped in to dominate the Diet and convinced German states in the north to join in a trade pact, or Zollverein. This organization promoted industrialization and economic growth during the nineteenth century and fostered a sense of political unity.

German national aspirations were expressed most forcefully in the democratic revolution of 1848. Inspired by attempts at democracy throughout Europe, German nationalists assembled in Frankfurt and Berlin not only demanded free elections and a parliament but also began writing the constitu-

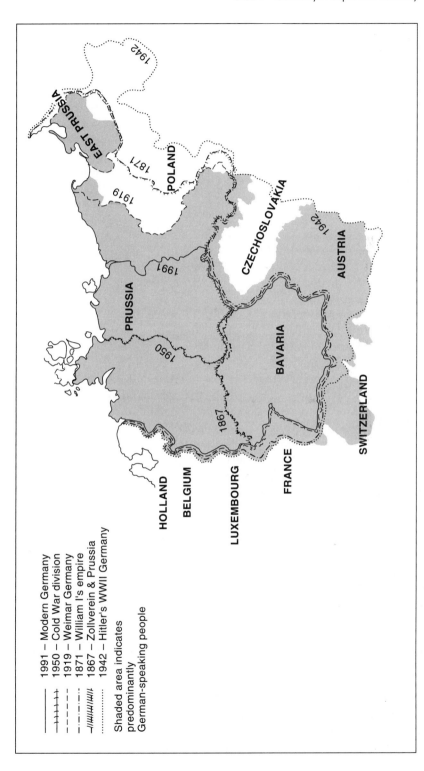

Map 1.1 German territory and German-speaking peoples
Source: William Carr, *A History of Germany, 1815–1985* (London: Edward Arnold, 1987).

tion of a united German state. The conference foundered on the question of Austria's role, and there was strong disagreement on the nature of Germany's future government. Austria rejected the proposal to include only its German-speaking territories because it wanted a dominant voice. Republicans, Marxists, and monarchists failed to find a suitable leader to champion their cause. Within months, the delegates' enthusiasm had dissipated. The conference ultimately disbanded in failure, but not without securing reforms from Prussia's monarchy, including the creation of Germany's first popularly elected parliament, the Reichstag.

In 1862, Otto von Bismarck emerged as the dominant political voice in Prussia and set about to achieve Germanic unity through more traditional means. He had already concluded that the small and scattered German states were ripe for military conquest. As Bismarck put it, "Not by speeches and majority votes are the great questions of the day decided—that was the mistake of 1848 and 1849—but by blood and iron." Prussia first allied with Austria to seize territories claimed by Denmark and then in 1866 decisively defeated Austria's army, thereby securing complete Prussian control of northern German provinces. France, an uneasy bystander to this display of Prussian military prowess, found itself in a diplomatic wrangle with Prussia over the question of Spanish royal succession. The spat spilled over into war, and in 1870 Prussia soundly defeated France's ill-prepared army. The victory allowed the German princes to proclaim the unification of the German Reich and to pledge their loyalty to Prussian ruler William I.

For the next twenty years, Bismarck reassured his European rivals that Germany was "sated" and had no further territorial ambitions. By 1890, however, the new kaiser, William II, was eager to make Germany a global power. After Bismarck's retirement, William II dramatically expanded the German navy and army and undertook imperial conquests in Africa. Around 1900, liberal German nationalists cooperated with authoritarian romanticists and began to stir up xenophobic and chauvinistic feelings. (Note that these attitudes were prevalent throughout Europe at the time. See Hildebrand 1989, 236.) Germany, along with the rest of Europe, prepared diligently for a war that by 1910 seemed inevitable. It formed an alliance with Austria-Hungary against France and Russia and developed a strict plan for mobilization and deployment of troops against France.

The assassination of Archduke Ferdinand in Sarajevo in the summer of 1914 precipitated a chain of events over which political leaders seem to have had little control (see especially Tuchman 1962). By August, all of Europe was embroiled in a war that would prove to be the deadliest in history. The result was a bloody three-year stalemate ultimately broken by the Russian Revolution and the entry of the United States into the war in 1917. In October 1918, the kaiser was ousted in a democratic revolution and Germany capitulated. The Treaty of Versailles severely punished Germany, laying the blame for war on its doorstep. Germany's war machine was dismantled, the Bundesbank was required to pay heavy reparations, and portions of German territory were either carved up or occupied.

Europeans welcomed the new democratic federal government that was established at Weimar, with the Social Democratic Party—a center-left party that favored social reform—at the helm. However, almost as soon as German nationalists learned of the humiliating treaty terms, conservative and fascist parties sprang up in Germany, including Adolf Hitler's fledgling National Socialist (Nazi) Party in Bavaria. A traditional nationalist party—the Volkspartei—was created by former imperial supporters and became part of the ruling coalition government in the mid-1920s. The German economy, saddled with debt because of the reparations and heavy reconstruction costs, stagnated during the 1920s, and the Wall Street crash plunged it into deep depression in 1929. Radical parties on the right and the left flourished, while none of the mainstream parties could solve the crisis. Violence in the streets spread as unemployment reached new highs. For several years, the politicians in the Reichstag failed to organize a stable government, and between 1930 and 1933, more and more Germans became disenchanted with democracy. In January 1933, figurehead President Paul von Hindenburg reluctantly asked the leader of the now-powerful Nazi Party to join the Volkspartei in a coalition with Hitler as the nominal chancellor. Hitler immediately demanded of the Reichstag the power to rule by decree, which was granted out of desperation in March.

Hitler's dictatorship in Germany is well known. Suffice it here to say that he applied his extreme conception of German nationalism in the eradication not only of Jews, Gypsies, and other minorities but also of any Germans deemed inferior (namely, the handicapped and mentally ill). Hitler imported so-called Aryan bloodstock and attempted to build a race of superhumans capable of controlling the world. Even his highest generals were shocked by the extent of his ambitions. Several attempts were made on his life, and during the mid-1930s, his ruthless government forced scores of Germany's scientists and artists to flee persecution.

Hitler methodically acted to reverse the most objectionable aspects of the Treaty of Versailles by rebuilding Germany's military, regaining control over lost territory, and refusing to pay war reparations. These actions, though illegal, met with little international resistance because British and French officials surmised that it might be wiser to grant Hitler what he demanded in the hopes that he could be sated, as was Bismarck. This effort to avoid confrontation by accommodating Hitler was called "appeasement."

Hitler further demanded the incorporation of all German-speaking peoples into the Third Reich—a policy that was at first glance consistent with the general goal of self-determination but that would have resulted in a lopsided advantage for Germany in comparison to other continental powers (see the discussion of "balance of power" in Case 3). Hitler pressed his claims in Austria and Czechoslovakia, in particular. When Austria threatened to become an autonomous (rather than subservient) authoritarian state in early 1938, Hitler invaded and put his political allies in power. In Czechoslovakia, demands for autonomy by German-speaking Sudetens were rejected by Czech central authorities. Hitler mobilized his troops in preparation for an apparent invasion, prompting Neville Chamberlain of Great Britain to agree to Hitler's demands for Sudeten autonomy at a conference in Munich.

In 1939, Hitler used racist rhetoric to justify the invasion and annexation of non-German areas of Poland, Scandinavia, and much of Eastern Europe, claiming that the German people required far more space to flourish. In 1941, it became clear that this "Lebensraum" knew no limit, as Hitler declared war on the Americans and Soviets. By 1942, he had achieved dominance in all of Europe except Britain and in all of North Africa except Egypt.

Hitler's fortunes changed in the snows around Stalingrad in 1943. By 1944, with the Axis armies in full retreat, the Allied nations were already planning postwar Europe. Perhaps the most important move made by Josef Stalin, Winston Churchill, and Franklin Roosevelt was the decision at Yalta to permit two vast spheres of influence in Europe, roughly equivalent to the regions liberated by the Soviet armies in the east and by the American, British, and French armies in the west. Germany itself would be temporarily divided and administered by the two groups. With the end of the war in May 1945, Germany lost its independence and became a divided nation.

After Germany's capitulation, the occupying powers began to apply their very different philosophies to governing the areas under their jurisdiction. The Soviets dismantled German industrial equipment and transported it to the Soviet Union as payment of war reparations. British and American occupiers began laying the groundwork for a liberal and independent democracy. By 1949, West Germany had a constitution (Basic Law) that promoted liberal democratic principles and human rights, while Communists in East Germany declared the nation to be a socialist state and outlawed rival parties. By 1950, both nations had become fully committed to the political goals of their sponsors.

Konrad Adenauer emerged as the leader of the Christian Democratic–led coalition government in 1949 and advocated a firm anti-Communist policy. Under Adenauer, the Federal Republic of Germany (its official name) withheld diplomatic recognition of the German Democratic Republic (East Germany) on the grounds that the division was illegitimate (the "Hallstein doctrine") and that Germans everywhere had a right to citizenship in the West (a policy that attracted many immigrants from East Germany from 1949 to 1961 and then again in the late 1980s). Adenauer brought West Germany into the North Atlantic Treaty Organization (NATO) and the European Community (EC) and made his country a model western state. By the end of his chancellorship in the early 1960s, the Federal Republic was more prosperous and solidly democratic than nearly all of its European neighbors.

Soviet officials were determined to transform the German Democratic Republic (GDR) into a prosperous socialist state. The rapid success of the West far exceeded the significant gains of the East, however, and its citizens could not resist the temptation to migrate. At two different junctures—1948 and 1953—Soviet and East German officials intervened with force to prevent the exodus, which by August 1961 had prompted one out of six East Germans to leave. The divided city of Berlin was an especially troublesome question because many used it as an open doorway to the West. Finally, the decision was made not only to outlaw emigration but also to construct a physical barrier of wire and stone. The Berlin Wall, which encircled the western half of the city, long stood as a symbol of socialism's failure.

With the emigration problem solved, the Socialist Unity Party government gradually responded to East Germans' demands for a higher standard of living. Soon, the GDR grew at remarkable rates and did in fact become the model of socialism, complete with heavy industry, guaranteed employment, cradle-to-grave security, and relatively high incomes. By the end of the 1960s, Walter Ulbricht began to boast that the GDR's socialist industrialization was superior to the Soviet policies at home. He also criticized the Soviet foreign policy of détente (or relaxation of tensions) with the West. In 1971, he was ousted by Soviet-sponsored conspirators and replaced by Erich Honecker.

Meanwhile, the political scene in the Federal Republic of Germany (FRG) went into a period of flux after Adenauer's resignation until the Social Democratic Party of Germany (SPD) won elections in 1969 and organized a coalition government with Willy Brandt as chancellor. Brandt immediately initiated a series of actions aimed at improving relations with the East. In particular, he signed a new "Basic Treaty" with pro-détente Honecker, which reversed the Hallstein doctrine and extended diplomatic recognition to the GDR. His opponents at home deplored the abandonment of the goal of unification but applauded the reduction of Cold War tensions. Each Germany was permitted to fill a seat in the United Nations for the first time in 1973.

With this newfound recognition, both German governments began to move in a more independent political direction. West Germans were ambivalent about their role on the front line of the Cold War and largely rejected the renewal of tensions during the first term of U.S. President Ronald Reagan. Both Helmut Schmidt and later Helmut Kohl found it difficult to accommodate both public opinion and NATO demands. Likewise, East German officials found more to gain from working with the West Germans than with the Soviets in the early 1980s. Honecker attempted to instill in the Germans of the GDR a distinct "East German nationalism" that would discourage emigration by building pride in socialism. During this period, both Germanys signed a variety of treaties pledging economic and political cooperation. Both government leaders and opposition parties formulated joint statements concerning cooperation and the need for détente between the superpowers. The 1987 U.S.–Soviet Intermediate-Range Nuclear Forces Treaty and the talks on reducing conventional forces in Europe were strongly supported by both the FRG and the GDR.

Thus much was already in place when, with the tacit approval of Mikhail Gorbachev in Moscow, all of Eastern Europe abandoned first strict emigration policies and then Communist control in 1989. What began as a small crack in the Iron Curtain at the Austria–Hungary border soon grew to a huge breach as East Europeans traveled west. From August to October, 1989, East German leaders faced increasingly militant crowds demanding free emigration and the dismantling of the Berlin Wall. Gorbachev, on October 7, suggested to Honecker that "life itself punishes those who delay" in responding to historical forces, and Kohl promised substantial economic aid in exchange for free elections ("A Chronology of Events" 1990, 195). Finally, after a record-setting crowd of 500,000 demonstrated in East Berlin on November 8, Honecker opened the border to the West the next day. East Germany quickly experienced its first democratic elections, followed by diplomatic negotiations on a reunification timetable, and concluded by formal unification and relinquishing of Allied powers on October 3, 1990. Germany occupied a single seat in the United Nations in 1991.

The German "Nation"

Is German nationalism as coherent and aggressive as many outsiders believe? Recent studies indicate that it is a much more fragmented and limited phenomenon than many have claimed. In particular, it is important to understand that three different nationalist forces exist in Germany and that they rarely work as a united movement (Hughes 1988).

Since the early nineteenth century, many German intellectuals have yearned to create a country that would encompass all German speakers. As expressed in a famous poem by Ernst Moritz Arndt (1769–1860), typical of romantic German nationalism:

> What is the German's fatherland?
>
> Come, name for me this mighty land!
>
> As far as the German tongue resounds
>
> And from God in heaven song abounds:
>
> There it must be!
>
> That, noble German, belongs to thee!
>
> (Grass 1990, 77)

Romantic nationalists yearn for a German "Golden Age"—a mythical period roughly equivalent to the reign of Frederick the Great in Prussia (1740–1786). Bismarck and William I made frequent references to this period in their efforts to garner public support for wars against Denmark, Austria, and France. Since World War I, romantic nationalists have continued to support a traditional, militaristic Germany based on Prussian traditions of hard work, discipline, and loyalty to the state. Contemporary Christian Democrats tend to lean in this general direction, and although Kohl's reunification of Germany was done in the name of democracy, traditionalists strongly endorsed the move. The recent ceremonial reburial of Frederick the Great in the former GDR exemplifies the symbolic activities of traditionalists today.

In southern Germany—Bavaria in particular—and among lower classes, nationalism has taken a more simple, xenophobic tone. Rather than taking pride in the real or imagined glory of a past Germany, xenophobes emphasize the dangers and threats of Germany's enemies. *Xenophobia* refers to the fear and loathing of things "foreign." In the years leading up to World War I, William II exploited these sentiments in an effort to galvanize support for the coming war effort (Carr 1987). Hitler's philosophy stressed fear of aliens (Jews in particular) and mobilized violent demonstrations called "pogroms." Today, neo-Nazi groups in Germany, organized as the Republican Party, are looked upon as a nuisance, an embarrassment, and an ill omen. Since the reunification of Germany, Republican activities have increased and they have been joined in the political fight by new reactionary parties.

A third form of German nationalism has been a liberal democratic idealism based on the work of Immanuel Kant and other Enlightenment philosophers. This philosophy led to the 1848 revolution and dominated the Weimar Republic. The SPD and many German intellectuals have seen Germany as part of a wider Western culture, rather than as a separate entity following a "special path" or *Sonderweg* (Hildebrand 1989, chap. 10). Modern German attachment to the European Union institutions and participation in the international economic system are consistent with this approach, although conservative German politicians have not always embraced the participatory democracy promoted by liberal nationalists.

At any given point in Germany's history, a mixture of these tendencies has resulted in a special form of behavior. Bismarck eagerly manipulated the mass media to intensify Germans' xenophobia and pursue traditional goals of the Prussian elite (Hughes 1988, 118). Hitler likewise combined xenophobia and traditionalism after the failure of the liberalism of the Weimar Republic. Hitler was unique, however, in his extreme emphasis on racist explanations of German superiority (Kershaw 1985). Certainly his crude and ruthless genetic engineering and genocide are looked upon with shame by most Germans today.

Many worry that German nationalism will reemerge as a destructive force (Bertram 1990). For this to happen, German democracy would need to be replaced by a more authoritarian structure, given the many checks on central authority and the strong popular commitment to a peaceful foreign policy in Germany today. Although the despair and resentment following the reunification of Germany have caused many in the former GDR to oppose the Kohl administration, there is little indication that even the most dissatisfied people want a return to authoritarianism of any shape. Flag-waving, saluting, jingoism, and attacks on foreigners, though practiced by a few, remain far from the ordinary German's mind.

Some have wondered whether the official recognition of Polish control over formally German territory will placate the desires of some to unite with their homelands. Some 15 million German-speakers left Poland and other East European nations after World War II, although they still consider those regions home. On this subject, Kohl said:

The truth is—and this should not be suppressed on a day such as this— the expulsion of the Germans from their native regions was a grave injustice. There was no justification, either moral or legal. Nor can we say decades later that it was legitimate. . . . [Nonetheless] we . . . forgo revenge and reprisal. This is our serious and heartfelt resolve in remembrance of the untold suffering that the past . . . . has inflicted on mankind. (Bundestag speech, June 21, 1990)

Such assurances are comforting, but it is also true that at least for another generation, there will be some in Germany who long for their home across the border.

The German State

The German state has changed dramatically over the years in both dimension and governing arrangements. As illustrated in Map 1.1 and Table 1.1, the size of the German state spread from a loose confederation in the early nineteenth century to a large empire covering much of central Europe. At its zenith in 1942, German authority extended over all of Europe and Scandinavia (excluding Great Britain, Italy, and the Balkans) and large parts of Africa and the Soviet Union—territory that obviously extended far beyond lands inhabited by German-speakers. At the end of the war, Germany had lost all political autonomy and was controlled by its occupiers. To a large extent, Germany's borders have been decided by non-Germans. German unification in 1990 represents the first time the German people as a whole were given a voice in determining their country's borders.

In addition to changing the country's territorial dimensions, German governments have dramatically altered the regime style over the years. These changes correlate with the three forms of nationalism discussed previously. In addition, the question of concentration of power in the center has varied over the years.

The first unification of the German nation in 1871 was, as explained by Carr, "the uneasy compromise between the forces of conservative federalism, the liberal unitary principle and the military might of Prussia. . . . The Empire did not emanate from the will of the people" (1987, 119). It was not until the Weimar Republic that the principle of popular sovereignty was officially enshrined in the 1919 Constitution. In spite of liberals' attachment to centralized democracy, the Laender (provinces) retained much of their traditional authority over education, social policy, police, and church activity. The retention of the official title "Reich" acknowledged, as explained by Hugo Preuss, author of the Constitution, "the tradition of centuries, the entire yearning of a divided German people for national unity are bound up with the name Reich and we would wound the feeling of wide circles without reason and to no purpose if we gave up this designation" (255).

Hitler's concentration of power in Berlin is an exception to the tradition of federalism in Germany, although the GDR's administrative structure showed some similarities. As put in a recent government publication, "Germany always had a decentralized structure until its catastrophic experience

Table 1.1   German Governmental Structures Since 1815

Period	Regime Type	Power Distribution
1815–1848	German Confederation	Competition between Austria and Prussia. Federal Diet made up of princes.
1848–1850	Revolution	Constitutional convention creates weak Reichstag, grants civil rights.
1850–1867	German Confederation	Growing Prussian dominance. Federal Diet, Reichstag weakened.
1867–1881	North German Confederation	Prussian-dominated federation. Popular Reichstag given more power.
1871–1918	Second Reich	Prussian-dominated federation. Federal Bundesrat and popular Reichstag.
1918–1933	Weimar Republic	Constitutional democracy. Reichstag dominates various Laender (provinces).
1933–1945	Third Reich	Unitary totalitarian state.
1945–1949	Occupied Germany	Soviet and U.S./U.K. control.
1949–1990	Federal Republic	Constitutional democracy with popular Bundestag, federal Bundesrat.
1949–1990	Democratic Republic	Unitary dictatorship when legislature weakened.
1990+	Federal Republic	FRG institutions applied to GDR.

with centralism in the form of the National Socialist dictatorship from 1933 to 1945. The delegation of political authority to the regions is part of the legacy of German constitutional history" (Reuter 1991, 1). What the article ignores is the tension between federal pressures rooted in traditional notions of the sovereignty of principalities and duchies that made up the Reich, and centralist pressures emanating from liberal conceptions of popular sovereignty. Add to that an autocratic Prussian tradition, and it is easy to see why the structure of German government has changed so much over the years.

Despite their extremely varied histories and relatively recent incorporation in the German federation, the Laender have not pressed for political independence. The lack of secessionism in Germany may be a result of both the general consensus on what constitutes German nationality in recent years and the federative governmental system that grants to the Laender significant administrative and some policy-making roles. Allied forces carved up the prewar Laender—especially by partitioning Prussia—and thereby created new units and loyalties to the German people. The new generation of leaders has a vested interest in maintaining the current structure, so it will likely endure. In fact, rather than separatism, the current trend is for German-speakers to freely seek annexation to the German state. A plebiscite in the French-dominated regions of the Saar in 1957 favored annexation, which came to pass in 1959. In 1990, an overwhelming majority of East Germans voted in favor of reincorporation into a single federal state.

Although the German state today is a benign and cooperative international presence, it is possible that a united Germany, by attracting population and wealth, could become a threat to European stability, if only because Germany's neighbors have a tradition of mistrust. In the next section, we will consider ways European powers have dealt with this problem.

German Nationalism as an International Problem

Clearly the most troublesome problem related to the German nation-state is the tension among self-determination, civil rights, irredentism, and balance of power in Europe. On the one hand, is the objective of nation building and self-determination outweighed by the security demands of neighbors? Specifically, at what point should the demand of German nationalism take precedence over the balance of power in Europe? On the other hand, should irridentist claims be granted if the government in question is violating human rights? Should Hitler's demands have been met, given the treatment of German citizens already under his control? Does German unity today have a different significance simply because the government is democratic?

In the nineteenth century, much of European diplomacy was dominated by the effort to cooperate in the resolution of continental conflicts. The Concert of Europe system began to break down with the Crimean War and the rise of Germany in the middle of the century. By then, the kingdoms of Austria-Hungary, Turkey, and Russia were beginning to show their weaknesses, while Germany and Italy were on the rise. Not only were they growing in territory through unification, but Germany in particular experienced unprecedented economic and military growth during the latter half of the nineteenth century. By 1890, the German economy ranked only behind that of Britain in total size. By 1913, Germany was producing more manufactured goods than Britain. On the eve of World War II, Germany was spending more on military hardware than the United States and Soviet Union combined (Kennedy 1987, chap. 5).

To contain this rapid growth, European powers first resorted to traditional balance-of-power tactics. With Britain and Russia uninvolved, cooperation between France, Denmark, Austria-Hungary, and Italy was far from adequate to contain German expansion. After the defeat of France in 1871, Britain began to exert more pressure on Germany, but it was not until the 1890s that a concerted anti-German alliance began to form. By then Britain and France were far outstripped, and Russia—the other coalition partner—was on the verge of revolution.

World War I demonstrated the dramatic changes in warfare that had occurred over the preceding half-century. With massive new weapons (aerial bombardment, mobilization of troops by rail, machine guns, chemical weapons, tanks) and the strategy of "total war" in which there was no safety for civilians, millions were slaughtered in a slugging match that dragged on for four years. At its conclusion, 16 million were dead, two empires were dissolved, and Lenin had taken control in Moscow.

Although the Treaty of Versailles lays the blame for the war squarely on Germany's shoulders, several interesting alternatives to this theory have been offered. In particular, Tuchman (1962) argues that the war was essentially preventable, in that unwise and impetuous leaders blundered into conflict by allowing minor incidents to escalate into major crises. In a sense, Tuchman would blame all the European leaders collectively. Choucri and North (1975) present a statistical case for the argument that the war was inevitable and without villains because the long-term economic and demographic forces at work were beyond anyone's control. With so much growth and so few new outlets, confrontation was inevitable, they claim.

Containment of Germany was bought at a frightening price, and the formation of the League of Nations was motivated largely as an alternative to war. The Treaty of Versailles was punitive but was quickly reinterpreted. At the Locarno Conference of 1925, Britain and France made it clear that Germany would be welcomed back as a full European power. French Prime Minister Aristide Briand and Britain's Chamberlain went out of their way in the late 1920s to accommodate Germany's legitimate demands and attempt to form economic and political ties that would bind Germany to the rest of Europe.

To a large extent, diplomacy succeeded; until Hitler arrived, German behavior was basically consistent with larger European goals. The Great Depression, the onslaught of fascism, and the militarism of Hitler obviously reversed this trend. However, rather than reacting forcefully, British and French officials maintained their accommodating stance vis-á-vis new, more daring German demands. The remilitarization of the Saar, the renunciation of postwar reparations, the dramatic increase in military capability (German military spending nearly doubled each year between 1934 and 1939), and the annexation of Austria were met with little resistance. Not until Hitler attempted to annex the Sudetenland by force did Britain and France present forceful opposition. The Munich Conference was considered a major diplomatic achievement at the time, although Chamberlain quickly regretted his approval of Sudeten annexation. The invasion of Poland was the last straw and the war began—although somewhat hesitantly after Warsaw's fall. It took several months before Germany's armies directly confronted Allied forces, meeting little resistance.

Were British and French officials wrong to grant Hitler's government the retraction of certain objectionable features of the Versailles Treaty? One may perhaps question their motives: Were they driven by fear of confrontation or did they seek greater respect for human rights? What started out as a sincere desire to integrate Germany into a new Europe (French officials already envisioned a version of the Common Market including Germany) became a desire to avoid war at all costs. This delay naturally provided Hitler time to build up Germany's war-fighting capability.

After World War II, the Allied powers attempted to solve the German Question through partition and continued occupation. Integration of East and West Germany into the alliance systems of the USSR and United States was aimed not only at offsetting the power of the superpower rival but also at keeping German power in check. The strategy worked for forty-five years, albeit at the expense of German freedom and self-determination. Where nineteenth-century Europeans generally favored German unification at the expense of European stability (perhaps unintentionally), the superpowers did not hesitate to sacrifice German integrity for the sake of the balance of power.

Conclusion

Germany's reunification was to a large extent a diplomatic achievement. As put by Kaiser, "German unification, brought about by a multitude of bilateral and multilateral negotiations and arrangements, represents one of the greatest triumphs of leadership and diplomatic professionalism in the postwar period" (1990/91, 179). George H.W. Bush quickly endorsed early proposals for unification by Helmut Kohl, although France and the Soviet Union expressed reservations. Events were propelled by the strong East German demands for reunification, and within three months of the Berlin Wall's collapse, the two Germanys had agreed on a diplomatic process to end partition in cooperation with the four World War II powers. The resulting "two-plus-four" talks centered on whether the Soviet proposals for German neutrality (or dual alliance membership) would be met and what to do about foreign forces based in Germany. The solution reached ultimately granted the new Germany full sovereign rights to join whatever alliance it chose, but Germany agreed to a gradual repatriation of Soviet military located in the former GDR.

Thus far, the various approaches to the German Question—diplomacy, war, and partition—have failed to satisfy both the demands of the German people and the security needs of Germany's neighbors. Perhaps a strong, democratic, united Germany—which is tied inextricably to the world economy and European security arrangements—offers the best hope of achieving these otherwise irreconcilable objectives.

How does the German case help us understand the concept of the "nation-state"? Clearly, nationalism is not as concrete as many have been led to believe. In some cases, and in Germany in particular, it is perhaps mostly a contrivance rather than an abstract reality. The existence of other German-speaking peoples and the lack of cultural unity across the various German Laender challenge the view that all Germans are culturally homogenous. The same is true of almost every "nation," for that matter. On the other hand, the emergence of Germany's state lay at the heart of many of the world's major conflicts since 1850 and has been discussed at length in the case study.

The German case could lead one to conclude that the concept of "nation-state" should perhaps be set aside in favor of the separate concepts of "state" and "nation." It may well be that the broader term is more confusing and misleading than helpful. It can also be used for propaganda purposes by states in search of a nation of loyal citizens. Furthermore, the German case shows that the "nation-state" concept can be used to justify aggression, irredentism, and separatism.

Debate Topic

When German leaders first proposed unifying East and West in 1990, other European powers and Russia were confronted with a question: Will a united Germany rediscover its chauvinistic past and behave aggressively toward its neighbors? With the benefit of a decade of hindsight, consider the arguments for and against this prospect.

PRO

According to this position, Germany presents a potential threat to the rest of Europe and Russia for the following reasons: (1) Germany's economy has continued to grow despite spending $1 billion on rehabilitating East Germany, to the point that it is clearly the dominant economic force in Europe. (2) Germany has taken advantage of its economic strength to consolidate its status in the European Union, in particular by making sure that its philosophy of monetary policy is the one used with respect to the euro, the new European currency unit. (3) Fascist tendencies reemerged during the 1990s and have yet to be brought fully under control. (4) Germany has been eager to extend its influence in the Balkans and NATO, indicating a less-than-passive view of its own importance.

CON

Germany, according to this perspective, is no threat to its neighbors for these reasons: (1) Germany continues to demonstrate its commitment to peaceful resolution of disputes and multilateral approaches to crisis management. (2) Germany's deep involvement in European institutions will make it increasing difficult for it to behave either aggressively or unilaterally. (3) Former East Germans are becoming increasingly assimilated into West German culture, thus expanding the spread of democratic principles.

Are there other facts or ideas that might support one position or the other, based on this casestudy or other research you have conducted?

Questions to Consider

1. Germany's reunification obviously presents new problems—not only internal to Germany but also international. Will Germany's economy so dominate Europe that it will cause resentment and hostility?

2. Will a united Germany rediscover its chauvinistic past and begin to make new demands on its neighbors?

3. Will a strengthened Germany remain loyal to Western security objectives, or will it chart a new foreign policy path?

4. How will Germany resolve its immigration problem? Will it continue to impose new restrictions?

5. How will Germany deal with increasing discontent and unemployment in the East? Will a social revolution be the outcome?

Websites

German history page: **www.sedelmeier.com/history1.htm**
Documents in German history project: **www.ncl.ac.uk/~nhistory/germany.htm**
Contemporary German history: **web.uccs.edu/!history/index/germany.html**
German history links: **h-net2.msu.edu/~german/links.html**

References

Bertram, Christoph. "The German Question." *Foreign Affairs* 69 #2 (Spring 1990):45–62.

Carr, William. *A History of Germany, 1815–1985* (London: Edward Arnold, 1987).

Choucri, Nazli, and Robert North. *Conflict Among Nations* (New York: W. H. Freeman, 1975).

"A Chronology of Events." *World Affairs* 152 #4 (Spring 1990):195–197.

Grass, Gunter. *Two States–One Nation?* Trans. by Krishna Winston (New York: Harcourt Brace Jovanovich, 1990).

Hildebrand, Klaus. *German Foreign Policy from Bismarck to Adenauer*. Trans. by Louise Willmot (London: Unwin Hyman, 1989).

Hughes, Michael. *Nationalism and Society: Germany 1800–1945* (London: Edward Arnold, 1988).

Kaiser, Karl. "Germany's Unification." *Foreign Affairs* 70 #1 (1990/91):179–205.

Kennedy, Paul. *The Rise and Fall of the Great Powers* (New York: Random House, 1987).

Kershaw, I. *The Nazi Dictatorship: Problems and Perspectives* (London: Edward Arnold, 1985).

Reuter, Konrad. "Sixteen States, One Country: The Political Structure of the Federal Republic of Germany." *Inter Nationes*, Special Report (1991 manuscript).

Tuchman, Barbara. *The Guns of August* (New York: Macmillan, 1962).

2

Pearl Harbor

INTELLIGENCE

Introduction

Intelligence is a word pregnant with intrigue and mystery. In fact, *intelligence*, as used in government circles, simply means the gathering and analysis of information on foreign policy problems. The vast majority of intelligence is gathered and analyzed the same way research papers are written—by informed observers using public documents. It is common knowledge in Washington, D.C., that the *New York Times* routinely provides better information about unfolding events than the Central Intelligence Agency (whose job it is to know what is going on). Some more unusual sources of intelligence include spying, electronic surveillance, and satellite reconnaissance. As technology has advanced, the significance of electronic information gathering has increased, typically at the expense of traditional spying.

Today, analysts rely increasingly on electronic intelligence, including telephone intercepts (both cellular and ground-based), e-mail and Internet traffic monitoring, and other electronic communications. The National Security Agency, along with the CIA and various defense and diplomatic intelligence-gathering organizations, monitors and catalogues millions of conversations and e-mails each day in dozens of languages. Such intercepts have allowed U.S. federal agencies to discover various terrorist plots in advance. However, the flow of information is often overwhelming and takes days—even weeks—to translate and interpret. Such delays may have prevented the U.S. government from identifying pre-September 11, 2001, communications that could have prompted a heightened state of alert.

Many intelligence experts complain that electronic intelligence is supplanting human intelligence as the principal source of information, even though it is relatively easy for an organized threat to come together without relying on communications that could be monitored. The case of Pearl Harbor shows what can happen when officials rely too heavily on one particular type of information—in this case, the ability to crack diplomatic messages between officials in Tokyo and Japan's representatives in Washington.

The Pearl Harbor story also tells us something about how intelligence is organized. Because of their separate sources of information, the Army and the Navy were expected to share—but often they did not. A similar observation was noted in the investigations following September 11, when it was discovered that the Immigration and Naturalization Service had files on several of the terrorists, the NSA had some intercepted conversations, and other agencies had additional bits of information that, if placed side-by-side, might have led an analyst to infer that an attack was imminent.

PEARL HARBOR
KEY FIGURES

Franklin Roosevelt—U.S. President, 1933–1945. He embraced a more internationalist role for the United States in world affairs and supported Britain during the early months of World War II. He reacted swiftly to Japan's attack on Pearl Harbor and presided over the country's war efforts until his death a few days before Germany's surrender.

General Hideki Tojo—Japanese Premier, 1941–1944. The dominant militarist in the Tokyo government, he is broadly considered the mastermind of Japan's aggression in the 1930s and 1940s. He was later executed as a war criminal.

Admiral Husband Kimmel—Commander of the U.S. Pacific Fleet, stationed at Pearl Harbor in 1941. He, along with Army General Short, was blamed for inadequate preparation for the Japanese attack.

General Walter Short—Commander of the Hawaiian Sector of the U.S. Army. His unwillingness to work with Admiral Kimmel was cited as a cause for the military's lack of preparedness for the Pearl Harbor attack.

Cordell Hull—U.S. Secretary of State, 1933–1944. He spearheaded Roosevelt's internationalist policy and was awarded the 1945 Nobel Peace Prize.

Prince Fumimaro Konoye—Japanese Premier, 1937–1939 and 1940–1941. He was known for his attempts to block the political rise of the military.

Admiral Kichisaburo Nomura—Japanese Ambassador to the United States in 1941.

PEARL HARBOR
CHRONOLOGY

1931
Japan attacks Manchuria. U.S. Secretary of War Henry Stimson succeeds in pressing a policy of nonrecognition by the United States

1933
Japan leaves the League of Nations under protest, following imposition of sanctions.

(continued)

1937

Japan launches war on China.

1935–1939

The United States passes the Neutrality Acts.

1939

July	The United States cancels its bilateral trade agreement with Japan.
September	Germany attacks Poland; France and Britain declare war—World War II begins.
November	Neutrality Act of 1939 commits the United States to sell arms to belligerents on a cash-and-carry basis.

1940

June	France falls to Germany.
September	Congress enacts the draft by one vote. Germany, Italy, and Japan sign the Tripartite Pact, pledging mutual support in the event any of the three is attacked.
December	U.S. President Franklin Roosevelt receives an urgent request for lend-lease aid from British Prime Minister Winston Churchill in violation of the 1939 Neutrality Act.

1941

January	Congress approves the lend-lease following Roosevelt's reiteration of formal neutrality. Pearl Harbor is placed on high alert following rumors of a Japanese attack.
March	U.S. Secretary of State Cordell Hull and Japanese Ambassador Kichisaburo Nomura negotiate in Washington over continued Japanese conquests in China and Japan's adherence to the Tripartite Pact.
July	The Japanese Imperial Conference endorses policy of military conquest in the Pacific.
July 24	Japan moves into Indochina after pressuring the pro-Nazi Vichy government in France to relinquish its colonial holdings.
July 26	The U.S. government freezes Japanese assets and takes control of trade. Some argue that cutting off Japan from American oil and markets forced it to go to war.
August 6	Japan offers concessions on China issue in exchange for an end to the U.S. freeze on assets—the United States rejects the offer. Japan begins plans for an attack on Pearl Harbor. They are ready by late October.
August 9–14	Roosevelt and Churchill meet in Newfoundland and issue the Atlantic Charter, which includes U.S. support for the British and Chinese fight against Japan in the Pacific and rejection of Japanese domination of Manchuria.
August 17	The United States warns Japan of a possible American resort to force to implement the Atlantic Charter.
August–September	Japanese Prime Minister Fumimaro Konoye meets with Churchill.
September–October	U.S. destroyers are attacked in the Atlantic. Roosevelt adopts a shoot-on-sight policy against German U-boats.
September 6	Konoye offers the proposal for the summit with Roosevelt. U.S. Ambassador to Japan Joseph Grew warns that the Konoye government may fall if the United States rejects the offer.
October 2	The United States rejects Konoye's proposals and defers the summit meeting. Negotiations show no further progress from this point on.
October 16	Hideki Tojo, leader of the Japanese War Party, becomes prime minister when the moderate Konoye cabinet falls.
November 3	Ambassador Grew warns that the Japanese may be planning a secret attack and urges conciliation in Washington.
November 5	Army Chief of Staff George Marshall and Harold Stark, chief of naval operations, recommend to Roosevelt that all support short of war with Japan should be given to China, but reiterate that Germany is the "most dangerous enemy." Roosevelt approves the proposal.
November 7	The United States rejects the Japanese Imperial Conference's "Proposal A." Cordell Hull warns in an earlier Cabinet meeting that Japan may be planning a secret attack.

(continued)

November 17	By a thin margin, Congress passes amendments to the Neutrality Act to allow convoy escorts into war zones.
November 17	Special Japanese envoy Saburo Kurusu joins Nomura in Washington to begin negotiations (with a secret Japanese deadline of November 30).
November 20	The United States receives Japanese "Proposal B." It again demands an end to Japanese actions in the Pacific and China.
November 22–26	Hull weighs and rejects "modus vivendi" based on Proposal B in a ten-point note offering new proposals. Meanwhile, a Japanese carrier force leaves Japan for Hawaii under radio silence.
November 27	The United States Army and Navy send secret war alerts to Pacific bases.
November 29–Dec.1	Japanese cabinet secretly rejects ther U.S. proposals, although this response will not be conveyed until December 7.
December 2	The order to commence the Pearl Harbor attack given to carrier groups: "Climb Mount Nitaka."
December 5–6	The Japanese destroy codes in their embassy and move troops south from Indochina.
December 6	Roosevelt sends an urgent message of peace to Emperor Hirohito.
December 6	Roosevelt receives part of the Japanese rejection of the November 26 offer through code breaking; Roosevelt interprets it as a sign that war is imminent.
December 7	Cryptographers in Washington intercept Japanese instructions to their ambassador in the United States to deliver a declaration of war to Roosevelt by 1:00 p.m., Washington time. The message is not conveyed to Pearl Harbor prior to attack. Washington learns of the Pearl Harbor attack at 7:55 a.m., Hawaii time, but a Japanese legate fails to convey the declaration of war until after the attack has already started.
December 8	Roosevelt delivers his "day of infamy" speech, after which Congress unanimously approves a declaration of war on Japan. Germany and Italy declare war on the United States within a week.

Prologue

In the pre-dawn hours of Sunday, December 7, 1941, a Japanese task force under the command of Vice Admiral Chuichi Nagumo bore down upon Oahu. His formidable armada centered around six aircraft carriers. Upon reaching a point some 220 miles north of the island, they launched two successive waves totaling 350 aircraft—40 torpedo bombers, 78 fighter aircraft, 103 high-level bombers, and 129 dive bombers. Their targets were the ships of Admiral Husband E. Kimmel's U.S. Pacific Fleet at moorings in Pearl Harbor. . . . Before a single shot had been fired, Commander Mitsuo Fuchida, leader of the air strike, knew that the Japanese had achieved total surprise, and so advised the flagship, Akagi, by the code word Tora! Tora! Tora! (Tiger! Tiger! Tiger!). At 0750 Fuchida signaled for the general attack. Approximately four hours later, his aircraft, the last to leave the scene, touched down on Akagi's flight deck. He and his men left behind a devastating sight. They had sunk, capsized, or damaged in varying degrees a total of eighteen warships—eight battleships, three light cruisers, three destroyers, and four auxiliary craft. The U.S. Navy's air arm had lost eighty-seven aircraft of all types. The Japanese had also destroyed 77 aircraft of [the Army's] Hawaiian Air Force. . . . An additional 128 aircraft had been damaged. . . . Worst of all, 2,403 personnel of the Army, Navy, Marine Corps, and civilians had been killed, were listed as missing, or died later of wounds, while those wounded but not killed totaled 1,178. (Prange 1986, xxxi–xxxii)

The overwhelming reaction to the events at Pearl Harbor was shock and anger—shock that the United States could be so unprepared for such an attack and anger at those responsible, principally Imperial Japan. The unity and resolve that Pearl Harbor instilled in the American people carried them through four years of bloody conflict across the globe. Shortly before the war ended, however, probing questions arose concerning who in the U.S. government was responsible for the obvious lapses that made Pearl Harbor possible, if not likely. Before we turn to these issues, a brief overview of the antecedents to the attack on Pearl Harbor is essential (see the Chronology).

Pearl Harbor—The Controversy

As early as 1944, with World War II nearly over, isolationists and Republicans in Congress and elsewhere began to question openly the origins of American involvement in the war. Roosevelt himself was mistrusted by many Americans who took his affable, confident demeanor to be a mask for an otherwise unscrupulous character. Roosevelt's desire to enter the war in support of Britain was well known, and his critics surmised that he had twisted and perhaps even precipitated events in such a way that the American people would ultimately come around to his side. To the cynic, Pearl Harbor was not only avoidable, but also contrived.

During the 1940 election campaign, Roosevelt promised to keep the country out of the war then raging in Europe and Asia. At the same time, he confided to his close advisors that he wished to quickly bring the American people around to supporting his quasi-alliance with Britain after the election. In October 1940, he told Admiral James Richardson, commander of the Pacific Fleet (before being replaced by Admiral Husband Kimmel in January 1941), that he expected war to start with a Japanese "error" (Theobald 1954, 192). According to Bailey:

> Franklin Roosevelt repeatedly deceived the American people during the period before Pearl Harbor. . . He was like the physician who must tell the patient lies for the patient's own good. . . . The country was overwhelmingly non-interventionist to the very day of Pearl Harbor, and an overt attempt to lead the people into war would have resulted in certain failure and an almost certain ousting of Roosevelt in 1940, with a consequent defeat of his ultimate aims. (Bailey 1948, 11–13, in Chamberlin 1965, 3)

Roosevelt quickly abandoned his campaign promises after his third electoral victory. Even before his inauguration, Roosevelt responded to British pleas for military aid by pushing through Congress the lend-lease program, waiving the provisions of the Neutrality Act. Roosevelt secured congressional support in part by promising that the United States would not be pulled into war, although at the same time his closest advisor Harry Hopkins was secretly assuring Churchill that the country would stick with him come what may (Chamberlin 1965, 5). Roosevelt implemented lend-lease with enthusiasm—not only allowing the provision of weapons on credit, but also protecting the delivery convoys to Britain with warships. This policy led to attacks on U.S. vessels in the Atlantic in the fall and Roosevelt's order to retaliate and ultimately to shoot "enemy" ships on sight in October. As early as May, Roosevelt exaggerated the German threat, warning that the U.S. coasts were vulnerable to invasion in an effort to heighten public fears. The Atlantic Charter, signed in August, so fully committed the United States to cooperate with Britain that it amounted to an alliance.

Some have interpreted Roosevelt's actions as deliberately provocative to the Japanese, to the point of recklessness. The negotiations with Japan during 1941 involved little of the give-and-take typically associated with diplomacy. Japan, on its side, sought U.S. approval (or at least tolerance) of its conquest and annexation of much of China, with the possibility of U.S. support for a complete occupation of the country. For its part, the United States wanted to see Japan's exit from China (and later Indochina) as well as its abrogation of the Tripartite Pact—an alliance signed with Germany and Italy in September 1940. The United States also sought assurances that Japan would no longer threaten the Philippines, a U.S. stronghold, and British and Dutch colonies in the South Pacific and Southeast Asia (these included Burma, Singapore, Malaya, Indonesia, Papua New Guinea, and Australia). Virtually every Japanese and U.S. proposal focused on these mutually exclusive demands.

What made American policy threatening, according to Roosevelt's critics, was the economic embargo on Japan, imposed gradually beginning with the refusal to renew a rather bland trade agreement in 1939 and culminating in the much more damaging July 26, 1941, sanctions that cut off vital oil exports (Theobald 1954, 193). These actions, according to revisionist critics, forced the Japanese to take the offensive in Asia in search of alternative sources of fuel and raw materials.

As the negotiations dragged on through 1941, the Japanese repeatedly urged American negotiators to open trade again, offering various, if minor, concessions on China. During the fall, Japanese Ambassador Admiral Kichisaburo Nomura and special envoy Saburo Kurusu, following a number of unsuccessful talks, proposed a summit meeting between Roosevelt and Japanese Premier Prince Fumimaro Konoye. The preconditions imposed by the United States were unacceptable to Japan, however, and the meeting never took place. Revisionist historian Charles Beard asked: "Did the Japanese proposal offer an opportunity to effect a settlement in the Pacific and were the decisions [U.S. officials] made in relation to it actually 'looking' in the direction of peace?" (Beard 1965, 51). Both diplomatic intercepts and the Ambassador to Japan Joseph Grew indicated that the Japanese were sincere and should be heeded. Grew advocated "constructive conciliation" and warned that failure to work with the Konoye government might lead to its downfall (Rauch 1965, 58).

The talks stalemated in spite of repeated attempts by the Japanese to keep them going. Even after the Konoye administration was replaced by the militaristic government of General Hideki Tojo, Tokyo put forward at least two more proposals for a temporary arrangement that would secure U.S. recognition of Japan's position in China and a removal of the economic sanctions in exchange for assurances of no further Japanese conquests or attacks in the Pacific. Secretary of State Cordell Hull dismissed these proposals perfunctorily and in his final message of November 26, largely perceived as an ultimatum shrouded in veiled threats, left only the weakest hint of further concessions (Trefousse 1982, 35).

Not only did this diplomatic intransigence indicate a willingness (if not eagerness) to go to war over China and Southeast Asia, but the military deployments of 1941 seem to have been calculated to invite a surprise attack—the sort of attack Roosevelt had already indicated would be necessary to turn the American people around. In late 1940, Roosevelt ordered the Pacific Fleet to be docked in Pearl Harbor rather than in California to serve as a deterrent. Admiral Richardson opposed this plan on the grounds that it would leave the fleet too exposed, and he lost his job for his protests. Admiral Kimmel was more willing to support this forward basing despite the increased vulnerability it involved, and he was given the command. Then, in the spring of 1941, Roosevelt ordered a sizable portion of the Pacific Fleet reassigned to duty in the Atlantic to fight German submarines. This decision left the outpost even less defended than before. These moves could have only one purpose, according to Theobald: "The retention of the Fleet in Hawaii, especially after its reduction in strength in March 1941, could serve only one purpose, an invitation to a surprise Japanese attack" (Theobald 1954, 195).

In the days preceding the attack on Pearl Harbor, Washington officials failed to convey to officers in the field all they knew about the seriousness of diplomatic tensions with Japan. This lapse, though excused by Roosevelt's supporters, is consistent with the reckless policy of a war-bent Roosevelt. Intelligence reports indicating that November 30 was the deadline for diplomatic settlement set by Japan were not clearly conveyed to Hawaiian commanders, nor were the signs of December 3–7 showing that the Japanese were in the final stages of breaking diplomatic relations and declaring war. Instead, the news was either kept in Washington or transmitted through the slowest of means, almost as if to ensure that the island would be unprepared for an attack (Theobald 1954, 197). Some have even hinted that Roosevelt knew the silent fleet was en route to Pearl before the fact (Coox 1990, 121).

In fact, the conspiracy theory seems to assume that Roosevelt had far more information and control over events than is logically conceivable. As pointed out by Morison:

> Even if one can believe that the late President of the United States was capable of so horrible a gambit, a little reflection would indicate that he could not possibly have carried it off. He would have needed the connivance of Secretaries Hull, [Republicans] Stimson and Knox, Generals Marshall, Gerow, . . . Admiral Stark, and many of their subordinates, too—all loyal and honorable men who would never have lent themselves to such monstrous deception. (S. Morison 1965, 94)

Not only would such a conspiracy have required the involvement of even the lowly radar men in Oahu who mistook the Japanese invasion force for a group of B-17s returning from California, but it would have required all these individuals to knowingly put at risk the largest concentration of military power in the Pacific—hardly the sort of behavior possible from those who would be expected to fight the war in the ensuing months and years (Kahn 1991/92, 149). Unless one goes so far as to opine that Roosevelt wanted us not only to be in the war but to lose it as well. . .

Likewise, the point that the United States actually provoked a war with Japan through diplomatic confrontation is overblown. Although several diplomatic cables indicated a certain sincerity on the part of the Japanese negotiators, the overwhelming majority of their instructions were bellicose. As put by Feis:

> [L]eaving Konoye to go on with his talks with the United States, the Army and Navy threw themselves at once into the plans for action [in August 1941]. The Operations Section of the Army began to get ready to capture Malaya, Java, Borneo, the Bismark Archipelago, the Indies, and the Philippines; it was to be ready by the end of October. The Navy finished its war games. These included the surprise attack on Pearl Harbor and the American fleet there. At the end of the games the two general staffs conferred on the result and found it satisfactory. By the end of September these steps towards war—if diplomacy should fail—were well under way. . . If Konoye was ready and able—as Grew thought—to give Roosevelt trustworthy and satisfactory promises of a new sort, he does not tell of them in his "Memoirs." Nor has any other record available to me disclosed them. He was a prisoner, willing or unwilling, of the terms precisely prescribed in conferences over which he presided. . . . It is unlikely that he could have got around them or that he would have in some desperate act discarded them. The whole of his political career speaks to the contrary. (Feis 1965, 39–41)

Once the Japanese war plans were in place, the country made ridiculous demands on Washington, tantamount to U.S. surrender in the Pacific (Rauch 1965, 62). War, to the Japanese planners, was the expected outcome. It is no surprise, therefore, that talks were allowed to fail; even the negotiators themselves were kept in the dark about these war plans lest it diminish their appearance of sincerity (Levite 1987, 52). If there was a conspiracy for war, it could be found more easily in the Imperial Conference than in the Kitchen Cabinet.

To a certain extent, the Roosevelt and Truman administrations fueled the popularity of conspiracy theories of Pearl Harbor, in that the initial investigations so alarmed senior officials that they attempted to shift the blame to subordinates: "The administration created scapegoats who then attracted the attention of those who wished to discredit Roosevelt and his supporters" (Melosi 1977, 162). The eventual dismissal of Admiral Kimmel and Hawaiian sector army commander General Walter Short created deep resentment among those who felt they had been left in the dark. Successive investigations in Hawaii, the White House, and Congress did little to clear up the confusion.

Looking elsewhere for an explanation of the lapse that made Pearl Harbor possible, one can cite a large number of instances of organizational failure and poor judgment on the part of both senior and midlevel officials. Perhaps the most direct comment in this regard is made at the conclusion of Wohlstetter's major work on the subject:

> The fact of surprise at Pearl Harbor has never been persuasively explained by accusing the participants, individually or in groups, of conspiracy or negligence or stupidity. What these examples illustrate is rather the very human tendency to pay attention to the signals that support current expectations about enemy behavior. If no one is listening for signals of an attack against a highly improbable target, then it is very difficult for the signals to be heard. (Wohlstetter 1962, 392)

In 1941, particularly after the January warning of a potential attack on Pearl Harbor turned out to be a false alarm, American military planners were preparing for a possible surprise attack in the South Pacific. Roosevelt was well aware of Japanese tendencies for dramatic gestures and had made sure that American commanders in the Philippines and around Indochina were alerted to the possibility of attack. This was the logical place for a Japanese attack because a victory there would not only damage American capabilities but more than likely bring territorial gains as well. Military planners in Washington doubted the Japanese ability to cross the Pacific and attack Hawaii—something Secretary of War Stimson later acknowledged publicly (E. Morison 1965, 70). Based on the tendency to look to Asia rather than Hawaii, war warnings emphasized the former region. Even the last war warning delivered on November 27 by the navy mentioned only "the Philippines, Thai or Kra peninsula, or possibly Borneo" as likely targets of Japanese aggression (Trefousse 1982, 173). As put by Prange:

> The human inclination to believe what one wants to believe, to see what one wants to see, no doubt played a part in the Pearl Harbor drama. . . This lack of genuine, gut-level belief [in the threat of Japanese attack], as opposed to a cool, academic setting forth of theoretical possibilities, was the fundamental cause of the United States being caught flat-footed on December 7, 1941. All other sins of omission and commission were its sons and daughters. (Prange 1986, 525, 529)

Thus many signals pointing to Hawaii were either dismissed or ignored (we will say more about this later). More importantly, many critical developments were simply never conveyed to the commanders stationed at Pearl Harbor. In an angry article written after the war, Admiral Kimmel listed the bits of information that were in the hands of Washington planners and intelligence officials but were never transmitted to him: (1) details of intercepted diplomatic cables proving the deterioration of negotiations—especially Japan's rejection of Hull's ten-point note received on December 6 and 7; (2) information on Japan's strong efforts to secure detailed information on the facilities and ships at Pearl Harbor; and (3) specific deadlines announced by the Japanese, including the 1:00 p.m. Washington time deadline (7:00 a.m. Hawaii time) on December 7 when relations were severed. As he put it: "I cannot understand now—I have never understood—I may never understand—why I was deprived of the information available in the Navy Department in Washington on Saturday night and Sunday morning" (Kimmel 1965, 77). About the failure to transmit this information, Trefousse commented:

> Why this information was never forwarded to Pearl Harbor is a more serious question. If anybody should have known about Japanese interest in the anchorage of the Pacific Fleet, it was obviously Admiral Kimmel. Yet he neither received the messages nor any summary of them—a good example of the poor dissemination of intelligence information at the time. (Trefousse 1982, 47)

Washington planners were reluctant to communicate too much of the information drawn from the decoded signals so as to minimize security leaks. If the Japanese suspected their codes had been broken, they would have immediately changed them. Furthermore, because intelligence was gathered separately by the army and the navy, interservice rivalry led to some delays in sharing crucial information (Clausen 1992). In addition, some communications were given higher priority for decoding based on assumptions about Japanese behavior. Thus the flood of cables from Tokyo to the Japanese embassy was handled expeditiously, while the trickle of messages from the Hawaiian consulate was almost ignored, even though it was the channel through which the detailed schemas of the Pearl Harbor facilities were being transmitted (Levite 1987, 53). Finally, Washington commanders feared that sending too much information might devalue the importance of each item and lead to complacency. This was a special concern with war warnings, which were sent with some regularity from January to December 1941 (Trefousse 1982, 71).

The ability to transmit vital information was further hampered by an apparent lack of anxiety in some circles in the Washington bureaucracy, culminating in the absence of several key individuals—not to mention whole departments—over the weekend of December 6 and 7. Secretary Stimson was unavailable, and his Chief of Staff George Marshall was riding horses on Sunday morning in Washington (while it was still night-time in Hawaii). They were not available to respond vigorously to the 1:00 p.m. deadline. Admiral Harold Stark, chief of naval operations, did not take the warning very seriously. As a result, the only response to the direct threat was sent to Hawaii at 12:18 p.m., Washington time, and was not received until after the bombs had started falling (Trefousse 1982, 69).

On November 27, two crucial messages were transmitted to commanders in Hawaii. They were the army and the navy's war warnings, which called upon all American forces in the Pacific to go on extreme alert, as can be seen in the army's version:

> Negotiations with Japan appear to be terminated to all practical purposes with only the barest possibilities that the Japanese Government might come back and offer to continue. Japanese future action unpredictable but hostile action possible at any moment. If hostilities cannot, repeat cannot, be avoided the United States desires that Japan commit the first overt act. This policy should not, re-

peat not, be construed as restricting you to a course of action that might jeopardize your defense. Prior to hostile Japanese action you are directed to undertake such reconnaissance and other measures as you deem necessary but these measures should be carried out so as not, repeat not, to alarm civil population or disclose intent. (Trefousse 1982, 174)

Although the warning seems unambiguous in retrospect, General Short and Admiral Kimmel complained later that the messages were confusing. They seemed to indicate that alertness should be heightened, but it should be done almost secretly, so as not alarm the locals. This was clearly not possible if by defensive measures the Washington commanders envisioned deployment of the fleet in the high seas. As a consequence, Kimmel and Short did little to change their ordinary routine over the next week. General Leonard Gerow, who received Short's rather bland response to the warning, failed to understand that he had not grasped the seriousness of the situation, and so the matter was dropped (E. Morison 1965, 70).

The importance of this failure of leadership and judgment is debatable. At no time did Washington officials have any hard evidence that Japan intended to attack Pearl Harbor on December 7 (Levite 1987, 71). Prange explained the Japanese preparations:

We have seen how meticulously the Japanese perfected their planning; how diligently they trained their pilots and bombardiers; how they modified weapons to achieve maximum damage; how persistently they dredged up and utilized information about the U.S. Pacific Fleet. They balked at no hazard, ready to risk a wild leap to achieve their immediate ends. (Prange 1981, 736)

A useful analogy might be that a homeowner would take seriously a rumor of burglars in the neighborhood but dismiss reports of terrorists driving tanks!

A point rarely made about war preparedness at Pearl Harbor is that the fleet may have been in even greater danger had it been alerted and deployed. After all, within ten minutes of the attack, all the navy's shipboard antiaircraft guns were manned and firing, but with little effect (Clausen 1992, 9). Had the fleet been at sea, it still would have been outgunned and even more vulnerable to attack. Pearl Harbor provided the benefit of a shallow berth. Though not eliminating the risk of aerial torpedo attack, as the local commanders learned with chagrin, it did allow salvage of almost all the ships that were hit and even sunk, not to mention the rescue of the crews (Wallin 1968, 283). The most serious lapse was in the air force, which left its planes wingtip to wingtip at every airfield on the island. Had planes been airborne (in itself a departure from procedure), the Japanese planes might have been sighted and engaged sooner. At any rate, given the overwhelming military might brought to bear on the area by a committed Japanese force, Pearl Harbor was destined to be a bloodbath, warning or no.

The classic question remains: How much did Washington know and when did it know it? This query refers to the intelligence capabilities of the U.S. government in 1941. Resources that are common today, such as spy satellites, electronic eavesdropping devices, night-vision goggles, and aerial reconnaissance, were either not available or of limited utility due to the primitive nature of the devices. Aerial reconnaissance, though used during World War II, was of little value to a remote outpost such as Pearl Harbor, given the range and altitude capabilities of existing aircraft. Even radar, which was available, was a novelty that even its operators did not understand. Given these technological constraints, the means available for gathering intelligence on the Japanese consisted of only (1) public sources (newspapers, tourists), (2) diplomatic communications (ambassadors' analyses), (3) espionage (human intelligence), and (4) signals intelligence (intercepting coded radio messages).

By 1940, public sources of information from Japan were severely limited due to heavy censorship imposed by the government. Although reporters generally had a good idea of what was going on, they could not print it. What was worse, at the turn of the decade many of the most seasoned analysts were reassigned and replaced with far more inexperienced staff (Levite 1987, 46). With the economic sanctions imposed in July 1941, the many American traders, seamen, and investors who had previously kept in touch with Japan turned their attention elsewhere and were no longer available as a public intelligence source.

Ambassador Joseph Grew exerted considerable energies not only to acquire information on the Japanese government's intentions, but also to convey his impressions and analysis to the secretary of state. He was the one who predicted the collapse of the Konoye administration and shared the Pearl Harbor attack rumor nearly a year before its occurrence. Unfortunately, because of his tendency to speculate without hard evidence, the Washington team discounted his opinions in favor of what they saw as the most important "hard intelligence": signals intercepts. That the government did not rely on espionage, as would be expected, is explained this way:

> In sharp contrast to Great Britain, Germany, Japan, and the Soviet Union, which were investing, at the time, a lot of resources in espionage, the United States deliberately refrained from engaging in this type of intelligence activity due to moral, political, and budgetary considerations. (Levite 1987, 50)

The key element of U.S. intelligence on Japan came through the extensive message decoding operation known as MAGIC. Through it the army, under the direction of the Signals Intelligence Section (SIS), was able to intercept and translate almost all Japanese diplomatic cables to the United States and Hawaii from 1937 to 1941 (except for an eighteen-month period in 1939–1940 when a newly introduced code had to be broken). In fact, the U.S. decoding efficiency was so high that American diplomats and senior officials often had copies of the cables before the Japanese delegates themselves. Clearly, U.S. negotiators benefited greatly by knowing precisely how much latitude the Japanese delegates were permitted by their home office. Americans also could follow the changing tone of the messages to gauge the increasing likelihood of war (Kahn 1991/92, 143).

Important interceptions obtained via MAGIC included the following: the announcement that the Imperial Conference had approved a strategy of aggression in the South Pacific in July 1941; a conciliatory message wedged between numerous belligerent ones on November 15, 1941; a self-imposed Japanese deadline of November 22 (later extended to November 29) for a settlement with the United States following which "things are automatically going to happen"; instructions to embassies to destroy documents and codes on December 3; the fourteen-part message rejecting Cordell Hull's ten-point note on December 6–7; and the December 7 announcement that relations would be severed at 1:00 p.m., Washington time (Trefousse 1982, 48). In addition, military planners in Washington were vaguely aware of messages to Japanese spies in Hawaii, also intercepted and interpreted through MAGIC. A controversial message over Tokyo radio known as the "winds execute" signal was detected by army intelligence on December 4 but never conveyed to Hawaiian commanders. This signal was a coded announcement that relations with the United States were being severed.

Although some have complained that these diplomatic communications were not relayed quickly enough to the commanders in Hawaii, the truth is they did not provide a consistent and coherent picture of Japanese plans in and of themselves. According to Wohlstetter, this was because of the overabundance of "noise":

> In short, we failed to anticipate Pearl Harbor not for want of the relevant materials, but because of a plethora of irrelevant ones. Much of the appearance of wanton neglect that emerged in various investigations of the disaster resulted from the unconscious suppression of vast congeries of signs pointing in every direction except Pearl Harbor. (Wohlstetter 1962, 388)

Because the diplomatic corps was not privy to the details of war plans, even this exhaustive source was not adequate. For its part, navy intelligence was working on breaking the military codes. But due to lack of staff, most of whom were working in the Signal Corps (collecting communications) rather than cryptography, the navy was unable to crack the essential military codes and was forced to rely on mere traffic patterns to keep track of the Japanese fleet's deployment. By simply monitoring which ships were in radio communication at different times, it was possible to locate them with some precision. At various times, some ships went silent, but typically only when they were close to the mainland and captains could receive instructions by hand.

As of December 1941, the bulk of the Japanese fleet was detected moving south toward Indochina and Indonesia—with the exception of one large carrier group, which could not be located due to radio silence (Kahn 1991/92, 145). Intelligence analysts naturally assumed a repetition of the previous pattern and did not bother to alert Hawaii about this "lost fleet" (something that particularly annoyed Hawaiian commanders after the fact). In fact, the fleet was bound for Hawaii with lengthy and detailed orders that earlier had been hand-delivered in Japan. Thus the fleet was able to maintain radio silence in spite of their distance. This situation also made diplomatic intervention to stop the fleet impossible without revealing its location and thereby causing a major incident.

The last line of intelligence gathering—on site in Hawaii—also proved inadequate. Navy radar operators on Oahu spotted a large blip on their screens early on the morning of December 7 indicating a large group of aircraft some 135 miles offshore. They were puzzled and a bit suspicious of this signal and called in to their base for clarification, only to be told that the blip was probably a group of army B-17s coming from the coast and to "forget it." No one bothered to check with the army to confirm the planes' estimated time of arrival. The radar operators, having already worked a half-hour past quitting time, then shut off the machines and left (Trefousse 1982, 77).

To answer the question of how much the "U.S. government" knew is not the same as determining how much different individuals within the government were aware of. As we mentioned, intelligence details were shared grudgingly between the army and the navy, and the difficulty in processing the flood of signals forced the cryptography staff into a sort of intelligence triage, passing along only those messages they considered most vital. Many errors of judgment and cooperation were therefore made, although it is difficult to place blame on any one person.

Wohlstetter maintains that never before had the United States collected so much information on a potential belligerent, implying that the government did have the capacity, by pooling all of these facts and figures, to predict that an attack on Pearl Harbor on December 7 was likely (Wohlstetter 1962, 382). Kahn and Levite take exception to this conclusion by arguing that even if all the information had been centralized, the resulting picture would still have been ambiguous and confusing (Kahn 1991/92; Levite 1987). As put by Levite:

> The United States was indeed poorly equipped, organized, and deployed to collect information regarding Japan's intentions and capabilities in general, and their preparations for attack on Pearl Harbor in particular. In fact, the overall picture is one in which the United States not only lacked systematic coverage of the Japanese military, but its sources were actually drying up in the period immediately preceding the Pearl Harbor attack. . . It would seem that under the collection conditions prevailing prior to the Pearl Harbor attack, it would have taken an incredible stroke of luck for the United States to obtain concrete advance warning of Japan's intention to launch the attack. (Levite 1987, 60)

Conclusion: The Lessons of Pearl Harbor

Because one cannot assume that intelligence gathering will ever yield the "smoking gun" proving an adversary's intent, the lesson of Pearl Harbor is not primarily to increase intelligence gathering efforts. These will always be inadequate in some way. Instead, there are two principal lessons of Pearl Harbor. First, intelligence, once gathered, should be centralized, to allow analysts with a global perspective to assess the meaning of the material, and then disseminated as rapidly and widely throughout the government as security permits. Second, decision makers should think creatively about an adversary's possible tactics and strategies. Rather than assume a particular chain of events is inevitable, they should assume it is merely "likely" and consider other less probable scenarios.

Debate Topic

The story of Pearl Harbor pits two different questions related to intelligence against each other. Was the debacle mostly about poor intelligence-gathering techniques, or was it a matter of organization and information analysis? Those who favor the first position will be designated "pro."

PRO

Points that favor the "pro" position include the following: (1) Radar operators knew aircraft were incoming, but could not distinguish friend from foe. (2) Diplomats knew the Japanese were communicating hostile messages through their Washington office, but could not access the critical final page quickly enough to warn the President. (3) The United States did not have adequate early-warning tools in place, such as ships at sea or patrol aircraft, to see the Japanese attack force.

CON

Points favoring the "con" position include the following: (1) Radar operators failed to confirm the identity of the incoming aircraft because of poor communication—not because no one knew where the American planes were. (2) The diplomatic intelligence analysts failed to provide the military with everything they knew, so a complete picture of the threat was never assembled. (3) Anecdotal evidence of Japanese intentions, collected through various governmental and nongovernmental means (including a Dutch fishing vessel that spotted the armada), were not correctly interpreted or communicated to those responsible for policy.

Questions to Consider

1. To what extent has the U.S. government attempted to remedy the organization and attitudinal problems revealed by the Pearl Harbor disaster? Could such a disaster happen again?

2. Who or what is most to "blame" for Pearl Harbor? Roosevelt? Interservice rivalry? Tojo? Inept radar operators? Admiral Kimmel and General Short? Inadequate technology?

3. To what extent did the Pearl Harbor experience influence American military strategy in the postwar era? How has it affected nuclear strategy, for example?

Websites

Pearl Harbor on The History Place: **www.historyplace.com/worldwar2/timeline/pearl.htm**
Let's Find Out site: **www.letsfindout.com/subjects/america/pearl.com**
Roosevelt's "day of infamy" address: **www.nara.gov/education/teaching/fdr/infamy.html**
Links page: **www.sperry-marine.com/pearl/pearlh.com**

References

Bailey, Thomas A. *The Man in the Street* (New York: Macmillan, 1948).
Beard, Charles A. "Appearance and Realities" in Waller, ed., *Pearl Harbor*, 48–56.
Chamberlin, William Henry, "Roosevelt Maneuvers America into War" in Waller, ed., *Pearl Harbor*, 1–13.
Clausen, Henry, with Bruce Lee. *Pearl Harbor: Final Judgement* (New York: Crown Publishers, 1992).
Coox, Alvin D. "Repulsing the Pearl Harbor Revisionists: The State of Present Literature on the Debacle" in Hilary Conroy and Harry Way, eds., *Pearl Harbor Reexamined: Prologue to the Pacific War* (Honolulu: University of Hawaii Press, 1990), 119–126.
Feis, Herbert. "The Road to Pearl Harbor" in Waller, ed., *Pearl Harbor*, 31–47.
Kahn, David. "The Intelligence Failure of Pearl Harbor." *Foreign Affairs* 70 #5 (Winter 1991/92): 138–152.
Kimmel, Husband. "Admiral Kimmel's Story" in Waller, ed., *Pearl Harbor*, 72–79.
Levite, Ariel. *Intelligence and Strategic Surprises* (New York: Columbia University Press, 1987).
Melosi, Martin V. *The Shadow of Pearl Harbor: Political Controversy over the Surprise Attack, 1941–1946* (College Station: Texas A&M University Press, 1977).
Morison, Elting E. "An Unanswerable Question" in Waller, ed., *Pearl Harbor*, 68–72.
Morison, Samuel E. "Who Was Responsible?" in Waller, ed., *Pearl Harbor*, 94–98.
Prange, Gordon W. *At Dawn We Slept: The Untold Story of Pearl Harbor* (New York: McGraw-Hill, 1981).
Prange, Gordon W., with Donald M. Goldstein and Katherine V. Dillon. *Pearl Harbor: The Verdict of History* (New York: McGraw-Hill, 1986).
Rauch, Basil. "Principle in International Policy" in Waller, ed., *Pearl Harbor*, 57–68.
Theobald, Robert A. *The Final Secret of Pearl Harbor: The Washington Contribution to the Japanese Attack* (New York: Devin-Adair, 1954).
Trefousse, Hans. *Pearl Harbor: The Continuing Controversy* (Malabar, FL: Krieger Pub, 1982).
Waller, George, ed. *Pearl Harbor: Roosevelt and the Coming of the War* (New York: D. C. Heath, 1965).
Wallin, Homer Norman. *Pearl Harbor: Why, How, Fleet Salvage, and Final Appraisal* (Washington, DC: Naval History Division, 1968).
Wohlstetter, Roberta. *Pearl Harbor: Warning and Decision* (Stanford, CA: Stanford University Press, 1962).

3

Sino–Soviet– American Relations

THE BALANCE OF POWER

Introduction

As major powers seek security in international affairs, they have several options: increase their military capability beyond the level of any potential adversaries, declare neutrality, or align with other countries to combine their military strengths. The last option is the essence of the balance of power: As nations seek security by forming alliances, the international system will be composed of coalitions that balance one another. This is not to say that every state will remain in a given coalition, but that overall the arrangement of alliances will tend toward a stalemate. Advocates of the balance of power emphasize that this arrangement is both inevitable and beneficial because it prevents any one state from conquering the world. Opponents point out that the balance of power has failed to prevent world wars in the past and that it is based on the amoral principle that "might makes right."

In the past, the story of world affairs has often been told as the story of great power alliances. European history, in particular, consists largely of a string of strategic and tactical agreements between monarchs and emperors, cemented through treaty, marriage, territorial transfers, and so forth. Rarely did any question of whether a particular alliance was "moral" or "right" arise— just whether it was advantageous or prudent. The result has been a string of strange pairings between democracies and dictatorships, kingdoms and republics.

This situation began to change at the beginning of the twentieth century, when ideology began to emerge as an important defining trait of states. With the entry of the United States into World War I, President Woodrow Wilson could claim (however speciously) that the struggle pitted freedom against oppression (he conveniently ignored the fact that Great Britain, France, and the United States were on the same side as the despotic Tsarist

Russia). Since then, it has become increasingly important for alliances to have a greater purpose than to merely offset the power of a threatening state. Rather, they must also advance some overarching cause, such as democracy, socialism, or divine destiny. Pragmatic realists seem to be on the defensive in their advocacy of alliances of convenience.

Throughout the Cold War, the three major powers—the United States, the Soviet Union, and the People's Republic of China (PRC)—were often torn by the desire to make alliances meaningful while at the same time behaving pragmatically to defend against would-be enemies. The result has been a series of often surprising alignments.

SINO–SOVIET–AMERICAN RELATIONS
KEY FIGURES

Josef Stalin   Soviet Communist Party leader, 1928–1953. He introduced collectivization and industrialization policies in tune with his view of socialism. Stalin allied with Nazi Germany at the beginning of World War II, then with the Allies after Hitler's attack on Russia in 1942. After the war, his actions in Eastern Europe and elsewhere contributed to the emergence of the Cold War.

Mao Zedong   Leader of the Chinese Communist Party and the Chinese Revolution in 1949. He led China from 1949 to 1976, taking it through various phases of development and crisis.

Harry Truman   U.S. President, 1945–1953. He presided over the outbreak of the Cold War. His "Truman Doctrine," defending pro-U.S. and democratic regimes with force, shaped U.S. policy toward the Soviet Union and China for many years.

Nikita Khrushchev   Leader of the Soviet Communist Party, 1953–1964. He undertook a number of economic and political reforms that liberalized life in Russia to some extent while also challenging the West.

John F. Kennedy   US President, 1961–1963. He dealt with repeated Soviet challenges to U.S. power in Cuba, Berlin, Vietnam, and elsewhere. He helped inaugurate détente after the Cuban Missile Crisis.

Richard Nixon   U.S. President, 1969–1974. Although an ardent anti-Communist as a member of the House of Representatives and Vice President, he adopted a pragmatic, strategic approach while in office. He is credited with consolidating détente and establishing relations with China.

Leonid Brezhnev   Soviet Communist Party leader,1964–1982. He enjoyed a businesslike relationship with Richard Nixon, although the USSR's relations with China soured during his rule.

Mikhail Gorbachev   Soviet Premier, 1985–1991. He undertook radical political and economic reforms that resulted in the introduction of a pro-Western democratic government in Moscow, democratization of Eastern Europe, the end of the Cold War, and the collapse of the Soviet Union.

Deng Hsiao Ping   Leader of the PRC beginning in 1976 with the death of Mao. While maintaining strong Communist Party control over China, he introduced market reforms that helped accelerate the country's development and opening to the rest of the world.

Jimmy Carter   U.S. President, 1977–1981. He formally recognized the PRC as the only government of China and signed the SALT II arms control treaty with the USSR. The Soviet invasion of Afghanistan in 1979 prompted him to impose sanctions on Russia and increase U.S. military spending.

(continued)

Henry Kissinger   Senior U.S. foreign policy maker under Presidents Nixon and Gerald Ford, serving as National Security Adviser and Secretary of State. His realist approach to international affairs guided a pragmatic, unsentimental U.S. foreign policy that improved relations with both the Soviet Union and China.

Ronald Reagan   U.S. President, 1981–1989. A well-known anti-Communist, Reagan imbued his first term with anti-Russian and anti-Chinese rhetoric, expanded the military, and eschewed arms control. During his second term, he presided over a more conciliatory approach that contributed to major arms control agreements with Moscow, the collapse of the Berlin Wall, and the end of the Cold War.

SINO–SOVIET–AMERICAN RELATIONS
CHRONOLOGY

1945
At the close of the Second World War, Russia, the United States and China are victorious allies.

1945–1947
The Soviet Union conspires with local Communist Eastern Europe to install sympathetic regimes across the region.

1947
In response to threats from Communist rebels against pro-U.S. forces in Greece and Turkey, Harry Truman announces his plans to provide direct military and economic assistance. This new policy is dubbed the "Truman Doctrine."

1948
West Berlin is cut off from the rest of Germany by a road and rail blockade. Over 18 months, the United States supplies the city by air.

1949
The Soviet Union successfully tests an atomic bomb. Mao Zedong's People's Liberation Army takes power in Beijing as the Nationalist government begins its exile in Taiwan. NATO is formed. The Warsaw Pact is formed shortly thereafter.

1950
North Korea, with Soviet encouragement, invades South Korea in hopes of unifying the country under communism. China later joins the fight on the side of the North Koreans.

1953
The Korean War armistice ends the fighting without resolving the conflict.

1954
The PRC shells the Taiwanese islands of Quemoy and Matsu. The United States threatens nuclear retaliation. The incident is repeated in 1958.

1956
Soviet military forces invade Budapest and replace the West-leaning government of Hungary.

1959
Sputnik, the first human-made satellite, is launched by the Russians, prompting a decades-long "space race."

1961
The East German government erects a concrete wall around West Berlin to prevent East Germans from emigrating.

(continued)

1962

Cuba allows the deployment of Russian nuclear weapons, prompting a U.S. blockade of the island. The weapons are withdrawn after tensions come close to the breaking point. Mao Zedong repudiates the Soviet version of socialism.

1963

A U.S.–Soviet "hotline" is installed to prevent lapses in communication during a crisis.

1964

The Tonkin Gulf Resolution inaugurates a period of significant U.S. military involvement in Southeast Asia. China tests an atomic bomb.

1968

The USSR deploys troops to Prague to suppress reformist movements in Czechoslovakia.

1968–1969

China and Russia engage in sporadic border clashes.

1969

SALT I is signed by the United States and Soviet Union, signaling the beginning of détente.

1971

Nixon visits China.

1979

The United States and Soviet Union sign SALT II. The United States formally recognizes the PRC. The Soviet Union invades Afghanistan.

1981

Ronald Reagan assumes office. He refers to the Soviet Union as an "evil empire" and begins a dramatic increase in military spending.

1983

Reagan unveils the military's Strategic Defense Initiative, dubbed "Star Wars" by the press.

1985

Mikhail Gorbachev becomes Chairman of the Communist Party of the Soviet Union and almost immediately begins a series of economic and political reforms at home and in Eastern Europe. Russia announces a unilateral moratorium on nuclear testing.

1987

The United States and Russia sign the Intermediate-Range Nuclear Forces Treaty, the first nuclear arms reduction treaty.

1989

Gorbachev signals to Eastern European governments that political reforms are acceptable. In rapid succession, following the dismantling of the Berlin Wall in November, each socialist government in Eastern Europe falls amid protests and street demonstrations. The Warsaw Pact is dissolved.

1990

A coup attempt in Moscow is thwarted by Russian President Boris Yeltsin, and Mikhail Gorbachev is reinstalled as his ally. They negotiate the dismantling of the Soviet Union into its fifteen republics. The Soviet flag is lowered on December 25, 1990.

1991

The United States and Soviet Union are allies in the Persian Gulf War.

2002

Russia joins NATO as a junior member.

The Superpower "Triangle" and Alignments

John Stoessinger opined:

> Machiavelli would have taken considerable pleasure in the dynamics of Sino–Soviet–American triangular relations in our time. During the 1950s, China and the Soviet Union were allies, and the United States feared the menace of a monolithic Sino–Soviet threat. In the 1960s, after the Cuban missile crisis had ushered in a détente between the Soviet Union and the United States, China began to fear the specter of Soviet–American collusion. And in the 1970s, the Soviet leaders began to worry that the Chinese and Americans might be getting along too well. Each of the three powers has had its turn at being frozen out by the other two. (Stoessinger 1990, 257)

The tenuousness of superpower relations is symptomatic of the balance of power. To understand changes in relations among these countries, it is not enough to know the ins and outs of diplomatic language, protocol, and individual personalities. It is also not enough to understand the cultural heritage, historical habits, and ever-changing perceptions of world leaders. Instead, one should focus on how each nation has tried to increase its security by adjusting its relations with a pair of enemies. This adjustment is the essence of the balance of power.

Little naturally links the United States, the Soviet Union, and the People's Republic of China (PRC). In fact, it was not until the twentieth century that meaningful contacts developed among the three nations, at a time when each was already a major global power. The historical circumstances that have forced these three nations to take on the burden of world leadership seem to have been largely beyond their control. Because of this fact, the response of the countries' leaders to these political choices can be more clearly attributed to strategic concerns than to habit, tradition, or heritage.

Each of the three nations has viewed itself as a model for the rest of the world. China's sense of cultural superiority was boundless until the twentieth century, when Western barbarians began to exact humiliating concessions for trade. The Russian empire has consistently viewed itself as a model of efficiency and sophistication, although its views of the West have been generally sympathetic. The United States, with its feelings of "Manifest Destiny," has long considered its role as a model of democracy and scientific progress to be unquestioned. The Communist revolutions in Russia and China had the effect of accentuating ideological differences and feelings of uniqueness and superiority.

At the turn of the century, the United States attempted to mediate a dispute between Western powers intent on trading with China and anti-Western Boxers with its "Open Door" policy, but in the end it sided with the Westerners (Stoessinger 1990, 25). The United States refused to accept the outcome of the October 1917 Bolshevik Revolution and joined an international force to overthrow the new Russian regime in 1919. The Chinese were largely uninterested in Russia, although the Great Wall provided little insurance that the influence of the northern barbarians could be contained for long.

By the 1930s, however, relations among the three nations had grown generally warm. The Soviets provided support for both the Nationalist government in Beijing and the Communist Party forces under Mao Zedong. In 1933, after the Soviet Union had demonstrated political and economic resilience through the Great Depression and America had not, the United States was more favorably disposed toward working with the socialist behemoth on equal terms. Their budding friendship was temporarily strained by Stalin's decision to sign a nonaggression pact with Hitler in 1939. Americans actively supported the beleaguered Chinese National government in its failed efforts to prevent conquest of Manchuria (northern China). When Hitler invaded Russia in 1941 and Japan attacked Pearl Harbor a few months later, the three superpowers-to-be suddenly and quite unexpectedly found themselves on the same winning side in World War II.

The story of how these three World War II allies evolved into a nuclear triangle is the great diplomatic saga of our time.

Major Incidents

Outbreak of the Cold War and U.S.–PRC Tensions

On March 12, 1947, President Harry Truman addressed a joint session of Congress and requested $400 million to support regimes in Greece and Turkey against Soviet-backed insurrections. Without explicitly naming the Soviet Union, Truman declared:

> It would be an unspeakable tragedy if these countries, which have struggled so long against overwhelming odds, should lose the victory for which they sacrificed so much. Collapse of free institutions and loss of independence would be disastrous not only for them but for the world. Discouragement and possibly failure would quickly be the lot of neighboring peoples striving to maintain their freedom and independence. (McCormick 1986, 59)

With that statement, all pretense of cordial postwar relations with the Soviet Union was dropped and the Cold War began in earnest. The 1945–1947 period had witnessed the "gradual disengagement" of the Soviet Union from its Cold War alliance with the United States (Ulam 1971, 102). Fueled by a persistent fear of invasion from Europe, Soviet leaders acted to consolidate control over the Eastern European territories liberated by the Red Army in the closing months of World War II. The response from the West was slow; the Truman administration held out a great deal of hope for the United Nations to act as a vehicle for restoring postwar order.

Soviet attitudes toward the United Nations were disturbing. The "Baruch Plan" to bring all nuclear weapons under international control was rejected by the Soviets in 1946, as were countless resolutions in the Security Council, where the Soviet veto prevented action. Americans deeply resented this frustration of a great cause and began to question Soviet commitment to peaceful coexistence. The fact that Stalin was carrying out an extraordinarily intense reindustrialization program at the time did little to comfort the West.

Soviet forces and pro-Soviet leaders in East Germany became alarmed during 1948 at the collapse of the East German mark specifically and the vulnerability of the economy generally. In response, Soviet forces were dispatched to seal off West Berlin from Western products and prevent emigration by rail or road. The United States then embarked on an eighteen-month airlift that supplied so much food and other materials that prices for the goods fell below East Berlin levels. The worst fears of Soviet intentions were confirmed, and events demonstrated the importance of American leadership, technology, and boldness. The Soviet decision not to shoot down the aircraft also illustrated the limits to Soviet power and belligerence.

At that time, U.S. policy was heavily influenced by the thoughts of George Kennan, a senior expert on Russia, who coined the word *containment*. Kennan's call for diplomatic maneuvering to undermine the Soviet bloc suggested ways to pull apart the East European coalition through selective pressure, enticements, and determined resoluteness. He added the recommendation to act quickly to shore up collapsing pro-U.S. governments in Western Europe by providing massive economic aid and a strong military presence. In 1948, the Marshall Plan aid from the United States, which amounted to some $12 billion over five years, became available to West European. In 1949, the United States helped to form the North Atlantic Treaty Organization, (NATO) a military alliance aimed at preventing further Soviet expansion in Europe. NATO members moved quickly to restore German sovereignty and military might, and thousands of American soldiers were deployed to Germany. The Soviets responded by organizing the Warsaw Pact and maintaining a large military force in the East European theater.

In September 1949, the Soviet Union detonated its first atomic weapon, thereby ending the U.S. nuclear monopoly. The effect of this event was primarily psychological, in that the Soviets then lacked the means to deliver the weapon to a target. It was at this time that the U.S.–Soviet nuclear arms race began, however.

The Chinese Revolution in 1949 represented the culmination of a fifteen-year Communist insurrection that had weathered assassinations, mass arrests, a "Long March" to regroup forces, and Japanese invasion. Mao Zedong received Soviet support, although he had sought American backing, and almost immediately turned to the Soviet Union once victory was achieved. The Soviets responded by providing large numbers of military, economic, and industrial advisors, whose aim was the establishment of a large-scale industrial plant in China and the inclusion of the Chinese Communist Party in the Soviet-dominated Comintern—the umbrella organization of all Communist parties worldwide. Mao was quick to embrace Soviet support and formed what appeared to be a united front against imperialist capitalism. For its part, the United States denounced the Cultural Revolution and preserved formal diplomatic ties with the exiled Nationalist government, now based on the island of Taiwan.

The formation of what appeared to be a united Communist bloc covering the entire Eurasian continent from Warsaw to Beijing gave a special urgency to the U.S. containment strategy. The document designated NSC-68 took the original ideas of Kennan and tilted them toward a blatantly military strategy of direct confrontation (Gaddis and Diebel 1987, 6). The result was a readiness on the part of the United States to respond to Soviet "mischief" with proportional force. This primarily reactive policy prompted U.S. interventions in Korea, Vietnam, and Cuba over the next fifteen years.

The jury is still out on the question of who started the Cold War. Soviet behavior in Eastern Europe can easily be interpreted as aggressive, especially when combined with Soviet support for the Western European Communist parties that came close to taking power in the late 1940s. Given Soviet apprehensions about the vulnerability of the USSR's western borders, however, the policies are easy to explain and even justify. From the Soviet perspective, U.S. attempts to shape the world through the United Nations, the Marshall Plan, and the rearming of Germany seemed no less threatening. After all, the United States had delayed its entry into the European theater by two years in World War II (Soviets expected an American landing by 1942), it had detonated an atomic weapon and in the process cut the Soviets out of the peace process in the Far East, and it had participated in an invasion of the Soviet Union in an attempt to reverse the Bolshevik Revolution.

Much as in a family feud, the question of who started the conflict may be immaterial once the fight is on. We can, however, gain some interesting insights into the nature of the balance of power. One can easily argue that when two powers exist on the world stage without rival, they will tend to fear each other and therefore each will protect itself against the other (Waltz 1979). Once this process has begun, it is nearly impossible to distinguish "prudent preparations for potential conflict" on the one hand, from "openly hostile actions" on the other. One cannot tell by looking at it whether a nuclear missile is "offensive" or "defensive" after all.

Cold War I: 1949–1962

With the stage set for an enduring three-way conflict among the United States, the Soviet Union, and China, all three nations were preparing for a possible outbreak of hostilities. On June 25, 1950, equipped with Soviet-made weapons and supported politically by China, North Korean forces crossed the postwar dividing line of the 38th parallel to invade and ultimately annex the U.S. ally South Korea. The United States called for multilateral action against the North Koreans, which was organized in the United Nations (the Soviet delegation was boycotting the Security Council to protest the continued occupation of the China seat by the Taiwanese Nationalists and so was not able to veto the proposal). American ships were already on their way and within days began pushing back North Korean forces, which had taken control of roughly seven-eighths of the total South Korean territory. General Douglas MacArthur led the counteroffensive and, with the dramatic invasion at Inchon behind the front lines, succeeded in pushing back the invaders to the original frontier by late September. After

MacArthur's demand for surrender went unheeded, the General Assembly authorized the invasion of North Korea by UN forces.

With the tables turned, the North Korean forces quickly fell back until the UN armies threatened to enter China, Korea's neighbor. Despite Chinese threats not to approach the border, UN forces came within miles of China and prompted the People's Liberation Army to enter the fray. Chinese intervention in the Korean War raised the very real possibility of full-scale world war in late 1950. MacArthur was sacked by President Truman precisely because he had ignored Truman's warnings to avoid accidental escalation. The front moved back into South Korean territory and eventually stabilized near the 38th parallel. Peace talks dragged on as both sides hoped for a military breakthrough. An armistice was eventually signed on July 27, 1953, after some 450,000 casualties on the South Korean side, of which 150,000 were Americans, and an estimated 2 million casualties on the North Korean/Chinese side (Chai 1972, 86).

In the beginning of the Korean War, U.S. ships were maneuvered into the Formosa Straits between mainland China and Taiwan to discourage would-be aggression by the PRC against the Nationalist government on the island. Throughout the 1950s and 1960s, both governments remained adamant in their claims that the other side had no right to govern any part of China. The United States repeatedly acted to prevent aggression, but by so doing precipitated bellicose responses from Beijing. The U.S.–Taiwan Mutual Defense Assistance Agreement of 1951 confirmed China's fears that the United States sought domination of the entire Asian continent from this foothold (Camilleri 1980, 32). With the formation of the South-East Asian Treaty Organization (SEATO), which encircled China, Beijing had sufficient evidence to seek a preemptive strike to reassert its control over the region.

China began shelling some of the Taiwanese fortresses on the islands in the Formosa Straits in late 1954. In response, the United States demanded a cessation of hostilities, implicitly threatening U.S. intervention with atomic weapons. This U.S. policy of "brinkmanship" surfaced again in 1958 after Chinese shelling was renewed. The Chinese, meanwhile, were ambivalent. In 1956, China declared its interest in improved relations with the West in the context of the Third World Bandung Conference. The goal of disengaging the United States from the region had clearly failed, but concerns about precedents and appearances prevented a public capitulation on the issue. The result was simmering Sino–American hostility, which was exacerbated by the U.S. entry into the Vietnam War in the mid–1960s.

During the 1950s, the U.S.–Soviet Cold War was in full swing. Although the Eisenhower administration offered tentative olive branches (his "Open Skies" proposal would have permitted free access by each nation's reconnaissance aircraft to the other's airspace), confrontational rhetoric dominated the debate. John Foster Dulles, the U.S. secretary of state, strongly advocated a "perimeter containment" strategy, which led to the formation of numerous regional alliances (containment) in areas surrounding the Soviet Union. Minor skirmishes were to be treated as major tests of resolve. The enemy was seen as an insidious, pervasive, single-minded force bent on world domination. This perspective was codified in the 1957 "Eisenhower Doctrine" declaring U.S. support for any victim of "armed aggression from any country controlled by international Communism" (Spanier 1988, 101). We should note, however, that U.S. intervention stopped short of helping nations already within the Soviet sphere, such as Hungary in 1956, where an anti-Soviet uprising was quelled with tanks.

The Soviets, on their side, viewed any American efforts at self-defense as inherently provocative. The rearmament of Germany beginning in 1950, the establishment of anti-Soviet alliances, the dramatic Korean War–era U.S. military buildup, and the detonation of the hydrogen bomb in 1952 all seemed to convey the attitude that the United States was preparing to conquer the world. With the economic aid provided to Western Europe in the context of European integration and the isolation of the Soviet economy, Moscow had evidence that the United States also aimed to cripple the socialist world financially.

By 1960, Americans were close to panic following a chain of Soviet achievements: the Soviet detonation of a hydrogen bomb in 1953, the test of the first intercontinental ballistic missile in 1957, and the shocking success of the Sputnik satellite in 1957. Fidel Castro's successful revolution in Cuba in 1959 prompted the United States to intervene in what would be later called the "perfect failure"—the Bay of Pigs. A group of U.S.-backed Cuban exiles attempted an amphibious invasion to overthrow Castro's regime, only to be captured at great public embarrassment to the Kennedy administration (Higgins 1987). The downing of a U-2 reconnaissance aircraft in 1960 scuttled an important peace conference being planned at the time, and the Berlin Wall crisis of 1961 severely tested the mettle of newly elected President John F. Kennedy.

This is not to say that the entire period was a catastrophe. On the contrary, many felt that with the death of Joseph Stalin in 1953, his successor Nikita Khrushchev would bring a new warmth to U.S.–Soviet relations. A number of early summits and agreements confirmed this hope. Khrushchev became the first Soviet leader to visit the United States when he attended a summit there in 1959. Talks concerning the disposition of Germany continued throughout the decade, albeit with no resolution. American intervention to prevent the fall of Egypt's left-leaning Gamel Nasser during the 1956 war with Israel did much to convince Third World revolutionaries that the United States was capable of impartiality.

The culmination of these Cold War tensions was also the crucible for change. The Cuban Missile Crisis, which took place over a two-week period in October 1962, brought the two superpowers to the brink of full-scale nuclear confrontation (see Case 4). Kennedy estimated at the height of the crisis that the chances of all-out war were "between one out of three and even" (Allison 1999, 1). Ostensibly an attempt by the Soviet Union to offset the tremendous American advantage in nuclear weaponry, the deployment of Soviet medium-range nuclear missiles in Cuba was deemed provocative by the Kennedy administration, and their removal became the object of a tense confrontation. The Soviets demanded, after stonewalling for a week, U.S. assurance that Cuba would never again be attacked and that U.S. weapons deployed in Turkey would be dismantled. Kennedy placed a naval blockade around the island in an attempt to buy time and prevent completion of the missile project, only to find that by day 13 the missiles were apparently operational. An American reconnaissance aircraft was shot down over Cuba, and the United States prepared to implement plans for an all-out attack and invasion against Cuba. Only at the last moment did word come from Moscow, in the form of conflicting cables, that the Soviets would accept a settlement.

While the world breathed a sigh of relief, the immediacy of nuclear war led leaders on both sides of the Cold War to seek new arrangements and agreements to prevent a serious confrontation from happening again. From 1963 through 1979, the United States and the Soviets (later joined by the Chinese) entered a period of relative "détente" or relaxation of tensions. Although the Vietnam War interrupted this trend, the pattern is nonetheless visible (Stoessinger 1990, 207).

Détente I: 1963–1979

Almost as soon as the Cuban Missile Crisis was over, Kennedy and Khrushchev (soon to be replaced by Lyndon Johnson and Leonid Brezhnev) began to build bridges. The "hotline" was established in 1963 as a permanent communication link between the United States and the Soviet Union (although a Norwegian's plow once severed it!), and the problem of rapid communication in times of crisis was essentially solved. An above-ground nuclear Test Ban Treaty was also signed, ending the environmentally catastrophic practice of testing nuclear weapons in the atmosphere.

Perhaps the most significant development during this period, aside from the gradual rapprochement between East and West, was the severing of relations between erstwhile comrades in the Soviet Union and the PRC. Although the Sino–Soviet alliance had clearly been as much a marriage of convenience as an ideological alliance, the breakup largely resulted from differences in philosophy and priority. Mao's revolutionaries had long placed Third World liberation ahead of all other international objectives and did not hesitate to burn bridges with the United States in their efforts to liberate colonies and spread socialism. The Soviet Union, on the other hand, had learned that it was partly dependent on Western support and goodwill to succeed in the world and was inclined to favor warmer relations. This difference in attitude became more pronounced after the Cuban Missile Crisis, when China found itself allied with more and more radical regimes in the Third World as decolonization moved into full swing and as the Soviets mended fences with the West.

Another key factor in the rupture was China's resentment of the influence exerted on its political and economic life by a Soviet Union long intent on reproducing itself. Soviet economic advisors urged Chinese leaders to implement a full-scale industrialization program based on steel, machines, and other heavy industry. This plan collided with the largely agrarian context in which the Chinese Revolution had flourished. The Great Leap Forward, a program of intense modernization of the Chinese economy, was initiated as much to achieve economic objectives as to assert Chinese autonomy. Furthermore, Mao objected to the rather tentative Soviet reforms under Khrushchev, which introduced more market-oriented policies. Chinese leaders felt that the Soviets had essentially sold out the revolution and that China alone held the torch of true socialism.

In 1962, Mao declared that the leaders of the Soviet Union were now "revisionists"—a withering attack from an ideological perspective that aimed at undermining Soviet leadership of international communism. In 1963, China condemned the Test Ban Treaty, which pointedly left it out as a "non-nuclear power." In 1964, the country tested its first atomic weapon, as if to thumb its nose at what it saw as a U.S.–Soviet alliance forming against it (Yahuda 1982, 30). By the late 1960s, the Soviets and Chinese engaged in border skirmishes that threatened to escalate as the Soviets spoke of preemptive strikes against Chinese nuclear installations. Ultimately, it was the United States that intervened to defuse the conflict.

The Vietnam War created new tension in what by the mid-1960s was clearly a three-way relationship. American support for the South Vietnamese government deeply troubled China, although China's relations with the North Vietnamese were cool at best, stemming from Hanoi's rejection of Chinese claims on Vietnamese territory. The Soviet Union, having supported Ho Chi Minh and the North Vietnamese revolution, was forced to provide support for China again throughout the Vietnam War. China was thus in the enviable position of watching its two enemies fight it out with each other, all the while hoping the violence could be contained to a modest level. During this period of relative security, the Cultural Revolution was begun to purify China's society of Western influences, although the result was the elimination of many of the nation's most accomplished intellectuals. The events so disgusted Western observers that Chou En-Lai felt forced to render a weak explanation six years later on the occasion of Henry Kissinger's first visit to China (Kissinger 1979, 751).

The escalation of U.S. involvement in Vietnam from a handful of troops and advisors in 1964 to more than 500,000 personnel by 1969 was so gradual that it never, in and of itself, constituted a serious threat to global stability. It was not until the war began to wane, following Lyndon Johnson's decision in 1968 to begin troop withdrawals, that uncertainty entered the picture. Richard Nixon's attacks on Cambodia; the "Vietnamization" of the war, through which poorly motivated South Vietnamese soldiers were put in charge of the fighting; the popular unrest at home; and the on again–off again peace talks in Paris combined to give the closing years of the Vietnam War an unreal dimension that was separate from the "real" world of superpower diplomacy. An illustration of this was Beijing's crucial invitation to the United States to send a high-level representative in 1971. Henry

Kissinger went to Pakistan and secretly on to China (absent on the pretense of catching the flu!), where preparations were made for Nixon's historic trip. All of this activity took place against the backdrop of intensified American air attacks in North Vietnam and a secret invasion of Cambodia.

Nixon's visit to China came in late February 1972 and resulted in a rather ambiguously worded statement known as the Shanghai Communique. The statement pledged an effort toward normalization of relations and supported the notion of "One China," although it left unclear who should govern this entity—the PRC or Taiwan (Kissinger 1979, 1085). Nixon's visit to China was followed in May by the first-ever visit by an American president to Moscow, where the Strategic Arms Limitation Talks (SALT I) were accepted in principle. Each of these agreements came in spite of ongoing disputes between the superpowers over conflicts with China, India, and Pakistan; between North and South Vietnam (although the Paris Peace Accords ended U.S. involvement in the war in January 1973); between Israel and Arab nations (Anwar Sadat expelled Soviet advisors from Egypt in July 1972, five years after they had supported his country during the Six-Day War); and in Cambodia and elsewhere.

The period of détente was perhaps best known for the general warming of relations between all Western nations and the East. Willy Brandt, Chancellor of West Germany during the mid-1970s, established solid ties with the German Democratic Republic to the East. (See Case 1.) The Helsinki Accords were signed in 1975 and pledged all European nations, East and West, to safeguard human rights and civil liberties. The United States, under Jimmy Carter, continued these trends by strengthening the arms control agreements made under SALT I and extending full diplomatic recognition to the PRC, now under the leadership of Western-oriented Deng Hsiao Ping in 1979. In short, there seemed to be every reason to hope that the United States had established an era of understanding and cooperation.

Cold War II: 1979–1985

The year 1980 stands out as a critical turning point in the Cold War because it was in January of that year that the Soviet Union for the first time invaded a neutral country with its own troops. It would be another nine years before the troops were withdrawn, and during this period East–West relations slipped back into Cold War patterns.

Following the Afghanistan invasion, Jimmy Carter declared, "My opinion of the Russians has changed more drastically in the last week than in the previous two and a half years" (Stoessinger 1990, 232). Soviet motives for the invasion remain difficult to understand, although the immediate reason was to shore up an embattled ally in a strategic region. The fall of the Shah of Iran in 1979 had facilitated the spread of radical Islamic fervor throughout the region and jeopardized Russia's long-term quest for a warm-water port, access to oil reserves, and proximity to Pakistan and India. Perhaps also the Soviets estimated that the benefits of U.S. rapprochement were at a zenith and could only go downhill. The Soviet Union imposed martial law in Poland in response to worker unrest, and with the election of President Ronald Reagan in late 1980, détente was over. The Carter Doctrine, which pledged U.S. action against any attempt by an "outside power" to control Middle East oil, was the new agenda. (The Carter Doctrine later formed the basis for George H.W. Bush's Gulf War actions.)

The Reagan administration chose this time to strengthen U.S. power at home and to improve ties with Beijing abroad. Sino–American relations were never better. China imposed diplomatic sanctions against Moscow and joined the United States in its containment of Soviet expansionism (Stoessinger 1990, 106). Reagan expanded the arms buildup begun by Carter, even at the cost of an overwhelming fiscal deficit, and engaged in military interventions in Nicaragua, Lebanon, and Afghanistan. SALT II was abandoned and Reagan's aggressive rhetoric ("evil empire," "plan for Armageddon") alarmed Europeans without chasing away their support. Margaret Thatcher and Helmut Kohl were united in condemning Soviet aggression and, acting against extraordinary public pressure, permitted the deployment of a new generation of medium-range nuclear missiles in Europe.

Reagan offered rather unrealistic arms control proposals, which resulted in a stalemate and ultimately a Soviet walkout at the Strategic Arms Reduction Talks (START) and Intermediate-Range Nuclear Forces (INF) talks. The Strategic Defense Initiative (SDI) was proposed in 1983 with the goal of enveloping the United States in a protective shield of high-tech weapons aimed at incoming Soviet missiles. Reagan proposed repeatedly to abandon the research program in exchange for deep unilateral Soviet arms cuts.

It was not until the emergence of Mikhail Gorbachev on the world scene that Cold War II began to change course.

Détente II: 1985–1991

The story of the second wave of détente, culminating in the collapse of the Soviet Union itself, is probably familiar and so bears only a cursory review. Suffice it to say that Reagan embraced the new, youthful, and apparently open-minded Soviet leader with open arms. He noted that Gorbachev was not a typical Communist, but rather someone with whom the United States could work (Nathan and Oliver 1989, 483). A number of summits were arranged, and by 1987 the INF Treaty, the first-ever arms reduction agreement, was signed.

Strategic arms talks took much longer to resolve, with Gorbachev repeatedly asking the United States to abandon SDI unilaterally. It was not until the Soviet empire was crumbling during the Bush administration's watch that a far-reaching strategic arms reduction treaty was signed. Before the ink was dry (and prior to ratification by the Senate), a new, more profound agreement was signed with the new Russian Republic under the leadership of Boris Yeltsin. Other agreements to dramatically cut chemical weapons stockpiles and ban their production, implement significant cuts in conventional (non-nuclear) weapons deployed across Europe, and form an eventual U.S.–Soviet "alliance" against Iraq in the Persian Gulf War of 1990–1991 demonstrated an entirely new era of cooperation. With the Soviets leaving Afghanistan and releasing control over all East European states in 1989, thereby permitting the reunification of Germany in 1990, the Cold War was well and truly over. Rehabilitation of the defeated erstwhile enemy became the pressing issue of peacetime, much as it was had after the defeat of Nazi Germany and Imperial Japan in 1945.

What was the Chinese orientation to the Americans and Russians in this new context? The well-known Tienanmen Square massacres of 1989 dealt a serious blow to the emerging democracy movement that had swept across China under Deng. The immediate result was the imposition of sanctions against China by the United States and Western Europe, although most of these were either allowed to lapse or reversed by 1992. Chinese relations with the Soviet Union improved significantly during the Gorbachev era. The Soviets supported a UN-mediated withdrawal of Soviet-backed Vietnam from China-backed Cambodia—a process that has not entirely succeeded at this writing. A Sino–Soviet summit took place in 1989 (the first since 1956) as "Russia wooed and China cooed" (Rourke 1990, 44). China became concerned about the closeness of U.S.–Soviet relations during the Gulf War but stopped short of vetoing a critical UN resolution permitting armed intervention against Iraq.

Post–Cold War Era: After 1992

Since the breakup of the Soviet Union in 1991, the strategic triangle has been far more difficult for analysts to understand. Economic factors seem to predominate now. It is thus increasingly difficult to know which pair of countries is experiencing strain or harmony because trade and investment not only serve as indicators of good relations but also generate friction and can be used as potential weapons. Russia received billions in aid from the West, particularly through the International Monetary Fund (too much, according to both Russian and IMF accounts). This largesse generated considerable resentment, however: In Russia, nationalists and Communists objected to the "neo-imperialism" implicit in this economic dependence; in the West, officials grew increasingly impatient with the inefficiencies and corruption of the Yeltsin regime. For China, economics has become the focal point of national planning, which has produced annual growth rates of close to 10 percent for much of the 1990s. Maintaining a strong trade relationship with the United States has significantly helped China control its balance of payments. Americans have shown increasing resentment of the unbalanced trade relationship with China, and Congress resisted granting the country "normal trade relations" status until 2000. Considerable doubt remains as to whether China will become a full-fledged member of the World Trade Organization. China's mixed record in human rights further complicates U.S. willingness to work closely with Beijing.

On the security front, the relationship among the three countries is also ambiguous. Officially, relations are good, but at the same time each country is acutely aware of the potential threat that the others pose. Consequently, the game is more "shadow boxing" than outright rivalry. Each country is engaged in efforts to enhance its military preparedness, although Russia is clearly lagging in this regard. During the 1990s, China detonated a number of nuclear warheads, resisted cooperating in the nonproliferation regime, openly threatened Taiwan's election campaign in 1999 (to which the United States at times responded with military deployments of its own), and was involved in illicit military technology transfers—both by spying on U.S. nuclear facilities and by selling technology to Pakistan and other Asian countries. The United States has maintained high levels of defense spending in the past ten years, although it has also dismantled a number of bases and units and has moved forward to implement START II nuclear weapons reductions (along with Russia, although both have encountered resistance in their respective legislatures). In addition the United States has continued to improve weapons based on stealth technology and has undertaken a new initiative to improve its antiballistic missile defense capability, purportedly to protect against isolated attacks from rogue states such as North Korea. Dramatic U.S. support of regional military intervention, particularly in Yugoslavia (both Bosnia and Kosovo), was resisted by Russia. Perhaps most directly threatening was the decision taken by the United States in 1995 to expand NATO by including Poland, Hungary, and the Czech Republic, a move that met with considerable Russian opposition ("Eastern Cheers" 1997, 5). Yeltsin spoke of a "cold peace," and at a summit meeting in mid-2000 ("At CSCE Summit" 1995, 8), both Russian and Chinese leaders warned the United States of the dangers of generating tensions through its antiballistic missile defense plans.

Although it is too early to say that the United States is becoming isolated by Russia and China and that the latter are forging a strong alliance, those developments would hardly be surprising. Realists would predict that the second- and third-ranking powers in any international system would naturally unite to offset the power of the preeminent state. As China becomes more economically powerful and Russia regains its financial footing, we can expect to see both act with considerably less deference to Washington's wishes. In the spring of 2001, for example, the United States deployed one of many spy planes along the Chinese coast to intercept various electronic communication signals. Unlike in past incidents, the Chinese air force intercepted one plane and accidentally made contact, forcing it to land in Chinese territory. Rather than return the plane and simply write off the incident, Beijing opted instead to castigate the United States for recklessly violating its territory and proceeded to detain the crew and dismantle the aircraft. After weeks of negotiation, the United States agreed to issue a "quasi-apology" for the incident and the crew was released. The plane was later returned–in several crates. . . .

The September 11, 2001 terrorist attacks altered the superpower relationships, at least temporarily. Both Moscow and Beijing made it very clear that they viewed the attacks as a threat to civilization itself and pledged unlimited support for the United States. They all joined in the war against terrorism, with the United States leading the way in Afghanistan. Except for a United States decision to withdraw from the Anti-ballistic Missile (ABM) Treaty, which was greeted with dismay by Russian President Vladimir Putin in early 2002, there are few signs that the latest era of good feelings has diminished significantly. Naturally, this could all change should the George W. Bush administration go forward with its threat to invade Iraq.

The Balance of Power Triangle

As we mentioned, the balance of power theory assumes that major powers, in the pursuit of increased security and influence, will combine forces with other nations that share the same enemies. These alliances will shift frequently over time as different nations develop greater capacity to wage war and thereby become a new threat. Overall, no single country will rise above the rest, and every major power's essential identity will be preserved (or at least the basic number of major players will remain stable).

Does this pattern of behavior hold true in our case? First, we will discuss the nature of a three-way balance of power, usually referred to as tripolarity. Four alliance patterns are possible in a tripolar system, as illustrated in Figure 3.1: (1) a very cordial "ménage à trois," in which all major powers cooperate with one another; (2) the "unit veto" system, in which none of the players cooperates; (3) the intermediate stages of a "marriage," in which one player ("odd man out") is positioned against the other two; and (4) the "romantic triangle," in which one player ("pivot") has good relations with each of the others, which are antagonistic to each other (Dittmer 1987).

Figure 3.1 also gives examples of the possible alliances in a tripolar system. The "marriage" and "romantic triangle" arrangements have numerous examples and deserve more attention. Segal and the contributors to his volume (1982) generally credit China with best understanding the nature of the "triangle" and with taking the most active role in changing its nature over time. After all, it was China that attempted to mend fences with the Eisenhower administration and ultimately invited Nixon to Beijing. And it was China that severed relations with the Soviets against Moscow's wishes.

The United States demonstrated some diplomatic sophistication beginning in the mid-1960s, particularly during the Nixon administration, when it abandoned twenty years of ideological principles in favor of an improved strategic position by warming up to China and working with the Soviets (perhaps trusting them both too much). One can hardly imagine two more unlikely individuals to meet with Chinese leaders in Beijing than Richard Nixon and Ronald Reagan, both passionate Cold Warriors from the outset!

Under Gorbachev, the Soviet Union maneuvered itself into something close to a pivot position when it continued to work closely with the Chinese during the Tienanmen Square period as U.S.–Chinese relations cooled significantly. This move represented a departure for the Soviets, who tended to view the "China Factor" with some contempt—particularly in the presplit days when the Chinese were viewed as mere pupils.

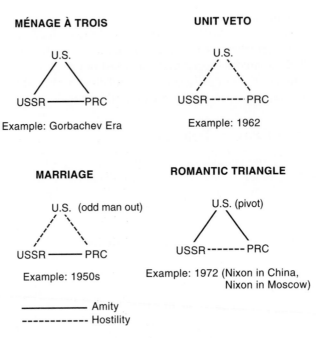

Figure 3.1 The tripolar system's possible configurations
Source: Adapted from Lowell Dittmer, "The Strategic Triangle: A Critical Review" in J. Kim Ilpong, ed., *The Strategic Triangle* (New York: McGraw-Hill, 1987).

Conclusion

By the 1960s, all superpowers were clearly cognizant of the tripolar dynamics in which they were enmeshed and made some effort to jockey for the best position—namely, the pivot role. Barring diplomatic success, each player at least attempted to avoid being locked in the least desirable position—"odd man out." For example, one can attribute China's eagerness to open diplomatic relations with the United States in the late 1960s to Beijing's perception of significantly improved U.S.–Soviet relations and the fear of being "left out"—even if its actions resulted in giving extraordinary influence to the United States. Likewise, Gorbachev knew that combining his good relations with the United States with improved ties to China could ultimately put him in the pivot position, although this scenario never materialized.

Debate Topic

Ultimately, the key issue in this case study is whether international politics is best approached from a pragmatic, unsentimental perspective (or whether values and ideology should play a part).

PRO

Those who support a realist approach have made the following points: (1) "Ideologies change— interests don't." It is best to always be practical because beliefs and attitudes might change at any moment. (2) Ideology gets in the way of useful relationships—both economic and strategic. (3) Ideology can drive a state to greater degrees of violence and aggression than mere pragmatism.

CON

Those who challenge the "balance of power" make the following arguments: (1) The point of politics should be to make life better for individuals; engagement with human rights violators is therefore wrong. (2) International relations based only on convenience are inherently unstable and unpredictable, carrying a greater risk of violence. (3) International affairs is evolving toward a more principled approach based on law; the balance of power means regression.

Questions to Consider

1. What does the future hold for this great power triangle? With the demise of the Soviet Union and the end of East–West antagonism in the European theater, is China the ultimate "odd man out" from here on? Or will the United States now play that role as China and Russia strive to balance power?

2. To what extent were forces other than balancing power significant in determining alignment choices by the superpowers? Did ideology make a difference? What about perceptions?

3. To what extent were the needs of humanity served by the tripolar relationship? Were people on the planet safer? More free? Better fed? What does this tell us about politics and morality?

Websites

Several universities and NGOs maintain websites with background material on security-related matters.

George Washington University National Security Archive: **glws.circ.gwu.edu/~nsarchiv**

American Foreign Policy Council: **www.afpc.org**

National Center for Policy Analysis: **www.ncpa.org**

Center for American–Eurasian Studies and Relations: **www.eurasiacenter.org**

References

Allison, Graham. *Essence of Decision: Explaining the Cuban Missile Crisis,* 2nd ed. (New York: Addison Wesley Longman, 1999).

"At CSCE Summit, Yeltsin Warns of 'Cold Peace.'" *Current Digest of the Post-Soviet Press* 46 #49 (January 4, 1995): 8–9.

Camilleri, Joseph. *Chinese Foreign Policy: The Maoist Era and Its Aftermath* (Seattle: University of Washington Press, 1980).

Chai, Winberg. *The Foreign Relations of the People's Republic of China* (New York: Putnam's Sons, 1972).

Dittmer, Lowell. "The Strategic Triangle: A Critical Review" in J. Kim Ilpong, ed., *The Strategic Triangle* (New York: MacGraw-Hill, 1987): 17–33.

"Eastern Cheers, Russian Jeers, American Silence." *Bulletin of the Atomic Scientists (January/February 1997): 5–7.*

Gaddis, John Lewis, and Terry L. Diebel, eds. *Containing the Soviet Union (New York: Pergamon-Brassey's, 1987).*

Higgins, Trumbull. *The Perfect Failure: Kennedy, Eisenhower and the CIA at the Bay of Pigs* (New York: Norton, 1987).

Kissinger, Henry. *White House Years* (Boston: Little, Brown, 1979).

McCormick, James M., ed. *A Reader in American Foreign Policy* (Itasca, IL: Peacock, 1986).

Nathan, James A., and James K. Oliver. *United States Foreign Policy and World Order*, 4th ed. (Glenview, IL: Scott, Foresman, 1989).

Rourke, John T. *Making Foreign Policy: United States, Soviet Union, China* (Pacific Grove, CA: Brooks/Cole, 1990).

Segal, Gerald, ed. *The China Factor: Peking and the Superpowers* (New York: Holmes & Meier, 1982).

Spanier, John. *American Foreign Policy Since World War II*, 11th ed. (Washington, DC: Congressional Quarterly Press, 1988).

Stoessinger, John G. *Nations in Darkness: China, Russia, and America*, 5th ed. (New York: McGraw-Hill, 1990).

Ulam, Adam B. *The Rivals: America and Russia Since World War II* (New York: Viking, 1971).

Waltz, Kenneth. *Theory of International Politics* (Reading, MA: Addison-Wesley, 1979).

Yahuda, Michael. "China and the Great Power Triangle" in Segal, ed., *The China Factor*: 26–41.

CASE

4

The Cuban Missile Crisis
RATIONALITY

Introduction

When making a decision, we typically know in advance what we want. We consider the facts at hand, come up with a few alternative courses of action, imagine what might happen if we pick each one, and then choose the alternative that gets us what we wanted in the first place. This is the epitome of what is meant by rationality. Any other method is not purely rational, although the result is not necessarily wrong or bad. We sometimes make choices based on habit or tradition, or we feel driven by our emotions. Our analysis of the situation and consideration of alternatives may be cursory. Anyone who has ever worked on a committee knows that groups rarely make decisions based on a careful calculation of costs and benefits—they typically go for the least common denominator. And this tells us nothing about putting the decision into practice.

Scholars have learned that if they assume rationality on the part of the people they study, it is possible to predict how different decision makers will address similar situations, which in turn allows us to anticipate numerous events. The field of game theory attempts to explain how rational actors interact with one another. When an actor faces a decision the outcome of which depends on what another actor decides, it is often possible to design a matrix that shows the range of outcomes. You can select the alternative that each actor will choose based on these outcomes and the goals each actor brings. For example, where two players face the option of cooperating or not cooperating, but where cooperating opens up the possibility of losing something of considerable value, one can predict that the actors will likely shun that option (this helps to explain everything from an international arms race to marital infidelity).

With respect to the Cuban Missile Crisis, we see two sets of actors. On the one hand, we have the "game" of superpower relations where each country plays a game of "chicken" with the other. On the other hand, we have the interactions between domestic decision makers within each country (presidents, advisors, generals, and so forth). As we explore the story of the Cuban Missile Crisis, consider whether the various players are behaving "rationally"—that is, identifying goals, exploring options, selecting the "best" option, and seeing it fully implemented.

THE CUBAN MISSILE CRISIS
KEY FIGURES

John F. Kennedy   U.S. President, 1961–1963. It was his responsibility to set U.S. policy with respect to detection and removal of Soviet missiles in Cuba in 1962.

Nikita Khrushchev   Soviet Premier, 1953–1964. He led the Soviet Union to both deploy and withdraw nuclear missiles in and from Cuba.

Fidel Castro   Leader of the Cuban government since 1959. He sought Soviet protection following the failed Bay of Pigs invasion.

John Scali   American newsman. He was used for back-channel negotiations with Aleksandr Feklisov.

Aleksandr Feklisov (Fomin)   Soviet KGB operative based in Washington, D.C.

Anatoly Dobrynin   Soviet Ambassador to the United States, 1962–1986.

Selected Members of ExComm

Robert F. Kennedy   Attorney-General of the United States, 1961–1964. As the brother of President Kennedy, he always had influence in shaping national policy in many areas. He conducted the meetings of the Executive Committee.

Dean Rusk   U.S. Secretary of State, 1961–1963.

George Ball   Undersecretary of State, 1961–1966.

John McCone   Director of Central Intelligence Agency, 1961–1965.

McGeorge Bundy   National Security Advisor, 1961–1966.

Robert McNamara   U.S. Secretary of Defense, 1961–1968. He discounted the threat presented by the Russian missiles.

Llewellyn Thompson   Ambassador-at-Large, 1962–1966. Former U.S. Ambassador to the Soviet Union, he was the only Russia expert on ExComm.

THE CUBAN MISSILE CRISIS
CHRONOLOGY

1959

Fidel Castro takes power in Cuba at the head of a Communist revolution.

(continued)

1960

John F. Kennedy is elected to be the youngest president in U.S. history.

1961

The Kennedy administration withdraws support for Cuban exiles who suffer defeat at the Bay of Pigs. Castro demands additional military support from the Soviet Union to defend against future U.S. attacks.

1962

June	Soviet Premier Nikita Khrushchev comes away from his summit meeting with Kennedy unimpressed.
September	The Soviet Union begins deploying nuclear missiles in Cuba.
October 15	American U-2 aircraft detect Soviet activity in Cuba.
October 16–20	ExComm deliberates, ultimately recommending a blockade first, and an invasion second.
October 22	Kennedy announces his plan to the nation by televised address.
October 23	Kennedy orders the blockade against Cuba. Later that day, Adlai Stevenson presents photos of the Cuban sites to the UN Security Council.
October 24	Russian vessels turn away from the blockade, prompting George Ball's "eyeball to eyeball" comment.
October 26	A conciliatory message is sent by Khrushchev, followed shortly thereafter by a more intransigent demand for the withdrawal of U.S. missiles from Turkey.
October 27	The "Trollope Ploy" is formulated in response to two conflicting Russian messages. The conciliatory message is treated as a genuine compromise and largely accepted.
October 28	Khrushchev agrees to withdraw the missiles from Cuba. Kennedy secretly agrees to withdraw U.S. missiles from Turkey.
November 19	Removal of Soviet missiles from Cuba is complete.

Rationality and the Cuban Missile Crisis

Almost as soon as it was resolved, the October 1962 Cuban Missile Crisis became the object of scholarly attention. It was one moment, suspended in time, when the earth's survival hung in the balance. President John F. Kennedy himself is reported to have estimated that the chances of a nuclear war were "between one out of three and even" (Allison 1999, 1). Fidel Castro felt the odds were 20:1 that a U.S. invasion of Cuba was virtually inevitable, and he urged Nikita Khrushchev to launch a full-scale nuclear strike in retaliation. Given the extreme danger and risk of the situation on the one hand and its successful conclusion on the other hand, this episode in world history has become a popular case study of conflict management and crisis decision making. Because of the ease of hearing from actual participants in the crisis, particularly since the end of the Cold War, and the voluminous documentary evidence available to scholars (including secret tapes of White House meetings), analysts have considerable details to study.

We will focus on what the Cuban Missile Crisis teaches us about how policy is developed and implemented in a crisis. A crisis, as defined by Charles Hermann (1969), is a problem that combines the elements of surprise, salience, and urgency. In other words, the problem erupts with little warning, directly threatens a high-priority value, and must be resolved quickly to avoid negative consequences. From another point of view, a crisis is "coercive diplomacy" used by an adversary to blackmail or intimidate a nation into submission without the direct use of force (Craig and George 1990). Avoidance of bloodshed is the primary concern in such situations, even though the risk of war is usually extremely high.

Hermann assumes that in a crisis situation, decisions are made at the top levels in a bewildering "pressure cooker" environment. Issues of lesser importance are set aside, all energy is put into gathering facts and alternatives, and stress levels are high. Conditions are ideal for intensive and creative problem solving as the combined energy and talent of some of the most able men and women in the country are brought to bear on a single issue. Of course, the reverse can also happen when decisions based on few facts must be made quickly by people with a great deal to lose. The actual outcomes depend on many factors, including the personalities, perceptions, and decision-making styles of the key participants, the degree of contingency planning that preceded the crisis, and the organization of the decision-making unit itself. To the extent that information is made available, options and objectives are clearly and creatively articulated, and the implications of various choices are thoroughly understood, the likelihood of a sound decision increases.

Before determining whether the decisions made during the Cuban Missile Crisis meet our ideal standard, we will review the history of the event.

The Cuban Missile Crisis

Precursors

In 1960, John F. Kennedy ran for president on a platform of narrowing the "missile gap" between the USSR and the United States. Upon reaching office, he was surprised to learn that, according to the CIA, the missile gap was larger than he expected—but it was in America's favor. Soviet leaders were acutely aware of the U.S. advantage in number, quality, and deployment of nuclear missiles, however, and were considering options to achieve a balance.

In 1959, Fidel Castro became the leader of Cuba and in 1961 declared himself unabashedly Marxist, to the dismay of American defense planners. His presence in the hemisphere represented a "bridgehead of Sino–Soviet imperialism and a base for Communist agitation" (Ferrell 1985, 362). U.S. agents made several attempts on Castro's life in these early years, and in 1961, the United States helped orchestrate a failed amphibious invasion of Cuba aimed at overthrowing the regime. Conservatives in Congress accused Kennedy of being "soft on Communism."

These events, combined with a disastrous U.S.–USSR summit meeting in June 1962 that gave Khrushchev the impression that Kennedy was a political lightweight, set the stage for the Soviet decision to deploy nuclear missiles in Cuba in May 1962 (Fursenko and Naftali 1997, 179). By deploying missiles, Khrushchev hoped to achieve a nuclear balance, protect Cuba from

U.S. invasion, and keep Castro in the Soviet camp (rather than defecting to the more radical China). He wanted to deploy several medium-range missiles, along with defensive antiaircraft batteries, between May and November 1962 without revealing his plans to the United States. Once the installations were in place, Khrushchev hoped the United States would feel obliged to accept this change in strategic balance (Gartoff 1989, 23; Trachtenberg 1985, 163).

U.S. officials suspected Soviet intentions and tried to get information through both open and secret channels. Each time they met with firm denials. It was not until October 15, 1962, that the United States had proof of Soviet activities: photographs of Soviet nuclear installations in Cuba taken by an American U-2 spy plane. The Cuban Missile Crisis had begun.

The Crisis Erupts

Early the next morning, Kennedy was presented with the information from the photographs by his national security advisor, McGeorge Bundy, who stressed the seriousness of the situation: The Soviets now had the capability to attack more than half of the United States, including Washington, D.C., with only a few minutes' warning. The president was astonished by the report. As put by Robert Kennedy, the president's brother and U.S. Attorney General, "[T]he dominant feeling was one of shocked incredulity" (Kennedy 1969, 27). President Kennedy determined during that first meeting that some forceful response was incumbent upon the administration, although not all agreed. (Secretary of Defense Robert McNamara wondered aloud whether this discovery constituted, in and of itself, a mortal danger.) Nonetheless, given the political climate at home and worldwide, Kennedy determined that this situation qualified as a crisis.

By that evening, a group that came to be known as the ExComm (Executive Committee of the National Security Council—even though it included individuals who did not belong to the council) was organized by the president and was generating options for responding to the news. Potential actions included blockade or quarantine, surgical air strike followed by invasion, diplomatic overtures and negotiation, talks with Castro, and leaving things alone (Sorenson 1965, 735). Although everyone acknowledged that air strikes followed by invasion were the only means of being sure the missiles were removed, most did not want to pursue that option as a first alternative. The diplomatic option was ruled out as too timid and passive. Ultimately, the air strike/invasion option and the blockade option were deemed the only viable responses, and the blockade was considered far weaker under the circumstances.

For nearly a week, the ExComm deliberated to develop a final operational plan that could win unanimous approval. As time went on, the air strike option was set aside for two principal reasons. First, if done without warning, an air strike would be seen by the rest of the world as a "Pearl Harbor in reverse" (as put by John McCone, the director of the CIA—Fursenko and Naftali 1997, 226) or as an unprovoked attack against an unprepared enemy. Second, the air strike option was never guaranteed success by military planners, in part because no air strike is ever guaranteed and because the missiles were considered "moveable targets" and therefore able to be relocated without warning. The blockade, in its favor, was a less "final" solution. The United States could rather easily escalate its response if a blockade failed. Also, a blockade was considered a fairly forceful reaction—an act of war according to international law. It might be enough to force the Russians to back down and negotiate a settlement. A blockade could not, in itself, remove the missiles, however. And the ExComm had to consider what to do if the Russians attempted to run the blockade. The crisis might simply be relocated rather than solved.

By Friday evening, October 20, President Kennedy had made the decision to impose a blockade, citing the advantage of giving Khrushchev more time to consider the implications of the situation (Sorenson 1965, 691). Kennedy readily acknowledged that "there isn't a good solution . . . but this one seems less objectionable" (National Archives 1988, 7). The decision was made formal on October 22, when Kennedy spoke to the nation in a televised address. He announced the existence of the missiles, his intent to see them removed, and the approach he intended to use to do that. He made sure to keep his options open. He underlined the gravity of the problem for both American and Soviet audiences:

> My fellow citizens: let no one doubt that this is a difficult and dangerous effort on which we have set out. No one can foresee precisely what course it will take or what costs or casualties will be incurred. . . . The path we have chosen for the present is full of hazards, as all paths are—but it is the one most consistent with our character and courage as a nation. (National Archives 1988, 10)

The Blockade Aftermath

Over the next four days, the situation worsened. Khrushchev, alarmed to learn that the Americans had discovered his missiles, was relieved when he learned of the blockade. He considered the blockade the policy of a weak leader, and he intended to take advantage of it. He ordered the Cuban installations accelerated and instructed ships carrying nuclear equipment to move quickly to beat the blockade. Only at the last minute, once the blockade was in place, were other Russian ships ordered to halt (prompting Secretary of State Dean Rusk to make the famous remark: "We're eyeball to eyeball and I think the other fellow just blinked!"). At the same time, Khrushchev moved to ensure his direct control over the nuclear missiles that were operational to prevent an accidental launch (fearing Castro's impulsiveness).

Meanwhile, the United States began a diplomatic assault against Russia in the Organization of American States (OAS) and the UN Security Council, where virtually every nation approved the U.S. response and demanded a withdrawal of Soviet missiles (Blight 1990, 17). Robert Kennedy undertook back-channel negotiations through Georgi Bolshakov as well as front-door meetings with Anatoly Dobrynin, the USSR's envoy in Washington, both to determine Russian thinking and to communicate American resolve (Fursenko and Naftali 1997, 249–252). Perhaps most important, the Kennedy administration mobilized active-duty and reserve personnel and moved a half-million troops with accompanying equipment into the south Florida area. It sent every possible signal that an invasion force was prepared to act at any moment. (This helps explain Castro's alarm.)

Khrushchev also used a variety of channels to communicate his intentions. He communicated through an American businessman in Moscow, through journalists, and through KGB agents in Washington. Ultimately, a letter was delivered through Alexander Fomin (a code name for Aleksandr Feklisov) to John Scali, a reporter with ties to the Kennedy administration. The initial proposal involved removal of the missiles by the USSR in exchange for a promise to respect Cuban sovereignty by the United States. While the ExComm was formulating a response to this message, it received a second message via Radio Moscow adding the caveat that Jupiter missiles—American medium-range missiles based in Turkey—also be removed.

The administration did not know what to believe after receiving conflicting proposals at almost the same time. If they had known that Fomin was acting on his own initiative, the confusion would have been even greater (Garthoff 1989, 80). Add to this the downing of an American U-2 over Cuba at the same time (October 27, 1962), and it was frankly impossible to know what was taking place. (The downing was not even authorized by Moscow—Garthoff 1989, 91.) For that matter, the United States was guilty of sending mixed signals of its own. It had ordered the constant overflight of the Arctic region by bombers with nuclear weapons, and one of them strayed into Soviet airspace at about this time. In fact, Khrushchev was very personally involved in the formulation of proposals, and the second proposal to remove missiles from Turkey came when he considered an invasion of Cuba less likely (Garthoff 1989, 82).

Negotiating the Resolution

The ExComm made two decisions on Saturday, October 27. The first was to make final preparations for an invasion of Cuba to begin on Monday (Blight 1990, 18), and the second was to draft a formal response accepting the conditions detailed in Khrushchev's first proposal. This latter move was suggested by Soviet expert Llewellyn Thompson and was nicknamed the "Trollope Ploy." Thompson also exerted considerable energy to convince a downhearted President Kennedy to implement the plan. In addition to drafting a message to be sent to Khrushchev, Kennedy dispatched his brother Robert to present the American position as well as to offer a "sweetener": secret removal of the Jupiter missiles over a five-month period.

On October 28, Khrushchev's response accepting these terms was received at the White House. The Cuban Missile Crisis was at an end. By November 19, much to Castro's chagrin, the missiles had been dismantled and removed.

Analysis of the Decision to Blockade Cuba

Although several critical decisions were made at various points prior to and during the crisis, two are easiest for American audiences to study: (1) Kennedy's decision to reveal the existence of the missiles and impose a blockade and (2) Kennedy's decision to accept the terms of the first Khrushchev letter and ignore the second message. To determine whether these two decisions by Kennedy were "rational," we should consider his goals, assess the quality of the search for options and their respective outcomes, and check whether the final choice promised to achieve his original goals. To the extent that the decision-making process comes close to this ideal model, we can say that it was rational (Allison 1999, 33).

The decision to impose a blockade was reached after roughly four days of intensive deliberations in the White House. Within twelve hours of learning about the missiles, Kennedy had assembled a collection of individuals chosen for their authority over certain key areas of foreign policy and their subject-matter expertise. He called in the secretaries of state and defense, the director of the CIA, the national security adviser, and the joint chiefs of staff (chaired by Maxwell Taylor). Douglas Dillon, secretary of the treasury; Theodore Sorenson, presidential counsel; Pierre Salinger, press secretary; and Robert Kennedy were also included, though more for their relationships to President Kennedy than for their policy roles. Six other men from the State and Defense Departments were brought in for their expertise, and Lyndon Johnson, the vice president, was permitted to join the group. The Ex-Comm met regularly, sometimes for ten hours at a time (not all members met all the time). The group had no obvious seniority system, although Robert McNamara and Robert Kennedy informally led the discussions.

The ExComm structure has been praised as a nearly ideal form for crisis decision making, in that the individuals were present, as Sorenson later put it, "on our own, representing the President and not individual departments" (Sorenson 1965, 679). Furthermore, as the days wore on, the group met without the president, divided into smaller caucuses, and otherwise ignored traditional rank and protocol as they deliberated. Robert Kennedy commented, "It was a tremendously advantageous procedure that does not frequently occur within the executive branch of the government, where rank is often so important" (Kennedy 1969, 46). Specifically, the arrangement minimized the tendency for peer pressure to lead group members to take a more hard-line approach than would normally be the case ("groupthink"—see Janis 1972). It also worked against any bureaucratic struggle over turf.

Perhaps the first decision required was to determine whether the placement of missiles in Cuba was indeed a threat to national security. In fact, that question did not even come up until the evening of October 16, and then at the instigation of McGeorge Bundy—not the president. McNamara made it clear that he did not consider the new missiles a threat. The joint chiefs unanimously disagreed ("White House" 1985, 184). Note that a decision to ignore the threat of the missiles would have simply eliminated the crisis because one of the key ingredients in every crisis situation is a threat to salient values. Kennedy dismissed McNamara's assessment, although he did not necessarily agree with the joint chiefs either. He was more concerned about conservatives in Congress who, he felt, would likely have him impeached if he ignored the missiles.

Once the problem was identified, the process of clarifying the goals and options began, though not necessarily in that order. Early on, Kennedy determined, with general approval, that the missiles must be removed but that the use of force should be a last resort. Kennedy weighed not only U.S. security concerns but also the response of the American public and NATO allies. The Europeans, he surmised, would not be especially alarmed at the presence of Soviet missiles in Cuba because they lived every day with the prospect of a Soviet attack from the Ukraine and eastern Russia. Kennedy kept in mind that a tradeoff of Cuban missiles for Jupiter missiles would seem eminently reasonable to U.S. allies ("October 27, 1962," 1987/88, 58). As the crisis evolved, avoiding global nuclear war was likely the highest priority on Kennedy's mind and shaped his willingness to ignore Soviet provocations.

McNamara was the first to clearly articulate three options for dealing with the crisis: (1) a "diplomatic" option involving public declarations, consultations with allies, UN resolutions, and other gestures aimed at condemning and publicizing the Soviet move; (2) a "middle course" of aggressive surveillance and interdiction (read: blockade) of new weapons bound for Cuba; and (3) a "military" option with several variants ranging from air strikes on narrowly selected targets (missile launchers and installations) to a broad-ranging series of attacks on all Cuban military facilities followed by an amphibious invasion ("White House" 1985, 182). Other ideas were mentioned, including taking retaliatory measures, doing nothing at all, and somehow persuading Castro to expel the weapons (Sorenson 1965, 682). Beyond these general categories of action, the ExComm questioned the specific implementation of each approach at length. Should an air strike be preceded by a public ultimatum, or should it be a surprise? Should diplomatic initiatives include a specific ultimatum and a deadline for withdrawal? Should an exchange of missiles in Turkey (which President Kennedy had once ordered removed) be offered up front to persuade the Soviets to settle the problem quickly? Should the nuclear arsenal be put on alert and forces mobilized? What contingencies should be made for a likely Soviet move in Berlin?

Transcripts and personal accounts indicate that discussion of these questions was thorough and uninhibited, although certain voices and ideas clearly dominated. By the evening of October 16, the choices seemed to have been whittled down to two: blockade and diplomacy versus air strikes and invasion. McNamara was the most methodical thinker and speaker in the group. He generally favored the blockade option, although he acknowledged that it would not suffice to remove the missiles. At one point, when the president seemed to be leaning toward an air strike, McNamara essentially halted the discussion: "I think tonight we ought to put down on paper the alternative plans and probable, possible consequences thereof in a way that State and Defense could agree on, even if we disagree and put in both views. . . . [T]he consequences of these actions have not been thought through clearly" ("White House" 1985, 189). His suggestion was accepted, and the group split into two committees, each drafting the pros and cons of different options. Heavy emphasis was placed on extrapolating the outcomes and implications of each action, including the variations of the actions. Exactly how will oncoming ships be treated at the blockade perimeter? What about submarines? Will the OAS, NATO, and UN support the United States? Should classified information regarding the missiles be divulged? How and where will the Soviets respond to air strikes? Will Berlin be affected? (It is interesting that the joint chiefs initially anticipated that there would be no Soviet response to a U.S. air strike—a scenario Kennedy rejected.) Note this emotional exchange about the implications of an air strike between Undersecretary of State George Ball and McGeorge Bundy:

> BALL: This [surprise attack scenario] just frightens the hell out of me as to what's going beyond. . . .
>
> BUNDY: . . . What goes beyond what?
>
> BALL: What happens beyond that. You go in there with a surprise attack. You put out all the missiles. This isn't the end. This is the beginning. . . . ("White House" 1985, 194)

This process of deliberation, development of options, extrapolation of possible outcomes, and assessment of risks, reactions, and secondary options proceeded for three full days, before a decision was made. At one point, the ExComm actually organized a sort of "moot court," assigning certain members to be advocates for particular policy options while others "cross-examined" them to identify weaknesses. The blockade ended up as the most attractive option. It at least had a chance of resolving the crisis, and at minimal cost. Deputy Secretary of Defense Roswell Gilpatrick explained, "Essentially, Mr. President, this is a choice between limited action and unlimited action, and most of us think that it's better to start with limited action" (Sorenson 1965, 693–695).

In reconsidering this decision-making ordeal, we see that the participants self-consciously and painstakingly went out of their way to be rational. Although the initial decision to declare the problem a crisis may have been rather poorly thought out, the decision to impose a blockade resulted from a very systematic, impartial, and thorough process. An alternative point of view is that President Kennedy manipulated the process from behind the scenes, and some evidence indicates that Robert Kennedy played the role of president-in-abstentia. Also, one can ask whether the consideration of only a half-dozen alternatives to a situation that threatened the future of humankind was adequate. Herbert Simon and James March argue that in the best of all worlds, the most we can expect of organizational decision making is "satisficing": selecting the first option that satisfies the key elements of a solution, even though other options might have met a wider range of objectives (March and Simon 1958).

Response to the Soviet Offers

Several days of rancorous debate in the UN Security Council and a number of close calls on the high seas east of Cuba preceded the exchange between the U.S. and Soviet governments of what seemed to be genuine offers at settlement. Three messages in particular arrived at the White House on Friday, October 26, and Saturday, October 27. Adding information about the downing of the U-2 on Saturday morning, one could say that four messages were delivered. The ExComm had to decide which of these conflicting messages to take seriously.

The most significant message delivered on Friday was a lengthy, disjointed letter from Khrushchev. After a spate of editorials and speeches in the United States about the imminence of nuclear war and a warning of an impending U.S. invasion of Cuba, Khrushchev wrote about the risks of nuclear war. He compared the crisis to a knot that he and Kennedy were pulling tighter and tighter each day. Unless they reversed their course, the only way to undo the knot would be to cut it. Buried in this message was the "germ of a reasonable settlement: inasmuch as his missiles were there only to defend Cuba against invasion, he would withdraw the missiles under UN inspection if the U.S. agreed not to invade" (Sorenson 1965, 712). At roughly the same time this message was received and translated, Alexander Fomin was communicating a similar proposal to John Scali on his own authority, although later reports indicate Fomin thought Scali was the one who put forward the proposal (Fursenko and Naftali 1997, 265). Combined, the two messages offered a way out of the crisis.

On Saturday morning, the Soviet news agency TASS announced that the USSR would be willing to withdraw its missiles from Cuba if the United States dismantled its missiles in Turkey. Although the message was sent publicly over the airwaves, Khrushchev did not intend to put any particular pressure on the United States; the channel was chosen simply to accelerate communication of the message (Fursenko and Naftali 1997, 276). Nevertheless, Khrushchev was well aware that this proposal was more demanding than the earlier one. It was simply a gamble on his part, though one based in part on informal talks between Robert Kennedy and Dobrynin. The effect of the second message was despondency at the White House. The growing sense of alarm and urgency was based in part on the mistaken notion that the Cuban weapons were not yet operational but soon would be. The White House feared that local Cuban commanders might take it upon themselves to order a launch without Moscow's approval.

The transcript of the ExComm meetings make it clear that President Kennedy was deeply shaken by Khrushchev's second letter:

> . . . We're going to be in an unsupportable position on this matter if this [the trade] becomes his proposal. In the first place, we last year tried to get the missiles out of [Turkey] because they're not militarily useful. . . . Number 2, . . . to any man at the United Nations or any other rational man this will look like a very fair trade. . . . I think you're going to find it very difficult to explain why we

are going to take hostile military action in Cuba against these sites—what we've been thinking about. The thing that he's saying is, "If you'll get yours out of Turkey, we'll get ours out of Cuba." I think we've got a very tough one here. ("October 27, 1962," 1987/88, 366–367)

The president's advisors, arguing against the tradeoff, pointed out that it would be undercutting a NATO ally and might undermine the entire alliance. This debate engendered a search for alternatives, although the pressure of time seems to have constricted the number of options considered. McNamara and others pushed for an immediate cessation of work on the missile sites and some form of warning and implicit threat to the Soviets to remove the missiles within forty-eight hours. From that point, it seems to have been assumed that air strikes would have to begin by Tuesday at the latest.

As the ExComm prepared a reply to the messages, the option of simply ignoring the second message was raised. The following pivotal exchange occurred between Llewellyn Thompson and President Kennedy:

JFK: . . . [W]e're going to have to take our weapons out of Turkey. I don't think there's any doubt he's not going to retreat now that he's made that public, Tommy—he's not going to take them out of Cuba if we . . .

THOMPSON: I don't agree, Mr. President. I think there's still a chance that we can get this line going [i.e., ignore the second letter].

JFK: He'll back down?

THOMPSON: The important thing to Khrushchev, it seems to me, is to be able to say, "I saved Cuba—I stopped an invasion." . . . ("October 27, 1962," 1987/88, 59)

Some in the administration surmised that the second letter might have been written by the alleged "hawks" in Khrushchev's Politburo and that ignoring it might effectively elevate Khrushchev's status in his own government. We now know that this was merely wishful thinking and Khrushchev was, in fact, in firm control of the government at this time.

At any rate, the ExComm decided to issue a response that simply did not mention the Turkish missiles. At the same time, secret communications relayed in a meeting between Robert Kennedy and Dobrynin indicated a willingness by the United States to remove the Jupiter missiles at a later time. The ExComm continued to make detailed preparations for an air strike/invasion policy. The starting time for the attack was given as Thursday at the latest. The decision to ignore the U-2 downing was another U.S. effort to postpone the military option as long as possible.

The delay proved felicitous because Khrushchev's response arrived on Sunday morning. Was Khrushchev's cooperation the result of U.S. prudence, or were Kennedy administration officials simply lucky? In retrospect, much hinged on some communications that no one at the White House was aware of. A KGB agent who worked as a bartender at the National Press Club overheard a number of conversations between American journalists, including speculation by Warren Rogers that a U.S. invasion of Cuba was imminent. This information was communicated to Moscow along with reports of hospitals in Florida being warned to prepare for casualties and other rather disconnected observations that convinced Khrushchev on Friday that war was imminent (Allison 1999, 350). Although he had changed his mind in the interim, the downing of the U-2, unauthorized as it was, further alarmed Khrushchev and prompted him to accept the American response. He doubtless feared that the situation was spiraling out of control. Two recent revelations support this view. One is that Castro had actively encouraged the local Soviet commander to launch the missiles against the United States without seeking prior authorization from Moscow. The other is that on October 27, the commander of a Soviet submarine armed with nuclear weapons was seconds away from firing a nuclear-tipped torpedo at an American sub destroyer in retaliation for dropping depth charges when he was persuaded by his senior officers to desist (*Chicago Tribune* 2002). Khrushchev may have felt it was only a matter of time until a nuclear accident would force Washington's hand.

Conclusion

Thus, although the White House was operating on largely false assumptions and the messages that seem to have mattered most to Moscow were not the ones the administration deliberately sent, the outcome was a peaceful one. We should continue to ask whether the decision-making process was rational, however. Clearly, the White House believed that no action that could be seen as "final" ought to be taken if at all possible. This stalling ultimately proved to be the most prudent deliberate move. This policy was as much the result of Kennedy's frazzled emotional condition and fear of commitment, however, and could easily be considered "nonrational."

Much of the Kennedy administration's decision-making process was based on flawed intelligence and therefore faulty assessments of Soviet behavior and intentions. This stemmed in part from the organizational structures and processes in place at the time. In addition, once decisions were made, they were often not carried out according to plan. The implementing agencies frequently filtered the instructions from the White House through their own standard operating procedures and institutional cultures.

As it happens, the most significant actions that the administration took involved the substantial preparations for war that were telegraphed to Moscow on a daily basis. In retrospect, it was perhaps this state of readiness that made the deepest impression on the Soviet leadership and prompted them to take the other messages coming from Washington seriously. Warnings, blockades, speeches at the UN, and so forth, carried a powerful punch when placed against the backdrop of hundreds of thousands of Marines and soldiers gathering in Florida.

Interestingly enough, the Cuban Missile Crisis signaled the beginning of a long and winding process of superpower détente. Having faced a nuclear exchange, both Moscow and Washington took steps over the next few years to prevent such a crisis from reoccurring. The "hotline" was installed in 1963 to allow the heads of each government to communicate at any time. Major arms control agreements and military safeguards were negotiated during both Lyndon Johnson's and Richard Nixon's administrations between 1963 and 1972. Thus, although the world can fault the superpowers for bringing it to the brink of annihilation, we can take comfort from the fact that important lessons were learned and acted upon.

Debate Topic

His handling of the Cuban Missile Crisis catapulted John F. Kennedy to heroic status. Does he deserve the credit he has been given?

PRO

Kennedy apologists routinely cite the following points: (1) Kennedy single-handedly promoted the blockade solution as a way of helping the Soviets save face. (2) Kennedy overcame objections from both the military and the diplomatic corps (including his brother Robert) to maintain this course once adopted. (3) Kennedy carefully constructed a decision-making structure that promoted brain-storming and "buy in."

CON

Those who question Kennedy's stature point out the following: (1) The blockade solution actually heightened risks by alerting the Soviets to U.S. intentions without removing the missiles in itself. (2) Kennedy did not assert control of intelligence gathering and the implementation process until after serious mistakes were already made. (3) Kennedy was the beneficiary of numerous strokes of luck that were beyond his control (and even knowledge).

Questions to Consider

1. To what extent were decision makers during the Cuban Missile Crisis motivated by habit, prejudice, emotion, or other nonrational impulses? Would other people in the same situation have reached the same decisions?

2. To what extent did group dynamics and social pressures influence the Ex-Comm's decision making? Would these individuals have reached the same decisions alone?

3. How did the stress and pressure of crisis decision making affect the search for alternative options? Would the players have come to the same conclusions if they had had several weeks or months to think them through?

4. How effectively were the decisions implemented? Did any unanticipated outcomes follow from the decisions taken?

Websites

Audio recordings of ExComm meetings: **www.hpol.org/jfk/cuban**
National Security Agency's record: **www.nsa.gov:8080/docs/cuba**
Documents on the crisis: **www.mtholyoke.edu/acad/intrel/cuba.htm**
More crisis documentation: **www.gwu.edu/~nsarchiv/nsa/cuba_mis_cri/index.html**
Overview of the crisis: **www.hyperion.advanced.org/11046/days.htm**

References

Allison, Graham. *Essence of Decision: Explaining the Cuban Missile Crisis,* 2nd ed. (New York: Addison Wesley Longman, 1999).

Blight, James G. *The Shattered Crystal Ball: Fear and Learning in the Cuban Missile Crisis* (Savage, MD: Rowman and Littlefield, 1990).

Chicago Tribune, October 14, 2002, p.3

Craig, Gordon, and Alexander George. *Force and Statecraft* (New York: Oxford University Press, 1990).

Ferrell, Robert, ed. *The Twentieth Century: An Almanac* (New York: World Almanac, 1985).

Fursenko, Aleksandr, and Timothy Naftali. *"One Hell of a Gamble": Khrushchev, Castro and Kennedy, 1958–1964* (New York: W. W. Norton, 1997).

Garthoff, Raymond. *Reflections on the Cuban Missile Crisis,* rev. ed. (Washington, DC: Brookings Institute, 1989).

Hermann, Charles. "International Crisis a Situational Variable" in James Rosenau, ed., *International Politics and Foreign Policy* (New York: Free Press, 1969): 113–137.

Janis, Irving. *Victims of Groupthink* (Boston: Houghton Mifflin, 1972).

Kennedy, Robert. *Thirteen Days: A Memoir of the Cuban Missile Crisis* (New York: W. W. Norton, 1969).

March, James, and Herbert Simon. *Organizations* (New York: Wiley and Sons, 1958).

National Archives. *The Cuban Missile Crisis: President Kennedy's Address to the Nation, October 22, 1962* (Washington, DC: U.S. Government Printing Office, 1988).

"October 27, 1962: Transcripts of the Meetings of the ExComm." *International Security* 12 #3 (Winter 1987/88): 30–92.

Sorenson, Theodore. *Kennedy* (New York: Harper & Row, 1965).

Trachtenberg, Mark. "The Influence of Nuclear Weapons in the Cuban Missile Crisis." *International Security* 10 #1 (Summer 1985): 135–163.

"White House Tapes and Minutes of the Cuban Missile Crisis." *International Security* 10 #1 (Summer 1985): 171–203.

5

The Military–Industrial Complex

DEFENSE SPENDING

Introduction

To what extent are military spending and the accumulation of weapons matters of foreign or domestic policy? Defense planners almost always justify their latest and greatest inventions in terms of national security, but considerable evidence indicates that with or without a foreign enemy, the military would look pretty much the same. Some see this as a sign of bureaucratic inertia, insider politics, or even economic pump priming (see, respectively, Sandler and Hartley 1995; Ward and Davis 1992; Cusack 1992). Others see the effects of politics and election-year intervention at work in determining the type and size of spending (Stoll 1992; Mayer 1992). We will focus on one particularly popular perspective on military spending—the iron triangle.

The Iron Triangle

Washington insiders know that many national policies are developed, determined, and implemented by a rather narrow set of self-interested individuals. The policy-making elite tend to respond to special interests, and the more obtuse and complex the issue, the more special interests (rather than public opinion) tend to dominate. Many analysts have used the term iron triangle to describe one type of cooperative network. As explained by Dye and Zeigler:

> Once the bureaucracy takes over an issue, three major power bases—the "iron triangles"—come together to decide its outcome: the executive agency administering the program; the congressional subcommittee charged with its oversight; and the most interested groups, generally those directly affected by the agency. The interest groups develop close relationships with the bureaucratic policy makers. And both the interest groups and the bureaucrats develop close rela-

tionships with the congressional subcommittees that oversee their activities. Agency–subcommittee–interest group relationships become established; even the individuals involved remain the same over fairly long periods of time, as senior members of Congress retain their subcommittee memberships. (Dye and Zeigler 1993, 283)

The military-industrial complex is a special and significant example of an iron triangle. Since the end of World War II, defense contractors, Pentagon procurement specialists (buyers), and congressional subcommittees charged with appropriating funds for weapons have come together in a "you scratch my back, I'll scratch yours" arrangement (Adams 1982, 24–26). Some see the Department of Defense as a "captured regulator" that has the industry's interest rather than the public's interest at heart (Leitzel 1992). One could even apply a radical Marxist perspective and conclude that the business classes and the government elites are working together at the expense of taxpayers and working people (Barnet 1969).

This is not to say that the relationships among Congress, the Pentagon, and defense contractors have always been cordial. At various times, reform efforts have been instigated following disclosures of waste, fraud, and political intrigue in defense procurement. A reform effort was initiated in the mid-1980s, although it had not shown clear results before the end of the Cold War dramatically changed the equation.

Department of Defense–Industry Cooperation

We will look at the military-industrial complex by considering each of the three relationships in the triangle. Then we will consider the changes and pressures on this system that have developed in the last twenty years.

The relationship between the Department of Defense (DoD) and defense contractors is special. On the surface, the Defense Department depends on contractors to manufacture weapons for war, while the defense contractors depend on the Pentagon for much of their business. The relationship goes beyond this simple exchange, however.

To begin, a great deal of valuable insider information and special expertise is exchanged between industry and defense contractors through the regular rotation of personnel. Because military officers may retire after only twenty years of service, many with experience in procurement and weapons purchasing leave the Pentagon to work for contractors, who pay them well for their connections and background. In 1960, for example, 691 retired officers were working for defense contractors; in 1968, that figure had risen to 2,072 (Donovan 1970, 54). The benefits are obvious, as explained by Adams:

> The contractors obtain many benefits from the movement of personnel: information on current and future DoD and NASA plans, especially in research areas; access to key offices in Federal agencies, technical expertise for weapons development and marketing, skilled personnel with an intimate knowledge of both sides of contracting. (Adams 1982, 79)

Understanding the Pentagon's intentions and procedures is naturally vital to defense contractor planning. To a certain extent, most defense contractor–Pentagon relations involve contractors' efforts to secure as much information about future weapons and strategies as possible. Some of these efforts have become routine. Defense Science Boards bring together Pentagon and defense contractor officials "at the earliest possible stage, well before Congress or the general public are aware of" future programs (Adams 1982, 168). This effort to obtain information has also been at the heart of some of the most serious fraud cases in the procurement process. Raytheon, manufacturer of the Patriot missile, was charged with fraud in 1990 for illegally obtaining documents that gave it an unfair bidding advantage in 1983. The court ruled that a pattern of such behavior had existed from 1978 to 1985 (Donahue 1991, 28–29).

Defense contractors are eager to have guidance through the bureaucratic maze of Pentagon procurement (Reppy 1983, 25). The specifications for the Amraam missile in the late 1980s were 500,000 pages long (Huey and Perry 1991, 36). As put by Korb with regard to procurement in the 1980s:

> The laws and regulations governing acquisition were extremely cumbersome. For example, there are some 400 different regulatory requirements that are pegged to some 60 different dollar thresholds. . . . [D]efense contractors were forced to spend more time dealing with inspectors and auditors than working on the project. DoD proudly proclaimed that it performed in excess of 10,000 audits of defense contractors per year. (Korb 1988, 36–37)

Not only do defense contractors struggle for information about the Pentagon (to the point that they risk breaking the law to get it), but Defense Department planners in turn rely heavily on defense contractors for information about new weapons systems, testing results, and so on, in their efforts to secure funding from Congress (Reppy 1983, 27). Defense contractors are happy to supply this information because of their dependence on the Pentagon's representation and advocacy.

Many defense contractors have few alternative customers other than the Pentagon for their products. In the late 1980s, six of the top ten defense contractors made a majority of their sales to the Pentagon. Lockheed sold more than nine-tenths of its products to the Department of Defense. The other 10 percent went to NASA, the U.S. Postal Service, and other government agencies. Even corporations that are primarily civilian-oriented, such as General Motors and Boeing, have grown especially eager to maintain and expand their government contracts as their civilian sales have faltered.

A list of normal business expenses includes such things as capital investments (buildings, factories), machinery, storage, research and development, and market research. These expenses and other "start-up costs" are generally borne by the firm. Executives are under pressure to turn a profit quickly to begin paying off the debts incurred in this beginning phase. If a new product fails, the business must either suffer losses, lay off workers, or both. Such is the life of the ordinary business.

For defense contractors, many of these risks are either shared with or borne entirely by the government. As a result, doing business with the Pentagon can be addictive, as explained by Reppy:

> It is likely that the defense-oriented firms invest less in plant and equipment than other comparable firms. The contractual forms used by the DoD discourage capital investment by covering all allowable costs on cost-plus contracts and by giving only a low weight to a firm's investment in new plant and equipment in negotiated profit rates. (Reppy 1983, 39)

A 1976 Defense Department study concluded that defense contractors reinvested only 35 percent of their sales, while comparable commercial firms typically reinvested 63 percent. That the Pentagon routinely covers overhead expenses normally borne by the firms is a clear advantage to selling to the Pentagon. It isn't so clear that Marx would describe this as capitalist collusion.

Perhaps the most significant advantage of doing business with the Pentagon is that it shares research and development costs. The Defense Department covers much of the research and development costs for weapons construction, which put together make up the bulk of research and development expenditures for all American industry. For the top defense contractors in the 1970s, the Defense Department covered more than three-fourths of Grumman's research and development, two-thirds for Northrop, roughly half for Lockheed and General Dynamics, and one-third for Rockwell (Adams 1982, 97). Overall, three-fourths of defense industry research and development was covered by the Department of Defense (Reppy 1983, 31).

The Defense Department not only partly covers research related to officially approved programs but also provides seed money for promising proposals. As put by Cypher:

> Large arms contractors regularly bombard the Pentagon with "unsolicited proposals" (known in the trade as Independent Research & Development and Bid and Proposal Programs—IR&D/B&P). Thousands of such proposals pour into the Pentagon, and 7,000 or more are funded every year. (Cypher 1991, 11)

Research and development is the key component of some programs. In the case of the Strategic Defense Initiative (SDI), a massive, high-tech antiballistic missile system, more than 80 percent of Defense Department expenditures was devoted to research and development alone. As the technological component of weapons systems has grown, the research and development share of total costs has increased, roughly doubling from 1965 to 1985.

Another important dimension of Pentagon–contractor relations is the "follow-on imperative." The follow-on imperative is described in some detail by Kurth, with specific reference to the aerospace industry:

> About the time a production line phases out of one major defense contract, it phases in production of a new one, usually within a year. Since new aerospace systems require a considerable period of development before production, the production line normally is awarded the contract for the new system about three years before production of the old one is scheduled to phase out. (Kurth 1989, 199)

For political reasons we will review later, the pressures to maintain a production line for these major industries is very strong. Few major firms lose successive bids as a result (Reppy 1983, 28). The survival rate of defense firms is therefore very high. Lockheed, General Dynamics, McDonnell Douglas, Grumman, and other major contractors have been primary suppliers to the Defense Department since before World War II.

This propensity to preserve a contractor seems to transcend concerns about inefficiency and even illegal behavior in the past. Following the Pentagon's decision to cancel General Dynamics' A-12 aircraft project due to cost overruns, the Department of Defense demanded the return of $1.9 billion originally advanced. General Dynamics appealed the demand on the grounds that this would bankrupt the firm, and the Defense Department relented, citing the need to "safeguard the nation's industrial base" (Cypher 1991, 10). Twenty-five of the nation's top defense contractors have been convicted of procurement fraud but are still awarded new contracts.

Sometimes follow-on contracts seem to be awarded as a sort of compensation for failure to win or preserve another program. In the 1960s, Rockwell was given the Apollo spacecraft contract shortly after the cancellation of the B-70. It was awarded the Space Shuttle contract after the B-1 was halted during the Carter administration (Kurth 1989, 204).

In addition to exchanging information, covering overhead and research and development costs, and providing follow-on contracts, the Pentagon has almost guaranteed the profitability of defense contractors by tolerating inefficiency on a large scale. In 1969, Senator William Proxmire (D-Wisconsin) focused attention on the tendency for defense contractors to seriously underestimate total costs in their bids to the Pentagon. He lamented:

> What is so discouraging about both the past and the future is the cavalier way in which increases and overruns are shrugged off by the military. . . . What appalls us is the uncritical way in which these increases are accepted by the military. To be consistently wrong on these estimates of cost, as the military has been consistently wrong, should bring the entire system of contracting under detailed scrutiny. But there is not the slightest indication that this is being done by the military. In fact, when such questions are raised, we find the services far more defensive than they are eager to improve the system. (Proxmire 1971, 85–86)

More than twenty years later, industry experts were repeating the refrain:

> Contractors are often rewarded for higher-than-planned costs with contributions to overhead, increased sales, and profits. And government managers are often rewarded for placing a higher priority on gaining congressional approval to begin a new weapon program (or to obtain additional funding for an ongoing program) than on controlling costs for existing programs. The acquisition cost problems of the 1970s and 1980s are not aberrations; they are the result of many government and industry participants reacting in perfect accord with the rewards and penalties that are inherent in the acquisition process. (Fox 1989, 155)

The net result of Pentagon tolerance of inefficiency seems to be high overall profit rates for defense contractors. Using return on investment (as opposed to percentage of sales), we find that defense contractors earned roughly 30 percent higher profits than comparable commercial manufacturers as of 1980. A study commissioned by the Navy in 1986 revealed that from 1977 to 1985, defense industry profits were higher than those of commercial firms (two and one-third times higher on average), and during the recession years of 1982 and 1983, they were three and four times higher, respectively (Cypher 1991, 10).

The Defense Department also arranges for the sale of weapons to foreign governments. Foreign arms sales to developing countries (roughly half of the total) have ebbed and flowed in inverse proportion to the size of the defense budget. Just as the follow-on imperative helps preserve production lines, DoD-arranged arms sales make up for drops in new weapons purchases by the Pentagon. As explained by Cypher:

> Through the Pentagon's Defense Security Assistance Agency, the U.S. government approves billions of dollars a year in foreign arms sales. In 1989, officially acknowledged arms sales totaled $15 billion. . . . [In 1990], Deputy Secretary of State Lawrence Eagleburger sent a memorandum ordering [the State Department] to "get on board by helping open doors for U.S. defense vendors." (Cypher 1991, 11)

Rockwell and other defense contractors proudly trumpet their success in foreign arms sales in their annual reports, with no reference to weapons proliferation or regional wars. Skeptics have pointed out that when the Defense and State Departments criticize China and France for spreading weapons illegally, they are really trying to create new markets for U.S. defense contractors. Some analysts have encouraged the expansion of overseas arms sales to save U.S. jobs (Bajusz and Louscher 1988). After the Gulf War, President George H.W. Bush approved a $21 billion sale of F-14 fighters, Apache helicopters, M-1 tanks, Patriot missiles, and rocket launchers to Saudi Arabia. "One congressional aide described the proposed sale as the 'defense relief act of 1990'" (Cypher 1991, 11).

In exchange for its consideration and support, the Defense Department is well rewarded. Each decade brings a new generation of increasingly sophisticated and impressive weapons with which to fight wars against increasingly weak adversaries. Defense industry officials are able to respond to Defense Department concepts and also stimulate new ideas about future weapons by showing research on what is possible. SDI is an example of DoD-driven research, whereas Stealth technology was largely the result of industry-driven research.

Each branch of the armed forces competes for the fanciest new innovations to better encroach on the others' turf. Certain contractors have developed strong linkages with certain services (Grumman with the Navy, Lockheed with the Air Force) on the presumption that their needs are so specialized that no other firms could satisfy them (Kurth 1989, 198). Past efforts by Pentagon officials to increase the compatibility of weapons across services (persuading the Air Force to use the Navy's F-14, for example) have not often been successful. The Navy has refused to consider reequipping Air Force jets for aircraft carriers, and the Air Force opposes sharing the A-10 "Warthog" attack aircraft with the Army.

Just as defense contractors welcome former Pentagon officials into their ranks, there is some movement of defense contractor personnel to the Pentagon, usually as "seconded" staff on temporary assignment. Such cross-fertilization gives "useful insights into the contractors' way of doing business" (Adams 1982, 79).

Defense contractors maintain large Washington offices, which are natural conduits for information, much of which is passed on to Pentagon associates. Sometimes the Department of Defense is able to get a better sense of what is happening on "the Hill" (in Congress) from industry lobbyists than through direct channels (Adams 1982, 131).

Overall, both the Pentagon and defense contractors have strong incentives to maintain close relations. The ties are intimate, to the point that sometimes it is difficult to know where the private sector leaves off and the public sector begins.

Industry–Congress Cooperation

Because almost all Defense Department spending must be approved by Congress, defense contractors and Pentagon officials alike have learned to hone their lobbying skills and to cultivate good relations with the ever-changing cast of characters on the Hill. Likewise, because defense-related industries are a crucial component of many home districts' economies, politicians on the Hill have learned to look out for the interests of defense industries. A symbiotic relationship has developed.

Candidate Bill Clinton learned the importance of the electoral clout of defense industry workers during the Connecticut primary in 1992, where the future of the SeaWolf submarine being built in New London was a key issue. Clinton had originally proposed scrapping it but then changed his mind in favor of finishing one of the two units planned. There were simply too many jobs (and votes) at stake.

During the 1991–1992 recession, it became apparent that dismantling (or "converting") the defense industry at a time of slow overall economic growth is nearly impossible without increasing unemployment. Even the closing of numerous military installations across the country has had a significant impact on many communities. The adjustment period afterward proved to be more difficult than previously imagined.

The concentration of defense-related jobs (and votes) has likewise affected the lobbying strategies of defense contractors. In California, for example, a half-million people work directly for the Department of Defense, and $29 billion was spent on weapons contracts in 1985 alone. Some 70,000 jobs in the Silicon Valley are directly connected to defense spending (Beers 1990, 30). In New York, more than $11 billion was spent on defense contracts in

1985, of which nearly $4 billion went to Grumman alone. When presented with a choice between converting the defense industry and funding the Grumman F-14, Congressman George Hochbruechner (D-New York) went against his principles and chose Grumman. "We had to do this one, the F-14, because this is the bread-and-butter aircraft for Grumman. That's the one that makes the money" (Beers 1990, 66).

As if they did not already have enough influence, defense contractors spend considerable sums on lobbying in Washington. To move specific bills forward, "[t]he Washington staff enlists the support of employees, shareholders, and the local communities dependent upon the economic well-being of their plants" (Adams 1982, 134). Defense contractors contributed in excess of $2 million to the Democratic members of the House and Senate Armed Services and defense-related appropriations subcommittees in 1988 (Beers 1990, 67).

> The Washington office staff . . . weaves a network in Congress, starting with the Representatives and Senators on committees that are important to the company—Armed Services, Appropriations, Science and Technology—and from districts and states in which the company has plant locations. In general Washington staffers tend to visit and encourage friends, rather than try to sway opponents of a program. (Adams 1982, 131)

The promotion of defense industries and the military by some members of Congress borders on fawning. One former chairman of the House Armed Services Committee "claims he was never fortunate enough to serve in the military but he has managed to be captivated by the military leaders and serves them with undaunted loyalty. He has done more than most generals to advance the interests of the nation's military" (Donovan 1970, 47). Even after it was proved that McDonnell Douglas illegally obtained classified documents to unfairly secure the ATA (Stealth attack aircraft) contract in 1987, Senator Sam Nunn (D-Georgia) supported leaving the contract with the firm so as not to disrupt construction. Particularly during the Reagan administration, many members of Congress bent over backward to appear pro-defense. Korb and Daggett described congressional attitudes in 1988:

> Among the Democrats, the centrist stance is defined by support for the Midgetman missile and opposition to a ban on missile flight tests. The moderately liberal position is to oppose defense waste and mismanagement and to favor conventional arms. The very liberal position is to criticize the growth of military spending at the expense of social programs. Among Republicans, the major issue appears to be who is more vigorously in favor of SDI. (Korb and Daggett 1989, 60)

Politicians often join one of the service associations and participate in social activities sponsored by defense contractors and the Pentagon. "The major problem with contractor entertainment is that it reinforces the closed-circuit of policy-making in the 'iron triangle.' It contributes to shared perceptions of the present and expectations about the future, to the view that critics are the enemy of both industry and Government" (Adams 1982, 176). Richard Barnet has argued that there is no need to look for a conspiracy in the close relationships among Congress, the Pentagon, and defense contractors. Those involved have such common interests, backgrounds, and perspectives that they simply reinforce one another's natural tendencies (Barnet 1969).

The Reform Movement and the Persian Gulf Renaissance

If the situation we have described seems as undemocratic as it is beyond remedy, it should be balanced with a discussion of other developments in defense spending and procurement.

After the end of the Vietnam War, defense spending on new weapons declined by one-third, and many firms struggled to survive. Although foreign arms sales made up for much of the decrease, the Carter administration's cost cutting and program reduction placed the defense industry in a serious situation. Defense spending declined not only in absolute terms but also as a share of total government spending and of the gross national product. Many deplored what was seen as a drop in American defense preparedness and a widening gap with growing Soviet arsenals.

This situation came to an end with the election of Ronald Reagan in 1980. Programs that had been canceled, such as the B-1 bomber and the MX missile, were resurrected and given unprecedented support. Several California firms reaped windfalls (Kurth 1989, 205), and new firms such as TRW and Raytheon became heavy hitters in the high-tech world of SDI. During the period 1981–1986, defense spending on new weapons increased by 75 percent, and research and development grew by 86 percent in real terms (Sullivan 1985, 55).

On the heels of this growth came new pressures to combat inefficiency and fraud. As discouraging test results and alarming cost overruns came to the attention of Congress, a new mood of reform swept Capitol Hill. The Bradley fighting vehicle was a target in the early 1980s when tests showed that it could not float, as originally advertised, and that its "armor" could not stop much more than gunshots—a fact that led to its exploding in a ball of flame when hit with an antitank shell (Main 1991, 54). Other weapons, such as DIVAD, the Sergeant York, and the B-1B, proved unable to carry out their assigned missions.

These reports, combined with stories of widespread fraud, led to a major reform movement in Congress and even at the White House. Commissions were formed, investigations launched, and hearings held. A new Defense Procurement Fraud Unit was set up but soon proved to be mere window dressing and did little to attack corruption in the procurement process. The relationships among Congress, the Pentagon, and the defense contractors grew increasingly bitter as each shifted blame for the problems onto the others (Korb 1988).

Determining whether the reform movement has changed the military-industrial complex in any permanent way is difficult. The end of the Cold War and the relative decreases in military budgets have certainly made it clear to the defense industry that conversion is no longer desirable, but essential. Congress cut SDI research in half in the 1990s, and the Defense Department demonstrated a more aggressive attitude against waste by canceling the Navy's A-12 attack aircraft project in 1990 (Huey and Perry 1991, 36). More than one-third of all procurement contracts are now based on "fixed-price" calculations of parts and machinery, which aim at containing costs (Cypher 1991, 10). The result seems to be greater efforts to contain costs and experimentation with a team approach to management in such firms as McDonnell Douglas and Rockwell. The F-117A Stealth fighter was proudly delivered in record time and below cost in 1990 (Perry 1991, 48).

The reform movement may have been cut short by the war in the Persian Gulf. Almost as soon as the bombs fell and the Stealth fighters and cruise missiles flew into Baghdad, criticism of the Defense Department's penchant for high-tech weaponry melted away. Senator John Warner said, "I think you'll find the members of Congress voicing much less criticism with respect to high-tech weapons. The investment in these weapons systems has paid off" (Huey and Perry 1991, 34). As put by Cypher:

> The smooth transition from Cold War to global militarism highlights the extent to which military interests have developed their own momentum within the United States. And while no one argues that the United States spearheaded the war against Iraq solely to benefit arms contractors, they may emerge as the biggest winners from the conflict. (Cypher 1991, 9)

Consolidation, Conversion, and "Cashing Out"

The post–Cold War era has presented a key test of the "military-industrial complex" perspective on defense expenditures because for the first time since the 1930s, the United States has no obvious, threatening enemy (see Cases 3 and 8). If, in fact, the defense establishment's purpose is to protect the country from threats, then the 1990s should have been a period of considerable dismantling of hardware, closure of bases, and disruption among defense contractors. In fact, much of this occurred, though perhaps not to the extent one might expect. The persistence of much of the defense establishment seems to confirm at least in part the predictions of "iron triangle" theorists.

As shown in Figure 5.1, defense spending has been trending downward since 1987 in terms of its share of national government spending. In 2000, defense spending accounted for less than 15 percent of the federal budget for the first time since before World War II.

Much of the story of the defense industry in the 1990s involved mergers. More than $70 billion in mergers occurred in the defense industry between 1993 and 1997 (Weidenbaum 1997). Almost all of 1990's top ten defense con-

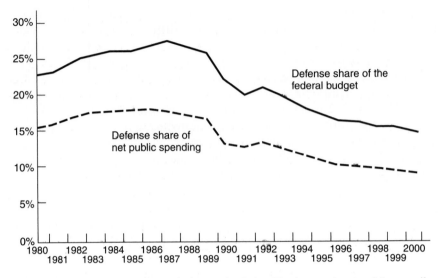

Figure 5.1 Defense spending relative to the federal budget and net public spending
Source: Department of Defense defenselink website, August 2000.

tractors were involved (see Table 5.1), resulting in a greater concentration of ownership and substantial layoffs (the aerospace industry lost 500,000 jobs between 1989 and 1996). General Dynamics' Plant 4 in Fort Worth, Texas, is a case in point. The factory employed 31,000 in the mid-1980s when it built the F-16 fighter jet. It was in line to receive a new contract for the A-12 when President George H.W. Bush canceled it. General Dynamics sold the plant to

Table 5.1 Top Ten Pentagon Contractors, 1997–2001
(contract value in current $ billion)

Rank		Company Name	Contracts	
1997	2001		1997	2001
1	1	Lockheed Martin	11.6	14.7
2*	2	Boeing Company	9.6	13.3
16	3	Newport News Shipbuilding	0.7	5.9
5	4	Raytheon	2.9	5.6
3	5	Northrup Grumman	3.5	5.2
4	6	General Dynamics	3.0	4.9
7	7	United Technologies	1.8	3.8
14	8	TRW	0.8	1.9
11	9	Science Applications International	1.1	1.7
8	10	General Electric	1.7	1.7

*In 1997, Boeing acquired McDonnell Douglas, which was ranked number 2 in 1996.
Source: Directorate for Information Operations and Reports, Statistical Information Analysis Division, DOD, 2002: www.dior.whs.mil/peidhome/peidhome.htm.

Lockheed in 1993 at about the same time its missile division was acquired by Hughes Aircraft, leaving the company with a global payroll of only 43,000. Lockheed began cutting staff, to the point that Plant 4 now employs only 10,000 people (and employee numbers continue to drop). Lockheed itself merged with Martin Marietta in 1995 in response to a direct recommendation (with federal assistance) from the secretary of defense (Greider 1998, 57).

Of course, defense contractors have tried to adjust to this new environment and have buttressed their earnings in new areas. Lockheed Martin now sells roughly one-fifth of its output to overseas buyers, and it has diversified its product line to the point that defense contracts account for less than half of the company's total sales. (In 1989, defense contracts accounted for 75 percent of Martin Marietta's sales and 90 percent of Lockheed's sales.) Lockheed Martin has also relocated much of its activity overseas to take advantage of both lower wages and easier access to local markets, and it now has facilities in fifty-six countries (Hartung 1999). Increases in overseas sales are nothing new, given the historic pattern of increasing foreign arms sales when domestic contracts have fallen off (Brzoska and Ohlson 1987). A key difference now is that no one believes the current pattern is just a temporary setback. Overall, the defense industry is reshaping itself to look increasingly like any other corporate sector in a globalized economy (see Case 20). Conservatives have even expressed concern that the United States may be jeopardizing its military preparedness by allowing the defense industry to shrink (Weidenbaum 1997).

The George W. Bush administration interpreted its election as a mandate to strengthen the military preparedness of the nation, and submitted a budget for 2002 that was $32.6 billion (11 percent) higher than the 2001 budget. After the terrorist attacks of September 11, 2001, the military drew up new requirements, which added another $10.1 billion to a 2003 proposal that would have been $40 billion higher than the 2002 budget anyway. The $355 billion budget, as ultimately approved, provides $72 billion for new weapons–an 18 percent increase over 2002 levels—and $7 billion for antimissile systems (DoD 2002). Even though many big-ticket weapons are of questionable value (the F-22, B-1, and V-22 aircraft and the Comanche helicopter have been singled out, along with the Crusader self-propelled artillery system), none has been eliminated. On the contrary, after September 11, the Defense Department issued a blanket invitation for new weapons proposals that might help in the fight against terrorism (Knickerbocker, 2002).

Conclusion

The days of automatic, large contracts seen during the Cold War seem to be over, and the defense budget remains low relative to the total size of the U.S. economy. This is not to say that the country is demilitarizing. U.S. defense spending levels are still high relative to those of other countries. The United States accounts for 34 percent of global defense spending, while Russia accounts for only 8 percent and China less than 5 percent. If all defense spending by NATO allies is added to that by the United States, the total accounts for 62 percent of global defense spending. The United States alone supplies more than half of the world's weapons (Hartung 1999). Although the United States has promoted a reduction in strategic weapons, its lack of commitment to conventional arms control was illustrated by its refusal to sign the land mine ban (see Case 24) and by its decision to abrogate the Anti-ballistic Missile Treaty in 2002 (see Case 3).

The post–September 11 environment will likely mean good times for defense contractors for the foreseeable future. If anything, the Bush administration's plans to maintain a large presence in Afghanistan and Iraq mean a steady stream of orders. The 2003 budget is more than one-fourth larger than the 2001 budget, and it is unlikely that 2004's budget will show flat growth. It is too soon to say that this trend is resulting in waste, but some caution seems warranted given the scale of spending.

Debate Topic

Should defense contracts be the exclusive domain of private firms? Should it be part of the government itself, as in France?

PRO

Those who support the private nature of defense contracting make several points: (1) The competitive bidding process increases the likelihood that the best weapons will be made at the lowest cost. (2) The past success of private contractors, and the clear superiority of U.S. weapons compared to those of other countries, provides clear evidence that the system is working. (3) So many individuals and communities depend on existing defense firms that abandoning the system would create considerable hardship unnecessarily.

CON

Those who believe weapons should be built by government agencies make the following arguments: (1) Private firms are notorious for using deceptive, dishonest, and wasteful practices to win and get the most from government contracts. (2) Private firms are largely redundant, and consolidation in a public agency can generate great savings. (3) There is no reason to think that layoffs or hardship would be necessary, since existing facilities could be used for future production, regardless of ownership.

Questions to Consider

1. What factors seem to best explain trends in defense spending? Are internal or external forces the most important causes?

2. To what extent is defense spending a result of lobbying by contractors and their cozy relationships with policy makers? Is it possible that de-

fense spending is more a function of national priorities than parochial self-interest?

3. How have changes in defense spending affected you and your community? Is your state home to defense contractors? Has unemployment risen as a result of base closings or contract termination? How do you feel about that?

Websites

Government Sites
Department of Defense Fact File: **www.defenselink.mil/factfile/rl**
House Armed Services Committee: **www.house.gov.hasc/rl**
Senate Armed Services Committee: **www.senate.gov/committee_detail.cfm?/COM-MITTEE_ID=408rl**

Defense Contractors
General Dynamics: **www.gd.com**
Litton Industries: **www.litton.com**
Lockheed Martin: **www.lmco.com**
Northrup Grumman: **www.northgrum.com**
Rand Corporation: **www.rand.org/natsec**

Interest Groups
Center for Defense Information: **www.cdi.org/issues/mic.html** (Note its exhaustive links page.)
Center for Strategic and International Studies: **www.csis.org**
Institute for Defense Analysis: **www.ida.org/index.html**
Institute for Global Communications: **www.igc.org/infocus/papers/micr.html**
Project on Defense Alternatives: **www.comw.org/pda/index.html**
Stockholm International Peace Research Institute: **www.sipri.se**

References

Adams, Gordon. *The Politics of Defense Contracting: The Iron Triangle* (New Brunswick, NJ: Transaction Books, 1982).

Bajusz, William D., and David J. Louscher. *Arms Sales and the U.S. Economy: The Impact of Restricting Military Exports* (Boulder, CO: Westview Press, 1988).

Ball, Nicole, and Milton Leitenberg, eds. *The Structure of the Defense Industry: An International Survey* (New York: St. Martin's Press, 1983).

Barnet, Richard. *The Economy of Death* (New York: Atheneum, 1969).

Beers, David. "Brother, Can You Spare $1.5 Trillion?" *Mother Jones* 15 #5 (July/August 1990): 28–33, 66–68.

Brzoska, Michael, and Thomas Ohlson. *Arms Transfers to the Third World, 1971–85* (New York: Oxford University Press, 1987).

Cusack, Thomas. "On the Domestic Political-Economic Sources of American Military Spending" in Mintz, ed., *The Political Economy of Military Spending in the United States,* 103–134.

Cypher, James M. "The War Dividend." *Dollars & Sense* #166 (May 1991): 9–11, 21.

Department of Defense, "2003 Defense Budget Is Investment in Transformation," Press release, February 4, 2002.

Donahue, Jim. "The Patriots at Raytheon." *Multinational Monitor* 12 #3 (March 1991): 26–29.

Donovan, James A. *Militarism, USA* (New York: Charles Scribner's Sons, 1970).

Dye, Thomas R., and Harmon Zeigler. *The Irony of Democracy: An Uncommon Introduction to American Politics* (Belmont, CA: Wadsworth, 1993).

Fox, J. Ronald. "Obstacles to Improving the Defense Acquisition Process" in Kruzel, ed., *American Defense Annual*, 145–160.

Greider, William. *Fortress America: The American Military and the Consequences of Peace* (New York: Public Affairs, 1998).

Hartung, William. "Military-Industrial Complex Revisited: How Weapons Makers Are Shaping U.S. Foreign and Military Policies." Available on the website of the Institute for Global Communications, June 1999.

Huey, John, and Nancy J. Perry. "The Future of Arms." *Fortune* (February 25, 1991): 34–36.

Knickerbocker, Brad. "Return of the 'Military-Industrial Complex'?" *Christian Science Monitor* (February 13, 2002).

Korb, Lawrence. "The Department of Defense, Defense Industry and Procurement: Fatal Misconception" in Herbert L. Sawyer, ed., *Business in the Contemporary World* (New York: University Press of America, 1988), 35–42.

Korb, Lawrence, and Stephen Daggett. "The Defense Budget and Strategic Planning" in Kruzel, ed., *American Defense Annual*, 43–65.

Kruzel, Joseph, ed. *American Defense Annual*, 1989–1990 (Lexington, MA: D. C. Heath, 1989).

Kurth, James R. "The Military-Industrial Complex Revisited" in Kruzel, ed., *American Defense Annual*, 195–216.

Leitzel, Jim. "Competition in Procurement." *Policy Sciences* 25 #1 (February 1992): 43–56.

Main, Jeremy. "FMC Profile." *Fortune* (February 25, 1991): 50–56.

Mayer, Kenneth. "Elections, Business Cycles, and the Timing of Defense Contract Awards in the United States" in Mintz, ed., *The Political Economy of Military Spending in the United States*, 15–32.

Mintz, Alex, ed. *The Political Economy of Military Spending in the United States* (New York: Routledge, 1992).

Perry, Nancy. "Lockheed Profile." *Fortune* (February 25, 1991): 47–48.

Proxmire, William. "The Costs of Military Spending" in Kenneth S. Davis, ed., *Arms, Industry and America* (New York: H. W. Wilson Co., 1971), 82–89.

Reppy, Judith. "The United States" in Ball and Leitenberg, eds., *The Structure of the Defense Industry*, 21–49.

Sandler, Todd, and Keith Hartley. *The Economics of Defense* (London: Cambridge University Press, 1995).

Stoll, Richard. "Too Little, but Not for Too Long: Public Attitudes on Defense Spending" in Mintz, ed., *The Political Economy of Military Spending in the United States*, 52–64.

Sullivan, Leonard. "The Defense Budget" in George Hudson and Joseph Kruzel, eds., *American Defense Annual*, 1985–86 (Lexington, MA: D. C. Heath, 1985), 53–75.

Ward, Michael, and David Davis. "Risky Business: U.S.–Soviet Competition and Corporate Profits" in Mintz, ed., *The Political Economy of Military Spending in the United States*, 65–102.

Weidenbaum, Murray. "The Changing Threats to National Security." Address to the National Association of Business Economists, St. Louis, MO, September 17, 1997.

CASE
6

Vietnam Homefront
PUBLIC OPINION

Introduction

Until several major powers became democratic, public opinion was important only to the extent that soldiers were willing to fight and citizens were willing to pay taxes without excessive pressure from the state. By the turn of the century, however, it was widely accepted that public opinion was crucial, even to nondemocratic governments. One can distinguish between fundamental and short-term public attitudes. Nationalism, a sense of duty toward the state, a feeling of community with compatriots, and confidence in the rightness of the national course tend not to vary significantly from month to month or year to year. These represent what may be called the "national character." On the other hand, public opinion polls demonstrate that the national mood and opinions about specific policies change dramatically from month to month—even minute by minute during a crisis. A successful leader will distinguish between these two and learn how to use them to his advantage. An unsuccessful one will kick against mass opinion at his peril.

War in a democracy is a hazardous endeavor for any politician seeking reelection. Although a democratic nation united in battle is an awesome force, democracies are uniquely prone to discouragement when wartime sacrifices seem to outweigh promised benefits. Politicians have been forced to break off an unpopular fight to save their political skins. Many argue that this is precisely what took place in the Vietnam era in the United States. Even today, Americans continue to experience a sense of deep personal ambivalence with regard to Vietnam. Could we have won the war? Was our cause just? Who was to blame for our failure? These doubts and questions were at the root of the public opposition to the war, which in turn contributed to the fall of two presidents and a dramatic change in our foreign policy priorities. As put by former Secretary of Defense George Ball:

We have never recovered from the anger and divisiveness of the latter 1960s, and I find increasing evidence of the baleful mark left by our Vietnam experience on almost all aspects of American life. . . (Ball 1982, 467)

To better understand both how public opinion was formed during the war and how this opinion may or may not have affected policy, we will briefly review the key events of the Vietnam War itself. U.S. involvement in Vietnam's civil war dates back at least to World War II and began in earnest in 1954, when the French colonists withdrew from Vietnam after their defeat at Dien Bien Phu. Ho Chi Minh, leader of the Vietcong Communist guerrillas since 1941, became the leader of the provisional North Vietnamese government in Hanoi, while a succession of largely unpopular governments emerged in Saigon with U.S. support. The rest of the story can be told most quickly with the simple chronology.

VIETNAM HOMEFRONT
KEY FIGURES

John F. Kennedy U.S. President,1961–1963. He supported expanding U.S. military assistance to South Vietnam, although he became disillusioned with its government.

Lyndon Johnson Vice-President, 1961–1963, and U.S. President, 1963–1969. He presided over the dramatic increase in U.S. military involvement in Vietnam, based in part on the Tonkin Gulf Resolution he persuaded Congress to pass. He eventually chose not to run for reelection in 1968 because of public opposition to his Vietnam policies.

Richard Nixon U.S. President,1969–1974. He completed the American withdrawal from Vietnam and negotiated, with Henry Kissinger, the Paris Peace Accords. He also directed a series of massive bombing campaigns in Vietnam and Cambodia.

Henry Kissinger Senior advisor to Presidents Nixon and Gerald Ford as National Security Advisor and Secretary of State. He promoted a pragmatic approach to Vietnam that included both escalation and withdrawal.

Robert McNamara U.S. Secretary of Defense, 1963-1968. An early supporter of military intervention in Vietnam, he later testified before Senator Fulbright's committee that the effort was failing.

Dean Acheson U.S. Secretary of State, 1949-195. He offered objections to the war beginning in 1967.

Clark Clifford U.S. Secretary of Defense, 1968-1969. He encouraged President Johnson to withdraw troops from Vietnam.

Ho Chi Minh Leader of the Vietnamese Communist Party, he governed North Vietnam from 1949 to 1969.

Nguyen Van Thieu South Vietnamese President, 1967–1975.

Ngo Dinh Diem Leader of South Vietnam from 1955 until his overthrow in 1963.

William Fulbright U.S. Senator from Arkansas. He helped pass President Johnson's Tonkin Gulf Resolution in 1964 and later conducted hearings critical of Johnson's conduct of the Vietnam War.

(continued)

Barry Goldwater Unsuccessful U.S. presidential candidate in 1964. He believed Lyndon Johnson was not going far enough to support South Vietnam.

Hubert Humphrey U.S. Vice-President, 1963–1969. He was an unsuccessful presidential candidate in 1968.

William Westmoreland Commander of U.S. forces in South Vietnam, 1964-1968.

Eugene McCarthy Unsuccessful U.S. presidential candidate in 1968. He opposed U.S. involvement in Vietnam.

Robert F. Kennedy Former U.S. Attorney General and candidate for president in 1968. He opposed the war and was assassinated in 1968.

George McGovern Unsuccessful U.S. presidential candidate in 1972. He opposed U.S. involvement in Vietnam.

Daniel Ellsberg Defense Department official who resigned, and then released the Pentagon Papers to the *New York Times* in 1971.

Abby Hoffman Antiwar activist.

Tom Hayden Antiwar activist.

Walter Cronkite Eminent news anchor. He came out against the war in Vietnam in 1968.

Martin Luther King, Jr. Eminent civil rights leader. He came out against the war in Vietnam in 1968.

VIETNAM HOMEFRONT
CHRONOLOGY

1955

January	U.S. military advisors begin training the South Vietnamese army.
July	The Soviet Union and China begin providing aid to North Vietnam.
October	Ngo Dinh Diem becomes president.

1956

Diem begins a crackdown on Communist sympathizers (Vietminh).

1957

May	Diem and Eisenhower meet in Washington, D. C.
October	The North Vietnamese government helps organize a guerrilla army (Vietcong) in South Vietnam.

1959

May	The Ho Chi Minh Trail, running through Laos and Cambodia from Hanoi into South Vietnam, becomes an operational supply route for matériel for the Vietcong.
July	The first Americans die in Vietnam fighting.

1960

April	Universal military conscription is imposed in North Vietnam.
November	An unsuccessful coup attempt against Diem occurs amid growing protests over the regime in South Vietnam.
December	Civil war erupts in Laos, with Soviets supplying the rebels.

(continued)

1961

May	The Geneva Conference on Laos leads to the creation of a neutral government. Lyndon Johnson returns from a visit to South Vietnam with a recommendation for more aid to the Diem regime.
October	Maxwell Taylor and Walt Rostow recommend covert military aid after a visit with Diem, but Kennedy opts for more financial support.

1962

February	The United States organizes formal military support in South Vietnam and increases the number of advisors there from 700 to 12,000.

1963

January	The Vietcong score victories in battles with the South Vietnamese army; army unrest increases in the South.
May–June	Some Buddhist demonstrators are shot and others commit suicide by self-immolation.
August	The United States urges Diem to change his repressive policies and warns of a coup attempt.
November	General Duong Van Minh overthrows Diem in coup; Diem is assassinated.
December	U.S. advisors in South Vietnam number 15,000; U.S. aid in 1963 equals $500 million.

1964

January	General Nguyen Khanh seizes power in Saigon.
June	Robert McNamara and Dean Rusk encourage more support; the U.S. military plans a bombing raid against North Vietnam.
August	The Tonkin Gulf incident, involving purported North Vietnamese attacks on U.S. intelligence ships off the coast, leads to passage of the Tonkin Gulf Resolution, giving Lyndon Johnson significant powers to respond.
Autumn	Johnson rejects retaliatory bombing following Viet Cong raids against U.S. installations.

1965

February	Operations Flaming Dart and Rolling Thunder begin systematic bombing of North Vietnam. General Khanh is removed by Phan Huy Quat in Saigon.
March	The first Marines land at Da Nang airfield.
June	Nguyan Cao Ky becomes the new prime minister, with Nguyan Van Thieu as South Vietnam's president.
July	In light of the defeats for the South Vietnamese army, Johnson authorizes the deployment of forty-four more battalions.
December	Johnson suspends the bombing campaign over Christmas to induce the North Vietnamese to negotiate. U.S. troop strength reaches 200,000.

1966

January	Bombing of North Vietnam resumes.
Spring	The battles of Hue and Da Nang give the South Vietnam–U.S. forces major victories.
December	U.S. troop strength reaches 400,000.

1967

Spring	Johnson secretly corresponds with North Vietnamese officials on peace options; the North Vietnamese demand a halt to bombing prior to beginning negotiations.
August	McNamara testifies before Congress that the bombing campaign is ineffective.
October	A massive antiwar protest takes place at the Pentagon.
November	General William Westmoreland exudes confidence during a trip in the United States.
December	U.S. troop strength reaches 500,000.

1968

January	The Tet offensive involving Viet Cong and North Vietnamese attacks on South Vietnamese cities, is repulsed but demonstrates the strength of the North Vietnamese forces to a surprised American audience. *(continued)*

March	Johnson decides to halt the war escalation and announces he will not run for reelection.
April	Paris peace talks begin between the United States and North Vietnam.
July	The Democratic convention in Chicago is the scene of antiwar demonstrations.
October	Johnson halts the bombing.
December	Troop strength peaks at roughly 540,000.

1969

January	South Vietnam is included in the Paris peace talks.
March	President Richard Nixon begins secret bombing of Cambodia.
June	Thieu and Nixon announce the withdrawal of 25,000 U.S. troops under the rubric of "Vietnamization."
October	A massive antiwar demonstration takes place in Washington.
November	The My Lai massacre is revealed.
December	U.S. troop strength is down to 480,000.

1970

April	Nixon reveals the covert attacks against Cambodia.
May	Four students are killed in an antiwar protest at Kent State University.
Autumn	Nixon explores the possibility of simultaneous withdrawal with the North Vietnamese.
December	Troop strength is down to 280,000.

1971

March	Lieutenant William Calley is convicted of murder in connection with the My Lai massacre.
June	The Pentagon Papers are published, leading to an investigation of Daniel Ellsberg.
December	Troop strength is down to 140,000.

1972

January	Nixon reveals the secret talks between Kissinger and North Vietnamese officials (dating back to February 1970).
March	The North Vietnamese army attacks across the frontier.
April	Nixon approves the bombing of Hanoi.
August	Paris negotiations continue in spite of South Vietnamese resistance.
October	The United States and North Vietnam reach an accord; Thieu opposes it.
December	After the collapse of talks, the bombing raids resume.

1973

January	The peace accords are signed in Paris.
March	The last U.S. troops leave South Vietnam.
August	Congress forces the Nixon administration to halt the bombing of Cambodia.
November	Over Nixon's veto, Congress passes the War Powers Act.

1974

| January | War is initiated again. |

1975

January	The final North Vietnamese push begins.
March	Hue falls.
April	Saigon falls; South Vietnam ceases to exist.

*Karnow (1983, 670–686) provides the best chronology available.

Public Opinion and Vietnam

The American public generally favors presidents who deal decisively with foreign policy crises, even when their efforts fail. In the case of Vietnam, public support was not only strong but sustained until 1968. Following the

Tet Offensive, the domestic consensus on the rightness of the U.S. war effort in Vietnam underwent a palpable shift, which directly affected the way the White House fought the war. To better understand this shift, we need to look at the chain of events that preceded and followed it.

Tonkin Gulf and Rally 'Round the Flag

The Kennedy administration came to office with a call to sacrifice in the fight against communism. Kennedy referred to a "New Frontier" of progress and leadership. In the aftermath of to the Sputnik shock, the "missile gap" scare, the fall of Cuba to communism, and other deeply troubling events, however, the country seemed to be on a war footing. Although Kennedy met with a setback in the failed invasion of Cuba at the Bay of Pigs, he captured the country's imagination with his firm stand against Moscow over the Cuban missiles (Kattenburg 1980, 210). Thus, for reasons of national pride and compassion for the citizens of "captive nations," as well as out of simple fear, the American public was favorably disposed in the early 1960s to undertake a crusade on distant shores (Levy 1991, 16). Although Vietnam had not yet entered the public consciousness, Kennedy and Vice President Lyndon Johnson could feel assured of the public's latent support.

After Kennedy's assassination in November 1963, Johnson came to power in the White House. His attitude was far less patient than that of Kennedy, who had tolerated the overthrow of South Vietnam's leader Ngo Dinh Diem after refusing to support the unpopular president. Johnson was more eager to score victories on the battlefield, where the Communist Vietcong insurgents, funded and supplied by North Vietnam, were making significant progress. Looking for a popular rationale for deploying more troops to the region, Johnson seized upon an incident in the Gulf of Tonkin. Two U.S. patrol boats had exchanged fire with North Vietnamese warships near the coast, prompting an outcry from the White House that was echoed on Capitol Hill. Johnson asked Senator William Fulbright to shepherd a resolution giving Johnson broad powers to retaliate immediately and in the future. The Tonkin Gulf Resolution was passed on August 7, 1964, by a vote of eighty-eight to two. As pointed out by Herring:

> From a domestic political standpoint, Johnson's handling of the Tonkin Gulf incident was masterly. His firm but restrained response to the alleged North Vietnamese attacks won broad popular support, his rating in the Louis Harris poll skyrocketed from 42 to 72 percent overnight. He effectively neutralized [hawkish Republican presidential hopeful Barry] Goldwater on Vietnam, a fact which contributed to his overwhelming electoral victory in November. (Herring 1986, 122)

Kattenburg explained, however, that this support was largely naive because the American public did not fully understand the nature of the war that was under way.

> [T]he American people wanted to believe [the New Frontier rhetoric], and believe they did. When the number of U.S. military men increased from under

1,000 to about 15,000 in Vietnam in a little over six months, few people realized that the New Frontier had in effect started the process of extending U.S. borders to those of Indochina with Thailand. (Kattenburg 1980, 209)

Lyndon Johnson won an overwhelming victory against Goldwater in 1964, campaigning as the peace candidate (a position he reversed shortly after the election—Kattenburg 1980, 251). Support for the war was at 65 percent by late 1965, and with news of the bombing campaigns, public opinion was supportive (Mueller 1973, 119). This "spike" in public support is an illustration of the "rally 'round the flag" phenomenon, whereby large segments of the public express support for the president's policies in any crisis situation, regardless of the substance of the policies. Leslie Gelb argued that in spite of the emergence in 1965 of an antiwar movement, "the widespread belief that South Vietnam should not be lost to communism generated and sustained that war" (Gelb 1976, 103). Nevertheless, letters opposing the bombing campaign poured into Capitol Hill offices following the announcement (Herring 1986, 133). Overall, the signals sent by the public in the early stages of the war were contradictory and confusing. Political leaders could and did read into them what they wanted.

Growing Skepticism

During 1966 and 1967, Johnson's policy of escalation was in full swing. By the end of 1967, nearly half a million troops were deployed and nearly 10,000 had fallen in combat. Sustained bombing of the North, coupled with CIA covert operations, supported the Marines in the field. Vietnam was very much on the minds of Americans, to the point that it was viewed as the single most significant issue of the day by 1967. However, as the fight wore on, three different groups of Americans began to question the rightness of the war.

The first to defect was a group of already disenchanted individuals who later came to form the core of the antiwar movement across college campuses. We will say more about the peace movement later, but by 1965 it largely consisted of pacifists, leftists, and radicals but also included a growing number of housewives, moderate academics, and various celebrities. By mid-1965, antiwar groups could muster crowds of 15,000 and more (Levy 1991, 126). In November 1965, a major march in Washington, D. C., which hoped to appear aimed at being respectable by including major mainstream figures, nonetheless deteriorated into a circus of sorts. It was not until the Fulbright hearings of early 1966 that dignified opposition could be articulated.

Of much greater significance to Johnson than antiwar demonstrations was the defection of several high-level policy advisors and members of Congress, who had previously supported the policy of escalation. Senator Fulbright began hearings on the war in the spring of 1966 with Senate Majority Leader Mike Mansfield's tacit support (Herring 1986, 172). At the hearings, the Senate Foreign Relations Committee questioned senior officials as well as prominent outsiders to the administration to make the point that the war had no clear objective or plan of action. In August 1967, Secretary of Defense Robert McNa-

Table 6.1 Classification of Attitudes on Vietnam

When the war first became an issue	Toward the end of U.S. involvement			
	I tended to favor a complete military victory	I tended to feel in between these two	Not sure	I tended to favor a complete withdrawal
I tended to favor a complete military victory	SUPPORTERS (n = 363, 15.9%)	AMBIVALENT SUPPORTERS (n = 346,15.2%)		CONVERTED CRITICS (n = 867, 38.0%)
I tended to feel in between these two	CONVERTED SUPPORTERS (n = 128, 15.6%)	AMBIVALENTS (n = 128, 5.6%)		
Not sure				
I tended to favor a complete withdrawal		AMBIVALENT CRITICS (n = 63, 2.8%)		CRITICS (n = 378, 16.6%)

Source: Ole Holsti and James Rosenau, *American Leadership in World Affairs* (Boston: Allen & Unwin, 1984).

mara gave the committee much ammunition by stating that the intensive bombing campaign in the North not only was failing to achieve its objective of halting the supply of matériel to the South but likely would never succeed.

A group of senior unofficial advisors to Johnson, including such respected figures as former Secretary of State Dean Acheson, advised him privately in mid-1967 and publicly thereafter that the war could not be won and that he should look for a way out. The newly appointed Secretary of Defense Clark Clifford consistently encouraged Johnson to begin troop withdrawals and a general program of "Vietnamization"—turning over the prosecution of the war to local South Vietnamese forces (Karnow 1983, 559–562).

Most of these defections were by individuals who were firmly committed to U.S. leadership in the fight against communism. It wasn't that they opposed the New Frontier; they simply felt that Vietnam, with its largely illegitimate government, ill-defined battle fronts, and ambiguous context, ought not be the test case (Gelb 1976, 111).

Overall, as documented by Holsti and Rosenau (1984), elite opinion in the United States shifted dramatically against the war. Table 6.1 shows that 38 percent of the elites in the country began by favoring the war and ended by opposing it; only 16 percent consistently supported the war effort. If one adds the "ambivalent supporters," whose enthusiasm for the war clearly wanes, to the "critics," "converted critics," and "ambivalent critics," then three-fourths of the elites in the country were either critical or tending to be more critical of the war at its end than at its outset (Holsti and Rosenau 1984, 33). This kind of pressure from individuals who tended to play an active role in politics was overwhelming for Johnson.

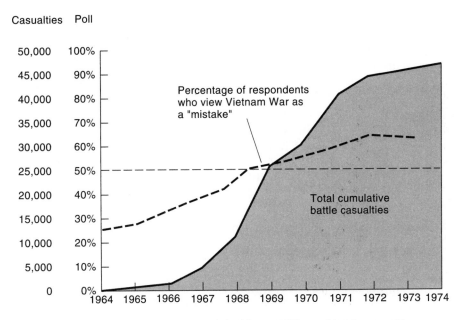

Figure 6.1 Americans' attitudes toward the Vietnam War and battle casualties.
Sources: Various issues of Gallup Poll annual editions.

The third group that became disenchanted with the war was the "general" public—that poorly organized mass of opinion that pollsters constantly seek to measure and plot. Although the nature of public opinion prior to 1968 was uncertain, it seems that the U.S. public's perception changed slowly after 1965 from an initial and fairly general understanding that external aggression was being resisted by the South Vietnamese, to a largely unexpressed image of Vietnamese, both southern and northern, resisting the imposition by U.S. means of a type of U.S.-made order upon Vietnam (Kattenburg 1980, 244).

The press played some role in all of this. As early as 1963, it was reporting on the confusing nature of the war. Stanley Karnow criticized the corrupt regime of the Diem family in the mainstream magazine *Saturday Evening Post* (Levy 1991, 52), and visual reports from televised news media brought home the brutal and ugly nature of this conflict. The question of a "credibility gap" between official military projections and the reality of televised reports became the focal point of the debate on the war by 1968. Ultimately, the Tet Offensive tipped the balance ever so slightly against the war (see Figure 6.1 on public opinion).

Tet Shock and Johnson's "Resignation"

During the January 1968 lunar new year celebrations (called Tet) in Vietnam, the Vietcong and North Vietnamese Army (NVA) took advantage of a general lull in the fighting to launch an all-out offensive on every conceivable target in South Vietnam. The "Tet Offensive" brought Vietcong and NVA troops as far south as Saigon, outside the U.S. embassy complex there. Cities, airfields, and fuel depots were all targeted by the most visible and dramatic military operation of the war.

All of this was covered in painful detail and was exaggerated to melodrama by the American media (Levy 1991, 145). Although the military engagement was clearly won by U.S.-led troops, the psychological effect of the event was to shock the American public into a realization that this war was far from over. Walter Cronkite, "the most trusted person in America," said on February 27, 1968, following an analysis of Tet, that it seemed "more certain than ever that the bloody experience of Vietnam is to end in a stalemate" (Karnow 1983, 547). Shortly thereafter, Martin Luther King, Jr., declared his opposition to the war. A majority of Americans for the first time agreed that U.S. involvement in Vietnam was "a mistake," although there was no consensus on how the country should extricate itself from the conflict (roughly half of those who opposed current policy felt the United States should escalate the war to finish the job, and roughly half felt troops should simply withdraw—Karnow 1983, 546). By 1968, the U.S. public seemed to agree that preserving South Vietnam was not vital to U.S. national interest (Kattenburg 1980, 244).

On the political front, the Tet Offensive coincided with the beginning of the 1968 presidential campaign. Although Johnson was assumed to be the party's nominee, he had failed to file as a candidate in time for the New Hampshire primary in March. A relatively unknown senator named Eugene McCarthy, running on an antiwar platform, inundated the state with an army of clean-cut college students and managed to secure just 300 votes less than write-in candidate Johnson in what was seen as the political upset of the decade. Certainly, all those who voted for McCarthy were not doves (three out of five, in fact, believed the United States should escalate the effort in Vietnam—Kearns 1976, 354), but the event galvanized opposition to Johnson within the Democratic Party. Within a week, Senator Robert Kennedy had announced his candidacy for the presidency and declared his opposition to the war as the key issue of the race (Karnow 1983, 559). As put by Roche:

> The defection of Robert Kennedy was a decisive event in the anti-war saga. At last the anti-war forces had a senior, legitimate political figure who could not be written off as a Hanoi stooge or some species of eccentric. (Roche 1976, 131)

Lyndon Johnson had suddenly become what he feared most—the "war candidate." Furthermore, his visceral antipathy toward Robert Kennedy knew no bounds. He was haunted by Kennedy in his dreams (Kearns 1976, 264). Johnson immediately set out to draft a full-blown peace proposal, to be announced before the next round of primary elections in April. Finally, on March 31, Johnson announced a halt to the bombing of North Vietnam, a beginning of troop withdrawals, and his own decision not to run for reelection. The Tet Offensive, though failing to topple the South Vietnamese government, succeeded in felling a U.S. president.

During this stage, Johnson clearly was heavily influenced by public opinion. As stated by advisor William Bundy:

> My own impression—for what it is worth—is that the thrust of professional civilian advice would probably have been toward the most limited possible force increases, but that the change in bombing policy was greatly influenced— particularly in Secretary Clifford's actions and recommendations—by a sense of the progressively eroding domestic political support that was so dramatically evident to us all during the month of March. (Schandler 1977, 329)

The combination of elite and mass opinion (as expressed most concretely in New Hampshire) had a significant impact on the president's decision. What is less clear is the impact, if any, that the by-now large antiwar/peace movement was having.

The Peace Movement

The antiwar demonstrations of the 1960s and 1970s were among the most dramatic outpouring of public sentiment on a foreign policy issue in U.S. history. Roughly half a million people gathered in Washington, D.C. for the Vietnam Moratorium in October 1969. During the student protests following the Kent State/Cambodia incidents, 450 college campuses across the country were closed (Levy 1991, 155–159). In fact, the peace movement was strong among veterans of the war and even soldiers in Vietnam. Desertions rose to some 500,000 over the course of the war, and toward its end, many officers were reluctant to assign dangerous missions because of numerous incidents of "fragging" (assassination by another soldier) (Kattenburg 1980, 284). Estimates are that nearly 10 million of the 27 million draft-eligible men deserted, fled to another country, or obtained legal deferments to avoid service.

In general terms, the resistance of the youth of the country to the war effort went far to debilitate its prosecution but did not in and of itself alter government policy. In fact, Herring concludes:

> Anti-war protests did not turn the American people against the war, as some critics have argued. . . Public opinion polls make abundantly clear, moreover, that a majority of Americans found the anti-war movement, particularly its radical and "hippie" elements, more obnoxious than the war itself. In a perverse sort of way, the protest may even have strengthened support for a war that was not in itself popular. (Herring 1986, 173)

According to Gelb:

> Passionate opposition and intellectual arguments, in the end, counted for very little and changed few minds. The argument that finally prevailed at the end of the Johnson Administration was the weight of dead Americans. (Gelb 1976, 112)

The antiwar movement was never centralized. It consisted of a wide variety of interests organized primarily at the local level at certain major universities and cities. The San Francisco Bay area, with the University of California at Berkeley as the focal point, was early on a key hub of the movement. The principal elements of the movement were pacifist, radical, and anarchist in the early stages. Even the early leaders disagreed over methods and aims. It seems in retrospect that the only thing they shared was a disgust with the war. This problem would come back to haunt the more moderate elements of the movement in later years because it became apparent that antiwar activists were successful only to the extent that they focused exclusively on Vietnam (Levy 1991, 48).

Some of the important organizations associated with the antiwar movement were the Students for a Democratic Society (which later spawned a small terrorist group known as the Weathermen), the National Mobilization Committee to End the War, the Vietnam Moratorium Committee, and the National Peace Action Coalition. Important leaders included Tom Hayden, Jerry Rubin, Abby Hoffman, David Dellinger, and later Daniel Ellsberg, Dr. Benjamin Spock, Jane Fonda, Joan Baez, Bella Abzug, and even Tony Randall (Kattenburg 1980, 274). As further evidence of the disparate interests at work in the peace movement, the individuals listed above had very different, even contradictory, interests. For example, when an effort was made to organize a massive antiwar demonstration in front of the Pentagon in October 1967, many were content to sing folk songs and sign petitions, while others in the group physically assaulted the military police (Levy 1991, 136).

This split became especially pronounced during the 1968 election campaign, when a large number of activists joined forces with Eugene McCarthy and Robert Kennedy to work for gradual change. In the meantime, anarchists and radicals, who called for an overthrow of the political system itself through civil disobedience and even violence, became more active (Brown 1976, 122). The contrast was vividly displayed during the tumultuous 1968 Democratic convention in Chicago.

On the floor of the convention, for those delegates whose credentials were approved—the fight, though acrimonious—was relatively formal. For the better part of a day, the convention delegates debated inclusion of an antiwar plank in the party platform, which was quickly countered by a plank supporting administration policy. When the vote was finally tallied, it demonstrated a profound split: 1,568 in favor and 1,041 against the pro-administration policy (Levy 1991, 149). The absence of Robert Kennedy, who was shot in California in June, meant that anti-administration forces were unprepared to counter the nomination of Vice President Hubert Humphrey, who reluctantly advocated the administration's positions (Karnow 1983, 568).

Outside the convention hall, a large number of antiwar protesters assembled to confront, before a live television audience, the aggressive Chicago police force. As put by Shils:

> Hippies, pacifists, socialists, propagandists for a North Vietnamese and Vietcong victory came together and challenged the Chicago police. The provocation was deliberate and successful. The police responded as they were desired to respond, and the television services showed the entire country what the establishment was like—heavy-handed, monstrous, brutal, and incompetent. (Shils 1976, 57)

In a famous moment, the crowd, recognizing the cameras were rolling, began chanting "The whole world is watching!" Viewers at home were generally repelled by both sides of this confrontation, and it generated little sympathy for the antiwar movement.

The Nixon administration continued the policy of rapid troop withdrawal begun by Johnson in April 1968, and the peace movement lost some momentum. The urgency of changing government policy dissipated, and the movement returned to its more radical roots as moderates lost interest. The revelations in April 1970 that the administration had escalated the war by launching large-scale bombing raids in Cambodia and Laos, however, stirred a new enthusiasm for protest. Almost no campus was prowar by this time (Shils 1976, 56). Unrest broke out, most notably at Kent State University, where National Guardsmen, under the direction of Governor James Rhodes, fired into an unruly crowd with live bullets, killing four students. The outrage that followed the incident paralyzed the educational system of the country. For the first time, the public's sympathy was with the demonstrators (Kattenburg 1980, 278).

Did the peace movement change policy? Lyndon Johnson never appreciated the message that the activists conveyed, and he always felt unable to communicate with them. They did not seem to understand the feelings of self-sacrifice, devotion to country, and dread of communism that were so important to Johnson's generation. Likewise, Johnson feared the freedom, tolerance, and moral outrage spoken of by the students and activists.

Divided in values and assumptions, they went their different ways, the peace movement to the streets, Johnson to the refuge of his adamant convictions. Perhaps for the first time in his life, he could not even fathom the position of the other side. No longer the mediator, he had become a righteous if ineffective advocate of his own inflexibility. (Kearns 1976, 343)

Even leaders of the antiwar movement recognize that they achieved few of their goals regarding changing public policy (although this may be a function of unrealistic expectations). Activist Sam Brown gave a postmortem of the movement after the war and found that the split in leadership and excessive reliance on the college community (rather than a larger population of workers, professionals, and minorities) hindered the movement's ability to grow. Furthermore, litigation aimed at defending Daniel Ellsberg and the militant "Chicago Seven" cost the movement $2 million, which could have gone toward organizing efforts (Brown 1976, 124). This said, the antiwar movement set a precedent that was followed in the early 1980s by the nuclear freeze movement as well as protests against every military intervention since then.

The Nixon Era and Congressional Reassertion

Richard Nixon at one point claimed to have a "secret plan" to end the war in Vietnam. Just as Johnson had misled the public in the 1964 election, Nixon's claims were deceptive. The only plan was to escalate the violence while pursuing confidential contacts with the North Vietnamese (Levy 1991, 152). In fact, Nixon ended up dropping even more bombs on Indochina than Johnson had (Roche 1976, 135).

The reality that the war was not ending soon prompted an intensification of general opposition to the war. "Lou Harris observed that 'a literal race' was on between successive Nixon announcements of further troop withdrawals and a growing public appetite for faster and faster removal of troops from Vietnam" (Levy 1991, 161). Twenty-six percent of respondents thought that troop withdrawals were progressing too slowly in late 1969. In May 1971, that figure was up to 45 percent, and in November 1971 it had reached 53 percent. This increase in opposition paralleled the growth in cumulative casualty figures and mounting financial costs of the war. The mid-1971 publication of the Pentagon Papers, a collection of classified documents related to prosecuting the war, revealed a pattern of deception and secret escalation on the part of successive administrations (*New York Times* 1971, xi). The Cambodia revelations and the My Lai massacre of Vietnamese civilians by Lieutenant William Calley's unit all combined to create a new public consensus—this time in favor of rapid withdrawal regardless of the implications for South Vietnamese sovereignty (Kattenberg 1980, 258).

Nixon's general plan of "peace with honor" finally came to fruition shortly after the 1972 election with the Paris Agreement of January 1973. By then the public felt no remorse over the "loss" of Vietnam—only relief at the end of the conflict. When Saigon fell in mid-1975, President Gerald Ford did nothing to prevent it.

Congress had grown increasingly restive, adopting a variety of tactics to limit presidential prerogative. Following the Fulbright hearings in 1966–1967, several other committees followed suit—taking testimony from witnesses, traveling to Vietnam on fact-finding missions, and ultimately issuing antiwar resolutions aimed at curtailing the length and scope of the war. The Tonkin Gulf Resolution was repealed in late 1971, although an effort to prevent further military operations pending a formal declaration of war was defeated. Following a string of resolutions calling for withdrawal by a given deadline, Congress passed a bill banning all further military operations in Vietnam in 1973 (after the troops had already been withdrawn). In an effort to prevent future unilateral executive military interventions, Congress passed the War Powers Act over President Nixon's veto. The net result of congressional reassertion was a collapse of much of the power that had accreted to the White House over the period following World War II. The question of presidential war powers is still one the most hotly debated constitutional issues of our time (note the Senate debate on the Gulf War in 1991).

Conclusion: Can the Public Shape Policy?

The experience of Vietnam can teach several lessons to those wondering about the role of public opinion in foreign policy. At least as many questions are left unanswered, however.

The Vietnam experience demonstrates the limited impact of street activism in influencing national policy. To a certain extent, the reason for its ineffectiveness is that those who resort to mass demonstrations tend to be those who lack institutional power. That a large number of college students, many of whom could not even vote, failed to alter national policy through protest marches is therefore not surprising. Instead, the Vietnam experience demonstrates the significance of elite opinion in shaping national policy as well as the potential role of "mass opinion" in at least limiting the options a president might otherwise choose. The attentiveness with which successive presidents studied public opinion as well as their considerable efforts to shape it (including deception, obfuscation, and misrepresentation) are testament to the significance politicians attach to this amorphous social entity.

Because the Vietnam War created a moral conflict in the American public, opposition was never unambiguous. Those who favored continuing the war generally deplored its cost, while those who had come to favor withdrawal often regretted the loss of face and prestige it would cause. Congressional ambivalence throughout most of the war reflected this tension and prevented it from taking control. One could argue that even congressional assertion as expressed in the War Powers Act did more to legitimate presidential assertiveness than to limit it, particularly because the act has done little to hinder presidential freedom since 1973.

Debate Topic

Perhaps the most lasting legacy from the Vietnam War era is the changed relationship between the Congress and the White House with respect to waging war. The War Powers Act of 1974 was designed to curtail presidential power to deploy troops, while increasing congressional oversight. Is this good for the country?

PRO
Supporters of increased Congressional oversight stress three points: (1) The United States is, first and foremost, a democracy, with the people exercising sovereign control over elected officials, typically through other elected officials such as Congress. The people cannot shirk this duty. (2) Presidents have often made strategic and tactical errors in choosing to deploy troops. Additional congressional involvement might enhance the quality of policy. (3) Presidents sometimes are able to deceive the public at large, but have more difficult time deceiving Congress, given the greater access to information and expertise on Capitol Hill.

CON
Opponents of increased Congressional oversight argue these points: (1) Questions of national security necessarily require some degree of secrecy. Increasing access to classified materials, which congressional involvement would entail, might put American lives at risk. (2) Foreign policy aims sometimes require stealth and surprise, both of which would be undermined by increased congressional involvement. (3) Members of Congress represent individual constituencies and often cannot see the "big picture" of the national interest.

Questions to Consider

1. What was the relationship between the peace movement and society in general? Between the peace movement and the White House? How much influence did it really have over policy and shaping alternatives?

2. To what extent did Nixon and Johnson misjudge fundamental American attitudes? What are the apparent limits to patriotism in the United States?

3. What are the lessons of Vietnam in terms of the role of public opinion? How did the lessons of Vietnam shape later military operations (Grenada, Nicaragua, Panama, Persian Gulf, Somalia, . . .)?

Websites

Vietnam War Internet Project: **www.lbjlib.utexas.edu/shwv/vwiphome.html**
The Sixties Project: **lists.village.virginia.edu/sixties**

References

Ball, George. *The Past Has Another Pattern* (New York: W. W. Norton, 1982).
Brown, Sam. "The Defeat of the Antiwar Movement" in Lake, ed., *The Vietnam Experience*, 120–127.
Gelb, Leslie. "Dissenting on Consensus" in Lake, ed., *The Vietnam Legacy*, 102–119.
Herring, George C. *America's Longest War: The United States and Vietnam, 1950–1975*, 2nd ed. (Philadelphia: Temple University Press, 1986).
Holsti, Ole R., and James N. Rosenau. *American Leadership in World Affairs: Vietnam and the Breakdown of Consensus* (Boston: Allen & Unwin, 1984).
Karnow, Stanley. *Vietnam: A History* (New York: Viking Press, 1983).
Kattenburg, Paul. *The Vietnam Trauma in American Foreign Policy, 1945–1975* (New Brunswick, NJ: Transaction Books, 1980).
Kearns, Doris. *Lyndon Johnson and the American Dream* (New York: New American Library, 1976).
Lake, Anthony, ed. *The Vietnam Legacy: The War, American Society and the Future of American Foreign Policy* (New York: New York University Press, 1976).
Levy, David W. *The Debate Over Vietnam* (Baltimore: Johns Hopkins University Press, 1991).
Mueller, John. *War, Presidents, and Public Opinion* (New York: John Wiley & Sons, 1973).
New York Times. The Pentagon Papers (New York: New York Times Co., 1971).
Roche, John P. "The Impact of Dissent on Foreign Policy: Past and Future" in Lake, ed., *The Vietnam Legacy*, 128–138.
Schandler, Herbert Y. *The Unmaking of a President: Lyndon Johnson and Vietnam* (Princeton, NJ: Princeton University Press, 1977).
Shils, Edward. "American Society and the War in Indochina" in Lake, ed., *The Vietnam Legacy*, 40–65.

SALT I and Its Aftermath

ARMS CONTROL

Introduction

This case study is intended to illustrate the concept of arms control. Arms control is any effort by nations to negotiate future levels of weapons. It can involve expenditure limits, restrictions on testing, ceilings on deployment, and/or prohibitions on new types of weapons. Arms control need not result in arms reduction; in fact, it may lead to an overall increase in the amount of weapons in existence. In general, arms control agreements demonstrate that nations are aware that an open-ended arms race is inherently dangerous and needs to be channeled by political leaders.

In Case 4 (on Cuba), we mentioned "game theory," which can allow us to predict to some extent what two rational actors will do when faced with a decision, the result of which is contingent on the other's action. Arms control—or the lack thereof—can be explained by the prisoner's dilemma game. In it, we assume two individuals who committed a crime together are interrogated separately by the police. Each is given the opportunity to either confess (thereby betraying the partner in crime) or to stay silent (and remain loyal). The police explain that, given the sketchy evidence at their disposal, only a confession from one of the prisoners will allow them to charge one of the two with a serious crime, otherwise, they will have to settle for a lesser charge. Naturally, if each prisoner is loyal, the outcome will be much less painful than if either one confesses to the police, and the choice seems obvious. But here is the catch: If one prisoner confesses, the police will let that person go free while only the partner is charged with a very serious offense. Knowing that your partner is being offered the same option, what would you do? Loyalty now carries very serious implications and will give you a desirable result only if it is reciprocated. Given the fact that most of us go through life in the hope of minimizing risk (the entire insurance industry is based on this premise!), it is easy to predict that most people would betray their partner and confess to police, with the result that many obtain a less-than-ideal result.

Scholars have found, however, that a few measures can be taken to minimize this outcome. First, if partners have the chance to communicate their choices as they make them, they are more likely to remain loyal. Also, if the partners can expect to be in similar situations again in the future (i.e., their relationship is stable), then they will be more likely to remain loyal—for fear of being a victim in the future. Also, if the number of such interactions is assumed to be virtually infinite (a closely related scenario), cooperation is more likely. Many game theorists therefore propose that it is not the game itself that matters but the context in which it is played.

This situation lies at the heart of arms control. In the case of the Soviet Union and the United States at the end of the 1960s, each side had the capability to inflict overwhelming pain on the other. What was more serious was that new technologies, procurement programs, and deployment patterns created a very real risk that nuclear war might break out by either accident or impulse. To minimize the risk of accidental or precipitous nuclear attack, as early as 1962 the nations entered into agreements on such things as enhanced capital-to-capital communication (the "hotline"), increased security of nuclear arsenals (the nonproliferation agreement and sharing of fail-safe technology), and a cap on overall nuclear arsenals (the Strategic Arms Limitation Talks, or SALT I and SALT II). Still, each side was eager not to close off future opportunities to gain some advantage.

Were the SALT negotiations a useful step in lessening tensions between the superpowers, or did they simply become yet another contentious issue? Did they lead to the results for which the negotiators hoped, and were these expectations mutually compatible? How did the SALT experience prepare each side for the dramatic arms control and disarmament breakthroughs of the 1990s?

An arms control agreement may be stabilizing or destabilizing, but much depends on the sincerity of each side's desire to control an arms race. On the one hand, if each wants to dupe the other into thinking it has slowed its rate of arms procurement so as to cheat and thus gain a unilateral advantage, no agreement of any type will stabilize the relationship. On the other hand, if each party is sincere, certain types of weapons should be encouraged or at least tolerated if the agreement is to prove stabilizing.

> A stable strategic weapon should be capable of delayed response; it should be invulnerable; and it should be unambiguously deprived of what is called a first-strike, or damage-limiting, capability. Put differently, it should not be able to disarm some portion of the other side's forces, or diminish them appreciably. Measured by these standards, the least-stable element of America's triad is the Minuteman [ICBM] force. (Newhouse 1989, 20)

Against this standard one should judge the SALT negotiations of the 1970s. But before we proceed, some definitions are in order. In 1970, nuclear weapons could be delivered to a target in three ways: intercontinental ballis-

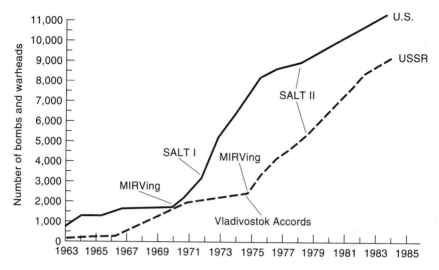

Figure 7.1   U.S. and Soviet strategic nuclear delivery vehicles, 1965–1985
Sources: David Barash, *The Arms Race and Nuclear War* (Belmont, CA: Wadsworth, 1987), and Thomas W. Wolfe, *The SALT Experience* (Cambridge, MA: Ballinger, 1979).

tic missiles, based on land (ICBMs); submarine-launched ballistic missiles (SLBMs); and strategic bombers carrying traditional gravity bombs (and later cruise missiles capable of hugging the ground and evading radar). By 1970, the United States had begun to change the traditional nature of a nuclear-capable missile by placing multiple warheads (the nuclear device itself) in the nose cone of the missile, and it further refined this development by inventing a booster and guidance system that would allow the operator to aim each warhead (also known as a reentry vehicle) at a different target (see Figure 7.1). This innovation, called a multiple, independently targeted reentry vehicle (MIRV), dramatically changed the nature of offensive nuclear weapons by increasing the number of targets that could be knocked out by the launch of a single missile. The larger the missile, the larger the "throw-weight," the larger the payload it could deliver, and the more MIRVed warheads it could carry. As of 1970, only the United States was close to deploying MIRVed missiles, but the Soviets were far ahead in throw-weight.

Nuclear defenses—particularly popular in the Soviet Union—included standard antiaircraft guns, which could be used to knock out bombers, as well as a variety of missiles capable of intercepting incoming ballistic missiles, much like the Patriot missile of Persian Gulf War fame. The Soviet antiballistic missile (ABM) defenses seemed to U.S. planners to increase the likelihood that Moscow would survive an American nuclear attack with enough operational missiles to devastate the United States (second-strike capability), which in turn prompted the Americans to push for MIRVing, to overwhelm these defenses, and deployment of American ABMs. It was this dynamic that ultimately led to the beginning of arms negotiations in 1971.

SALT I AND ITS AFTERMATH
KEY FIGURES

U.S. Presidents

John F. Kennedy   U.S. President, 1961–1963.

Lyndon Johnson   U.S. President, 1963–1969.

Richard Nixon   U.S. President, 1969–1974.

Gerald Ford   U.S. President, 1974–1977.

Jimmy Carter   U.S. President, 1977–1981.

Ronald Reagan   U.S. President, 1981–1989.

George W. Bush   U.S. President, 2003–present.

Other U.S. Officials

Robert McNamara   U.S. Secretary of Defense, 1961–1968

Henry Kissinger   U.S. National Security Advisor, 1969–1975; U.S. Secretary of State, 1973–1977.

Williams Rogers   U.S. Secretary of State, 1969–1973.

Gerard Smith   Director of the Arms Control and Disarmament Agency, and head American delegate to the SALT negotiations.

Soviet Leaders

Nikita Khrushchev   Soviet Premier, 1953–1964.

Leonid Brezhnev   Soviet Premier, 1964–1982.

Other Soviet Officials

Aleksey Kosygin   Senior Soviet leader, 1964–1980.

A. F. Dobrynin   Soviet Ambassador to the United States, 1962–1986.

Vladimir Semenov   Head Soviet delegate to the SALT negotiations.

SALT I AND ITS AFTERMATH
CHRONOLOGY

1945
The Trinity Test ushers in the atomic age.

1949
The USSR tests a fission bomb.

(continued)

1952

The United States tests a fusion bomb.

1955

The USSR tests a fusion bomb.

1960

France tests a fission bomb.

1961

The United States begins an open debate on setting a ceiling on its nuclear arsenal following the "missile gap" hoax of the 1960 presidential campaign.

1964

China tests a fission bomb.

1967

Lyndon Johnson proposes a ceiling on nuclear weapons and antiballistic missile systems at the Glassboro summit.

1968

U.S. and Soviet negotiators, along with those of dozens of other nations, conclude the Non-Proliferation Treaty, limiting the number of new nuclear-weapons countries. The Soviet invasion of Prague delays arms control talks.

1969

The Nixon administration begins formal nuclear arms control talks with Russia.

1971

"Back-channel" negotiations between Kissinger and senior Soviet officials produce a breakthrough in the SALT talks.

1972

The United States and the USSR sign both the ABM treaty and the "Interim Agreement" (SALT I), thereby limiting the number of antimissile defense systems and the total number of nuclear weapons launchers (missiles, bombers, and submarines).

1973

Negotiations begin on what will become SALT II

1974

Agreements are reached on some aspects of MIRVs in Vladivostok.

1979

SALT II is signed.

1980

After the Soviet invasion of Afghanistan, Jimmy Carter withdraws SALT II from Senate consideration and the treaty remains unratified.

1987

The Intermediate-Range Nuclear Forces treaty is signed. For the first time, the total number of nuclear missiles drops.

1989–1992

The end of the Cold War makes nuclear arms reduction easier as the START I and START II treaties are concluded and ratified in quick succession.

(continued)

2002

George W. Bush abrogates the ABM treaty over Russian objections on the ground that the treaty imposes too many limits on U.S. efforts to defend itself against "rogue" states that might launch a small number of missiles.

Antecedents to SALT

The Johnson administration saw the military balance in the mid-1960s as extremely volatile. The United States was in a generally antimilitary mood. Secretary of State Robert McNamara had concluded that the United States had too many nuclear missiles and was pressing for a ceiling of roughly 1,000 ICBMs for the foreseeable future, contrary to a Republican proposal to double the Minuteman ICBM force. McNamara's conclusion was based on the fact that the United States needed only 400 missiles to devastate the Soviet Union. With 900 ICBMs to the Soviet Union's 250, the United States could easily survive a nuclear attack with the capacity to deliver a crushing blow to the USSR. Given the rising costs of the Vietnam War, ceilings on missile procurement also made good financial sense (Newhouse 1989, 57). In addition, the United States was concerned about the wisdom of ABM systems because their effectiveness in battle was suspect, they would cost inordinate sums to be deployed around every major city and missile installation, and they might provoke the Soviets to build even more missiles.

Although this attitude made sense in the context of a steady Soviet force, it no longer worked when the Soviets began building new missiles and ABM systems at an impressive rate after 1965. By 1966, the Soviets were moving quickly to enlarge their ICBM force and deploy an ABM system around Moscow, while the Johnson administration's buildup was leveling off (Labrie 1979, 4). Between 1964 and 1969, Soviet nuclear forces tripled while American forces increased by half. After 1969, American forces remained level (delivery vehicles only) while Soviet forces doubled. Numerical parity was achieved in 1972. Assuming reasonable accuracy for the Soviet weapons, this force size virtually nullified the solid second-strike capability that was the foundation of McNamara's strategy (Payne 1980, 13). There were even indications as early as 1967 that some Soviet planners were anticipating the day when the USSR could so disable the United States with a first strike that no retaliation could be mounted (Payne 1980, 15).

Two alternatives presented themselves: mounting a massive U.S. arms buildup or negotiating with the Soviets to agree on a freeze of nuclear weapons at current levels. In January 1967, President Johnson proposed to Soviet Premier Aleksey Kosygin a freeze on offensive and defensive systems at current levels. The response was tepid at best. From the Soviet perspective, the proposal seemed to freeze its forces into inferiority and therefore had little appeal. In June 1967, at the Glassboro, New Jersey, summit, the United States made the appeal again, this time with Robert McNamara issuing warnings about the implications of continued ABM deployment in the

Soviet Union. He painted a dark picture of the escalation that would result from the move, which would necessitate deployment of an American ABM as well as a dramatic increase in the offensive nuclear arsenals (he withheld information on the MIRV program then being tested) (Newhouse 1989, 95).

The speech made little impression on Kosygin, but the U.S. announcements of MIRVing and deployment of the Sentinel ABM system in late 1967 seemed to have a more profound effect. Beginning in January 1968, the Soviet Union began working toward serious arms control negotiations aimed particularly at controlling American ABMs (Newhouse 1989, 102). By June 1968, the Politburo had issued a lengthy document, provided to the United Nations, which committed the nation to a wide range of both improbable and potentially significant arms control and disarmament objectives. Among the more interesting was a proposal to limit the total number of nuclear delivery vehicles (ICBMs, SLBMs, and bombers). The gesture convinced U.S. policy makers to commence strategic arms negotiations, which were announced formally at the signing of the Non-Proliferation Treaty (NPT) on July 1, 1968. The NPT was likely an important ingredient to Soviet cooperation because it prohibited always-threatening Germany from acquiring nuclear weapons (Payne 1980, 16).

Talks were scheduled to begin in the fall of 1968. The day before that announcement was to be made, however, Moscow sent tanks into Prague, Czechoslovakia, prompting a U.S. protest that included shelving the talks. The Soviets were eager to begin again the SALT process to rehabilitate their image but were unable to make progress with the Johnson administration. The Nixon administration, victorious in the November elections, undertook a thorough review of the SALT concept and waited until November 1969 to resume talks (Wolfe 1979, 3).

Several factors contributed to the agreement to begin the negotiations. First and foremost was the attainment in 1969 of effective nuclear parity by the Soviet Union (see Figure 7.1). As put by Payne:

> The most important reason for the Soviet agreement to begin the SALT negotiations in 1969 was the Soviet Union's attainment of strategic parity with the United States. By mid-1969 the Soviet Union was close to attaining this goal and by mid-1970 had virtually as many strategic nuclear missiles as the United States. The was recognized in both countries as a fundamental factor. President Nixon said in retrospect: "The approaching strategic parity provided an opportunity to achieve an overall agreement that would yield no unilateral advantage and could contribute to a more stable strategic environment." A Soviet commentator described 1968 as "one of those rare moments in history when both sides are ready to admit equality in the broadest sense and to look on it as a starting point for achieving agreement on limiting and eventually reducing armaments," and urged political leaders "not to let this chance slip away." (Payne 1980, 18–19)

Secondary factors included improvements in satellite reconnaissance, which by the late 1960s made verification of a nuclear agreement possible without resorting to on-site inspection (Newhouse 1989, 70). The Nixon administration hoped to use the talks to link U.S. acceptance of Soviet parity with a Soviet agreement to cooperate on a number of international "hot spots," including the Middle East and Vietnam (Labrie 1979, 8). On purely military terms, the United States hoped it could avoid the next round of the arms race, including a new Soviet MIRV threat and a U.S. ABM buildup (Newhouse 1989, 21). Finally, the hope was that by accomplishing all of these goals, the international system would enter into a more stable and predictable, if not necessarily fair, period. Failure to enter into an agreement carried the very real threat of an uncontrolled and volatile arms buildup in which each side would be forced to develop large numbers of first-strike weapons (Pfaltzgraff 1973, 17).

Objectives, Tradeoffs, and Outcomes of SALT

The SALT negotiations began on November 17, 1969, in Helsinki, Finland, under extraordinary media glare. The talks went on until May 26, 1972, when the ABM treaty and an "Interim Agreement" on strategic arms were signed in Moscow. The location of the negotiations alternated between Helsinki and Vienna, cities chosen for their relative neutrality and experienced hosts. The U.S. delegation was led by Gerard Smith, head of the Arms Control and Disarmament Agency, although by January 1971, the negotiating process was largely controlled by Henry Kissinger, Nixon's national security advisor. On the Soviet side, the Politburo remained actively engaged behind its negotiator, Vladimir Semenov.

The principal objectives have already been outlined, but it is interesting to note that early on, the Nixon administration chose to ignore possible linkages between the SALT negotiations and other international problems (Bowie 1973, 128). For their part, the Soviets quickly rejected a tentative U.S. proposal to ban MIRVs and MIRV testing. Thus the talks focused on ABM systems and numerical limits on missiles (Newhouse 1989, 181).

In general terms, the United States sought firm, binding, specific agreements that could be verified, while the Soviets were more attracted to broad statements of intent that allowed maximum flexibility of implementation (Wolfe 1979, 9).

> Initially, the U.S. suggested possible approaches involving both numerical and qualitative limitations on strategic offensive and defensive systems, including MIRVs. We also put forward an alternative comprehensive approach which would not constrain MIRVs, but would involve reductions in offensive forces in order to maintain stability even in the face of qualitative improvements. The Soviet Union, for its part, submitted a general proposal which diverged from ours in many respects, including a major difference on the definition of strategic systems. (Bowie 1973, 135)

This difference of approach led to significant difficulties, particularly when definitions (of "heavy missiles," for example) were central to the agreement.

The main subjects of discussion in the early stages of SALT I were the ABM systems each nation would be permitted and the possible limitation of total delivery vehicles of nuclear warheads. The two sides reached early agreement on the notion that any ABM system should be well short of countrywide. Thus the options of a national capital area (NCA) defense with or without deployment of ABMs to protect missile installations emerged as the most promising. The U.S. negotiators presented several ABM proposals in quick succession (which may have contributed to Soviet confusion and overconfidence—Newhouse 1989, 191). Meanwhile, the Soviets were adamant about their most contentious demand—conclusion of an initial ABM agreement without specific commitments to offensive missile limits (Labrie 1979, 12).

During 1970, the talks stalemated. As put by participant Newhouse, "At best, it was an impasse. At worst, SALT was having a perverse effect, planting doubts and uncertainties instead of promoting some understanding on each side of the other's position. Suspicion and mistrust were being fed, not dissipated" (Newhouse 1989, 195).

In early 1971, several developments broke the deadlock at SALT. First, Henry Kissinger met secretly in Washington and in Moscow with Soviet Ambassador A. F. Dobrynin and Politburo members to work out a compromise for SALT. This "back-channel" negotiation produced a tentative settlement in May 1971. The key element involved acceptance by the Soviets of a temporary offensive missile ceiling, in combination with an ABM treaty, which would be renegotiated shortly after the conclusion of the first round of talks. In addition, the United States accepted an unequal ceiling for the Soviet Union (Newhouse 1989, 204). As put by Henry Kissinger:

> This is why at crucial moments in these negotiations there had been direct contacts between the President and Soviet leaders which led by mutual agreement to breakthroughs—the first on May 20 of 1971, in which there was an agreement that broke the deadlock that had developed between the Soviet insistence that an agreement cover antiballistic missile systems only and our view that an agreement involved as well the offensive weapons. The compromise was that the initial treaty would deal with ABMs and that this would be accompanied by a freeze on certain categories of offensive weapons. (Kissinger 1979, 33)

This agreement was facilitated by the elevation of Leonid Brezhnev, a committed arms control supporter, to supreme party chief in March (Payne 1980, 75).

Critics of SALT focus on the way Kissinger operated. The U.S. SALT delegation head, Gerard Smith, has challenged the wisdom of one American taking on the entire Soviet establishment in face-to-face talks. The result, he points out, was a largely outmaneuvered and often disoriented Kissinger. Kissinger was so distrustful of his colleagues that he refused to use American interpreters to go over the Russian drafts of the agreement (Smith 1980, 223, 407). The operation did much to undermine the delegation's confidence as well. "I thought the whole episode a sad reflection on the state of affairs in the Administration. Kissinger and the President went the Soviets one better. At least in the Soviet Union, the whole Politburo was consulted, on several occasions. The bulk of the American national security leadership was never consulted. It was informed after the fact" (Smith 1980, 234). As a result, several concessions made or implied in the May 1971 agreement were later rescinded or modified.

The unequal missile ceiling anticipated by this May 1971 agreement led to much contention in U.S. circles. The most celebrated opposition came from Senator Henry Jackson, who was able to place a condition on eventual Senate ratification of the treaty, insisting that any future agreement provide for equal ceilings. In fact, the unequal ceilings could be justified on several grounds. First, the Soviets agreed to exclude "forward-based systems"—nuclear missiles located in Europe but under American control. Second, U.S. targeting and MIRV technology gave its missiles much more punch in comparison to the less accurate, single-warhead Soviet missiles. Third, U.S. submarine-launched missiles were much more difficult to detect, given their quieter drive mechanisms and the fact that they also enjoyed the MIRVing and targeting advantages of their ground-based counterparts. Finally, the U.S. bomber fleet was much larger than the Soviets', with the result that the United States had a larger number of more-accurate warheads and bombs, even if it had fewer missiles (Barash 1987, 223).

Although the May 1971 statement set the stage for the conclusion of negotiations the next year, many points were left unresolved. On the ABM front, the Soviets ultimately moved in the direction of U.S. support for missile defense systems and, after considering alternatives, settled on a one-plus-one arrangement that would allow a missile defense system and an NCA arrangement, each limited to 100 missiles (Newhouse 1989, 232). In addition, both sides agreed to ban "exotic" ABM systems, such as space-based missiles.

The offensive missile ceilings were far more complex, in that little in the arsenals of the two nations was directly comparable. Small MIRVed missiles seemed to the Soviets a greater threat than their large single-warhead missiles, although American negotiators were quick to point out that the Soviet missiles, with their larger throw-weight (capacity to lift larger warheads), could carry a very large number of MIRVed missiles in the near future (see Figure 7.2). American efforts to limit the size of Soviet missiles ended in an agreement in principle to a cap of 313 "heavy missiles," although the United States was forced to define "heavy missile" without Soviet concurrence (Nitze 1979, 12). The Soviets also accepted in principle the U.S. proposal to limit enlargement of existing silos, although the expanded dimensions would still accommodate the newest generation of heavy missiles.

The final agreement on offensive land-based missiles provided for a ceiling of 1,054 ICBMs for the United States—equal to its existing inventory—and 1,618 for the Soviet Union—slightly more than it controlled at the time. Both limits provided for continued modernization and improvement of the

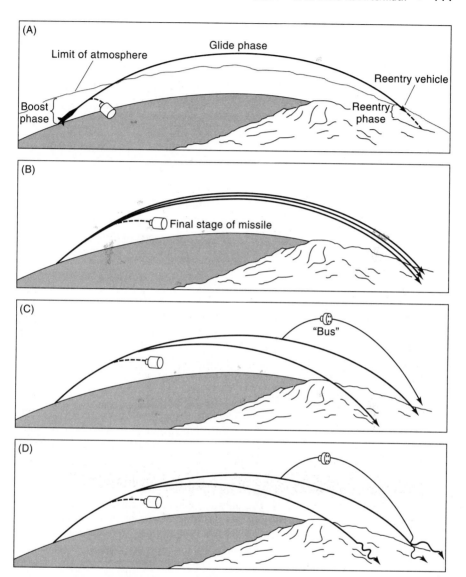

Figure 7.2 The flight phases of an ICBM, also showing different reentry vehicle patterns: (A) A single-warhead missile with one RV. (B) A MRVed missile, with three RVs that are not independently targeted. (C) A MIRVed missile carrying three RVs, each of which is aimed at a different target. The "bus" delivers the first RV to target 1, reorients itself to permit the second RV to go to target 2, and so on. (D) A MIRVed missile carrying three RVs that are independently targeted and also maneuver prior to reaching their target.
Source: David Barash, *The Arms Race and Nuclear War* (Belmont, CA: Wadsworth, 1987).

missiles, meaning that MIRVing would be unimpeded. The Soviets agreed to destroy 210 obsolete missiles to make way for newer ones, while the United States destroyed only 54.

In the final stages of the talks, the question of submarine-based missiles moved to center stage. Particularly at the final round during the Moscow summit, a number of proposals and counterproposals were reviewed. The Soviets were eager to achieve a very high ceiling on total submarines because the country was in the process of manufacturing many more each year. They sought and obtained a limit of 62 submarines (or six additional) versus 44 for the United States (or three additional). The number of SLBMs controlled by the Soviets in 1972 was a subject of debate until the final hours of the talks—the Soviets claimed a high number of 768, whereas U.S. intelligence estimates pegged the number at 640. Nixon and Brezhnev agreed on 740 as the benchmark, to which the Soviets could add 210 additional SLBMs (Labrie 1979, 13). This compared with 710 SLBMs from a baseline of 656 for the United States.

Perhaps the most interesting feature of the agreements signed in May 1972, from an international law perspective, was the establishment of a Standing Consultative Commission to interpret the treaty (Wolfe 1979, 11). In fact, the commission has been approached several times for clarification of the agreement. Furthermore, the agreements provided an opt-out clause—made explicit in the case of the ABM treaty and implied by the five-year duration of the Interim Agreement.

Assessments of SALT I are largely a reflection of expectations (Van Cleave 1973, 327). The administration sought a means to control the accelerating pace of Soviet arms acquisition. Both Kissinger and Secretary of State William Rogers agreed that the threat of a spiraling arms race was very high in 1969 and that threat was largely abated. As put by Kissinger:

> [T]he question to ask in assessing the freeze is not what situation it perpetuates but what situation it prevents. The question is where we would be without the freeze. And if you project the existing building programs of the Soviet Union into the future, as against the absence of building programs over the period of the freeze in either of the categories that are being frozen, you will get a more correct clue to why we believe that here is a good agreement and why we believe that it has made a significant contribution to arresting the arms race. The weapons are frozen, as we pointed out, in categories in which we have no ongoing programs. (Kissinger 1979, 34)

Although he objected to the way the agreement was reached, Smith concurred that the SALT I Treaty was an honest beginning to an ongoing process of arms control (Smith 1980, 34).

Critics on the left pointed out how SALT provided for considerable increases in nuclear weapons on both sides, through either MIRVing old missiles or building new ones. As shown in Figure 7.3, which provides warhead and bomb counts, SALT I seems to have done more to propel the warhead race than to slow it down. As put by Bowie:

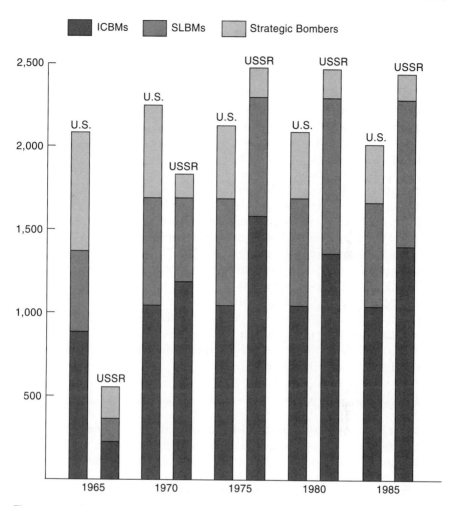

Figure 7.3   Numbers of bombs and warheads, 1965–1985
Source: David Barash, *The Arms Race and Nuclear War* (Belmont, CA: Wadsworth, 1987).

In practice, neither side has suspended its weapons programs. Throughout the period of the SALT the Soviet Union has continued to install SS-9s and other missiles at a rapid rate, to build Polaris-type submarines at the rate of eight per year, to test multiple warheads and improved ABMs, and to dig nearly one hundred new silos. The United States has likewise gone forward with missiles equipped with MIRVs for the modified Polaris submarines and for Minuteman ICBMs, and with the revised ABM Safeguard systems. . . . There is no evidence that the weapons actions by either side have impeded the SALT. Indeed, it can be argued that unilateral suspension of planned improvements would remove one of the motives for Soviet agreement to restrictions in the SALT. (Bowie 1973, 136)

Some feared that such a weak agreement would actually exacerbate the arms race by encouraging development of new technologies that could fit in existing missiles. Defense Department officials campaigned vigorously in 1972 and 1973 for new generations of submarine-and land-based weapons as well as the B-1 bomber program, justifying them as legal, if not essential, under SALT (Labrie 1979, 82). Furthermore, MIRVing programs and other innovations were viewed as potential bargaining chips in future negotiations, much as the ill-conceived ABM system proved to be in the SALT I process (Newhouse 1989, 78).

Critics on the right expressed strong concern about the headroom issue as well as the question of verification. They objected to exclusive reliance on "national means" of checking Soviet compliance (satellite photography) on the grounds that the USSR had every reason to cheat in spite of its promises. Given their throw-weight advantage, existing ABM systems, and incipient MIRVing, the Soviets had the capacity to achieve first-strike capability by the end of the decade, according to conservatives (Labrie 1979, 153).

Claims of success in SALT are certainly justified. It achieved a degree of confidence and predictability that failure to negotiate would have made impossible (Wolfe 1979, 14). Parity was acknowledged and enshrined, mutual deterrence legitimated, and uncontrolled arms acquisition and improvement discouraged. From the Soviet perspective, the SALT elevated the country's status as nothing else could in 1972, while excluding China. Furthermore, it consolidated the power within the Soviet Union of Brezhnev and supporters of détente (Payne 1980, 77).

Maneuvering in SALT

Much has been written about the ill-fated SALT II process, which began six months after SALT I was signed and ended with Jimmy Carter's withdrawal of the signed treaty from Senate consideration after the Soviet invasion of Afghanistan in 1980. Although the failure of SALT II is interesting in itself, we will limit ourselves to a more general overview of the SALT II process and its implications for arms control and disarmament in the 1990s.

The Soviet Union approached the SALT II negotiations with greater confidence and perhaps more stubbornness than during SALT I. The Soviets were convinced that the "correlation of forces" was moving in their favor, meaning that when all dimensions of power were taken together—military, diplomatic, economic, moral, ideological—the Soviet Union was on the verge of overtaking the United States (Wolfe 1979, 95). In such a situation of rising power, concessions are generally counterproductive and patience is by far the greatest virtue.

The talks stalemated rather quickly, primarily because of Watergate and Richard Nixon's resignation in 1974. But the talks would not have progressed far in any case because the questions of headroom, Euro-missiles, MIRVing, bombers, and so, on had already delayed an agreement by the mid-1975 deadline. The prospect of a permanent offensive missile treaty was dim at best (Barash 1987, 227). In particular, on the MIRVing question, the Soviets were emboldened by their successful tests of 1973 and their plans for deployment in 1974–1975. Some Soviet planners imagined the possibility of deploying as many as 15,000 independently targeted warheads, given the throw-weight of their land-based missiles (Wolfe 1979, 98).

Other new developments undermined the prospects for an early conclusion of SALT II: the development of the cruise missile and the Soviet Backfire bomber and the emergence of Ronald Reagan as a force in the Republican Party. Albeit for very different reasons, both challenged previous assumptions. Cruise missiles, while in existence during SALT I, were not included in the discussions. Whether to include them or the medium-range Backfire bomber was a troublesome issue, largely because of questions about whether the missiles' limited range but forward deployment classified them as "strategic" weapons. The cruise missile complicated negotiations doubly because its capacity to evade radar detection made it an ideal first-strike, and therefore destabilizing, weapon (Barash 1987, 227).

The Republican Party was torn apart by a split between the moderate, pro-SALT wing and the conservative wing dominated by Reagan and such groups as the alarmist Committee on the Present Danger. The strong showing of Reagan during the 1976 Republican primary elections undermined then-President Gerald Ford's efforts at détente with Moscow. The split ultimately damaged the administration's political viability and allowed the election of a political newcomer, Jimmy Carter, in November.

In spite of these obstacles, a significant agreement in principle was reached at Vladivostok in 1974. This agreement became the foundation of the eventual SALT II of 1978 and, therefore, deserves special consideration. Early in the SALT II process, in response to the Jackson Amendment concerning strategic parity, the Nixon administration proposed ceilings on all strategic weapons, including bombers. Given U.S. numerical superiority in strategic bombers, this move alone went far to achieve the target of overall strategic parity (Nitze et al. 1979, 12).

The question of MIRVing was addressed next, with the United States proposing an overall throw-weight ceiling and the Soviets countering with a limit on the total number of MIRVed missiles. Given the small size of U.S. missiles, a throw-weight ceiling would have given it the opportunity to build a much larger number of individual, MIRVed missiles. The Soviet counterproposal preserved its advantage in throw-weight (Wolfe 1979, 100–102).

It was clear by mid-1974 that a permanent offensive weapon agreement was beyond reach, so both sides focused on achieving another interim settlement, this one to last until 1985. An additional agreement was achieved in late 1974 when the Soviets dropped their demand that American-controlled Euro-missiles be included in the accord. Cruise missiles and the Backfire bomber were also excluded from the framework agreement. After these concessions, a general agreement was relatively easy.

The Vladivostok Agreement signed by President Ford and Secretary Brezhnev provided for an overall ceiling of 2,400 delivery vehicles, with each bomber counted as one delivery vehicle. This figure provided for a small increase in the U.S. forces (of 1,258) and a slight reduction in the Soviet forces (of 299). The treaty made a modest effort to constrict MIRVing by providing a sublimit of 1,320 MIRVed missiles or cruise-missile–carrying bombers. This limit was much higher than the 1,000 ceiling originally proposed by the Soviets. Perhaps the most interesting feature of the treaty was the "freedom to mix" provision, which meant that each nation could choose its nuclear emphasis. For example, the United States or the USSR could deploy more land-based missiles or bombers, so long as it reduced its sea-based missiles by the same number (Barash 1987, 225). Other provisions of the Interim Agreement (SALT I) were extended (Wolfe 1979, 174). In addition to the offensive weapons agreement, the Vladivostok Summit produced a refinement of the ABM treaty, cutting the number of ABM systems allowed to only one.

Supporters of the agreements noted the virtue of placing unambiguous ceilings on overall strategic weapons. Opponents on the left were quick to emphasize the high level of this ceiling, which provided for a continued arms race, both quantitative and qualitative (Barash 1987, 225). Critics on the right charged that the throw-weight imbalance canceled out the numerical parity and inadequate verification provisions made considerable cheating possible.

The Carter administration entered the fray in 1977 with optimistic proposals that were treated with disdain by the Soviets. Quickly the talks returned to the cautious give-and-take that had become the pattern for SALT. The ultimate SALT II agreement signed in 1979 bore close resemblance to the Vladivostok Accords of 1974. They provided for a slightly lower overall ceiling (2,250) and included cruise missiles. While allowing "freedom to mix" in principle, SALT II included sublimits on MIRVed weapons (of the 1,320 total, no more than 820 MIRVed ICBMs and 1,200 total MIRVed ICBMs and SLBMs) (Panofsky 1979, 820).

The debate over SALT II echoed previous debates, with the complicating factor that although the Vietnam War was finally over, Soviet adventurism in developing countries was on the rise. The situation was further complicated by Carter's rather weak influence over the Senate and his ambivalence about Soviet human rights violations. By the time the Senate was about to formally consider the treaty for ratification—a doubtful prospect at best—the Soviets had invaded Afghanistan, prompting Carter to withdraw the treaty to both sanction the Soviets and avoid a defeat in the Senate (Barash 1987, 228).

Conclusion: Implications of SALT

The SALT experience shows clearly that arms control is quite different from disarmament. Throughout the SALT process, arms acquisition continued at a rapid pace, particularly in terms of warhead accumulation. In only a few instances were older missiles retired—something that may well have been done without an agreement. The objective of SALT was clearly not a reduction in the number of weapons but a change in the arms race dynamic. SALT was intended primarily as an effort by the United States to prevent the Soviets from developing first-strike capability by rapidly improving their arsenal at a time when the United States was unwilling to invest in continued improvements.

It was not until the United States launched a costly and risky arms buildup in the early 1980s that genuine disarmament became possible. With the collapse of the Soviet economy in the mid-1980s and the emergence of Mikhail Gorbachev, the United States found a willing negotiating partner at a time when its arsenal was clearly excessive. Just as the Sentinel ABM system provoked the Soviets to enter into negotiations, the Star Wars program (an alleged violation of the ABM treaty) prompted them to renew the suspended START (Strategic Arms Reduction Talks) process. Disarmament treaties came in rapid succession in the late 1980s: the Intermediate-Range Nuclear Forces (INF) Treaty in 1987, the Conventional Forces in Europe (CFE) Treaty in 1990, the first START agreement in 1991, and a second START agreement in 1992 (signed before the Senate had completed review of the first treaty, and later ratified by Ukraine and Belarus).

Whether the lessons of SALT bear any relation to the successes of START is an open question. Some have argued that arms control is possible only when it is no longer necessary. Presidents George H.W. Bush and Bill Clinton announced unilateral arms cuts that exceeded those negotiated in 1992 and 1993 (see Case 3). Mikhail Gorbachev induced U.S. participation in arms talks by imposing a unilateral ban on weapons testing for eighteen months in 1986. These actions imply that when political conditions are ripe, arms control is simply one of many symptoms of warmer relations. On the other hand, when tensions are high, arms control alone cannot be expected to solve the problem. This reflects predictions we find in the prisoner's dilemma game presented at the beginning of the chapter.

Strangely enough, in spite of a decade of progress on arms reduction, the United States has recently back-pedaled on the issue. The skepticism displayed toward the landmine ban is discussed in Case 24. On the nuclear side, the George W. Bush administration made it clear from the outset that it rejected the constraints imposed by the ABM treaty in the present context. With countries such as North Korea and Iraq striving to develop nuclear capability, U.S. officials considered the country to be at risk of an isolated, but potentially devastating attack. Only a network of antiballistic missile defense systems would be able to protect against these "rogue states" (including perhaps China), so the treaty would have to be renegotiated abrogated. As Vladimir Putin, President of Russia, was not interested in renegotiation, Bush unilaterally withdrew from the treaty in early 2002. From his point of view, however, this had nothing to do with disloyalty to Russia, but rather represented a response to a change in the nature of the game and its players.

Debate Topic

Because arms control, in itself, neither diminishes weapons stockpiles nor solves international conflict, one could argue that the enterprise is largely pointless. Realists generally are skeptical of promises made in arms control negotiations, while idealists and liberals believe they are the basis for a more civilized relationship.

PRO

Those who believe in arms control generally make the following points: (1) Arms races tend to exacerbate underlying tensions, making conflicts more difficult to solve. If arms control can change the course of an arms race, it is worth the risk. (2) Arms control has generally produced agreements that have been honored, indicating that the risk of noncompliance is low. (3) Even partially flawed arms control agreements allow states to divert resources away from military spending and toward more productive investments, thereby making it easier to spend more on weapons in the future if need be.

CON

Opponents of arms control make the following arguments: (1) Arms races are never the product of peaceful relations, so arms control is possible only if the conflict has abated, making it superfluous. (2) If the relationship is marred by mutual suspicion, it likely that arms control agreements will be violated secretly, creating a prisoner's dilemma situation all over again. As in the prisoner's dilemma game, the treaty-abiding country runs the risk of being victimized by the cheating country. (3) Arms control negotiations often merely redirect the arms race in a new direction, creating a false sense of security for the citizens of each country.

Questions to Consider

1. What factors seem to have precipitated arms control negotiations? To what extent did they steer the content of the talks thereafter?

2. To what extent did expectations contribute to the decision to engage in arms control talks? Were these expectations fulfilled?

3. How did domestic debate affect the progress of arms control? Is it possible for world leaders to remain unaffected by such things?

Websites

Government Agencies
Arms Control and Disarmament Agency: **www.acda.gov**
Department of Defense: **www.dtra.mil/inspection/ost**

Nonprofit Agencies
Institute for Defense and Disarmament Studies: **www.idds.org**
Stockholm International Peace Research Institute: **www.sipri.se**
Center for Arms Control, Energy,and Environment (Russia): **www.armscontrol.ru**

References

Barash, David P. *The Arms Race and Nuclear War* (Belmont, CA: Wadsworth Publishing, 1987).

Bowie, Robert R. "The Bargaining Aspects of Arms Control: The SALT Experience" in Kintner and Pfaltzgraff, eds., SALT, 127–140.

Kintner, William, and Robert Pfaltzgraff, eds. *SALT: Implications for Arms Control in the 1970s* (Pittsburgh, PA: University of Pittsburgh Press, 1973).

Kissinger, Henry. *White House Years* (Boston: Little, Brown, 1979).

Labrie, Roger P., ed. *The SALT Handbook: Key Documents and Issues, 1972–1979* (Washington, DC: AEI, 1979).

Newhouse, John. *Cold Dawn: The Story of SALT* (New York: Pergamon-Brassey, 1989).

Nitze, Paul H., James Dougherty, and Francis Kane. *The Fateful Ends and Shades of SALT: Past . . . Present . . . and Yet to Come* (New York: Crane, Russak, 1979).

Panofsky, W. K. H. *Arms Control and SALT II* (Seattle: University of Washington Press, 1979).

Payne, Samuel B., Jr. *The Soviet Union and SALT* (Cambridge, MA: MIT Press, 1980).

Pfaltzgraff, Robert L., Jr. "The Rationale for Superpower Arms Control" in Kintner and Pfaltzgraff, eds., SALT, 3–20.

Smith, Gerard. *Doubletalk: The Story of the First Strategic Arms Limitation Talks* (New York: Doubleday, 1980).

Van Cleave, William R. "Implications of Success or Failure of SALT" in Kintner and Pfaltzgraff, eds., SALT, 313–336.

Wolfe, Thomas W. *The SALT Experience* (Cambridge, MA: Ballinger, 1979).

8

U.S. Role After the Cold War
THE NATIONAL INTEREST

Introduction

"National interest" is an incredibly elastic concept—capable of stretching to encompass any potential foreign threats for which an overzealous internationalist wants to prepare. It can also shrink to cover only life-threatening dangers on your doorstep. Because of the concept's malleability, we could easily dismiss it as a mere rhetorical flourish. Beneath the rhetoric, however, lies a fundamental question of what really matters in American foreign policy. Drawing the line between vital interests and peripheral preoccupations is the great question of our time.

Historically, "national interest" has come to include increasingly more issues. In the early days of the nation-state, it was possible to say the national interest was nothing more than the monarch's interests: "I am the state," Louis XIV once declared to no one's objection. As states came to be based on popular sovereignty, however, the interests of the citizenry as a whole had to be taken into account. The happiness of the people—which included economic vitality, agricultural prosperity, a sense of confidence and security, and so forth—became the principal end of national policy. It even extended to the security of citizens living outside the territory of the state. Most powerful states have been quick to intervene—often militarily—when their citizens come under attack overseas (see Cases 13 and 19). The most powerful ones even try to anticipate potential threats, taking steps to mitigate them in advance, perhaps by creating a "buffer zone" of friendly governments along the border or by moving troops overseas to facilitate quick deployment at great distances.

Each time a state expands its definition of the national interest, it must face a cost-benefit calculus: How much happiness and security do my people demand, and how much can they afford? Chances are high that no state will be able to do everything it takes to make its citizenry absolutely secure, so compromises are inevitable. In the history of the United States, decisions about these compromises have occasionally become a matter of broad and heated debate, as we will see.

U.S. ROLE AFTER THE COLD WAR
KEY FIGURES

Dwight D. Eisenhower U.S. President, 1953–1961. He promoted an internationalist policy but generally eschewed the United Nations.

George H.W. Bush U.S. President, 1989–1993. He involved the UN in U.S. policy more deeply than had past U.S. Presidents.

Bill Clinton U.S. President, 1993–2001. He maintained the multilateralist policies of George Bush.

James Baker III U.S. Secretary of State, 1989–1993. He cautioned George W. Bush against a unilateral, preemptive strike against Iraq.

George W. Bush U.S. President, 2001–present. He has generally promoted a unilateralist approach.

Charles Krauthamme Syndicated columnist. He is known as a supporter of the "hegemonic imperative."

Ross Perot Businessman, frequent presidential candidate, and supporter of the "national interest" approach.

Patrick Buchanan Journalist, frequent presidential candidate, and supporter of the "national interest" approach.

Jesse Helms U.S. Senator from North Carolina, 1972–2003, and Chairman of the Senate Foreign Relations Committee. He often opposed multilateralism.

Joseph Nye Harvard University political scientist who has promoted multilateralism.

Bruce Russett Yale University political scientist who advocates multilateralism.

The "Great" Debate

Americans have not always accepted the U.S. role as leader of the free world. Prior to the entry of the United States into World War I, for example, most opinion makers in the country agreed that the United States should remain aloof from European troubles. After the war, U.S. membership in the League of Nations and the establishment of a standing army were rejected by Congress. Meanwhile, the White House and State Department had grown attached to American leadership and repeatedly advanced its necessity. At the heart of this debate was the question of whether American idealism—its quest for peace and justice—should push the country into a leadership role in world affairs (exporting idealism, as it were) or whether it should avoid all "entangling alliances" (to use George Washington's phrase). This debate was ultimately resolved with the Japanese attack on Pearl Harbor.

After the collapse of the Berlin Wall, the dismantling of the Warsaw Pact, and the dissolution of the Soviet Union, the U.S. foreign policy establishment found itself without a clear purpose. The question of what to do in the next century gripped policy analysts in a dramatic way. Such publications as *Foreign Affairs, Foreign Policy, National Interest, National Review,* and the *Atlantic Monthly,* to name but a few (see also Kegley and Wittkopf 1992; Schmergel 1991; Lynn-Jones 1991; Lynn-Jones and Miller 1992), devoted considerable space to a single question: What should be the guiding principles of U.S. foreign policy in this new era? We will review the major points of this debate by organizing the various proposals into three general categories: the "national interest" approach, the "hegemonic imperative" school, and the "multilateralist" position.

National Interest

The "national interest" position, often espoused by politicians seeking the votes of unemployed steel or textile workers, aims at defining national interest in narrow terms. John F. Kennedy's pledge on behalf of the American public in 1961 to "bear any burden" in the cause of freedom rings hollow to analysts who see a declining U.S. economy and an urban and even suburban social infrastructure in shambles, where problems of the outside world seem trivial at best. To the 1972 McGovern Democrats' call of "Come Home America," many neoconservatives add the refrain "America First." As put by Charles Krauthammer, "[T]he internationalist consensus is under renewed assault. The assault this time comes not only from the usual pockets of post-Vietnam liberal isolationism (e.g., the churches) but from a resurgence of 1930s-style conservative isolationism" (Krauthammer 1990/91, 23).

Republican Patrick Buchanan and Democrat Tom Harkin made "American First" a prominent campaign theme during the 1992 presidential election, and numerous analysts have written extensively about the need for relative retrenchment in U.S. foreign policy. Alan Tonelson argued that the George H.W. Bush administration's attachment to Cold War activism was misguided and neglected the simple fact that U.S. power must be founded on a strong domestic society and economy. "The contrast between American victories in the Cold War and the Gulf War, and growing domestic social and economic decay shows that the traditional benchmarks for evaluating United States foreign policy are sorely inadequate" (Tonelson 1992, 145). William Pfaff argued that, as the world system becomes more complex and unpredictable, U.S. capability will be based as much on inner strength and resistance to instability abroad as on the ability to project power beyond the country's borders (Pfaff 1990/91). Paul Kennedy and Arthur Taylor, in testimony on Capitol Hill, argued that the only way to stop the decline of U.S.

strength is by redirecting resources from international commitments to domestic retooling and reinvigoration (U.S. Congress 1990).

Most national interest authors emphasize the need for the United States to withdraw from nonessential international obligations. The *Atlantic Monthly's* July 1991 cover story criticized the failures of internationalism, which, in the authors' view, was out of step with the American public and had led to wasting billions of dollars on problems of only remote importance to the U.S. citizenry (Tonelson 1991). They urged a renewed emphasis on programs that directly benefit the United States, although they did not dismiss all international activities. "An interest-based foreign policy would tend to rule out economic initiatives deemed necessary for the international system's health if those initiatives wound up siphoning more wealth out of this country than they brought in" (Tonelson 1991, 38).

In the tradition of avoiding "entangling alliances" (Hendrickson 1992), the new national interest would exclude international commitments that involve long-term and open-ended obligations, on the grounds that these limit U.S. flexibility and self-reliance. Such analysts see no further need for our involvement in NATO given the dissolution of the Warsaw Pact, as well as U.S. maintenance of military bases across the world, and call for a large-scale withdrawal of troops. Furthermore, they question the merits of an overwhelming nuclear missile deterrent in the face of the collapse and democratization of the United States' principal nuclear adversary, the Soviet Union, and call for unilateral disarmament (Krasner 1989).

During the 1990s, the national interest position focused on U.S. involvement in UN activities and payment of dues to the agency. Following the gruesome deaths of U.S. Marines in Somalia, Senator Jesse Helms of the Senate Foreign Relations Committee blocked U.S. participation in other UN missions (Sterling-Folker 1998, 287). Congressional leaders also blocked the payment of UN dues until the United States nearly lost its voting rights (Tessitore and Woolfson 1999, 300).

Some national interest advocates emphasize the need for reducing oil dependency and import dependency generally, while others focus on the need to control foreign investment flows into the country to preserve U.S. control of critical resources, industries, and even symbolic entities such as Rockefeller Plaza and the Seattle Mariners. Protectionism, investment controls, export promotion, and maintenance of an undervalued currency are among the international economic policies consistent with this approach.

Analysts who accept the national interest approach emphasize the primacy of American sovereignty; however, liberals and conservatives disagree on what in America needs fixing. Liberal neo-isolationists stress repairing urban decay, alleviating poverty, fighting racism, and rebuilding schools. Neoconservatives, in contrast, seek reductions in government regulations and handouts to the poor, and a reversal of the decline of "family values." Conservatives dismiss liberal isolationism as merely a ploy "to spend the maximum amount of money on social programs at home and the minimum abroad" (Kristol 1990, 20).

Although the national interest approach seems particularly appealing during tough economic times, the Bush administration and liberal internationalists outside government argued strongly against it. Such retrenchment, so the logic goes, will take us down the well-worn path toward isolation, xenophobia, and ultimately the collapse of the modern world order. Richard Nixon argued that the choice between domestic resurgence and international activism is a false one. "We do not face a choice between dealing with domestic problems and playing an international role. Our challenge is to do both by setting realistic goals and by managing our limited resources" (Nixon 1992, 277–278). Anti-isolationists argue that even a limited retrenchment from international obligations, whether collective or unilateral, could lead to an increase in America's insecurity as renegade states, reactionary dictatorships, and protectionism abroad flourish and undermine U.S. interests.

Hegemonic Imperative

Many feel that the United States is still, both by duty and by right, the leader of the free world. With the collapse of the Soviet Union, we no longer need to worry about an overwhelming threat to our security. But with that collapse go much of the order and stability of the international system and the risk of new, unforeseen dangers (Gaddis 1987; 1991). As pointed out by Chairman of the Joint Chiefs Colin Powell, none of the troop deployments during the George H.W. Bush administration (Panama, Persian Gulf, Somalia) were anticipated at the time of his inauguration—a fact that reinforces the need for the country to be prepared for threats to peace, no matter how remote they may seem (U.S. Congress 1992, 367).

Many like-minded authors argue that the United States has the capability to lead and lacks only the will. Joseph Nye, an antideclinist, disagrees with President Bush's lament that the United States lacks not the will but the wallet by saying that the reverse is true: In terms of what we can afford as a nation, we are far too tight-fisted in dealing with global problems (Nye 1990). Richard Cooper argued before Congress that the United States must not shrink from global responsibilities for fear of what it will cost (U.S. Congress 1990). Alexander Haig echoed the sentiment, pointing out that it is up to the executive to promote a domestic consensus about the need for American leadership abroad and then to act on that consensus (Haig 1991).

There is a further sense from many authors that the United States has the right not only to lead but also to act unilaterally. Although they pay some lip service to multilateral institutions, they imply that the United States has the best ideas, the strongest institutions, and the natural gifts required to create world order. Charles Krauthammer pointed out: "American preeminence is based on the fact that it is the only country with the military, diplomatic, political and economic assets to be a decisive player in any conflict in whatever part of the world it chooses to involve itself" (Krauthammer 1990/91, 24). Coupled with this assumption of preeminence comes a disdain for the cumbersome mechanisms of the United Nations and the assumption that the UN will never have effective enforcement powers. This tone has been criticized as vain "triumphalism."

During the 1990s, U.S. dominance came to be seen almost as a birthright. The Clinton administration worked to preserve U.S. power through a variety of maneuvers aimed at rewarding countries that had accepted a subordinate position and co-opting those that had not (Mastanduno 1997). The United States, furthermore, has returned to some old, romantic notions of spreading democracy worldwide (Ikenberry 1999). Foreign aid, military deployments, and other initiatives are increasingly designed to strengthen liberal regimes and punish autocrats. Many governments have begun to fear that the United States is "throwing its weight around" with no regard to the implications of its actions. This attitude was at the heart of the debate over U.N. authorization of the American attack on Iraq in 2003.

Some analysts suggest that the U.S. leadership role is merely an extension of old Cold War attitudes and behaviors, as if the Soviet Union had never collapsed. Richard Lugar declared, "Americans must demonstrate staying power and the ability to master and prolong the peace" (Lugar 1992). Many call for maintaining alliances, defense spending, and nuclear weapon arsenals at roughly constant levels in anticipation of future conflicts.

In their exuberance, some have gone so far as to declare the end of international conflict. With the end of the Cold War, so the thinking goes, we are at the conclusion of the grand struggle between liberalism and authoritarianism—the "end of history" itself (Fukuyama 1989). Given this situation, we may find ourselves well and truly in an age without the threat of global war. Naturally, some have steered clear of such dramatic predictions and contented themselves with pointing out the unique nature of America's position in the world, with a call for continued leadership and international engagement (Huntington 1989).

The "errors of endism" are probably obvious enough but bear repetition here. Sanders has warned that attachment to a "unipolar myth" will quickly lead to frustration by those who ignore the reality of the diffusion of power in the last few years. This frustration with America not always getting its way may in turn lead to nationalist retrenchment, with equally serious consequences (Sanders 1991).

In economic affairs, the question is whether the United States is using its position of dominance for good or for ill. An established tradition in international relations literature holds that for the world to enjoy open markets and free flows of ideas and money across international borders, it takes a "hegemon." A hegemon, in this context, is a powerful, benevolent nation that can provide money, markets, and technology to weaker countries as an inducement to them to lower international barriers (Gilpin 1987). In 1944, the Bretton Woods system was set up by the United States and the United Kingdom as a framework for this sort of bargain. The United States was successful in persuading most nations of the world to join the pact but in the 1980s began increasingly to ignore its provisions (see Case 23).

In the 1990s, even though the U.S. economy was growing at the rate of nearly 4 percent per year, the Clinton administration adopted a fairly combative approach to international trade and economics generally. It cut back on foreign aid, negotiated the North American Free Trade Agreement, (NAFTA), which took advantage of the United States' strong position relative to Canada and Mexico, and repeatedly pressured Japan to allow increased amounts of U.S. imports with specific targets for market shares in semiconductors, autos, and automobile parts (Mastanduno 1997). Although the United States concluded the Uruguay Round negotiations of the General Agreement on Tariffs and Trade (GATT) in 1994, it did so by employing very harsh tactics, threatening to pull out at several junctures if its demands were not met. The United States increasingly makes use of dispute settlement panels and threats of unilateral sanctions against what it considers unfair trading partners, even at the expense of security agreements (Maswood 1997, 534). Throughout, U.S. policy makers stress that they are merely trying to promote liberal economics through U.S. leadership—the essence of hegemony.

More subtle are the debates among would-be supporters of U.S. hegemony concerning the goals of U.S. leadership. On the one hand, some feel that U.S. internationalism should be firmly rooted in American idealism and that the nation should devote its energies to supporting and sustaining democracy and human rights. For example, candidate Bill Clinton argued for, among other things, sanctions against China for its repression of students in 1989; support for Somalis, Kurds, and Bosnians fighting against authoritarian enemies; and admission of Haitian refugees into the United States on humanitarian grounds (see also DLC 1991).

On the other hand, many feel that the United States need not be a crusader. Its international engagement should be based on a sort of expanded self-interest, they argue. A stable world order is good for America because it minimizes surprises, allows for methodical planning, and usually results in economic prosperity. The object of U.S. foreign policy should be to discourage instability by supporting the status quo, particularly where existing regimes are already pro-United States. Krauthammer and others stress that the great enemy is no longer an organized opposition but rather disorder itself. They emphasize the need to contain this "chaotic sphere" in international relations by controlling the spread of weapons, intervening in civil wars before they spread, maintaining existing troop deployments in an effort to respond more rapidly to crises, and otherwise taking on the burden of enforcing international law—unilaterally if necessary (Krauthammer 1990/91; Gaddis 1991). Nowhere in this discussion, however, is there any mention of U.S. compliance with international law if such compliance undermines U.S. interests.

The George W. Bush administration has begun to formulate what has been dubbed the "Bush Doctrine." Simply put, it means that, particularly where terrorist threats are concerned, the United States should not wait until the attacks occur to retaliate, but rather seek out plotters and strike preemptively. This philosophy underpins the decision to attack Iraq in advance of its attacking U.S. interests directly. Presumably, this action would be taken not by seeking international approval through the UN, but as part of America's role as global hegemon. As put by Director of Policy Planning in the State Department, Richard Haass:

> We're not looking to turn international relations in 2002 into the Wild West. We understand that restraint and rules still need to be the norm. But there may well be a place for exceptions. You have to ask yourself whether rules and norms which have grown up over hundreds of years in one context are adequate to changing circumstances. (*Chicago Tribune*, September 4, 2002)

We have already discussed the neo-isolationist critique of this traditional approach to U.S. foreign policy. We will now turn to the multilateralist response.

Multilateralism

The differences between the multilateralist and hegemonic approaches are rather subtle but nonetheless profound. To begin, most multilateralists are skeptical of the argument that the United States has either the capability or the prerogative to lead the world. Foremost among their concerns is the fact that the world is no longer bipolar and will never be unipolar. At best, the world is tripolar, with Germany, Japan, and the United States at three opposite poles (Tarnoff 1990). With the end of the Cold War, raw military might has become largely obsolete. We live in an age of economics. As pointed out by Fred Bergsten, "The central task in shaping a new American foreign policy is to set priorities and select central themes. Those choices must derive from America's national interests, which have shifted sharply in the direction of economics" (Bergsten 1992, 4).

The economic issue has led many to urge a collaborative U.S. policy based on close cooperation among the United States, Japan, and Europe (via Germany) (U.S. Congress 1990). The tripartite arrangement will go the farthest to promote open markets, liberal monetary policy, and free investment activities (Tarnoff 1990). Analysts emphasize the need to work through multilateral institutions, such as GATT and the International Monetary Fund (IMF), and to create yet more, stronger rules and enforcement mechanisms to preserve open markets (Aho and Stokes 1990/91). They assume that a failure to continue expanding free trade will lead quickly to a rapid retreat into protectionism.

This urge to "go multilateral" stems not only from an acceptance of the U.S. decline into parity (or at least the rise of Europe and Japan), but also from a hope that security concerns will continue to remain back-burner issues in the future. Some have pointed out that democracies do not go to war with each other, concluding like the "endists" that the threat of global conflict is virtually over (Jervis 1992). War has become less likely because of the nature of states, and it has become less profitable and therefore less attractive to rational actors interested in maximizing gains over losses (Kaysen

1991). The implication of these developments is that we have reached a point when collective security may finally be a feasible method for dealing with all international conflict—a solution that would eliminate the need for American unilateralism. Russett and Sutterlin feel that now is the time to give the UN the authority and capability to intervene actively in conflict situations not only to "keep" the peace but also to "make" it. The success of the UN in the Persian Gulf War

> can enhance the United Nations' ability not just to restore the status quo as it existed prior to a breach of the peace, but also to change the parameters of the global order to something more favorable than existed under the prior status quo. In this it may even go beyond the vision of the U.N. founders. (Russett and Sutterlin 1991, 82)

In the Clinton administration, Secretary of State Madeleine Albright and Vice President Al Gore were noted for their enthusiasm for the multilateral approach. Their propensity to urge an assertive U.S. leadership role, including a military one, has been described as "assertive multilateralism" (Sterling-Folker 1998, 284). A draft presidential directive—PRD-13—called for a broader and more dynamic UN role, including a standing UN army and a willingness to place U.S. troops under UN command. Though no longer U.S. policy as early as 1994, this position was assailed by Republican critics and remained an issue into the 1996 presidential campaign.

Although it is assumed that the UN will continue to be supportive of U.S. goals of promoting democracy, spreading free trade, and enforcing international law, there is an implicit acknowledgment that in the future the United States must accept that it will not always get its way. Former U.S. envoy to the UN Daniel Patrick Moynihan deplores the fact that the United States has a bad habit of giving lip service to the letter of international law without complying with its spirit. We sign the Optional Clause of the World Court, thereby showing our support for rendering its decisions binding, and then we deny their validity on technical grounds when they go against us. We draw up a UN Charter that pledges our support for establishing a UN-commanded standing military force, and then we refuse to allow U.S. troops to participate in peacekeeping operations. It is time, so the multilateralists say, to play by all the rules, not just those we like (Chace 1992).

It may seem ironic that multilateralists, while accepting the fact of American decline, believe that American idealism can now be adopted as the global standard. The hope is that, given the core values of fairness and tolerance, a weaker United States will actually live in a manner closer to its own rhetoric. On the down side, multilateralists fear that American decline and increased great power parity may create an urgent need to institutionalize idealism quickly. Failure to do so may lead to a collapse of the precarious consensus we now enjoy.

Critics of multilateralism come from many corners. Neo-isolationists fear that multilateralism will become yet another way to "sell the farm" to foreign interests. Yielding to international pressures does not come naturally to most

Americans, particularly those who deny any automatic or inevitable international role for the United States. They do not see the need for continued international involvement as a prerequisite for national renewal, and they see multilateral institutions as an impediment to national strength, not a help.

Unilateralists deny the inevitability of U.S. decline and feel that multilateralism, though acceptable when applied to other nations, should not be U.S. policy. They point to the economic troubles experienced by Europe and Japan in the second half of 1992 as evidence that nothing is inevitable about their ascendance. They further point to the paralysis of the European Community in the face of full-scale civil war in Yugoslavia as evidence that the United States should not expect international leadership from Brussels or Berlin. The UN has been incapable of enforcing international law, and international economic institutions have more often than not provided a cover for unfair trading practices by the United States' economic rivals, so the logic goes. Thus, although the unilateralists share the multilateralists' internationalism, they emphasize leadership. Furthermore, they share with the neo-isolationists the view that the United States should never voluntarily submit to international law if this law is dysfunctional and runs contrary to U.S. interests (however defined).

Conclusion

If you, the reader, are still a bit uncertain about where you stand on the question, do not be dismayed. Even the experts have to hedge a bit. Secretary of State James Baker, a unilateralist at heart, emphasized the need for the United States to share both burdens and powers with its allies via multilateral institutions (U.S. Congress 1992). Joseph Nye likewise seems to straddle the fence on whether the United States should take control of global institutions or be more of a team player (U.S. Congress 1990). Even military analysts who seem most readily inclined to accept unilateralism have paid lip service to the UN.

Some neo-isolationists are still quick to acknowledge that there might be a role for some U.S. troops overseas (as a trip wire, perhaps) and caution against the dangers of a too-rapid demobilization (Hyland 1990; Brzezinski 1991). They will accept that although weapons manufacturing is no longer essential, maintenance of production lines, jobs, and even technological research may continue to have a place in a peacetime economy. Even the threat of protectionism is seen by many as merely a bargaining strategy to persuade other nations to open their markets and embrace true free trade.

The record of the Clinton administration was mixed, and the door remains open to future presidents to adopt any number of courses of action. Although assertive multilateralism is on the shelf for now, given George W. Bush's basic skepticism of UN intervention, the United States has a record of supporting multilateral ventures.

The disasters that took place on September 11, 2001, prompted a strong and virtually unanimous response from policymakers and legislators on both sides of the aisle. The war against terror became the new, defining focus of U.S. foreign policy, playing much the same role as anti-communism during the Cold War (*Chicago Tribune*, September 6, 2002). The United States was determined to lead the fight, without direction from the rest of the world (although U.S. officials were careful to obtain UN approval first). Operation Enduring Freedom in Afghanistan was very much an American operation, as was the establishment of the Karzai government after the defeat of the Taliban.

It was not until the summer of 2002, when Bush administration officials leaked plans to invade Iraq and replace Saddam Hussein, that some voices of dissent and concern were raised. Perhaps most troubling to Bush was the opposition of loyal Republicans who served in the Senate and had previously supported his father. James Baker opined that a military strike, while well intentioned, was ill advised without a UN resolution to back it up (Baker 2002). Senior Democrats have gone on record against the proposal. Even after the war's successful outcome in April 2003, some question whether ignoring international law was necessary.

Thus a new debate has begun, focused on the limits of the Bush Doctrine of unilateral, preemptive strikes. It seems to be having some effect, since in September 2002 the White House indicated some willingness to consider a debate in Congress and at the UN prior to launching an attack. It may be useful to dust off the pages of the Great Debates of the past as the United States attempts to find its way through a post–September 11 world.

Debate Topic

Is the current war against terror best carried out as a multilateral or unilateral strategy?

PRO

A supporter of the multilateralist approach would likely argue as follows: (1) Because terrorism violates the rules of civilization itself, fighting it is inherently multilateral. Only supporters of terrorism would object. (2) Because terrorism is ubiquitous, only a global approach will be successful. (3) The United States is a relative newcomer in the fight against terrorism, and it could benefit from undertaking joint operations with states such as the United Kingdom, Germany, Italy, and Israel which have far more experience.

CON

Supporters of a unilateral approach have pointed out: (1) The September 11 attacks were aimed solely at the United States, so it is incumbent on the United States to respond directly, with or without the rest of the world's support. (2) Only the United States has the capability of projecting force worldwide, and it will therefore be expected to lead an antiterror campaign. (3) Because so many countries sponsor and tolerate terrorism, it is best not to depend too much on international collaboration, but to move forward unilaterally.

Questions to Consider

1. If you were an advisor to the president, what would you recommend?

2. What basic values can you identify in relation to each of the perspectives on post–Cold War U.S. policy? With which values are you most comfortable and why?

3. Can one make a "rational" decision about such issues when so much is tied up in values, perceptions, beliefs, and assumptions? Or are these part of rationality itself?

Websites

Well-Known Foreign Policy "Think Tanks"
The Brookings Institution: **www.brook.edu/fp/fp_hp.htm**
Council on Foreign Relations: **www.cfr.org**
Foreign Policy Association: **www.fpa.org**
Foreign Policy Institute: **www.sais-jhu.edu/centers/fpi/index.htm**
Heritage Foundation: **www.heritage.org**
Institute for Policy Analysis: **www.ifpa.org**
United Nations Association of the United States: **www.unausa.org**

References

Aho, Michael, and Bruce Stokes. "The Year the World Economy Turned." *Foreign Affairs* 70 #1 (1990/91): 160–178.

Baker, James, "The Right Way to Change a Regime," *New York Times,* August 25, 2002.

Bergsten, Fred. "The Primacy of Economics." *Foreign Policy* 87 (Summer 1992): 3–24.

Brzezinski, Zbigniew. "Selective Global Commitment." *Foreign Affairs* 70 #4 (Fall 1991): 1–20.

Chace, James. *The Consequences of the Peace: The New Internationalism and American Foreign Policy* (New York: Oxford University Press, 1992).

Chicago Tribune, September 4, 2002.

Chicago Tribune, September 6, 2002.

Democratic Leadership Council. *The New American Choice: Opportunity, Reponsibility, Community.* Resolutions Adopted at the DLC Convention, Cleveland, Ohio, 1991.

Fukuyama, Francis. "The End of History?" *National Interest* 16 (Summer 1989): 3–18.

Gaddis, John Lewis. *The Long Peace: Inquiries into the History of the Cold War* (New York: Oxford University Press, 1987).

Gaddis, John Lewis. "Toward the Post–Cold War World." *Foreign Affairs* 70 #2 (Spring 1991): 102–122.

Gilpin, Robert. *The Political Economy of International Relations* (Princeton, NJ: Princeton University Press, 1987).

Haig, Alexander. "The Challenges to American Leadership" in Schmergel, ed., *U.S. Foreign Policy in the 1990s,* 34–46.

Hendrickson, David. "The Renovation of American Foreign Policy." *Foreign Affairs* 71 #2 (Spring 1992): 48–63.

Huntington, Samuel. "No Exit: The Errors of Endism." *National Interest* 17 (Fall 1989): 3–11.

Hyland, William. "America's New Course." *Foreign Affairs* 69 #2 (Spring 1990): 1–12.

Ikenberry, John. "Why Export Democracy?" *Wilson Quarterly* #3 (Spring 1999): 56.

Jervis, Robert. "The Future of World Politics: Will It Resemble the Past?" in Lynn-Jones and Miller, eds., *America's Changing Strategy*, 3–37.

Kaysen, Carl. "Is War Obsolete? A Review Essay" in Lynn-Jones, ed., *The Cold War and After*, 81–103.

Kegley, Charles, and Eugene Wittkopf, eds. *The Future of American Foreign Policy* (New York: St. Martin's, 1992).

Krasner, Stephen. "Realist Praxis: Neo-isolationism and Structural Change." *Journal of International Affairs* 43 #1 (1989): 143–160.

Krauthammer, Charles. "The Unipolar Moment." *Foreign Affairs* 70 #1 (1990/91): 23–33.

Kristol, Irving. "Defining Our National Interest." *National Interest* (Fall 1990): 16–25.

Lugar, Richard. "The Republican Course." *Foreign Policy* # 86 (Spring 92): 86–98.

Lynn-Jones, Sean, ed. *The Cold War and After: Prospects for Peace* (Cambridge, MA: MIT Press, 1991).

Lynn-Jones, Sean, and Steven Miller, eds. *America's Changing Strategy in a Changing World* (Cambridge, MA: MIT Press, 1992).

Mastanduno, Michael. "Preserving the Unipolar Moment: Realist Theories and U.S. Grand Strategy After the Cold War." *International Security* 21 #4 (Spring 1997): 49–88.

Maswood, Javed. "Does Revisionism Work? U.S. Trade Strategy and the 1995 U.S.–Japan Auto Dispute." *Pacific Affairs* 70 #4 (Winter 1997): 533–555.

Nixon, Richard. *Seize the Moment: America's Challenge in a One-Superpower World* (New York: Simon & Schuster, 1992).

Nye, Joseph. *Bound to Lead: The Changing Nature of American Power* (New York: Basic Books, 1990).

Pfaff, William. "Redefining World Power." *Foreign Affairs* 70 #1 (1990/91): 34–48.

Russett, Bruce, and James Sutterlin. "The U.N. in a New World Order." *Foreign Affairs* 70 #2 (Spring 1991): 69–83.

Sanders, Jerry. "Retreat from World Order: The Perils of Triumphalism." *World Policy Journal* 8 #2 (Spring 1991): 227–250.

Schmergel, Greg, ed. *U.S. Foreign Policy in the 1990s* (New York: St. Martin's, 1991).

Sterling-Folker, Jennifer. "Between a Rock and a Hard Place: Assertive Multilateralism and Post–Cold War U.S. Foreign Policy Making" in James Scott, ed., *After the End: Making U.S. Foreign Policy in the Post–Cold War World* (Durham, NC: Duke University Press, 1998), 277–304.

Tarnoff, Peter. "America's New Special Relationships." *Foreign Affairs* 69 #3 (Summer 1990): 67–80.

Tessitore, John, and Susan Woolfson, eds. *A Global Agenda: Issues Before the 54th General Assembly of the United Nations* (Lanham, MD: Rowman and Littlefield, 1999).

Tonelson, Alan. "Prudence or Inertia? The Bush Administration's Foreign Policy." *Current History* 91 #564 (April 1992): 145–150.

Tonelson, Alan. "What Is the National Interest?" *The Atlantic Monthly* (July 1991): 35–52.

U.S. Congress, House. *The Future of U.S. Foreign Policy in the Post–Cold War Era.* Hearings before the Committee on Foreign Affairs, 102nd Congress, 2nd Session, 1992.

U.S. Congress, House. *U.S. Power in a Changing World.* Special Report 28-802 prepared for the Committee on Foreign Affairs, 101st Congress, 2nd Session, 1990.

CASE

9

The Persian Gulf War
CAPABILITIES AND INFLUENCE

Introduction

Central to the debate over the best definition of power is how a nation's power capabilities are converted into actual influence. A nation is often described as "powerful" when it has a large military establishment, sizable natural resources, and a large and well-educated population, among other things. These features are more properly described as "capabilities," and they may or may not translate into "influence" in terms of changing or preserving the international system. An army two million strong and several thousand nuclear warheads did not bring American victory in the Vietnam War, and many feared that the overwhelming advantage of the U.S.-led coalition in the Persian Gulf War would likewise be for naught. Control of oil was an advantage for Iraq, but, paradoxically, control of oil consumption turned out to be a more significant asset for the United States and the West.

Resources are certainly vital to a nation's power. As pointed out by Rothgeb, they provide (1) the impression of power (which may be enough in and of itself to bring about compliance with your wishes), (2) expanded vehicles for influencing others (bribery, boycotts, invasions, and so forth), and (3) resistance to others' efforts at influencing your own policies (oil stockpiles protect against embargoes, for example) (Rothgeb 1993, 192).

This is not to say that capability is sufficient to generate influence. Much depends on how this power is utilized in day-to-day, dynamic situations. Military threats that are not credible or are poorly communicated will probably not deter undesired action. If a nation's capabilities are exaggerated, then the country may enjoy a false sense of security until a crisis unravels everything.

The reader is invited to pay especially close attention to the way power is used in a crisis where stakes are high and "all necessary means" are brought to bear. The number of players in the Gulf War was quite large, and their interests and power varied dramatically. To what can we attribute George H.W. Bush's success in assembling an anti-Iraq coalition with countries in Western Europe, the Middle East, and many other regions? How significant was the UN's involvement? Could this alliance have occurred in different circumstances? Most important, was war inevitable? Why did the coalition win?

THE PERSIAN GULF WAR
KEY FIGURES

Saddam Hussein   Iraqi President, 1979–present. His armies invaded Kuwait on August 2, 1990.

George H.W.Bush   U.S. President, 1989–1993. He organized the coalition that liberated Kuwait on February 28, 1991.

Boutros Boutros–Ghali   UN Secretary-General, 1992–1996. He served as a mediator between the Security Council and Iraqi officials.

General Norman Schwartzkopf   U.S. Commander, Central Command, at the time of the Gulf War. He led the military offensive to retake Kuwait.

Tariq Aziz   Iraqi Foreign Minister during the Gulf War. He acted as Saddam Hussein's representative at the UN.

Eduard Schevardnadze   Soviet Foreign Minister during the Gulf War. He pressed for a diplomatic settlement.

Mikhail Gorbachev   Soviet Communist Party Chairman, 1985–1991.

THE PERSIAN GULF WAR
CHRONOLOGY

1932
Great Britain draws the boundaries between Iraq and Kuwait as part of its dismantling of the Ottoman Empire.

1961
Kuwait is granted its independence over Iraq's protests.

1979
Saddam Hussein becomes President of Iraq.

1980
The Iran–Iraq War begins with Iraq's invasion of Iran in retaliation for its destabilization efforts in southern Iraq.

1988
The Iran–Iraq War ends.

1990

July	The Iraqi government challenges Kuwaiti policies and sovereignty.
August 2	Iraqi forces attack and defeat Kuwaiti defenses.
August 5	U.S. forces are deployed to Saudi Arabia.
November 6	President Bush announces a large increase in troop strength.

(continued)

| November 29 | The UN Security Council sets a deadline for Iraqi withdrawal from Kuwait. |

1991

January 17	Coalition forces launch air strikes against Iraqi forces in and around Kuwait.
January 20	Coalition forces achieve air superiority.
January 26	Iraqi forces begin releasing Kuwaiti oil into the Persian Gulf.
February 23	Coalition forces launch a ground strike against Iraqi forces.
February 28	Iraqi forces surrender.
May	U.S. troops are withdrawn from Kuwait. Kurds rebel against Saddam Hussein's regime. A "no-fly" zone is created in northern Iraq to discourage Iraqi attacks against rebels.

1992

A "no-fly" zone is created in southern Iraq. UN weapons inspectors are rebuffed in Baghdad.

1998

The United Kingdom and the United States launch air strikes against Iraqi weapons installations. Iraq bars UN weapons inspectors.

2002

The United States proposes an invasion of Iraq to overthrow Saddam Hussein's regime.

2003

British and American forces invade Iraq and remove the regime of Saddam Hussein.

Antecedents to War

On August 2, 1990, the Iraqi army, fourth largest in the world, led by more than 4,000 tanks, poured across the Kuwaiti border to overrun a nation roughly the size of Connecticut. Moral outrage, fear of what might happen next, and a desire to test the post–Cold War environment eventually led to an overwhelming military defeat for Iraq and the liberation of Kuwait. One might ask, given this ultimate outcome, why did Saddam Hussein do it? To answer this question, one must understand both the circumstances of the invasion and the character of the Iraqi regime and its leader.

A long-time member of the Baathist political movement, Saddam Hussein began his career as a torturer for the short-lived Baathist regime that governed Iraq from 1958 to 1963. Upon its return to power in 1968, the party rewarded Hussein's loyalty and energy with the position of deputy chairman of the Revolutionary Command Council, where he set about ensuring that the party would never again be victimized by factional infighting as it had in 1963. Within a few years, he emerged as the de facto leader of the state and, with the wealth he derived from oil following the 1973 price hike, covered himself with riches and power. He assumed the presidency in 1979 and immediately purged the upper ranks of the party, often carrying out the executions personally and with great publicity (Miller and Mylroie 1990, 45).

The legacy of Hussein's rule is well known. Several villages populated by ethnic Kurds in the northern regions of Iraq were attacked with chemical weapons during the 1980s on the grounds that they sought a separate statehood. The Shi'a Muslim majority of Iraq (as opposed to the minority Sunni to which Hussein belonged) were frequent targets of Saddam's internal attacks because of their support for the radical Ayatollah Khomeini in neighboring Iran. During the Iran–Iraq War (1980–1988), Hussein was accused of aggression because his tanks crossed the border into Iran and his Scud missiles fell on Iranian urban centers (although the World Court was unable to determine who actually "started" the war).

Throughout his reign, Hussein frequently attacked Israeli "Zionism" as a racist threat to Arab unity, although his own attachment to the Arab cause seems to have been more contrived than genuine. His relations with Kuwait, Syria, and Saudi Arabia were always tense, and he often threatened to take matters into his own hands when unable to negotiate on his terms. Organization of Petroleum Exporting Countries (OPEC) matters were especially problematic, given Iraq's dependence on oil exports and the tendency of smaller OPEC members to undercut the organization through overproduction. At various OPEC summits, Hussein challenged the Arab nations to display greater solidarity and anti-Israeli unity. Iraq's $70 billion war debt, accumulated during the Iran–Iraq War, created an especially urgent financial problem for the country and prompted its demands for debt forgiveness (Kono 1990, 37), particularly from Kuwait, to which Iraq owed billions.

To understand why Iraq was willing to invade a neighboring Arab country in spite of pan-Arabism, we need to look at Kuwait's image in the Arab world. Kuwait had a reputation for arrogance borne of its record-breaking wealth. Many Arabs resented the Kuwaiti practice of hiring other Arabs for the most menial jobs they were not willing to do themselves and then denying the workers any political or civil rights. It was widely believed that Kuwaitis were siphoning oil from the Rumaila oil field in Iraqi territory (*New York Times*, September 3, 1990, A7). And Kuwait regularly exceeded its OPEC-imposed production quota to reap unfair profits at OPEC's expense. All this Saddam Hussein knew full well. He also knew that millions of Arabs in cities from Morocco to Pakistan would delight in the humiliation of Kuwait and that these throngs would put pressure on their governments to support Iraq in this apparently noble quest—especially if the call was issued with religious imagery and symbols.

Iraq has had territorial claims against Kuwait for decades and especially since 1932, when the current borders were established as the British and French carved up the Ottoman Empire. When Kuwait gained its independence in 1961, the Iraqi government once again explicitly stated its perpetual claim on Kuwaiti territory (Miller and Mylroie 1990, 197). In particular, Iraq felt it needed definitive control of the Euphrates River estuary and the Kuwaiti islands of Bubiyan and Warbah, critical choke points controlling access to Basra and Umm Qasr, the country's only ports.

In spite of all this, Iraq and Kuwait were actually on the same side during the Iran–Iraq War, although Kuwait adopted an officially neutral position. Kuwait shipped Iraq millions of dollars in aid and suffered through numerous terrorist attacks from Iranians. Its tankers were reflagged and protected by American ships in 1987, a move that preserved the flow of roughly 1.5 million barrels of oil per day from Kuwait. Paradoxically, Kuwait had even joined Iraq in strident anti-Israeli rhetoric during the early 1980s. This rather ambivalent and mixed relationship between Iraq and Kuwait may help to explain the shock Kuwaitis and others felt at the savagery of Hussein's surprise attack. There were as many reasons against an attack as there were those in favor of one.

One can see Iraq's policies in 1990 in terms of balance of power politics (Sayigh 1991) and anti-Zionism. After Egypt was neutralized by the Camp David Accords, Saudi Arabia and the Gulf States tilted ever more to the West, the Soviet Union became unwilling to support radical regimes, and Iran moved toward a moderate position, Hussein saw Iraq as the last of the militant anti-Israeli Arab states. In addition, Iraq had the largest military in the region and was challenged in that regard only by Israel, Iran, and Syria. The desire to lead the anti-Zionist elements in the Middle East (including the masses in Jordan and elsewhere) and the opportunity to position Iraq as the primary challenger to Israel may have been important factors in Hussein's decision to invade Kuwait.

Throughout the 1980s, the United States had a rather ambivalent position vis-à-vis Iraq and Kuwait. Although it tilted toward Iraq in its war with Iran, the United States shipped relatively few weapons to the country. Evidence from UN inspection teams who arrived after the Gulf War indicated that the United States played a part in Iraq's nuclear weapons program. Also, some U.S. grain credits offered to Hussein seem to have been diverted for military purchases. The United States sold Iraq $240 million worth of military equipment in 1987 and 1988 (Hippler 1991, 28–29). It should be emphasized, however, that 53 percent of Iraqi weapons purchases in the 1980s were of Soviet origin, and most of its military's foreign training took place in the Soviet Union (a fact that caused no small amount of second-guessing in Moscow after the war, when the poor performance of these weapons was amply demonstrated—*New York Times*, March 1, 1991, A11).

In the months leading up to the invasion, the U.S. position was especially mixed—a problem that dogged George Bush during his 1992 presidential reelection campaign. The U.S. envoy to Iraq, April Glaspie, was accused of telling Saddam Hussein in June that territorial disputes between Arab neighbors were strictly a regional matter, hinting that the United States would stand on the sidelines. Although this has been denied (*New York Times*, March 21, 1991, A17), rumors persisted through 1992. At any rate, in testimony on Iraq's human rights record in April 1990, U.S. State Department officials downplayed abuses and applauded the improvements they saw. According to a CIA official, however, the United States knew as early as January 1990 that Iraq was prepared to attack Kuwait (*New York Times*, September 25, 1991, A1). It was not until Iraq spoke openly in July 1990 of military action against both Kuwait and the United Arab Emirates, following failed attempts to negotiate for lower oil production, that the United States signaled its willingness to intervene by deploying combat ships to the Persian Gulf (*New York Times*, July 25, 1990, A1).

Nevertheless, White House officials claimed to have been entirely surprised by Iraq's invasion of Kuwait (Davis and Arquilla 1991). Likewise, Saddam seems to have been taken off guard by the vigorous U.S. response. Even after the invasion occurred, President Bush felt the need to consult his top military advisors to determine whether this constituted a real threat to the United States (*New York Times*, August 12, 1990, A1).

The Diplomatic Phase: August 2, 1990–January 16, 1991

Within a week of the invasion of Kuwait, Iraqi forces began to mass on the Saudi Arabian border to the south. To deter an Iraqi attack on the enormous Saudi oil fields, the United States sought and obtained permission to deploy the 82nd Airborne Division along the border. With this "trip-wire" force in place, the United States began to expand its forces in the region to withstand an assault in case Iraq decided to attack after all. At the same time, President Bush sought the support of other countries, focusing especially on powerful European allies and Arab countries most directly threatened by Iraq in the hope of pressuring Saddam Hussein to withdraw from Kuwait.

The UN Security Council was active in the days and weeks following the invasion, passing a dozen resolutions that included issuing sweeping condemnations of the Iraqi "breach of the peace," demanding a restoration of the situation to pre–August 1, 1990, conditions (Resolution 660), and setting up extensive economic and diplomatic sanctions in the hope they would force Iraq to leave Kuwait (Resolution 661). These sanctions were to be enforced by the U.S.-led coalition through sea power (Resolution 665). Ultimately, in a dramatic show of unity, the foreign ministers of the Security Council members approved Resolution 678 on November 29, 1990, which authorized nations to enforce all preceding sanctions "by all necessary means"—a clear signal that military intervention had the UN's blessing. Resolution 678 in a sense signaled of the failure of diplomatic efforts by James Baker of the United States, Tariq Aziz of Iraq, and Eduard Schevardnadze of the USSR to reach a settlement on the Kuwaiti problem.

In the early weeks of the crisis, a central issue was the treatment of foreign nationals trapped in Kuwait at the time of the invasion. Several thousand Westerners were residing in Kuwait in August 1990 and were captured by Hussein's forces during the invasion. They were relocated at sensitive military installations throughout Iraqi territory to discourage a surprise attack from the West (*New York Times*, August 10, 1990, A1) and to force a U.S. withdrawal from the region (*New York Times*, August 20, 1990, A1). Called "guests" by Hussein, these hostages created an unnerving twist in what was becoming a very different sort of war. The taking of civilian hostages by a government at war was a clear violation of the 1948 Geneva Convention and gave a strong indication that Iraq did not intend to be bound by international law in the treatment of civilians (as if invading Kuwait had not been persuasive enough). In what Iraq called a "gesture of goodwill," the hostages were permitted to leave the country in time for Christmas (*New*

York Times, December 8, 1990, A6). In the meantime, the Iraqi government cut off all food and water to the embassies of coalition members in Kuwait, leaving hundreds of diplomats stranded. American diplomatic personnel staged a heroic last stand in spite of rapidly deteriorating conditions and the departure of other diplomatic teams. Ultimately, they were withdrawn, and by the new year all Westerners who wished to leave Kuwait were gone.

Until late October, American and European diplomats held out hope that some compromise might be reached between Iraq and Kuwait that would avert the need for further war. These efforts revolved around putting pressure on Iraq through economic sanctions, pressure on Kuwait to accept the possibility of future concessions, and pressure on other powers to support the U.S. decisions. Economic sanctions held surprisingly well throughout the period, although some leaks at the Iraq–Jordan border were noted. According to Tucker, "Those sanctions were almost completely successful in stopping Iraqi oil exports, and Iraqi imports were reduced by 90 percent. Iraq's GNP fell almost immediately by 40 percent. In their severity, these economic sanctions were unprecedented in modern history" (Tucker and Hendrickson 1992, 101). In spite of these costly penalties, Iraq's position hardened during the period. Not only did Iraq not withdraw from Kuwait, but it officially annexed it and moved to terrorize the local inhabitants and suppress any hint of rebellion.

Other diplomatic efforts centered on both consolidating an anti-Iraq military coalition and planning for an eventual post-crisis political realignment in the Persian Gulf. President Bush, drawing on his extensive personal contacts with European leaders, was able to blunt reservations expressed by French and Soviet diplomats. By late August, the Western powers, Japan, and the Soviet Union were essentially speaking with one voice. Germany and Japan were pressed to provide substantial financial support to the exercise—a move that placed the Japanese government in a very awkward position at home. Tokyo's initial offer of $1 billion was judged inadequate by Washington, but the next offer of $4 billion for the U.S. and regional allies was barely accepted in Japan's parliament. Ultimately, the Japanese provided even more funds, although a constitutional provision prevented the government from deploying troops in the Gulf region (the so-called Peace Constitution, largely inspired by U.S. occupation forces in the 1940s, prohibits such deployments). In Germany, a similar clause in the Basic Law limited the government's options to financial support and endorsement of NATO's role in the crisis. Countries that contributed troops to the coalition included the United Kingdom, France, Canada, Saudi Arabia, and Egypt—twenty-eight nations all together. By the end of September, 250,000 troops from this combined force were deployed in Saudi Arabia.

The Soviets, unwilling to join the coalition itself, were especially active in seeking a compromise between the parties in the crisis. Foreign Minister Eduard Schevardnadze, special envoy Yevgeny Primakov, and Primakov's aide Serge Kiripitchenko undertook their own shuttle diplomacy. On September 5, one month after the invasion, Iraqi Foreign Minister Tariq Aziz visited with Soviet President Mikhail Gorbachev to determine whether any diplomatic movement in Iraq was possible. Instead of new flexibility, the Soviets heard old demands that Israel withdraw from Palestinian occupied territories in exchange for Iraqi withdrawal from Kuwait (*Middle East Insight*, 1990). The Soviets indicated a willingness to consider new political arrangements in the Gulf region after Iraqi withdrawal, which included acknowledging Iraq's prewar demands. Up to the day before the beginning of the ground offensive, Soviet emissaries continued pressing for a deal that would prevent war. In the end, Iraqi leaders went so far as to promise to withdraw from Kuwait and release all prisoners of war. Because the proposal included demands for ending sanctions before the withdrawal was complete and did not stipulate Iraqi reparations to Kuwait, it was rejected by the United States and replaced with tougher demands the next day, in spite of Soviet objections. When these were finally rejected by Hussein, the ground offensive began (*New York Times*, February 23, 1991, A1).

One can question Iraqi and U.S. sincerity during these diplomatic exchanges. Iraq clearly was interested only in dividing the coalition by appealing to Arab unity and anti-Israeli sentiments in the Middle East. One can also see Soviet diplomatic efforts as a vehicle for Hussein to undermine coalition unity. "Although the American-led coalition had the capability to do as it threatened, the Iraqi government apparently believed that it possessed the military muscle needed to neutralize any moves by the coalition. Thus, Iraq largely ignored the American threats made in the fall of 1990 and the winter of 1991" (Rothgeb 1993, 101).

American demands, which were more modest in the early weeks of the crisis, became increasingly inflexible as the U.S. military presence grew. Bob Woodward of the *Washington Post* has argued that the decision to rely entirely on military force was made as early as late October and that all diplomatic moves from that point were largely posturing and rhetoric (Woodward 1991). Others have argued that, given White House priorities, the military option was considered far preferable to either maintaining the sanctions or withdrawing, even though the Cabinet was divided on the question (Mintz 1993). Withdrawal would naturally give a victory to Iraq and make the United States appear weak. But sanctions also carried serious risks, because they might take too long, fail to persuade Iraq to withdraw, and give Bush's political opponents in Washington a political victory of their own.

On November 6, a few days after the midterm election, George Bush announced his decision to essentially double U.S. troop strength in the Gulf, from roughly 250,000 to more than 500,000—half of America's active-duty combat forces (Stork and Wenger 1991, 12). The decision to rely on military solutions, as fate would have it, soon revealed itself to be irreversible—and perhaps this was the intention of the president. It became clear that sustaining a military force of 500,000 in the harshest climate on earth, where merely providing water took extraordinary measures, could not last very long. When combined with the coming of the summer months, when temperatures would rise to 120 degrees Fahrenheit, the prospects for a peaceful resolution were even dimmer. In addition, placement of these forces in Saudi Arabia presented a political dilemma for local Arab leaders, because it sent a clear message that the United States had gained control of the situation and that all talk of an Arab-led alliance was mere rhetoric. Finally, the systematic destruction of Kuwait by Iraqi forces and reports of atrocities put extraordinary pressure on the coalition to use these forces to put an end to it all (*New York Times*, December 16, 1990, A1).

At home, the debate was raging over whether to permit sanctions to do the job of getting Iraq out of Kuwait without resorting to war. The debate in the Senate in early January was heated and passionate. At issue was a resolution supporting the UN's "all necessary means" language (while stopping short of a declaration of war). For some, such as Republican minority leader Bob Dole, support of the president's foreign policy program was reason enough to vote for the resolution. Others, such as Democrat Al Gore, felt that the chances of Iraqi withdrawal without war were slim and that the resolution merited their vote. Forty-five Democrats and two Republicans voted against it, primarily on the grounds that sanctions had not been given enough time to work, although they were often quick to add that military intervention should not be ruled out entirely.

Throughout the nation, most citizens expressed a willingness to support their president, although lingering doubts about the justice and necessity of the war were frequently voiced. Former National Security Advisor Zbigniew Brzezinski, no pacifist, joined others in support for continued reliance on sanctions (Brzezinski 1990; Elliott et al. 1990). Neo-isolationists, such as Patrick Buchanan, joined with pacifists and radicals in academia in calling for a withdrawal of U.S. forces from the Middle East. Stories of the army placing a rush order for 16,000 body bags in December alarmed many friends and relatives of Gulf War soldiers and confirmed fears of a bloodbath. In the final analysis, the Senate vote reflected the ambivalent attitudes of the nation at large, and George Bush took "a divided nation into battle," according to Representative Ron Dellums (*New York Times*, January 13, 1991, A1).

Thus it was, with a UN-imposed deadline for Iraqi compliance with all UN resolutions of January 15, 1991, that the region was poised for war. Estimates at the time indicated that some 550,000 troops were in place on the Iraqi side, although more recent figures put the total at closer to only 380,000 (Tucker and Hendrickson, 1992 75). Five thousand Soviet-made tanks, several hundred Scud missiles (thought to be carrying chemical or nuclear weapons), 600 combat aircraft, and some 2,000 artillery pieces rounded out the Iraqi army's resources in the region (Stork and Wenger 1991, 24). It was generally assumed that the Republican Guard troops, deployed deep inside Kuwait, posed the greater threat, and that their sand dune defenses would make for tough slogging after the initial thrust into the country.

On the U.S./coalition side, at least 470,000 ground troops from fifteen countries were deployed mostly just south of the Kuwaiti border. These troops were armed with roughly 6,500 tanks and supported by 2,200 combat aircraft—including the new Stealth fighter and Patriot missiles. In addition, some 50,000 marines were stationed offshore in the Gulf itself, preparing for a possible amphibious invasion. In the Gulf and the Mediterranean, the United States and the United Kingdom deployed 6 aircraft carriers, along with more than 25 additional attack craft, which were loaded with in excess of 700 nuclear bombs and missiles (Stork and Wenger 1991, 25). The stage was set for the "mother of all battles," as put by Saddam Hussein. Iraqi leaders hoped to inflict thousands of casualties on what they considered a weak-willed coalition force, while the Bush administration hoped that advanced technology would prevent such an event and deliver victory (Freedman and Karsh 1993).

The Air War Phase: January 17–February 23, 1991

Those who watched the events unfold on television will long remember the beginning of the air war on Baghdad early in the morning of January 17, 1991 (3:00 a.m. local time). Memories of anxious foreign correspondents—CNN's Bernard Shaw, Peter Arnett, and Wolf Blitzer; NBC's Arthur Kent—are burned into the national consciousness from watching hour upon hour of special reports. It was a moment of collective action, which is rare in contemporary society. As put in a dramatic *New York Times* essay, "Suddenly, in public places where cacophony is the norm, there was an unusual silence, eerie rather than giddy. Grand Central Terminal in Manhattan—where even whispers can take on an echoing, high-decibel intensity—was quiet" (*New York Times*, January 17, 1991, A1). President Bush appeared on television in his "warrior mode" and declared the beginning of the attack as well as its purpose, making frequent references to the U.S. invasion on D-Day 1944: "The liberation of Kuwait has begun."

The tactic in the air war was fairly simple: destroy all targets that could conceivably support the Iraqi war effort. As a result, not only radar installations, military airfields, and bunkers, but also electrical power plants, highways, water treatment facilities, and commercial airports, were on the list of targets. Within a week of bombing, Baghdad had no water or electricity (*New York Times*, January 20, 1991, A1). Early attacks were carried out primarily by Tomahawk cruise missiles and Stealth fighters, which were launched from ships offshore and could hug the ground and pass below radar. Although Iraq eventually responded with antiaircraft artillery, the defense of Baghdad was anemic at best. After the first few hours, Iraqi air defenses were essentially "blind" (*New York Times*, January 17, 1991, A1). Estimates indicated that more than 150 targets in Iraq were hit after the first night of bombing, although later revisions on these and other estimates brought these figures down over the course of the war (Godden 1994).

Iraq responded the next day with Scud attacks on Israel, a move aimed at widening the war and undermining Arab support for the United States. In an unprecedented show of restraint, Israel refrained from retaliating against Iraqi targets. U.S. bombers attempted to destroy Iraqi Scud launchers with only partial success. More remarkable was the ability of U.S. and Israeli troops to fend off Scud attacks with the Patriot antimissile system, which seemed to consistently knock down incoming missiles (again, kill estimates were revised downward after the war).

By January 20, U.S. forces had achieved air superiority. Iraq's radar installations were inoperative, and many Iraqi combat aircraft were fleeing into Iran. The A-10 Thunderbolt II "Warthog" was now brought in for its slow, low-level flying abilities, and the operations moved toward destroying the Republican Guard and other ground troops in Kuwait (*New York Times*, January 20, 1991, A1). The successes did not come entirely without costs, though; the Scud attacks continued to threaten Israel and the viability of the coalition. Also, several aircraft were shot down and seven American prisoners captured by Iraq were paraded before television cameras and forced to make anti-American statements. These sacrifices fell far short of what many feared, however, and by the end of the first week, the war began to take on a surrealistic feeling. Emphasis on technical details of missile targeting led some to describe it as the "Nintendo War" (Florman 1991). Daily reports of targets destroyed and images from cameras mounted on missile nose cones seemed like so many graphics from a video game (see Map 9.1).

During this time, as well as before, the United States felt compelled to turn a blind eye to other problems in the world. Syria invaded Lebanon in the fall, ending a bloody civil war with martial law, with little criticism from Washington. On January 20, Soviet commandos stormed a building controlled by Latvian independence forces in an unsuccessful attempt to quell the growing movement toward separation. The need to keep the coalition together prevented President Bush from responding.

Scud attacks continued to rattle the nerves of Israelis, although the repeated donning of gas masks proved unnecessary, given that none of the warheads contained chemical weapons. Twenty-seven U.S. soldiers were killed when a random Scud fell on a barracks in Riyadh, Saudi Arabia. This incident caused the single largest loss of American life during the war.

On January 26, Hussein's forces opened valves on numerous Kuwaiti oil wells and spilled millions of gallons of crude oil into the Gulf, clogging desalination plants in Saudi Arabia and devastating the natural surroundings. Although the act may have made an amphibious invasion less convenient, it seemed to have no discernable military purpose (*New York Times*, January 26, 1991, A1). One can only conclude that it was a gesture of spite and defiance. Only hours before the ground offensive, Iraqi troops set fire to many of the oil wells they had previously opened, as well as to numerous ponds filled with petroleum. More than 150 wells were aflame by the time of the invasion and continued to burn throughout the war and for months afterward.

Reports of the air war's effects on Iraq were sketchy at best and propagandized at worst. U.S. military spokesmen routinely underestimated civilian casualties. They were defensive when clear evidence was presented that several hundred were killed in a bomb shelter, accusing the Iraqi government of deliberately planting civilians in a known military target area (*New*

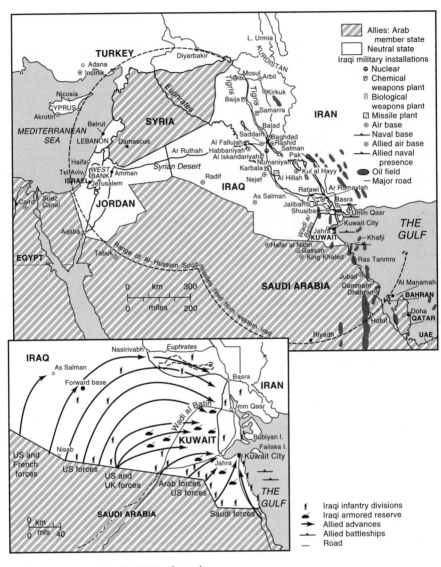

Map 9.1 Map of the Gulf War (1991)
Source: Michael Dockrill, *Atlas of Twentieth Century World History* (New York: HarperPerennial, 1991), 114–115.

York Times, February 14, 1991, A1). Estimates of Iraqi civilian casualties vary, but the general consensus is that 7,000 were killed as a direct result of the bombing (Hooglund 1991, 4). Troop losses during this phase of the war seem to have numbered around 75,000. The condition of Iraqi soldiers captured and of refugees coming into Jordan gave visible evidence of widespread disease and malnutrition in the Iraqi capital and on the front lines. Neither side wanted to admit at the time that the situation in Iraq was near the breaking point; Hussein feared loss of morale and Americans feared overconfidence in the troops. It was clear by the end of the air war, however, that the outcome of the war was no longer in doubt. This may explain Iraq's newfound willingness to make diplomatic concessions and Bush's eagerness to press the war to its conclusion.

The Ground War Phase February 24–February 28, 1991

In the middle of February, new deadlines were set, new ultimata laid down, and new battle plans set in motion. On February 24 (4:00 a.m. local time), U.S.-led troops and tanks stormed southern Iraq and Kuwait in a dramatic sweep from the west through miles of barren desert (see Map 9.1). In what was dubbed the "Hail Mary" operation—an allusion to a last-ditch pass by a football quarterback into a crowd of receivers in the end zone—U.S. General Norman Schwartzkopf ordered the deployment of troops originally massed on the Kuwaiti border to positions stretching 150 miles westward along the Saudi–Iraqi border. Marine forces were kept in the waters off Kuwait City, forcing the Iraqis to maintain a strong presence and leave their rear relatively unguarded. With French forces unfurling a protective cover in the extreme left flank of the operation, U.S. and U.K. divisions stormed into the desert, performing a pivoting maneuver at and around Kuwait, thereby completely isolating Iraqi troops stationed in the area. The tank battle that ensued was extremely lopsided, in that only American tanks were equipped with targeting systems that allowed them to fire while moving at full speed and through dust and smoke. "We're meeting the enemy, and we're not having any trouble destroying him," said a military spokesman on Tuesday after thirty-six hours of fighting (*New York Times*, February 26, 1991, A1).

Within forty-eight hours, nearly all of southern Iraq and most of Kuwait were in coalition hands, and Iraqi soldiers were surrendering by the battalion. The Iraqi news agency announced the country's decision to withdraw immediately from Kuwait, although this offer was considered unconvincing because the statement was not made by Hussein himself. In effect, this declaration gave tacit approval to what would become one of the saddest retreats in modern history. Tens of thousands of fleeing Iraqi troops lined the road leading northward out of Kuwait City, many of them with Kuwaiti hostages. Coalition jets targeted the troops as if they were still part of the fighting.

The retreat created a column twenty-five to thirty miles long, three or four abreast in places. Except for a few surface-to-air missiles, the troops were defenseless against the F-15, F-111, and F-16 fighter-bombers that came at them, wave after wave, along with Navy planes. In the wind and the driving rain, "it was close to Armageddon," an air force officer said (*New York Times*, February 27, 1991, A1).

In the waning hours of the campaign, Soviet and Iraqi delegates pressed the United Nations for a cease-fire to no avail. The allied attack penetrated deep into Kuwait City, where the Republican Guard crumbled after a vain but fierce battle. The most serious problem for American commanders was the disposition of prisoners of war, who numbered nearly 100,000 by war's end, and burying the Iraqi dead, estimated at 20,000 (Hooglund 1991, 4). After 100 hours of fighting on the ground and the expulsion of Iraqi forces from Kuwait, President Bush officially announced a cessation of hostilities on February 28, 1991.

Since the war, considerable ink has been spilled on the question of why the victory was comparatively easy for the coalition forces. The first arguments point to the lack of challenge presented by the Iraqis, who from the very beginning compounded strategic errors with tactical mistakes. We have already discussed the lack of prudence in moving into Kuwait militarily and refusing to back down once the coalition was formed. From the beginning, the Iraqis had an inadequate troop strength to conduct the type of war they were provoking (Record 1991). They were poorly deployed as well. For example, despite the fact that they were operating in an almost perfectly flat desert, the Iraqi military deployed its tanks behind large mounds of sand. Not only did this tactic give away their positions, but the sand was no match for tank shells that made short order of the Iraqi tanks (Biddle 1996). They were also pointed in what proved to be the wrong direction, as the coalition forces attacked from the west rather than the east. Entire Iraqi divisions were simply pointed the wrong way and were not a factor. Perhaps more serious was the extremely low morale of the troops, who saw the advancing coalition forces more as liberators than as enemies (Mueller 1995).

The principal alternative point of view stresses the technological advantages enjoyed by coalition forces, as well as their superior training and leadership. There is no question that the victory in the air war was a forgone conclusion given the tremendous superiority of coalition aircraft and pilots—something that became so clear to Iraqi pilots that they decided fleeing to Iran to avoid contact would be the best way to protect themselves. American tanks, with their ability to fire while traveling thirty miles per hour—even at night—were frighteningly effective and made the ground war's outcome entirely predictable (Inman, et al. 1992). Add to this the remarkable strategy of General Schwartzkopf, and the victory proved overwhelming (Friedman 1993).

Winning the Peace

A wide range of problems became the responsibility of the coalition governments with the end of the war, and most of these have yet to be resolved a decade later. Saddam Hussein's forces destroyed oil tanks and set 500 oil wells on fire, leading to an oil spill of some six million barrels (twenty times the amount released in the 1989 Exxon Valdez accident) and a smoke plume that spread to Kashmir, 1,500 miles away (Canby 1991, 2). Iraqi forces moved to suppress uprisings in Kurdistan and in Shi'a-dominated cities in the south. The Kuwaiti regime took far longer to reestablish itself than expected and encountered determined opposition from forces that favored a liberalization of the regime. Finally, the questions of Iraqi weapons and the country's general compliance with UN resolutions dealing with war reparations and boundary guarantees are yet to be finally resolved.

The environmental catastrophe following the Gulf War served to destroy not only the region's wildlife but also the Kuwaiti regime's credibility. Countless delays, largely the result of bureaucratic incompetence in Kuwait, prevented the speedy extinguishing of fires at the 500 wells. It took a total of fifteen months to finally put out all the fires—but at least five months of this time were largely wasted. The regime has struggled with the question of restoring its stature ever since, the most recent development being the formation of a strong anti-monarchy movement in the parliament, a move that may be throttled by a regime still unsure of its tolerance for dissent.

As it turned out, the environmental impact of the oil spill and fires could have been far more serious. For example, five times more animals died in the *Exxon Valdez* incident. Nearly half of the oil spilled simply evaporated as it floated down the Gulf. Also, desalination plants were protected, and oil recovery efforts netted roughly 20,000 barrels each day (Canby 1991, 25). The contaminated air in Kuwait City itself was dangerous and numerous cases of smoke inhalation and bronchitis occurred throughout the Gulf. Nevertheless, the air above Kuwait had sulfur dioxide concentrations that fell within tolerable limits, according to U.S. health standards.

U.S. troops left the region by May, although the humanitarian crisis in northern Iraq following the displacement of thousands of Kurds reached epidemic proportions shortly after the end of the war. Some 300,000 Kurds were killed by Iraqi troops, both before and after the war, through systematic razing of Kurdish villages. As put by Tucker, "The Shi'a and Kurdish peoples within Iraq, who mistook the president's call to overthrow Saddam Hussein as a pledge of support and protection and who rose up in response, were then left alone to suffer the might of Saddam Hussein's fury" (Tucker and Hendrickson 1992, 194). Ultimately, to protect and provide for these people, a portion of Iraq north of the 36th parallel (roughly 20,000 square miles) was declared a sanctuary by the UN and patrolled by peacekeeping forces (*New York Times*, May 19, 1991, A8). There is little prospect of any change in this arrangement so long as Hussein remains in power. This is not to say that the UN will always intervene in such cases, but rather that the Kurdish situation is extreme (Mayall 1991, 421).

To the south, Shi'a Moslems rebelled against Hussein and were suppressed, not only immediately after the war but throughout 1991. Not until the summer of 1992 did the UN impose a no-fly zone over the southern regions of Iraq (south of the 32nd parallel). This had the effect of eliminating the more wanton aspects of Iraqi reprisals, and it also led to a more permanent role for U.S. pilots charged with enforcing the rule.

The destruction of Iraqi weapons precipitated several violent and nearly disastrous encounters between Iraqi officials and UN inspectors throughout 1992. Given the task of destroying all Iraqi weapons of "mass destruction" by the Security Council, the UN inspectors went where angels fear to tread—into Iraqi nuclear weapons laboratories and other extremely sensitive sites. In July 1992, a team of inspectors, under the name UNSCOM (United Nations Special Commission), sought access to the Agriculture Ministry building in Baghdad in pursuit of documents relating to Iraq's nuclear weapons program; they were denied entry. After a two-week standoff, punctuated by increasingly strident threats by the West, the government finally relented, but not before it had ample opportunity to remove documents, if there were any (*New York Times*, July 25, 1991, A1).

Similar experiences have occurred numerous times, most recently in late 1998, when Hussein refused to permit UNSCOM inspectors access to military and intelligence facilities. After several months of cat-and-mouse maneuvers, the United States and United Kingdom ultimately launched punitive air strikes in December. The result was that UNSCOM was permanently barred from access to facilities that would have allowed it to do its job. Added to this were reports that UNSCOM had been collaborating with U.S. intelligence services, sometimes unwittingly, which spelled the end for the inspection regime. Many took heart that Iraq's war-fighting capability had been severely curtailed during the 1990s, but news that Hussein had managed to obtain the necessary materials to assemble three nuclear warheads in spite of it all was troublesome (Tessitore and Woolfson 1999, 49).

By the late 1990s, the coalition that had organized the Gulf War counteroffensive had splintered. Russia and China were joined by France in their efforts to end the economic sanctions against Iraq, which had already cost the country tens of billions in lost oil revenues and were increasingly linked to deteriorating health and nutrition levels among Iraqi children. A growing number of nonprofit organizations began to mobilize against the sanctions, including the Iraq Action Coalition, which posted a website and began a petition drive in the United States. Ramsey Clark, former U.S. attorney general, founded the International Action Center and joined UNICEF and the UN's Food and Agriculture Organization to deplore the effects of sanctions on children (Clark 1998). As of mid-2000, the stalemate between the pro-sanctions and antisanctions forces seemed unbreakable.

Perhaps the most significant question, in the context of the discussion of power, is whether resorting to war was necessary or was a sign of weakness on the part of the United States. Many have argued that the U.S. instructions to Iraqi representative April Glaspie were simply too ambiguous to be effective in deterring an Iraqi attack against Kuwait prior to the war. An issue during the 1992 presidential race (the so-called Iraqgate question) also stressed the significance of U.S. aid to Iraq prior to the invasion and the degree to which these funds were channeled into military hardware. Independent congressional inquiries determined that this funneling of funds probabl did not occur, and the Bush administration vehemently denied it. Also, whether U.S. funds were diverted is a moot point because the provision of aid freed up the Iraqi budget for other activities.

One might argue that the fact that Saddam Hussein chose to intervene is sufficient evidence that the United States failed to give clear signals of its intentions. But this conclusion assumes Hussein was rational and riskaverse. Throughout the Gulf War, even after it was clear that the United States was indeed serious about its intentions to remove Iraqi forces from Kuwait, Hussein made almost no effort to extricate himself from the situation. He took measures to protect himself and his family, but he did little else. It appears that he relished his role as underdog and welcomed the possibility of defeat. This posture was also a strategy aimed at preserving his own power. Charles Tripp wrote:

> The importance, as far as Saddam Hussein is concerned, of maintaining a determined and decisive image cannot be overstressed. To vacillate is dangerous because it suggests to those who have hitherto supported him that he is losing his touch. The fear will arise that others will act upon this signal, seizing their opportunity to attempt the overthrow of Saddam Hussein and his patronage network. (Tripp 1990, 9)

In early 2003, the Bush administration offered numerous rationales for setting aside the U.N. sanctions-and-inspection program as ineffectual. The regime, Bush argued, was directly involved in supporting international terror, was engaged in large-scale programs to produce weapons of mass destruction, and continued to be a direct threat to its neighbors, as well as the United States itself. All this in spite of the tough international supervision. As a result, only force could work. Six months of negotiations in the U.N. Security Council provided a great deal of diplomatic drama, but little agreement. The ultimate refusal of France, Russia, and Germany to endorse the plan prompted the U.S., with Britain and a handful of other countries, to launch the attack without U.N. approval (in contrast to the first Gulf War). On March 19th, a dramatic series of precision bombings was begun, followed the next day by a massive ground war. Within a week the troops were fifty miles from Baghdad and two weeks later Saddam Hussein's regime was gone.

Conclusion

What does the Gulf War story tell us about the nature of power, as understood in terms of both capability and influence? Much depends on one's assessment of the extent of coalition victory. Clearly the immediate aims of dislodging Iraq from Kuwait were achieved, although only by resorting to force. In spite of Iraq's almost complete dependence on oil exports, the sanctions did not have the immediate effect of changing the government's policy in Kuwait (although no one will ever know whether they might have eventually worked). Likewise, sanctions and weapons inspections have not ended Iraq's various weapons programs. In fact, at this point the coalition is as divided as ever over whether to maintain these sanctions and require new inspections.

On the other hand, the formation of the coalition in and of itself was a remarkable victory, given the disparate and often conflicting aims of the various members. Building a coalition that included France, Israel, Egypt, Saudi

Arabia, the United States, and the United Kingdom is perhaps unprecedented, and proved to be short-lived. But it survived long enough to complete the military mission of the day (thanks in part to Saddam's provocative acts—Cooper, et al.1991). Likewise, the effectiveness of the military operation, even though not the first choice among all possible options, demonstrated the benefits of technological sophistication, strong leadership and communication skills, and outstanding training of those facing the enemy. The coalition also enjoyed a degree of political legitimacy that is rare thanks to the approval of UN bodies throughout the operation (Russett 1994). In this sense, one sees a congruence between various types of capabilities, culminating in the final result.

Debate Topic

Did the coalition forces "win" the Persian Gulf War?

PRO
Those who are satisfied with the outcome of the war point out: (1) Kuwait regained its sovereignty, which was the fundamental mission. (2) Saddam Hussein was weakened and contained—at least for more than a decade. (3) In spite of being in a position to conquer Iraq, the coalition showed restraint by limiting its advance to that authorized by UN resolutions, thus honoring the law (a victory in itself, according to some).

CON
Those who are dissatisfied with the result of the Gulf War make the following arguments: (1) Kuwait's liberation should not have been the primary objectives; Saddam Hussein's removal would have been a true victory. (2) Hussein's continued efforts to build weapons of mass destruction mean that the coalition lost the peace, if not the war. (3) The suffering of innocent Iraqi civilians means that the coalition has lost the moral high ground it enjoyed at one time.

Questions to Consider

1. Was the Gulf War a legitimate and/or moral use of American power? What did international observers (UN, press, foreign governments) say about this issue?

2. To what extent was resorting to military force a sign of weakness or strength?

3. Did the Gulf War achieve the political objectives of the Bush administration? To what extent were international and domestic public opinion a deciding factor in how Bush prosecuted the war?

4. Does the Gulf War case help you to decide when military force should and should not be used? Are there causes worth fighting for?

Websites

General Gulf War information: **www.arab.net/kuwait/history/kt_gulfwar.html,
www.desert-storm.com, www.historyoftheworld.com/soquel/gulfwar.htm**
Advocacy groups: www.iraqaction.org, **www.iacenter.org**

References

Biddle, Stephen. "Victory Misunderstood: What the Gulf War Tells Us About the Future or Conflict," *International Security*, 21 #2(Fall 1996) 139–180.

Brzezinski, Zbigniew. "Patience in the Persian Gulf, Not War." *Washington Post*, October 7, 1990.

Canby, Thomas Y. "After the Storm." *National Geographic* (August 1991): 2–35.

Clark, Ramsey, ed. *The Children Are Dying: Reports by the UN Food and Agriculture Organization* (New York: International Action Center, 1998).

Cooper, Andrew, Richard Higgott, and Kim Nossal. "Bound to Follow? Leadership and Followership in the Gulf Conflict" *PSQ* 106 (1991) 391–410.

Davis, Paul, and John Arquilla. *Deterring or Coercing Opponents in Crisis: Lessons from the War with Saddam Hussein* (Santa Monica, CA: Rand, 1991).

Elliott, Kimberly, Gary Hufbauer, and Jeffrey Schott. "The Big Squeeze: Why the Sanctions on Iraq Will Work." *Washington Post*, December 9, 1990.

Florman, Samuel. "Engineers and the Nintendo War." *Technology Review* 94 #5 (July 1991): 62.

Freedman, Lawrence, and Efraim Karsh. *The Gulf Conflict, 1990–1991: Diplomacy and War in the New World Order* (Princeton, NJ; Princeton University Press, 1993).

Friedman, Norman. *Desert Victory: The War for Kuwait* (Annapolis: Naval Institute Press, 1993).

Godden, John, ed. *Shield and Storm: Personal Recollections of the Air War in the Gulf* (London: Brassy's, 1994).

Hippler, Jochen. "Iraq's Military Power: The German Connection." *Middle East Report* (January–February 1991): 27–31.

Hooglund, Eric. "The Other Face of War." *Middle East Report* (July–August 1991): 3–13.

Inman, Bobby, Joseph Nye, William Perry, and Roger Smith. "US Strategy After the Storm," in Joseph Nye, and Roger Smith, eds. *After the Storm: Lessons from the Gulf War*, (New York: Madison Book, 1992) 267–289.

Kono, Tom. "The Economics Behind the Invasion." *Middle East Insight* 7 #4 (December 1990): 36–41.

Mayall, James. "Non-intervention, Self-determination, and the New World Order." *International Affairs* 67 #3 (1991): 421–429.

Middle East Insight (December 1990): 11–17.

Miller, Judith, and Laurie Mylroie. *Saddam Hussein and the Crisis in the Gulf* (New York: Random House, 1990).

Mintz, Alex. "The Decision to Attack Iraq." *Journal of Conflict Resolution* 37 #4 (December 1993): 595–619.

Mueller, John. "The Perfect Enemy: Assessing the Gulf War." *Security Studies* 5 #1 (Autumn 1995): 77–117.

Record, Jeffrey. "US Lousy at Zeroing in on Third World Prowess." *Houston Chronicle*, September 8, 1991.

Rothgeb, John G., Jr. *Defining Power: Influence and Force in the Contemporary International System* (New York: St. Martin's Press, 1993).

Russett, Bruce. "The Gulf War as Empowering the United Nations," in John O'Loughlin, Tom Mayer, and Edward Greenberg, eds. *War and Its Consequences: Lessons from the Persian Gulf War.* (New York: HarperCollins, 1994), 185–197.

Sayigh, Yezid. "The Gulf Crisis: Why the Arab Regional Order Failed." *International Affairs* 67 #3 (1991): 487–507.

Stork, Joe, and Martha Wenger. "From Rapid Deployment to Massive Deployment." *Middle East Report* (January–February 1991): 12–26.

Tessitore, John, and Susan Woolfson, eds. *A Global Agenda: Issues Before the 54th General Assembly of the United Nations* (Lanham, MD: Rowman and Littlefield, 1999).

Tripp, Charles. "The Gulf Crisis and the Politics of Iraq." *Middle East Insight* (December 1990): 4–10.

Tucker, Robert W., and David C. Hendrickson. *The Imperial Temptation: The New World Order and America's Purpose* (New York: Council on Foreign Relations, 1992).

Woodward, Robert. *The Commanders* (New York: Simon & Schuster, 1991).

10

The United Nations and the Use of Force

COLLECTIVE SECURITY

Introduction

For those who feel that international relations should be governed by something other than "might makes right," international law has a strong appeal. But the question of enforcement must still be resolved: Once you decide what may and may not be allowed, how can you make countries comply? At the turn of this century, the answer was to bring a united, global force to bear against the law breaker until it ceased the offending policy. This concept was named "collective security," and it still animates the United Nations Security Council.

In its essence, collective security involves several basic steps. First, war must be outlawed. Naturally, this is easier said than done, for the question then becomes "What is war?" Traditionally, states have reserved the right, even under collective security, of self-defense. Thus "war" means "aggression," or the resort to violence without it being in retaliation for a direct attack. Even here, most aggressors have claimed to be acting in self-defense, so the question is often left to the judgment of other states. This said, once general agreement is reached on the offending behavior, states next undertake to pledge to one another their unqualified support in the event one of their number becomes the victim of aggression. In a sense, states join an open-ended alliance, because no one knows in advance who the enemy will be—or even who the ally will be (except that it will be one of many signatories to the agreement).

For this system to work, wide-spread disarmament is a useful step as well, as it will make it easier for the world to confront an aggressor. Collective security would not work very well if the one aggressive state also happened to have enough weapons to defeat the entire world combined. If every state is at least somewhat equal, collective security may serve as a deterrent. Finally, it would help for states to establish an agency that will make judgments about whether aggression has occurred and what steps are warranted. Naturally, for all of these steps to be taken, special circumstances must pertain. Usually, collective security becomes a popular idea only when the balance of power has proved utterly disastrous, such as immediately after a global conflict costing millions of lives.

During the Persian Gulf War, observers were given the impression that the whole world had united in righteous indignation against a criminal state. Diplomacy was portrayed more as a "plea-bargaining" exercise than as a negotiation among equals. Saddam Hussein was given ample opportunities to repent and make restitution, but he failed to do so and therefore suffered the consequences.

This scenario is a far cry from that of many other wars fought over the years. Karl von Clausewitz, a nineteenth-century German military writer, argued that war is merely diplomacy by other means (Vasquez 1990, 298). Clausewitz's contemporaries, German Chancellor Otto von Bismarck and his European counterparts, agreed that there was no reason a nation should hesitate to attack a rival as long as the fight could be won. Such callous cynicism is characteristic of the "realist" approach in world politics.

What George Bush and his Gulf War coalition partners were trying to convey was a sense of legality and rightness to their cause. The United Nations went far to legitimate the operation, although it stopped short of actually conducting the war. The conflict cuts to the heart of the debate on collective security. Should nations be held accountable when their actions violate another nation's legal rights, and how should the international community respond? The answer will go far to determine what type of future we will see in world politics. Should the superpowers withdraw from the unilateral use of force and yield instead to a multilateral approach, or should nations always rely on themselves for defense and security? Should the UN become an international law enforcement agency, complete with global police/military forces, international tribunals, prosecuting attorneys, and penitentiaries? Or would such a change bring more, rather than, less instability?

THE UNITED NATIONS AND THE USE OF FORCE
KEY FIGURES

Woodrow Wilson U.S. President, 1913–1921. He is credited with developing the concept of the League of Nations and spearheading its formation.

Franklin Roosevelt U.S. President, 1933–1945. He developed a pragmatic approach to post-war institutions, including the United Nations.

Harry Truman U.S. President, 1945–1953. He helped finalize the U.S. entry into the United Nations and ordered American troops to defend South Korea in 1950 with UN sponsorship.

Douglas MacArthur U.S. military commander during the Korean War.

(continued)

George H.W. Bush   U.S. President, 1989–1993. He sought UN support for U.S. actions in the Persian Gulf.

Dag Hammarskjold   UN Secretary-General, 1953–1961. He is credited with developing the concept of peacekeeping.

Boutros Boutros-Ghali   UN Secretary-General, 1991–1996. He urged world leaders to expand the power of the UN to intervene in crisis situations.

Mikhail Gorbachev   Premier of the Soviet Union, 1985–1990. He was the first Soviet leader to work closely with the West in multilateral security operations.

Saddam Hussein   President of Iraq, 1979–present. He has defied the UN repeatedly.

Norodom Sihanouk   Ruler of Cambodia, 1993–present.

Hun Sen   Leader of Cambodia under Vietnamese domination, 1979–1993. He remained as the Second Prime Minister following the election of Norodom Ranariddh. In 1997, he ousted Ranariddh and in 1998 was elected sole Prime Minster in a tainted vote.

THE UNITED NATIONS AND THE USE OF FORCE
CHRONOLOGY

1919
Woodrow Wilson plays a key role in establishing the collective security provisions of the League of Nations.

1945
Franklin Roosevelt plays a role similar to Wilson's with respect to the founding of the United Nations.

1947
The growing Cold War tensions between the superpowers stifle the functioning of the UN Security Council.

1950
The UN Security Council invokes the collective security provisions of its charter in its intervention in Korea. The Soviet Union's representative is absent when the critical votes are cast. He returns later to block subsequent collective security resolutions.

1956
The first UN peacekeeping mission, UNEF I, is deployed, applying Dag Hammarskjold's notion of an international buffer force to deter renewed fighting where a cease-fire has been declared.

1964
The UN operation in the Congo is opposed by the Soviet Union, which threatens the agency with bankruptcy.

1990
The Security Council authorizes a military response to Iraq's invasion of Kuwait, invoking collective security principles.

1992
UN and U.S. operations in Somalia begin, fail, and are withdrawn a few years later. UNPROFOR begins operations in Bosnia, to be replaced in 1995 by NATO forces. UNTAC is deployed in Cambodia.

1999
NATO intervenes to stop Serbian operations in Kosovo. UN forces under Australian leadership are deployed in East Timor.

Evolving Role of Collective Security

The United Nations has been at the center of the debate on collective security. After the League of Nations failed to prevent the Japanese invasion of Manchuria, the Italian war in Ethiopia, and the outbreak of World War II, world leaders wanted to create an organization that had the same philosophical roots but much stronger enforcement powers. The anti-Fascist alliance formed during World War II was seen as the first successful effort at collective security, and the alliance became formally known as the "United Nations" (Riggs and Plano 1988, 15). Franklin Roosevelt envisioned a political future without "the system of unilateral actions, exclusive alliances and spheres of influence and balances of power and all the other expedients which have been tried for centuries and have always failed" (Kaufmann and Schrijver 1990, 57).

The UN Charter provides for two forms of enforcement against outlaw states: negotiated settlement of disputes (Chapter VI) and collective security, including sanctions (Chapter VII). The power to both identify and deal with a breach of international peace was vested in the Security Council. Article 42 states that "the Security Council . . . may take such action by air, sea, or land forces as may be necessary to maintain or restore international peace and security." Such legal "teeth" were expected to give the UN real power to prevent and stop all conflict. However, as succinctly pointed out by Weiss and Chopra, "the onset of the Cold War and victory by Mao Zedong over the Chinese Nationalists prevented the kind of unanimity among the five permanent members upon which the logic of the Charter was based" (Weiss and Chopra 1992, 4).

The Security Council is an organ of the UN that deserves a more detailed description. The council consists of fifteen members, five of which are permanent. When the charter was signed, it provided that any of the five permanent members (United States, USSR, United Kingdom, France, and China) could halt any action by simply voting no, known as the "veto." The other ten members of the Security Council are determined by election and geographical distribution. A certain number of seats are earmarked for particular regions (two for Latin America and three for Africa, for example) and filled by members of those regions electing representatives for two-year staggered terms. As a result, each year ten Security Council members from the previous year are joined by five new members. A resolution passes the Security Council if it is approved by at least nine members and it is not opposed by any of the "Perm-5" (five permanent members).

Given the extreme hostility of some Perm-5 nations toward the others, the concept of collective security became the first casualty of the Cold War. Although the Korean War was initially sponsored by the United Nations in 1950, the sponsorship was the result of a diplomatic fluke. After the Chinese Revolution in 1949, the United States refused to recognize the government of Mao ZeDong (for thirty years!) and with its veto blocked its accession to the China seat on the Security Council. The Soviets, in fit of a diplomatic pique and an effort to demonstrate socialist solidarity, boycotted the Security Council meetings for a month. It was during this month that North Korea crossed the 38th parallel and came dangerously close to overrunning the entire peninsula. American troops were already on their way to support South Korea when the UN addressed the issue and voted to sponsor a collective security action. Even with UN involvement, the United States continued to lead the action and provided more than 90 percent of the troops. The UN became almost entirely marginalized after the Soviets ended their boycott and began vetoing efforts to maintain the support in Korea, and the action was pushed to the General Assembly for safekeeping. President Harry Truman acted alone in removing General Douglas MacArthur from duty in 1951. The UN was not involved in the peace negotiations in any substantive way, and in every other respect the Korean operation was merely a unilateral American conflict (Riggs and Plano 1988, 130).

The end of superpower unanimity resulted in increased tensions and hostility worldwide and an ever-greater need for efforts to resolve these conflicts. The UN struggled for many years to find its role in maintaining and creating peace but was largely frustrated. The Soviet Union adopted the position described as "Mr. Nyet," which included the following responses:

- Rejection of any form of supranational decision making in favor of the dogma of absolute national sovereignty
- Frequent use of the veto in the Security Council
- Opposition to a broad interpretation of the powers of the secretary general
- Refusal to pay its share of the costs of peacekeeping operations
- Arms control initiatives projected to discredit Western policies
- Support of radical developing country positions in the General Assembly combined with refusal to implement them (Kaufmann and Schrijver 1990, 90)

U.S. attitudes toward the UN were somewhat less strident, but it was clear by the time John Foster Dulles became secretary of state and began to direct U.S. policy with a rigid anti-Communist ideology that multilateralism and the UN would never be the centerpiece of American action.

Peacekeeping

In these circumstances, "middle powers" such as Austria, Norway, Canada, and the Netherlands began to search for an alternative to what had become gridlock in the Security Council. Trygve Lie, the first UN secretary general, proposed the formation of standing UN police forces to patrol areas where competing territorial claims had not been resolved (Luard 1979, 24). He developed the idea of "observer missions" to simply monitor development in "hot spots." Lester Pearson, soon to be prime minister of Canada, urged Secretary General Dag Hammarskjold to find a role for the UN independent of the superpowers (Harrelson 1989, 77). The concept of a sort of "referee for the world" emerged and was embraced by the secretary general (Gordenker 1967). Hammarskjold envisioned his role as a mediator and honest broker with a duty to anticipate conflicts and intervene personally before they escalated to violence. Furthermore, he felt that the charter provided the authority to dispatch troops to a trouble spot to keep the peace once a cease-fire was accepted. As currently defined in UN documents, peacekeeping is "an operation involving military personnel, but without enforcement powers, undertaken by the United Nations to help maintain or restore international peace and security in areas of conflict" (UN 1990, 4).

In 1956, the UN took its first action as a peacekeeper. Egypt declared sole ownership of the internationally managed Suez Canal, and after several months of failed negotiations, Britain, France, and Israel mounted a joint military operation to reclaim control of the canal on October 19, 1956. Dag Hammarskjold called for a cease-fire, which was supported by both the United States and the USSR, although France and Britain vetoed efforts to pass a Security Council resolution condemning the invasion. The General Assembly took up the issue in keeping with the Uniting for Peace resolution, which granted that authority to the assembly in the event the Security Council is deadlocked, and passed resolutions calling for a cease-fire, withdrawal of foreign troops, and introduction of a peacekeeping force to monitor the situation and prevent new hostilities. On November 7, a cease-fire was signed and the United Nations Emergency Force (UNEF I) was deployed progressively to the Sinai peninsula between Egyptian and Israeli troops. As explained in a UN document:

> The creation of UNEF . . . represented a significant innovation within the United Nations Organization. It was not a peace-enforcement operation, as envisaged in Article 42 of the Charter, but a peacekeeping operation to be carried out with the consent and the co-operation of the parties to the conflict. It was armed, but units were to use their weapons only in self-defense and even then with restraint. Its main functions were to supervise the withdrawal of the three occupying forces and, after the withdrawal was completed, to act as a buffer between the Egyptian and Israeli forces and to provide impartial supervision of the cease-fire. (UN 1979, 79)

Peacekeeping troops were deployed only into territory where the government was willing to accept them, and their costs were paid by the parties to the conflict and other UN members (although several nations routinely refused to pay if they voted against the operation, even after the World Court ruled that was part of their UN mandatory obligations). In the case of UNEF, for example, when the political situation deteriorated in the Middle East again in 1967, its troops were withdrawn prior to the outbreak of hostilities to prevent UN soldiers from being caught in the cross-fire. Shortly after the so-called Yom Kippur (or Ramadan) War in 1973, UNEF II was organized and deployed until 1979, when the Camp David Accords settled the question of the Sinai peninsula and there was no longer a need to monitor developments.

The UN's experience with peacekeeping is long and checkered. Until 1987, the UN was forced to address only those conflicts that were not vital to the superpowers or other permanent members of the Security Council. As a result, many major conflicts came and went with minimal UN involvement, such as the Vietnam War, the Hungary and Czechoslovakia invasions by the Soviet Union, and the Falklands War between Great Britain and Argentina. Even wars in which the superpowers had not firmly taken sides, such as the Iran–Iraq War, raged on for years before the UN could intervene. Table 10.1 lists UN operations that can clearly be called "peacekeeping" rather than merely "observation missions."

UN peacekeeping operations, including observer missions and humanitarian activities, have totaled 53 to date. Several deserve more attention as examples of how UN operations address the opportunities and obstacles they encounter. Perhaps the most famous cases of peacekeeping are in the Middle East.

The UN has been actively engaged in the Middle East, sometimes in spite of itself, since Israel's declaration of independence in 1948 (and even before). The Arab–Israeli conflict is discussed in Case 18, but here we will review the role of peacekeepers in the Middle East. It is important to understand that for most of Israel's history, all of its Arab neighbors have considered its very existence illegal and immoral. Israeli settlers for years encountered determined opposition from Palestinian and other Arab populations, manifesting itself in numerous armed clashes. The decision by the General Assembly in 1948 to partition Palestine was rejected at the time by all parties and was never implemented (although it remains a legal touchstone in Mideast peace talks). Instead, Israel declared its control of the entire Palestinian area in 1948, following which several Arab neighbors declared war. After the withdrawal of troops and the securing of new territory by Israel, Jordan, and Egypt, the UN Truce Supervision Organization was deployed in 1948 to serve as a liaison between the parties. This force of 500 is still present.

Over the years, the UN established peacekeeping groups at various points along the Israeli border: in the Sinai (UNEF I and II), the Golan Heights (UNDOF), and Lebanon (UNOGIL and UNIFIL). In each case, UN troops were deployed to supervise and monitor a withdrawal of Israeli forces from a particular region following a serious battle. For example, in 1978 PLO commandos claimed responsibility for an attack against targets in northern Israel, near the Lebanese border. In retaliation against this and previous incidents, Israel invaded Lebanon to take control of PLO staging camps and civilian installations. A week later, the Security Council responded to Lebanon's protest by calling upon Israel to withdraw immediately and established UNIFIL for a six-month period. UNIFIL was never able to restore Lebanese sovereignty over the entire region and conceded a strip of land along the border to Israeli-supported troops. PLO installations operated with little impediment, and as a consequence, Israel invaded again in 1982 through the UNIFIL forces, which posed little obstacle. In the words

Table 10.1 Major UN Peacekeeping Missions

Operation	Location	Duration	Peak Troop Strength	Objective
UNEF I	Sinai	11/56–6/67	3,400	Protect buffer zone between Israeli and Egyptian forces
ONUC	Congo	6/60–6/64	20,000	Preserve Congo's independence during civil war
UNFICYP	Cyprus	3/64–	6,400	Monitor cease-fire line
UNEF II	Sinai	10/73–7/79	7,000	See UNEF I
UNDOF	Golan Heights	6/74–	1,500	Monitor buffer zone between Israeli and Syrian forces
UNIFIL	Lebanon	3/78–	7,000	Monitor Israeli troop withdrawal and promote Lebanese independence
UNTAG	Namibia	4/89–3/90	8,000	Monitor Namibian transition to independence
ONUCA	Central America	8/89–7/92	1,000	Monitor and implement peace agreements
UNIKOM	Kuwait	4/91–	1,500	Monitor Iraq–Kuwait border
UNTAC	Cambodia	3/92–9/93	15,000	Monitor Cambodian transition to democracy
UNPROFOR	Former Yugoslavia	3/92–12/95	14,000	Protect safe havens and prevent humanitarian crises
UNISOM I, II	Somalia	4/92–3/95	21,000	Prevent humanitarian crises and help restore order and central government
UNMIBH	Bosnia	12/95–	3,500	Assist IFOR in postconflict peace building
UNMIK	Kosovo	12/96–	7,300	Assist NATO in post-conflict peace building
UNAMSIL	Sierra Leone	10/99–	12,200	Restore stability and order in civil war
UNTAET	East Timor	10/99–	9,700	Restore stability and order in civil war
MONUC	Congo	12/99–	600 (5,500 authorized)	Restore stability and order in civil war

Source: UN Department of Public Information.

of the UN: "This invasion changed UNIFIL's situation drastically. For three years, UNIFIL in its entirety remained behind the Israeli lines, with its role limited to providing protection and humanitarian assistance to the local population . . ." (UN 1992).

Prior to and during the period of Israeli dominance, the capital city of Beirut was devastated, with opposing militias and governments vying for control of small sections of the city. Shortly before the Gulf War, in 1990, Syria gained control of most of Lebanon and established a stable government. Israel withdrew from Lebanon in 2000, but UNIFIL has yet to complete its full mission. UNIFIL was a financial millstone around the UN's neck, given the fact that the United States, the Soviet Union, and the parties to the dispute themselves never provided consistent support. UNIFIL was continually in jeopardy as each six-month renewal was the target of intense debate. In 1991, total unpaid contributions to UNIFIL equaled almost two years' worth of costs. Given the tasks that UNIFIL was assigned, this general lack of support seems almost forgivable.

The UN peacekeeping forces have been ill equipped to solve international disputes. This objective has clearly been on the minds of UN leaders, but the difference between a cease-fire and a settlement has proven substantial. Obstacles such as financial difficulties, superpower opposition, the intractable nature of many regional conflicts, and the practical difficulties of mounting an effective peacekeeping operation have led to some despondence over the chances of using the UN to resolve conflict (Haas 1983). It was not until the 1980s that the UN was able to compile a record of performance that gave observers some optimism.

Resurgence of UN Enforcement Role

In 1987, Mikhail Gorbachev officially announced to his staff at the UN that the Soviet Union would cease its obstructionist behavior and seek accommodation and compromise on the Security Council. The mood at the UN immediately changed. Combined with a greater tolerance for multilateralism on the part of the United States and a tempering of rhetoric in the developing countries, the Soviet action went far to restore some of the lost effectiveness at the organization.

This new orientation was never more apparent than when the Security Council became directly involved in enforcing the end of the Iran–Iraq War and the withdrawal of Soviet troops from Afghanistan, where they had fought the mojahedin resistance for ten years. Although the Soviet Union approved the use of UN troops, the force proved ineffective in bringing about a settlement to what became a chaotic situation as the Soviet-supported Afghan government held off an increasingly divided resistance movement backed by the United States and Pakistan (Tessitore and Woolfson 1991, 44). Naturally, the collapse of the Soviet Union in 1991 and the eventual success of the Afghan resistance made much of the UN's work irrelevant, but at least a precedent was set for involving the UN in matters that directly affected the superpowers.

The active role of the UN in supervising peaceful elections in Nicaragua in mid-1990 was further evidence of superpower tolerance of UN involvement in vital problems. For nearly a decade, the United States had funded opposition guerrillas (named Contras) in and around Nicaragua who were trying to overthrow the Soviet-backed Sandinista government. After repeated efforts by the countries of the region, led by Mexico and Venezuela, a general settlement was finally reached for the withdrawal of superpower support to the Nicaraguan combatants as well as other players in the area. In connection with this effort, a UN monitoring group was deployed in November 1989 to check on compliance with the agreement. A UN team was sent to supervise the elections in Nicaragua, where a conservative, pro-U.S. coalition won the presidency. Both developments received support from the United States and the Soviet Union, testimony for the new spirit of cooperation that had developed.

Three more cases are worthy of note because they put the UN in new situations, using new enforcement tools: the Persian Gulf War, Yugoslavia, and Cambodia. Ample detail on the Gulf War is provided in Case 9. Suffice it here to say that the UN was drawing on some rarely used provisions of the charter and reinterpreting still others. Article 4(2) prohibits the use of force by UN members for the settlement of disputes. Chapter VI provides for economic and diplomatic sanctions, however, and Chapter VII anticipates their enforcement. Only in the case of South Africa and Rhodesia were widespread mandatory economic sanctions put in place prior to the actions against Iraq following its invasion of Kuwait on August 2, 1990. Within a week, the Security Council had approved mandatory sanctions on Iraq, and by August 25, it had approved the use of force in carrying out these sanctions. The instrument to be used was the military force of the nations patrolling the waters near Iraq, not the UN itself. By late September, the mandatory sanctions were expanded to cover all transportation flows in and out of Iraq and were applied to nations that were not members of the UN, such as Switzerland (Kaufmann et al. 1991, 13).

In all this enforcement activity, the UN was broadening its interpretation of Article 4(2) without explicitly invoking provision under Articles 41 and 42 calling for direct UN control. When the Security Council passed Resolution 678 in November, it went still further by authorizing the use of force to implement all UN resolutions relating to Iraq, although it did not organize a UN-commanded force. Instead, it merely gave its blessing to those armies already assembled on Kuwait's behalf. Only a loose interpretation of Article 51 offers a legal underpinning for the UN's action—it provides for nations taking actions in self-defense or organizing an alliance for defensive purposes (Kaufmann et al. 1991, 25). In legal terms, this simply means that the UN relinquished control of the enforcement of sanctions and authorized a self-existing military coalition to act to protect an ally. Though far from mere balance of power politics, it is clear that this is also far from strict collective security as envisioned by the UN's founders.

The situation in Yugoslavia proved far more resistant to solution than the problem in the Persian Gulf (although the charge to eliminate all of Iraq's weapons of mass destruction has been quite a challenge, prompting George

W. Bush to seriously contemplate an invasion). The problem in Yugoslavia defied description by traditional diplomatic terms (see Case 15). The parties to the dispute were not entirely nation-states and thus lacked diplomatic standing in the UN. Bosnia had such little control over its territory that its diplomatic standing was relatively hypothetical, while Serbia had been expelled from the organization. The role of outside actors in Bosnia was extremely complex, in that the Serbian government not only supplied matériel to the ethnic Serb fighters in Bosnia but also commanded troop movements. The only consensus in the Security Council was on the need to provide humanitarian relief to besieged cities such as Sarajevo, the capital of Bosnia, but even this action raised serious questions because Serb troops blocked most of the access routes and shot down relief planes. The UN officially admitted it had failed to prevent genocide in Srebrenica in 1995, for example, and had it not been for NATO intervention, the killings probably would have continued. It is significant that it was NATO, not UN, troops that arrested Serb officer Radislav Krstic for war crimes in that city and brought him to justice at the Hague. Ultimately, it was the Serbian people who can be thanked for bringing the crisis in the region to a close by overthrowing their leader, Slobodan Milosevic, and sending him to the Yugoslav War Crimes Tribunal in 2002.

The Cambodian situation is also unique in that for the first time the UN took full responsibility for governing a nation. The UN has at times intervened in a major way to quell civil disturbances (Congo, West Irian), but as a result of the Paris Accords of 1990, the UN has been plunged into the center of a most complex situation. To begin, at least four major parties have an immediate stake in Cambodia and some legitimate claim on the government: conservative Prince Norodom Sihanouk and his supporters (backed by the United States), the radical Khmer Rouge (backed by China), the more mainstream Khmer People's National Liberation Front headed by Sihanouk's son Son San (backed by China as well), and the sitting government of Hun Sen (backed by Vietnam and the Soviet Union). All of the opposition parties formed a government-in-exile in Thailand and have occupied the Cambodia seat at the UN, although they strongly disagree over the future of the country and possible power-sharing arrangements.

For several years, coinciding with the decision by Vietnam to withdraw from Cambodia and the Soviet withdrawal of support to Vietnam, the parties to the Cambodian disputes held periodic discussions. Not only did the Cambodians themselves meet, but the Perm-5 and other Asian observers also held concurrent meetings in Paris to work out a compromise coalition government that gave all the players a share of power. Naturally, the United States and Soviets opposed the Khmer Rouge, while China balked at a major role for Prince Sihanouk. After several false starts, Australia proposed a UN-dominated transitional government that would disarm the factions and supervise elections after a one-year cooling-off period. This became the core of the arrangement ultimately accepted by the various parties (Tessitore and Woolfson 1991, 55).

UNTAC was deployed in March 1992 with a total of nearly 22,000 personnel, including several police contingents, public administrators, military forces, and technical advisors (*UN Chronicle,* June 1992, 10). The central effort of UNTAC has been to disarm the various factions on the ground, an effort that had come up against serious resistance by Khmer Rouge guerrillas. Prince Sihanouk has been approved as the nominal head of the new Cambodian regime, buttressed by UN officials serving at high levels throughout the government, but he has yet to establish a strong degree of central authority over the entire nation (and may never do so). At any rate, the UN Charter has once again been interpreted loosely in response to a consensus by the Perm-5 to remedy a serious problem. In May 1993, elections were held in spite of a Khmer boycott. More than fourth-fifths of eligible Cambodians braved sniper fire and threats of civil war to go to the polls. The result was a fair election of a centrist government under the loose leadership of Prince Sihanouk. The commander of UNTAC credits its success to the decision not to expand the mandate of the mission but instead stick to a purely neutral and limited role (Sanderson 1998).

The mission's success was tainted by the refusal of Han Sen, the loser in the election, to step down and make way for Norodom Ranariddh, the winner. He was given the title of "Second Prime Minister," but overthrew Ranariddh in 1997 and secured the post of prime minister alone by way of a tainted election in 1998. His regime is stable, but marred by corruption. Prince Sihanouk continues to serve as a figurehead monarch.

In Somalia, a UN operation begun officially in April 1992 was actually initiated by the deployment of U.S. Marines in December 1991, which was designed to stem the humanitarian catastrophe that followed the complete collapse of the country's central government. The complexities of Somali political life were generally lost on the peacekeepers, however, and their actions contributed to intensified interclan violence. In particular, Mohammed Farah Aidid was targeted by U.S. and UN troops as a criminal, but efforts to hunt him down led to tragic ambushes and the deaths of dozens of peacekeepers and nearly one hundred U.S. Marines in 1993–1994 (Schraeder 1998, 345). The United States withdrew its forces shortly thereafter, and the mission was left to founder. UN forces later withdrew, leaving the country mired in interclan fighting and still with no central government (Mazrui 1998). The experience has been compared to a movie Western gone bad (Debrix 1999).

In Rwanda, the UN did nothing to halt some of the worst ethnic violence in history, in spite of the presence of UNAMIR, a UN observer mission. Roughly half a million Tutsis were hacked to death by Hutus, who in turn fled the country into neighboring Burundi and Zaire (now the Congo). The international neglect was so profound that the Organization for African Unity has demanded reparations (Tessitore and Woolfson 1999, 13). The experience highlighted the wariness on the part of the major powers to make large commitments in nonstrategic parts of the world and thereby undermined the legitimacy and impartiality of the UN.

Whither the UN: Peacekeeper or Peacemaker?

Many UN critics have seen the institution as merely a talk shop or even a threat to the peace. More recent discussion of the future of the Security Council and collective security has been far more optimistic. Not only have the Soviets pledged to do more to promote the organization and its principles, but the United States has also made a number of concrete proposals that will result in substantial increases in UN powers. In his September 21, 1992, address to the General Assembly, George Bush spoke warmly of an expanded enforcement role for the UN, although he stopped short of committing U.S. troops to the effort as called for in the charter (*Christian Science Monitor* 1992). He discussed the possibility of providing U.S. bases to train and U.S. air transport to move UN troops during operations.

In a report drafted at the request of the Security Council (entitled *Agenda for Peace*), Boutros Boutros-Ghali suggested five possible roles for the UN in security affairs:

- Peacemaking: This involves the fairly well-known practice of mediation and nonviolent conflict resolution to bring about a peaceful settlement.
- Preventive diplomacy: This complements peacemaking with the addition of confidence-building measures, including fact-finding missions and possibly "preventive deployment" of UN troops where violence is likely.
- Peacekeeping: Peacekeeping involves the deployment of neutral troops in a buffer zone between forces that have declared an armistice.
- Peace enforcement: The most controversial of the approaches, this involves the deployment of troops to protect civilians, to reverse aggression, or otherwise to enforce Security Council decisions without a cease-fire being in place.
- Post-conflict peace building: The UN would intervene to help the new administration establish the rule of law, a healthy economy, and promotion of human rights through police training, election monitoring, and so forth.

The lesson of Somalia and Yugoslavia, where the UN deployed a total of 35,000 troops and spent roughly $2 billion, was that the UN is simply not equipped to enforce peace without direct leadership by a major power (read: the United States). Beginning in 1994, the Security Council sought ways to pull the UN out of these types of missions, either by simply closing them down or by transferring responsibility to another agency. "Peacekeeping by proxy" (Tessitore and Woolfson 1999, 2), whereby the UN allows and/or encourages regional security agencies to carry out a Security Council mandate, became increasingly popular. In Bosnia, for example, NATO took on the post-conflict peace-building role following the Dayton Accords in 1994. In 1999, NATO, frustrated with failure by the Belgrade government to withdraw from Kosovo in spite of Security Council demands and considerable evidence of widespread atrocities, launched air strikes against Serb targets with increasing ferocity over more than two months, which proved both destructive and controversial but ultimately successful (see Case 15). A less successful venture is under way in Sierra Leone and Liberia, where African peacekeepers from ECOMOG have struggled to prevent the spread of local civil wars.

By comparison, the election-monitoring and post-conflict peace-building missions in Central America and Cambodia have proved remarkably successful. Even in East Timor, where a rapid and dramatic rise in civil unrest and an Indonesian military intervention in 1999 precipitated a flood of refugees, the quick deployment of a UN peacekeeping mission created a zone of relative peace and autonomy for the local population. Also, the UN deployment in Macedonia has blocked what most likely would have been a Belgrade intervention at some time in the last six years.

Conclusion

Large-scale UN peacekeeping operations fell out of favor between 1994 and 1999, and existing missions faltered with a lack of funds. As of early 1999, more than $1 billion was owed to UN peacekeeping operations (two-thirds by the United States), and the organization faced yet another year of financial crisis. In spite of this "peacekeeping fatigue," four major new missions were approved during 1999 involving a total authorized troop strength of 34,000 and a 2000 budget of $1,680 million. Most of these missions are of the post-conflict peace-building type. One exception is a major mission in East Timor, an island formerly claimed by both Portugal and Indonesia, where a pro-independence referendum was suppressed by Indonesian forces in 1999. Australia led a military force to oust Indonesian troops from the area and help establish an East Timorese government. The operation was dramatically successful, and in 2002, East Timor became the newest member of the United Nations.

Debate Topic

Should a major power, such as the United States, be obligated to wait for international approval before deploying military forces into conflict situations overseas?

PRO

Idealists and legalist (see the discussion of multilateralism in case 8) generally see the rule of law as paramount and support this position: (1) Only when powerful states agree to comply with inconvenient laws does the world have order. It is therefore in the self-interest of the United States to refrain from aggression. (2) Most military operations require considerable international cooperation to be successful, so it is better, from an operational standpoint, to wait for support. (3) The United States and other great powers hold considerable sway in the UN and other bodies that control collective security decisions, so there are few risks in working with them.

CON

The unilateralist approach (see case 8) stresses the right and capacity of great powers to act unilaterally: (1) As a sovereign state, the United States answers to no one and should not create a precedent for international interference in policymaking. (2) International participation often leads to confused and undisciplined policy that would be far better pursued in isolation. (3) American values are not always shared abroad, so decisions to deploy U.S. forces should not be subject to foreign control.

Questions to Consider

1. Is "collective security" the best description of what the UN is engaged in? To what extent is this merely "great-power policing"?

2. How could UN operations be improved? What obligation do UN members have to support and direct peacekeepers?

3. What are the rights of nations where peacekeepers operate? How might these be violated?

Websites

The United Nations home page: **www.un.org**
The UN's student-oriented site: **www.un.org/Pubs/CyberSchoolBus/**
Several NGOs with links to UN agencies: **www.conferenceofngos.org**

References

Christian Science Monitor, September 23, 1992, 1.

Debrix, Francois. *Re-envisioning Peacekeeping: The United Nations and the Mobilization of Ideology* (Minneapolis: University of Minnesota Press, 1999).

Gordenker, Leon. *The UN Secretary-General and the Maintenance of Peace* (New York: Columbia University Press, 1967).

Haas, Ernst. "Regime Decay: Conflict Management and International Organizations, 1945–1981." *International Organization* 32 #2 (Spring 1983).

Harrelson, Max. *Fires All Around the Horizon: The UN's Uphill Battle to Preserve the Peace* (New York: Praeger, 1989).

Kaufmann, Johan, Dick Leurdijk, and Nico Schrivjer. "The World in Turmoil: Testing the UN's Capacity." *ACUNS Reports and Papers 1991-4,* 1991.

Kaufmann, Johan, and Nico Schrijver. "Changing Global Needs: Expanding Roles for the United Nations System." *ACUNS Reports and Papers 1990-5,* 1990.

Luard, Evan. *The United Nations: How It Works and What It Does* (New York: St. Martin's, 1979).

Mazrui, Ali A. "The Failed State and Political Collapse in Africa" in Aloara Orunnu and Michael Doyle, eds., *Peacemaking and Peacekeeping for the New Century* (Lanham, MD: Rowman & Littlefield, 1998), 233–244.

Riggs, Robert, and Jack Plano. *The United Nations: International Organization and World Politics* (Chicago: Dorsey Press, 1988).

Sanderson, J. M. "Dabbling in War: The Dilemma of the Use of Force in United Nations Intervention" in Olara Otunnu and Michael Doyle, eds., *Peacemaking and Peacekeeping for the New Century* (Lanham, MD: Rowman & Littlefield, 1998).

Schraeder, Peter. "From Ally to Orphan: Understanding U.S. Policy Toward Somalia After the Cold War" in James M. Scott, ed., *After the End: Making U.S. Foreign Policy in the Post–Cold War World* (Durham, NC: Duke University Press, 1998), 330–357.

Tessitore, John, and Susan Woolfson. *Issues Before the 45th General Assembly of the United Nations* (Lexington, MA: Lexington Books, 1991).

Tessitore, John, and Susan Woolfson. *Issues Before the 54th General Assembly of the United Nations* (Lexington, MA: Lexington Books, 1999).

United Nations. *The Blue Helmets: A Review of United Nations Peacekeeping* (New York: UNDPI, 1990).

United Nations. *Everyone's United Nations,* 9th ed. (New York: UNDPI, 1979).

United Nations. "United Nations Peacekeeping Operations: Information Notes." *UNDPI,* January 17, 1992.

UN Chronicle, June 1992, 10.

Vasquez, John A. *Classics of International Relations,* 2nd ed. (Englewood Cliffs, NJ: Prentice-Hall, 1990).

Weiss, Thomas, and Jarat Chopra. "United Nations Peacekeeping: An ACUNS Teaching Text." *ACUNS Reports and Papers 1992-1,* 1992.

CASE
11

The Kyoto Protocol
COLLECTIVE GOODS

Introduction

As a result of increasing human activity and economic growth, a growing number of issues cross national boundaries. Refugees, ocean pollution, space exploration, pandemics, ozone depletion, and global warming are but a few examples. These problems, while the product of specific actions in specific states in most cases, affect much of the planet. Once in place, they are not easily solved by just one or two countries, but require collective action from numerous players.

A "pure" collective good is one that does not belong to any one player, nor could it. Once in place, it cannot be withheld from any one player, but is available to all (in practice, very few things fit this description, but many come close). This is not to say that a collective good is free, however. Typically, collective goods require considerable sacrifice and expense, and the story of the creation of collective goods comes down to the fight over who will pay for it. A simple example would be how a group of four roommates divides up the bill for a pizza. One simple solution would be to split the bill equally. But suppose one person goes to pick up the pizza and feels that his time and gas are worth something—and makes the argument that his share of the bill should be lower. What if one person is carbo-loading for a marathon and plans to eat more than one-fourth of the pie—should he pay more? What if one person is short of cash that day—can he pay less and work it off by doing everyone's dishes? Perhaps you've had this experience. Because we're dealing with roommates, where no one has ultimate authority, the solution will probably be negotiated (unless one is a weight-lifter and simple knocks a few heads to get his way . . .).

This situation emerges in international affairs where sovereign states have problems that are inherently trans-boundary in nature. Sometimes, governments agree on the need for a collective good, such as rules to govern chlorofluorocarbon (CFC) emissions to prevent depletion of the ozone layer (which protects living things on earth from some of the sun's harmful ultraviolet rays). Acknowledging the need for a collective good is merely the first step, however. Questions may arise regarding the source of the CFCs, for example, and states may insist that those who have caused the most damage historically should be expected to pay the most for the repair now. If these states are willing to make the contribution, then all will be well—but such is often not the case. It is more likely that, unless some actors emerge as leaders who are willing to shoulder the bulk of the costs of the collective good, no solution will emerge (Olson 1965). A widely held belief is that the creation of a collective good requires a single player able and willing to absorb most of the costs of its creation and maintenance. Such an actor is called a *hegemon* (Kindelberger 1986).

Once the collective good is in place, how does one maintain it? Because it isn't possible to deny the good to anyone, one cannot simply "charge admission" (although, as mentioned earlier, this idea rarely holds in practice and so states are, in fact, "charged admission."). Suppose governments agree to strict guidelines on CFC emissions, for example, and a few states are willing to make deep cuts. What if other countries decide to renege on their commitments and revert back to CFC production? The benefits of the program will probably still occur, and the "free-riders" will enjoy the same benefits as the burden-carriers. Only if a major player refuses to go along is the collective good jeopardized (such an actor is called a "spoiler"). The incentive to cheat is clearly high. But if there are enough free-riders, problems could arise. If nothing else, those carrying the burden will grow to resent their sacrifice and the unfairness of the arrangement. There will probably need to be some sort of penalties for noncompliance, but these may be difficult to design and enforce given the inability to deny benefits to cheaters.

The story of the creation of the rules on global-warming gases is illustrative of the problems inherent in collective goods.

THE KYOTO PROTOCOL
KEY FIGURES

Bill Clinton   U.S. President, 1993–2001. He supported the basic framework of the Kyoto Protocol, although his administration sought ways to give the U.S. separate rules.

George W. Bush   U.S. President, 2001–present. His administration rejected the Kyoto Protocol.

Al Gore   U.S. Vice-President, 1993–2001. The author of *Earth in the Balance*, he was a strong supporter of stricter pollution controls.

John Prescott   British Deputy Prime Minister, 1997–present. As the country's senior environmental policy official, he has been instrumental in pressing for the Kyoto Protocol's conclusion.

(continued)

Mikhail Kasyanov   Russian Federation Prime Minister. He announced the country's plans to ratify the Kyoto Protocol in 2002.

Raul Estrada   Chairman of the FCCC meetings leading to the Kyoto Protocol.

Timothy Wirth   Under U.S. Secretary of State for Global Affairs, 1993–1997. He was the principal U.S. negotiator at the Kyoto meetings.

THE KYOTO PROTOCOL
CHRONOLOGY

1988
The Intergovernmental Panel on Climate Change (IPCC) is formed by UNEP and WMO. Officials in Toronto recommend a reduction of CO_2 emissions by 20 percent by 2005.

1990
IPCC issues a report declaring its certainty that human activity is resulting in pollutants that will intensify the greenhouse effect. The panel predicts that the earth's temperature will increase by one degree Celsius by 2025.

1992
The UN Conference on the Environment and Development is held in Rio de Janeiro. It results in the Framework Convention on Climate Change (FCCC), among other agreements.

1995
Signatories to the FCCC meet in Berlin to outline specific targets on emissions.

1997
Signatories agree to the broad outlines of emissions targets in Kyoto, Japan. The United States dissents.

2000
Efforts to accommodate American and Australian objections to the Kyoto draft agreement fail at a meeting of signatories in The Hague.

2001
George W. Bush withdraws U.S. endorsement of the Kyoto Protocol and goes back on a campaign promise to reduce reliance on coal-burning power plants. Following important breakthroughs in Bonn in June, participants in the November Marrakesh meetings finalize the provisions of the Kyoto Protocol without U.S. support.

2002
Russia and Canada ratify the Kyoto Protocol to the FCCC, bringing the treaty into effect.

Global Warming

As we all know from the tremendous precautions taken by astronauts to protect themselves against the cold of space, the earth would become a frigid wasteland without a capacity to trap solar energy as it bounces off its surface. Misnamed the "greenhouse effect" (actual greenhouses operate on a different principle of physics), this is accomplished by the thin layer of atmosphere that covers the globe. A few substances, including carbon dioxide and methane, are able to absorb and trap ultraviolet rays from the sun and thereby assist in preventing heat from escaping into space (Sparber and O'Rourke 1998, 2).

Another well-known fact is that the planet's average surface temperature has gone through rather dramatic swings over its long history. Most recently, it was nearly ten degrees cooler during the great Ice Age that resulted in the spread of Northern Hemisphere glaciers well south of the current Canada–U.S. border.

Two more facts are known as well. First, since the Industrial Revolution at the end of the eighteenth century, humanity—especially the peoples of the West—has been burning fossil fuels at a tremendous rate, in contrast to the entirety of human experience to that point. Second, earth's surface temperature has been moving inexorably higher over the past one hundred years.

Noting these facts, observers—both scientists and amateurs—began expressing concern in the early 1980s over the possibility that human activity was intensifying the greenhouse effect to the point that the earth was experiencing human-induced global warming. As put by Breidenich and her coauthors;

> most scientists believe that anthropogenic [human-generated] emissions of greenhouse gases increase the heat-absorbing capacity of the atmosphere and will result in a corresponding increase in the global average temperature. This warning is predicted to have various global impacts, including the melting of the polar ice caps; rising sea levels; increased intensity and frequency of storms; changes in amounts and timing of precipitation; changes in ocean currents; and an enlarged range for tropical diseases such as malaria, cholera and dengue fever. (Breidenich et al. 1998, 316)

Conservative estimates indicate that the planet may continue warming at the rate of three or four degrees per century unless some intervention occurs to reverse the trend. While this may not sound like much, it is useful to recall that during the Ice Age, the earth's temperature was a mere seven degrees cooler than today on average. One group of environmental organizations has created a website (Global Warming: Early Warning Signs, www.climatehotmap.org) that maps specific, local events (updated regularly) that are harbingers of global warming around the planet.

Among the specific alerts: The polar ice caps are beginning to melt and break up. A piece of the Antarctic ice shelf the size of Rhode Island (1,260 square miles) broke off and floated out to sea in March 2002. Scientists attribute this and other breakups of Antarctic ice to a nearly five-degree (Fahrenheit) warming of the area since 1945. Watery patches have appeared in the Arctic where the ice has not melted in the past. The area covered by sea ice has declined by roughly 6 percent since 1980. Glaciers in the Himalayas have shrunk dramatically (close to one hundred feet per year), leading some to predict the loss of all central and eastern glaciers by 2035. In Spain, half of the glaciers present in 1980 are now gone. Partly as a result of ice melting, sea levels are rising at three times the normal rate, resulting in increased flooding in low-lying areas from Bangladesh to the Chesapeake Bay. Mangrove forests in Bermuda's coasts are dying off due to rising sea water levels.

In addition, global weather patterns are likely to change significantly. For example, the temperate zones of the planet will shift northward, resulting in longer growing seasons in Scandinavia and Canada, and more tropical climates in China and Missouri. For countries that are already tropical, the resulting changes in rainfall, could lead to desertification of some areas. Ocean temperatures will rise, contributing to intensification of tropical storm and hurricane activity, along with unusual phenomena such as El Niño. To illustrate, high temperatures in Great Britain are increasingly rising above sixty-eight degrees Fahrenheit (more than twenty-five days per year in the 1990s versus fewer than five days per year in the 1770s). Severe heat waves were common in 1998 and 1999, resulting in hundreds of fatalities in cities such as Chicago. Changes in Indonesia's temperatures have contributed to a spreading of malaria into higher elevations (Telesetsky 1999).

These changes will, in turn, bring about important socioeconomic changes, including a redistribution of the world's agricultural centers, and increased food scarcity in some areas, both of which will contribute to large-scale movements of populations in search of food security. This migration could contribute to shifts in global power distributions and an increase in local conflicts. It is probably enough to offer this list of potential problems (and a few opportunities).

Global warming remains an extremely controversial issue. One reason is the continuing disagreement among scientists about it. Although an overwhelming majority of climatologists are on record stating that human activity is contributing to global warming, a small minority rejects this conclusion as premature. The existence of the merest dispute has been seized upon by politicians and firms that are predisposed to resist the standard remedies for global warming. The George W. Bush administration, for example, has explained its resistance to cuts in carbon dioxide emissions in terms of continuing doubts among scientists. According to Lindsay, "uncertainty also explains why global warming has not yet emerged as a burning issue in the United States. . . . Few Americans list global warming as a top environmental concern . . . and by a two-to-one margin they say it will not pose a serious threat during their lifetime" (Lindsay 2001, 27).

Creating Rules on Global Warming Gases

Global warming is controversial largely because of the types of solutions that exist. When it comes to reducing the biggest culprit—carbon dioxide—what is required is a reduction in the burning of fossil fuels and an increase in carbon-absorbing forests. At this point, however, considerable resistance emerges to seeking alternatives to fossil fuels. Two important factors are coal-burning power plants and the internal combustion engine. They are the predominant contributors to the 30 percent increase in CO_2 concentrations in the atmosphere since 1750 (Telesetsky 1999, 781). Dramatic changes would require auto manufacturers, utility companies, highway contractors, and most mining companies to either drastically curtail production or undertake considerable research to develop new products. Some, including former Vice President Al Gore, have suggested that nothing less than the replacement of the internal combustion engine will be enough to begin to solve to problem (Gore 1993).

While these emissions occur mostly in the developed West, the developing South is industrializing at a rapid rate and is expected to emit a large share of global-warming gases (the name for all gases that contribute to the phenomenon, including carbon dioxide and methane). In addition, developing countries are guilty of removing one of the key natural defenses against carbon dioxide concentrations by cutting large portions of the planet's forests. Young trees are especially effective recyclers of CO_2 because they absorb it through their leaves and convert it to oxygen. Deforestation has cost the earth a large fraction of its forests in recent years, and relatively little of it has grown back. The forests are being eliminated in part to provide farmland to the growing populations of the developing world, which also increases demand for fossil fuels. The problem is thus exacerbated doubly.

Getting to Kyoto

In the late 1980s, governments around the world began debating whether and how the problem of global warming could be tackled. In 1988, a panel of scientists and government officials proposed reducing carbon dioxide levels by 20 percent by 2005 as a starting point (Barrett 1998). That same year, the UN General Assembly invited the UN Environmental Programme and the World Meteorological Organization to form the Intergovernmental Panel on Climate Change—a collection of 2,000 climatologists from more than one hundred countries—to study the facts regarding global warming. They reported in 1990 that human-induced emissions were, in fact, contributing to the earth's gradual warming.

The issue was placed on the agenda of the United Nations Conference on the Environment and Development, scheduled for June 1992 in Rio de Janeiro, Brazil. The meetings were intended to be a dramatic, high-level event where the world's leaders would address and develop answers for a wide range of environmental problems, from desertification to ocean pollution. What emerged from the meetings was a series of broad agreements—mostly on principles—and a laundry list of policy goals. Buried in the mix was the UN Framework Convention on Climate Change that called upon sponsoring states to keep emissions of global-warming gases to 1990 levels to prevent acceleration of temperature increases in the years to come. But little more was spelled out at that time, and the signatories agreed to meet again to hammer out the details in the form of a "protocol" of legally binding measures (Breidenich et al. 1998, 318).

The states met again in Berlin in 1995, with the goal of putting some precision in their promises. Although all agreed that 1990 emission levels were high enough, and that the planet as a whole should cap output, considerable disagreement arose concerning which states should make the deepest cuts. As put by Lindsay,

> global warming poses a collective goods dilemma. Countries know that pursuing virtuous global warming policies makes little sense if no one else follows suit. Any individual reduction on their part will be swamped by emissions from others. Indeed, going first could be economically lethal . . . Fairness issues exacerbate the collective goods problem. (Lindsay 2001, 27)

Four groups of states emerged early on, and most of the negotiations involved tradeoffs between them. First and foremost was the European bloc, led by Germany and France, which called for the deepest cuts in emissions. These countries were driven by both ideological and practical considerations. On the one hand, pollution in Europe had prompted the emergence of a strong and active environmental movement that considered global warming a "clear and present danger," the substance of which was beyond debate (Gelbspan 2002). These states also were in a position to explore alternatives to fossil fuels by virtue of the fact that most countries were concerned about their dependence on foreign oil and had already begun efforts to wean themselves off it. France had begun a massive nuclear power program in the 1960s and had significantly reduced its reliance on coal-burning plants, for example. It also introduced numerous energy-saving initiatives and fuel taxes to encourage efficiency. By 2000, per capita energy use in Europe was half that of the United States—a fact that has bred deep resentment of the United States' efforts to give itself exceptions from the Kyoto Protocol (Mathews 2001). The European states were consistently the most forceful advocates for deep cuts and strong legal commitments.

The second group consisted of mature, developed economies that, for a variety of reasons, were not yet ready to make the deep cuts Europe proposed. This group, labeled "industrialized laggards" by European analysts, consisted of Canada, Japan, and Australia, and was led by the United States (Oberthur and Ott 1999, 17). The U.S. position remained consistently skeptical throughout the 1990s. Even at Rio de Janeiro, the George H. W. Bush administration refused to endorse the full array of agreements reached, preferring to adopt a "wait-and-see" approach. The Clinton administration, prodded by Vice President Gore, warmly welcomed the Rio agreements on principle, although it found its hands were tied when it came to making specific, legal commitments. Members of the U.S. Senate, in particular, expressed their deep concern with any treaty that might result in economic stagnation or unemployment. They also opposed any agreement that would treat developing countries more leniently than Western countries. In 1997, the Senate unanimously passed a resolution prohibiting the White House from signing any global warming agreement that did not remedy these issues (Barrett 1998, 22).

The nations in this group worked to minimize mandatory cuts in emissions. Australia managed to negotiate an increase for itself, for example. The United States sought permission for moderate reductions in emissions by offsetting them with increases in the size of its carbon dioxide-absorbing forests ("carbon sinks"). This group also promoted various emissions-trading schemes that would allow high polluters to reduce their exposure by exchanging credits with low-polluting countries in a variety of ways.

The third group was the Eastern European states in economic transition. Although they were known to be very heavy polluters, their difficult economic transitions created a pollution windfall. High failure rates for their heavy industries meant that many smokestacks were idled, and pollution levels plummeted even as unemployment lines swelled.

Finally, the developing countries sought special protections during the negotiation of the Kyoto Protocol. They argued that, given their dependence on industrialization for economic growth, it was unfair to ask them to set aside poverty-alleviating development for the sake of the environment. Besides, they pointed out, global warming was almost entirely the fault of Western industrialization in the past—hence the need for Western states to carry the bulk of the cost of emissions controls. They pointed out that, on a per capita basis, developing countries produced very little pollution (for example, China emits one-tenth the carbon dioxide emitted by the United States per capita—Oberthur and Ott 1999, 21). Oil-exporting countries pleaded for rules that would not jeopardize their export levels, lest they collapse economically and politically. Only the small island states in the developing world felt strongly that global warming should be halted (given their special vulnerability to rising ocean levels).

Pollution Trading at Kyoto

One of the first steps undertaken at Kyoto was the establishment of an emissions baseline against which future rules would be measured. This goal was achieved with relative ease, because it is possible to measure carbon dioxide emissions with considerable precision, and thereby estimate the total volume of global-warming gases coming from each country. The negotiators developed a table that listed the total amount of emissions and each country's share (see Table 11.1). Special attention was given to the so-called Annex I countries that were responsible for the overwhelming majority of pollution—namely, the industrialized West.

Once the baselines were established, the pollution trading began in earnest. Almost every participant in the Kyoto negotiations entered the discussion with the goal of minimizing costly reforms. Even the Europeans sought ways to permit some European Union members to have small reductions, or even increases, in CO_2 emissions. The three principal ways of reducing the emissions reduction targets were to (1) plead "special circumstances," (2) exchange emissions with lower-polluting countries, and (3) devise offsetting mechanisms involving improvements to the environment. The first strategy was taken up by many developing countries and most of

Table 11.1   1990 Emissions Baseline for Kyoto Protocol Signatories

	Total CO2 Emissions for 1990 (thousands of gigagrams)	Share of Annex I Country Totals
United States	4,957	36.00
European Union	3,289	24.05
France	367	2.68
Germany	1,014	7.24
Italy	429	3.14
United Kingdom	577	4.22
Australia	289	2.11
Canada	463	3.38
Japan	1,155	8.45
Economies in Transition	3,364	24.60
Russia	2,389	17.47
Poland*	415	3.03

*Poland and a few other economies in transition were allowed to utilize 1988 or 1989 levels as the baseline (slightly higher than 1990).

Source: UN Framework Convention on Climate Change, www.unfccc.int.

Table 11.2   Kyoto Targets for 2002–2012, Relative to 1990 Base Year*

United States	93%
European Union	92%
France	92%
Germany	92%
Italy	92%
United Kingdom	92%
Australia	08%
Canada	94%
Japan	94%
Economies in Transition	103%
Russia	100%
Poland*	108%

*Poland and a few other economies in transition were allowed to utilize 1988 or 1989 levels as the baseline (slightly higher than 1990).

Source: UN Framework Convention on Climate Change, www.unfccc.int.

the U.S.-led bloc. Australia was perhaps the most successful, negotiating for itself the right to increase its carbon dioxide emissions to 8 percent above its 1990 baseline. (see Table 11.2).

The second strategy was also promoted by the U.S. delegation against the resistance of the Europeans. The Americans argued that, since the goal of the Kyoto meeting was reduction of global levels of global-warming gas levels, so long as one country's increase was offset by another country's decrease, the total objective could be met. They proposed to create a "market for emissions," whereby countries would be allowed to convert some of their emissions into a "budget" that they could sell to countries that were well ahead of global emissions averages. In particular, the United States was interested in taking advantage of the collapse of East European emissions resulting from economic depression and deindustrialization, which created "hot air" opportunities (Barrett 1998). At the end of the day, this arrangement was approved by the signatories, although it was not enough to satisfy the U.S. negotiators. Even the Europeans negotiated a special arrangement whereby their emissions were counted as a whole. As a consequence, Germany and France's deep emissions cuts would allow increases in emissions in Spain and Greece ("joint implementation").

The third strategy was promoted by the United States and some developing countries. The U.S. delegation pressed especially hard for a more generous treatment of so-called carbon sinks. Given the carbon-absorbing character of forests, and given the United States' commitment to reforestation, the government believed it should get credit for reductions in emissions as a result of forest absorption (Barrett 2001). Some have estimated that approval of this strategy could allow the United States to cut in half the reductions it must make against the 1990 baseline (Telesetsky 1999, 805).

Developing countries pressed for arrangements that, like the World Bank's Global Environmental Facility, would give developed countries credit for helping a developing country lower its global-warming gas emissions. Special projects and initiatives under the so-called Clean Development Mechanism would be graded according to the degree of emissions reduction they produced, and the donor country would have its emissions for the year cut by a similar amount (Coghlan 2002, 168–171). This tactic is intended to use market incentives to cause states to do good (Breidenich et al. 1998, 325).

As these provisions were negotiated and (mostly) adopted at Kyoto, more general issues were debated as well. The United States pressed for a more flexible deadline for reducing emissions than the drop-dead deadline proposed by the Europeans. Ultimately, compromise was reached on the establishment of a five-year period rather than a single date for achievement of the targets. The average emissions per year for the period 2008–2012 would be the ultimate test of compliance with Kyoto—meaning that the final day of reckoning would not come until 2012. So long as targets were reached, on average, during this period, countries would be considered compliant. Further, the United States insisted on lax enforcement mechanisms with respect to noncompliance. Other than regular reporting to the FCCC Secretariat, no specific set of enforcement mechanisms was created, although the parties to the Kyoto have agreed to consider this question in the future (Breidenich et al. 1998, 330). With the United States' ultimate rejection of the treaty, it is possible that the Europeans will insist on tougher enforcement measures (Gelbspan 2002).

As a way to prevent adoption of a meaningless treaty, the negotiators agreed that it would not come into force until it was ratified by at least 55 states responsible for at least 55 percent of the world's global warming gasses. This meant that almost all of the world's major polluters would have to come on board before the Kyoto Protocol would take legal effect.

Impasse at The Hague

The Kyoto meetings ended in passage of the Kyoto Protocol, signed by the United States, European states and more than one hundred other participants, albeit not without the dramatic and personal intervention of Al Gore, the Japanese Prime Minster, and other high-ranking diplomats. The meetings also benefited from the able chairmanship of Raul Estrada of Argentina, who had led previous FCCC meetings and knew the participants well (Reiner 2001, 38).

The meetings were declared a victory by environmentalists, but it was a hollow victory at best. The agreement, after all, faced almost unanimous Senate opposition and left many contentious issues unresolved. As put by Reiner, "The Kyoto Protocol, prepared in December 1997, had masked irreconcilable differences among participants by papering over many fundamental disagreements among and within the negotiating parties" (Reiner 2001, 36).

History was not working in favor of resolving global warming. Most countries, including the United States, continued to expand carbon dioxide emissions during the 1990s. In the United States, the proliferation of sport-utility vehicles, which emit up to five times more global-warming gases than their passenger-car counterparts, made achieving reductions difficult. Even in the Netherlands, where the government implemented tough emission-reducing policies, emission levels did not fall. Those countries that had reduced emissions had done so largely because of reasons beyond their control. Germany benefited from the collapse of heavy industry in the East after reunification, and the United Kingdom was able to reach its targets by using its newly discovered North Sea oil to convert coal-burning power plants to less-polluting oil-burning ones (Reiner 2001, 37).

The signatories gathered again at The Hague in November 2000 with the goal of eliminating ambiguities and "agreements in principle" left over from Kyoto. Since little had changed in the U.S. position and the Senate's attitude, there was little expectation of success. The practicalities of the negotiations were also hampered by the U.S. presidential election and its notorious "Florida fiasco" that kept Al Gore and other Clinton administration officials away from the meetings at critical times. The apparent opposition of candidate George W. Bush did nothing to improve the mood at the meetings.

Even as American negotiators felt compelled to be cautious, newly elected Green politicians in the German (and French) delegations felt emboldened to press for deeper concessions, including cutting back the emissions trading schemes. The result was an agreement to disagree. While the United States did not block approval of the agreements by other states, it refused to endorse the result. As put by the chief U.S. negotiator at The Hague;

[European countries] ignored environmental and economic realities, insisting on provisions that would shackle the very tools that offer us the best hope of achieving our ambitious target at an affordable cost . . . Some seem to have forgotten that [emissions trading] is a fundamental feature of the Kyoto Protocol— accepted by all parties as a legitimate means of meeting our targets . . . Some of our negotiating partners also chose to ignore physical realities of our climate system, depriving parties of another important [tool] by refusing them credit for carbon [sinks] . . . And finally, they ignored the political reality that nations can only negotiate abroad what they believe they can ratify at home. (Frank E. Loy, Department of State press release, November 25, 2000, in AJIL 2001, 648)

Decisions on outstanding issues were postponed until meetings to be held in Bonn and Marrakech over the next year.

The Current Situation

The new Bush administration, which was led by two former oil men, had an ideological and political antipathy toward the Kyoto Protocol. It mistrusted the scientific basis for the sacrifices being required of the United States, was strongly wedded to market schemes that would permit the country to reduce its exposure, and was antagonistic toward any enforcement mechanisms that would punish noncompliance. This said, candidate Bush had promised to shrink the role of coal-burning power plants in the United States during his tenure, but was forced to back-peddle shortly upon taking office under pressure from utility companies.

Seeing no way to accommodate both the demands of the European and developing countries and the interests of conservatives and industry in the United States, the Bush administration formally rejected the Kyoto Protocol in March 2001. Environmental Protection Agency chief Christine Todd Whitman was charged with making the announcement that the Kyoto treaty was "dead" as far as the United States was concerned.

Nevertheless, the United States sent representatives to the Bonn and Marrakech meetings later in the year, and even succeeded in winning considerable concessions from chastened Europeans eager to bring the United States back into the process. Negotiators in Bonn agreed to most of the U.S. demands regarding carbon sinks and emissions trading, for example (AJIL 2001, 649). The United States also watched from the sidelines as the negotiators reached final agreement on the provisions of the Kyoto Protocol in Marrakech in November 2001.

The latest position of the Bush administration is that it will not interfere with efforts by other countries to implement the Kyoto Protocol, and will work toward reducing what it calls "greenhouse gas intensity"— emissions per unit of economic activity (total emissions divided by GDP). The target of 18 percent reduction by 2011 will result, admittedly, in an overall increase in emissions (AJIL 2002, 487).

Meanwhile, countries have ratified the Kyoto Protocol (dubbed "Kyoto Lite" because of the concessions made to the United States, albeit to no avail). The Framework Convention on Climate Change maintains a running tally of ratifications by number of countries and the proportion of total emissions they represent (see its website, www.fccc.int). As of October 2002, that chart showed ninety-five ratifications by countries that, together, were responsible for 37.1 percent of global emissions of greenhouse gases. However, at the 2002 Johannesburg Summit on Sustainable Development, the governments of Russia and Canada announced that they were moving ahead with ratification, meaning that the 55 percent target would likely be exceeded. Russia's Prime Minister, Mikhail Kasyanov, told the conferees on September 3, "Russia has signed the Kyoto Protocol and we are now preparing its ratification. We consider that ratification will take place in the very near future" (Lean 2002).

The Russian and Canadian ratifications present the United States with an odd situation. As with the cases of the International Criminal Court, the Convention on the Rights of the Child, and the Landmine Ban, new international rules and institutions are being created without it. In fact, many American firms wonder why they do not have the opportunity to participate in emissions trading and other schemes like the Europeans and Japanese. As far as whether this means the problem of global warming is now under control, we should recall that it is "Kyoto Lite" that was adopted, and that even the original Kyoto Protocol was not particularly robust. The treaty provides numerous exceptions, exemptions, and exclusions that may well make it a less-than-effective tool for solving the original problem.

Conclusion

The Kyoto Protocol to the United Nations Framework Convention on Climate Change will become international law in 2002, but without U.S. support. This case helps to demonstrate several important aspects of collective goods that might come as a bit of a surprise. First, this process calls into question the widely held assumption that a "hegemon" is needed to create a collective good (Kindelberger 1986). U.S. leadership was clearly beside the point after a critical mass of countries had reached agreement on Kyoto. Furthermore, even if all the signatories work hard to implement the agreement (an unlikely scenario given the temptation to cheat), little change in global warming trends will probably occur. So long as Americans continue to produce more than one-third of the world's total global-warming gas emissions, other states' efforts may be negligible. Ultimately, the collective good of maintaining (or lowering) the earth's temperature will likely not be achieved in spite of the treaty.

Second, the story of the Kyoto Protocol illustrates the way in which economics and international law intersect. The schemes to trade emissions, in particular, were clever ways of using the market to achieve socially beneficial results. While innovative, the schemes were seen by some as merely a shell game that would ultimately allow heavy polluters to delay needed reforms.

Finally, the Kyoto Protocol story illustrates the difficulty of achieving agreements on economic sacrifices in the face of even slightly ambiguous science. In contrast to the Montreal Protocol, which brought about strict, binding limits on CFC emissions in the face of unanimous scientific agreement on their deleterious effects on the ozone layer, the Kyoto Protocol failed in part because a few scientists were unwilling to endorse the majority view concerning global warming (Lindsay 2001). From another perspective, this case shows how science can be manipulated by self-interested politicians and industrialists (one is reminded of how cigarette manufacturers misrepresented scientific findings on the links between smoking and cancer).

Debate Topic

Should the United States ratify the Kyoto Protocol?

PRO
The United States should ratify the agreement for the following reasons: (1) It is the best mechanism available for solving the problem of global warming. (2) The United States needs to be engaged in the process of implementation to protect its interests in the future. (3) The United States is expected to take a leadership role and appears short-sighted by not ratifying the treaty.

CON
The United States need not ratify the agreement for these reasons: (1) The Kyoto Protocol would cost American jobs and cause bankruptcies. (2) The agreement gives China and India carte blanche to pollute for years to come. (3) Current American laws are doing an adequate job of limiting carbon dioxide emissions while giving the government maximum flexibility.

Questions to Consider

1. Can financial incentives be used to induce reductions in carbon dioxide emissions? If so, how?

2. To what extent do ethical values govern the decision to pollute?

3. On the basis of what principles should the cost of pollution abatement by distributed?

4. What part are you playing in global warming?

Websites

Governmental Sites
U.S. Environmental Protection Agency: **yosemite.epa.org/global warming.nsf/ content/index.html**
NOAA: **www.ngdc.noaa.gov/paleo/globalwarming/home.html**

United Nations Framework Convention on Climate Change: **www.unfccc.int**
Other Organizations
The Cooler Heads Coalition: **www.globalwarming.org**
Global Warming: Early Warning Signs: **www.climatehotmap.org**
Sierra Club: **www.sierraclub.org/globalwarming**
Union of Concerned Scientists: **www.ucsusa.org/warming/env-home.html**
A Skeptical View
Still Waiting for Greenhouse: **www.vision.net.au/~daly**

References

AJIL. "U.S. Rejection of Kyoto Protocol Process." *American Journal of International Law* 95 #3 (July 2001): 647–650.

AJIL. "Bush Administration Proposal for Reducing Greenhouse Gases." *American Journal of International Law* 96 #2 (April 2002): 487–488.

Barrett, Scott, "Political Economy of the Kyoto Protocol." *Oxford Review of Economic Policy* 14 #4 (Winter 1998): 20-43.

Breidenich, Clare, Daniel Magraw, Anne Rowley, and James W. Rubin. "The Kyoto Protocol to the United Nations Framework Convention on Climate Change." *American Journal of International Law* 92 #2 (April 1998): 315–331.

Coghlan, Matthew. "Prospects and Pitfalls of the Kyoto Protocol to the United Nations Framework Convention on Climate Change." *Melbourne Journal of International Law* #1 (May 2002): 165–184.

Gore, Al. *Earth in the Balance: Ecology and the Human Spirit* (New York: Plume, 1993).

Gelbspan, Ross. "Beyond Kyoto Lite: The Bush Administration's Absence from the Global-Warming Talks Could Actually Lead Other Nations to Pursue a Bolder Approach." *The American Prospect* (February 25, 2002): 26–29.

Kindelberger, Charles. *The World in Depression, 1929–1939* (Berkeley: University of California Press, 1986).

Lean, Geoffrey. "Russia and Canada Shock Summit with Plans to Ratify Kyoto Treaty." *New Zealand Herald*, April 9, 2002.

Lindsay, James M. "Global Warming Heats Up: Uncertainties, Both Scientific and Political, Lie Ahead." *Brookings Review* 19 #4 (Fall 2001): 26–30.

Mathews, Jessica T. "Estranged Partners." *Foreign Policy Magazine* (November/December 2001): 48–53.

Oberthur, Sebastian, and Hermann E. Ott. *The Kyoto Protocol: International Climate Policy for the 21st Century* (Berlin: Springer, 1999).

Olson, Mancur. *The Logic of Collective Action* (Cambridge, MA: Harvard University Press, 1965).

Reiner, David. "Climate Impasse: How the Hague Negotiation Failed." *Environment* 43 #2 (March 2001): 36–43.

Sparber, Peter, and Peter E. O'Rourke. "Understanding the Kyoto Protocol." *Briefly: Perspectives on Legislation, Regulation, and Litigation* 2 #4 (April 1998).

Telesetsky, Anastasia. "The Kyoto Protocol." *Ecology Law Quarterly* 26 #4 (November 1999): 797–814.

12

The Nuremberg Trials
INTERNATIONAL LAW

Introduction

International law is a collection of principles, rules, and procedures designed to govern international affairs—particularly relations among nation-states. It is derived from a wide variety of sources: treaties, conventions, protocols, traditions, scholarly writings, customs, habits, and so on. Although international law aims at creating the sort of order in international society that exists in domestic society, it lacks a crucial element: centralized enforcement. Because there is no world government, international law can be applied only by the consent of members of the international community. Historically, international citizens have been reluctant to take the risks required to enforce international law militarily, so wars come and go as always. An important exception to this rule was the disposition of Nazi war criminals in 1945.

States dominate the character and implementation of international law. To a large extent, it is a system of rules under which actors other than states (e.g., firms, international organizations, individuals, minority groups) have little voice or standing. For example, the premier international tribunal — the International Court of Justice—restricts its contentious proceedings to states. Only if a government chooses to promote the cause of some other actor may that figure's case be heard (this has happened very rarely). Thus crimes by and against private individuals have almost always been prosecuted in national, not international, courts.

Where the behavior of individual soldiers and officers in combat is concerned, states have been careful to prevent even national courts from exercising jurisdiction. Military justice permits officers of a nation's defense force to judge individual soldiers and sailors, granting them limited rights to defend themselves. The Hague and Geneva Conventions create international standards of conduct in wartime, but provide no automatic enforcement by way of an international tribunal. Governments have resisted creating such a permanent arrangement, as was seen recently in the United States' objections to its service men and women being brought before the newly formed International Criminal Court.

How should the world community respond to the systematic slaughter of six million Jews, some 2 million Soviet prisoners of war, thousands of handicapped persons, and still more Gypsies, Poles, and other ethnics? How do civilized nations respond to one regime's ruthless plan for global domination? How does one punish behavior that was never before imagined?

These questions faced American, British, French, and Soviet military and diplomatic leaders in the waning months of World War II and ultimately led to the war crimes trials at Nuremberg. Looking back, we can ask: On what basis were the leaders of a nation judged as criminals? Were these charges and the ensuing judgments justified? Have these actions and decisions set any precedent for the bloody acts of scores of other countries in dozens of other wars since that time? Are we a more civilized world after the Nuremberg Trials?

THE NUREMBERG TRIALS
KEY FIGURES

Hermann Göring (Goering)   Founder of the Gestapo (secret police) and second-ranking Nazi after Hitler (although he plotted his overthrow in the waning months of World War II). He was the most prominent defendant at Nuremberg.

Rudolf Hess   Deputy Fuhrer (third most powerful leader) in the Nazi regime and senior defendant at Nuremberg. He flew to England in 1941 in a bizarre attempt to negotiate peace. He was held captive until the Nuremberg trials.

Ernst Kaltenbrunner   Leader of the Nazi elite military branch and a defendant at Nuremberg.

Arthur Seyss-Inquar   Leader of the Austrian Anschluss and a defendant at Nuremberg.

Albert Speer   Organizer of industrial production under Hitler and a defendant at Nuremberg.

Fritz Sauke   Organizer of concentration camp labor under Hitler and a defendant at Nuremberg.

John Jackson   U.S. Supreme Court Justice, who served as chief prosecutor at Nuremberg.

Francis Biddle   Senior American judge of the Nuremberg tribunal.

Lord Geoffrey Lawrence   British judge of the Nuremberg tribunal.

I. T. Nikitchenko   Russian judge of the Nuremberg tribunal.

Donnedieu de Vabres   French judge of the Nuremberg tribunal.

Adolf Eichmann   Nazi war criminal convicted in Israel.

Slobodan Milosevic   Leader of Serbia and defendant at the Yugoslav War Crimes Tribunal.

1907

The Hague Convention on legitimate military tactics is signed.

1919

The League of Nations Covenant is signed. It provides for prohibitions against aggression.

1924

The Geneva Convention on treatment of prisoners of war (POWs) is signed.

1925

The Kellogg-Briand Pact outlawing aggressive war is signed.

1933

Hitler's Nazis burn the Reichstag building to create panic and secure emergency powers.

1935

The Nuremberg Race Laws against Jews are decreed, removing German citizenship from Jews.

1938

Germany invades Austria, declaring "anschluss" (unification) of the two countries. Anti-Semitic laws are extended.

1939

Germany attacks Poland, starting World War II.

1942–1945

Nazis kill roughly six million Jews, Slavs, and others in the Holocaust.

1944

Murray Bernays of the U.S. State Department proposes a war crimes tribunal after the war.

1945

January	Eighty American POWs are murdered by Nazi guards, prompting Franklin Roosevelt to endorse a war crime trial in principle.
May 8	Germany capitulates in May. Subsequently, Nuremberg defendants are arrested by American, British, and Russian troops.
November 20	The Nuremberg Trials open. Prosecution begins its case.

1946

March	The defense stage of trial begins.
September	Judges deliberate and render verdicts.
October 16	Defendants sentenced to death are hanged.

2002

The International Criminal Court begins operation.

Organizing the Trials

Early on, the behavior of Hitler's Germany in World War II was described as criminal. Statements by Roosevelt, Churchill, and later Stalin condemned the aggressive acts of a ruthless dictator, the mistreatment of prisoners of war, and the systematic slaughter of millions (although the full extent of the atrocities did not become clear until concentration camps were liberated and documents examined). Clearly, this was no gentleman's war, and the objectives of the Allied forces quickly escalated far beyond a simple return to the status quo. Nothing less than the eradication of Nazi institutions and ideology would suffice to avenge the atrocities and restore world order.

In this context, it is understandable that radical measures were conceived regarding the planned treatment of the leaders of the Nazi regime after the war. Churchill and much of the British government favored the summary execution of Nazi leaders upon their capture by Allied troops. Henry Morgenthau, the U.S. secretary of the treasury, strongly advocated the execution of Nazi leaders, the deportation of former SS officers, and the total deindustrialization of Germany. He even contemplated arresting the children of senior German officials in an effort to purge the society of all real and potential Nazi influence (Smith 1981, 40). Soviet leaders advocated a purge of all senior and mid-level Nazis (roughly 50,000 in all).

When Henry Stimson, the powerful U.S. secretary of war, began to promote the notion of a public legal proceeding, some individuals in Washington began planning for such an event. From the start, the idea of a trial was highly controversial because it necessitated breaking new diplomatic, military, and legal ground. Which laws had the Nazis broken? Which individuals were truly responsible? Who should gather documents and on what basis? What forum should be used for this trial? How could the procedure be anything other than a "high-class lynching"?

In late 1944, Stimson used a proposal developed by a mid-level officer, Murray Bernays, to flesh out his idea and gather support from other cabinet officers. He found the road very hard; even the Joint Chiefs of Staff were skeptical of his proposal. Once the controversial questions were raised, the proposal was nearly dropped. "After six weeks in which the plan had repeatedly been examined, debated, and revised, only to be challenged once more, not a single government department had formally approved it" (Smith 1981, 112).

As was common in wartime planning, policy decisions were swept along by events on the battlefield. In January 1945, reports from Belgium described the slaughter of eighty American prisoners of war by Nazi guards apparently acting under specific orders. The act so directly violated the 1924 Geneva Convention on the treatment of POWs that Roosevelt was prompted to formally endorse the idea of a war crimes trial. By March, American officials were speaking in favor of a wide-reaching war crimes trial and ultimately managed to persuade and cajole British and Russian diplomats to accept their viewpoint.

The key sticking points until the finalization of the plan in June were the notion of a German conspiracy to commit aggressive war and the prosecution of organizations themselves. Both were new ideas to the Europeans because conspiracy trials are uniquely American inventions. The definition of "aggressive war" not only was weak at the time but continues to elude the

United Nations to this day. Finally, proving the guilt of an entire organization was never attempted at even the domestic level, and serious questions were raised about whether it was possible or appropriate. After all, not all members of an organization have equal culpability if the organization becomes involved in crimes. And only individuals can be accused of crimes, not social institutions. These questions were ultimately left unresolved, and it would be up to the judges at Nuremberg to determine the merits of the charges separately. Perhaps most important, the actions of the victorious Allies were never held up for judgment. Allied leaders knew that the firebombing of Dresden and the atomic annihilation of Hiroshima and Nagasaki would not stand up very well to objective legal analysis (Taylor 1993).

The organization of the trial was based on the four-member alliance that had defeated Germany. American, British, Soviet, and French judges were named, along with an alternate for each one. They heard all the documentary, film, and oral testimony about the crimes of twenty-two men chosen for their prominence, breadth of experience in different aspects of the Nazi regime, and direct participation in war crimes. Prosecutors from each country gathered documents, interrogated witnesses and defendants, and undertook cross-examination. Each defendant was allowed a German defense attorney of his choosing, and all materials were made available in German and English, with the hearings simultaneously translated into English, French, German, and Russian (a first for IBM).

The defendants in the Nuremberg Trials were all notorious in their own right, although as would become clear during the proceedings, they differed dramatically in their degree of participation and control over the commission of atrocities and war crimes. Hermann Goering and Rudolf Hess were perhaps the closest to Adolf Hitler himself, although Goering's influence had waned and Hess was profoundly schizophrenic. Other prominent organizers of Nazi rule gathered at Nuremberg included Ernst Kaltenbrunner (SS), Hans Frank (governor-general of Poland), Arthur Seyss-Inquart (Anschluss organizer), Alfred Rosenberg (theoretician/East Europe commander), Julius Streicher (prominent anti-Semite), Baldur von Schirach (Hitler Youth leader), Konstantin von Neurath (member of the "secret cabinet"), Albert Speer (production/labor organizer), Fritz Saukel (labor), and Hans Fritzsche (propagandist). In addition, leaders of the military (Admiral Karl Doenitz, Admiral Erich Raeder, General Alfred Jodl, Field Marshall Wilhelm Keitel), the economy (Walter Funk, Hjalmar Schacht), and the formal government (Franz von Papen) were assembled.

Each defendant was charged with one or more of the following counts: (1) conspiracy to commit aggressive war, (2) crimes against peace, (3) war crimes (traditional), or (4) crimes against humanity (see Smith 1977, chap. 1). Count 3—traditional war crimes—was the easiest to establish because clear treaty provisions already existed. The Hague Convention of 1907 and the Geneva Convention of 1924 clearly prohibit the harsh treatment of prisoners of war, the use of chemical and bacteriological weapons, and deliberate attacks on defenseless noncombatants. Of the eighteen men charged with traditional war crimes, only two (Hess and Fritzsche) were acquitted. The German high command, the Nazi Party organization, and other supporting organizations had left behind an unambiguous paper trail detailing the planning and perpetration of abuses of rules of war as codified in the treaties. German leaders often went to great lengths to conceal their actions by burning the bodies of their victims and inventing gross lies to explain away deaths—acutely aware that "the world would hold the Wehrmacht (German military) responsible for such outrages and killings," as put by a senior aide to Jodl (Conot 1983, 189). Even as they attempted to hide the facts of these atrocities, however, they carefully preserved a record on film and on paper.

The other counts raised serious problems of ex post facto prosecution. As put in the final judgment at Nuremberg: "It was urged on behalf of the defendants that a fundamental principle of all law—international and domestic—is that there can be no punishment of crime without a preexisting law . . ." (Falk et al. 1971, 97).

To be sure, the notion of a crime against humanity, though intuitively appealing, had never been mentioned or discussed prior to Nuremberg. The concept was put forward originally by the Soviet judge, Generak I. T. Nikitchenko, as a way to punish the Nazis for the Holocaust. In light of the doctrine of sovereign immunity, which allows a government to treat its own citizens in any way it pleases, there was no traditional international law against Germans killing Jewish Germans. "Crimes against humanity" was a device to make such prosecution possible. Given the fact that such a law did not exist in 1939, the defense charged that new laws were being invented and applied retroactively to their clients.

To meet this objection, lawyers for the prosecution argued that even though the law had not been codified on paper, there existed in 1939 an international moral consensus against genocide (the deliberate slaughter of a race of people). As put by Robert Jackson, the American prosecutor:

> It is true, of course, that we have no judicial precedent for [these charges]. But International Law is more than a scholarly collection of abstract and immutable principles. It is an outgrowth of treaties and agreements between nations and of accepted customs . . . . The real complaining party at your bar is Civilization. (Falk et al. 1971, 84, 87)

Sir Hartley Shawcross, the British prosecutor, expressed the idea more directly:

> The rights of humanitarian intervention on behalf of the rights of man, trampled upon by a state in a manner shocking the sense of mankind, has long been considered to form part of the recognized law of nations. . . . If murder, rapine, and robbery are indictable under the ordinary municipal laws of our countries, shall those who differ from the common criminal only by the extent and systematic nature of their offenses escape accusation? (Conot 1983, 180)

The judges at Nuremberg determined during the trial that Nazi atrocities were so far beyond what could be considered civilized behavior, even in time of war, that they upheld the charge of "crime against humanity." Documents indicating the desperate speed with which extermination camps carried out the "Final Solution" to exterminate all European Jews clearly pointed to a complete abandonment of any pretense at humanity in the waning years of the war.

The crime of conspiring to commit aggressive war involved at least four different legal problems:

> It was submitted that ex post facto punishment is abhorrent to the law of all civilized nations, that no sovereign power had made aggressive war a crime at the time the alleged criminal acts were committed, that no statute had defined aggressive war, that no penalty had been fixed for its commission, and no court had been created to try and punish offenders. (Falk et al. 1971, 97)

The Kellogg-Briand Pact of 1928 was a lofty pledge by the world's major powers never to resort to war. The signatories (which included Germany) declared "in the names of their respective peoples that they condemn recourse to war for the solution of international controversies, and renounce it as an instrument of national policy in their relations with one another" (Falk 1971, 46). The judges at Nuremberg determined that this treaty by itself was sufficient to show that international law prohibited the initiation of war (although very narrow provisions existed in which preemptive war was permissible). Through the course of their deliberations, the judges settled on the fact that Germany planned its attacks far in advance, that the Nazis attacked neutral nations, and that they did so without regard for international law. Hitler himself offered the most telling comment when he said, with regard to his plan to attack France via neutral Belgium and Holland; "Breach of the neutrality of Holland and Belgium is meaningless. No one will question it when we have won" (Conot 1983, 191).

The existence of a conspiracy was all-important to the Americans. Collusion and organized crime were not considered separate offenses in Europe, so the French judges in particular had great difficulty with this concept, as well as with the notion of charging whole organizations with crimes. As it happened, however, the charge of conspiracy could be proven thanks to the meticulous recordkeeping of the Third Reich. At several meetings, with attendance recorded, Hitler, Goering, and others explained plans to annex first Austria and then Czechoslovakia and later to invade Poland. Plans to breach the Moscow Pact and attack the Soviet Union in 1941 were clearly articulated at a number of secret gatherings, along with the program to exterminate all Jews in Europe (the "Final Solution"). The guilt of an individual defendant could have easily been determined by his presence at such meetings, but the judges showed leniency if the defendant later acted to delay or scale back the implementation of the plans.

The question of whether the Nuremberg Tribunal had the authority to prosecute heads of state for war crimes was—and still is—a tricky legal problem. After all, the court derived its authority from the military occupation forces and was not directly connected to the United Nations or the International Court of Justice. To a large extent, it could be said that such a trial was merely a complicated way for victorious nations to seal their success. On the other hand, the Allies' position of power permitted them to treat their prisoners with far more harshness than they actually used. Under the circumstances, the Allies that organized the trial felt they were offering the accused far more respect, compassion, and fairness than they deserved. The alternatives of a "show trial," summary executions, and a widescale purge were rejected on the grounds that none of these gave the criminals any opportunity to defend themselves. The process would have appeared entirely political and idiosyncratic. (The Russians made it clear they looked forward to executing any apparent war criminal who fell into their hands, whereas the French favored greater leniency.) As put by Robert Jackson:

> If these men are the first war leaders of a defeated nation to be prosecuted in the name of the law, they are also the first to be given a chance to plead for their own lives in the name of the law. Realistically, the Charter of this Tribunal, which gives them a hearing, is also the source of their only hope. . . . Despite the fact that public opinion already condemns their acts, we agree that here they must be given a presumption of innocence, and we accept the burden of proving criminal acts and the responsibility of these defendants for their commission. (Falk et al. 1971, 82)

It is clear, in retrospect, that although one might quibble about the impartiality of a tribunal of victors judging the actions of a vanquished government, and although one might ask whether the full array of legal protections accorded under any given country's legal system was offered to the Nuremberg defendants, the accused did receive relatively fair treatment. The judges were clearly disposed to give each defendant the benefit of the doubt and often ruled against the prosecution's requests—particularly in granting defendants' rights of reply. During the trial, each defendant was permitted not only to have a defense of his own choosing but also to call witnesses (the vast majority of witnesses were German themselves—and often senior aides to the defendants during the war), review documents, and speak on his own behalf at several junctures. It was possible to appeal sentences (although none of these efforts was successful). Whatever bias emerged during the trial tended to be in favor of social status—the judges showed a marked penchant to give intellectuals and professionals leniency—rather than political views. As put in a *New York Times* editorial written at the conclusion of the trial, "In short, the international tribunal had meted out what it was supposed to mete out—stern and exact justice, but justice, not vengeance" (Conot 1983, 435).

Courtroom Drama

The trial itself was largely tedious and disorganized, involving primarily a rambling discussion of documents (many were read out loud in their entirety) and enumeration of countless minor incidents, obscure characters, and secret meetings. During the final weeks of the trial, as the warm and humid Bavarian sun beat down on the poorly insulated courtroom, the judges themselves had great difficulty staying awake! In contrast, graphic films of concentration camp victims, angry confrontations between prosecutors and defendants during cross-examination, and the coldly frank discussion of mutilation, crematoriums, and experiments on human specimens could not help but hold the attention of the international audience.

The trial opened on November 20, 1945, after eight months of gathering documents, interrogating defendants and witnesses, and registering the charges. The judges of the tribunal were Francis Biddle and John Parker of the United States, Lord Goeffrey Lawrence and Norman Birkett of the United Kingdom, I. T. Nikitchenko and A. F. Volvchov of the USSR, and Donnedieu de Vabres and Robert Falco of France. The dominant voices on the tribunal were Birkett and Nikitchenko, who were involved in drafting the charter of the court. De Vabres spoke consistently for leniency in sentencing, and Lawrence did much to promote orderliness and efficiency during the proceedings.

The first three months of the trial presented a detailed account of the crimes committed by the defendants and the broader Nazi regime. The prosecution used some 5,000 different documents, which had been translated from German, to show the planning and execution of the Nazi leadership's goal of world domination, starting with the subversion of the Weimar Republic in 1931 and the famous Reichstag fire, which propelled the Nazis into full control of a police state (an event that was later proven to be the fault of Goering himself). The establishment of a system of state-sponsored terrorism, the placing of the economy on a war footing, and the beginnings of abuses against Jews came next.

From then on, the narrative became somewhat haphazard as prosecutors took advantage of the availability of witnesses when convenient. They attempted to prove that a wide array of German institutions and agencies were implicated in the atrocities. For example, the Reichsbank (central bank of Germany) laundered the considerable amount of jewelry, watches, and even gold teeth through its official accounts during the heyday of Jewish exterminations after 1942. The Hitler Youth organization was so effective in shaping the next generation that Hitler was known to tell regime opponents that he cared little for their complaints because he already "had" their children. The army's blind obedience made the invasion of Germany's neutral neighbors possible, and Gestapo and SS repression prevented internal uprisings. Even the industrial system was intertwined with atrocities as millions of POWs and Jews were put to work in weapons-making factories and other programs. Evidence was laid out in painful detail through testimony, documentary films, and written records.

By mid-March of 1946, the defense had its turn to present its case. As put by Conot:

> Since in the minds of the defense as well as of the prosecution, there was little doubt that the essence of the Nazi regime's criminality had been proved, the task of the individual accused in attempting to show his innocence or mitigate

his guilt was to disassociate himself from the group, to demonstrate that he had not participated in the alleged "common plan" and had not been involved in violations of international law or crimes against humanity. (Conot 1983, 330)

Nearly all the defendants took the stand during the trial, which gave rise to the most interesting and dramatic moments. Goering was first. After he articulated his basic position that he was in fact heavily involved in all of the Third Reich's highest bodies, he went on to explain that, according to international law, his actions were not criminal. In a heated cross-examination by Jackson, Goering pointed out that bombing campaigns by the Luftwaffe, which were categorized as part of his war crimes, were no worse than Allied attacks on Dresden and other German cities and that most charges against him were ex post facto. Jackson was disarmed by Goering's able self-defense (Conot 1983, 338). Even Jackson's sympathetic biographer acknowledged that Goering had the upper hand (Gerhart 1958, 394). The judges permitted Goering considerable latitude to give speeches while explaining his answers, according to observers. While this infuriated Jackson, it did not especially help Goering either, and Jackson was able to argue a strong case on the major charges. Goering was found guilty on all four counts and sentenced to death. He avoided the noose only by taking a cyanide capsule before his execution.

Few defendants had the arrogance of Goering. Some were apologetic and remorseful, but most waffled about their prominence and responsibility. Keitel admitted his guilt from the stand: "I cannot make white out of black." Schirach and Frank also admitted complicity, with the latter exclaiming, "A thousand years will pass and still this guilt of Germany will not have been erased!" In his final statement, Saukel said, "In all humility and reverence, I bow before the victims and the fallen of all nations, and before the misfortune and suffering of my own people, with whom I alone must measure my fate." Many Nuremberg defendants excused their behavior on the grounds that they were either ignorant of the regime's worst offenses or not senior enough to have set policy, or else they were simply "doing their job." Jodl, the stern military man, said, "As for the ethical code of my action, I must say that it was obedience." Rosenberg weakly rationalized his participation in the Holocaust by pointing out that the Jewish Talmud itself says Gentiles are inferior, and therefore it is no crime to treat Jews as inferiors. The capacity for Nazi self-justification was so great that it has prompted numerous psychological studies of complicity in institutionalized violence. (Note the famous Milgram experiments in which college students willingly administered apparently lethal levels of electric shock to their peers because a scientist in a lab coat told them to do so.)

For many defendants, the documentary evidence was overwhelming, establishing attendance at key meetings and certain knowledge and authorization of atrocities. Where documents were not enough, the prosecution was usually able to bring German eyewitnesses to testify against their former superiors. Ribbentrop's secretary, Margaret Blank, inadvertently gave the prosecution vital evidence of his close ties to Hitler even though she had been called as a defense witness! The commander at Auschwitz testified that Kaltenbrunner, contrary to his own testimony, was fully aware of the large-scale gassing at the extermination camp.

In general terms, the prosecution was assisted by the relatively weak performance of the defense attorneys. The judges' efforts to give the defendants leeway in answering questions and in utilizing and translating documents made the task of the prosecution difficult nonetheless. The general consensus on the part of most observers—German and Allied—was that the trial gave all parties ample opportunity to present their cases in the best possible light. Jackson offered in summation: "Of one thing we may be sure, the future will never have to ask, with misgiving, what the Nazis could have said in their favor. The fact is that the testimony of the defendants has removed any doubt of their guilt" (Conot 1983, 469).

The Judgment

The eight justices met during most of September 1946, immediately after the conclusion of the trial, and quickly handed down sixteen convictions. For example, the justices were unanimous in their decisions on the guilt of Goering, Ribbentrop, Kaltenbrunner, and Streicher and debated only briefly the convictions of Keitel, Jodl, Rosenberg, Frank, Frick, Saukel, and Seyss-Inquart. On the grounds that these individuals played an active and direct role in the planning and execution of Nazi war crimes, each was sentenced to be hanged.

Regarding the other defendants, the judges debated vigorously. Three were sentenced to life in prison: Hess, Funk, and Raeder. Because Funk and Raeder were judged to be outside the inner circle of Hitler advisors and Hess was clearly only marginally competent, they received lighter sentences. The moderate sentences of Doenitz (ten years), Speer (twenty years), Neurath (fifteen years), and Schirach (twenty years) were based not so much on guilt on specific charges but rather on extenuating circumstances and compromises among the judges. Bradley Smith argues that the personal background of the defendants had much to do with their sentences because professional types were consistently treated more kindly that the uneducated ruffians in the group (Smith 1977, 305).

Three defendants were acquitted largely due to a fluke of rules. Early on, the judges determined that unless a defendant was convicted by a clear majority (three countries against one), that individual should be acquitted. Out of a total of seventy-four individual charges, there were twenty-two acquittals—a surprisingly high failure rate, considering that the defendants had been carefully selected for their obvious culpability. In the case of von Papen, the Russians called for the death penalty, as they had throughout the proceedings for nearly all the defendants, and the French called for a light sentence on principle. The British and American judges were unconvinced by the evidence and called for acquittal. Thus, although the French and

Russian judges disagreed about the penalty, their agreement on the need for conviction led to Papen's acquittal by producing a 2–2 stalemate. After considerable discussion, the judges decided to go back to the previous convictions of Fritzsche and Schacht and acquit because of the remarkable similarities in the cases of all three men.

The charges against certain Nazi and German organizations were upheld. Rather than urging the prosecution of any member of these groups, however, the judges instructed future prosecutors to ascertain on a case-by-case basis the individual culpability of each member. The result was a cumbersome and ultimately short-lived legal process that resulted in only a few hundred prison sentences over the next two years. The urgency of the Cold War pushed World War II business to the back burner everywhere but in Israel, where World War II war crimes trials continue to this day.

On October 16, 1945, the defendants sentenced to death were hanged outside the courtroom (with the exceptions of Goering and Bormann, who had already died). Their bodies were later cremated and their ashes scattered near Munich. Thus the birthplace of Nazism became its grave.

Implications of the Nuremberg Trials

The Nuremberg Trials offer a significant and rich example of international law in all of its aspects: as a general body of values and principles, as a set of codified treaties, and as a feature of domestic law. Also, in these trials we see both the development and application of international law—a rare opportunity. Finally, the Nuremberg Trials offer a legacy that is very much alive today, as illustrated by George Bush's call for the prosecution of Saddam Hussein on war crimes charges in 1991.

A crucial problem becomes clear when we consider the Nuremberg Trials—that is, the dilemma of applying law that is not yet codified in treaty form. German defendants and later critics have argued that the law applied at Nuremberg was ex post facto, especially insofar as crimes against peace and humanity are concerned. Linking the concept of aggressive war with the unenforceable Kellogg-Briand Pact created further difficulties. Nothing in existing international law (as of 1939) expressly forbade a head of state from launching any sort of war under penalty of death. On the contrary, given the heritage of colonialism with all its bloody dimensions, the many minor and major wars fought throughout the nineteenth and early twentieth centuries, and the escalation in weaponry and tactics, it could easily have been inferred that the type of war Germany contemplated was perfectly legal according to existing legal codes and customs.

So why was the effort made to prosecute the Nazi leadership? As Jackson and others put it, the nations that held the power at the time agreed to establish a new standard for international behavior. They could do that most quickly by establishing a judicial precedent at Nuremberg—in spite of the absence of formally codified laws (see Harris 1954, 491). International law was viewed as a sort of global common law—an ad hoc collection of rules and judgments that are handed down to future generations for their own interpretation. Although this view is certainly convenient, the general trend since World War II has been to codify explicit declarations—worded generally—as a precursor to more specific and binding treaties. Thus the Universal Declaration on Human Rights of 1949 has served as a backdrop for the more recent Declaration on the Rights of the Child, which in turn will permit more forceful agreements on child labor laws and health standards. Perhaps the most significant result of the Nuremberg proceedings was not the convictions themselves but the articulation of general principles.

Since the trials, several new treaties have been drafted that articulate specific crimes related to the Nazi actions. The Geneva Convention was updated in 1949 to cover a wider array of acts against prisoners of war and noncombatants. The United Nations established in 1950 the International Law Commission, which has as its mission the codification of existing rules and principles. An important first step was the drafting of the Genocide Convention in 1949, which prohibits any attempt to destroy a "national, ethical, racial or religious group" and clearly makes all individuals involved in such crimes responsible and punishable "whether they are constitutionally responsible rulers, public officials or private individuals" (Articles II and IV) (see Woetzel 1960).

The so-called Nuremberg Principles were accepted by the United Nations in 1950 and offer legal justification for the actions of the tribunal. For example, Principles I and II state:

> Any person who commits an act which constitutes a crime under international law is responsible therefor and liable to punishment. The fact that internal law does not impose a penalty for an act which constitutes a crime under international law does not relieve the person who committed the act from responsibility under international law.

This notion of personal responsibility has also been written into domestic laws, including the Constitution (Basic Law) of Germany and the field manuals of the U.S. Army. The principles further specify that all accused persons have a right to a fair trial and list specific crimes that warrant prosecution: crimes against peace, war crimes, and crimes against humanity. These terms were applied in the Tokyo War Crimes Trials and the Adolf Eichmann trial of 1961. They also became the touchstone for a growing number of war crimes tribunals in the 1990s.

In 1993, the UN Security Council established the first international war crimes tribunal not related to World War II to investigate and prosecute charges of genocide in Bosnia. The next year, the council set up a panel to deal with the atrocities in Rwanda. There is some discussion about doing the same in Cambodia to prosecute those responsible for the genocide in the 1970s (Tessitore and Woolfson 1999, 279). In each case, the appointment of judges, the treatment of defendants, and the list of crimes were drawn almost directly from the Nuremberg experience. A major difference is that the laws utilized at Nuremberg have now been codified in the Nuremberg Principles, the Genocide Convention, the International Covenant on Civil and Political Rights, and other treaties that deal with the rights of minorities, refugees, women, and children. The scope of the charges is now broader and includes such crimes as the use of rape as a weapon of war. Furthermore, these laws have been incorporated into the constitutions of most countries. No one can claim ignorance of these fundamental standards of conduct.

The Yugoslav and Rwandan war crimes tribunals have functioned continuously since their founding, although they have not met with unqualified success. The Rwandan court was plagued with inefficiencies and other flaws, and it did not hand down its first conviction until 1999. Nevertheless, the judges on the court succeeded in establishing the guilt of a prominent local official in Rwanda on the charge that failure to use his authority to stop the massacres was tantamount to participation. In the Yugoslav court, the number of indicted individuals continues to rise along with the status of the defendants. In mid-1999, the leader of the Yugoslav Republic, Slobodan Milosevic, was indicted.

Perhaps the greatest honor paid to the Nuremberg prosecutors was the decision taken by more than one hundred nations on June 17, 1999, to approve the Rome Statute for an International Criminal Court by a vote of 120–7, with 21 abstentions, after nearly ten years of negotiation. The scope of the new court will be almost the same as that of the Nuremberg Tribunal. Eighteen judges will render decisions based on a formal trial. The court officially opened for business in July 2002, although the United States has opted out. As put by Tina Rosenberg, "Such a court would be a fitting heir to the tribunals, which, after fifty years, still represent what chief U.S. prosecutor at Nuremberg Robert Jackson called 'one of the most significant tributes that Power has ever paid to Reason'" (Rosenberg 1995, 691).

Conclusion

To what extent have the Nuremberg Principles and new treaties affected the actual conduct of international affairs, and the conduct of war in particular? A complete answer is impossible here. The press usually begins the debate by considering acts committed during wartime. During the Vietnam War, it became clear by the late 1960s that atrocities were being committed both deliberately and inadvertently as a result of U.S. military operations. The "carpet bombing" missions of hundreds of B-52 bombers saturating large sections of North Vietnam with heavy bomb payloads resulted in thousands of civilian casualties. Several U.S. officers were accused of and formally charged with violations of military law as a result of large-scale attacks on unarmed civilians.

The villages of My Lai and Son My were attacked by American forces at the height of the Vietnam War. Villagers were rounded up and shot in a particularly brutal way by American servicemen under orders to maximize their "body count" of Vietnamese casualties. It is clear from the testimony delivered at the court-martials of those involved, including Lt. William Calley, that many prisoners of war were killed and many villages razed to increase body count statistics, and these actions were tolerated and even implicitly encouraged by commanders. Calley seems to have played the role of scapegoat for a system that was fundamentally corrupt (Falk et al. 1971, 226).

Perhaps more serious, war criminals who win wars are unlikely to be charged, let alone prosecuted. Not only will the victors still have the protection of their government, but they will also have a hand in deciding the parameters of war crimes themselves. The Russians during the Nuremberg Trials were careful to prevent the judgment from encompassing their own misdeeds during the war. As the saying goes, "If the traitors are victorious, none dare call it treachery."

Terrorism is a quasi-military action against primarily civilian targets. Although the acts of terrorists are not explicitly covered by existing international law, they are clearly violations of the domestic law in places where they occur. The Reagan administration prosecuted terrorists through domestic U.S. courts if they had been involved in attacks on American citizens. In some cases, bringing the terrorists into custody has involved some reactive military and diplomatic maneuvers, such as the recent case involving the United States, the United Kingdom, and Libya over the release of individuals held in Libya and wanted for the downing of Pan Am flight 103 over Lockerbie, Scotland, in 1988. The suspects were ultimately released, a trial conducted, and convictions were handed down against two Libyan operatives.

Perhaps most impressive has been the trial of former Serbian leader Slobodan Milosevic (see Case 15). The Yugoslav War Crimes Tribunal was established to try war criminals and those charged with genocide in connection with the wars in Croatia, Bosnia, Kosovo, and Serbia in the 1990s. After his removal from office in 2001, Milosevic was turned over to the tribunal for prosecution. He has been charged with aggression, genocide, and various war crimes. He took the stand in 2002 and has mounted his own defense, charging that the entire proceeding is illegitimate. The outcome is in doubt as of this writing, but the fact of the trial reaffirms the principles first articulated at Nuremberg.

Overall, the Nuremberg Trials served many important purposes, although they clearly fell short of the ambitious goal to prevent future war crimes. Without the trials, much of the information we now have about the Holocaust would have remained unorganized. Without the trials, German leaders likely would have been shot summarily and treated very differently depending on which country had captured them. The trials prevented the martyrdom of Nazi leaders as well as a popular uprising against the occupation forces. They went far in helping Germany establish firm anti-Nazi laws and a constitutional government. The elevation of what were perhaps subconscious moral principles to the level of international law has also served an important moral purpose, if not becoming a cure-all for the world's evils. As put by Harris, "It has become a test of faith that the victors now live by the rules of law they used to condemn and punish the leaders of Hitler's Germany" (Harris 1954, 560).

Debate Topic

Were the Nuremberg Trials merely "victors' justice"? In other words, was the outcome a foregone conclusion, given the thirst for revenge on the part of the victors of World War II?

PRO
Those who agree argue as follows: (1) The courtroom was presided over only by judges from the victorious nations. (2) These nations established the procedural and substantive rules for the trial, based mostly on martial law. (3) Nazis with equally dubious war records were often exonerated and invited to work for the Allies because of their unusual scientific skills.

CON
Opponents of this view point out: (1) Defendants were provided competent legal counsel at no cost. (2) British and Russian officials complained that the defendants were granted too many rights. (3) The "bottom line": several defendants succeeded in persuading the judges of their innocence, and not all were sentenced to death.

Questions to Consider

1. Were the Nuremberg Trials really a legal undertaking or merely window dressing for what was essentially the spoils of victory? How can such trials be governed purely by law?

2. To what extent is the Nuremberg experience a precedent? In law? In morality? In social interaction? How could the Nuremberg Principles be applied in Yugoslavia? In Somalia? In Chicago?

3. How effective were the Nuremberg Trials in ending fascism and genocide?

Websites

Detailed Nuremberg Sites Run by Universities and NGOS:
www.yale.edu/lawweb/avalon/imt/imt.htm,
www.ess.uwe.ac.uk/genocide/wwwzres.htm,
www.holocaust.history.org/works/imt/01/htm.c001.htm
Nuremberg Higher Superior Court: **www.justiz.bayern.de/olgn/imte-more.htm**

References

Conot, Robert E. *Justice at Nuremberg* (New York: Harper & Row, 1983).

Falk, Richard, Gabriel Kolko, and Robert Jay Lifton, eds. *Crimes of War: A Legal, Political-Documentary, and Psychological Inquiry into the Responsibility of Leaders, Citizens, and Soldiers for Criminal Acts in Wars* (New York: Random House, 1971).

Gerhart, Eugene C. *America's Advocate: Robert H. Jackson* (New York: Bobbs-Merrill, 1958).

Harris, Whitney R. *Tyranny on Trial: The Evidence at Nuremberg* (Dallas: Southern Methodist University, 1954).

Rosenberg, Tina. "From Nuremberg to Bosnia." *The Nation* 260 #19 (May 15, 1995): 688–691.

Smith, Bradley F. *Reaching Judgment at Nuremberg* (New York: Basic Books, 1977).

Smith, Bradley F. *The Road to Nuremberg* (New York: Basic Books, 1981).

Taylor, Telford. *The Anatomy of the Nuremberg Trials* (New York: Little, Brown, 1993).

Tessitore, John, and Susan Woolfson, eds. *A Global Agenda: Issues Before the 54th General Assembly of the United Nations* (Lanham, MD: Rowman & Littlefield, 1999).

Woetzel, Robert K. *The Nuremberg Trials in International Law* (New York: Praeger, 1960).

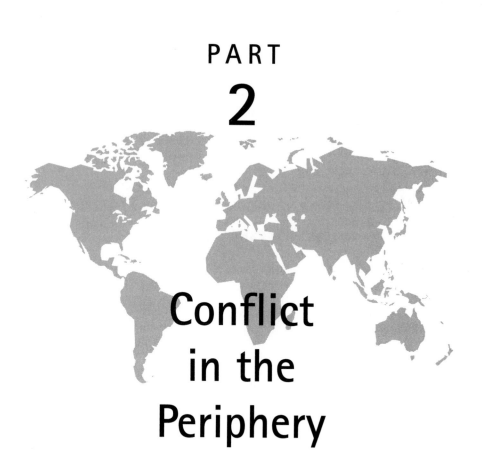

PART

2

Conflict
in the
Periphery

CASE
13

Decolonization in Africa
DECOLONIZATION

Introduction

Since 1960, more than 100 states have secured membership in the United Nations, thus fulfilling the nationalist dreams of billions of people. Perhaps the most dramatic example of growing nationalism is the decolonization of Africa. Statehood means membership in an elite club that brings with it such perks as diplomatic recognition and the opportunity to join countless international organizations, declare war, attend state dinners, and so on. By definition, a state is any government that has control over a territory and population, but inclusion in the club of nations is the legal capstone to self-determination. As we discuss African decolonization, consider whether statehood was a means to an end or an end in and of itself.

In the space of less than ten years at the end of the nineteenth century, the great powers of Europe took control of nearly 90 percent of the African continent. In the 1960s, thirty-one African states (out of a present total of fifty-one) gained membership in the United Nations as independent, sovereign states. The story of this colossal transfer of power from the weakest to the strongest, and back again, is one of the great chapters in twentieth-century history. The problem of establishing political authority and identity following decolonization in Africa is far from resolved.

Although many have written about decolonization in Africa as a whole, the process was as varied as the geography and as diverse as the cultures involved. Algeria's and Angola's bloody wars of independence bear little similarity to the relatively peaceful changing of the guard in Tanganyika, Kenya, and Nigeria. UN intervention ended the injustice of South Africa–supported apartheid in Namibia, quite unlike the difficult and costly UN activities in the Belgian Congo. To lump together all African nations is a great injustice, so we will make every effort to highlight differences across the continent after briefly reviewing the international context of decolonization.

DECOLONIZATION IN AFRICA
KEY FIGURES

King Leopold II   Ruler of Belgium, 1865–1909, and strong advocate of European colonialism in Africa.

Dag Hammarskjold   Secretary-General of the United Nations, 1953–1961. He died in the Congo when his plane crashed during a peace mission.

Richard Trumbul   British governor of Tanganyika at the country's independence.

Charles deGaulle   President of France, 1959–1969.

Julius Nyerere   Leader of the Tanganyika African National Union and later President of Tanganyika (later Tanzania) President, 1961–1985 (except for a brief hiatus in 1962).

Ahmed Ben Bella   Leader of Algerian FLN and first President of Algeria, 1963–1965.

Ferhat Abbas   Leader of Algerian FLN.

Gamal Abdel Nasser   President of Egypt, 1956–1970, and strong advocate of decolonization in Africa.

Mobutu Sese Seko   Leader of the Congo (Zaire), 1965–1997. He was known for his corruption and brutality.

Patrice Lumumba   Leader of the Congo in early-1960s.

Joseph Kasavubu   Leader of the Congo in the early 1960s.

Moise Tshombe   Rival to various leaders of the Congo in the 1960s.

DECOLONIZATION IN AFRICA
CHRONOLOGY

1830s
France establishes sovereignty over Algeria.

1870s
Belgium's decision to claim inland regions of Africa sets off the "scramble."

1888
At the Berlin Conference, European diplomats draw up a map of Africa delineating their possessions.

1905
The Maji Maji rebellion against German rule in Tanganyika is put down by massive force.

1919
The League of Nations is established. It introduces the notion that European governments should help colonial protectorates attain self-government.

1929
The Tanganyika African Association, precursor to TANU, is founded.

1945
Revolt in the Algerian city of Setif is put down by French authorities.   *(continued)*

1953

Julius Nyerere is elected to lead the TAA. He founds TANU.

1954

The Algerian revolution begins.

1956

Nasser's rise to power in Egypt offers a model for anticolonial African leaders.

1957

Belgium sponsors the first of several elections, only to find no coherent Congolese parties form.

1958

TANU candidates sweep elections for the national legislature. Nyerere is installed as Prime Minister.

1959

The French government in Algeria collapses in part due to pressure from white residents. Charles de Gaulle establishes military rule before ushering in the Fifth Republic.

1960

De Gaulle begins peace negotiations with Algerian independence leaders. The Belgians grant the Congo independence. Congolese troops riot, three rival governments emerge, and Belgian and UNOC troops are deployed to restore order.

1961

Tanganyika achieves independence peacefully. Nyerere is installed as the first president. Dag Hammarskjold is killed in a plane crash in the Congo.

1962

De Gaulle recognizes Algerian independence. Ahmed Ben Bella becomes Algeria's first president.

1964

Zanzibar agrees to local autonomy under a federation with newly formed Tanzania.

1965

Mobutu assumes leadership in a coup in the Congo (later renamed Zaire).

The Context of African Decolonization

Europeans have been in control of parts of Africa since antiquity, but the modern phase of European colonialism began in the Age of Discovery, when African ports were first used and then claimed by various seafaring European states. Throughout the age of early imperialism (eighteenth century), Europeans contented themselves with strengthening their foothold on coastal areas of the continent through treaties (typically imposed upon local chieftains). It was not until the late nineteenth century that the inland expanses of Africa came under direct European control as a result of the "scramble for Africa"—a period of intense European rivalry for control over raw materials and potential markets. Belgian King Leopold II decided to claim a vast expanse of central Africa as a Belgian possession in the 1870s, setting off a contest over control of Africa's interior. France and Britain nearly went to war over the Sahara, and Germany used subterfuge to assert its claims in East Africa (Hargreaves 1988, 26). By 1900, Europeans had laid claim to nearly all of Africa (except for parts of the Sahara, Liberia, and Ethiopia), and white Afrikaners and British South Africans were heading toward a bloody fight called the Boer War. The scramble for Africa was over. The consolidation of colonial rule was under way.

In general terms, Portuguese, Belgian, French, and, to a lesser extent, German colonialists undertook a policy of "assimilation" of their colonies into the political life of the mother country. This led to efforts to dismantle and destroy local ethnic identities and cultures. The British, by contrast, allowed for some local autonomy by ruling indirectly through local chiefs. Both policies failed to win over native peoples to European ways, and by the 1920s, African nationalism was becoming increasingly more pronounced (Oliver and Crowder 1981, 193).

The two world wars led to introspection among European imperialists. The League of Nations and the United Nations instituted a system of caretakership, whereby colonial rule was deemed legitimate only as a vehicle for eventual independence (Bennett 1991, 351, 356). To prevent unrest and to make the colonies more profitable and self-reliant, administrators began economic development projects in many colonies during the 1930s (Hargreaves 1988, 42). The Great Depression both slowed down these efforts, given the lack of funds in the mother countries, and demonstrated to the native populations the potential weakness of their Continental masters. The collapse of many European powers during World War II further galvanized nationalist aspirations. Finally, the eye-opening experiences of many Africans who served their colonial masters at war underscored their lack of opportunities at home and exacerbated the feelings of injustice that were already growing (Oliver and Page 1988, 191).

Shortly after the war, African nationalist parties began to spring up across the continent for different reasons and with different purposes. A few prominent individuals capitalized on a sort of hero worship, while other independence movements were based more on ideology (Hargreaves 1988, 68). At the same time, unrest boiled over into anticolonial violence. In the early 1950s, the Mau Mau in Kenya and the Arabs in Algeria attacked their white patrons with reckless abandon. The results of these actions were rather extreme. On the one hand, a weakening of imperial resolve occurred, as in Egypt, Ghana, and Sudan, where independence was achieved early on. On the other hand, the military instrument was strengthened, as in Kenya, Algeria, and Angola, where imperialists brutalized native peoples. In South Africa, white nationalists introduced a virulent form of antiblack racism known as apartheid and attempted to enforce it beyond their borders. Egypt, under Gamal Abdel Nasser, became a model for radical pan-Arab anticolonialists. A key factor in predicting the type of imperial response to nationalist pressures was the size of the white European community in the colony and their attachment to dominance. The larger and more determined the white population, the more difficult the transition.

The influence of the United States and the USSR during the early years of decolonization was mixed. While the Soviet Union tended to promote anti-imperialist movements, its resources were limited and it was not a key player in most cases. The United States weighed carefully the concerns of its imperialist allies, but it tended to undermine colonialism with its support of certain independence movements. During the Suez Crisis of 1956, for example, both the Soviets and the Americans joined in persuading the British, French, and Israeli forces that occupied Nasser's canal to withdraw or face serious consequences. It was not until the 1970s that Africa became a serious Cold War battlefield. Struggles in unstable countries such as Angola and Ethiopia were far more violent as a result of the American and Soviet arms that flowed to the warring factions.

Rather than make any further generalizations, we will now look at three specific cases of decolonization in Africa. We choose Algeria, Tanzania, and Zaire primarily because they illustrate differences in how African states achieved independence. For an overview of African decolonization, see Map 13.1.

Cases in African Decolonization

Algeria: Civil War in Two Countries

Algeria is a region of northern Africa originally inhabited by a variety of rulers and tribes with little connection to one another. Largely because of the French decision in 1830 to conquer, populate, and ultimately annex the territory to France, the nation of Algeria gained a political identity. As late as 1936, only eighteen years before the start of the war of independence, prominent Algerian Arab Ferhat Abbas declared, "I will not die for an Algerian nation, because it does not exist. I have not found it" (Horne 1987, 40).

For the first one hundred years of French involvement in Algeria, the region was dominated by the 1.5 million so-called pieds noirs of French, Spanish, and Italian descent. Europeans from across the Mediterranean flocked to this country of warm sun and relatively fertile soil. Major cities grew with strong links to Europe but a clear identity. The pieds noirs felt themselves inferior in many ways to their continental counterparts, but they were also fiercely proud of their dominance in this new region. They were nonetheless dependent on the "metropole" to repress periodic unrest among the overwhelming majority of 9 million Arabs who lived in Algeria.

Various programs instituted by Paris and aimed at industrializing and modernizing Algeria had some success. Attempts at liberalizing the political system to extend more civil rights to Arabs met with tenacious resistance by the pieds noirs. By the beginning of World War II, the best Arabs could hope for was participation in a rump assembly especially designated for them. In contrast, the white population enjoyed direct representation in Paris and almost complete dominance over political structures in Algeria, where colonial officers continued the century-old system of direct control. This situation did not change in any appreciable way throughout the period of French dominance in Algeria. What was worse from the perspective of the Arab nationalists was that Arabs who were permitted a role in government were almost always handpicked yes-men ("Beni-Oui-Oui") who would parrot the pieds noirs party line (Tlemcani 1986, 43).

At the end of World War II, during V–E day celebrations, Algerian Arabs revolted. At the town of Sétif, a massive spontaneous uprising resulted in the death of more than one hundred pieds noirs—particularly individuals who represented the French government. Although this event was shocking in and of itself, the official reaction to the events was extremely violent, culminating in the deaths of between 15,000 and 40,000 Muslims. The action eliminated any resistance for a decade, but the emotional and political impact on Algeria was irreversible. From that time on, a moderate solution to the Algerian question was virtually impossible.

In response to Sétif, a variety of incipient Algerian independence movements began to organize underground. The Movement for the Triumph of Democratic Freedoms (MTLD), later renamed the Algerian Nationalist Movement (MNA)—all acronyms are based on the French versions—under Messali Hadj began developing a program for revolutionary independence, while moderate Ferhat Abbas organized the Democratic Union for the Algerian Manifesto (UDMA) in an attempt to bring about democratic reforms in Algeria under the auspices of French governance. A combination of strong personalities, imprisonments, financial difficulties, and ideological and tactical disputes led to the eventual splitting of the MTLD into a more moderate faction and a radical National Liberation Front (FLN) wing, which would later grow to encompass all Algerian nationalist movements (in 1955, Ferhat Abbas himself joined the FLN) (Tlemcani 1986, 59). In 1954, the first deliberate attempt to organize armed resistance came about with a group known as the Revolutionary Committee of Unity and Action (CRUA), which included those who would become the core of Algeria's revolution: Balkacem Krim, Ahmed Ben Bella, and Hocine Ait Ahmed. Unlike other African revolutionary groups, however, Algeria's FLN lacked consistent leadership centered on a particular individual. One can attribute this fragmentation to the efficiency of the French police, who managed to imprison most FLN leaders.

The Algerian Revolution began "officially" on November 1, 1954, when the CRUA mounted a series of attacks on urban pieds noirs targets across Algeria. Simultaneously, a declaration called for full independence for Algeria, full civil rights for all inhabitants of Algeria, and international endorsement of the declaration. The CRUA and FLN never wavered in their demands as the revolution dragged on, a strategy that, according to Horne, ultimately led to their overwhelming success in the face of growing French ambivalence (Horne 1987, 145).

For the next three years, after a very weak beginning, the French progressively reasserted control over Algeria. Various French leaders in Algeria attempted reforms but without success; only the military approach seemed to reap benefits. The violence of the war was particularly appalling, as

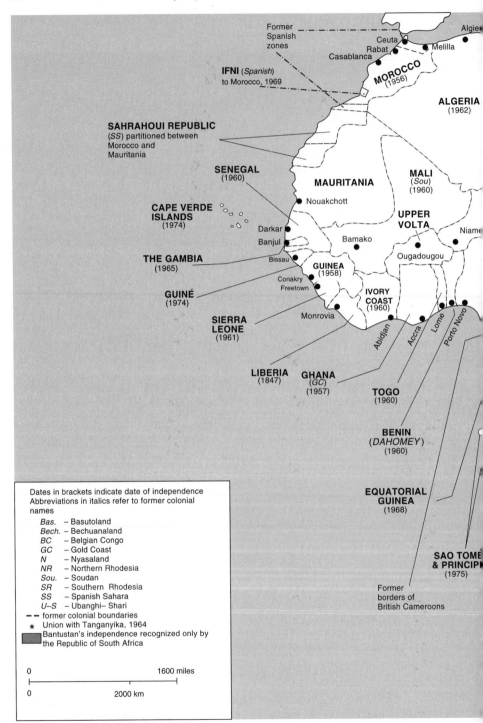

Map 13.1 Map of African decolonization providing dates of independence and former colonial names. Source: John Hargreaves. *Decolonization in Africa* (New York: Longman, 1988).

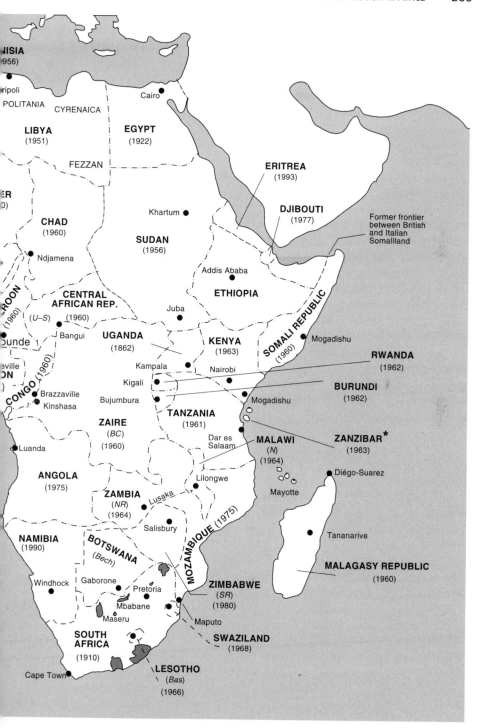

NISIA
(1956)

ripoli

POLITANIA   CYRENAICA

LIBYA
(1951)

FEZZAN

Cairo

EGYPT
(1922)

ERITREA
(1993)

Khartum ●

DJIBOUTI
(1977)

Former frontier
between British
and Italian
Somaliland

ER
0)

CHAD
(1960)

● Ndjamena

SUDAN
(1956)

Addis Ababa ●

**CENTRAL
AFRICAN REP.**

(U–S)   (1960)

● Bangui

Juba ●

ETHIOPIA

UGANDA
(1862)

KENYA
(1963)

SOMALI REPUBLIC
(1960)

● Mogadishu

RWANDA
(1962)

Kampala ●

Nairobi ●

BURUNDI
(1962)

Kigali ●

Bujumbura ●

Mogadishu ●

eville
N

CONGO (1960)

● Brazzaville
● Kinshasa

ZAIRE
(BC)
(1960)

TANZANIA
(1961)

Dar es
Salaam

MALAWI
(N)
(1964)

ZANZIBAR*
(1963)

● Luanda

ANGOLA
(1975)

ZAMBIA
(NR)
(1964)

Lusaka

Lilongwe

Diégo-Suarez ●

Mayotte

NAMIBIA
(1990)

BOTSWANA
(Bech)

Salisbury

MOZAMBIQUE (1975)

Tananarive ●

MALAGASY REPUBLIC
(1960)

Windhoek ●

Gaborone ●

Pretoria ●

ZIMBABWE
(SR)
(1980)

Mbabane ●

Maseru ●

Maputo ●

SWAZILAND
(1968)

**SOUTH
AFRICA**
(1910)

LESOTHO
(Bas)
(1966)

Cape Town ●

Algerian rebels resorted to terrorism, mutilation, and eventually reprisals against Arab collaborators in their effort to galvanize support. By 1957, FLN strength was so great that its leadership called for direct confrontation with the French in the capital city of Algiers. The Battle of Algiers was, in fact, a fairly brief campaign of bomb attacks and general strikes that was suppressed by an increasingly organized French military, led by paratroopers and counterinsurgency teams. Their techniques included widespread use of "bleus"—Algerian collaborators, including former FLN members—and torture, which ultimately led to a backlash among French liberals at home. In 1957, the military approach almost eliminated the FLN's leadership. In addition, internal dissent in the FLN reached a crisis point (Horne 1987, 128).

This is not to say the FLN was failing entirely. On the international front, the FLN was gaining reputation, support, and experience. The Non-Aligned movement had publicly embraced the FLN, and the United Nations had added Algerian independence to its agenda. Egypt's Nasser was slowly but surely beginning to provide logistical and diplomatic support, and even such prominent Western politicians as John F. Kennedy endorsed Algerian independence. These moves culminated in the declaration of the provisional government of the Republic of Algeria by FLN leaders in exile, under Ferhat Abbas.

Beginning in 1958, relations between whites in Paris and Algiers would prove to have far more significance for Algeria's future than battles between paratroopers and the FLN. A massive revolt of pieds noirs in Algiers brought down the governor-general responsible to Paris and led to a temporary military government. The ensuing chain of events led to the temporary abandonment of constitutional democracy. When Charles de Gaulle returned to power in May, he governed by decree for six months, after which the constitution for the French Fifth Republic was approved by the National Assembly.

De Gaulle was troubled by the international and domestic disapproval that the Algerian Revolution had heaped on the French government. While trying to maintain good relations with the pieds noirs, he took many steps to end the conflict. He dispatched a new military commander to replace the dangerous Massu and Salan and encouraged an end to the war first by military means. He also initiated peace talks beginning with a first meeting in Melun, France, in June 1960. The talks proffered no solution as the FLN stuck with its initial demands from 1956 to 1957. Two major revolts—first of civilian pieds noirs against the military in 1960 and later of the military against Paris in 1961—rocked Algiers. In each case, de Gaulle was able to restore order by appealing directly to the rebels in televised addresses. The combination of this unrest, a nearly successful assassination attempt on de Gaulle himself, and ever-increasing international pressure (the UN endorsed Algerian self-determination in December 1960) culminated in the decision by de Gaulle to sue for a settlement in Algeria on the FLN's terms (Horne 1987, 465). The peace accords signed on March 18, 1962, called for a referendum on independence and a cease-fire in Algeria. Although the white backlash was substantial, by June the pieds noirs had signed a truce with the FLN. On July 1, the referendum yielded a 6 million to 16,000 majority in favor of independence. On July 3, 1962, de Gaulle recognized Algerian sovereignty. Beginning in August, nearly 1.5 million pieds noirs left Algeria—only 30,000 stayed behind.

The Algerian Revolution was a highly wrenching experience for France and one of the bloodiest wars of independence in Africa. By the end of the war, the French government had experienced the fall of one constitution, a succession of military coup attempts, and civilian unrest on a large scale. European deaths amounted to 18,000 French soldiers and 10,000 pieds noirs, while roughly 300,000 Arabs were killed (of whom nearly 100,000 died at the hands of FLN vigilantes). The French recovered from the experience and went on to a prosperous period of European prominance, but the Algerians were forced to transplant an entire government-in-exile, complete with internal dissent and personal rivalries (Tlemcani 1986, 84). Although Algeria has had the trappings of democracy, it has yet to develop a healthy two-party system with tolerance for opposition movements. The country's economy, thanks in large part to its oil reserves and aggressive government intervention, has been vibrant, if largely one-dimensional. Given a recent rise in Muslim fundamentalism, Algeria's political stability is now in question, however.

Tanzania: Nyerere's Statesmanlike Revolution

The Tanzanian and Algerian independence movements are a study in contrasts. Tanzania never had a large expatriate community, the British government never intended to create a transplant white government, and it had little interest in defending its state with force. Whereas the Algerian Revolution lacked a single leader, Julius Nyerere was from the beginning an important focal point in Tanzanian independence. Whereas the Arab Algerians were continually excluded from government, Africans were courted actively by the British and even controlled the government in the waning days of the colony. The international community, only somewhat interested in Algeria, played an active and direct role in Tanzania.

Like Algeria, Tanzania was composed of a variety of chieftains and kingdoms that had little in common until the first Europeans arrived in the sixteenth century. Portuguese explorers were followed by French and British immigrants as well as travelers from the Middle East. The first major attraction to the region was its people—as a commodity. The slave trade lasted until the mid-nineteenth century, when British interests intervened to halt the practice in favor of free trade, which redounded to British advantage. By the 1850s, the British were entrenched on the island kingdom of Zanzibar, off the coast of Africa, and British, German, French, and even American companies had operations in so-called Tanganyika on the mainland. It was never a particularly lucrative colony, so no single power sought control of the area until the scramble for Africa began. In 1885, the Germans presented other European leaders with a variety of dubious and often laughable "treaties" with local rulers (who were often illiterate) as evidence of their supremacy in the region. Germany was able to play off tensions between France and Britain in making its move.

Germany governed what is now Tanzania until after World War I, during which time it attempted to consolidate its authority. Germany was never able to completely pacify the region, however, and throughout its rule uprisings were common. In 1905, the Maji Maji rebellion prompted Germans, who feared that it would spread to better-organized tribes, to slaughter the rebels with machine guns.

In World War I, the Germans lost the colony to Great Britain, which was granted legal stewardship over the area through a League of Nations mandate. The British were expected to provide annual reports on the state of the people in the colony, particularly with regard to social progress. The League took no action to shape British policy, however. By 1926, the British had instituted a sophisticated system of local rule involving tribal leaders and government appointees dispersed throughout the country. The British also instituted somewhat broader educational opportunities for Africans, although the number of college graduates never rose beyond a few hundred until the 1960s.

British governors in Tanganyika tended to be fairly enlightened in their efforts to give Africans a voice in government. Donald Cameron approved the formation of the Tanganyika African Association (TAA) in 1929—an organization that would later create the independence-minded Tanganyika African National Union (TANU) under Julius Nyerere. Richard Trumbull, governor during the late 1950s, played a crucial part in the nation's independence by treating Nyerere as a spokesman for Tanzanians and deferring to him on matters of national policy. The British governors helped instill a sense of national unity for Africans by recognizing African-led national organizations (Hatch 1972, 91).

The period before and after World War II was a painful one for Tanzania; it felt the effects of the Great Depression, Nazi Germany made claims on the territory, and border skirmishes were common. Educational opportunities dried up, production was reemphasized, and Britain rejected out of hand a UN proposal to grant the colony independence by 1975 (Taylor 1963, 82).

It was in this context that, beginning in 1950, the TAA was transformed into a political movement to press the governor for reforms—political, social, and economic. In 1953, Nyerere, an educated son of a lesser chieftain, was elected to lead the TAA. He called for the creation of TANU as a free-standing political party. Nyerere consistently favored reform of the Tanganyikan political system rather than its overthrow, and he was generally successful in calming the voices of militants. He was convinced that only by working through the British legal system could genuine independence be achieved. TANU was endorsed by various UN officials who visited the country and grew to be the focal point of disaffected Africans throughout the country. TANU was strengthened by a decision to exclude whites and

Asians from the organization at the outset. In a short time, TANU was a force to be reckoned with for then-governor Edward Twining (who generally favored limiting power for blacks). Within TANU, each regional office had considerable autonomy, and little effort was made to indoctrinate the masses (Yeager 1982, 19).

By 1957, with the independence of Ghana and the nearing of the end of Governor Twining's term of office, the die was cast. In a series of elections, Nyerere's TANU party fielded candidates (against the wishes of many radical TANU members who favored boycotts—see Taylor 1963, 163) and posted impressive victories. The party benefited from an absence of serious opposition and the gradual incorporation of many nonblack TANU supporters. In October 1958, elections were held for a new multiracial assembly in which all seats were up for grabs, regardless of race (previously the seats had been split evenly among Europeans, Asians, and blacks). TANU won every seat in this new legislature and Nyerere became its leader (Hatch 1972, 123). The speed of independence was greatly accelerated by the cooperation of the newly appointed Governor Turnbull, who pushed forward scheduled election dates, including the election in August 1960 that resulted in Nyerere forming his own cabinet. The governor was then responsible for foreign policy only. The biggest problem facing Tanganyika's African leaders seems to have been arrogance on the part of many elected officials and apathy on the part of the electorate, who had already come to expect huge electoral victories (Hatch 1972, 128). On December 9, 1961, under the sympathetic eye of Governor Turnbull, the Union Jack was lowered and the Tanganyikan flag was raised for the first time.

Militants and unionists dogged the early years of Nyerere's regime, which had become a one-party state against his wishes. Maintaining the populist character of the TANU party led to strict guidelines on membership by Nyerere and eventually the enunciation of a socialist doctrine that would serve as a model for African Marxists. An important development—which is largely separate from TANU-led politics—was the decision to form a federation with politically unstable Zanzibar off the coast at the sheik's request (Yeager 1982, 23). In 1964, the two nations merged as Tanzania, with Zanzibar retaining substantial autonomy through the 1970s.

Zaire: The Congo in Turmoil

Zaire, known originally as the Belgian Congo, is in the heart of what Stanley and Livingstone called "darkest Africa." For many years it served as a private hunting reserve for the flamboyant Belgian King Leopold II. In 1879, Leopold determined to secure European recognition of Belgium's control of the region. "Probably it was Leopold, more than any other single statesman, who created the 'atmosphere' of scramble" (Oliver and Page 1988, 161).

Belgian rule over the Congo epitomized the worst of colonialism. The entire country was converted into a vast resource extraction operation. Railways were built at the cost of hundreds of lives, plantations flourished with slave labor, and eventually great mining companies operated with reckless abandon in the Katanga region in the southeast. All this activity was directed by a 10,000-strong Belgian colonial administration and a sizable expatriate community, which eventually reached 100,000 shortly before independence. Although some Belgian officials embraced the "white man's burden" of Kipling fame with paternalistic authority ("Control to serve" was one administrator's slogan), the result was not only the pillaging of the country but also a reduction in the size of the native population (Young 1965, 60).

The Congo consisted of numerous regional groupings, ethnic identities, and social classes. Educated Africans in the capital sought civil rights equal to those of the Europeans. The mining region of Katanga felt confident of its ability to govern itself and sought independence. Other regions, particularly the northeast, were remote, poorly organized, and easily cut off from the capital. All these factors became extremely important in the years following independence.

Although sporadic violence against Belgian rule was common throughout the century, it was not until well after World War II that anything approximating an independence movement became evident. Belgians were quick to address African grievances in the hope of reaching a quick solution based on association of whites and blacks (Young 1965, 40). When African demands became more coherent in the mid-1950s, Belgians quickly abandoned these dreams to avoid a revolution. Elections were held in 1957, although no African political parties had been formed. Even with the election of a self-governing body in 1959, no truly national Congolese parties existed. Spontaneous riots in the capital of Leopoldville (now Kinshasa) precipitated what can only be described as a helter-skelter independence process, culminating in national elections in early 1960 and Belgian withdrawal in June. To a large extent, nothing approximating a state was in place with the granting of independence. This failure to prepare for self-rule led to five of the most turbulent years of recent African history.

The first leader of the Congo was Patrice Lumumba, a native of the northeastern region who had embraced a form of pan-African Marxism only a few years before independence. As the leader of the Chamber of Deputies, he was empowered to organize a government, although the high degree of splintering in the parliament led to the formation of a weak coalition government. Lumumba was never especially secure in his position, particularly because the capital was located in an area dominated by his political rivals. Joseph Kasavubu, long a prominent African in the Congo, became president of the country with rather uncertain powers of appointment and censure. Given Kasavubu's political rivalry with Lumumba, the struggle over these powers would prove the undoing of the country's constitution.

Less than a week after independence was granted, Congolese troops rebelled against their Belgian officers who had remained in transition. A short time later, groups of angry soldiers began brutally harassing Belgian expatriates in an effort to humiliate them (Young 1965, 321). This prompted the Belgian government to request direct military intervention to protect its nationals. Although this action was not opposed by Lumumba, it led to a severing of diplomatic ties between the two nations. The mineral-rich province of Katanga declared its independence under the leadership of Moise Tshombe. Belgian troops openly supported Tshombe's government and encouraged the recruitment of foreign mercenaries, much to the chagrin of Lumumba, who contacted Nikita Khrushchev after breaking with Brussels. By this point, 80,000 Belgians had fled and most of the country was in disarray.

It was in this context that Lumumba petitioned the UN to intervene in support of his country's territorial integrity and unity. Secretary General Dag Hammarskjold strongly endorsed UN intervention and used his powers of persuasion to obtain Security Council approval for the deployment of peacekeepers (Franck 1985, 124). Within two weeks of independence, UN troops were deployed into the Congo under the auspices of UN Operation in the Congo (ONUC) and charged with the task of restoring public safety and political stability. In the beginning, UN forces refrained from taking sides in the Katanga rebellion and merely acted to prevent bloodshed. As the crisis wore on, however, the UN found this position increasingly untenable. In fact, Hammarskjold interpreted ONUC's mandate very broadly, and by the end of the crisis the UN troops were actively engaging secessionist forces.

In September 1960, Kasavubu revoked Lumumba's authority as prime minister and appointed Joseph Ileo in his stead. Meanwhile, Lumumba revoked Kasavubu's authority, while himself under house arrest (Young 1965, 328). The legal wrangle that ensued was finally resolved when Mobutu Sese Seko, a military commander, suspended the constitution in a coup d'état. The parliament was suspended, and Ileo left his position on an interim basis. Lumumba's forces organized a rival Congolese government based in the northeast around the person of Antoine Gizenga. When the Kisai region in central Congo declared its independence in mid-1960, the country could count four different governments. This chaotic state of affairs continued for roughly a year while the UN struggled with the issue of which government to support.

The Congo's politics became more coherent in August 1961, when the leaders of the major rival governments (Tshombe excepted) settled on a compromise candidate for prime minister. Cyrille Adoula, former minister of the interior under Kasavubu, received unanimous approval. The initial effort at reunification of the country was centered on the Gizenga regime. Lumumba was assassinated in February and Gizenga himself was arrested in January 1962. With Kisai's forced and bloody reentry into the Leopoldville-centered regime, the country was left with only one outstanding conflict (Young 1965, 338).

The role of the UN dramatically expanded during 1962 and 1963 as officials on the ground engaged in frequent, if largely fruitless, negotiations with the Tshombe regime. The Security Council approved Hammarskjold's request for expanded authority, and the ONUC went on the offensive against the Katanga rebels. Operation Rumpunch in August netted hundreds of foreign mercenaries who were deported (O'Brien 1962, 220).

Tshombe sued for peace, only to break yet another truce once his forces had regrouped. During the middle of these difficult times, Hammarskjold himself intervened in the negotiations by flying to meet with Tshombe. His plane was shot down by Katangan forces and crashed into a mountain (at the time it was thought the crash was accidental).

Tshombe eventually accepted the terms for reintegration into the Congo proposed by Adoula, but later he violated the agreement. The new UN Secretary General, U Thant, proposed still other terms, which were again accepted—and broken. It wasn't until UN forces were successful in capturing key military and government installations in Katanga that Tshombe finally called off the rebellion in January 1963 (Young 1965, 343). The ONUC was withdrawn as quickly as possible thereafter.

The Congo continued to experience profound political instability for many years. Constitutional government was abandoned following another coup d'état by Mobutu in 1965, which set in place the most corrupt African regime in modern history. In the newly renamed Zaire, Mobutu undertook systematic pillaging and self-aggrandizement that defy description. Analysts have been forced to place the regime in an entirely new category of political phenomenon: the "cleptocracy" (Callaghy 1984). Mobutu was eventually overthrown in 1997 by Laurent Kabila, following which the country was renamed the Democratic Republic of Congo. It has continued to experience widespread unrest and numerous border clashes.

Conclusion: Colonialism and Independence

If few generalizations can be drawn from these cases, it is by design. It is difficult to predict how an independence movement will come into being, how it will make its demands on the established colonial administration, and what the outcome will be. In Algeria and the Congo, overzealousness to retain and/or relinquish the colony proved disastrous to a future of constitutional democracy. In Tanzania, the presence of one man played an extraordinarily important role—an accident of history, perhaps. It is difficult to identify the ingredients necessary for successful separation from a mother country.

An important issue for all newly independent countries is how to establish both administrative services and political legitimacy so as to develop a relationship of trust and responsibility with the society at large. Where democratic institutions were already in place, as in Tanzania, this process was greatly facilitated. Where unifying ideologies existed, as in Algeria, success was more likely. But where the idea of nationhood was a largely artificial construct, as in the Congo (and perhaps in all African states), the task was made more difficult. At this point, in many African nations, legitimacy—the belief that the government has a right to govern—is seriously in question. From the Congo to Somalia, where at the time of writing there simply was no government, the average citizen wonders whether there is a central government or simply an aristocratic elite that enjoys international recognition.

Debate Topic

Would Africans be better off under a new form of colonialism?

PRO

This controversial proposal has a few advocates, who make the following points: (1) Although colonialism may have been wrong, independence has proved even more devastating to the people of Africa. Western states have the obligation to take responsibility for the situation by becoming directly involved in African governance. (2) Many African leaders do not promote either development or human rights, while many Western leaders have worked diligently to improve living conditions in former colonies. (3) African leaders do not have the resources to build up their countries, while Western, developed states do.

CON

The mainstream position holds that independence is worth preserving: (1) Self-determination is one of the cardinal rules of international politics, and it cannot be set aside simply because some people disapprove of how a country is governed. (2) The West can provide the resources and support to alleviate much of the pain in Africa without reasserting direct control. (3) African leaders have scored many great victories and deserve a chance to succeed.

Questions to Consider

1. Why was statehood an important goal for the Algerians, Tanzanians, and Zairians? What did they hope to accomplish by achieving this goal? Did statehood bring peace or prosperity to the people of Algeria, Tanzania, and Zaire?

2. Who really wanted statehood? Who benefited most from statehood? Were there secessionist tendencies in the new states? Did the subnational groups achieve statehood?

. What role did diplomacy play in the quest for statehood? Did international organizations, diplomatic conferences, or great powers intervene to grant recognition at crucial times?

Websites

Africa chronology: **www.campus.northpark.edu/history/WebChron/Africa/Africa. html**

British Empire historical archives: **landow.stg.brown.edu/victorian/history/empire/empireov.html**

The Africa Summit (nonprofit organization): **www.africasummit.org**

References

Bennett, A. LeRoy. *International Organizations: Principles & Issues* (Englewood Cliffs, NJ: Prentice-Hall, 1991).

Callaghy, Thomas. *The State-Society Struggle: Zaire in Comparative Perspective* (New York: Columbia University Press, 1984).

Franck, Thomas M. *Nation Against Nation: What Happened to the U.N. Dream and What the U.S. Can Do About It* (New York: Oxford University Press, 1985).

Hargreaves, John D. *Decolonization in Africa* (New York: Longman, 1988).

Hatch, John. *Tanzania: A Profile* (New York: Preager, 1972).

Horne, Alistair. *A Savage War of Peace: Algeria 1954–1962*, rev. ed. (New York: Penguin Books, 1987).

O'Brien, Conor C. *To Katanga and Back: A UN Case History* (New York: Simon & Schuster, 1962).

Oliver, Ronald, and Michael Crowder, eds. *The Cambridge Encyclopedia of Africa* (New York: Cambridge University Press, 1981).

Oliver, Ronald, and J. D. Page. *A Short History of Africa* (New York: Facts on File, 1988).

Taylor, J. Clagett. *The Political Development of Tanganyika* (Stanford, CA: Stanford University Press, 1963).

Tlemcani, Rachid. *State and Revolution in Algeria* (Boulder, CO: Westview Press, 1986).

Yeager, Ridger. *Tanzania: An African Experiment* (Boulder, CO: Westview Press, 1982).

Young, Crawford. *Politics in the Congo: Decolonization and Independence* (Princeton, NJ: Princeton University Press, 1965).

CASE
14

Apartheid in South Africa
HUMAN RIGHTS

Introduction

"Inalienable rights," a notion fundamental to the American system, means that people enjoy certain privileges simply by virtue of being human, and no government has the right to take those privileges away. Where the rights originated matters little; "inalienable" means that they came before governments were ever established. When we speak of "human rights" in international affairs, we are generally referring to those inalienable rights. They include not only the familiar freedom of speech, freedom from slavery and discrimination, and the right to participate in public life, but also rights with unique importance on the global level: self-determination, prohibition against genocide, and the right to peace. Over time, a consensus has developed on these and still other economic and social rights, such that countries that routinely and wantonly violate them are frequently the object of international censure.

This consensus has been expressed in the form of several important documents, the most celebrated of which is the Universal Declaration of Human Rights. This statement (not a binding law) was drafted shortly after World War II by representatives of more than fifty countries under the leadership of Eleanor Roosevelt, Franklin Roosevelt's widow. In it, governments agree that such fundamental civil rights as freedom of speech, thought, and assembly are paramount and that no government should restrict them without a strong public purpose. The document also declares that democracy and all its ancillary characteristics (elections, a free press, due process in the courtroom, and so forth) are the ideal form of government. The document further urges states to attend to the economic, social, and physical needs of their citizens, and it declares that all people have a right to such things as an education, housing, food, and employment.

Over the years, the rights enumerated in the Universal Declaration have been expanded upon and made more binding, such that today governments have gone so far as to intervene militarily to overthrow regimes that have repeatedly violated fundamental human rights in egregious ways (see Case 10). At the very least, many governments that have violated basic human rights have been subjected to diplomatic and economic penalties and sanctions. South Africans understand this relationship better than most.

> Either the white man dominates or the black man takes over. I say that the non-European will not accept leadership—if he has a choice. The only way the Europeans can maintain supremacy is by domination. . . . And the only way they can maintain domination is by withholding the vote from the non-Europeans. (Dr. Daniel F. Malan, South African Prime Minister, 1948–1954)

> We, the people of South Africa, declare for all our country and the world to know that South Africa belongs to all who live in it, black and white, and that no government can justly claim authority unless it is based on the will of all the people . . . that only a democratic state based on the will of all the people can secure their birthright without distinction of colour, race, sex or belief . . . . (Freedom Charter of the African National Congress, 1955)

These two quotes present the essence of the struggle in South Africa. Unlike the civil rights movement in the United States, South Africa pitted a minority in power against an overwhelming but largely powerless majority. That minority controlled most of the wealth, schools, businesses, and property of the country against the will of the majority. Moreover, that minority became more and more determined, during the middle part of this century, to maintain not only its power but also its exclusive right to citizenship in an ever more narrowly defined state.

Many misconceptions exist about the nature of apartheid, the policy of separation of the races in South Africa. Furthermore, there is much ignorance about the origins and basis for this national policy. Although the history that follows is extremely brief, we hope it will shed some light on this vital and burning issue of international politics.

APARTHEID IN SOUTH AFRICA
KEY FIGURES

Hendrik Verwoerd   Prime Minister of South Africa, 1958–1966. An avowed white supremacist, he was the principal architect of the apartheid laws.

P. W. Botha   Prime Minister of South Africa, 1979–1989. He began the process of dismantling the apartheid laws after imposing martial law.

F.nW. de Klerk   Prime Minister of South Africa, 1989–1994. He ended apartheid.

Daniel Malan   Prime Minister of South Africa, 1948–1954, and former Dutch Reformed Church minister.

Sol Plaatje   Founder of the African National Congress in 1912.   (continued)

Nelson Mandela   Leader of the African National Congress, he was imprisoned for 27 years under apartheid. He became the first president of post-apartheid South Africa, 1994–1999.

Steve Biko   Black Consciousness activist and founder of SASO. He was arrested and died in prison in 1976.

Mangasuthu Buthelezi   Ruler of the KwaZulu nation and leader of the Inkatha Party.

Walter Sisulu   A leader of the ANC.

Allan Boesak   Founder of the United Democratic Front in 1983.

Jan Smuts   Afrikaner general in the Boer War, and later political leader and Prime Minister of the Union (later Republic) of South Africa, 1919–1924.

Desmond Tutu   Roman Catholic Archbishop in South Africa. He fought apartheid and led the Truth and Reconciliation Commission under Mandela.

APARTHEID IN SOUTH AFRICA
CHRONOLOGY

1652
South African area is claimed and settled by Dutch.

1815
The British purchase the Cape Colony and establish a governmental presence. They begin discriminating against native African tribes and Dutch-born Boer settlers. A dispute leads to the killing of British troops and the hanging of their Boer attackers at Slachter's Nek.

1837
Thousands of Boers migrate inland in the beginning of the Great Trek.

1838
Piet Retief's Boers defeat a large Zulu army. Afrikaners see it as a sign of God's protection.

1867
Diamonds and other minerals are discovered in Kimberly.

1875
The first apartheid laws exclude blacks from diamond mine ownership. Later, they would exclude blacks from gold-mining profits in Johannesburg in the 1880s.

1899
British settlers under Alfred Milner begin a war to displace Afrikaners. The Boer War lasts until 1902, when Afrikaners surrender.

1910
The Union of South Africa under British dominance is formed.

1912
The African National Congress is formed to protect fast-eroding rights for nonwhites.

1918
Black workers strike and are arrested en masse.

1922
Two hundred Afrikaner miners were killed in government attempts to quell labor unrest.

(continued)

1924

Afrikaner politicians gain significant electoral victories, speeding up passage of antiblack legislation.

1936

Blacks are no longer allowed to vote.

1948

Afrikaners control the South African government for the first time. They issue a Declaration of Grand Apartheid.

1950s

The government of Prime Minister Daniel Malan passes a series of apartheid laws, including the Population Registration Act, the Separate Amenities Act, the Bantu Authorities Act, and the Prohibition of Mixed Marriages Act.

1952

The ANC leads a series of antiapartheid demonstrations that turn violent.

1955

The Freedom Charter is passed at the Congress of the People. Many ANC leaders are imprisoned

1960

The ANC is outlawed. A Pan-African Congress demonstration is suppressed in what is known as the Sharpeville Massacre.

1968

The South African Student Organization is founded by Steve Biko.

1973

The UN General Assembly passes the International Convention on the Suppression and Punishment of the Crime of Apartheid.

1976

Soweto riots result in 600 deaths. Steve Biko is killed while in police custody.

1977

The Sullivan principles are articulated, urging multinational corporations operating in South Africa to promote racial justice in the workplace.

1983

Outdoor meetings of blacks are banned.

1984

Two nonwhite national assemblies are created under a new constitution. Unrest in Sharpeville prompts the government to declare a state of emergency in 1985.

1985

Struggling under international economic sanctions, South African business leaders openly support the black franchise.

1987

Liberal whites form the National Democratic Movement in response to the increasingly hard-line attitude of the Afrikaner Conservative Party.

1989

P. W. Botha resigns the prime minister's post. F. W. de Klerk becomes prime minister and begins dismantling the apartheid laws.

1990

Nelson Mandela is released from prison after 27 years.   *(continued)*

1992

The ANC is fully legalized. CODESA begins planning a new constitution.

1993

CODESA produces a draft constitution that is accepted by the Parliament. Mandela and de Klerk win the Nobel Peace Prize.

1994

Nelson Mandela is elected president of South Africa.

1996

The New South African Constitution is formally signed into law by Nelson Mandela in Sharpeville.

1998

The Truth and Reconciliation Commission issues its final report.

1999

Thabo Mbeki is elected to succeed Mandela.

2002

South Africa hosts the United Nations Conference on Racism.

Origins of South Africa: 1652–1910

Beginning in the days of Magellan, the Cape of Good Hope was recognized as a useful waystation for travelers between Europe and India. The Dutch first decided in 1652 to establish a permanent claim and settlement under the leadership of Jan van Riebeeck. He almost immediately set about establishing a viable farming colony populated by "freeburghers" (pioneer farmers), which extended into the neighboring territory. Native black tribes opposed this encroachment, which prompted van Riebeeck to assert white superiority by force. Within fifty years, black slaves from other African territories were imported to expand the farming capacity of the colony (they are the ancestors of the modern-day "coloreds" in South Africa). "Thus he persuaded the company to take the four decisions that shaped South Africa: to found the colony, to settle freeburghers, to establish superiority over the local tribes and to import slaves" (Lapping 1986, 4).

By the end of the eighteenth century, the Dutch were unable to control overseas territories because they were under attack by Napoleon's France. The British first protected and then purchased the Cape Colony in 1815, dispatching a colonial administration to govern the settlement. They introduced "pass laws" for the first time, which obliged the nomadic African Khoikhoi to carry a written "pass" proving their association with a particular Dutch settler. The British presence was resented from the start by the now-independent Dutch settlers, or Boers ("farmers"), particularly when British administrators began issuing legal judgments in favor of native African tribesmen. In 1815, while carrying out an arrest order against several Boers, a British detachment was attacked. The offending Boers were arrested and later hanged at Slachter's Nek—an event that served as a symbol of British authoritarianism (Lapping 1986, 10).

British officialdom became ever more ubiquitous as English-speaking missionaries attempted to establish schools for both Afrikaner (descendants of Dutch settlers) and black children. Ultimately, the Boers decided that they could no longer tolerate the imposition of British culture and power, and they embarked on one of the great migrations of people in history: the Great Trek. In 1837, some 6,000 Afrikaners began moving both eastward along the coast and some 800 miles northward into largely unpopulated wilderness to found a new homeland for themselves. The principal concentrations were in the area south of the current city of Johannesburg in the Orange Free State and along the coast near modern-day Durban in Natal province. By 1854, some 10,000 Afrikaners and an equal number of colored and black servants had migrated from Cape Colony toward what would become the heart of South Africa.

White South African propaganda maintains that the Boers arrived in an unpopulated territory where blacks later migrated (in part drawn by the prosperity of the whites) (Republic of South Africa 1973, 10). In fact, not only does ample archaeological evidence reveal a substantial African presence before the Great Trek, but the Zulu nation under Shaka Zulu had already advanced far into the same territory and engaged in several bloody skirmishes with the advancing Boers. The most famous skirmish involved trekker Piet Retief who, after being tricked by a Zulu interpreter, was cornered along with his pioneers by several thousand Zulu warriors on December 15, 1838. By virtue of their position against a mountain pass, the Boers were able to protect their rear and face the Zulus with overwhelming firepower. While 3,000 Zulus were killed, not a single Boer perished. Many Afrikaners attribute the Boers' success to a covenant with God entered into the day before, offering Afrikaner devotion and piety in exchange for victory (Lapping 1986, 16). (They also promised to build a church, which was later converted to a stable.)

The Boers eked out a living during the first years after their trek, but in 1867 mineral discoveries began to rapidly alter the character of their nation. Rapid population growth following the discovery of diamonds in Kimberly, in the western Orange Free State, overwhelmed the underequipped British authorities, who quickly moved in en masse to administer the territory. Famous explorers, financiers, and speculators from across the empire converged on the area and made easy fortunes. Cecil Rhodes became one of the richest men in the world by purchasing numerous apparently dry wells from impatient excavators—the holes actually contained billions of dollars worth of diamonds.

Within ten years, the British government, with Afrikaner urging, established race-based laws to govern the ownership of diamond mines. As put by Brown: "The momentous step in the development of apartheid occurred in 1867 when diamonds were discovered along the Orange and Vaal rivers. . . .

[I]n 1875 the right to own and operate a diamond concession was permitted only to whites" (Brown 1981, 59). From 1875 on, the blacks of South Africa were effectively excluded from profiting from the most promising opportunity to come to the African continent until the oil strikes in Libya. Instead, they were relegated to the status of mere laborers. The same was true for gold mining after it started around Johannesburg in 1880.

A radical interpretation does not seem out of place:

> Whenever superior races settle on lands where lower races can be profitably used for manual labour in agriculture, mining and domestic work, the latter do not tend to die out, but to form a servile class. This is the case, not only in tropical countries where white men cannot form real colonies, working and rearing families with safety and efficiency, and where hard manual work, if done at all, must be done by "coloured men," but even in countries where white men can settle, as in part of South Africa and of the southern portion of the United States. (Hobson 1965, 258, in Magubane 1979, 8)

As further explained by Magubane:

> South Africa is not a plural society; it is a society with a dual labor market: a primary (white) market of relatively secure, well-paid jobs, and a secondary (black) market of insecure, filthy, low-paid jobs. African workers are confined to a marginal, yet indispensable, role by fraud, violence, and a system of institutionalized racism that protects "the white masters of the world." (Magubane 1979, 17)

As the end of the century neared, the struggle for control of gold and diamonds in the heart of South Africa continued to intensify. Although the British were able to establish clear control in the Kimberly area, Afrikaners held out in the Orange Free State and farther to the north in the Transvaal, where the plucky Boer Paul Kruger retained control in 1899 after three abortive British seizures. In 1899, a new British governor, Alfred Milner, embarked on a systematic, all-out effort to dislodge the independent Afrikaners from the Transvaal and elsewhere in the north by deploying a large British army into the region. The Boer War that ensued lasted nearly three years and caused tens of thousands of casualties. In particular, the British introduced "concentration camps" by capturing thousands of women and children and interring them in tent cities across the region, where disease and malnutrition took some 26,000 civilian lives. In the countryside, the British practiced a "scorched earth" policy to deprive the Boer guerrillas of finding sustenance from the land (Lapping 1986, 31).

After the Boers finally surrendered in 1902, the British moved to consolidate their gains by inviting more British settlers into the country and establishing a united federal state with the consent of the Afrikaners in the Transvaal and the Orange Free State (a form of expansive home rule tantamount to independence was offered as an inducement). A new generation of Afrikaner politicians, led by Jan Smuts and Louis Botha, embraced the British offers. In 1910, the Union of South Africa was proclaimed a part of the British Empire.

Establishment and Consolidation of Apartheid: 1910–1965

Part of the deal made with the Afrikaners involved British concessions on social policy. A series of race-related laws guaranteeing Afrikaner superiority was implemented in the 1910s. Before discussing the details of these and other laws, we will look at the philosophy and social norms that undergird apartheid.

The Afrikaners held that their presence in South Africa was more than merely a coincidence of human migration—rather it was the product of divine intervention on behalf of the white race. Dr. Daniel Malan, prime minister in 1948–1954 and former Dutch Reformed Church minister, declared:

> We hold this nationhood as our due, for it was given us by the architect of the universe. His aim was the formation of a new nation. The last hundred years have witnessed a miracle behind which must lie a divine plan. Afrikanerdom is not the work of men but the creation of God. . . . Not because we Afrikaners are tremendously good people, but because God, the Disposer of the lot of the nations, has a future task for our People. (Lapping 1986, 66)

From this perspective, Afrikaner tribulations represent the punishments of a just and loving God working for their betterment. Their separate development from the Africans is required not only for economic reasons but also to preserve the white race. By the 1940s, it was difficult to distinguish Afrikaners' talk of their destiny from the anti-Jewish rhetoric of the Nazis in Germany. Malan "made the attempt with as ambitious—or ridiculous—a claim as any politician has ever made: that God's destiny for the Afrikaner people, the reason he had chosen them, punished them, saved them, was to preserve the white race" (Lapping 1986, 71).

For many years after apartheid had become established, the South African government justified the policy not just on religious but also on human rights grounds:

> A policy designed to avoid group conflicts cannot be said to run counter to civilized conceptions of human rights, dignities and freedoms, irrespective of race, colour or creed. On the contrary, the Government's fundamental aim with self-determination for all the country's peoples is the elimination of the domination of one group by another. . . . The principle of self-determination to which the Government is committed, leaves the way open for each population group eventually to make its own choice regarding its political future. (Brown 1981, 74)

To the extent that either the religious or the human rights argument was accepted, there could be little room for negotiation or compromise.

Shortly after the consolidation of the republic, the Transvaal and Orange Free State enacted a number of restrictive racial policies. In particular, new pass laws forced blacks, "coloreds", and a growing Indian immigrant population to carry identification cards at all times. Failure to produce the pass when confronted by a police officer typically resulted in incarceration. Controls on physical movement were combined with continued restrictions on property ownership, and severe limitations on nonwhite suffrage prompted protests and petitions by certain educated blacks, four of whom formed the African National Congress (ANC) in 1912. These Africans asked little more than a retention of certain rights they had been granted prior to 1910 as British subjects. They failed to get a hearing with the king when they traveled to London in 1913 under the leadership of Sol Plaatje. In the meantime, the Native Lands Act, which the ANC had warned against in London, passed, thereby creating a system of reservations for blacks—some 7.3 percent of South Africa's poorest land was designated for the more than 60 percent of the population that was black. Rather than alienate the newly pacified Afrikaners, the monarchy and Parliament in London refused to reverse the policy. When World War I broke out, the ANC leaders pledged the support of Africans for the British war effort in the hopes of obtaining rights on the basis of being veterans and loyal subjects, even though they knew this would alienate the generally pro-German Boers.

An important parallel development occurred in the Indian community, where Mohandes Gandhi, the advocate of nonviolent resistance and future leader of India, organized a series of demonstrations against pass laws and property restrictions. Although for a time he was successful in securing a softening of pass law enforcement, the effort was fairly short-lived (Lapping 1986, 49).

In the 1920s and 1930s, relations among Africans, Afrikaners, and the English deteriorated. Black worker strikes in 1918, born of frustration with the failure of the ANC accommodation, led to massive arrests. The ANC was shaken by the reversal and for the next twenty years drifted almost leaderless. Meanwhile, the Afrikaner workers protested and struck over the limited promotions some black mine workers received (some whites were passed over by British managers), and in 1922 Prime Minister Jan Smuts ordered troops to quell the disturbance. Some 200 Afrikaner miners were killed in the ensuing action. The event led to an electoral victory for pro-Afrikaner militants in 1924, which in turn led to strengthened white worker rights and eventual removal of the limited black electoral franchise by 1936.

Black workers began to adopt an increasingly militant style in the 1940s. By 1944, Anton Lembede had organized the Youth League, loosely affiliated with the ANC, and began training what would become the next generation of ANC leadership: Nelson Mandela, Walter Sisulu, and Oliver Tambo (Lapping 1986, 82). They adopted a more consciously pro-black, anticapitalist philosophy and urged violence and widespread action against the white government.

A variety of conservative Afrikaner politicians felt that their time had finally come in the 1930s. They latched onto the misery of the Depression with its attendant anti-British and anti-Jew fearfulness and the symbolism surrounding the centennial of the Great Trek to catapult themselves into power in the 1948 elections—the first to produce an all-Afrikaner cabinet. The importance of the 1948 election cannot be exaggerated. At the same time the United States was working to desegregate the military, schools, and all public facilities, the Afrikaner government in South Africa embarked on a program to introduce and intensify racial separation. In 1950, Prime Minister Malan appointed Dr. Hendrik F. Verwoerd minister of native affairs. Verwoerd, in this position and later as prime minister until his assassination in 1966, was the single most important architect of apartheid (Lapping 1986, 106).

Verwoerd's legislative strategy displayed a systematic approach to separation of the races. The Population Registration Act set out to classify every resident of South Africa by race. It then "empowered the government to mark off areas for residence, occupation and trade by the different races and then to move each race into its own area, by force if necessary" (Lapping 1986, 105). Some 100,000 disputed their racial classification, which was based on "appearance, general acceptance and repute" (Omond 1985, 22). This basic classification was refined and clarified over the years, although as recently as 1985, nearly 800 people had their racial classifications legally changed. The Prohibition of Mixed Marriages Act ensured racial purity in mainstream family relations, while the Immorality Amendment Act of 1957 outlawed any intercourse whatever between individuals of different races.

Verwoerd was famous for his promotion of the status and symbolic powers of black tribal leaders across South Africa. He promoted himself as the great "Bantu" (Native African) chief of chiefs and joined the tribal leaders in elaborate ceremonies reaffirming their legitimacy as rulers of black nations. The South African government began to emphasize differences among the various black tribes:

> In a nutshell, the inescapable feature of the South African situation is that South Africa is a country of many nations: Four million whites of European origin, four million Xhosa, four million Zulu, two million Tswana, two million Sotho and so on. Each group is a minority—there is in fact no single majority group. (Republic of South Africa 1973, 29)

Verwoerd hoped to accomplish the dual goal of undermining black solidarity and creating a vast network of black supporters of the white Pretoria regime. In this context, the Bantu Authorities Act of 1951 designated specific homelands for each of ten major African tribes that resided in South Africa (see Map 14.1). Regardless of where members of these various tribes happened to be living at the time, the government expected that they would migrate to their areas and away from white cities: "The Bantu in the cities are not distinct from the Bantu in the Native Reserves. . . . Their roots are in the Native Reserves. The opportunities for them to enjoy rights, whether they be social or political rights, are available in their home areas" (Lapping 1986, 113). In these territories, the black leaders were permitted control of certain governmental functions (subsidized often to the tune of 75 percent of their budgets by Pretoria) and "tribal citizens" could exercise their right to vote. South African citizenship was denied, however. In the late 1960s, a few of these homelands were granted independence by the Pretoria government (Transkei in 1976, Bophuthatswana in 1977, Venda in 1979, and Ciskei in

Map 14.1   The Homelands
Source: Anthony Lemon, *Apartheid in Transition* (Boulder, CO: Westview Press, 1987).

1981), although this move did little to change their government other than reinforce the separate legal status of homelands residents. As put by one of Verwoerd's successors in a speech before Parliament:

> If our policy is taken to its logical conclusion as far as the black people are concerned, there will not be one black man with South African citizenship. . . . Every black man in South Africa will eventually be accommodated in some independent new state in this honourable way and there will no longer be a moral obligation on this parliament to accommodate these people politically. (Omond 1985, 102)

In this context, Verwoerd argued that education was to be strictly controlled and segregated:

> Native education should be controlled in such a way that it should be in accord with the policy of the state. . . . If the native in South Africa today in any kind of

school in existence is being taught to expect that he will live his adult life under a policy of equal rights, he is making a big mistake. . . . There is no place for him in the European community above the level of certain forms of labor. (Omond 1985, 80)

Lemon has pointed out that South Africa is one of the only countries where the educational system for a majority of its citizens is specifically designed to restrict, rather than create, opportunities by limiting them to a homeland-specific training (Lemon 1987, 52). This policy was later extended to the university level.

In the homelands, medical services, agrarian support, infrastructure development, and the like were severely limited. The total welfare support for all blacks in the homelands was less than half that provided to the minority whites, who were at any rate relatively affluent and protected by private forms of insurance (Omond 1985, 67). In general terms, living conditions for blacks were deplorable, so the government had to adopt very aggressive measures to force as many Africans as possible to relocate to their respective homelands.

Verwoerd pressed forward with relocating blacks from white neighborhoods in Johannesburg and Pretoria. Over a five-year period, many thousands of blacks were moved out of white neighborhoods. The elderly and infirm were specifically targeted for removal. As put by one of Verwoerd's successors in 1967:

It is accepted government policy that the Bantu are only temporarily resident in the European areas of the Republic for as long as they offer their labour there. As soon as they become, for one reason or another, no longer fit to work or superfluous in the labour market, they are expected to return to their country of origin or the territory of the national unit where they fit ethnically. (Lapping 1986, 154)

By 1980, roughly half of black Africans were residing in the Bantustans—the end result of thirty years of government effort (Lemon 1987, 199). Estimates indicated that as many as 3.5 million people were relocated in connection with the Native Lands Act during the 1980s, with another 1.8 million being vulnerable to future expulsion (Omond 1985, 114).

At the same time that the government worked to deport as many blacks as possible from the more restricted territory of white South Africa, actions were taken to remove other nonwhites from white neighborhoods in major cities. "Townships" near Johannesburg, Port Elizabeth, and other towns were created in the 1950s to eliminate "black spots" (integrated neighborhoods). A variety of laws, including restricted property rights, intensified pass laws, and the Separate Amenities Act of 1953, which prohibited multiracial use of public facilities, were passed and enforced with great vigor. Once these townships were formed, blacks who were productive laborers were "encouraged" to migrate in much the same way that the less productive were encouraged to migrate to the homelands and Bantustans. For example, Sophiatown, a Johannesburg neighborhood of 58,000, was entirely emptied over a five-year period in the 1950s—first through inducements, then by intimidation, and finally with force (Lapping 1986, 119).

These actions created a large migrant worker population in South Africa. The mere relocation of workers did little to spur the relocation of the workplace. In 1970, some 1 million blacks were forced to migrate to work. That figure had increased to 1.4 million by 1982 (Lemon 1987, 199). Such an imposed lifestyle wreaked havoc on the black family:

> From the standpoint of the homelands and their people, the economic and social disadvantages of the migrant labour system are overwhelming. Socially, the break-up of family life and impediments to normal sexual relationships affect some of the most basic human needs . . . illegitimacy, bigamy, prostitution, homosexuality, drunkenness, violence and the breakdown of parental authority [are] direct effects of the system, whilst venereal disease, tuberculosis, malnutrition and beriberi are some of the indirect results of the lifestyle of migrant laborers. Men are degraded by a system which deprives them of a family role, whilst women are left behind feeling lonely and helpless, anxiously waiting for letters and money from their husbands. (Lemon 1987, 200)

The migration pattern resulted in an indirect subsidy to white areas by the homelands. Some 80 percent of migrant workers' incomes were spent in white neighborhoods. Migrant workers were paid less than comparable white labor on the grounds that black workers did not need to pay for family housing. And although blacks continually increased their skills over the course of their careers, promotions were forbidden so that business owners could use increasingly more efficient labor without paying the price. The Native Labour Act of 1953 also prevented blacks from organizing labor unions, declaring that no black could be classified as an "employee" (Omond 1985, 90).

Not all blacks accepted the new order passively or sought to take advantage of it for their own aggrandizement. The ANC attracted an increasingly diverse assortment of followers—coloreds, Indians, Communists, academics—with a leadership under growing pressure to radicalize the movement. Albert Luthuli, ANC leader in the 1950s, was cautious about radical demands and worked to keep the ANC legal and able to work with the government. In 1952, the ANC initiated what was expected to be a series of peaceful demonstrations and civil disobedience gestures as part of this moderate approach. The campaign degenerated into a series of melees between police and passersby untrained in nonviolent techniques. The government cracked down on ANC leaders, restricting their travel to their own neighborhoods. Although the ANC consequently lost stature with the government, its membership grew from a mere 7,000 to some 100,000 (Lapping 1986, 119).

In 1955, through the efforts of new ANC members working as messengers and organizers, and in spite of warnings of police intervention, the organization held a momentous Congress of the People to protest apartheid laws and draft a plan of action. The Freedom Charter was the result of the Congress's desire for a democratic, multiracial South Africa. In addition to civil rights, the Freedom Charter called for land reform, labor rights, and redistribution of wealth to "the people as a whole." It represented the most radical and united statement by blacks in South Africa's history and became a rallying cry for all opponents of apartheid. Beyond South Africa's borders, nations began to take notice. The government of India repeatedly raised the question of apartheid at the United Nations until UN condemnation of this social system became one of the strongest bonds of developing countries' solidarity.

The South African government, dismayed at the apparent power of the ANC as an alternative political order, responded ferociously. The leaders of the ANC were declared traitors to the state and were imprisoned. As a direct consequence, the world's attention was drawn even more sharply to the plight of blacks in South Africa. Newspaper accounts sympathetic to the government flowed from Pretoria even as contributions from around the world flowed into the ANC's accounts. A lengthy and bitter trial ensued under the glaring eye of international public opinion. The government's prosecutor bungled the charges of treason and Communist sympathies, instead creating ideal opportunities for the ANC leaders to make their own case publicly, clearly, and eloquently. Nelson Mandela presented himself as the indignant lawyer and future leader of the ANC with this scathing attack on the legitimacy of the proceedings:

> Firstly, I challenge it because I fear that I will not be given a fair and proper trial. Secondly, I consider myself neither legally nor morally bound to obey laws made by a parliament in which I have no representation. In a political trial such as this one, which involves a clash of the aspirations of the African people and those of whites, the country's courts, as presently constituted, cannot be impartial and fair. In such cases, whites are interested parties. To have a white judicial officer presiding, however high his esteem, and however strong his sense of fairness and justice, is to make whites judges in their own case. . . . The white man makes all the laws, he drags us before his courts and accuses us, and he sits in judgment over us. . . . I feel oppressed by the atmosphere of white domination that lurks all around in this courtroom. Somehow this atmosphere calls to mind the inhuman injustices caused to my people outside this courtroom by this same white domination. (Mandela 1990, 134)

In the end, all of the accused were acquitted, primarily because of prosecutorial incompetence.

Having failed to achieve its goal through the use of laws then on the books, the government, now under Verwoerd himself, adopted new laws. The ANC was included among outlaw organizations under the 1960 Unlawful Organization Act. By 1963, such prominent ANC leaders as Walter Sisulu, Nelson Mandela, Robert Sobukwe, and Oliver Tambo were imprisoned or forced into exile, along with some 14,000 other blacks who had demonstrated in Sharpeville and participated in bombing and sabotage under the rubric of "Umkonto"—an underground vigilante group. These leaders would not see freedom for a quarter of a century.

The 1960 Sharpeville Massacre was a case of police impatience. The Pan-African Congress, a black organization with more radical objectives than the ANC, organized a demonstration of 5,000 people in what was thought to be a model township. However, unemployment, dissatisfaction with the pass laws, and forced migration had created intense hostility with the white government. The marchers surrounded a police station, where they waited for most of the day. Then a scuffle broke out, the crowd surged forward, and the police began shooting into the throng. Nearly 100 blacks were killed—most of them in the back—in the ensuing chaos. Luthuli called for a day of work stoppage and peaceful protest, which the government in turn repressed by arresting 18,000 strikers across the country. New laws permitted the government to detain suspects indefinitely with a judge's approval and to detain for interrogation anyone the police wanted. The Public Safety Act allowed the government to declare a state of emergency and thereby suspend most of the few remaining civil rights in specific areas for limited but renewable periods of time (Omond 1985, 158). By 1963, South Africa was reviled in international circles as the worst human rights violator on the planet.

Stalemate: 1965–1988

The period from 1965 to 1988 can be described as a stalemate between a galvanized but largely leaderless black community and an increasingly ambivalent white government unable to maintain both social domination and economic prosperity. The inflexible apartheid of the Verwoerd era was inherently unstable. While it protected the white population from association with blacks, it deprived the nation of its most important asset: black labor and intellect. At best, black Africans were learning to manipulate the system for their own ends—hardly the basis for legitimate government (Lambley 1980, 125). Even more serious was the impact of increasingly strict international economic and diplomatic sanctions on the vitality of the South African economy. These objective conditions would ultimately force the white government to reverse most of apartheid's structures during the 1980s and begin the process of democratizing the country in the 1990s.

A leaderless black community drifted for much of the 1960s, when new philosophies and organizational structures began to emerge. Steve Biko, a black medical student in Natal province, having failed to convince the white leaders of multiracial student organizations of the need for greater black participation and influence, worked to form an all-black student group known as the South African Student Organization in 1968. Steve Biko put it eloquently:

> Black Consciousness is an attitude of mind and a way of life. . . . Its essence is the realization by the black man of the need to rally together with his brothers around the cause of their oppression—the blackness of their skin—and to operate as a group to rid themselves of the shackles that bind them to perpetual servitude. It is based on a self-examination which has ultimately led them to believe that by seeking to run away from themselves and emulate the white man, they are insulting the intelligence of whoever created them black. This philosophy of Black Consciousness therefore expresses group pride and the determination of the black to rise and attain the envisaged self. . . . (Fatton 1986, 78)

In the context of the spread of this Black Consciousness movement, black students across South Africa protested their forced education in Afrikans in the 1970s. In Soweto, an overcrowded township near Johannesburg where many black intellectuals resided, feelings were particularly strong and spilled over into large demonstrations. In June 1976, protests swelled to involve tens of thousands. Police fired into the crowd, which then went on a rampage through neighboring black and white areas for several days. In the end, nearly 600 black protesters were killed and some 3,000 wounded. The police incarcerated and beat numerous individuals, not the least of whom was Steve Biko himself, who died following police beatings. As explained by Lapping, "Steve Biko's death may have been no worse than several dozen others. It was merely the one that attracted world attention and can therefore be described in most detail. Biko was never found guilty of any crime, never arrested for inciting violence, never accused of it" (Lapping 1986, 160).

Government repression intensified even as leaders of the Nationalist Party, which ruled South Africa for most of the century, began to reconsider the long-term viability of apartheid. Executions of blacks increased from roughly 50 each year in the mid-1970s to 125 per year in 1977–1980 (Omond 1985, 144). Outdoor meetings were banned selectively at first and then outright in 1983. Declarations of states of emergency became more common and travel restrictions intensified. The border with radical black African neighboring states became a virtual war zone, complete with intensive patrols, periodic incursions against ANC members in exile, and strictly enforced prohibitions against foreign aid to what had by 1978 become an openly militarized outlaw ANC.

The new prime minister, P. W. Botha, began to seriously consider relaxing apartheid laws as early as 1979 in the face of growing opposition in the South African business community. Business leaders pointed out that the economy would thrive best if the work force—largely black—was stable and content (100 strikes in 1979 steadily increasing to 1,000 strikes in 1989 proved otherwise—ILO 1990, 31) and if blacks could become affluent enough to provide a market for goods made in South Africa (St. Jorre 1986, 63). Foreign firms operating in compliance with the voluntary pro–civil rights standard known as the "Sullivan principles" were proving that a policy of racial equality in the workplace could increase both productivity and profitability.

The hope that traditional tribal leaders could undermine black support for the ANC proved entirely baseless. Even the practice of recruiting blacks to serve in the police force and township government backfired; black officials became targets of black hatred rather than legitimate representatives to their communities. Much of the black-on-black violence that occurred in the 1980s was the result of the failure of these government efforts at cooptation. Some form of democratic participation was clearly in the offing, even as the police, soon to be joined by the military, intensified their enforcement of old apartheid laws.

In the early 1980s, several regulations were passed that loosened some of the more "purely irritating" aspects of apartheid, including the laws against interracial marriage. The number of blacks admitted to white universities increased, restrictions on black job advancement relaxed, and pass laws became more permissive (Omond 1985, 47, 85). In 1984, a new constitution provided for the election of two new nonwhite assemblies—one for Indians and one for coloreds. The government hoped that even if its chances of gaining support from blacks (who were still legally attached to their homelands rather than to Pretoria) were remote, it might secure the backing of other racial groups in an effort to legitimate white rule. Indians and coloreds stayed away from the polls in large numbers (only 10 to 15 percent of those eligible voted). Reverend Allan Boesak of the newly formed United Democratic Front (UDF), a loose coalition of moderate antiapartheid organizations, warned prospective Indian voters in 1983:

> Working within the system for whatever reason contaminates you. It wears down your defenses. It whets your appetite for power. . . . And what you call "compromise" for the sake of politics is in fact selling out your principles, your ideals and the future of your children. . . . (Lapping 1986, 171)

Likewise, other moves toward relaxation of apartheid did little to satisfy blacks. The ANC continued to grow in popularity and strength, subsuming the Black Consciousness movement in 1984 and attracting the endorsement of even the United Democratic Front moderates (Brewer 1986, 274). By 1984, the black opposition was clearly divided into the staunchly antiapartheid ANC and the more conservative accommodationist tribal leaders, including especially the Inkatha Party under Zulu leader Buthelezi (who had entirely sold out, however). Beginning with more incidents in Sharpeville in 1984, South African blacks were plunged into a protracted and ugly struggle for power between these major factions. Even worse, the government actively instigated and bankrolled Inkatha fighters to provoke anti-ANC fighting (*Europa Yearbook* 1993, 2453).

In Sharpeville in 1984, black residents protested proposed rent and bus fare increases by targeting black administrators in the area. Violence spread rapidly as many collaborators were subjected to the "necklace" (a tire, doused in gasoline, placed around the victim's neck and set on fire). Unable to control the unrest, the government declared a state of emergency (particularly around Port Elizabeth) in July 1985 (Lemon 1987, 339). Eight thousand people were arrested in the first year and more than 750 killed by police and army forces. The army quickly gained a reputation for brutality by beating and electrocuting detainees on their way to prison. Children were specifically targeted during this period—many of them shot in the back while fleeing the soldiers. Children incarcerated under the state of emergency were, like their adult counterparts, subjected to torture, beating, terror, and often death (Lawyers 1986, 6–8). Efforts to have children receive medical treatment at hospitals were frustrated by the police practice of arresting any injured patients—thus many died without treatment after being shot during a demonstration. Likewise, attempts by physicians to reveal the extent of prison violence were halted by official cover-ups. The state of emergency was extended several times until it began to be lifted piecemeal in 1989 and 1990. Thirty more antiapartheid groups were banned, including the UDF, and some 50,000 individuals were detained from 1985 to 1988.

White South Africans were divided to the breaking point over the pace and direction of reform. Racist Afrikaners broke with the National Party to form the Conservative Party, which soon became the major opposition in Parliament and activated a latent vigilante organization—the Afrikaner Resistance Movement. Conservative Party leader Andries Treurnicht defiantly declared:

> People who think that Mr. Botha's "crossing of the Rubicon" and his abdication of white government mean the end of the Afrikaner and broader white nationalism are making a big mistake. We will not allow the Oppenheimers and American pressure groups to create a potpourri of people or to establish a nonracial economic empire upon the ruins of a white Christian culture and civilization. A people is only conquered when it has destroyed its own spirit. We are not prepared to consider national suicide . . . no one will silence the awakening white nation. The battle for the return of our political self-determination has only just begun. (Treurnicht 1986, 100)

Liberal white politicians increasingly coalesced around a collection of antiapartheid parties—particularly after the state of emergency began in 1985. This culminated in the formation of the National Democratic movement in 1987. Botha's political support was thus threatened from both the left and the right until in 1989 he felt compelled to resign his post. The National Party under his successor F. W. de Klerk won less than half of the popular vote that year, although it retained a majority of seats in Parliament.

The Botha government had worked simultaneously and feverishly to dismantle apartheid, hoping not only to placate the uncontrollable black demonstrators but also to lessen the ever-increasing international sanctions and business opposition, while stopping well short of granting Mandela's demand of legalization of the ANC and democratic elections (St. Jorre 1986, 81). As it turned out, nothing short of the complete elimination of apartheid would satisfy these various communities.

International sanctions intensified during the mid-1980s, including disinvestment by numerous foreign firms operating the country. By the end of the decade, some $12 billion in foreign investment had been withdrawn or sold to local investors (in soft local currency that was of no use in repaying mounting foreign debts). International banks, bending to pressure from institutional depositors and shareholders and universities, city governments, and pensions, began to impose conditions of political reform on debt rescheduling. By 1989, the net effect of these sanctions was that the South African economy, according to local independent estimates, was 15 percent smaller than it should have otherwise been. The World Bank downgraded South Africa's economic status from "upper middle income" to "lower middle income" (ILO 1990, 9).

To express their dismay in 1985, 91 South African business leaders took out an ad in the country's largest newspaper, calling for "the granting of full South African citizenship to all our people." Still others met with Walter Sisulu, leader-in-exile of the banned ANC, at his headquarters in Zambia to discuss dismantling apartheid (Mann 1988, 81).

Dismantling Apartheid: 1989–1994

Following Botha's resignation in 1989, the new government of de Klerk moved aggressively to dismantle the most disturbing and fundamental aspects of apartheid, in spite of growing white violence and continuing black violence. The French call this a "fuite en avant" ("forward retreat"), whereby a desperate government makes itself radical for its own survival. In the case of the de Klerk government, the tactic worked.

Between 1989 and 1991, the legislative keystones of apartheid were removed one by one: the Group Areas Act, the Separate Amenities Act, the Population Registration Act, and various provisions barring peaceful political assembly and organization. The state of emergency was lifted throughout much of the country (although continuing unrest may well have justified retaining the provision in certain areas), and police powers were circumscribed. Perhaps most dramatic of all, Nelson Mandela was released from prison in February 1990, shortly after Walter Sisulu was released and less than a year before Oliver Tambo, president of the ANC, returned to South Africa after a thirty-year exile.

By 1992, the ANC enjoyed the full complement of leadership and unfettered rights to assemble, demonstrate, travel overseas, and eventually negotiate with the government as legitimate representatives of most blacks in South Africa. As put by Payne:

> By removing most of apartheid's legal underpinnings by June 1991, with the notable exception of black voting rights, South Africa had made a major and largely unanticipated first step toward creating a relatively egalitarian and nonracial society. The overwhelming white support in the March 1992 referendum for de Klerk's reforms underscored the commitment to change. Dismantling the more intractable social and economic components of a legal system of racial domination into which all South Africans had been socialized for almost half a century was clearly a more Herculean endeavor. Nonetheless, the vast majority of South Africans had embraced a hopeful but uncertain future. (Payne 1992, 149)

The political processes at work in South Africa centered on the Convention for a Democratic South Africa (CODESA), a constitutional convention that brought together nearly all black and most white parties and the homelands governments. Although some parties rejected the legitimacy of the exercise, it had the full backing of the government, the Inkatha Party, and the ANC. A referendum of white voters in February 1992 revealed that an overwhelming majority supported the CODESA efforts to establish a fully democratic government in South Africa. The result went far to marginalize white conservatives, who felt compelled to join the process. The funerals of Afrikaner nationalist Andries Treurnicht and black Communist leader Chris Hani in April 1993 were a study in contrasts, with tens of thousands mourning Hani and only a few hundred turning out for Treurnicht.

Events in September and October of 1993 dramatically changed the prospects for a peaceful transition to democracy for South Africa. The CODESA process reached its conclusion with the drafting of a federal-style constitution, which was expected to be ratified by the white-controlled Parliament. Prior to that, a "supercabinet" consisting of representatives from each party involved in the CODESA had been proposed, accepted by Parliament, and organized to control the National Party's cabinet during the transition (*New York Times,* September 24, 1993, A1). The "transitional executive council" (TEC) had the power to override de Klerk's government to assure fairness in the national elections set for April 27, 1994. These remarkable steps forward resulted in an end to the sweeping economic and diplomatic boycotts imposed on South Africa by the United Nations, the Organization for African Unity, the Commonwealth, and the European Community, not to mention the United States. Loans and investments were expected to flow freely into South Africa to take advantage of the end of sanctions (*Christian Science Monitor* 1993). As recognition for their achievement, Nelson Mandela and Frederick de Klerk were awarded the Nobel Peace Prize in mid-October.

These historic achievements were not just the beginning of South Africa's healing, but also marked an intensified and broader conflict. The ANC–Inkatha rivalry intensified as black-on-black violence resulted in an average of ten deaths each day. A short-lived show of solidarity by Mandela and Buthelezi collapsed into mutual recriminations as Buthelezi pulled his Inkatha Freedom Party out of CODESA. He demanded virtual autonomy for the Kwazulu region he governed—something Mandela was unwilling to grant. Blacks in Buthelezi's native Natal province were split in their support of the ANC and Inkatha, and many saw Buthelezi's efforts as a last-ditch attempt to retain some degree of power.

In April 1994, black, white, and colored South Africans voted in what was universally described as a peaceful, fair, and open election. The ANC won 63 percent of the vote. On May 10, 1994, Nelson Mandela was sworn in as South Africa's president.

Post–Apartheid South Africa

The inauguration ceremony of Nelson Mandela was a mixture of pomp and party. He declared:

> We enter into a covenant that we shall build a society in which all South Africans, both black and white, will be able to walk tall, without any fear in their hearts, assured of their inalienable right to human dignity—a rainbow nation at peace with itself and the world. . . . Never, never, never again shall it be that this beautiful land will again experience the oppression of one by another. . . . (Sparks 1999, 66)

Following Mandela's speech, jets and helicopters flew over the crowd, trailing the colors of the new flag to the tune of a new national anthem. Emotions ran high as the world witnessed a rare peaceful transition from authoritarian to democratic regime.

Six years have passed since that momentous event, and many report cards have been written about the Mandela period. First and foremost, he is given high marks for carrying out a peaceful and orderly change of government, particularly given the risks involved. He bent over backward to accommodate white concerns, particularly by using a consensus approach to decision making during the two-year period of Government of National Unity, when all major parties had a seat in the cabinet. He introduced a moderate budget, limited social welfare programs (which required considerable fine-tuning) to alleviate black poverty, and worked to open South Africa's economy to the world along liberal principles (Brent 1996). Gone were the threats of large-scale nationalization and Marxist policies. Political violence came to a virtual standstill. With his introduction of a Truth and Reconciliation Commission under the leadership of Desmond Tutu, Mandela also moved to resolve long-standing grievances of blacks and whites alike. The commission's report, issued in late 1998, offered a mountain of evidence from those who confessed to human rights abuses in exchange for amnesty that the National Party was guilty of systematic atrocities and abuses. But the black parties also came under attack—which prompted ANC and Inkatha Freedom Party leaders to condemn the report. Perhaps the greatest victory came on June 16, 1999, when Mandela's appointed ANC successor, Thabo Mbeki, won the presidency with 66 percent of the vote—a margin even greater than Mandela's. Pik Botha, a former apartheid enforcer, even announced his intent to join the ANC in early 2000.

Although the political achievements of Mandela and the ANC are breathtaking, serious problems persist and new ones have emerged. South Africa's economy, slated to grow at 6 percent by 2000, has slipped into the doldrums, in part because of the global repercussions of the Asian financial crisis. Unemployment of blacks approaches 50 percent in some communities, and there is a growing feeling of despair as the gap between wealthy whites and poor blacks continues to widen. In the transition to a post-apartheid regime, little attention was paid to structural problems in South African society, and it is likely that this weakness will catch up to the new Mbeki government (Statman 1997).

Visitors to South African black townships still see poverty, illiteracy, and poor living conditions, all compounded by dramatically increasing crime rates and the spread of the AIDS virus. Crime is in some ways a result of a combination of new freedom (drugs and guns now flow almost freely into South Africa thanks to reopened borders), poverty, and frustration, as well as a legacy of an apartheid-era police force that was trained to persecute rather than protect blacks (Gordon 1998). As a result, solving crime and other similar problems will require a multipronged policy strategy, and it is even possible that some tactics will be mutually contradictory. For example, rapid growth probably requires opening the market more, which will result in weak companies going bankrupt and laying off their workers, most of whom are likely to be black.

Conclusion

For all their troubles, the vast majority of South Africans are willing to support Mbeki and wait for better times (his popularity ratings are very high). For the moment, at least, they can clearly remember the pains of oppression, so the taste of freedom is deliciously sweet. It is doubtful, however, whether this situation will continue much longer. As of late 2000, Mbeki's popularity had slid to merely 50 percent amid economic troubles, rising crimes rates, and a spreading AIDS epidemic (*Mail & Guardian–Johannesburg*, October 20, 2000). The country's crime rate is now at an all-time high. South Africa's annual murder rate exceeds Colombia's at sixty per 100,000, and a violent crime is committed every 15 seconds somewhere in the country (BBC News, April 10, 2002). Since 1999, the government has considered fighting crime to be its top priority, but the crime rate still continues to rise.

Perhaps even more serious is the AIDS epidemic, which has swelled in significance in recent years. Nearly five million South Africans are HIV-positive (one in nine), and most victims are ostracized and even attacked by their neighbors. Mbeki's reaction has been somewhat puzzling, as he casts blame on multinational drug companies that refuse to offer low-cost AIDS drugs while simultaneously questioning the link between HIV and AIDS. The government, meanwhile, did not make antiretroviral drugs available to rape victims until mid-2002. As of late 2002, Mbeki's policies seemed to be growing more coherent and promised a more effective program (BBC News, April 24, 2002).

Overall, life is still filled with violence, poverty, and despair for the vast majority of South Africans. Children growing up in the townships are increasingly turning to gang culture for validation and survival. As put by Virginia Gamba of the Institute of Security Studies, "In twelve years time [2014] you'll have at least a quarter of a million orphans, with no role models to guide them. They won't care less, because they themselves are infected with HI . . . The escalation of violence could be so great that it becomes the only determinant of whether life is worth living. Such a future threatens democracy itself" (BBC News, April 10, 2002).

Who is to blame? Have the political and social freedoms that have been achieved by average South Africans been abused in some way? Are South Africans to blame for the increase in crime and disease, or are these merely normal social ills that afflict every advanced, liberal democracy? Is it possible that the white minority government would be facing the same challenges if it were still in office? Most South Africans seem to think so, because there is no talk of returning to the political "Stone Age" of apartheid.

This point leads us back to the original concept for this chapter—human rights. South Africa is posing an increasingly troubling question for observers: Are political freedom and social order somehow contradictory? The Universal Declaration provides for both civil and economic rights, after all. Most world leaders and human rights activists would find it disturbing to think that civil rights must necessarily bring social breakdown, although the precedent has already been set in Russia. Fascists have always claimed that freedom was antithetical to social order and economic progress, while liberals have pointed out repeatedly that liberty and the good society can coexist —and that they are mutually reinforcing.

At this point, South African leaders are working hard to achieve both social and economic progress and to consolidate democracy and civil rights. One can hope that they will soon turn a corner and be able to guarantee both for the average South African.

Debate Topic

Many African states continue to struggle with the status of minority groups in government. Is South Africa a model for other African states, such as Zimbabwe, Rwanda, and Namibia?

PRO
Supporters of the South African model point out: (1) The remarkable freedom for whites, blacks, and coloreds in the country allows free speech and free political activity for all. (2) Strong constitutional guarantees allowed a peaceful transition of government after Mandela's term of office ended. (3) South Africa now has a leadership role in international life and enjoys high regard at the United Nations and elsewhere.

CON
South Africa is not to be imitated, according to some: (1) South Africa is unique in many ways and enjoys special economic and resource advantages not shared by other African states. (2) The leadership in South Africa has not demonstrated the capacity to deal with serious social issues any more effectively than many other African governments. (3) South Africa has yet to fully empower the millions of poor and unemployed, with the result that the freedom is one-dimensional to a large extent.

Questions to Consider

1. To what extent has nonviolence succeeded where violence has not? Have Mahatma Gandhi's theories been validated by the South Africa experience?

2. How have human rights been perceived by various groups in South Africa? How have South Africans responded to international standards of human rights? To what extent did the international community succeed in changing the human rights policies of the South African government? Does the South African situation strengthen the case for economic sanctions?

Websites

The South African government's official website: **www.gov.za**
The ANC home page: **www.anc.org.za**
COSATU's home page: **www.cosatu.org.za**
South African politics site: **www.polity.org.za/default.htm**
The Universal Declaration of Human Rights: **www.un.org/Overview/rights.html**

References

BBC News, April 10, 2002

Brent, R. Stephen. "Tough Road to Prosperity." *Foreign Affairs* 75 #2 (March/April 1996): 113–126.

Brewer, John D. *After Soweto: An Unfinished Journey* (Oxford: Clarendon Press, 1986).

Brown, Godfrey N. *Apartheid: A Teacher's Guide* (New York: UNESCO, 1981).

Christian Science Monitor, October 1, 1993, 8.

Europa Yearbook 1993 (London: Europa Publishers, 1993).

Fatton, Robert, Jr. *Black Consciousness in South Africa: The Dialectics of Ideological Resistance to White Supremacy* (Albany: SUNY Press, 1986).

Gordon, Diana R. "Crime in the New South Africa." *The Nation* 267 #15 (November 9, 1998): 17–21.

Hobson, J. A. *Imperialism* (Ann Arbor: University of Michigan Press, 1965).

International Labor Organization. *Special Report of the Director-General on the Application of the Declaration Concerning Action Against Apartheid in South Africa and Namibia* (Geneva: ILO, 1990).

Lambley, Peter. *The Psychology of Apartheid* (Athens: University of Georgia Press, 1980).

Lapping, Brian. *Apartheid: A History* (New York: George Braziller, 1986).

Lawyers Committee for Human Rights. *The War Against Children: South Africa's Youngest Victims* (New York: Lawyers Committee, 1986).

Lemon, Anthony. *Apartheid in Transition* (Boulder, CO: Westview Press, 1987).

Magubane, Bernard Makhosezwe. *The Political Economy of Race and Class in South Africa* (New York: Monthly Review Press, 1979).

Mail & Guardian-Johannesburg, October 20, 2000.

Mandela, Nelson. *The Struggle Is My Life* (New York: Pathfinder, 1990).

Mann, Michael. "The Giant Stirs: South African Business in the Age of Reform" in Philip Krankel, Noam Pines, and Mark Swilling, eds., *State Resistance and Change in South Africa* (London: Croom Helm, 1988), 52–86.

New York Times, September 24, 1993, A1.

Omond, Roger. *The Apartheid Handbook* (London: Penguin, 1985).

Payne, Richard J. *The Third World and South Africa: Post-Apartheid Challenges* (Westport, CT: Greenwood Press, 1992).

Republic of South Africa. *Progress Through Separate Development: South Africa in Peaceful Transition* (New York: Information Service of South Africa, 1973).

Sparks, Alision. "The Status of the Dream." *The Wilson Quarterly* 23 #12 (Spring 1999): 66–67.

St. Jorre, John de. "White South Africa Circles the Wagons" in Mark A. Uhlig, ed., *Apartheid in Crisis* (New York: Vintage Books, 1986), 61–84.

Statman, James M. "No More Miracle?" *ReVision* 20 #2 (Fall 1997): 32–38.

Treurnicht, Andries P. "Conservative Party Congress Speech" in Mark A. Uhlig, ed., *Apartheid in Crisis* (New York: Vintage Books, 1986), 100–102.

CASE
15

Yugoslavia's Dismemberment
ANARCHY

Introduction

Anarchy is the condition that the world faces, according to most international relations scholars. Anarchy means the absence of a central, controlling, governing authority. Anarchy is not necessarily equivalent to chaos or violence, however. Peace and anarchy may exist simultaneously, which is generally the case in the international system.

Anarchy implies that if a state is to be safe, it must seek out its own allies, build up its own armies, and play the diplomatic game carefully. No one can be depended upon to rescue it from attack. This need for "self-help" explains much of the "balance of power" dynamic discussed in Chapter 3.

The opposite of anarchy is world government. In this condition, states need not fear for their safety, because a higher legal and political authority will come to their rescue. Inside states, we hope that no anarchy occurs, as it would indicate a breakdown of central authority (Somalia comes to mind). Internationally, a central government is mostly the vision of idealists. For all its symbolic presence, the United Nations is clearly not a world government. And for all the pressures against it, national sovereignty remains the rule in international life. Thus we live in a world of legal equals that have no overriding authority to settle disputes.

The case of Yugoslavia is useful for understanding anarchy not because of the high levels of violence found there, but because of the role that the international community played in recognizing new states and protecting their newfound independence as well as the rights of individuals living in the region facing extermination. As we will see, nothing that happened in Yugoslavia escaped international scrutiny, and the world community responded with all the resources it could muster, from economic sanctions to military intervention and a war crimes trial. Is it possible that Yugoslavia illustrates the end of anarchy?

For years, Yugoslavia was at the center of major power struggles for control over southern Europe. The Ottomans, Hungarians, and Austrians each took a turn at Balkan domination. Sarajevo entered the history books as the spot where World War I began. Much of the post–World War I settlement at Versailles was inspired by an international desire to provide justice and peace to the Balkans. The breakup of the Yugoslav Federation during the 1990s illustrated the limits of anarchy in some ways, even as it revealed the failures of international law. As civil war was transformed into international conflict with the secession and recognition of an increasing number of the country's republics, an ever-growing international military presence attempted to restore peace. At the same time, the international community used the Yugoslav experience to reinstate the principle of war crimes guilt, thus paving the way for the establishment of the first permanent International Criminal Court (see Case 12). Thus Yugoslavia is a case of both balance of power run amok and an international system attempting to create order.

The atrocities of the wars in the former Yugoslavia have been embedded in the international consciousness thanks to the work of war crimes prosecutors, journalists, and government- and UN-sponsored fact-finding missions. We have heard stories of summary executions of civilians, mutilations of enemy soldiers, concentration camps, and the use of rape as a weapon of war. These wars also included aerial bombardment of residential zones, economic sanctions, and diplomatic isolation imposed by Western forces, each painfully damaging in its own way.

YUGOSLAVIA'S DISMEMBERMENT
KEY FIGURES

Slobodan Milosevic President of Serbia, 1987–2000. He is generally considered responsible for the wars that took place in the Yugoslavian region during the 1990s. He is currently in the dock at the International Criminal Tribunal for the former Yugoslavia.

Josip Broz Tito President of Yugoslavia, 1946–1980.

Vojislav Kostunica President of Serbia, 2000–present. He won elections and international support, leading to Milosevic's resignation.

Louise Arbo Chief Prosecutor of the ICTY. She pursued Milosevic's arrest and prosecution.

Bill Clinton US President, 1993–2001. He deployed U.S. troops to Bosnia under NATO.

Richard Holbrooke U.S. diplomat who spearheaded the Dayton Accords.

Alija Itzebegovic Leader of the Bosnian Muslims.

Franjo Tudjman President of Croatia, 1990–1999.

Warren Christopher U.S. Secretary of State, 1993–1997.

Radovan Karadzic Leader of the Bosnian Serb, and an ICTY indictee

(continued)

Boutros Boutros-Ghali UN Secretary General, 1991–1996. He questioned Western interest in Yugoslavia in contrast to its neglect of Rwanda.

George H. W. Bush U.S. President, 1989–1993. He supported UN operations in Bosnia.

YUGOSLAVIA'S DISMEMBERMENT
CHRONOLOGY

1444
The Ottoman Empire defeats the Serbs at the battle of Varna.

1806
Serbians establish an independent kingdom. The Ottomans later reassert a degree of control.

1848
Croatia takes Austria's side in the rebellion against Hungary.

1871
A Croatian rebellion against Austria is unsuccessful.

1877
The Treaty of San Stefano establishes an independent Serbia and Montenegro.

1878
European powers revise the largely Russian San Stefano Treaty, leaving Serbia under Austrian rule.

1912
Balkan forces expel the Ottomans from the region, precipitating a two-year struggle for territory in the region.

1914
Austrian archduke Ferdinand is assassinated in Sarajevo by a Serbian nationalist, sparking the outbreak of World War I.

1918
The Kingdom of the Serbs, Croats, and Slovenes is proclaimed after the end of World War I.

1929
A dictatorship is imposed in response to ethnic unrest.

1941
The Nazis conquer the Balkans. Croat fascists (Ustase) join forces with them.

1946
Tito is elected leader of the newly proclaimed Yugoslav Socialist Republic under Soviet sponsorship.

1971
Tito suppresses a Croatian uprising.

1980
Tito dies, leaving a leadership void. Eventually, a rotating presidency is established that shares power among the various republics.

1981
The central government suppresses an Albanian uprising.

1990
Bosnia, Slovenia, Croatia, and Macedonia declare independence and hold elections.   *(continued)*

1991

Violence erupts as Serbian forces clash with Croatians. The war continues until 1992.

1992

Violence erupts in Bosnia between Serbs and Croat/Muslim forces. The war lasts until the Dayton Accords are signed in 1995.

1993

The International Criminal Tribunal for the former Yugoslavia founded.

1995

Serbs overrun Srebreniza, a UN-declared safe haven. NATO forces attack Serb artillery in Sarajevo.

November 21   The Dayton Accords are signed, ending the war and leaving Bosnia divided into Serb and Muslim sectors with NATO acting as a buffer.

1997

Kosovo Liberation Army forces attack Serb outposts. Serbia attacks.

1999

NATO bombs Serb installations to protect Kosovars. Serbia withdraws.

2000

Elections in September yield a victory for Milosevic's opponent, Kustunica. Street protests prompt Milosevic to resign.

2001

Milosevic is extradited to the ICTY.

2002

Milosevic's trial begins.

History to 1918

To a certain extent, the history of ethnic relations in Yugoslavia has followed a common pattern: increasingly mobilized linguistic and religious communities are overwhelmed by a foreign invader; the communities either collaborate or resist; the invader becomes increasingly unable to maintain control of the fringe territory; a new invader unseats the previous power, which gives the local community the opportunity to develop a new political arrangement (*Economist,* August 23, 1992, 36). In the process, differences among the communities become exaggerated and rivalries based on the different experiences emerge.

The earliest Balkan peoples arrived near the dawn of man and were organized at the family, clan, or tribe level. It was not until the early Middle Ages that nations became a force to be reckoned with. Bulgaria reached its zenith during the tenth century, Croatia dominated in the eleventh century, and Bosnia and Serbia were each independent kingdoms of some note in the fourteenth century. Although these moments of glory may seem quaint episodes from the modern perspective, they became embedded in the concept of "rightful heritage" that continues today: "In the nineteenth century the national leaders, looking back on this period, tended to consider the maximum extension of their medieval kingdoms as the natural historical boundaries for their nations" (Jelavich 1983 1, 27).

By the fifteenth century, the Balkans were the well-established battleground of empires, much like Poland to the north. Contact with numerous powerful empires left its imprint on Balkan society and spirit (see Map 15.1). In each region the population represented a fusion of original inhabitants with subsequent invaders, an amalgamation achieved through military conquest by a stronger group, the absorption of one people by another owing to the weight of numbers, or the acceptance of another language because of the cultural attraction offered by a more advanced civilization. (Jelavich 1983 1, 27)

The Ottoman Empire, an outgrowth of the great Muslim nation established by the prophet Mohammed, advanced into the Balkans and beyond in the fifteenth century and defeated the Serbs and their allies in 1444 at the battle of Varna (still cited as a dark day in Serbian history). By 1500, the Muslims had established firm control over the leaders of the Balkan peoples, forcing them to embrace Islam and submit to the "Porte," as the central government was called. The Ottoman hold continued through the seventeenth century, when Russian and Hapsburg (a central European dynasty embracing a wide variety of nationalities) armies threatened the Balkan territories. Christian dissent, both Orthodox and Catholic, was strengthened by these competing external forces, and in the eighteenth century, the Porte began to lose its authority in Croatia, Slavonia, and other fringe territories.

Some of the Ottoman domain was simply seized and controlled by Russia and the Hapsburgs. In other cases, such as Montenegro, the hostility of the terrain and people prevented any effective administration. In still others, such as Serbia, local Muslim strongmen emerged, exercising dictatorial powers without sanction from the Porte.

In Croatia, the Hapsburgs, though dominant, permitted the surviving Catholic elites to exercise considerable discretion and power over the domain. Orthodox Serbs remained considerably organized, thanks largely to geography and the tenacity of the Orthodox hierarchy. In Bosnia, most of the elites converted to Islam, but only one-third of the general population did so, thus leaving the Orthodox as the largest group.

During the second half of the eighteenth century, war raged across the region, particularly in Bosnia and Serbia, where local Serbs rebelled against despotic Muslim leaders with the Porte endorsement. By 1806, the Serbs, successful on the battlefield and far from the Porte's power, established an independent kingdom. Although the Ottomans were able to reassert some control, the Porte gave the Serbs considerable autonomy—a condition that would continue to some degree until World War I (Jelavich 1983 1, 196).

The Croats of the Hapsburg Empire were nominally subject to the Hungarian crown—a crown of thorns as it were. Croats repeatedly sought greater autonomy and status within the empire, demanding control of newly acquired territories to the south and east. An emerging Croat intelligentsia began to assert national ideals in the late seventeenth century and by

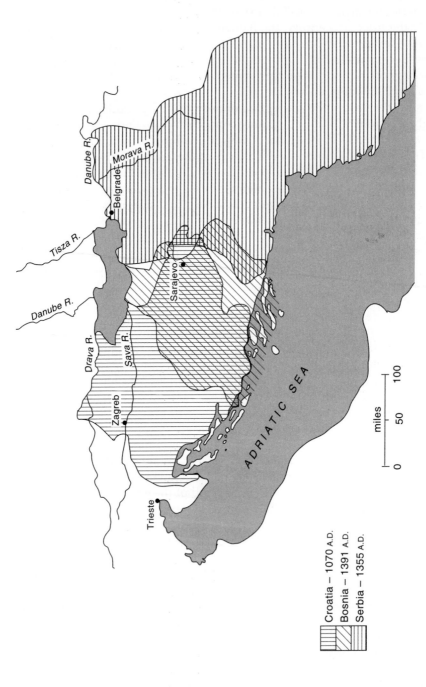

Map 15.1 Balkan medieval kingdoms with a breakdown of ethnic divisions

Source: Adapted from Barbara Jelavich, *History of the Balkans: 18th and 19th Centuries* (New York: Cambridge University Press, 1983).

1830 were caught up in the nationalist spirit of Europe. They demanded the right to educate their children in Croat (not Latin) and claimed the status of freemen in relation to Hungary. They resented Hapsburg attempts to "divide and rule" by offering some benefits to a few without extending them to the people at large (Cohen 1992, 369). The unrest boiled over into full-fledged rebellion in 1848, during the Hapsburg revolution, and Hungary, Zagreb, and Vienna went to war. Because Croatia fought against Hungary on the side of Vienna, it expected to gain more autonomy when Budapest fell. In fact, little changed and Croatia rebelled again in 1871. Although this disturbance was quelled, Croatia was granted additional powers (Jelavich 1983 1, 206).

Shortly after Croatia attempted to secure autonomy from the Hapsburgs in general and Hungary in particular, Bosnia and Serbia were in revolt against the Ottomans. The conflict was exacerbated by the active involvement of Russia, the Hapsburgs, and other continental powers that were eager to bring stability and their presence to a volatile, strategic region. The Treaty of San Stafano (1877), a largely Russian creation, provided for an independent Serbia and Montenegro as well as a huge Bulgaria under Russian occupation. The Congress of Berlin in 1878 was called by the other European powers to adjust this Russian power play and settled on a much smaller Bulgaria and Bosnia-Herzegovina's inclusion in the Hapsburg Empire (Jelavich 1983 1, 358). The problem of Macedonia was finessed by simply leaving it under Ottoman control—the last major bastion of Muslim power. Macedonia would prove to be a persistent bone of contention for Serbia (and Yugoslavia), Bulgaria, and Greece for the next century—and it is still a major diplomatic concern today (Stavrianos 1963, 95).

The late nineteenth century brought an increasing sense of frustration, borne of the mitigated success of each group. Increasingly Balkan peoples understood that they could achieve more by joining together, but the years of conquest and division had left profound animosities. Serbs considered Bosnia and Macedonia their rightful heritage, based largely on medieval and ethnic considerations. Croats felt largely the same way about Bosnia. The Muslim population of Bosnia was never considered "authentic" by Serbs or Croats, coming as it did as a product of Ottoman imperialism (Djilas and Mousavizadeh 1992, 26). Not only were these antagonisms ethnically based, but it soon became clear that concrete balance-of-power considerations made suspicion and apprehension rational attitudes. None of the Balkan states had the capacity to ensure its own safety, and any alliance between neighbors could tip the balance against a lone state. Hence competing experiences combined with outside powers, perceptions of national heritage, religion, language, and security concerns to prevent a lasting bond among the nations (Armour 1992, 11).

The great power game of continental Europe was being played with intensity by the turn of the century. Austria wanted to strengthen its southern borders and so decided to annex Bosnia outright, for which it received Russia's tacit blessing. This move naturally enraged Serb leaders, who felt betrayed by their erstwhile sponsors (Stavrianos 1963, 110). At about the same time, the traditional leadership in the Ottoman Empire was overthrown by the "Young Turk" revolt. These young colonels were determined to bring a sense of national unity to all the empire's colonies. The Balkan states saw the move as a concrete threat to their hard-earned independence and for the first time organized a strong alliance. The alliance was so confident that in 1912 it launched an attack against Turkish forces and succeeded in pushing them virtually off the continent.

Ironically, it was as a result of the alliance's success that the most tragic episode of Balkan relations began. The question of territorial compensation aroused intense disagreement because each nation felt its military victories had earned it more spoils of war than it was slated to receive. In particular, Russia's demand that a new Albanian state be formed from the former Ottoman territories angered Serbia because Serbia anticipated controlling the area itself. It sought an extra piece of Montenegro and Macedonia as compensation, which in turn infuriated the Bulgarians and Montenegrins. War broke out, and Serbian and Greek forces overwhelmed the Bulgarian army. Serbia then proceeded to annex most of Macedonia outright. The Treaty of Bucharest (1913) was signed in an effort to show that the problem was resolved, but it simply "papered over cracks for the time being. The period between the Balkan Wars and World War I was but a breathing spell during which Balkan states jockeyed for position. . . . From the Balkan point of view, World War I was essentially a continuation of the Balkan Wars" (Stavrianos 1963, 113).

World War I, made almost inevitable by a hair-trigger alliance network, long-standing grievances, gross imbalances of power, and the end of colonial opportunities, was sparked by a gunman in Sarajevo, a member of a Serbian nationalist group, who shot the Austrian Archduke Ferdinand in July 1914. (Many previous attempts had been made on Hapsburg royalty and representatives by both Serb and Croat nationalists.) Austria declared war on Serbia, Serbia allied with Russia, Russia declared war on Austria, Austria allied with Germany, and so on. Four years and 16 million deaths later, the war ended.

As the defeated Hapsburg and Ottoman Empires were dismantled, many new nation-states were formed. Even before the war ended, Croats and Slovenes were organizing a postwar united Yugoslavia, which could become the strongest nation in the Balkans and aspire to great power status in Europe. A Yugoslav Committee was formed which then prepared a draft constitution providing for Serbian participation. When the proposal was forwarded to the Serbian monarchy, it was accepted almost immediately. "Thus the organization of the Yugoslav state was primarily the work of national committees, and the initiative came from the Hapsburg South Slavs" (Jelavich 1983 2, 147). The proposal had to be validated in London, where the territory was formally mapped. On December 1, 1918, the Kingdom of the Serbs, Croats, and Slovenes was officially proclaimed (Cohen 1992, 369).

1918 to 1980

The first attempt at Yugoslav federation failed after ten years, when the largely nationality-based parliament demanded more autonomy for the various regions than the central government in Belgrade was willing to concede (see Map 15.2). Serbs in Belgrade hoped to instill a sense of national unity, but these efforts merely exacerbated tensions (Cohen 1992, 370). "The basic problem of the state was that, despite the hopes of some intellectuals and political leaders before 1914, a Yugoslav nationality did not come into existence" (Jelavich 1983 2, 151).

The principal rivalry in the kingdom was between Croats and Serbians because the smaller ethnic groups were able to bargain for concessions from the Serbs in exchange for support. Questions of language use, representation in the government, and self-rule became extremely intense in the late 1920s. In 1929, following violent demonstrations in Zagreb, King Alexander dismantled the parliamentary institutions and imposed a form of dictatorship on the country. He was assassinated in 1934, and his successor brought back some of the democratic structures, only to see his country overwhelmed by German Nazi forces in 1941.

The wartime experience of Yugoslavia has been suggested as a cause of the present antagonism. One reason is that the Catholic Croatian region was treated very differently than the Orthodox Serbian areas. Croatia was granted independence and membership in Axis-led international organizations. This diplomatic status and newfound autonomy, after years of failed attempts, was greeted warmly by many Croats. "A wave of enthusiasm pervaded Zagreb at this time, not unlike that which had swept through the town in 1918 when the ties with Hungary were severed" (Jelavich 1983, 2, 264). The Catholic hierarchy gave firm instructions to the clergy to serve the new rulers. In the words of the Zagreb archbishop: "These are events. . . which fulfill the long dreamed of and desired ideal of our people. . . . Respond readily to my call to join in the noble task of working for the safety and well-being of the Independent State of Croatia" (MacLean 1957, 88). The clergy worked with the fascist regime to force thousands of Orthodox Serbs to convert to Catholicism.

Croatia slipped into the fascist mode, and the new leadership worked closely with Italy. Moderate elements retired from the scene as the Ustase movement, a fascist Croatian group based in Italy, undertook a systematic and egregious rule of terror. Serbs who resided in Croatia were the primary targets, and they "suffered greatly at the hands of the Croatian fascists" (Cohen 1992, 371). According to the current Bosnian Serb leader, some 700,000 Serbs were killed from 1941 to 1945 at Croatian Catholic and Muslim hands, prompting him to vow, "We will never again be history's fools" (Karadzic 1992, 50).

Meanwhile, Josip Broz-Tito, leader of the outlawed Communist Party, organized a highly effective resistance movement in the mountains around Serbia and Bosnia. Because Yugoslavia's collapse had been swift, Germany never completely occupied the country, and many peasants with weapons

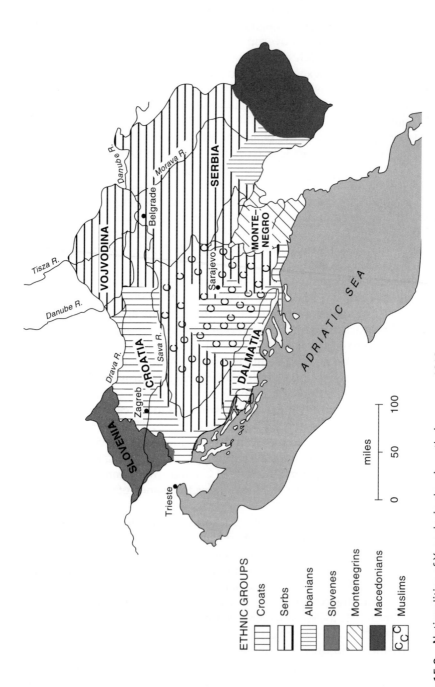

Map 15.2 Nationalities of Yugoslavia showing ethnic groups, 1919
Source: Barbara Jelavich, *History of the Balkans: 18th and 19th Centuries; 20th Century* (New York: Cambridge University Press, 1983), vols. 1 and 2.

were ready to take to the mountains, as their forefathers had done so many times before. A second substantial resistance movement, the Chetniks, formed, but because its aim was to restore the monarchy, the two rarely collaborated. Eventually, the Chetniks were found to have worked with the Nazis (Jelavich 1983 2, 267).

By the end of the war, tensions were extremely high among the various groups. Partisans regularly rounded up and shot Croatian fascists. One incident reveals the depth of animosity:

> As the Ustase were being led off to execution, a peasant woman rushed into the middle of them and began scratching and hitting at them, screaming all the time. The Partisans had difficulty pulling her off them. Then the shots rang out and she again rushed forward, this time among the corpses, dancing in the blood. "A-ah!" she gasped, dripping with sweat and blood. It seemed the Ustase had slaughtered all her sons. (MacLean 1957, 156)

Fearful of such reprisals, one particularly large group of Ustase surrendered to the British in the closing days of the war, only to be sent back to the partisans. Reports indicate that between 40,000 and 100,000 of them were killed within days (Jelavich 1983 2, 272).

Tito organized a government among the partisans, although a royal government-in-exile in London had the support of the United States and Great Britain. To consolidate his political support in Yugoslavia, Tito declared Macedonia, previously a province of Serbia, a full-fledged republic in the future Yugoslavia, a status that did and still does profoundly disturb Greece to the south and Bulgaria to the east. Tito received Soviet support and recognition and moved early after the war to join the emerging Soviet bloc as a socialist state. An ill-fated USSR-inspired attempt at a Balkan federation failed by 1948, which contributed in part to the eventual separation of Yugoslavia and the Soviet Union.

Tito embarked on a unique and solitary path toward socialism based on decentralized worker organizations, tolerance of nationalities, and intense socialist propaganda campaigns (Jelavich 1983 2, 388). He hoped that socialist solidarity and idealism, combined with dynamic economic growth and prosperity, would lead to a pan-Yugoslav nationalism. He put this nationalism into practice by leading the Non-Aligned Movement and working with the West at various junctures.

Tito's participation in international affairs was undercut by a growing national identification among writers and artists (Wachtel 1998, 175) and continued tension over the division of the political spoils among the national republics at home. In 1967, 1971, 1981, and indeed throughout all of Yugoslav history, ethnic tensions remained high. As put by Jelavich:

> With the loosening of the central bonds, more authority was transferred to the capitals of the republics, the majority of which had been, and still were, strongholds of fervent nationalist sentiments. When disputes arose over economic or political questions, the local leaders tended to dust off the old flags and symbols and return with enthusiasm to the battles of the past. . . . (Jelavich 1983 2, 388)

Tito and his government felt compelled in 1971 and again in 1981 to use force to suppress first Croatian and later Kosovo Albanian demands for greater autonomy and more national rights. Through it all, Tito continued to appeal to the people's socialist solidarity to overcome these political disputes. In the final analysis, however, Marxism failed as an integrative force in Yugoslavia (Braun 1983, 37). Tito died in 1980 without a clear successor. As would be seen in the 1990s, with the removal of the communist state, "all that remained was the nation, and the ideology of nationalism" (Hayden 1992, 43).

After Tito

The decade of the 1980s brought economic hardship and lack of central leadership in Yugoslavia, which together fostered nationalist demands in Croatia. The League of Yugoslav Communists failed to maintain cohesion, even though after forty years many party officials, military commanders, and government agents were firmly entrenched in the federal bureaucracy (Cohen 1992, 370). By 1987, Slobodan Milosevic emerged as the sole Serbian leader, resentful that Croatians and others had encroached on federal authority:

> Through his brash articulation of Serbia's political discontent, and particularly his populist mobilization of Serbian ethnic consciousness at mass rallies—sometimes referred to as "street democracy"—Milosevic challenged the oligarchic Titoist style of managing the "national question" and also provoked a sharp nationalist backlash from Yugoslavia's other republics and ethnic groups. (Cohen 1992, 371)

The winds of democracy swept through Yugoslavia in the tumultuous fall of 1989. Between April and December 1990, each republic held elections. In Slovenia, Croatia, Bosnia, and Macedonia, new democratic parties were elected, while former Communists were returned to power in Serbia, Montenegro, and Vojvodina.

> Although the elections of 1990 were an impressive exercise in regime transition, the results left the country even more politically fragmented than it had been during the last days of Communist rule. Thus, whether born-again Communists or non-Communists, both the newly elected political authorities and the bulk of the opposition forces in all regions of Yugoslavia were committed to programs of regional and ethnic nationalism that seriously challenged the power of the federal system. (Cohen 1992, 371)

Milosevic, following an undemocratic election, spearheaded efforts to preserve the federation with Serbia at the center and found considerable support among the federal power elite. He proposed a "modern federation," which would preserve the size of the military and the dominance of the Communist Party. In the meantime, he supported efforts by Serbs who resided outside of Serbia to exercise self-determination while maintaining their potential rights to citizenship in Serbia proper.

The question of ethnic rights for minorities came to a head later in 1990, when the Croatian assembly approved a constitution that failed to specifically mention protection of the rights of Serbs living in Croatia. This move was repeated across the nation. As put by Hayden:

> The solution found in the various Yugoslav republics was the creation of systems of a constitutional and legal structure that guarantees privileges to the members of one nation over those of any other residents in a particular state. (Hayden 1992, 41)

Serbians living in Krajina, a Croatian city where Serbs are in the majority, began demonstrating against Croatian authority and seized control of government bureaus and facilities. In early 1991, the Croatian government moved to suppress the unrest.

Warfare in Slovenia and Croatia

During the first part of 1991, Slovenia and Croatia moved toward outright independence, and the legitimacy of the shared federal presidency was challenged throughout the country. In March, when the Croatian delegate was scheduled to take his seat at the head of the table, the Serbian delegation protested his ascension and in May vetoed it altogether (*New York Times*, May 16, 1991, A1).

While attempts were made to preserve the federal structure, irreconcilable demands and fast action toward independence and diplomatic recognition in Slovenia and Croatia frustrated the efforts (*New York Times*, June 7, 1991, A5). Meanwhile, U.S. Secretary of State James Baker urged national leaders to preserve the federation, a statement that the military apparently interpreted as "a green light for military intervention should secession occur" (Cohen 1992, 373). When the Croatian and Slovene parliaments approved independence resolutions on June 26, 1991, the George H. W. Bush administration announced its "regret" for such "unilateral action" and warned of a "dangerous situation" (*New York Times*, June 27, 1991, A1). On June 28, Yugoslav army tanks battled Slovene troops that had taken control of border posts. Slovenia defeated the incursion and held firm to independence in spite of several offers for increased autonomy in the old federation. When Yugoslav troops began to make new inroads, European Community (EC) officials offered to mediate the dispute. By early July, EC mediators managed to identify the terms of a settlement, but when a cease-fire was accepted in August, it became clear that many soldiers in the field had no loyalty to the Belgrade government, prompting the EC mediators to declare that the Yugoslav army units were "out of control" (*New York Times*, August 30, 1991, A3).

In Croatia, violence first erupted in Zagreb and then quickly spread across the region inhabited by Serbs. Early on, the tactics used by both sides strayed far from traditional rules of war. Serb fighters used Croatian civilians as human shields when attacking Croatian outposts, forcing the defenders to shoot at relatives (*New York Times,* July 31, 1991, A1). On the other side, Serbian soldiers with Croatian relatives agonized over orders to shoot (*New York Times,* October 1, 1991, A1). The Yugoslav defense minister, Veljko Kadijevec, negotiated several cease-fires with the Croats during these months, only to be dismissed by an impatient Milosevic.

By the end of the initial phase of hostilities in March, some 10,000 were dead and 500,000 were homeless. The fighting intensified in the fall and continued through most of 1992. Vukovar was described as a "wasteland" in November after eighty-six days of shelling and aerial bombardment (*New York Times,* November 21, 1992, A1). By December, the military actions lost most of their strategic content and took on the form of vendettas. Reports of unconfirmed atrocities became commonplace by early 1992.

The international community was ill prepared to intervene in this situation, coming as it did during the collapse of the Soviet Union and the general restructuring of international institutions and practices. The EC wanted desperately for this situation to be resolved without military intervention, even of peacekeepers, and the EC lost several diplomats in the skies of Croatia in their efforts to mediate a peaceful settlement. NATO forces were unable to intervene because the treaty prohibited the use of the forces outside the member countries' collective borders. The CSCE (Council for Security and Cooperation in Europe) was untested and required unanimity in its decision making, and the UN was happy to let regional organizations take the first crack before intervening (Cohen 1992, 373). It was not until September that the Security Council began to issue a series of resolutions condemning Serbian and Yugoslav army support of Serbian militiamen in Croatia.

At any rate, the Western response was tepid at best. In spite of Germany's insistence, the EC did not officially extend diplomatic recognition to Croatia until January 1992 (nearly one month after Germany), and the United States waited until the spring. These delays hampered attempts to treat the problem as an international, rather than civil, conflict. Some have argued that this inaction helped bring on the war (Mastnak 1992, 11).

Over several months beginning in November, the UN Security Council deliberated a proposal to send a group of peacekeeping forces to monitor a future cease-fire in Croatia. This force, originally pegged at 10,000, was ultimately increased to 14,000 and was deployed strategically not only in the Serb-inhabited zones of Croatia ("pink zones") but also in Belgrade and Sarajevo. Wanting to assure himself that the UN troops would not be in serious danger, the new secretary general, Boutros Boutros-Ghali, waited until a cease-fire held for several days. This did not happen until March, following Croatian, Serb, and eventually Serb Croatian support (although in the case of Serbs living in Croatia, supporters of the peacekeeping operation had to force out an intransigent leadership—*New York Times,* February 22, 1992, A1). The troop arrival on March 16 marked the end of civil war in Croatia for the time being. Unrest erupted again in early 1993 but was contained.

Warfare in Bosnia

No sooner had peacekeepers arrived in Croatia than a full-scale war broke out in Bosnia-Herzegovina, which so dominated international affairs that the Croatian struggle paled in comparison. The war generated 2 million refugees and 140,000 dead or missing (11,000 died in Sarajevo alone). The scale of atrocities approachd World War II proportions, introducing a new concept in international discourse: "ethnic cleansing." Bosnian leaders declared their independence from the rest of Yugoslavia in October 1991, and a referendum was scheduled for early March 1992. Ethnic Serbs, who make up roughly one-third of the Bosnian population, protested the formation of an independent state where they would be outnumbered by their erstwhile enemies, and they boycotted the vote. On March 1, 1992, the country overwhelmingly approved independence. Within a month, Serb irregulars were fighting in the streets of Bosnia with the support of the local leader, Radovan Karadzic. After firing on pro-independence demonstrators, Serb sharpshooters were forced to flee the country, and a large guerrilla force formed in the mountains surrounding Sarajevo and beyond. Serbian leaders in Bosnia received considerable support from the Serbian government, which by late April had declared itself, along with Montenegro, Vojvodina, and a reluctant Kosovo, a new Yugoslav federation.

The international community acted swiftly to grant recognition to Bosnia and within one month had moved to include it in the community of nations, although some feared that this speed was as unwise as the delays had been vis-à-vis Croatia (Cohen 1992, 374). Discussion of deploying peacekeepers began almost immediately, but Boutros-Ghali slowed things down by pointing out that the level of violence in Bosnia posed a grave danger to any future deployment. He also rejected a call from Bosnian Muslim President Alija Itzebegovic for an "intervention force" on the ground that it would require "many tens of thousands" of troops in a very dangerous situation (*UN Chronicle*, September 1992, 8). In May, Boutros-Ghali withdrew most of the UN observers from Sarajevo, although he ultimately approved Cyrus Vance's recommendation to increase the force already there from 10,000 to 14,000.

The scale of destruction in Bosnia far exceeded that in Croatia. The artillery barrage against Sarajevo continued virtually uninterrupted for the next year, sometimes with as many as 3,000 shells falling on the city in a single day. Serbs moved quickly to gain control of Bosnian territory, and by summer, with only one-third of the population, Serbs controlled nearly three-fourths of the territory, cutting off access to several towns and villages populated by Muslims in the eastern region of the country. The refugee population grew at the rate of 30,000 per day in the early months of the war.

After some hesitation to take sides (particularly on the part of Russia—a historic Serbian ally), the UN Security Council began in May 1992 to condemn not just the war and its associated atrocities but specifically Serbia and the Serbs of Bosnia. The United States and EC nations imposed economic and diplomatic sanctions against Serbia and Montenegro in April, expanding them in May, and the French, British, and American representatives on the Security Council raised questions about Yugoslavia's continued membership in the UN (in September that membership was revoked, in spite of serious legal questions—"Current Development" 1992, 832). On May 30, the Security Council placed blame for the violence squarely on Serbia and called for sanctions on the basis of Chapter VII of the UN Charter (*New York Times,* May 31, 1992, A1).

The focus of UN efforts in Bosnia was to provide humanitarian assistance to the besieged Muslims in Sarajevo and other towns and villages that were cut off from food and fuel supplies. The Sarajevo airport, overrun by Serb gunmen, was eventually opened thanks to Security Council intervention and diplomatic activity, including a personal visit by François Mitterand, president of France (*New York Times,* June 29, 1992, A1). The Serbs continued to block access to more remote villages on the grounds that even humanitarian assistance had a concrete military impact, which prompted the Security Council to pass a resolution in late June allowing military escorts for humanitarian aid convoys. When this failed, the Security Council approved the use of "all necessary means"—a phrase taken from the Gulf War—to ensure that aid reached its destination (*Economist,* August 15, 1992, 37–38). Although the UN avoided direct confrontation, in March 1993 the rather innovative tactic of air drops delivered significant amounts of food. Perhaps the most heroic figure in the war was General Phillippe Morillon, commander of UN forces in eastern Bosnia, who made the saving of Srebreniza his personal quest. Entering the Muslim enclave despite shelling and inadequate food, he defied the Serbian troops to attack the helpless city. Even this effort largely failed, however, because many Muslims were eager to abandon the city (against Bosnian Muslim military leaders' hopes) and the secretary general was growing weary of Morillon's grandstanding (*New York Times,* April 8, 1993, A5).

Eventually, the UN became actively involved in evacuating Muslims from such cities as Srebreniza. UN intervention raised disturbing questions about its complicity with Serbian "ethnic cleansing," a practice that involved deliberate depopulation of Muslim-dominated regions. Ethnic cleansing involved not only simple removal of persons by the thousands but also mass executions and even large-scale rape to alter the gene pool of those who remained behind (*New York Times,* May 22, 1992, A1). The Serbs were soundly condemned by the Security Council, the General Assembly, and the Human Rights Commission. Reports of not only ethnic cleansing but also death camps prompted charges of "war crimes" and the approval in September of the creation of a war crimes tribunal along the lines of the Nuremburg Trials (see Case 12). In a conference held in London in August, Acting Secretary of State Lawrence Eagleburger warned Serb delegates:

> [W]e should, here at this conference, place squarely before the people of Serbia the choice they must make between joining a democratic and prosperous Europe or joining their leaders in the opprobrium, isolation, and defeat which will

be theirs if they continue on their present march of folly. (U.S. State Department, September 1992, 1)

It was not just one group that was guilty of atrocities, however; other developments took place during the first months of the war. To begin, Croats and Muslims were guilty of atrocities and ethnic cleansing as well. For example, in early June, Bosnian Muslims and Croats who lived in Bosnia were reported to have rounded up whole villages and killed the inhabitants. Radovan Karadzic, the Bosnian Serbs' leader, was convinced that Muslims were working for years to dominate the country through means of population control:

> The Bosnian Muslims want, ultimately, to dominate, relying on a very high birthrate. They even wanted to move some Turks from Germany to Bosnia to help build their Islamic society. Since such a strategy of domination would be at the expense of Bosnian Serbs, we have resisted it by protecting our own villages. . . . We have not been fighting to gain territory. We have been fighting for the principle that there will be three autonomous communities in Bosnia-Herzegovina in order that no one of the three dominates the other. . . . We are fighting to protect ourselves from becoming vulnerable to the same kind of genocide that coalition waged upon us in World War II when 700,000 Serbs were killed. Today, Serbs would be 60 percent of the population of Bosnia if this genocide had not been committed. We will never again be history's fools. (Karadzic 1992, 50)

In addition, numerous Serbs opposed violence. In late May, tens of thousands demonstrated in the streets of Belgrade against Slobodan Milosevic and called for his resignation. In the village of Gorazde, an ethnically mixed community, Serb residents were angry with Karadzic's policy of ethnic cleansing. When asked about his remarks that Serbs and Muslims are inherently hostile, they responded: "Remarks like that are simply stupid. . . . Serbs and Muslims have lived in the same valleys, used the same roads, worked in the same places, and intermarried throughout history. Now Karadzic wants to tear us apart" (*New York Times,* March 9, 1993, A5).

Serbian parliamentary leader Milan Panic, a long-time resident of the United States, pressed for a liberal solution to the Yugoslav problem and even ran a strong campaign for president until his defeat and eventual ouster in the fall. He portrayed the situation this way:

> I look at all this a little like a family feud. One family happens to be mine, the Serbs. They happen to live across the river in Bosnia. But they are my family, they are Serbs. To ask Serbs from one side of the river not to help Serbs on the other side is not fair. . . . Now I'm not saying send the army. But we need to help each other, to protect each other. (Panic 1992, 49)

The struggle in Yugoslavia was far from simple because it involved the mutually exclusive goals of territorial integrity and self-determination for a multiethnic state (Woodward 1992, 54). When past experience is overlaid on such a Gordian knot, it is no surprise that there are enough virtue and blame for all.

Peace negotiations under American and European auspices began in earnest in early 1993 with the so-called Vance–Owen plan (named after its diplomatic creators), which would have divided the country into ten more or less ethnically homogeneous areas. Negotiators representing the Muslim and Serb governments expressed strong interest in the plan, but it was ultimately rejected by the Yugoslav parliament in Belgrade under the leadership of Milosevic. Gradually, plans that focused on dividing the country along lines of actual military occupation seemed more realistic and became the foundation for the Dayton Accords.

In 1995, Serb forces stepped up their offensive in spite of NATO threats of retaliation. They overran two safe havens, Srebreniza and Zepa, in the summer and continued shelling Sarajevo. Negotiations for a peace settlement began in earnest in August, shortly before a mortar attack on Sarajevo cost the lives of nearly forty Muslims who were waiting in line at a market on August 28. Two days later, NATO followed through on its threat of aerial bombardment and maintained the shelling until September 14, at which time the tentative agreement to begin full-scale negotiations solidified (the bombing probably did not help move forward the peace process and ran the risk of backfiring—Malanczuk 1997, 414).

Beginning in late September, an extended, secret negotiation took place at Wright-Patterson Air Force Base near Dayton, Ohio. Alija Itzebegovic, Slobodan Milosevic, and Franjo Tudjman signed the agreement with U.S. Secretary of State Warren Christopher on November 21, 1995, signaling both an end to the fighting and the division of Bosnia into two quasi-states: the Serbian Republic centered in Pale and a Moslem-Croat Federation centered in Sarajevo. Although Bosnia is still formally a unified country and the Sarajevo regime is represented in the United Nations, in fact the country has been divided ethnically—one of the goals of the ethnic cleansers.

The Dayton Accords have been implemented primarily by NATO troops from France, the United Kingdom, and the United States, who divided the country into areas of supervision, much like Germany after World War II. The force of roughly 40,000 has encountered periodic resistance and has been criticized for failure to aggressively pursue those accused of war crimes, but in all it has performed as well as expected in preserving stability in the region.

Warfare in Kosovo

Ironically, the structure of the Dayton Accords inadvertently sowed the seeds of a new conflict in the Balkans, this time in Kosovo (Judah 2000, 125). Kosovo, formerly an autonomous republic inside Serbia, is inhabited primarily by ethnic Albanians who have fairly strong ties to the nation of Albania to the south (see Map 15.3). A Serb minority complained of abuse by Albanians in the late 1980s, and in response the Belgrade government rescinded the region's autonomy. Over several years, opposition groups began to coalesce in Kosovo, most aiming for at least a restoration of home rule if not independence, although they differed on the means to be employed to achieve either goal. Ibrahim Rugova, the Kosovar president elected in 1992,

Map 15.3 Yugoslavia after the Dayton Accords
Source: Viktor Meier, Yugoslavia: *A History of Its Demise* (New York: Routledge, 1999).

consistently favored a peaceful, negotiated settlement, whereas the Kosovo Liberation Army (KLA) took a more radical approach. After the Dayton Accords, Rugova and many Kosovars realized that a peaceful approach would never attract the attention of Western diplomats and was therefore doomed.

Beginning in 1997, KLA attacks against Serb military and police installations in Kosovo prompted retaliatory actions that began a tit-for-tat cycle of escalating violence. It is unclear to what extent the KLA was hoping for Serb reprisals, but it is easy to imagine that a lesson from the Bosnian experience was that Serb atrocities were likely to ultimately prompt NATO intervention (which was Kosovo's only real hope for independence—Ignatieff 2000, 28).

Western diplomats were slow to focus attention on Kosovo. In the meantime, the collapse of the Albanian government of Sali Berisha in 1997 created an opportunity for KLA fighters to consolidate their strongholds in Albania near the Kosovo border and to increase their stockpile of small arms (Judah 2000, 128). By 1998, sporadic violence was the norm in Kosovo. The United States ultimately dispatched Richard Holbrooke, the master diplomat who spearheaded the Dayton Accords, to forge a truce between the factions. In October, Milosevic, under threat of NATO aerial bombardment, agreed to pull back his police and military forces and allow international observers to monitor human rights conditions in Kosovo (*Economist*, October 17, 1998,

53). In January, however, a Serb reprisal that left forty-five ethnic Albanians dead brought an end to the deal. Western diplomats brought Milosevic to Rambouillet, near Paris, to force a peace treaty between Serbs and Albanian Kosovars, again under threat of bombing. The agreement called for NATO deployments in and around Kosovo and the withdrawal of Serb forces, while preserving the fig leaf of Serb sovereignty over the region. Ultimately, Milosevic considered this too great a violation of his country's independence and decided to take his chances on surviving a bombing campaign. As put by Judah, "He was going to risk the bombs and go for broke" (Judah 2000, 227). Milosevic was counting on the collapse of NATO resolve in the face of CNN reports of child victims and such. He also counted on Russian support in the corridors of power.

On March 22, 1999, NATO began a bombing campaign that intensified as it went on for 78 days. While the bombs fell, Serb police forced Albanians out of Kosovo in the hope of more easily exposing the remaining KLA fighters (Ignatieff 2000, 41). Nearly one million refugees flooded Albania, Macedonia (which was already protected by a UN force), and Bosnia (where Milosevic hoped war would break out again). The bombardment did little to protect the KLA, however, and Serbs regained control of numerous towns and roads. The Serbs were unable to completely dislodge the guerrillas, and the diplomatic collapse did not take place as Milosevic had predicted.

All his calculations had failed. NATO had not split, he was unable to spark new wars in Macedonia and Bosnia and, in the end, the Russians had proved unwilling or unable to help him. (Judah 2000, 279)

On June 10, 1999, following Milosevic's agreement to Western demands, the NATO bombardment was called off and NATO troops from neighboring Bosnia began to take up positions around the Kosovar capital with UN Security Council approval.

War Crimes Tribunal

In the background of the Yugoslav situation beginning in 1993 was the prospect that those responsible for atrocities would wind up on the docket in the Hague. The International Criminal Tribunal for the former Yugoslavia (ICTY), though starting slow, began to issue indictments for war criminals in 1994 and started its first trial in mid-1995. The first conviction was handed down for Dusko Tadic two years later. Gradually, during 1998 and 1999, an increasing number of those indicted (more than sixty, including leaders of the Pale and Belgrade governments) either surrendered or were captured and arrested by NATO forces in and around Bosnia. The pace of the trials and convictions picked up, and as of mid-2000, ten had been convicted and nearly forty were in custody awaiting imminent trial.

Critics point out that NATO forces have been slow to go after those indicted, often leaving them alone even when they know their whereabouts. Even more serious are charges of complicity by the Belgrade government in

providing asylum to many of those indicted. The indictments against Milosevic in May 1999 meant that he was a prisoner in his own country (the decision to issue the indictment was prompted in part by a fear on the part of
Chief Prosecutor Louise Arbour that Milosevic would flee to Belarus or
some other safe haven).

With the fall of the Milosevic regime in 2000, the new president, Vojislav
Kostunica, was pressured by the West to transfer him to the Hague Tribunal.
Under threat of aid being cut off, Kostunica relented and, in defiance of Serbian nationalists, surrendered Milosevic to the ICTY. The Tribunal finally
had its star suspect in custody. The trial itself began amid chaotic media attention on February 12, 2002, after a flurry of confusing and disjointed statements by Milosevic, who refused to recognize the authority of the trial. His
plea of "not guilty" was entered on his behalf by the Tribunal. The charges
against him include genocide, murder, extermination, torture, plunder, and
cruel treatment of civilians, stemming from Serbia's actions in Croatia,
Bosnia, and Kosovo.

At this writing (September 2002), the trial is still under way. Milosevic is
acting as his own attorney and has attempted to turn the attention away
from himself and on to NATO, which he accuses of war crimes for its bombing raids in Kosovo. Although disruptive, the charges do not seem to be
helping his case and the likelihood of conviction is high.

Conclusion: Whither Yugoslavia?

Have the great powers of the late twentieth century done any better at
bringing peace and justice to the Balkans, or have they simply manipulated
local conflicts for strategic ends? Although NATO intervention halted the
bloodletting in Bosnia and no doubt helped prevent the spread of warfare
during the Kosovo crisis, the conflict has always been on Western (specifically U.S.) terms. This has often meant delayed and minimal intervention.
The Bosnia conflict, after all, cost nearly 250,000 lives before NATO became
directly involved. Even the UN admits that the international community
failed in its effort to protect the citizens of Srebreniza and other safe havens
(United Nations 1999). Likewise, intervention in Kosovo did little in the
short run to protect ethnic Albanians but created instead an opportunity for
Serb aggression. Conversely, Western intervention has sometimes been precipitous for strategic reasons, as with Germany's sudden recognition of
Slovenian and Croatian independence without regard for the security implications. Even more uncharitably, one could interpret the entire Western initiative in the Balkans as an attempt to both shore up and extend NATO influence in southern Europe (Gervasi 1998, 20). Certainly an important loser
in all of this strategic jockeying has been Russia—an outcome not entirely
undesirable from a Western point of view.

The Western initiative has nevertheless been somewhat measured and
constrained compared to past great power machinations. The decision to act

through the UN to a considerable degree validates the norm of multilateralism. Likewise, the decision to establish a war crimes tribunal was intended to make clear that more than strategic considerations were at stake. As put simply by Senator Joseph Biden, "I think we did the right thing in our seventy-eight day air campaign, and we succeeded. The war against Milosevic was of great consequence" (Biden 1999). Is it possible that with respect to the Balkans at least, the international community has overcome international anarchy? This conclusion may be all the more intriguing when we consider the relative peace and prosperity we are currently witnessing in the new, democratic Serbia.

Debate Topic

Does Yugoslavia demonstrate the capacity of states to set aside power politics and instead ensure that "right" wins out over "might"?

PRO

Those who believe that the handling of Yugoslavia's problems bodes well for a future international system argue as follows: (1) Most major powers were reticent about becoming involved, but were persuaded to intervene to halt human rights atrocities. (2) The international community acted with considerable unity in a variety of institutions (UN, NATO, ICTY). (3) International actions in Yugoslavia helped set a precedent for other initiatives, including the ICC.

CON

Those who believe little has changed point out: (1) Americans and Europeans intervened only because Yugoslavia has strategic importance—unlike Rwanda. (2) Germany saw recognition of new former- Yugoslav republics as an opportunity to increase its influence in the region, in spite of European objections. (3) The West has been markedly unenthusiastic about pursuing known war criminals for fear of disrupting the strategic balance.

Questions to Consider

1. How does one judge the merits of a nation's demand for self-determination? At what point does such a demand become the concern of the international community? What criteria do the international community use to grant or deny the demand?

2. To what extent should justice take precedence over stability and peace? To what extent do the needs of ethnic communities justify the use of force to alter the political status quo?

3. What force ought to be used by the international community to remedy injustices? How much voice should the great powers have in deciding and implementing these choices?

Websites

The official website of the government of Yugoslavia: **www.gov.yu**
Official website for the war crimes tribunal: **www.un.org/icty/**
Updates on the Milosevic trial: **www.un.org/icty/glance/casestatus.htm**

U.S. Agencies That Maintain Information Updates
CIA: **www.odci.gov/cia/publications/factbook/bk.html**
State Department: **www.state.gov/www/regions/eur/**
Defense Department: **www.dtic.mil/bosnia/index.html**

Other Databases
www.kosovo.com
www.cco.caltech.edu/~bosnia/doc/history.html
www.bosnia-online.com
www.centraleurope.com

References

Armour, Ian. "Nationalism vs. Yugoslavia." *History Today* 42 (October 1992): 11–13.

Biden, Joseph. "Bosnia and Kosovo: Lessons for U.S. Policy." Director's Forum, Woodrow Wilson International Center for Scholars, July 22, 1999.

Braun, Aurel. *Small-State Security in the Balkans* (Totowa, NJ: Barnes & Noble Books, 1983).

Cohen, Leonard J. "The Disintegration of Yugoslavia." *Current History* 91 #568 (November 1992): 369–375.

"Current Development—UN Membership of the 'New' Yugoslavia." *American Journal of International Law* 86 #4 (October 1992): 830–833.

Djilas, Aleska, and Nader Mousavizadeh. "The Nation That Wasn't." *New Republic* (September 21, 1992): 25–31.

The Economist (August 15, 1992): 37–38.

The Economist (August 23, 1992): 36.

The Economist (October 17, 1998): 53.

Gervasi, Sean. "Why Is NATO in Yugoslavia?" in Sara Flounders, ed., *NATO in the Balkans: Voices of Opposition* (New York: International Action Center, 1998), 20–46.

Hayden, Robert. "Yugoslavia: Where Self-determination Meets Ethnic Cleansing." *New Perspectives Quarterly* 9 #4 (Fall 1992): 41–46.

Ignatieff, Michael. *Virtual War: Kosovo and Beyond* (New York: Metropolitan Books, 2000).

Jelavich, Barbara. *History of the Balkans: Vol. 1: 18th & 19th Centuries; Vol. 2: 20th Century* (New York: Cambridge University Press, 1983).

Judah, Tim. *Kosovo: War and Revenge* (New Haven, CT: Yale University Press, 2000).

Karadzic, Radovan. "Salvation Is a Serbian State—Interview." *New Perspectives Quarterly* 9 #4 (Fall 1992): 50–51.

MacLean, Fitzroy. *The Heretic: The Life and Times of Josep Broz Tito* (New York: Harper, 1957).

Malanczuk, Peter. *Akehurst's Modern Introduction to International Law*, 7th ed. (New York: Routledge, 1997).

Mastnak, Tomas. "Is the Nation-State Really Obsolete?" *Times Literary Supplement*, August 7, 1992, 11.

Meier, Viktor. *Yugoslavia: A History of Its Demise* (New York: Routledge, 1999).

New York Times, May 16, 1991, A1.
New York Times, June 7, 1991, A5.
New York Times, June 27, 1991, A1.
New York Times, July 31, 1991, A1.
New York Times, August 30, 1991, A3.
New York Times, October 1, 1991, A1.
New York Times, February 22, 1992, A1.
New York Times, May 22, 1992, A1.
New York Times, May 31, 1992, A1.
New York Times, June 29, 1992, A1.
New York Times, November 21, 1992, A1.
New York Times, March 9, 1993, A5.
New York Times, April 8, 1993, A5.
Panic, Milan. "The Future Is Forgetting—Interview." *New Perspectives Quarterly* 9 #4 (Fall 1992): 47–50.
Stavrianos, L. S. *The Balkans: 1815–1914* (New York: Holt, Rinehart & Winston, 1963).
UN Chronicle (September 1992): 8.
United Nations. "Kosovo: Recovering from Ravage." *UN Chronicle* #4 (December 1999): 54–55.
U.S. State Department Dispatch Supplement, September 1992, 1.
Wachtel, Andrew Baruch. *Making a Nation, Breaking a Nation: Literature and Cultural Politics in Yugoslavia* (Stanford, CA: Stanford University Press, 1998).
Woodward, Susan. "The Yugoslav Wars." *Brookings Review* 10 #4 (Fall 1992): 54.
Yugoslavia (Stanford, CA: Stanford University Press, 1998).

CASE
16

Kashmir and Nuclear War
BORDER DISPUTES

Introduction

At the center of most wars is a dispute over where to draw a line on a map. The line in question is the political boundary between two states. Where two states disagree on where that line should be drawn, we say that there exists a "territorial dispute." It may surprise the reader to know that dozens, if not most, countries have at least some part of their border with some neighbor that isn't quite what they feel is just and fair. Even the United States and Canada—famous for having the longest and most peaceful frontier in the world—had a dispute over where the line should be drawn. It took a judgment from the International Court of Justice to settle the matter.

More interesting than the question of *whether* a territorial dispute exists is the *whys* and *wherefores* of the dispute. After all, many territorial claims are entirely contrived. Hitler's claims on Czechoslovakia in 1938 were merely legal window-dressing for irredentist aggression (Case 1). Of the territorial disputes that are more genuine, most have one or more of the following rationales: nationality questions, economic opportunities, historical ambiguities, or strategic imperatives. Especially since the end of World War and the validation of "self-determination" as a basis for statehood, many states have found that the work of unifying a nation is still incomplete. In Africa, most states have boundaries that were drawn in Berlin by European diplomats and frequently placed parts of nations in different states. It is a wonder of modern diplomacy that there have been relatively few wars of irredentism (redrawing boundaries to include members of one nation into a single state). This issue was an important part of the conflict in Yugoslavia, where Serb politicians hoped to protect Serbs in Croatia and Bosnia (Case 15). As we will see, it is also an important factor in the war in Kashmir.

A territorial dispute may arise from genuine confusion over the rights of different states to a piece of land. In a famous International Court of Justice case, the United States and the Netherlands argued over control of some small islands—the Islands of Palmas—off the coast of Indonesia. Because of the maps the U.S. government had obtained from Spain showing its territorial claims, which the United States inherited after winning the Spanish–American War in 1898, Washington assumed the islands were newly won booty. In fact, the Spanish had never settled the islands in question, but had permitted the Netherlands to continue occupying and administering them. The court therefore ruled that they never belonged to Spain in the first place, so they could not belong to the United States. The International Court of Justice has heard dozens of similar cases involving legal confusion over where to draw boundary lines, especially in off-shore oceans where the rules are still a bit murky.

In most cases, the real issue is either power or money. Territorial disputes rarely arise over barren wastelands devoid of natural resources (Saudi Arabia, Yemen, and Iraq, for example, have left their borders undefined where they pass through uninhabited desert regions). Conversely, the possibility that there is oil in the South China Sea has prompted to no less than six nations laying claim to the otherwise uninteresting Spratley Islands. There seems little doubt that it was also oil that led Iraq to claim the Kuwaiti territory in 1990 rather than the faulty map-making of British colonial officials, as Iraq claimed (Case 9). Likewise, Libya attacked Chad in the hope of securing control over the Aouzou Strip mostly because of its alleged oil reserves. Military advantage is another reason for competition over land, as has occurred in the Middle East (Case 18). Israel continues to occupy the Golan Heights, claimed by Syria, because of their strategic importance as a high plateau overlooking northern Israel. China still claims Quemoy and Matsu—small islands located in the Straits of Taiwan—in part because they provide Taiwan with a beachhead near the Chinese coast.

Since conquest and gain are no longer justifications for war, states intent on using force to change their borders must come up with other rationales. Thus claims are usually made on the basis of legal ambiguity or nationalism and self-determination, however dubious those prospects. Nowhere is this more evident than in the complex and (perhaps) intractable dispute between India and Pakistan over the region known as Kashmir. Kashmir has already been at the center of two major wars between the parties, as well as numerous skirmishes and a decade-long civil war. Neither side shows any sign of backing down.

In the summer of 2002, Kashmir was in the headlines as tensions flared yet again. This time, though, the world's attention was riveted on the region for the simple reason that each of the two struggling parties possesses enough nuclear weapons to annihilate more than ten million people in a war. The fallout alone would likely contaminate not only Kashmir, but also most of northern India, Nepal, and Bangladesh. The stakes are clearly high. It therefore behooves us to have some idea of the origins of the conflict, the claims and complaints of the various parties, and the prospects for settlement. It would also be worthwhile to spend some time considering the degree of military buildup in the region to determine the degree of danger that the conflict presents to the rest of the world.

KASHMIR AND NUCLEAR WAR
KEY FIGURES

Jawaharlal Nehru   Indian Prime Minister, 1947–1964. Although an ethnic Kashmiri, he is widely considered the father of modern India. Inclusion of Kashmir was central to his vision of a secular state.

Indira Gandhi   Indian Prime Minister, 1966–1977, 1980–1984. She asserted her authority over Kashmiri leaders and fought wars against China and Pakistan.

Mohammed Ali Jinnah   Leader of the Muslim League, 1937–1948. He engineered a separate state for Muslims at the breakup of the British Raj. He also was the new country's first leader.

Maharaja Hari Singh Dogra   Hindu Prince of Kashmir, 1925–1949. He hoped to achieve independence for Kashmir, but instead acceded to India following a military incursion in 1947.

Sheik Mohammed Abdullah   Leader of the National Conference, an India-leaning Kashmiri party. His assent was requested by Nehru prior to the signing of the Accession Agreement in 1947. He led Kashmir from 1977–1982.

Mohammed Ayub Khan   Pakistani President, 1958–1969. He launched an ill-advised invasion of Kashmir in 1965.

Farooq Abdullah   Leader of the National Conference, an India-leaning Kashmiri party, and Chief Minister of Kashmir since 1983, with interruptions. He was imprisoned and then released in the 1980s when he won a widely criticized election to lead Kashmir. He narrowly escape an assassination attempt in mid-2002.

Pervez Musharraf   Pakistani leader, 1999–present . He was the chief of staff of the military under Prime Minister Nawaz Sharif.

Zulfikar Ali Bhutto   Pakistani President, 1971–1973. He signed the Simla Agreement with Indira Gandhi in 1972.

Atel Bihari Vajpayee   Prime Minister of India, 1996, 1998–present. He is leader of the nationalist BJP.

Gulab Singh   First ruler of Kashmir in 1846. He won his position by bargaining with the British.

Mian Nawaz Sharif   Prime Minster of Pakistan, 1990–1993, 1997–1999. He was overthrown by Pervez Musharraf.

KASHMIR AND NUCLEAR WAR
CHRONOLOGY

1846
Gulab Singh is granted control of Kashmir by the British in exchange for his support against the Sikhs to the south.

1929
Jawaharlal Nehru becomes President of the Congress Party, a position he holds at six different times.

1937
Mohammed Ali Jenna becomes the leader of the Muslim League.

1945
Great Britain announces its intention to withdraw from India.   *(continued)*

1947

Maharaja Hari Singh Dogra announces his intention to keep Kashmir independent. Pakistan imposes economic sanctions and provides support for Pashtun guerrillas in their rebellion against the maharaja. Under duress, he asks for Indian support, which is provided on condition of accession.

1949

A UN-sponsored cease-fire takes effect between India and Pakistan along a temporary cease-fire line, leaving Pakistan in control of one-third of the region.

1952

The Delhi Agreement is signed in August, resulting in the replacement of the maharaja by his son, Karan Singh, and a special status for Kashmir as a semi-autonomous province within India.

1953

Mohammed Abdullah is imprisoned for anti-Indian statements.

1954

The Kashmir constitution is formally accepted.

1962

China seizes control of the Aksai Chin from India in a decisive victory.

1963

Kashmiris demonstrate against Indian rule.

1965

The Pakistani leader, Ayub Khan, leads an attack into Indian-held Kashmir but is soundly defeated.

1966

The Tashkent Accords are signed in January to settle the 1965 war.

1971

India defeats Pakistan in the war of Bangladesh liberation.

1972

The Simla Agreement is reached between Indira Gandhi and Zulfikar Ali Bhutto, resulting in the acceptance of the line of control in Kashmir and Indian dominance over the subcontinent.

1974

India conducts a "peaceful" nuclear test.

1975

The Beg-Parthasarthi Accord puts an end to the plebiscite question in exchange for new authority for Kashmiri leaders.

1977

Mohammed Abdullah is elected to lead Kashmir.

1979

The Soviet Union invades Afghanistan, prompting the formation of the mujahaddin, funded in part by the United States. They later form the backbone of al Qaeda and the fundamentalist militants in Kashmir.

1983

Abdullah is succeeded by his son, Farooq Abdullah, after his death in 1982.

1987

Farooq Abdullah wins a tainted election that ties him closely to the New Delhi government.

(continued)

1989

An uprising led by the Jammu and Kashmir Liberation Front leads to large-scale violence. Farooq loses control of the Vale of Kashmir and is dismissed in 1990. India responds militarily with half a million troops, who become an army of occupation.

1997

Peaceful elections bring Farooq Abdullah back to power.

1998

Atel Bihari Vajpayee is elected Prime Minster of India. India and Pakistan carry out public tests of nuclear devices.

1999

Pakistan launches a series of probes in the Kargil area, forcing renewed Indian deployments, including air strikes. Violence also breaks out in the Siachen Glacier region. Perzev Musharraf seizes power in Pakistan.

2001

September 11 terrorist attacks improve Pakistan's relations with the United States and provide grounds for international support of India's fight with Islamic militants in Kashmir. Islamic militants attack the Indian parliament building in December.

2002

In June, Indian soldiers and civilians come under attack by militants in Kashmir. Farooq Abdullah narrowly escapes assassination. Pakistan and India mobilize one million troops in a tense face-off that is calmed by international diplomatic intervention. Election are held in Kashmir in September and October, resulting in a new ruling coalition coming to power.

History of India–Pakistan Border Disputes

Unlike other border disputes we review in this text, the India–Pakistan rivalry began relatively recently. In the 1920s, Pakistani and Indian leaders, then under the government of the British Raj, agreed on most of their political objectives (Rizvi 1986, 96). It was not until the 1930s that tensions began to brew between predominantly Hindu India and predominantly Muslim Pakistan. India aspired to become a multiethnic, secular state under the leadership of Jawaharlal Nehru after it gained its independence from Great Britain in 1947. Muslims recognized that they would end up a minority in such a unified state. When the differences became irreconcilable, the Hindu-dominated Congress Party and the Muslim League decided to take steps, under British tutelage, to divide the area into Muslim-dominated Pakistan and Hindu-dominated India.

The process of division proved to be controversial and difficult in some areas. Because there was no unified South Asian leadership, dozens of minor rulers were asked to choose which new country their regions wanted to join. Where disputes arose, the issue was left to a plebiscite of the people who lived in the area, and in almost every case, the result was acceptable to both the local ruler and his subjects. In two regions, however, a struggle erupted. Punjab, a fairly large area that straddles the current India–Pakistan border, was home to the Sikh religious community, which resisted incorporation into India. Ultimately, because the territory had a large number of Muslims in the west and Hindus in the east, a line was drawn down the middle by British overseer Cyril Radcliffe when local judges failed to reach a compromise solution. To this day, the Indian government has yet to resolve satisfactorily its relationship with the Sikh minority in its territory (Tinker 1977, 697).

Even more troublesome than the split of Punjab was the arrangement in Kashmir, a fairly large territory to the north of both India and Pakistan (roughly the size of Pennsylvania), located next to Tibet and Afghanistan (see Map 16.1). The area had come under unified political control only in the 1840s as result of British manipulation of local rivalries. The result was the installation of a one-time vagabond, Gulab Singh, as maharaja of the new territory of Kashmir. Once a sought-after resort for British colonialists and wealthy Indians to escape the summer heat, the region is famous for its beautiful vistas and rugged inhabitants. Roughly three-fourths of the population is Muslim, concentrated in the west and central valley around Srinagar. Hindus are the majority in the Jammu area to the southeast. The area is also home to a large number of Tibetan Buddhists and other ethnic and religious minorities (Thomas 2001, 205). In spite of this plurality, by the 1940s one could speak of a coherent Kashmiri identity (Ganguly 2001, 314).

In 1947, Kashmir was ruled by maharaja Hari Singh, a Hindu with Indian leanings. He made it clear that, in spite of British pressure to choose either Hindu India or Muslim Pakistan, he preferred to make Kashmir independent (in this endeavor, he was following the example of the leader of Hyderabad to the south). Neither India nor Pakistan accepted this approach, however, and Pakistan even imposed economic sanctions against the principality for the sake of the Muslim majority. The situation became a crisis when a Muslim uprising in the northwest regions of Kashmir resulted in the advance of a large army toward Srinagar (Oberoi 1997). Historians continue to debate the nature of this uprising. The Indian government and its sympathizers have argued that the uprising was actually an invasion of Paksitani Pathan tribesmen, Pakistani regular troops disguised as Kashmiris, and uniformed Pakistanis, all directed by Islamabad with the intent of annexing Kashmir (Hardgrave and Kochanek 2000, 419). The Pakistani version claims that indigenous Muslim groups rose up to seize control of the regime from the maharaja to prevent the country from being annexed by India (Baxter et al. 1998, 384). Recent scholarship has pointed out that these conflicting interpretations have developed their own mythology, to the point that neither side is especially eager to explore the facts for fear of undermining their position (Udayakumar 2001; Lamb 1985, 177). As put by Daanish Mustafa and Viren Murthy, "Historical narratives based on facts have been constructed supporting each of these positions, and it would be futile to determine which narrative is most 'true'" (Mustafa and Murthy 2001, 109)

In any event, with the armies closing in on his capital, the maharaja turned to India. Nehru seized the opportunity to ensure Kashmiri depen-

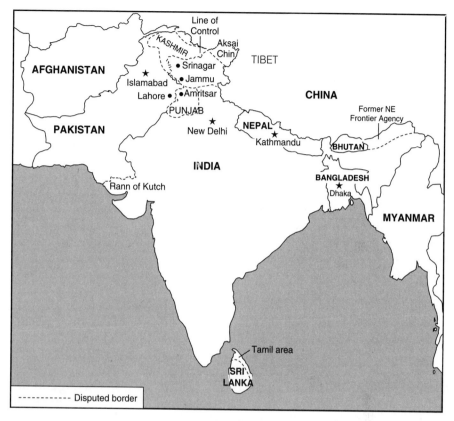

Map 16.1 South Asia, including disputed territory

dence on New Delhi by presenting him with a condition for India's support: sign an instrument of accession. Nehru, himself a high-caste Kashmiri native to Srinagar, had a good friend by the name of Sheik Mohammed Abdullah who was the Muslim leader of the National Conference, the largest political party in Kashmir. Abdullah supported Nehru's vision of a multiethnic, secular, socialist India, and gave his assent to the accession agreement (Thomas 2001, 205). The terms of the agreement provided for an eventual plebiscite (later demanded by the United Nations) so that all the people of Kashmir could vote on whether to become fully integrated in India. Such civilities would have to wait until after the crisis at hand could be resolved, however (Ganguly 2001, 312). The fact that this plebiscite was never held remains a bone of contention for Pakistan (Baxter et al. 1998, 384).

Immediately after India intervened, Pakistan dispatched troops to protect the Muslim majority. After several months of fighting, the two forces reached a stalemate at the so-called line of control and allowed the UN to step in and broker a cease-fire. A tentative cease-fire line was established on January 1, 1949. The line became essentially permanent over the years and was reaffirmed in 1972 in the Simla Agreement between India's Indira Gandhi (no relation to the Mahatma) and Pakistan's Zulfikar Ali Bhutto (Hardgrave and Kochanek 2000, 424).

Nehru was intent on keeping Kashmir within the Indian sphere of influence in part because it represented a validation of his notion of a secular state. Furthermore, "losing" Kashmir would likely result in the loss of other non-Hindu regions of the country, such as Assam to the northeast and Punjab to the west. Kashmir and its high plateaus also offered important strategic ground for the Indian military, since it put the forces within roughly two hundred kilometers of Islamabad. Conversely, control of the eastern portions of Kashmir could place the Pakistani army within less than five hundred kilometers of New Delhi by way of an easy route through a wide valley. And, of course, for Pakistan, the notion that Muslims could be content in Hindu-dominated India essentially negates Pakistan's reason for being. In a sense, then, Kashmir is as much a result as a cause of India–Pakistan tension (Hardgrave and Kochanek 2000, 418).

During the years following the first India–Pakistan war over Kashmir, New Delhi worked to forge a lasting relationship with the region that accommodated some of its nationalist aspirations. The final agreement, ratified in 1952, provided Kashmir with far more autonomy than other Indian provinces, but still subjugated its foreign policy and legal system to the center (Ganguly 2001, 314). Oddly enough, in spite of his close relationship with Nehru, Mohammed Abdullah was not part of the new Kashmiri regime, having been locked up along with other National Conference leaders for making anti-India statements. He was later released and led the government from 1977 until his death in 1982. His son, Farooq Abdullah, succeeded him. In general, the Kashmiri leadership has a reputation for corruption and ineptness, as well as toadying up to New Delhi (Farooq included). Although they have won numerous elections (which serve as a substitute for a plebiscite in India's mind), many of the elections have been tainted by both unlawful practices of Indian military pressure, such that none of the Kashmiri leaders has enjoyed full legitimacy (Bose and Jalel 1998, 226). In addition, Kashmir has consistently received less government support than other Indian provinces, and the level of poverty is among the highest in the country. These facts give the impression that many Kashmiri leaders have been looking out only for themselves. As we will see, this perception led to an explosive reaction in the late 1980s.

More fighting broke out in 1965, when Pakistan, hoping to prompt a Kashmiri uprising, launched an attack against Indian forces. India responded with counterattacks at several points along the border and quickly overwhelmed Pakistani forces. The hoped-for uprising did not materialize, demonstrating that Kashmiri discontent with Indian dominance does not equate with aspirations to merge with Pakistan. It is interesting to note that in those areas of Kashmir controlled by Pakistan, Kashmiris have not been permitted to govern themselves or hold elections (Ahmad 2000, 254).

Tensions between India and Pakistan remained high as Bangladesh obtained Indian support for its war of independence against Pakistan in 1971.

Agreements were reached in 1972 between India and Pakistan and in 1975 between India and Kashmir that brought a degree of stability (if not justice) to the region. Sheik Mohammed Abdullah was elected in the first of a string of ballots in 1977. In the 1980s, however, the election of Farooq Abdullah came as a result of back-room deals that tainted his government (Bose and Jalal 1998, 226). The election of 1987 was especially flawed, and it stimulated a violent response from a growing Muslim opposition within Kashmir. The unrest continues to this day.

Tension is greatest in the Srinagar valley (known as the "Vale of Kashmir"), where Muslims form a local majority and have never accepted Indian control. Beginning in 1989, the Muslim community, led by the Jammu and Kashmir Liberation Front, mounted another guerrilla campaign with covert support from Pakistan and the help of former Muslim militant fighters (known as "mujahaddin") from the war in Afghanistan. The conflict has generally consisted of Indian occupying forces taking action against guerrilla groups following small-scale attacks. The level of violence has become so great that many Hindus living in the Vale of Kashmir have fled to areas around Jammu or to India, where they live in resentment of the failure of Indian policy.

In early 1999, Pakistani forces faced off against Indian troops around Kargil and the Siachen Glacier (where more troops are dying from exposure than from bullets). At the same time, aircraft clashed in the southern region known as the Rann of Kutch, also a disputed area. Following the historical pattern, the two sides fought to a stalemate and ultimately withdrew to the status quo (Oberoi 1997).

After the attacks of September 11, 2001, Pakistan became a close ally of the United States in the war against al Qaeda. India, on the other hand, took advantage of the U.S. declaration of war against Muslim guerrillas, pointing out that the mujahaddin in Kashmir were closely tied to global terrorist networks. When attacks were launched against the Indian parliament in December 2001, India initiated raids into Kashmir. A series of reprisals followed, culminating in a large-scale attack against Indian military bases in Kashmir. Both Pakistan and India mobilized their forces, leading to one million troops facing off across the line of control. Given the fact that both countries possess nuclear capabilities, the entire international community became involved in mediating the dispute, which was ultimately achieved in July. The United States (rather than the UN, which India mistrusts when it comes to Kashmir) played a key role, although pressure from many quarters was extreme.

India–Pakistan Military Competition

To put the Kashmir situation in broader perspective, it is important to consider the increasing military capabilities of India and Pakistan.

Both India and Pakistan have, almost since their independence, felt a sense of inferiority with respect to their military adversaries. Following their separation in 1947 and the Indian acquisition of the lion's share of Great Britain's left-over military equipment, Pakistan began playing catch-up to India. Since 1962, however, India has felt inferior to its neighbor to the north. The sense of inferiority has led to a number of crash weapons programs over the years. Pakistan imported Western equipment during the 1950s and 1960s and Chinese equipment in more recent years. India has made a strong effort to reorganize its military forces and improve its domestic production capacity through a series of licensing arrangements with foreign defense contractors. India now has a flourishing indigenous missile development capacity, and both countries are essentially self-sufficient in munitions production. As shown in Figure 16.1, India and Pakistan have generally matched increases in military spending by the other, although these figures do not show whether one is responding to the other or to yet a third factor.

India, though primarily interested in Pakistan's military force, has also been concerned about China as it draws up its weapons budget. This concern arises because of not only China's size and obvious territorial ambitions on India but also its nuclear capability. In 1962, China successfully attacked India and secured control of the Aksai Chin territory. The attack galvanized the Indian military establishment and launched it on a course of research and development, expansion, and collaborative ventures with foreign defense contractors. India entered into contracts with French, German, Soviet, British, and Swedish companies to either build their equipment in India or subcontract Indian production to them. During the 1960s, India built or purchased MiG-21, Hunter, Su-7, and Marut jets, reaching the level of 1,000 aircraft by 1980 and expanding to roughly 1,500 by 1990. It purchased several hundred tanks from Britain and collaborated in building antiaircraft and 106-mm artillery. During the 1980s, India added more than 2,000 tanks to its armored arsenal and enjoyed a world-class navy of 36 attack craft (Thomas 1997).

Although the licensing arrangements with foreign firms helped India establish itself quickly as a strong fighting force, they did little to encourage an indigenous, diverse production capability. Little technology was transferred as a result of these arrangements (Thomas 1997, 112). In some respects, Pakistan's willingness to merely import much of its arsenal may give it an advantage over India (Husain 1997, 132).

Pakistan's conventional military posture is rather easily explained in relation to India. Almost its entire military is geared for border protection. Pakistan has emphasized fighter aircraft over bombers, tanks over helicopters, and patrol boats over long-range ships (Ahmed 1998, 349). Its troops are deployed along the border with India in a posture that could be described as offensive, whereas its navy is more defensive (the reverse of India's deployment—Arnett 1997, 20). As put by Ahmed:

> Because Pakistan's long history of conflict with India has created a "cold war" mind-set, the security thinking of its principal decision makers remains centered on India. They believe that the primary objective of policy must rest on ways of guarding Pakistan from India and of providing it with the ability to protect itself from the dangerous and hegemonistic designs of India. (Ahmed 1998, 351)

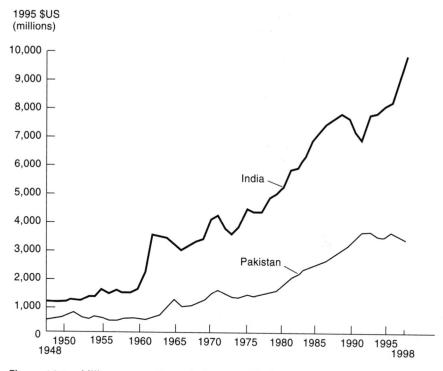

Figure 16.1   Military expenditures by India and Pakistan, 1948–1998 (estimated).
Source: Adapted from *SIPRI Yearbook of World Armaments and Disarmament* (London: Humanities Press and Oxford University Press, various years).

Pakistan almost immediately formed a close alliance with the United States. During the 1950s and 1960s, the United States transferred roughly $2 billion of equipment to Pakistan, including tanks and F-104 fighter jets. During the 1980s, the United States again became the principal arms supplier to Pakistan (although China's material continued to arrive) due to the increased strategic importance of the region after the Soviet invasion of Afghanistan in 1979. The United States provided dozens of F-16s and other advanced fighter aircraft, advanced guided missile systems, and helicopters, as did the French and British. By the 1990s, the Pakistani Air Force had nearly 500 advanced jets and other attack aircraft. Pakistan had also developed maintenance and repair capabilities through the facilities of the Pakistan Aeronautical Complex. Although the Indian Air Force had more than twice as many aircraft, they were mostly of Russian design and earlier origin. Pakistan's U.S. acquisitions did not continue, however, because the White House, under pressure from Congress, suspended all military transfers in 1990 when it could no longer guarantee that Islamabad did not have a nuclear weapons program (Cheema 1997, 153).

In the area of missile development, as mentioned earlier, both India and Pakistan are working hard to establish an internal capability. This project

Table 16.1   Missile Capability in India and Pakistan, 2000

India's missiles:

Prithvi	Deployed in 1995, range of 150 km, nuclear capable. 30 initially deployed near Lahore, now more central.
Prithvi II	In production, 250-km range, nuclear capable. 25 expected.
Prithvi III	Deployment by 2001, 350-km range, unknown nuclear capability. Sea-launched.
Sagarika	SLBM alleged to be in development, 300-km range.
Agni	In production, 2,500-km range, nuclear capable.
Agni II	Tested in 1999, 2,500-km range, nuclear capable.
Agni III	Alleged to have 3,500-km range and nuclear capability.
Agni IV	Under development, might have 8,000-km range.

Pakistan's missiles:

M-11	In production, 300-km range (?), nuclear capable. Unknown whether Pakistan has perfected the tritium detonator necessary to make the warhead explode.
Ghauri	In production, 1,500-km range, nuclear capable.
DF-2	Bomber-adapted missiles, nuclear capable.

Source: Joseph Cirincione, "Indian Missile Deployments and the Reaction from China." Working paper submitted to the Conference on the Nuclearization of South Asia, May 1999.

has been by far most successful in India. Table 16.1 shows India's and Pakistan's current and projected missile capability. If one is looking for evidence of an arms race between the two countries, it is most obvious in this area.

Nuclear Competition

In 1974, the Indira Gandhi government in India carried out what it called a "peaceful nuclear explosion." Few accepted the government's official explanation that the exercise was related only to India's nonmilitary use of nuclear energy, but New Delhi never admitted to having military nuclear capability. Generally speaking, most attribute India's quasi-nuclear test to its fear of China, not Pakistan. In 1962, a brewing border dispute between India and China erupted in large-scale warfare, with a resounding victory for Chinese forces and the loss of territory for India (the area, known as Aksai Chin, is located to the northeast of Kashmir). With its detonation of a nuclear weapon in 1964 and unresolved territorial disputes in eastern India, China represented an ongoing and serious threat to India's security. India hoped that by building a nuclear capability, it would deter future Chinese aggression.

In the process, however, India's nuclear test set off alarms in Islamabad, where the Pakistani government almost immediately launched a nuclear program of its own. By the mid-1980s, both India and Pakistan were reputed to have nuclear capability, although neither publicly admitted to it. One might ask why both countries kept their capability an open secret rather than either burying the information or making it public. By leaking the information, each country clearly hoped to achieve its principal goal: deterring an attack by a rival. To possess nuclear weapons in the 1970s was very controversial, however. In the mid-1960s, under U.S. and Soviet leadership, the vast majority of countries entered into the Non-Proliferation Treaty (NPT), which called upon states to limit the propagation of nuclear capability. Countries signed the treaty as either a nuclear or a non-nuclear power. Nuclear powers committed themselves to disarmament and tight oversight of their arsenals to prevent accidental launches of missiles. More importantly, they agreed not to share nuclear technology or material with non-nuclear states. Non-nuclear states, for their part, agreed to refrain from research and development or purchases of technology and material that could contribute to a nuclear weapons arsenal. The hope was that by capping the number of nuclear weapons states and encouraging arms control negotiations at the same time, the NPT could make the world more stable and avoid war. Both Pakistan and India declined to sign the nuclear Non-Proliferation Treaty (Chari 1995, 14–20).

Pakistan's nuclear program intensified after India's nuclear explosion in 1974. Pakistan began efforts to enrich uranium in 1976 and established its Engineering Research Laboratories secretly under the direction of A. Q. Khan. The country made contacts in Germany and elsewhere in Europe to obtain technology and parts for a gas centrifuge capable of enriching enough uranium to produce several bombs per year (Albright and Hibbs 1992). It sought support particularly from China, which was not an NPT signatory and had few reservations about assisting Pakistan's program (Kapur 2001, 327). China is alleged to have provided not only conventional weaponry but also missile technology, including important components and plans for the M-11, Pakistan's most advanced nuclear-capable ballistic missile (Joeck 1999). By the early 1990s, Western observers were certain that Pakistan was well on its way to both manufacturing nuclear weapons and installing them on medium-range missiles.

Pakistan began a series of test firings of its advanced weapons, which might have contributed to India's decision to become a public nuclear power in early 1998 (Koch and Sidhu 1998). In May 1998, India detonated a series of nuclear weapons and publicly reported the results. Pakistan followed suit within three weeks with tests of its own. This, in turn, explains the high degree of international involvement in resolving the Kashmir crisis in mid-2002, discussed earlier.

The Future of Kashmir

At the time of this writing, another election is under way in Kashmir. Although every effort is being made to ensure that it is free and fair, the boycott of the vote by the Jammu and Kashmir Liberation Front and various mujahaddin groups means that only pro-Indian candidates are running. It is therefore unlikely that the result of the voting will lessen the violence in the streets of Srinagar.

That said, the dispute continues to rage concerning whether Muslims in Kashmir deserve to be linked to Pakistan. It is debatable whether they would choose to do so if given the option, and it is not entirely clear that they would reject Indian ties, either. One thing is clear: The people of Kashmir have rarely been the focus of Indian or Pakistani attention in the ongoing struggle over control of the region. Some have argued that Kashmir has been treated as a mere "prize to be won" (Mustafa and Murthy 2001, 100; Ahmad 2000, 254). Much of the struggle involves status games, strategic positioning, and symbolism rather than a search for justice and peace. Given the lack of genuine interest in treating Kashmiris fairly, it is doubtful that any genuine settlement can be achieved by the Indian and Pakistani governments. The presence of weapons in the hands of Islamic militants will likely confuse the issue by intensifying a cycle of violence (Mustafa and Murthy 2001, 121).

A few positive developments have emerged. For one, India and Pakistan proved willing to back away from a dangerous military escalation in 2002. In addition, the two adversaries have engaged in some confidence-building measures in both the security and economic areas. For example, each state has pledged never to attack the nuclear facilities of the other, and both have agreed to a "no first use" policy for nuclear weapons. Both are active members of the South Asian Association for Regional Cooperation (SAARC), a regional economic body that has been meeting regularly since 1983. There is even talk of a free trade area for South Asia, building on the formation of the Preferential Trade Arrangement in 1995. India has clearly decided to become an active player in the World Trade Organization and expand its trade with the West. Finally, an election in Kashmir in the fall of 2002 resulted in the defeat of the National Conference party and the seating of a grass-roots opposition party more likely to demand concessions from New Delhi (*Chicago Tribune*, October 15, 2002, 3).

Conclusion

What does the Kashmir situation tell us about the nature of border disputes? To begin, it is clear that Kashmiri problem are multifaceted, and the facts are sometimes secondary to the myths. Neither India nor Pakistan agrees on the origins or substance of the conflict—only that it is irreconcilable. Likewise, it is clear that the disputing parties are more prone to focus on issues that resonate in the international community, such as self-determination and honoring international agreements, than on questions of power and wealth. In the case of Kashmir, Pakistan has made much of its support for the people's self-determination, even though it has taken steps to silence independence-minded Kashmiris living in regions under its control. Its support for Islamic mujahaddin in Kashmir now seems extremely reckless, given the war against terror. Likewise, India has based its rule on democratic processes, even though most of the elections of which it is so proud have been rigged. And New Delhi's tolerance of corruption among Kashmir's leaders has not gone unnoticed.

It is difficult to imagine how to achieve peace and justice in the region without changing the entire cast of players. The continued growth of military arsenals on both sides implies that the next fullscale war will have devastating effects. Thus the urgency of settling the question increases.

Debate Topic

Should the United States insist on a new plebiscite in Kashmir as a way of settling the problem?

PRO

Arguments in support of an active U.S. role in the region include the following: (1) The United States has a policy of promoting human rights everywhere. (2) The plebiscite is the best way to protect Kashmiri rights. (3) India and Pakistan are likely to acquiesce to a strong U.S. role, given their relationships.

CON

Arguments against such a role include the following: (1) The United States is unlikely to resolve this fifty-five-year-old dispute and should send its diplomats elsewhere. (2) The conflict is essentially strategic and a plebiscite will not resolve anything. (3) Only a basic settlement of the India–Pakistan conflict, including reconciliation between Muslims and Hindus throughout the region, will help bring about a solution.

Questions to Consider

1. Why is telling the basic story of Kashmir so contentious for India and Pakistan?

2. What role do nonregional and international players have in resolving the conflict?

3. What evidence suggests that an arms race in South Asia has caused or will cause increased violence?

Websites

AccessAsia Review: www.nbr.org/publications/review.html
U. C. Berkeley Library South and Southeast Asia collection: **www.lib.berkeley.edu/ SSEAL/\SouthAsia/nuclear.html**
Carnegie Endowment for International Peace **wyswyg://55/http://www.ceip.org/ programs/npp/indiapaper.htm**
Coalition to Reduce Nuclear Dangers: **www.clw.org/pub/clw/coalition/ctindia.htm**

References

Ahmad, Aijaz, Lineages of the Present: Ideology and Politics in Contemporary South Asia (New York: Verso, 2000).
Ahmed, Samina. "Pakistan: The Crisis Within" in Alagappa, ed., *Asian Security Practice: Material and Ideational Influences* (Stanford, CA: Stanford University Press, 1998), 338–366.

Alagappa, Muthiah, ed. *Asian Security Practice: Material and Ideational Influences* (Stanford, CA: Stanford University Press, 1998).

Albright, David, and Mark Hibbs. "Pakistan's Bomb: Out of the Closet." *Bulletin of the Atomic Scientists* (July/August 1992).

Arnett, Eric. "Beyond Threat Perception: Assessing Military Capacity and Reducing the Risk of War in Southern Asia" in Eric Arnett, ed., *Military Capacity and the Risk of War: China, India, Pakistan, Iran* (London: SIPRI/Oxford University Press, 1997), 1–24.

Arnett, Eric, ed. *Military Capacity and the Risk of War: China, India, Pakistan, Iran* (London: SIPRI/Oxford University Press, 1997).

Baxter, Craig, Yogendra K. Malik, Charles H. Kennedy, and Robert C. Oberst. *Government and Politics in South Asia*, 4th ed. (Boulder, CO: Westview Press, 1998).

Bose, Sugata and Ayesha Jalal. *Modern South Asia: History, Culture, Political Economy* (New York: Routledge, 1998).

Buzan, Barry, and Gowher Rizvi, eds. *South Asian Insecurity and the Great Powers* (New York: St. Martin's, 1986).

Chari, P. R. *Indo-Pak Nuclear Standoff: The Role of the United States* (New Delhi: Manohar Pubs., 1995).

Cheema, Pervaiz Iqbal. "Arms Procurement and Military Planning in Pakistan: Balancing the Needs for Quality, Self-reliance and Diversity of Supply" in Eric Arnett, ed., *Military Capacity and the Risk of War: China, India, Pakistan, Iran* (London: SIPRI/Oxford University Press, 1997), 148–160.

Chicago Tribune, October 15, 2002, 3.

Cirincione, Joseph. "Indian Missile Deployments and the Reaction from China." Working paper submitted to the Conference on the Nuclearization of South Asia, May 1999.

Ganguly, Sumit, "The Flash-Point of South Asia: Kashmir in Indo-Pakistani Relations," in Amita Shastri, and A. Jeyaratnam Wilson, eds. *The Post-Colonial States of South Asia: Democracy, Development and Identity.* (NewYork: Palgrave, 2001), 311–325.

Hardgrave, Robert L., Jr., and Stanley A. Kochanek. *India: Government and Politics in a Developing Nation,* 6th ed. (New York: Harcourt College, 2000).

Husain, Ross Masood. "Threat Perception and Military Planning in Pakistan: The Impact of Technology, Doctrine, and Arms Control" in Eric Arnett, ed., *Military Capacity and the Risk of War: China, India, Pakistan, Iran* (London: SIPRI/Oxford University Press, 1997), 130–147.

Joeck, Neil. "Nuclear Developments in India and Pakistan." *AccessAsia Review* 2 #2 (Fall 1999).

Kapur, Asok. "Pokhran II and After: Consequences of the Indian Nuclear Tests of 1998," in Amita Shastri, and A. Jeyaratnam Wilson, eds. *The Post-Colonial States of South Asia: Democracy, Development and Identity* (New York:: Palgrave, 2001), 326–346.

Koch, Andrew, and Waheguru Singh Sidhu. "Subcontinental Missiles." *Bulletin of the Atomic Scientists* 54 #4 (July/August 1998).

Lamb, Alastair. *Birth of a Tragedy: Kashmir 1947* (Hertingfordbury, UK: Roxford Books, 1985).

Mustafa, Daanish, and Viren Murthy, "'Faces of the Beloved': Rerouting the Tragic History of the Kashmir Issue," in S.P. Udayakumar, ed. *Handcuffed to History: Narratives, Pathologies, and Violence in South Asia* (Westport, CT: Praeger, 2001), 99–125.

Oberoi, Surinder Singh. "Kashmir Is Bleeding." *Bulletin of the Atomic Scientists* (March–April 1997).

Rizvi, Gowher. "The Rivalry Between India and Pakistan" in Barry Buzan and Gowher Rizvi, eds. *South Asian Insecurity and the Great Powers* (New York: St. Martin's, 1986): 94–114.

Shastri, Amita, and A. Jeyaratnam Wilson, eds *The Post-Colonial States of South Asia: Democracy, Development and Identity* (New York: Palgrave, 2001).

SIPRI, SIPRI Yearbook of World Armaments and Disarmament (London: Humanities Press and Oxford University Press, various years).

Thomas, Raju G. C. "Arms Procurement in India: Military Self-reliance Versus Technological Self-sufficiency" in Eric Arnett, ed. *Military Capacity and the Risk of War: China, India, Pakistan, Iran* (London: SIPRI/Oxford University Press, 1997), 110–129.

Thomas, Raju G. C. "The 'Nationalities' Question in South Asia," in Amita Shastri and A. Jeyaratnam Wilson, eds. *The Post-Colonial States of South Asia: Democracy, Development and Identity* (New York: Palgrave, 2001), 196–212.

S. P. Udayakumar, "Introduction" in, S. P. Udayakumar, ed, *Handcuffed to History: Narratives, Pathologies, and Violence in South Asia* (Westport, CT: Praeger, 2001), 1–22.

Tinker, Hugh. "Pressure, Persuasion, Decision: Factos in the Partition of the Ponjab." *Journal of Asian Studies* vol 36 #4 (August 1977): 695–704.

Global Terrorism and Al Qaeda
TERRORISM

Introduction

Before September 11, 2001, international terrorism was mostly an abstraction for many Americans—something the Israelis and British were forced to deal with, but not us. As long as we stayed home and minded our own business, we would be safe from international threats. After September 11, this illusion was shattered. Terrorism quickly became one of the country's top priorities. In the months following the September 11 attacks, as pointed out by President George W. Bush in his January 2002 State of the Union address, tens of billions of dollars of new spending were approved for homeland security, a vast international antiterror coalition was formed and new international laws adopted, and a war was fought and won in Afghanistan, resulting in the capture of thousands of al Qaeda operatives and the displacement of an entire regime (Bush 2002; *Christian Science Monitor* September 9, 2002, 1).

Defining terrorism seems easy when one considers such brazen acts of devastation. In practice, however, it is not always easy to categorize groups and actions neatly. Consider the following alternative definitions of terrorism:

> The unlawful use of force against persons or property to intimidate or coerce a government, the civilian population, or any segment thereof, in furtherance of political or social objectives. . . .

> Premeditated, politically motivated violence perpetrated against noncombatant targets by sub-national groups or clandestine agents. . . .

> The unlawful use or threat of violence against persons or property to further political or social objectives. It is generally intended to intimidate or coerce a government, individuals or groups or to modify their behavior or policies. . . . (Beres 1995, 3–4)

These definitions share several elements: 1. Terrorism involves violence—sometimes against civilian targets. 2. Terrorism has a political objective. 3. The terrorist expects that the political objective can be achieved by sowing fear. In most cases, terrorism is the act of an organized and politically motivated group that is expressing its profound dissatisfaction with the order of things, whether it be the occupation of territory by a foreign power, rule of a country by a racial minority, despotic government by a dictatorial regime, or something else.

Note that terrorism differs markedly from two other violent phenomena found in international life: international crime and warfare. International crime is conducted primarily for the purpose of accumulating wealth, and violence and political machinations are a means to that end. On the other hand, even where terrorists engage in garden-variety criminal activities, such as theft and drug-running, these actions are pursued to finance their political acts and agenda. Warfare involves state actors interacting with each other, and their actions are governed by codes of conduct and international law. Combatants must wear uniforms, refrain from targeting civilians, feed and protect prisoners, and so forth. The objective in war is to incapacitate the enemy, which is primarily a physical rather than a psychological goal (Tucker 1997, 67).

Terrorists share a great deal with guerrillas, who are usually better financed and organized but use many of the same tactics and have many of the same goals. Terrorists and guerrillas typically are both weaker than the governments they challenge and must therefore resort to hit-and-run attacks and other low-intensity tactics (bombings, assassinations, sabotage). Guerrillas differ in that they are always territorially based and are usually focused on seizing power to govern some land mass. Thus, the Peruvian Shining Path, the Tamil Tigers, and the ETA are interested in replacing existing governments in their homelands with their own members in Peru, Sri Lanka, and Spain, respectively. Their grievances are typically concrete and even understandable within the context of the state system and the goal of self-determination. Most countries in the world formed when some local group or nation sought to achieve independence from an alien government, and in almost all cases violence was part of the strategy. Many guerrillas who were successful have gone on to lead their countries as statesmen. Many of the prime ministers of Israel, for example, were guerrillas in their youth, as were Mao Zedong, Fidel Castro, and Nelson Mandela. One could even argue that George Washington was a guerrilla (he was portrayed as such by the British during the Revolutionary War).

Terrorists may also have concrete political goals, including replacing a government or controlling territory, but, as we have learned, this is not the only motivation. Terrorist organizations may have a broad set of goals that transcend controlling a particular state or region, and their membership may be drawn from many different nations. Their targets may include numerous states or nonstate actors across the globe, making them a genuine transnational threat.

Of the transnational terrorist organizations in the world, al Qaeda stands out and is therefore the focus of our study here. Al Qaeda is unusual in many respects, however, as we will make clear.

GLOBAL TERRORISM AND AL QAEDA
KEY FIGURES

Hasan al-Banna　1906–1949. He was the founder of the Society of Muslim Brothers in Egypt, a precursor to the Muslim Brotherhood that provided support to Osama bin Laden's al Qaeda in the 1990s.

Ayatollah Ruhollah Khomeini　1902–1989. He was the leader of the Iranian Revolution in 1978 that placed a revolutionary Shiite regime in power.

Sheik Omar Abdul Rahman　Leader of the Gama Islamiya (Islamic Group) in Egypt. With support from al Qaeda, his group carried out the first World Trade Center attacks.

Osama bin Laden　Born 1957. Heir to a business fortune and Afghan mujahaddin, he was co-founder of MAK in 1984 and al Qaeda in 1988. His organization claimed responsibility for the attacks on the U.S. embassies in Tanzania and Kenya on August 7, 1998, and on the *USS Cole*, He has also been blamed for the September 11 attacks in the United States.

Hasan al-Turabi　Islamic leader of Sudan since seizing power in 1989. He provided safe haven to al Qaeda from 1991 to 1996 and has carried out a bloody civil war against Christian and animist separatists in the south.

Ayman Mohammed Rabi' al-Zawahiri　Egyptian Islamic cleric who emerged as the dominant religious authority of al Qaeda after the assassination of Abdullah Azzam in 1989.

Muhammad Ibn Abdul Wahhab　Eighteenth-century Islamic cleric who developed a puritanical interpretation of Islam that became the foundation of the Saudi regime in Arabia.

Sheik Dr. Abdullah Azzam　1941–1989. A Muslim *ulama*, he was active in the Jordanian Muslim Brotherhood and founded the Afghan Service Bureau (MAK) with Osama bin Laden in 1984.

Mullah Mohammed Omar　Spiritual leader of the Taliban regime in Afghanistan. He worked closely with Osama bin Laden to impose an autocratic, puritanical rule on the country.

GLOBAL TERRORISM AND AL QAEDA
CHRONOLOGY

1744

Muhammad Ibn Abdul Wahhab joins forces with the future House of Saud, bringing a puritanical form of Islam to a position of power.

1916

The Sykes-Picot agreement between France and Great Britain consolidates European control over the Middle East, to the dismay of Arab leaders.

1928

Hasan al-Banna founds the Society of Muslim Brothers in Egypt.

(continued)

1932

The House of Saud establishes control over the Arabian peninsula and rules following the dictates of Wahhabism.

1942

The Society of Muslim Brothers forms a militant "secret apparatus."

1949

Al-Banna is assassinated by the Egyptian government following violent attacks by his followers.

1964

Ayatollah Khomeini is expelled from Iran for sedition.

1979

The Soviet Union invades Afghanistan, sparking a guerrilla war. Ayatollah Khomeini seizes power in a popular uprising and begins to support fundamentalist Islamic militants in the region.

1983

Sharia law is imposed in Sudan.

1984

Osama bin Laden and Abdullah Azzam found the MAK to provide support to the Afghan mujahaddin. They later create training camps for local and Arab guerrillas.

1988

Bin Laden, Azzam, Mohammed Atef, and Abu Ubaidah al Banshiri found al Qaeda as a base of support to mujahaddin in Afghanistan and elsewhere. They join fundamentalist militant organizations in Egypt and Sudan to found the International Islamic Front for Jihad Against the Jews and Crusaders.

1989

Taking credit for expelling the Soviet Union forces from Afghanistan, bin Laden returns to Saudi Arabia, where he opposes the Saud family.

1990

U.S. troops are deployed to protect Saudi Arabia from Iraq, prompting bin Laden to declare the House of Saud to be "apostates" of Islam.

1991

Bin Laden is expelled from Saudi Arabia and moves the headquarters of al Qaeda from Peshawar, Pakistan, to Khartoum, Sudan, where he develops a close and profitable relationship with the ruling National Islamic Front.

1992

The first al Qaeda attack occurs. It is a largely unsuccessful attempt to kill American troops en route to Somalia by way of Yemen. In Algeria, the government, fearing gains by the fundamentalist Islamic Salvation Front, cancels elections. The country plunges into violence.

1993

The first World Trade Center attack occurs in February under the direction of Ramsi Yousef and Sheik Omar Abdul Rahman. Attacks against American soldiers in Somalia are carried out by al Qaeda–trained militants.

1994

Saudi Arabia revokes bin Laden's citizenship.

1995

Al Qaeda attacks Americans based in Saudi Arabia.

1996

Al Qaeda issues the first of three fatawa declaring jihad against Americans, the House of Saud, and Westerners generally.

1998
On August 7, two truck bombs explode at the U.S. embassies in Kenya and Tanzania, killing 234 and injuring nearly 5,000.

1999
Governments in the West and Middle East begin a systematic crack-down on al Qaeda militants. Osama bin Laden is placed on the FBI's "Ten Most Wanted" list. Some anti-Taliban Afghan clerics issue a fatwa against bin Laden, authorizing his assassination. Reports emerge that bin Laden suffers from kidney and liver disease.

2000
October 5	Suicide bombers attack the *USS Cole* in Yemen, killing 17 sailors.
December	The UN Security Council passes Resolution 1333, imposing sanctions on the Taliban pending bin Laden's extradition.

2001
September 11	Four aircraft are highjacked by teams of suicide bombers. Three are flown into the World Trade Center and the Pentagon. One aircraft is recaptured by passengers and crashes in western Pennsylvania (it is believed its destination was the Capitol in Washington, D.C.). Nearly 3,000 people are killed. The next day, the UN Security Council approves a resolution authorizing "all necessary means" to neutralize the terrorists responsible.
October–November	Northern Alliance fighters, with ground and air support from the United States, remove the Taliban from power in Afghanistan, killing hundreds of Taliban and al Qaeda fighters and taking hundreds more captive. Many, including possibly bin Laden, flee to Pakistan and other locations.

2002
March	Abu Zubaydah, al Qaeda's second-in-command, is arrested in Pakistan.
October	Al Qaeda is linked to an attack against a French oil tanker in Yemen and the killing of American military personnel in Kuwait and the Philippines. A major attack in Indonesia kills more than 180. The U.S. Congress authorizes President Bush to employ force against Iraq, which is linked to international terrorism by the administration.

Islamic Fundamentalism

It is impossible to understand al Qaeda without knowing something of Islamic extremism. At its core, Islam is a conservative, family-centered, monotheistic faith that shares a great deal with Judeo-Christian religious tradition (Muslims generally feel a kinship with such "people of the book" and share a lineage to Abraham). Founded in the seventh century by the Prophet Mohammed (the story of his miraculous calling resembles in many ways the experiences of Moses and the Apostle Peter), Islam expanded quickly through the Middle East through both conversion and conquest. In its early days, its teachings on government and human rights were extremely progressive, since they encouraged democratic institutions, civil rights for women, and the empowerment of ordinary people (in contrast to the feudal and caste-based system of the day—al-Turabi 1987).

After the death of the Prophet and his immediate successors (the Caliphs), Islam experienced considerable splintering and decline. Today there is no single leader of the Muslim world (the *ummah*). Rather, numerous Islamic scholars (*ulama*), like theology professors or rabbinical scholars, spend their energies interpreting the Islamic holy writ (the *Qur'an*, giving revelations from the angel Gabriel to Mohammed, and the *Hadith*, stories and statements of Mohammed) and statements of earlier scholars.

A major schism occurred shortly after the death of the Prophet Mohammed and gave rise to two major Islamic movements: the Sunni and the Shi'a. From time to time, Islamic spiritualists (Sufi) and martyrs develop followings and become the source of other new schools and societies. The varieties of "Islams" are so diverse that what is permitted in some quarters is forbidden in others, sometimes leading to deadly arguments. Note, for example, the fact that every Muslim nation in the world (with the exception of the secular government of Saddam Hussein in Iraq) unequivocally condemned the September 11 attacks and hundreds of ulama went on record to declare terrorism to be an un-Islamic act (Schafer 2002, 18). This background is mentioned to make it clear that Islam is a varied and complex religious movement that defies easy generalization. One should add to this the fact that many Islamic traditions have adopted and incorporated social traditions from particular regions that existed long before Islam appeared. In Bangladesh, for example, Muslims continue to recognize Hindu castes in their day-to-day practice. The status and treatment of women varies dramatically across different Muslim communities, in part due to local traditions.

Among these myriad branches and sects, a few have developed relatively recently to challenge the mainstream. In the mid-1700s, in the wake of the European and Ottoman imperial conquests of North Africa and the Middle East, a few began to challenge the prevailing Muslim orthodoxy. They argued that Muslims had become lax and confused, having embraced too much of their Western invaders' ways and/or perverting the ways of the Prophet. They took it upon themselves to cleanse the society through teaching, organizing, and, in a few cases, violence. Muhammad Ibn Abdul Wahhab, for example, preached a puritanical form of Islam that he thought was practiced by Muslims at the time of the Prophet (Davidson 1998, 50). In 1744, he formed an alliance with the patriarch of the Saud family to defeat what they considered polytheistic heresy among other Muslims. The alliance succeeded for a time in conquering the Arabian peninsula and reclaiming the holy cities of Mecca and Medina, only to be driven out by the Ottomans (based in Turkey). The House of Saud reclaimed the territory over time, and by 1932 it was able to establish an Islamic monarchy that ruled using the Qur'an as its legal reference (*shariah* law). Osama bin Laden is a self-professed Wahhabi (Wright 2001, 264).

In Egypt, where Western influence was pervasive, Hasan al-Banna emerged as a teacher and activist. He organized the Society of Muslim Brothers in 1928 to urge fellow Muslims to return to the pure tenets of the faith. He aspired to restore not only the moral and social organization but also political structures of the earliest period of Islam. The movement proved extremely popular and received support from secular politicians, such as Gamal Abdel Nasser and Anwar Sadat, who took power in the

1950s. It attracted a following among Muslims who were radicalized by the creation of the state of Israel, although al-Banna was not especially militant himself. The Society he founded provided health care, education, and other services (even a Scouting program for youth) that were aimed at inculcating a respect for basic Muslim values.

The Society also had a secret, military organization that engaged in assassination, leading to the murder of al-Banna by Egyptian authorities in 1949 (Davidson 1998, 26). His successor also failed to restrain the violent tendencies of the Brotherhood, and during the 1960s the organization was repressed. From the 1970s, it grew in strength and served as an inspiration to so-called fundamentalist ("fanatically puritanical" might be a better term), anti-Western movements across the region. These sects included the Gam'a Islamiya (Islamic Group), led by the "Blind Sheik," Omar Abdul Rahman, who later collaborated with Osama bin Laden (Davidson 1998, 101; O'Ballance 1997, 19)

In 1978, Iran's Ayatollah Ruhollah Khomeini, a Shiite as well as a teacher and activist, led a popular uprising against the corrupt ruler Shah Reza Pahlavi. From his position at the helm of Iran, he was able to propagandize revolutionary Islamic fundamentalism by setting up Iran as a model, as well as provide shelter and direct support to revolutionary movements in the region and beyond (O'Ballance 1997). His regime was particularly instrumental in building Hezbollah (Party of God) in Lebanon in the early 1980s as a service organization with a strong military wing whose aim is the elimination of the state of Israel (Davidson 1998, 169).

Osama bin Laden and the Founding of Al Qaeda

It was in this context that Osama bin Laden came of age. One of the many children of a successful Saudi businessman, bin Laden studied engineering and Islamic law (his personal fortune has been conservatively estimated at $30 million—Gunaratna 2002, 19). In 1979, the Soviet Union invaded Afghanistan to establish a Communist regime on its southern border. Bin Laden was impressed by the strength of the resistance mounted by local Afghans, who came to be known as mujahaddin. He, along with Abdullah Azzam, began organizing various projects to bring relief supplies and war materiel to the mujahaddin in Afghanistan. In 1984, they organized the MAK (Afghan Service Bureau). They were part of a growing Arab presence in Afghanistan where, eventually, Islamic militants gathered from around the world (Huband 1998, 2). In the process of fighting together, these militants became increasingly radicalized as they saw the results of their struggle against the Soviet forces. When the Soviets withdrew in 1989, the mujahaddin, and bin Laden in particular, took full credit for their defeat (Wright 2001, 250). Furthermore, they took credit for the eventual collapse of the Soviet Union itself (bin Laden took personal offense at the West claiming credit for what was an Islamic victory—Gunaratna 2002, 22).

Hoping to capitalize on the energy of the Afghan movement, bin Laden and Azzam joined with Muhammed Atef and others to found al Qaeda (the

Base) in 1988 as a mechanism for keeping militants in contact with each other, coordinating their actions against anti-Islamic forces, and providing training and supplies for this purpose. By 1989, several militants had been sworn in as the first cadre of al Qaeda fighters (Gunaratna 2002, 23). They established their headquarters in Peshawar, Pakistan, with the help of the ISI (CIA-equivalent) of Pakistan.

Azzam's views of the organization were somewhat more moderate than those of bin Laden, who had started training guerrillas as early as 1986. In 1989, Azzam was murdered by Egyptian radicals who later became leaders of al Qaeda (Gunaratna believes bin Laden conspired with Ayman Mohammed Rabi' al-Zawahiri in the attack—Gunaratna 2002, 25). After 1989, the movement became more intransigent and active.

Three other important developments stimulated the growth and orientation of al Qaeda. In August 1990, U.S. troops were deployed in northern Saudi Arabia at the invitation of the Saud royal family to defend the area from the Iraqi forces that had just invaded Kuwait. After the defeat of Iraq, the American troops remained. Bin Laden believed that the willingness of the Saud family to allow infidels into Saudi Arabia—the home of the two holiest sites of Islam (Mecca and Medina)—was a betrayal of the Prophet and an abdication of their sacred duty to protect the shrines. He labeled them as apostates and called for their destruction (Wright 2001, 265).

In 1991, the Saudi regime expelled bin Laden for sedition, but the Sudanese government soon welcomed him and roughly 500 militants (Wright 2001, 251). After moving the headquarters of al Qaeda to Khartoum, bin Laden took advantage of the government's hospitality to build several prosperous businesses and sign lucrative contracts, thereby significantly increasing the organization's assets and cash flow. In 1996, however, the Sudanese asked bin Laden to leave under considerable pressure from the United States and other Western states. By this time, the Taliban had seized power in Afghanistan and offered him safe haven.

While in Afghanistan, bin Laden's stature and power rose considerably. He developed a close relationship with Mullah Mohammed Omar and became highly influential in the regime. It was bin Laden who encouraged the Taliban to destroy giant Buddha statues in Bamiyan, to international outcry (Gunaratna 2002, 43, 62). Al Qaeda provided 2,000 militants (055 Brigade) to help the Taliban fight the Northern Alliance during the late 1990s, earning the respect and gratitude of the regime. It was from here that bin Laden issued three fatawa proclaiming it the duty of all Muslims to destroy the Saudi regime and to kill Americans, and Jews, and any Westerners who were blocking the establishment of puritanical Islam (these can be found in the appendix of Alexander and Swetnam 2001). It was also from Afghanistan that al Qaeda launched its most notorious attacks, against two U.S. embassies in Africa in 1998, against the USS Cole in 2000, and against the World Trade Center and Pentagon in 2001. These attacks, along with other, minor strikes, killed a total of 3,300 individuals and injured more than 6,000.

The last attack, on September 11, 2001, began the most recent change in al Qaeda's fortunes. It prompted a massive retaliation by the United States and other states, including a global crack-down on al Qaeda's militants, finances, and sponsors, culminating in the defeat of the Taliban regime and the death and capture of thousands of militants in October and November of 2001.

Describing Al Qaeda

It is useful at this point to focus on the goals, structure, and financing of al Qaeda, so as to better illustrate the character of a major terrorist organization. It is important to underscore that al Qaeda is unique in several respects. To begin, it is uniquely transnational in structure and scope, including cells and operations in more than fifty countries with militants and financial backers in dozens of countries. It is also uniquely vitriolic in its orientation, surpassing even the militancy of other Islamic organizations (for example, the Saudi fundamentalist Advice and Reformation Committee announced that bin Laden's 1996 fatwa was a merely personal statement—Huband 1998, 115). It has been described as an "apocalyptic" organization, whose goal is primarily destruction and chaos in an attempt to usher in a new world, putting it on a par with Naziism (Herf 2002).

Al Qaeda's Goals

Bin Laden is a Wahhabi, taking an extremely puritanical approach to Islam. Only the Taliban embodied this view in its everyday practices, which included strict enforcement of dietary, moral, and other codes found in Islam. The Taliban, for example, viewed the place of women in society as extremely subordinate and inferior. Women were banned from schools and the business world and were not allowed to receive medical care from male doctors (since there were no female doctors, the implication was clear—Wright 2001, 264). Its absolutist view meant that not only were infidels from other faiths viewed as a threat, but even modern regimes that tolerated Western culture. Thus it is easy to understand why Anwar Sadat and Hosni Mubarak of Egypt were targeted by al Qaeda allies for assassination (the attempt was successful in the case of President Sadat). Likewise, attacks on Saudi leaders are consistent with this view.

The religious leaders of al Qaeda, especially Ayman Mohammed Rabi' al-Zawahiri, spend considerable energy working to legitimize their version of Islam to the world. This is done through religious instruction to the militants as well as through public pronouncements. The fatwa is used heavily as a religiously sanctioned call for action by all Muslims. Not only do al Qaeda clerics issue these from time to time, but in recent years bin Laden himself has been taking on the trappings of priesthood, naming himself "Sheik" and issuing fatawa (plural of fatwa) on his own authority (Wright 2001, 255). He has always endeavored to maintain a strict lifestyle so as to inspire piety and self-discipline in the ranks. Interestingly, bin Laden is one of the first Islamic militants to embrace terrorists of the Shiite school of Islam, in spite of the considerable hostility that has dominated Sunni–Shiite relations over the years. As a result, he has developed ties to both Iran and Lebanon's Ebola, much to the consternation of Western intelligence and defense agencies (Gunaratna 2002, case 3).

In "Join the Caravan," bin Laden urges all Muslims to take up the cause of jihad (struggle) against Jews and Christians (Zionists and crusaders) as an individual obligation (Gunaratna 2002, 87). Why join the jihad? (1) so that nonbelievers do not dominate; (2) because of the scarcity of manpower; (3) fear of hellfire; (4) fulfilling the duty of jihad and responding to the call of Allah; (5) following in the footsteps of pious predecessors; (6) establishing a solid foundation as a base for Islam; (7) protecting those who are oppressed in the land; (8) seeking martyrdom (Gunaratna 2002, 88).

A special problem for al Qaeda (and all Islamic militants) is the fact that the Qur'an and the Prophet's teachings specifically outlaw suicide and violence against innocents (particularly women and children). With respect to the ban on suicide, clerics have emphasized that the struggle requires the sacrifice of all things, including life itself. Those who take that ultimate step are assured "martyr" status and eternal bliss in heaven (there is even mention of women). Thus, it is not suicide at all, in a religious sense. With respect to killing innocents, they have argued that the end justifies the means, however. Since the goal is the eradication of opposition to Islam (defending the faith is one meaning of jihad, a central tenet of Islam), and since opposition includes whole nations of people, everyone is to some degree culpable. While women and children are not appropriate targets in and of themselves, they may be killed incidentally, according to al Qaeda's clerics (Gunaratna 2002, 76).

This religious underpinning explains why some have argued that the best weapon against al Qaeda may be a religious one. If moderate clerics, for example, can convince the puritanical fanatics that they are interpreting the holy writ incorrectly, they can undermine recruitment efforts (Miles 2002). Likewise, since the struggle is ideological and cultural, Western actors must convey the desirability of liberal democratic principles and the market (Berman 2001).

Al Qaeda's Organization

Al Qaeda differs from most terrorist organizations in that it is not territorially based but rather has a consciously global presence (Table 17.1). Its essential elements consist of a governing council (*shura majlis*) consisting of roughly one dozen bin Laden loyalists who help staff four policy committees (military, religious, financial, and public relations). These bodies behave in ways that resemble a philanthropic foundation by issuing overall purposes and guidelines, reviewing proposals for terrorist actions, and approving, funding, and sometimes organizing those actions. The proposals usually come from individual terrorist cells and regional offices.

Roughly 5,000 militants make up the rank-and-file of al Qaeda. They work in small, largely disconnected cells (called *anqud*—grape cluster) made

Table 17.1 Al Qaeda's Global Network

Countries with Islamic Militant Organizations Linked to Al Qaeda	Countries with al Qaeda Terrorist Cells (Working Alone)	Countries with Sources of al Qaeda Funding	Countries Where al Qaeda Attacks Have Occurred
Yemen	United States	United Kingdom	Yemen
Egypt	United Kingdom	Germany	Somalia
Algeria	Germany	Saudi Arabia	Egypt
Malaysia	France	United Arab Emirates	Saudi Arabia
Chechnya	Netherlands	Sudan	United States
Somalia	Belgium	Sweden	Philippines
Philippines	Canada	Denmark	Indonesia
Lebanon	Spain	Norway	
Iran	Canada	Algeria	
Tajikistan		Germany	
Uganda		United States	
Indonesia		Philippines	
China		Pakistan	
Eritrea			
Bosnia			
United Kingdom			
Palestine			
Uzbekistan			
Kashmir (India)			
Sudan*			
Pakistan*			
Afghanistan*			

*Former Al Qaeda headquarters.

Sources: Gunaratna 2002; Alexander and Swetnam 2002.

up of between two and fifteen individuals. The cells are relatively autonomous in their operations and are expected to be self-sustaining financially to a large extent (many cells rely on credit card fraud and theft). They are only vaguely aware of what other cells are planning and can organize their own operations with al Qaeda's blessing. Abu Zubaydah was responsible for coordinating their performance until his capture in March 2002 in Pakistan. The 055 Brigade, formed in Afghanistan, is organized along more traditional military lines and was the group encountered by coalition forces fighting in that country in October and November 2001.

Election to al Qaeda is a very high honor for an Islamic militant. Al Qaeda officials generally select only one out of every ten men who pass through their training camps. They are looking for "young Muslim men who are pure, believing and fighting for the cause of Allah" (Gunaratna 2002, 72). The key factors seem to be absolute loyalty and the willingness to sacrifice everything, including one's life, in the cause. In addition, al Qaeda fighters must be among the most highly skilled of those trained in the camps.

Terrorist attacks are generally carefully planned and executed, although they are not always successful. An attack was attempted against the *USS*

Sullivan, but failed when the boat loaded with explosives sank (it was overloaded). Likewise, assassination attempts against Hosni Mubarak, Bill Clinton, and Fidel Ramos (then president of the Philippines) were foiled for various reasons. Numerous terrorist attacks have also been detected and prevented, including a series of attacks planned on New York City landmarks (such as the UN and Holland Tunnel) in 1999. Detecting and linking attacks to al Qaeda is especially difficult because, unlike most terrorist organizations, the group rarely claims responsibility. In fact, it goes to great lengths to sow doubt about its role in the attacks, in part to add to the organization's mystique.

In the case of the September 11 attacks, planning began in the spring of 2000 under the direction of Mohammed Atta. Twenty militants were selected from several different cells, organized into four five-man teams, and allowed to secret themselves into the United States on student visas or across the Canadian border. This activity was followed by training at several flight schools around the country, the purchase of one-way business-class tickets, and other preparations.

Training covers the gamut of information that would-be terrorists might need to know, including religious indoctrination. A ten-volume (later eleven) "encyclopedia" of terrorism was written and published by al Qaeda in the mid-1990s (discovered by American intelligence agencies in 1999). It explains how to build explosives, how to use various weapons, how to organize paramilitary attacks, and how to build weapons of mass destruction. [bin Laden is believed to have purchased some fissile materials in his quest for an atomic weapon. He may already have the capability to launch an attack with a "dirty" bomb that would scatter radioactive material (Gunaratna 2002, 70).] The encyclopedia also provides training on how militants should blend into the host society, even if it means violating Islamic lifestyle codes (Gunaratna 2002, 70).

The geographic spread of al Qaeda is remarkable. Although its headquarters has moved between Pakistan, Sudan, and Afghanistan, its cells can be found in more than fifty countries. The countries with the largest number of militants are Algeria (where al Qaeda supports the Islamic Salvation Front), Egypt (where it has ties to the Muslim Brotherhood), and Yemen (where the *USS Cole* was attacked). There are still militants scattered across Pakistan, the Middle East, and Central Asia (al Qaeda left Bosnia in 1995 to the relief of local militants, who considered them too brutal). Al Qaeda has close ties with Islamic militants in Chechnya, Tajikistan, Iran, Pakistan, Palestine, Lebanon, western China, the Philippines, Saudi Arabia, and, increasingly, in Southeast Asia and Africa—notably Indonesia, Malaysia, Uganda, and Somalia, where al Qaeda–trained militants killed 18 American soldiers in 1992 (Gunaratna 2002, Chapters 3 and 4). Interestingly, Iraq and Libya are not known to have supported al Qaeda, although they have supported other terrorist organizations.

More troubling to Western audiences is the fact that al Qaeda has active cells and regional nodes in the United Kingdom, France, Germany, the

United States, and other developed states. Ramsi Yousef and Sheik Omar Abdul Rahman, who were loosely linked to al Qaeda, were based in a Brooklyn community center when they orchestrated the first World Trade Center bombing. In September and October 2002, the U.S. Justice Department arrested several individuals living in Buffalo, Portland, and Detroit on charges of conspiring with al Qaeda. Previously, cells had been identified in Washington, D.C., Chicago, New Jersey, and elsewhere in the United States. London has long been a principal hub of al Qaeda planning and financing, as are France and Germany, which has four known cells (Gunaratna 2001, 111–131).

The cells and regional offices maintain frequent contact by means of the most modern communications channels. In the past, they have used cellular telephones, satellite phones, encrypted e-mail, and secret websites to maintain contact with their worldwide membership. This fact enabled the FBI to eavesdrop on communication between al Qaeda headquarters and militants, thereby enabling agents to anticipate and break up several planned attacks in the late 1990s. In response, al Qaeda has switched to more traditional (and slower) methods of face-to-face communication. Given the lack of infiltrators, spies, and defectors, this trend may mean that future al Qaeda operations will be more difficult to detect.

Al Qaeda's Finances

Al Qaeda has a reputation for being very well financed, thanks to Osama bin Laden's fortune. However, it is estimated that the entire operation of al Qaeda costs only about $40 million per year and that bin Laden's fortune plays almost no part in its day-to-day funding. On the one hand, al Qaeda operations are generally very inexpensive. The September 11 attacks, the organization's most expensive by far, cost only $500,000 by most estimates. Local cells are expected to take care of their own finances to a large extent (the attackers in the first World Trade Center bombing had to get the deposit back on the truck that exploded to pay for their airfare home!). On the other hand, bin Laden has made several shrewd business decisions that have allowed al Qaeda to prosper from excellent returns on the investments. While in Sudan, in particular, he began several enterprises, including a bank, a large farming operation, a tannery, and a construction company, and he signed contracts to build a major highway and several buildings for the Sudanese government (Wright 2001, 251).

Al Qaeda also receives much of its funding from Islamic clerics and wealthy Muslim sympathizers in the Middle East. Saudi Arabia, for example, has uncovered a donation of $50 million from a group of fundamentalist clerics in 1999. Khalid bin Mahfouz, a wealthy Saudi banker, has transferred funds and facilitated other transactions over the years. The Dubai Islamic Bank in the United Arab Emirates has also been directly implicated (Alexander and Swetnam 2001, 29). Numerous nonprofit organizations, as well as banks, have been identified by law enforcement authorities in dozens of countries as front operations through which millions are transferred to al Qaeda. In reality, many of those who have handled al Qaeda funds were unaware of it because the monies typically pass through several legitimate businesses or organizations on their journey between source and destination (Wright 2001, 252).

Al Qaeda After September 11

As of September 10, 2001, bin Laden felt extremely sure of himself, it would seem. He had brought about the defeat and collapse of the Soviet Union in a mere five years. He had expelled the Americans from Somalia with a single attack. He had survived a full-scale cruise missile attack after the Africa attacks. He was beginning to feel powerful in the extreme. He had reached the conclusion that the United States was weak, tentative, and easily intimidated. He expected to remove them from Saudi Arabia in the future. It seems reasonable, given this view of his own importance, that bin Laden believed the September 11 attacks might bring down American democracy and capitalism once and for all.

The purpose of terrorism is outlined in terrorist manuals:

> [T]hey build a reserve of fighters by preparing and training new members for future tasks; they serve as a form of necessary punishment, mocking the regime's admiration among the population; they remove the personalities that stand in the way of the Islamic *da'wa* (call); they publicize issues; they help to reject compliance and submission to the regime and its practices; they provide legitimacy to the Islamist groups; they spread fear and terror through the regime's ranks; and they attract new members to the organization. (Gunaratna 2002, 75)

To this we could add that terrorism is also intended to provoke repression and over-reaction on the part of the target government, as this response breeds resentment, which in turns swells the ranks of militants.

It is unlikely, therefore, that the Bush administration surprised bin Laden with the forceful response provided by the United States, its allies, and the United Nations. In a matter of hours after the September 11 attacks, the UN General Assembly, the UN Security Council, and NATO had voted unanimously to approve war against al Qaeda. Thousands of Western troops were deployed to support the tens of thousands of Northern Alliance forces. Within a few weeks, in spite of stiff opposition, they broke through and seized control of Kabul and Kandahar, taking hundreds of prisoners.

In addition, the international community agreed to impose harsh penalties against al Qaeda, Afghanistan, and any private or public organizations affiliated with the terrorist group. To illustrate the degree of international commitment to the war against al Qaeda, even Cuba, which has had extremely poor relations with American governments over the years, agreed to help the United States by capturing and returning any prisoners who might escape from the various detention centers in Guantanamo Bay on Cuba's eastern coast. Al Qaeda's repudiation among Middle Eastern governments has been unequivocal and unanimous (with the exception of kind words from Iraq). In Pakistan, President Pervez Musharraf has purged Islamic fundamentalists from ISA and other government agencies, although the government has yet to establish clear control over the pro–al Qaeda regions in the north. The fight against Islamic militancy has become a defining feature of the post–September 11 international system, to the point that it has evolved into, to a large extent, the new "cold war."

Al Qaeda's position at this point is far weaker than it was before the World Trade Center and Pentagon attacks. It has lost in the neighborhood of 1,000 militants in Afghanistan, Pakistan, the Philippines, and elsewhere. Tens of millions of dollars in assets have been frozen. The organization has no headquarters, and many of its most closely guarded secrets are now in the hands of Western governments. However, this is not to say that al Qaeda has been defeated.

The organization has proved to be quite resilient in the past, having survived expulsion from two states during the 1990s. Given the cell structure of the organization, it is able to reconstitute itself rather quickly. Bin Laden has also made arrangements for his succession, (although the loss of his second-in-command, Abu Zubaydah, in March 2002 was a serious blow (Gunaratna 2002, 228). Thus there is reason to believe that the organization will continue to carry out attacks against Western targets. Attacks against a French tanker near Yemen and against American military personnel training in Kuwait and the Philippines, along with a massive attack against foreigners in Indonesia in the fall of 2002, signaled a renewed capacity to commit acts of terror (*Chicago Tribune*, October 15, 2002, 1).

In at least one area, the situation may be to al Qaeda's advantage. The destruction of the World Trade Center was greeted with celebration in many circles in the Arab world. It established al Qaeda as the most daring and single-minded challenger to the Western world. This sort of recognition will likely enhance the organization's recruitment efforts, because it adds to the prestige of those who share al Qaeda's goals. It is also likely that as governments move against al Qaeda militants and fundamentalist organizations, they will overreact and provoke a backlash that will further bolster the organization's recruitment.

Conclusion

What does the al Qaeda story teach us about terrorism generally? First and foremost, it is wrong to think that terrorists are always unorganized, unfocused or undisciplined. The al Qaeda example illustrates that they can be highly focused (even though the goals may border on the irrational), highly organized, and extremely disciplined (to the point of fanaticism). The degree of focus eliminates any possibility of self-doubt—a prerequisite of fanaticism. As a consequence, there may be no possibility of reasoning or negotiating with its members. This contrasts sharply with most terrorist organizations, which have at least a few reasonable objectives, or guerrilla movements, which generally seek only greater political power. Al Qaeda's quest to rid the Arab and Muslim world of Western influence is a political nonstarter, leaving no room for compromise.

Second, al Qaeda demonstrates that terrorist groups with disparate objectives can find common cause and collaborate with one another. This is not the first time this has happened: During the 1970s the Irish Republican Army, the Basque ETA, and other radical groups worked together. Never before has a global structure like al Qaeda's existed, however. Its defeat will, therefore, require a global response.

Al Qaeda demonstrates the destructive potential of terrorist organizations and raises the stakes. Although more people have been the victims of terrorist attacks over the history of the conflicts in Palestine, Northern Ireland, Kashmir, and other areas, never before has a terrorist organization carried out a single, massive attack that killed thousands in an instant. Potential victims must now take the terrorist threat as seriously as if they were defending against a state-sponsored military attack. Unfortunately, terrorists do not play by the same rules as states: They do not reside in one country, they do not wear uniforms, they do not march in columns and ranks, and they do not comply with the Geneva Conventions. Thus states may be faced with dilemmas with regard to appropriate and effective tactics and strategies. A military solution will likely go only so far, but a criminal approach may give the terrorists too many opportunities for escape.

This said, it would be prudent for Western states to consider seriously what types of actions might exacerbate the situation. Repression or over-reaction, for example, might increase recruitment, while half-measures might leave the organization too strong. Note the assessment of the Bush administration's plans for a preemptive strike against Iraq in early 2003. Iraq is not considered a serious sponsor of al Qaeda, so even military strategists and realists question whether overthrowing Saddam Hussein will make the United States less vulnerable to terrorism. Indeed, liberals argue that deploying more American troops in the Middle East is likely to provoke a fundamentalist backlash that could swell al Qaeda's ranks and precipitate increasing political instability (Lemann 2002).

Perhaps the most profound implication of al Qaeda's actions is the loss of the sense of security felt by most Americans before September 11. Although the nation has perfected the art of denial, the gnawing realization persists in the backs of people's minds that there is nowhere to hide. Such is life in the twenty-first century.

Debate Topic

Should the priority for the West be the arrest and imprisonment of existing al Qaeda leaders rather than a political settlement of the disputes that spur young men to join the organization?

> **PRO**
> Those pressing for arrest or military defeat of al Qaeda stress three points: (1) Al Qaeda presents a clear and present danger and must be stopped. (2) Many of al Qaeda's political demands are not feasible or not genuine and should not be addressed. (3) It would take too long to solve all of the world's injustices at any rate.
>
> **CON**
> Those arguing for addressing fundamental problems argue as follows: (1) Some grievances are legitimate, including the Palestinians' lack of a state. (2) U.S. interventionism has gone too far and should be pulled back. (3) The West's influence is too great, since it encompasses political, economic, and cultural areas.

Questions to Consider

1. Are there other terrorist groups that make use of other systems of religious teachings to justify their violence?

2. How does al Qaeda compare to the Nazis?

3. How much should the West curtail its civil liberties in its struggle against al Qaeda?

4. How do al Qaeda's structure and operation compare to those of other transnational organizations, such as NGOs or multinational firms?

Websites

Al Qaeda on U.S. Government Sites
FBI: **www.fbi.gov/terrorinfo/terrorism.htm**
CIA: **www.cia.gov/terrorism/faqs.html**
State Department: **www.usinfo.state.gov/topical/pol/terror/homepage.htm**

Competing Opinions on al Qaeda
Azzam: **www.azzam.com**
Anti-Defamation League: **www.adl.org/terrorism_america/bin_l.asp**
Institute for the Secularization of Islamic Society: **www.secularislam.org**
Federation of American Scientists: **www.fas.org/irp/world/para/ladin.htm**

References

Alexander, Yonah, and Michael S. Swetnam. *Usama bin Laden's al Qaida: Profile of a Terrorist Network* (Ardsley, NY: Transnational Pubs., 2001).

Al-Turabi, Hasan. "Principles of Governance, Freedom and Responsibility in Islam." *American Journal of Islamic Social Science* 4 #1 (1987): 1–11.

Beres, Rene Louis. "The Meaning of Terrorism: Jurisprudential and Definitional Clarifications." *Vanderbilt Journal of Transnational Law* 28 (March 1995): 239–256.

Berman, Paul. "Terror and Liberalism." *American Prospect* 12 #18 (October 22, 2001): 18–27.

Bush, George. "The President's State of the Union Address." Washington, D.C., January 29, 2002.

Chicago Tribune, October 15, 2002, 1.

Christian Science Monitor, September 9, 2002, 1.

Davidson, Lawrence. *Islamic Fundamentalism* (Westport, CT: Greenwood Press, 1998).

Gunaratna, Rohan. *Inside Al Qaeda: Global Network of Terror* (New York: Columbia University Press, 2002).

Herf, Jeffrey. "What Is Old and What Is New in the Terrorism of Islamic Fundamentalism?" *Partisan Review* 69 #1 (Winter 2002): 25–33.

Huband, Mark. *Warriors of the Prophet: The Struggle for Islam* (Boulder, CO: Westview Press, 1998).

Lemann, Nicholas. "The War on What?" *The New Yorker* (September 16, 2002): 36–44.

Miles, Jack. "Theology and the Clash of Civilizations." *Cross Currents* 51 #4 (Winter 2002): 451–460.

O'Ballance, Edgar. *Islamic Fundamentalist Terrorism, 1979–95: The Iranian Connection.* (New York: NYU Press, 1997).

Schafer, David. "Islam and Terrorism: A Humanist View." *The Humanist* 62 #3 (May–June 2002): 16–21.

Tucker, David. *Skirmishes at the Edge of Empire: The United States and International Terrorism* (Westport, CT: Praeger, 1997).

Wright, Robin. *Sacred Rage: The Wrath of Militant Islam* (New York: Touchstone Book, 2001).

CASE

18

The Camp David Accords*
DIPLOMACY

Introduction

Diplomacy is a general term used to describe any interaction among nations (or any other international actors for that matter). Traditional diplomacy has evolved into a heavily ritualized communication system—understandable only to the initiated. Diplomats are organized in ranks and offices, similar to officers in the military, and they employ formalistic language and procedures to communicate. Diplomacy can be conducted without diplomats, however, and it sometimes takes place directly between heads of state (summit diplomacy). States may also communicate through the media by issuing press releases and giving public speeches (public diplomacy). Finally, countries can communicate and negotiate through international institutions, such as the United Nations General Assembly (parliamentary diplomacy).

In addition to traditional diplomacy, nations and agencies often become involved in bilateral discussions as mediators. A mediator is any third party that is substantively involved in bilateral diplomacy, typically by providing suggestions and support. Mediation is often called for when two parties cannot communicate clearly with each other. This inability typically stems from mutual hostility, which may have resulted in mutual nonrecognition. For example, during the Iranian hostage crisis in 1979, when more than fifty American diplomats were held captive by the revolutionary government of Iran, the United States and Iran had no direct, official contacts. Ultimately, Algeria stepped forward to serve as a go-between. During the Persian Gulf crisis in 1990, this task fell to UN Secretary General Boutros Boutros-Ghali,

---

*This case includes substantial portions reprinted from Linda B. Miller, "Shadow and Substance: Jimmy Carter and the Camp David Accords," #433R Pew Case Studies in International Affairs, © 1988 by the Pew Charitable Trusts, revised 1992 by the Institute for the Study of Diplomacy, Georgetown University.

who was able to send messages between the United States and Saddam Hussein, albeit with far less successful results.

In general, mediation seems to work best when the parties are sincere in their search for solutions and when the mediator can offer something to "sweeten the deal." One of the classic stories of effective diplomacy and mediation is the Camp David negotiations between Anwar Sadat of Egypt, Menachem Begin of Israel, and Jimmy Carter of the United States. In this case, the success depended on the good will of Sadat and Begin, a unique stalemate that made the status quo undesirable to both parties, and an American president willing to put the country's reputation, military, and money on the line.

THE CAMP DAVID ACCORDS
KEY FIGURES

Henry Kissinger National Security Advisor, 1969–1975; U.S. Secretary of State, 1973–1977. He played a pivotal role in creating a stalemate between Egypt and Israel following the Yom Kippur/Ramadan War.

Jimmy Carter U.S. President, 1977–1981. He is credited with bringing Sadat and Begin together to work out a settlement to the Egyptian–Israeli conflict.

Menachem Begin Prime Minister of Israel, 1977–1983. A conservative who fought with Jewish guerrillas in the 1940s, his nationalist credentials made it easier for him to persuade the Israeli people of the benefits of the Camp David Accords.

Anwar Sadat President of Egypt, 1970–1981. He reversed the pro-Soviet policies of his predecessor and made overtures to the West and to Israel. He was assassinated by Muslim fundamentalists in 1981.

Golda Meir Prime Minister of Israel, 1969–1974.

Yitzhak Rabin Prime Minister of Israel, 1974–1977, 1992–1995. He reached a preliminary agreement with Yasser Arafat on Palestinian control of the occupied territories. He was assassinated in 1995 by Jewish nationalists.

Yitzhak Shamir Prime Minister of Israel, 1986–1992.

Shimon Peres Prime Minister of Israel, 1984–1986, 1995–1996. He served in numerous capacities in the Israeli government and repeatedly negotiated with its adversaries.

Yasser Arafat Leader of the Palestinian Liberation Organization and later the Palestinian Authority.

Benjamin Netanyahu Prime Minister of Israel, 1996–1999.

Ehud Barak Prime Minister of Israel, 1999–2001.

Ariel Sharon Prime Minister of Israel, 2001–present

Hosni Mubarak President of Egypt, 1981–present.

Bill Clinton U.S. President, 1993–2001. He helped sponsor the Oslo and Madrid Accords between Israel and the PLO and hosted Camp David II.

THE CAMP DAVID ACCORDS
CHRONOLOGY

1948
The State of Israel is declared. A war almost immediately ensues between the new Jewish government and surrounding Arab states.

1956
The Suez War pits Israel against Egypt over control of the Suez Canal.

1967
The Six-Day War takes place between Israel and its Arab neighbors.

1973
The Yom Kippur/Ramadan War between Israel, Egypt, and Syria ends in a stalemate. Henry Kissinger intervenes to negotiate a cease-fire and deployment of troops in a buffer zone.

1974
A cease-fire agreement between Israel, Egypt, and Syria is accepted by all parties.

1975
Preliminary and temporary agreements are signed by Egypt and Israel.

1977
Anwar Sadat meets Menachem Begin in Jerusalem.

1978
The Camp David negotiations begin. The apparent progress made earns Begin and Sadat the Nobel Peace Prize.

1979
Begin, Sadat, and Carter shake hands on the White House front lawn to celebrate the signing of the Camp David Accords, which provide for the gradual return of the Sinai peninsula to Egypt and guarantees of peace between Egypt and Israel.

1981
Anwar Sadat is assassinated. Hosni Mubarak succeeds him as president of Egypt.

1982
Israel invades and occupies southern Lebanon.

1987
The intifadah (Palestinian uprising) begins.

1988
The PLO renounces terrorism.

1991
The Persian Gulf War creates new alignments in the Middle East.

1992
Yitzhak Rabin is elected Prime Minister of Israel.

1993
The PLO and Israel accept the Oslo Peace Accords, which provide for a form of mutual recognition and phased transfer of land then under Israeli control to the new Palestinian Authority.

1994
Shimon Peres, Rabin, and Arafat are awarded the Nobel Peace Prize.   *(continued)*

1995

Yitzhak Rabin is assassinated.

1998

The Wye River Accords are signed in Washington.

1999

Camp David II ends in deadlock.

2000

The second intifadah begins. Palestinian suicide bombers attack Israeli cities.

2001

Islamic fundamentalists attack the World Trade Center in New York and the Pentagon in Washington, D.C., creating a shift in Middle East alliances.

2002

Israel seizes control of large segments of the West Bank that had been ceded to the Palestinian Authority, including Arafat's presidential compound.

Henry Kissinger and the 1973 War

Israel's lightning strike into Jordan, Syria, and Egypt in 1967 left Israeli troops and a growing number of settlers in power in the Golan Heights, the West Bank, the Gaza Strip, and the Sinai to the Suez Canal. None of these actions was recognized by the diplomatic community, and certainly not by the Arab states, which were determined to reverse Israel's gains. The Arab states seized their opportunity on October 6, 1973, during the Jewish Yom Kippur feast in Israel, when Egyptian and Syrian troops launched a coordinated surprise attack on Israel.

Unlike earlier Arab–Israeli wars, this battle did not produce a classic victory of West over East. To begin, Egypt had previously expelled its Soviet advisors in an ongoing effort to improve relations with the United States. ("Why has Sadat done me this favor?" Kissinger asked his aides—Sheehan 1981, 49.) Egypt was thus not acting as a Soviet surrogate. More important, the war did not go well for Israel. By the third day, it was clear that the Arab forces were well organized, were well armed, and were having moderate success. The Egyptians had reclaimed the Suez and a roughly ten-mile-deep adjacent strip in the Sinai. The Syrians reclaimed as much as one-third of the Golan, and Syrian forces pushed to within five miles of the Israeli border (Dockrill 1991, 109). Henry Kissinger took note of this rather unusual situation by endeavoring to "consolidate the stalemate":

I believed that only a battlefield stalemate would provide the foundation on which fruitful negotiations might begin. Any equilibrium—if only an equilibrium of mutual exhaustion—would make it easier to reach an enforceable solution. (Kissinger 1982, 496)

From October 10 to November 9, 1973, Kissinger exerted considerable pressure on Israel to accept a ceasefire and a negotiated settlement. On October 11, President Richard Nixon accepted Kissinger's recommendation to send an airlift of military supplies to Israel, having failed to secure Egyptian acceptance of an immediate cease-fire. Shortly afterward, Arab members of OPEC imposed an embargo on the export of oil to the United States along with a unilateral quadrupling of crude oil prices.

The oil embargo intensified Kissinger's efforts to reach a negotiated settlement of the war, and he sought the support of the Soviet Union. On October 22, UN Security Council Resolution 338, cosponsored by the two superpowers, demanded the immediate cessation of hostilities and the beginning of a peaceful settlement (along the lines of a two-state solution called for in UN Security Council Resolution 242). The resolution did not stop the fighting, and Israeli armies swarmed across the Suez, effectively cutting off Egypt's Third Army on the eastern bank. The Soviet Union came close to intervening directly to support Egypt, but American warnings and a dramatic rise in its nuclear preparedness (DEFCON) caused the Soviets to refrain. The United States simultaneously exerted pressure on Israel to pull back from the Egyptian front to allow Egypt's forces to be re-supplied. Israel was reluctant to agree, given the considerable diplomatic leverage on Egypt this military posture commanded.

With each passing day, Kissinger became more and more directly involved in negotiating a peaceful settlement of the Suez dispute. On November 7, while in Cairo, he secured the support of President Anwar Sadat of Egypt for a six-point program that provided for Third Army relief, prisoner exchange, and a future peace conference in Geneva. This has been considered a major turning point in Egyptian policy because it was the first time Sadat was willing to accept something less than full Israeli withdrawal to the 1967 lines (Kalb and Kalb 1974, 510). It was also the beginning of a break in the Arab alliance, although this outcome was more unintended than deliberate. On November 9, Israel agreed to the plan after the United States gave assurances that it would monitor the re-supply effort for the Third Army. The model of Israeli concessions conditional on major guarantees by the United States was repeated again and again during later talks.

Israel and Egypt were still far apart on two main issues: "nonbelligerency" and exchange of prisoners. The Israelis sought from Egypt a firm commitment to peaceful relations, whereas Egypt wanted to maintain strong ties to other Arab states. Egypt was also reluctant to engage in a full-scale exchange of prisoners until it could be assured that Israeli forces would withdraw from Egyptian territory west of the Suez Canal.

A third issue that still divided Israel and Egypt involved Palestinian rights and self-determination. Kissinger hoped to set this problem aside and move forward instead on bilateral arrangements between Israel and each of its enemies. Nonetheless, a conference was organized to study the general problem of the occupied territories as well as to finalize plans for troop disengagement in both the Sinai and the Golan. In this context, Kissinger sought the participation of Syria, Jordan, and Saudi Arabia as well as Israel and Egypt.

The December Geneva conference met with little enthusiasm. Although Israel, Egypt, and Jordan accepted invitations delivered jointly by the Soviets, Americans, and UN, Syria and Saudi Arabia declined on the grounds that Israeli withdrawal should precede any conference. Israel opposed UN participation, but the United States insisted, so Kissinger agreed to lessen the secretary general's role to that of symbolic figurehead. Israel refused to permit Palestinian representatives at the conference, which Egypt regretted but accepted. Throughout the preliminaries, all the Arab nations except Egypt seemed to assume that the United States was able to change Israeli attitudes with the wave of a hand—in reality, it seemed at times that the reverse was more accurate. Nevertheless, running throughout this process as a subtle prod to Arab attentiveness and flexibility was the implicit threat of U.S. military intervention.

The conference itself was largely symbolic rather than substantive, and it did not lead to any larger negotiations or even to talks between Israel and Jordan. In fact, by January what Kissinger hoped would become an ongoing negotiation process in Geneva was superseded by what became "shuttle diplomacy." On January 12, while meeting with Sadat in Cairo, Kissinger accepted Sadat's invitation to act as a gobetween to Israeli Prime Minister Golda Meir. The arrangement suited all the parties: not only did it give Sadat a superpower in Egypt's camp, but it also calmed Israeli fears that its concessions would make it more vulnerable. Kissinger himself received extraordinary publicity from the process.

The process of diplomacy led to a rather rapid reconciliation of the conflicting demands of the major parties. By mid-January, agreement was reached on an immediate Israeli troop withdrawal and Egyptian troop redeployment. On January 17, 1974, the agreement was signed, providing for a thin line of Egyptian forces on the east bank of the Suez Canal, while Israeli troops withdrew to a line roughly six miles to the east. Following a proposal by Israeli Defense Minister Moshe Dayan, a UN contingent was deployed in the narrow buffer zone between the forces, and troops near the buffer zone were lightly armed (Sheehan 1981, 65–66). This "five-zone" approach proved to be the recurring theme in all of the 1974–1975 disengagement talks involving Israel (see Map 18.1).

What role did Kissinger play in these negotiations? According to Touval, he

> was able to induce concessions without resorting to pressures. The incentives that the U.S. offered—economic aid to Egypt, and economic and military aid to Israel—do not appear to have been important causes for the parties' flexibility either. It was rather the pressure of circumstances in which Egypt and Israel found themselves that made them eager to conclude a disengagement agreement rapidly. The mediator's contribution was, however, essential in suggesting compromises and in arranging the indirect transaction of commitments. This procedure helped to reduce Sadat's vulnerability to criticism from the opponents of the agreement, which a direct commitment to Israel might have en-

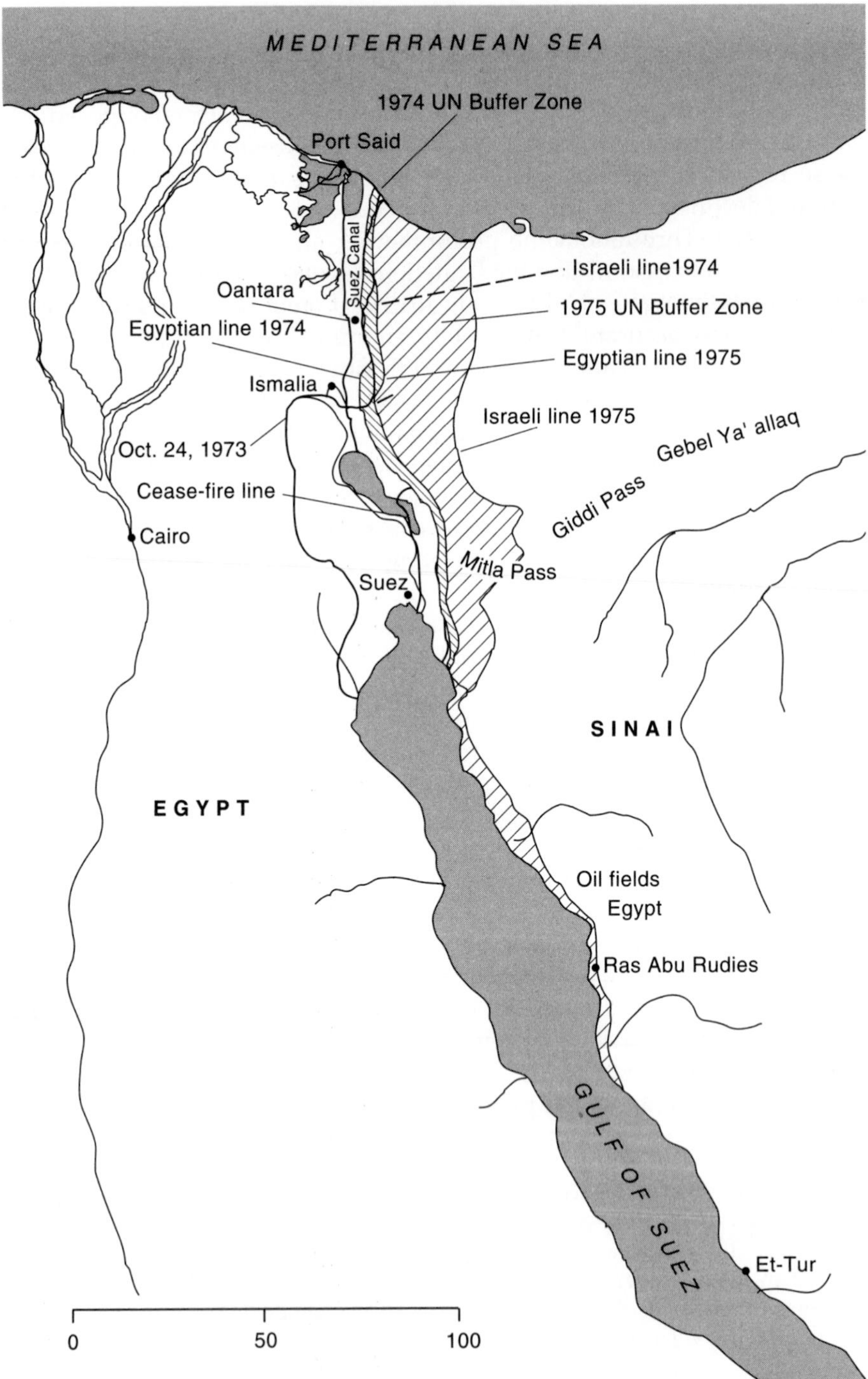

Map 18.1 1973–1975 Egyptian–Israeli troop withdrawal agreements
Source: Lester Sobel, ed. *Peace-Making in the Middle East* (New York: Facts on File, 1980).

tailed. And finally, by providing both parties with implicit and explicit guarantees, the mediator encouraged them to feel protected from some of the risks that
they believed that their concessions entailed. (Touval 1982, 248)

Following this relatively easy success, Kissinger was drawn into two
much more contentious processes: disengagement in the Golan and a second permanent Egyptian–Israeli disengagement in the Sinai. Because Syria
simply did not trust the United States, Kissinger found it far more difficult
to establish warm relations, unlike the rather easy warmth that developed
between Kissinger and Sadat on the one hand and the near-infatuation between Kissinger and Meir on the other (Sheehan 1981, 72). Kissinger's first
major contribution involved conveying prisoner lists to each party in late
February and privately assuring King Faisal of Saudi Arabia that he would
quietly work for Syria's interests. Formal talks were opened on March 18,
the same day the oil embargo was finally lifted (over Syrian objections).

The key issues in these talks were rather simple. On the one hand, Israel
did not want to withdraw its forces, which at the time were deep in Syrian
territory—twenty-five miles from Damascus—beyond the territory it had
occupied since 1967. On the other hand, Syria insisted on gaining considerable territory to prove that its war effort had been at least somewhat fruitful.
The debate focused on the eastern town of Kuneitra (El Quneitra), which Israel firmly controlled but which was once a regional administrative center
for Syria. Kissinger urged Israel to concede the city, or at least a sizable portion of it, and Israel relented. When it came to determining precisely where
the Israeli troops would be deployed, the talks nearly broke down because
Israel insisted on occupying three overlooking hills, to Syria's dismay. Israel
also insisted on allowing settlers to harvest their crops around the town.
Eventually, after Kissinger repeatedly threatened to walk out, the two parties settled on slightly deeper Israeli withdrawals in exchange for harvesting
rights and a fairly strong UN presence in a buffer zone around the town (see
Map 18.2).

On other issues, Syria refused to inhibit clandestine Palestine Liberation
Organization (PLO) raids into northern Israel, even though Israel refused
anything less than a guarantee that such attacks would cease. Kissinger intervened by pledging U.S. guarantees that any such attacks would be interpreted as a violation of the agreement, to which Israel could respond with
all necessary means. The United States also provided considerable aid as an
inducement (converting a $1 billion loan to a grant and sending military
hardware).

Perhaps most interesting in these talks is how Kissinger made himself
indispensable. He made the point that Israel would have a difficult time
finding a better interlocutor than a Jew from the United States. He demonstrated even-handedness with Syria to prove to Damascus that he was the
best available spokesman to Tel Aviv. He was able to keep the talks moving
forward simply by threatening to go home. On May 25, 1974, he went so
far as to coauthor with President Hafez al-Assad of Syria a communique

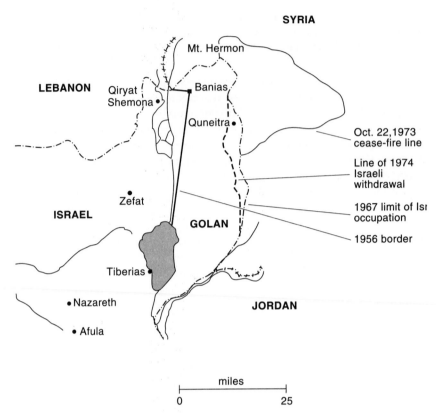

Map 18.2 1967–1974 Israeli–Syrian troop withdrawal agreements
Source: Lester Sobel, ed. *Peace-Making in the Middle East* (New York: Facts on File, Inc., 1980).

announcing the collapse of the talks and laying the blame on Israel (an important threat for Tel Aviv) when, on his way out the door, Assad said to him, "What a pity. We've come so far and not succeeded. Can't anything be done . . . ?" and urged him to try once more with the Israeli leadership (Sheehan 1981, 71). On May 29, Israel and Syria signed their disengagement treaty under Kissinger's watchful eye.

The second disengagement talks between Israel and Egypt stumbled from the start. The new government of Prime Minister Yitzhak Rabin was adamant about a peace treaty with Egypt, while Kissinger tried to convey the political dangers that such a move posed for Sadat vis-à-vis his Arab counterparts. Israel refused to abandon the strategic mountain passes Giddi and Mitla without guarantees. It sought access to Egypt's oil, U.S. aid, and U.S. weapons. Israel also wanted more participation in the rules surrounding the UN buffer troops. Israel's demands were so extreme and its position so obdurate that by the spring of 1975, Kissinger and other senior officials had concluded that the negotiations were dead. In a highly publicized "reassessment" of U.S. policy, Kissinger and President Gerald Ford implicitly accused Israel of stonewalling and threatening the talks. This ambivalence precipitated a "full-court press" by the Israeli lobby in the U.S. Congress, culminating in a letter signed by seventy-six members of Congress urging the Ford administration to maintain its commitment to Israeli security.

In this context, Israeli demands ultimately softened. Tel Aviv accepted the Egyptian offer of a "functional equivalent" to a peace treaty by pledging to solve all disputes by peaceful means. Egypt offered its oil to Israel at world market prices, and Israel was allowed a voice in decisions relating to the UN troops (particularly regarding their withdrawal, which in 1967 had been done unilaterally by Egypt). Israel also agreed to withdraw completely from the passes and allow U.S. and UN inspection of its deployment on the ground. Egypt explicitly (and Israel implicitly) agreed to abide by this treaty for at least three years, subject to annual review, thus creating de facto the Geneva conference arrangement Kissinger had originally hoped for. On September 1, 1975, the documents and corollary agreements were formally signed and Kissinger was hailed as a miracle worker.

In exchange for these agreements with Israel, the United States made what Sheehan describes as a "marriage": It promised to protect a wide range of Israeli interests, guarantee the security of Israel, and verify compliance with the treaties. The United States also promised to have no contact with the PLO so long as it did not renounce terrorism. Finally, the United States promised to veto any UN Security Council resolution that might undermine these various agreements. U.S. aid to both Israel and Egypt increased dramatically and proportionally.

Camp David

On September 5, 1978, President Anwar Sadat of Egypt and Prime Minister Menachem Begin of Israel and their delegations arrived at the U.S. presidential retreat in Maryland, Camp David, for a series of fateful meetings with President Jimmy Carter and his entourage. On March 26, 1979, the three leaders met on the front lawn of the White House to sign a peace treaty between Egypt and Israel. In the months that separated these widely publicized events, numerous obstacles between the countries arose and intensified; some crucial issues remained unresolved until the actual day of the signing. The entire undertaking was precarious at the time Carter reactivated his peacemaking initiative in August 1978 and remained so even after the documents were initialed and exchanged the next year. The story of these hopeful yet frustrating months is full of twists and turns that kept participants on the edge of failure and observers on the edge of their seats.

From the perspective of more than two decades after the accords were negotiated, the central issues that dominated the talks and their aftermath are clear. Would there be a bilateral accord between Egypt and Israel, linked vaguely (if at all) to an accord on the future of the West Bank and Gaza? Or would a comprehensive settlement address all facets of the Arab–Israeli conflict, from the status of Jerusalem and the Palestinians to elaborate security arrangements and normal relations among all the players (the approach Carter's advisors favored)? Furthermore, what should the United States offer and when should it secure the allegiance of Sadat and Begin to any agreements, as the two local leaders manipulated their own domestic constituents and the American public to gain better terms for themselves and their countries?

In November 1977, President Sadat paid his unprecedented visit to Jerusalem. His bombshell undercut U.S. plans for an international conference in Geneva. Carter was in danger of losing control over a process that had already aroused concerns in segments of the U.S. Congress and the American Jewish community. Some worried that Israel would be compelled to deal with the PLO or with a Palestinian state, and others were anxious about Syrian or Soviet meddling in the diplomatic process.

In the months of reassessment that followed Sadat's breakthrough trip, U.S. efforts concentrated on getting the Israelis and Egyptians to clarify their demands after bilateral talks at Ismailia stalled. Several of Carter's closest advisors "suggested moving toward a strategy of collusion with Sadat to bring pressure on Begin" (Quandt 1986, 163). Although Carter and Secretary of State Cyrus Vance flirted with this idea as a way of preventing the collapse of bilateral talks in the atmosphere of ill will and hostile rhetoric, they understood that it would not produce a lasting agreement and might worsen administration relations both with Begin and with the American Jewish community. Later, as America grew exasperated with Begin's rigidity, variations on this theme of U.S.–Egyptian collaboration reappeared in administration memos and dialogue. As 1978 proceeded, American officials became aware of the differing style of the two leaders: Sadat was eager for the dramatic gesture but not the tedious details of negotiations. Begin was insistent on dotting every *i* and crossing every *t* while lecturing his fellow politicians on Israel's security needs, its territorial claims, and the virtues of "autonomy" for the Palestinians rather than an independent Palestinian state or some form of federation of the West Bank and Gaza with Jordan.

Thus, in the second year of his administration, Carter, known for his own meticulous attention to detail, faced the choice of continuing to search for Israeli concessions on the West Bank and Gaza, perhaps more vigorously than Sadat himself would do, or striving to arrange a bilateral Egyptian–Israeli peace treaty based on the trade of Sinai for an end to belligerency. In seeking the second course—in deciding to work with Begin rather than against him—Carter adopted a posture consonant with the national objectives of Sadat and Begin and with public opinion on Resolution 242. When Carter issued his invitations to an unusual three-way summit in September 1978, he knew that he would have to promote interim arrangements for the thorniest issues—Jerusalem and the occupied territories.

Carter also knew that engaging the prestige of the U.S. presidency in such a venture was a high-risk enterprise that could backfire both domestically and internationally and might endanger other initiatives such as the SALT II agreement with the Soviet Union or congressional approval of the

Panama Canal treaties. Stresses and strains with Egypt and Israel mounted as Sadat and Begin pressed their respective cases with the White House, Congress, the press, and U.S. public opinion (Spiegel 1985, Chapter 8). Keeping the diplomatic game going as the administration prepared to submit a Middle East arms package to Congress was the biggest challenge, especially because Carter was also working on relations with China. The president's growing involvement with the minutiae of diplomacy meant that Middle East political figures would not be satisfied dealing with lesser U.S. officials. Each complicated exchange of questions and answers among Washington, Cairo, and Jerusalem seemed to offer Washington two choices: either confront the parties by submitting American-drafted texts or retreat from an active role, with the possibility that the enterprise would bog down and Carter personally would be blamed.

Inviting Sadat, Begin, and their closest advisors to Camp David to explore the possibilities of an accord was one thing; keeping them there long enough and secluded enough to develop a general formula or framework for negotiations together with supporting details was quite another. Although Carter believed that gaining and keeping the trust of the two leaders and their negotiating teams were crucial, he did not anticipate that moving beyond opening positions would take a full ten days or more, far longer than the initial three days, or at most a week, that he had planned to devote to the summit. One reason for the length of the negotiations was the expressed desire of both Begin and Sadat to structure agreements with the United States before or, at the very least, alongside any they might conclude with each other. As Carter reports in his memoirs:

> I knew it was a good negotiation tactic by either Sadat or Begin first to reach agreement with me and then to have the two of us confront the third . . . . I must admit that I capitalized on this situation with both delegations in order to get an agreement; it greatly magnified my own influence. (Carter 1982, 366)

Following ten days of successive one-on-one meetings with Begin and Sadat, Carter began to develop the essential feature of an agreement that would leave the Gaza and West Bank issues largely unresolved at Sadat's suggestion. On the eleventh day, Sadat threatened to leave—on the grounds that Israel would sign no agreements despite the tedious days of discussion and refining of terms. Impressed as he was with the efforts of two Israelis, Moshe Dayan and Ezer Weizman, to help bridge the gaps, Sadat nonetheless insisted that his advisors now counseled against signing an agreement with the United States alone if Israel could not be brought along. According to Carter's recollections, he approached Sadat, who was preparing to leave:

> I explained to him the extremely serious consequences of his unilaterally breaking off the negotiations: that his action would harm the relationship between Egypt and the United States, he would be violating his personal promise to me, and the onus for failure would be on him. I described the possible future progress of Egypt's friendships and alliances—from us to the moderate and then radical Arabs, thence to the Soviet Union. I told him it would damage one of my

most precious possessions—his friendship and our mutual trust . . . . I told Sadat that he simply had to stick with me for another day or two—after which, if circumstances did not improve, all of us simultaneously would take the action he was now planning. (Carter 1982, 392)

The experience was most likely more jarring for Sadat than Carter presents it here. National Security Advisor Zbigniew Brzezinski remembers Carter explaining that he told Sadat his departure would mean "an end to the relationship between the United States and Egypt" (Brzezinski 1983, 272). In the end, Sadat agreed to stay, in part because Carter assured him that any tentative concession he might offer at Camp David, if not part of a treaty agreement, would not be taken as a starting point for future talks with Israel.

Significantly, neither Carter nor Brzezinski mentioned any promises of massive U.S. economic aid or military assistance to Egypt that may have induced Sadat to stay at Camp David. The practicality of such a pledge would become clearer in the future. Carter next turned to Begin and the Israelis to try to resolve the remaining differences. As the talks neared the crucial phase on such issues as Sinai settlements, oil, and the demilitarized zones, together with the connections between Sinai and the West Bank or Gaza, Begin's stage presence, frequently overshadowed by Sadat's flair for surprise and presumed outrage, emerged.

The Likud Party leader, whose ideological predilections differed from those of the Israeli Labour Party leaders with whom U.S. officials were accustomed to dealing over the years, was careful to leave himself a loophole on the issue of removing Israeli settlements from Sinai by stating that he would submit the matter to the Israeli parliament (Knesset) for a vote. In view of what would happen in later phases of interpretation and implementation, Carter was perhaps too persuaded of his own skill as a mediator at this stage: "I told him again and again that this proposal was totally unacceptable to Sadat, who insisted on a commitment to remove all Israeli settlers from his territory before any other negotiations could be conducted" (Carter 1982, 396).

Begin finally agreed to an accelerated Knesset review without the requirement of party loyalty, thus freeing Knesset members to simply vote their conscience. This commitment was enough for Sadat, who tended to lack interest in other details of the agreement. The issues of the West Bank settlements and the status of Jerusalem were addressed with an oral agreement on Israel's part to halt the construction of new settlements until a more formal resolution could be reached. As Carter put it after the talks were through:

> After the Israelis left, Vance and I agreed that we had a settlement, at least for Camp David. There was no doubt that Sadat would accept my recommendations on the issues we had just discussed with Begin. What the Knesset might decide was uncertain, but I was convinced that the people of Israel would be in favor of the overall agreement, including the withdrawal of the settlers from the Sinai . . . . I intended to try in every way possible to shape world opinion and to get the American Jewish community to support this effort. (Carter 1982, 397)

Carter's persistence paid off. An agreement was reached, even though the final tradeoffs were specific only with reference to the Sinai and they downgraded the link between the bilateral accord and the future of the occupied territories, including Jerusalem. Begin could take pride in the arrangements calling for normalization of relations with Egypt. Sadat had attained what no other Arab leader had the courage to seek—the return of occupied territory through negotiations with Israel, even though the basic formula guaranteed Egyptian national aims at the expense of wider Arab demands concerning the Palestinians. Furthermore, Sadat had succeeded in having the United States play the role of "full partner." Ironically, the price he would pay for that accomplishment would be additional demands for concessions (see Map 18.3).

The thirteen days at Camp David had produced a framework outlining transitional arrangements for the West Bank and Gaza, an agreement by Egypt and Israel to sign a peace treaty within three months, and a specific plan for the return of the Sinai to Egypt with demilitarized zones and international policing of strategically sensitive areas. The issue of linkage might arise again, but for the time being, Begin's loose formulas had prevailed.

The post-conference haggling over who agreed to what, though predictable, threatened to heighten misunderstandings. Trust began to dissipate as the conflicting positions of Egypt and Israel hardened on the settlements and on linking a bilateral treaty to prospects for the West Bank and Gaza. Carter, sensing urgency, found it difficult to comprehend the domestic political problems Sadat and Begin faced. He was well aware of his own problems, with the midterm elections scheduled for November 1978. He was also aware that Begin was a master at using Israeli domestic constraints as a way to drag out the negotiations. Begin was often tougher than his advisors, whereas Sadat was often more accommodating. American policy makers openly considered an overture to the PLO as a way of pressing Israel harder, but Carter demurred, citing the 1975 U.S. pledges to Israel on the subject as a test of American credibility.

Perhaps more important as the months passed after Camp David, both Begin and Sadat knew that Carter's influence had peaked in 1978 and that as the 1980 U.S. presidential election approached, he would be entangled elsewhere. Begin sought a deceleration of the process to avoid granting Palestinians any additional rights, while Sadat hoped for a measured pace toward eventual linkage with independence for the occupied territories. Cyrus Vance approached Jordan and Saudi Arabia to enlist their support for some eventual Palestinian autonomy accord, although he was also aware that this had not been made explicit in the Camp David language.

In the context of these conflicting interpretations and hidden agendas, Carter learned of Israel's intention to increase the number of settlements in the West Bank, in violation of the oral agreement at Camp David:

> It [was] obvious that the negotiations [were] going backwards . . . . I told Cy [Vance] to withdraw from the negotiations at the end of this week, to let the technicians take over, and let the leadership in Israel and Egypt know that we

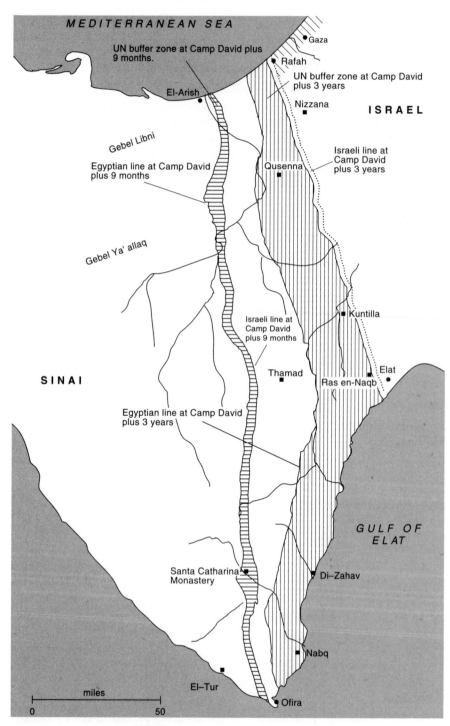

Map 18.3   1979–1982 Egyptian–Israeli troop withdrawal agreements
Source: Lester Sobel, ed. *Peace-Making in the Middle East* (New York: Facts on File, 1980).

are through devoting full time to this nonproductive effort. It [was] obvious that the Israelis [wanted] a separate treaty with Egypt; they [wanted] to keep the West Bank and Gaza permanently . . . and they [used] the settlements (on the West Bank) and East Jerusalem issues to prevent the involvement of the Jordanians and the Palestinians. (Carter 1982, 409)

By December 1978, Carter was close to throwing in the towel. The three-month deadline for an Egypt–Israel peace treaty set at Camp David would not be met. For Carter, the confluence of U.S. domestic politics—the 1980 election—and international politics—the tumultuous Iranian revolution then unfolding—meant that an Egyptian–Israeli peace treaty must come soon, if at all. "I decided to pursue with my top advisers the possibility of my going to Egypt and then to Israel—getting together with Sadat and making my strongest appeal to the Israelis. My main purpose would be to remind them what they would be giving up if the treaty were lost" (Carter 1982, 415).

Prior to the trip, Carter met with Begin in Washington and managed to create a treaty text that was "barely acceptable to the Israelis but did not quite comply with the key points on which Sadat was insisting . . . ." Upon hearing news of the treaty and Carter's upcoming trip to the Middle East, Sadat "was overjoyed" (Carter 1982, 416). Before leaving Washington, Carter was careful to prepare Sadat, who was delighted to welcome the president to Egypt. Carter warned him that additional concessions would be needed:

> The language may not be exactly what you want, but the target date issued and the "priority of obligations" issue are such that you can accept them and legitimately claim victory. You may or may not completely agree with me on the nuances of the exact words but, in any case, the differences are minimal when compared to the overall strategic considerations which you and I must address together. (Carter 1982, 417)

If the Camp David formula could be preserved, the details might be completed quickly while Carter was on the scene in the region. When Sadat did accept what the Israeli cabinet had approved, Carter was encouraged, yet Begin, in keeping with his previous modus operandi, told the president on his arrival in Israel that "he [Begin] could not sign or initial any agreement." As Carter wrote:

> I would have to conclude my talks with him, let him submit the proposals to the cabinet, let the Knesset have an extended debate, going into all the issues concerning the definition of autonomy, East Jerusalem, and so forth, and then only after all that would he sign the documents.
>
> I couldn't believe it. I stood up and asked him if it was necessary for me to stay any longer. We then spent about 45 minutes on our feet in his study. I asked him if he actually wanted a peace treaty, because my impression was that everything he could do to obstruct it, he did with apparent relish. He came right up and looked into my eyes about a foot away and said that it was obvious from the expression on his face that he wanted peace as much as anything else in the world . . . . (Carter 1982, 421)

The final breakthrough that permitted plans for signing of the treaty to go forward came when Carter returned to Cairo from Israel with agreements in hand that committed him to asking Congress for substantial aid in relocating Israeli bases from Sinai and provisions for the United States to compensate Israel for giving up Sinai oil. Also spelled out were steps to be taken if Egypt violated the treaty.

After Carter's return to Washington, amid preparations to receive Sadat and Begin in triumph, Vance, Dayan, and others strove to wrap up all the details in time for the signing. As Vance recalls, it was a close call:

> Inevitably, there were last-minute hitches. For several days prior to Begin's arrival I had discussions with Dayan on the U.S.–Israeli memorandum of agreement, as well as on the oil supply agreement and the U.S. financial and military assistance package that had been agreed to in Jerusalem. The President also met Sadat and Begin to work out the precise details of the accelerated Israeli withdrawal from that portion of the Sinai containing the oilfields.

The final details concerning Israeli access to Sinai oil remained an issue right down to the end. They were not finally resolved until Sadat and Begin agreed in a meeting in the residence of Ashraf Gorbal, the distinguished and extremely able Egyptian ambassador in Washington. At that time Sadat guaranteed to the Israelis the right to bid for Egyptian oil at the world market price on a permanent basis, thus removing the last major stumbling block to the signing ceremony. We did go down to the wire on one or two minor details . . . . (Vance 1983, 252)

On March 26, 1979, then, the signatures were placed on the document and an arduous process, begun by Henry Kissinger in 1973, was completed. The implementation of the agreement, including the continuation of discussion on Palestinian autonomy, was spotty. The Israeli army left the Sinai within the prescribed deadline—a remarkable example by Egypt of winning back territory through the pen rather than the sword. Autonomy talks for the Palestinians, however, were almost immediately overwhelmed by nationalist pressure in Israel and the revolution in Iran. More than a decade later, Camp David may seem to be less of an achievement than it was. If so, it is because Egyptian–Israeli peace is now taken for granted in the midst of rising political extremism in the region as a whole. That peace is perhaps the finest tribute to the thirtyninth president: other politicians come and go with less to show for their labors than Jimmy Carter.

Middle East Peace Since Camp David

With Carter voted out of office in November, the Middle East peace process halted. Egypt paid dearly for its peace with Israel. It was castigated by other Arab states. Sadat was assassinated in 1981, thus removing one of the most conciliatory Arab leaders in history. Israel invaded Lebanon in 1982, which precipitated the deployment of peacekeeping troops in Beirut by President Ronald Reagan, the evacuation of PLO headquarters, and the movement of thousands of troops across the Middle East. The PLO initiated the bloody "intifadah" in 1987—a mass uprising that continues to this day and in turn has spurred increased Israeli repression in the West Bank and Gaza. In 1988, the PLO renounced terrorism and quietly recognized Israel's right to exist, thus allowing the United States to undertake direct talks with PLO representatives. Throughout the 1980s, however, the Israeli position hardened and the United States found itself more and more at odds with Tel Aviv over everything from Israeli police repression in East Jerusalem to increased Soviet Jewish settlements in the West Bank.

It was not until the Persian Gulf War in 1991 that major shifts occurred in Middle East political alignments. During the war, many Arab countries sided with the United States and therefore implicitly with Israel. Israel also broke with precedent by not retaliating against Baghdad following repeated Scud missile attacks. Within a year of the war, the United States and the Soviet Union, under the leadership of Secretary of State James Baker and Foreign Minister Eduard Scheverdnadze, organized a new multilateral Middle East peace conference amid skepticism, ambivalence, and only a modicum of hope. The seating at the conference of a joint Jordanian–Palestinian delegation made possible the first direct talks between Israelis and Palestinians in forty-three years. In spite of this historic breakthrough, however, the negotiations plodded along unsuccessfully for nearly two years. Even the election in June 1992 of Yitzhak Shamir's Labour Party—traditionally more flexible on the issues of land for peace and Palestinian rights—had little effect.

On August 31, 1993, in the eleventh round of what seemed to be almost pointless negotiations, Israel and the PLO announced a surprise. As a result of extended secret talks, they had concluded a deal that provided for mutual recognition and self-rule for Palestinians in parts of the West Bank and Gaza. Within two weeks, Shamir and Arafat were shaking hands in front of the White House and American senators were dining with a former terrorist. President Bill Clinton was quick to take credit, if only by virtue of his intentions, even though the Norwegian government had a more direct role in facilitating the secret talks by discreetly providing good offices. More agreements signed in May and September of 1994 sealed the progress achieved. In October 1994, Jordan and Israel signed a peace agreement settling numerous outstanding issues.

Conclusion

The assassination of Yitzhak Rabin in Israel in 1995 and the subsequent election of Benjamin Netanyahu in mid-1996 derailed the peace process for another two years. Ultimately, in October 1998, at the Wye River complex near Washington, under the guidance of Secretary of State Madeleine Albright and President Bill Clinton, the Israelis and Palestinians committed to a timetable to complete the peace process—the withdrawal of Israeli forces from the West Bank and Gaza, the sovereignty of Palestine, and the disposition of Jerusalem. The process moved slowly until the election of Ehud Barak as Israel's prime minister in May 1999. He won on a campaign of bringing peace to the region and immediately began settling differences with his neighbors to the north (Israel withdrew its forces from Lebanon after an eighteen-year occupation and began peace talks with Syria) and his Palestinian rivals. Although an intense round of negotiations at Camp David in July 2000 (dubbed Camp David II) ended in failure, the process clarified what elements are needed for a final settlement—namely, resolution of the status of Jerusalem, compensation and repatriation of refugees, Israeli recognition of Palestinian statehood, and Palestinian security guarantees for Israel.

Today, the situation in the Middle East is as tense as ever. On September 28, 2000, Ariel Sharon, an Israeli leader much despised in the Palestinian community, paid a visit to the al-Aqsa mosque on the Temple Mount. The next day, Palestinians began systematically rioting and attacking Jewish targets, using both rocks and rifles. The Israeli government responded with rockets and missiles. In spite of intervention by Bill Clinton, the violence continued throughout the month of October until more than 300 Palestinians and Jews had been killed in what was dubbed the "al-Aqsa intifadah." By early November, the violence had begun to subside and Arafat and Barak were attempting to cement a cease-fire with President Clinton's help. Ehud Barak's failure to stem the violence or reach a settlement with the Palestinians contributed to his resounding defeat in elections in February 2001. The new prime minister, none other than Ariel Sharon, promised a hard line in talks.

Since the terrorist attacks on September 11, 2001, conditions in the Middle East have worsened considerably. Although Arafat was quick to condemn the attacks and continued to renounce terrorism, an increasing amount of violence was perpetrated on Jews in Israel and the West Bank. Suicide bombings became the favored tactic and cost hundreds of Israeli lives. With each attack, reprisals were administered by an increasingly belligerent Israeli government. The George W. Bush administration supported Sharon's policy as part of the war against global terrorism.

In March 2002, the Israeli government invaded Arafat's compound in Ramallah and proceeded to seize control of numerous Palestinian towns in the West Bank that had previously been turned over to the Palestinian Authority. Arafat remained holed up in his offices for days while Israeli soldiers swept the region for suspects. Although the troops were later withdrawn, the hostility between the two camps continues to be extremely high. As of this writing, there is no prospect of peace in Palestine.

What does this story tell us about the nature and effectiveness of diplomacy? Clearly, where hostility and mutual distrust are high, diplomacy may serve no other purpose than to enable the parties to launch charges and countercharges at each other, which typically adds to the tensions. In such a situation, perhaps the only constructive dialogue requires a mediator of some sort. The United States has generally been effective as a mediator between Egypt and Israel, but is less helpful where Israel and Palestine are concerned. In part, this stems from the fact that the United States is openly hostile to Yasser Arafat, having called for his resignation during the summer of 2002.

What may come as a surprise to the reader is how diplomacy and war seem at times to go hand in glove. Particularly where Egyptian–Israeli relations during the 1970s are concerned, we see that two nations turned from destroying each other's armies to signing lasting peace agreements almost overnight. Perhaps this tale tells us that the most dangerous move to make is to sever diplomatic relations, because it almost guarantees a lack of communication.

Debate Topic

Are diplomats important to resolving militarized disputes?

PRO
Liberals would argue that warfare is the problem and that diplomacy and negotiation are the only effective means to resolve difficult disputes. (1) Warfare creates its own consequences that make hostilities more intense. (2) Resorting to force does not resolve the question of justice and fairness, leaving the losing party resentful and bitter—and anxious to change the outcome at the first opportunity. (3) Diplomats are in a better position to clarify the core issues of a dispute and arrive at creative solutions.

CON
Realists see a place for diplomats, but believe many problems are amenable only to a military solution. (1) Where a dispute involves core principles of right and wrong, there is risk in negotiating, lest one surrender to injustice. (2) All negotiations take place against the backdrop of force, so denying its centrality is naïve. (3) A military stalemate can help move the parties toward a compromise at any rate.

Questions to Consider

1. What resources did Kissinger, Carter, and Clinton bring to bear on the negotiations by virtue of their position as U.S. leaders?

2. Did Kissinger and Carter make use of different personal, political, or diplomatic assets in their efforts? How did these affect the outcomes of their mediation?

3. To what extent did military matters and regional power relations affect the willingness of Israel, Egypt, and others to make concessions? Was this outcome predictable?

4. How do the experiences of the United States in the Middle East relate to Clausewitz's notion that war is merely the extension of diplomacy? Conversely, does it appear that "the pen is mightier than the sword"?

5. What makes for a good mediator, based on these experiences?

Websites

Several universities maintain websites about Middle East peace processes in general and Camp David in particular:

www.metalab.unc.edu/sullivan/CampDavidNegotiations.html
www.columbia.edu/cu/libraries/inciv/area/MiddleEast.htm
www.cfcsc.dnd.ca/links/wars/mid.html

The Conference for Middle East Peace provides useful information and links:
www.cmep.com

References

Brzezinski, Zbigniew. *Power and Principle* (New York: Farrar, Strauss and Giroux, 1983).

Carter, Jimmy. *Keeping Faith: Memoirs of a President* (Toronto: Bantam Books, 1982).

Dockrill, Michael. *Atlas of Twentieth Century World History* (New York: Harper-Perennial, 1991).

Kalb, Bernard, and Marvin Kalb. *Kissinger* (Boston: Little, Brown, 1974).

Kissinger, Henry. *Years of Upheaval* (Boston: Little, Brown, 1982).

Miller, Linda B. "Shadow and Substance: Jimmy Carter and the Camp David Accords." #433R Pew Case Studies in International Affairs, 1992.

Quandt, William B. *Camp David: Peacemaking and Politics* (Washington, DC: Brookings Institution, 1986).

Sheehan, Edward. "How Kissinger Did It: Step-by-Step in the Middle East" in Jeffrey Z. Rubin, ed., *Dynamics of Third Party Intervention: Kissinger in the Middle East* (New York: Praeger, 1981), 44–93.

Sobel, Lester, ed. *Peace-Making in the Middle East* (New York: Facts on File, 1980).

Spiegel, Steven. *The Other Arab–Israeli Conflict* (Chicago: University of Chicago Press, 1985).

Touval, Saadia. *The Peace Brokers: Mediators in the Arab-Israeli Conflict, 1948–1979* (Princeton, NJ: Princeton University Press, 1982).

Vance, Cyrus. *Hard Choices: Critical Years in America's Foreign Policy* (New York: Simon & Schuster, 1983).

CASE

19

U.S. Interventionism

COERCION

Introduction

Carl von Clausewitz argued that the use of military instruments—coercion—was simply an extension of the give-and-take of diplomacy, not its antithesis. As more powerful nations exert pressure on smaller states, they must sometimes flex their muscle to get what they want. The more powerful a nation, the less likely it will have to resort to violence. Instead, it will blackmail, persuade, induce, cajole, bribe, tempt, and even reward nations to influence their behavior. Naked coercion is normally a last resort but an extremely potent weapon in any nation's diplomatic arsenal. But is it diplomatic to kill people for political purposes?

As Americans consider their foreign policy choices in the post–Cold War era, a key question is whether the United States should play the role of global policeman. Should American troops be used to alter the domestic affairs of foreign nations? On the surface the obvious answer seems to be no, but in many instances in the past, the answer has been a resounding yes. Whether justified in terms of humanitarianism, enforcement of international law, or some strategic imperative, the United States has been rather quick to deploy its troops.

To better understand this interventionist tendency, we will look carefully at three very different cases drawn from the past thirty-five years. Before doing so, however, we will review various theories of intervention. The most obvious reason for U.S. intervention is strategic: The United States intervenes when its global interests are jeopardized (Deibel and Gaddis 1987). Given the way a great power strives for stability and preservation of the status quo, the temptation to intervene where the system is unstable can be irresistible. Some 2,500 years ago, when the small island of Melos petitioned Athens for respect of its neutrality, Athens refused, stating that it simply could not tolerate such an implicit challenge to its status as the dominant regional power. "The strong do what they can and the weak do what they must," was Athens' blunt reply.

Though not a particularly noble reason for intervention, its advocates often point to the need to preserve the balance of power and prevent enemies from encroaching on the American sphere of influence. The Monroe Doctrine of the early nineteenth century cautioned would-be imperialists in Europe from snatching colonial prizes in the Western Hemisphere. The Roosevelt Corollary to that warning had the military teeth to back it up and coincided with American intervention in Cuba, Nicaragua, Guatemala, Panama, Mexico, and across Latin America shortly after the turn of the century. Since World War II, various senior diplomats have justified U.S. intervention as simply preserving the status quo. George Ball, a former under secretary of state, pointed out that it is up to great powers—in this case the United States—to enforce international standards of peace and stability, unilaterally if necessary (Barnet 1968, 258).

Another key factor cited by many analysts to justify intervention is the fear of Communist ideology and despotism generally. Although fear of Soviet encroachment (a balance of power question) and fear of communism (an ideological issue) are often difficult to distinguish, many policy makers have been equally concerned about both. Certainly the idealism of the Woodrow Wilson, Franklin Delano Roosevelt, and Harry Truman administrations, as well as the intense anti-Communist passions displayed by Secretary of State John Foster Dulles under Eisenhower, demonstrate that democracy, freedom, and the free market were all key preoccupations of U.S. policy makers. Wilson drew up his "Fourteen Points" during World War I to map out a way to make the world "safe for democracy." As he put it when trying to persuade Congress to declare war on Germany in 1917:

> We have no selfish ends to serve. We desire no conquest, no dominion. We seek no indemnities for ourselves, no material compensation for the sacrifices we shall freely make. We are but one of the champions of the right of mankind. (Wilson 1990, 15)

Of course, much of the justification for entry into World War II was to halt the spread of totalitarian Germany and Japan. When Harry Truman challenged Congress in 1947 to fund the incipient Cold War offensive, he declared: "I believe that it must be the policy of the United States to support free peoples who are resisting attempted subjugation by armed minorities or by outside pressures." Presidents Lyndon Johnson, Ronald Reagan, and George H. W. Bush added their own doctrines, with the result that the United States gradually expanded the scope of unilateral intervention it considers justified. CIA Director Allen Dulles argued in the 1950s:

> [W]e cannot safely limit our response to the Communist strategy of take-over solely to those cases where we are invited in by a government still in power, or

even to instances where a threatened country has first exhausted its own, possible meager, resources in the "good fight" against Communism. We ourselves must determine when and how to act, hopefully with the support of other leading Free World countries who may be in a position to help, keeping in mind the requirements of our own national security. (Dulles 1963, 324, cited in Barnet 1968, 258)

The fear and loathing of the Communist threat reached a peak in the 1950s, during the era of Senator Joseph McCarthy's "witch-hunts" of suspected Communist sympathizers in the State Department, which were followed by John Foster Dulles's tenure as secretary of state, when his antipathy for communism reached epic proportions (Hoopes 1973). George Kennan argued in vain against what he considered kneejerk containment policies in the 1950s, which he felt lumped together all potential threats and gave them equal weight. He argued instead for a more case-by-case approach, which would enable policy makers to more selectively identify genuine threats to U.S. interests—regardless of the ideological context (Kennan 1947). Although Kennan failed to change U.S. rhetoric, his influence on policy was more profound.

Insurrections in the Third World were not unusual during the Cold War years, but only a few warranted U.S. intervention. It was those situations that combined evidence of Communist meddling with a threat to an existing U.S. alliance where intervention was most likely.

A final factor that has contributed to the U.S. decision to intervene is economic interest. Marxist interpretations of U.S. intervention have long stressed the role of major capitalist actors in the shaping of U.S. foreign policy. Harry Magdoff has probably gone as far as any Marxist to explain the dynamic. He argues that, although one may not find capitalists dictating policy to their political counterparts, the two groups have an unusual harmony of interest. American foreign investments bring large profits and extraordinary monopoly control for both business and government. American firms can control access to key raw materials, such as oil, which in turn are essential to the military—hence collusion between major capitalists and the Pentagon. These sorts of factors lead to a tendency for the state to intervene aggressively when foreign economic interests are threatened—which, as it turns out, usually involves attacking anticapitalist Third World rebels (Magdoff 1969).

Rather than attempt to assess the validity of these various perceptions of U.S. intervention, we will move into the case studies. The three cases of U.S. intervention are the Dominican Republic in 1965, Chile in 1973, and Panama in 1989. Although each case involved a Latin American nation, the methods, causes, and justifications of intervention were rather different. When combined with other cases of U.S. intervention discussed elsewhere in the text (Cuba, Vietnam, Iraq), they should provide a fairly balanced and general view of the issue.

U.S. INTERVENTIONISM
KEY FIGURES

Dominican Republic

Rafael Trujillo Absolute leader of the Dominican Republic, 1930–1961, serving at times as president. He was assassinated in 1961, opening the way for civilian rule.

Joaquin Balaguer President of the Dominican Republic, 1961, 1978. His election was made possible by the U.S. intervention in 1965.

Juan Bosch President of the Dominican Republic, 1961–1963. His left-leaning policies alarmed the United States and helped prompt intervention in 1965.

Donald Reid Cabral Leader of the Dominican Republic, 1963–1965. His junta overthrew Bosch, but was unable to bring stability.

W. Tapley Bennett US Ambassador to the Dominican Republic in 1965. He urged U.S. military intervention to prevent a radical take-over.

Hector Garcia-Godoy Leader of a caretaker government, 1965–1966. He sponsored elections that brought Balaguer to power.

Chile

Jorge Alessandri President of Chile, 1958–1964.

Eduardo Frei President of Chile, 1964–1970. His moderately progressive policies were encouraged by U.S. policy makers, but his failure at the polls made him less useful in preventing Allende's radicalization of Chilean policies.

Salvador Allende President of Chile, 1970–1973. His radical policies prompted the United States to push for his ouster.

Edward Korrey U.S. Ambassador to Chile during Allende's administration. He urged U.S. pressure on Chile.

Roberto Viaux Chilean general whose failed attempts to overthrow Allende resulted in his repudiation by would-be American supporters.

Augusto Pinochet President of Chile, 1973–1991. He led a violent coup against Allende that resulted in Allende's assassination. Pinochet's government was marked by police brutality.

Panama

Theodore Roosevelt U.S. President, 1901–1909. He supported Panama's independence from Colombia to help secure U.S. control of the Canal Zone.

Omar Torrijos President of Panama, 1968–1981.

Manuel Noriega President of Panama, 1981–1989. A staunch ally of the U.S. fight against communism, his corruption and autocratic style were no longer acceptable after the end of the Cold War.

Guillermo Endara President of Panama, 1989–1994. Noriega's refusal to accept his election was a key factor in prompting U.S. military intervention in 1989.

U.S. INTERVENTIONISM
CHRONOLOGY

1844
The Dominican Republic becomes independent.

1908
Panama becomes independent as the United States negotiates the purchase of the Panama Canal Zone.

1916–1924
American forces occupy the Dominican Republic.

1961
Rafael Trujillo is assassinated, Juan Bosch elected president in the Dominican Republic

1963
Bosch is overthrown by the military in the Dominican Republic.

1964
Eduardo Frei is elected president in Chile.

1965
The United States deploys troops in the Dominican Republic.

1966
Joaquin Balaguer is elected president in the Dominican Republic.

1968
Omar Torrijos seizes power in a coup in Panama.

1970
Salvador Allende is elected president in Chile.

1972
Chile struggles under American economic sanctions.

1973
Augusto Pinochet seizes power in Chile in a coup. Allende is assassinated.

1977
Panama signs a new canal treaty with the United States.

1981
Manuel Noriega rises to power in Panama following the death of Torrijos.

1988
Noriega is tied to the murder of a political opponent. The United States repudiates him.

1989
Elections give victory to Guillermo Endara in Panama. The results are rejected by Noriega, prompting U.S. military intervention to install Endara as Panama's president.

Dominican Republic: 1965

U.S. relations with the Dominican Republic epitomized for many years the imperialist impulse in U.S. foreign policy. Although it gained its independence from Spain in 1844, this island nation bordering Haiti remained vulnerable to outside interference—including a brief attempt at colonization by the United States. It had seen a succession of dictators before the first major U.S. military intervention—an occupation force that lasted from 1916 to 1924 and resulted in the strengthening of the country's army and a more hospitable climate for U.S. investment (Gleijeses 1978, 18).

That armed intervention set the stage for the second major intervention by the United States into the Dominican Republic in 1965. Rafael Leonidas Trujillo overthrew the constitutional government left behind in 1930 and began a thirty-year reign of terror (Barnet 1968, 155). Trujillo's principal virtue, from the American perspective, was that he provided a stable anti-Communist bulwark in the Caribbean. Trujillo also did much to give his country the appearance of growth and prosperity, although the image concealed a deeply divided society where incomes were extremely unequal, the established wealthy class mistrusted the newcomers—"nouveau riche"—and the overzealous Trujillo family, and the middle class was virtually nonexistent. Nonetheless, Trujillo reigned supreme until 1960, when his acts of terror against opponents at home and abroad caused even the conservative Catholic church in the Dominican Republic to repudiate him.

The United States, though supportive of conservative governments in the region, feared Trujillo would so oppress his people that he would precipitate Marxist revolution. Fulgencio Batista did just that in Cuba in 1959, and the United States faced an angry Castro only ninety miles from Florida. In mid-1960, the Eisenhower administration withdrew support for the Trujillo regime and endorsed economic sanctions favored by other Latin American states through the Organization of American States (OAS) (Gleijeses 1978, 21). Trujillo was assassinated on May 30, 1961, by a small group of coup plotters in the army, although their hopes of establishing a new regime were dashed as Trujillo loyalists moved quickly to preserve at least the form of power if not the content.

For the new Kennedy administration, the search was under way for a moderate democratic leader in the Dominican Republic, although the president acknowledged that failing that, a dictator would be better than a Communist (Barnet 1968, 158). The country went through a succession of quasi-military leaders, each receiving moderate U.S. support. The opportunistic Joaquin Balaguer, a former Trujillo cabinet member, held office with the support of Trujillo's family for a brief period following the assassination. Then the military, following the exile of Trujillo's son and brothers, took de facto control under General Pedro Echeverria (Gleijeses 1978, 57). Balaguer eventually resigned his post in favor of Rafael Bonelly, another former Trujillo official, who was even more eager to work with the United States (to the military's annoyance) (Yates 1988, 181). The United States and the OAS finally lifted the anti-Trujillo sanctions following the announcement of national elections scheduled for June 1, 1961. The Kennedy administration felt that it had finally found the path to what it sought, although there was intense disagreement over whether it could afford the risk of a Communist sympathizer winning the election.

The presidential elections included numerous candidates from across the political spectrum, although three parties dominated the campaign: the Revolutionary Dominican Party (PRD) under Juan Bosch; the National Civic Union (UCN), which already held sway in the transitional regime; and an assortment of leftist parties dominated by the June 14 movement. Contrary to its militant name, the PRD was a moderate left-of-center party with a reformist, anti-Trujillo agenda. In contrast to the June 14 movement, which included both armed and Castroite elements, the PRD seemed a viable alternative to the parties of the right (Gleijeses 1978, 39).

The elections were honest and fair, in spite of a never-ending atmosphere of violence and unrest that gripped the country after Trujillo's death. Juan Bosch and the PRD emerged victorious with well over half of the votes cast; Bosch received 59 percent of the vote—nearly twice that of his UCN rival (Gleijeses 1978, 86). The United States moved quickly to endorse the elections and support the Bosch administration, although U.S. ambassador John Bartlow Martin had strong reservations. He had grown accustomed to the former regimes and had become so heavily involved in Dominican policy making that even many conservative Dominicans had challenged his interference. Martin often criticized Bosch as a "divider" and even a "destroyer" because of his willingness to openly criticize and challenge U.S. policy in the region, including the regional aid program known as the Alliance for Progress (Barnet 1968, 166). Martin suspected Bosch of Marxist sympathies.

The Bosch administration was under pressure to carry out many reforms it had promised. After it began by introducing a new constitution, restoring some sense of integrity to the government, moving squatters and landless peasants onto their own plots, and taking steps to limit profit taking by foreign corporations, the conservatives began to organize concerted opposition to the regime. An important problem, from the perspective of affluent Dominicans and the military, was Bosch's failure to deport the known Marxists in the June 14 movement and other radical parties. Bosch argued that constitutional protection should be extended to all, regardless of their political coloration (Draper 1968, 29). This was the last straw, and in September 1963, the military took power. Bosch fled to Puerto Rico, and a three-man government was set up in his place. With the resignation of one of the "triumvirate" members in December, the new military government came under the dominance of Donald Reid Cabral and secured the support of the new Lyndon Johnson administration (Barnet 1968, 167). A feeble rebellion by the June 14 movement reduced the number of its armed guerrillas to less than one hundred. For the time being, the situation was stabilized and, from the perspective of ardent anti-Communists in Washington and Santo Domingo, more secure. In fact, the regime lasted little more than a year.

In spite of considerable support from the United States, the Reid regime was a failure from the start. Its attempts at economic development foundered amid corruption and falling sugar prices (Gleijeses 1978, 118). Its use of torture alienated the masses and spurred calls for reform and even revolution from both far- left and center-left sections (including the exiled

Bosch). The wealthy elite grew weary of the stagnant economy, and the military bristled at Reid's clumsy attempts to reform its ranks. By early 1965, some factions of the military were organizing a revolt in combination with former Bosch and Balaguer supporters, with the aim of returning constitutional government (Gleijeses 1978, 132). On April 24, the rebellion (officially termed a countercoup) erupted. On April 25, loyalists to the regime responded. The nation fell into civil war and chaos, with the heart of Santo Domingo at the epicenter.

Early on, the rebels scored impressive victories, leading to the resignation of Reid and the naming of former Bosch supporter José Rafael Molina Urena as provisional president. The victory was short-lived, however, and before the end of April, Urena was forced into hiding. In the meantime, poorly organized rebels took control of the streets of the capital amid rumors of atrocities. Reports of Communists taking over leadership of the rebellion were accepted without hesitation by CIA and embassy officials and the new ambassador, W. Tapley Bennett, who requested U.S. military forces to begin evacuating American civilians trapped in the city. Even after an initial wave of some 500 Marines arrived, Bennett concluded on April 28 that the situation called for still more dramatic U.S. intervention. He claimed that Americans were being shot at and that some 1,500 Communists were overrunning the capital (Barnet 1968, 171). Johnson was forced to respond on the grounds that Bennett's alarm could not be ignored, although he doubted the authenticity of the reports. The administration later chose to ignore Bennett's pleas (Yates 1988, 64).

By May 17, 1965, 24,000 troops had been deployed in and around Santo Domingo. U.S. troops were originally placed around neighborhoods where Americans lived and worked to evacuate them as rapidly as possible. Once this mission was accomplished, the operation moved to contain the rebellion by virtually surrounding the inner-city area of the capital with a belt of U.S. troops (Yates 1988, 75). This move effectively eliminated any prospect for a rebel victory and assured the loyalist military government, now under the command of Generals Antonio Imbert Barrera and Elias Wessin y Wessin, a relatively free hand in mopping up opposition to the regime. All the while, the U.S. troops proclaimed a policy of "neutrality" in the conflict.

The constitutionalist rebels regrouped after the initial shock of the U.S. deployment and found leadership under rebel Colonel Francisco Caamano Deno. Although not a Communist himself, he allowed several Marxists to play a role in leading the rebellion. There is some debate arose over the significance of these Marxists (Thomas and Thomas 1967), the consensus is that, contrary to the impression of embassy, CIA, and State Department staff at the time, the anti-U.S. rhetoric that poured out of rebel headquarters during much of the war was merely posturing. In fact, the vast majority of the rebels sought merely the return of the Bosch administration rather than some Castroite revolution (Barnet 1968, 173).

Once the situation was stabilized, the United States sought to create an effective multilateral presence in the city. The OAS organized a peacekeeping force that was deployed in mid-May and subsumed the U.S. presence. From that point onward, the emphasis of the operation was on finding a diplomatic solution to the crisis (Slater 1970). The U.S. troops played the role of genuine peacekeepers, not only containing the constitutionalist rebellion but also preventing the loyalist troops from entering their inner-city haven (Yates 1988, 145).

Ultimately, after months of effort and sporadic fighting between OAS forces and the rebels, a settlement was reached on September 3, 1965, which provided for a provisional government under the leadership of former Bosch official Hector García-Godoy. Caamano left the island for an overseas diplomatic post in January 1966, along with Urena. Marines were withdrawn from the island over the course of the year, with the last units departing on September 21 after a seventeen-month stay. The military was partially contained in the new regime, although it mounted several unsuccessful coup attempts later on. The García-Godoy regime sponsored elections on June 1, 1966, which returned Balaguer to power under a cloud of tainted voting.

Chile: 1973

Chileans elected a self-proclaimed Marxist to the presidency in 1970, much to the dismay of the White House and major U.S. firms that were operating in Chile at the time. The story of what they did to change the result of that election is an example of indirect and covert intervention.

Chile, unlike the Dominican Republic, enjoyed a tradition of democratic rule that extended, at least nominally, to the pre–World War II era. When President Jorge Alessandri, leader of the conservative National Party, was defeated by Christian Democratic Party (PDC) candidate Eduardo Frei in 1964, the government moved toward the type of progressive reforms the Kennedy administration had advocated. Though he was a nationalist who did not want to serve as lackey to U.S. interests, Frei was willing to accommodate U.S. business needs. In particular, he agreed to limit government intervention in the economy to those things that had the best chance of reversing the drastic inequality of income and wealth that had developed. In his dealings with such U.S. firms as Kennecott Copper and International Telephone and Telegraph (ITT), he generally negotiated new arrangements fairly and in good faith (Kissinger 1979, 657). The principal targets of his policies were the wealthy landowners, who were forced to relinquish property that was then redistributed to peasants (Sater 1990, 151). The policies of Frei were satisfactory enough to the Johnson administration that it secretly provided hundreds of millions of dollars for his party's election campaigns (Rojas Sandford 1976, 57).

Much of the support Frei received from the United States could be explained by the opposition he faced: Salvador Allende Gossens, leader of the newly formed Unidad Popular—a coalition party of leftist movements in Chile. His party represented the greatest challenge to Christian Democrats in 1962 and 1964 elections. The radical, anti-U.S. nature of his policies was seen as inimical to U.S. interests. In the September 1970 presidential elections, however, American observers and policy makers became convinced that he would do poorly against Alessandri and the PDC candidate Radomiro Tomic (Eduardo Frei was forbidden by the constitution to serve consecutive terms). Allende's election victory—which consisted of a 30,000-vote edge over Alessandri (out of 3 million votes cast)—came as a stunning shock in Washington (Kissinger 1979, 670). Henry Kissinger wished aloud that the United States had pumped more secret funds into the election, but he and Richard Nixon had been dissuaded by a State Department concerned about interference in domestic affairs (Kissinger 1979, 669). The ambassador, Edward Korrey, stated unequivocally that Allende's victory, though perhaps still reversible given certain provisions in the Chilean Constitution, was a serious blow.

Nixon was livid over the Allende victory and was desperate to prevent Allende from taking office in November. Nixon told CIA Director Richard Helms to ignore the State Department and do "whatever it takes" to reverse the outcome, offering up to $10 million for immediate actions (Kissinger 1979, 673). What transpired involved two "tracks" of intervention.

Track I was a fairly straightforward approach: Convince conservative members of the Chilean Congress to vote against Allende's bid—an option that seemed feasible given the narrow Allende win and Alessandri's decision to contest the election. To accomplish this, the United States warmly endorsed Alessandri's proposal to resign as soon as the Congress elected him president, thus forcing a new election six months later. The hope was that Frei, who could run for another nonconsecutive term, would be able to defeat Allende in a head-to-head race. Unfortunately, Frei was not interested in the scheme (Whelan 1981, 40; Sater 1990, 162).

At the same time, Nixon engineered an economic and financial embargo of Chile through private and government channels. He wanted the Chilean economy to "scream" (Kissinger 1979, 673). With the help of Chilean conservatives in the banking sector, rumors of Marxist excesses were spread, precipitating a run on several banks and a flight of some $50 million in private savings. All of these efforts went for naught, however, and the inevitability of an Allende presidency loomed large in Washington (LaFeber 1989, 620).

Track II intervention came into effect immediately before the late October congressional vote and involved a rather awkward attempted coup by the military with U.S. backing. Corporate executives of ITT, Pepsi-Cola, and other firms were eager to support a military takeover and lobbied the administration intensively throughout the Allende era (Sergeyev 1981, 138). At this initial stage, the coup attempt involved supporting General Roberto Viaux's attempt to kidnap the commander of the Santiago garrison, General Rene Schneider, and form a junta to replace the Congress. Weapons and funds were provided in early October but were cut off on October 15 after Viaux failed repeatedly (Kissinger 1979, 676). Viaux continued his efforts on his own and managed to capture the general, but Viaux killed him inadvertently in a skirmish. As a result, the conservative elements in Congress and the elite within the army closed ranks around Allende and the constitution and endorsed his election victory. He was sworn in as president in November.

The Allende administration was known above all for its rhetoric, which was consistently anti-American and anticapitalist. Allende made numerous contacts with Soviet Bloc countries and received modest financial support from Moscow and Eastern Europe as well as some sugar from Cuba. He moved rapidly, and often in violation of Chilean law, to nationalize not only large farms but also foreign businesses and factories (Rojas Sandford 1976, 95). Although resigned to the election's outcome at first, the Nixon administration later invoked the Gonzalez amendment and curtailed all multilateral lending to Chile pending just compensation for the seizures (LaFeber 1989, 620). Private U.S. banks dropped their lending to Chile from $219 million in 1970 to $32 million in 1971. Whereas in the 1960s Chile borrowed an average of $150 million each year from U.S. government sources, the figure slipped to $40 million in 1971 and to nothing in 1972 (Rojas Sandford 1976, 148). Many state-owned firms failed for lack of spare parts and capital due to this "invisible blockade."

In spite of his aggressive anti-U.S. stance, Allende tried to maintain a working relationship with his conservative Latin neighbors and Western financial institutions (Sater 1990, 165). After nationalizing Kennecott Copper (with the initial support of the opposition parties), Allende attempted to export copper to Europe (in contravention of international law). The executives at Kennecott tracked the shipments—allegedly with the help of the Navy—and brought lawsuits against Chile in whatever country they were delivered. With the collapse of the price of copper in 1972 and the growing reticence of Europeans to deal with Allende, the sales of copper grew perilously low. This factor, combined with a growing international debt, forced the Allende regime into an international crisis by 1972.

Allende, unable to secure adequate support from abroad, found his domestic programs were failing. His deficit spending program to stimulate consumption and reward his proletarian supporters quickly spurred inflation, which topped the 200 percent mark by 1973. Unable to satisfy workers whose purchasing power fell precipitously, Allende was in the uncomfortable position of dealing with an increasing number of strikes by his core supporters of the past. Truckers, copper miners, physicians, and others engaged in months-long walkouts to protest government policies, wreaking social chaos in the process. To preserve some semblance of stability, Allende invited military officers to his cabinet in 1972 and then again in 1973 (Whelan 1981, 6). When the generals came in the second time, they never left.

Beginning in August 1973, Allende faced pressure from an increasingly defiant military to address the civil disturbance in the country. On August 23, he accepted the resignation of his military commander, Carlos Prats Gonzales, who declared that he could no longer contain the pressure for a coup, and appointed Augusto Pinochet as his successor (Rojas Sandford 1976, 179). By September Pinochet had joined with the navy in a plan to overthrow the regime. On September 11, beginning with the occupation of the port of Valparaiso, the military attacked and seized the presidential offices at la Modena. By late afternoon, Allende was dead and one of the most brutal military regimes in Latin American history was in power.

Although one can argue that the fall of Allende was made possible only by three years of American pressure, it appears that the U.S. government did not have any direct hand in the coup itself. Even critics of U.S. policy acknowledge that the CIA and the White House learned about the coup at the same time as the rest of the world (Whelan 1981, 40).

Panama: 1989

The last of the three case studies offers an opportunity to analyze post–Cold War U.S. intervention. Although the Dominican and Chilean cases were clearly influenced by anti-Communist concerns, the Panama invasion of 1989 seems to have had no such ideological impetus. In fact, the strong desire on the part of the Reagan administration to preserve Panama as a listening post against the Nicaraguan Marxists (Sandinistas) led its members to overlook blatant narcotics trafficking, corruption, and despotism. When the Cold War was over and the Sandinistas were on their way out, the Panamanian government's indiscretions could no longer be tolerated (Conniff 1992, 166).

U.S. relations with Panama were as historically intimate and intrusive as its ties with the Dominican Republic. In 1908, President Theodore Roosevelt supported Panamanian independence from Colombia in an effort to work out a better Panama Canal treaty (Donnelly et al. 1991, 2). William Howard Taft essentially dictated presidential succession after the 1908 Panamanian elections, and under Woodrow Wilson the United States deployed troops and occupied the country after establishing a permanent military base (Conniff 1992, 76). By so doing, the Canal Zone became a sort of "micro-state"—an extension of U.S. territory abroad (Conniff 1992, 84).

Beginning in 1945, the Panamanian leadership became more and more determined to reclaim rights to the canal, or at least to profit more substantially from U.S. operations. Colonel Jose Antonio Remon pressed for a new treaty in the 1950s, and Roberto Chiari renegotiated the agreement in 1967. Anti-American demonstrations became gradually more intense over the years. Also, the democratic governments in Panama began to investigate corruption in the military. In 1968, to solve both problems, General Omar Torrijos and the elite Guardia Nacionale overthrew the popular President Arnulfo Arias (Donnelly et al. 1991, 4).

From the emergence of Torrijos in 1968 to the capture of Noriega in 1991, the story of Panamanian leadership was one of court intrigue, populist despotism, and narcotics trafficking. In 1969, an anti-Torrijos coup succeeded for a time until the general returned, accompanied by loyalist Manuel Antonio Noriega, to reconquer the capital (Conniff 1992, 126). Noriega, an important CIA contact in previous years, became even more significant as the newly appointed head of Panamanian intelligence. He later had regular contact with CIA officials, including CIA Director William Casey and Vice President George Bush. This relationship continued, in spite of the fact that he was identified as early as 1972 as the secret "Panama connection" in narcotics trade. Conniff has pointed out that U.S. blame for military rule in Panama

> began in 1968, when Washington's professed determination to promote civilian, democratic regimes in Panama weakened in the wake of the military coup. A decade later, U.S. policy seemed to be driven by the Senate's concern over the security of the canal. At the time, a stable Panama was more critical than a democratic Panama. This meant, among other things, greater involvement by the Panamanian military in the country's domestic politics. (Conniff 1992, 153)

The Panamanian government under Torrijos scored a major victory when it signed the ill-fated Panama Canal Treaty of 1977. The promise of a new relationship with the United States was largely frustrated by the death of Torrijos and the outbreak of the anti-Sandinista operation by U.S.-led "Contras" in 1981. General Manuel Noriega moved into position to lead a military triumvirate, illegally securing the election of a loyalist, Nicolas Ardito Barletta, to the office of president (Conniff 1992, 150). The United States endorsed the outcome and established extensive intelligence-gathering operations in Panama, including direct support and training for the renamed Panamanian Defense Forces.

After weeks of growing tension between Noriega, an increasingly democratic Barletta, and Noriega's military ally, General Dias Herrera, the situation began to unravel. The decapitated body of Noriega critic Hugo Spadafora was discovered in September 1988, and investigators quickly linked Noriega to the death. He tried to shift the blame to Dias Herrera, who launched a coup attempt in retaliation. Barletta was dismissed after threatening to publicly expose Noriega's role and was replaced by Eric Arturo Delvalle. For the first time, U.S. representatives issued Noriega a stern rebuke and a warning lest he abuse his power too blatantly (Donnelly et al. 1991, 10). Senator Jesse Helms held hearings in 1986 detailing Noriega's excesses, and the U.S. press began systematic attacks (Conniff 1992, 155). By now, Noriega was being compared to the likes of Libya's Muammar Qaddafi and Iran's Ayatollah Khomeini as a global pariah.

In June 1987, the situation took yet another dramatic turn. Dias Herrera turned down a Noriega offer of the ambassadorship to Japan and instead exposed sordid details of Noriega's atrocities to the Panamanian press (Donnelly et al. 1991, 11). The resulting outrage, which involved not only poor Panamanians in the barrios (slums) but also middle-class professionals, precipitated a violent repression. Noriega's troops fired into unarmed crowds and arrested U.S. servicemen (Conniff 1992, 156).

By the time drug indictments against Noriega were issued by two U.S. courts in February 1988, the United States had already begun to develop plans for military intervention. It formally imposed economic sanctions against Panama on April 8, 1988, by freezing $56 million in Panamanian assets in the United States, cutting off most trade, and putting severe restrictions on Panama's dollar-denominated money supply (Commission 1991, 23). In retaliation, Noriega stepped up harassment of U.S. military personnel and their families. The last opportunity for a negotiated settlement of the conflict came in May 1988, when President Reagan offered to drop the drug trafficking charges in return for Noriega's retirement. The offer was rebuffed (Donnelly et al. 1991, 35).

The May 1989 presidential elections, a farce by any democratic standard, provided a new focal point for the United States following the failure of the Reagan offer. The administration spent roughly $10 million on the campaign of progressive Guillermo Endara Galimany, who, according to reliable reports, received some 75 percent of the vote. Noriega, after failing to reverse the outcome through rigging, declared the election invalid and continued to govern the country. A coup attempt in October 1989 failed to dislodge Noriega in spite of participation by U.S. troops.

The question for the incoming Bush administration was how to intervene in Panama while minimizing casualties and maximizing legal justifications. Certainly the presence of some 10,000 American citizens, all of whom felt very much threatened by the growing civil violence and repression, could have been enough. Unfortunately, the argument that Noriega was a threat to international stability was hypocritical, considering the great lengths to which successive U.S. administrations had gone to build him up. Finally, on December 15 the opportunity came: Noriega declared that a "state of war" existed (and had existed for thirty months) between Panama and the United States (McConnell 1991, 281). He was then proclaimed head of state by a rump assembly of cronies, who naturally endorsed the declaration by a unanimous vote. As portrayed in the U.S. press, the statements seemed very much like a formal declaration of war, although in retrospect they seem more rhetorical than substantive. When still more harassment of U.S. troops followed, culminating in the death of a Marine, the Bush administration initiated Operation Just Cause.

The operation was intended as a "decapitating" strike against a limited number of military targets. Based on Colin Powell's notion of "overwhelming force," the Bush administration deployed 24,000 troops against a Panamanian Defense Force (PDF) of roughly 15,000, of which only 3,000 were combat-ready. The attacks began before dawn on December 20 and included strikes on the airport, a military academy, the prison where political opponents to the regime were held, a naval complex, and the Noriega headquarters, known as La Comandancia. The vast majority of the troops were deployed in Panama City, where they killed several hundred PDF soldiers guarding various installations. Although the Comandancia was captured early in the fighting, Noriega slipped away, as he did on some forty other occasions before he finally sought refuge in the papal nuncio (Donnelly et al. 1991, 105).

In the midst of the fighting, Guillermo Endara and his two vice presidents were gathered into a secure location in the Canal Zone and sworn in as the legitimate leaders of the country. Washington immediately granted diplomatic recognition to the new Endara administration and offered $50 million in reconstruction aid (Conniff 1992, 164). Within a few weeks, the Bush administration renegotiated the canal treaty so that it provided for a significantly extended period of U.S. presence.

International reaction to the invasion was mixed. The OAS was clearly pleased to see Noriega gone, but it decided to "deeply regret" the U.S. intervention. For many Latins, the action seemed similar to the pre–Cold War policies of Teddy Roosevelt. In the United Nations, sentiments were also split. Although the United States won a slim majority for a resolution favoring the change of government, its victory came only because a large number of countries abstained. At home, the operation was over too quickly to precipitate any organized resistance.

U.S. troops were accused of causing large numbers of civilian deaths, although estimates vary widely (between 1,000 and 4,000). The Defense Department was clearly eager to minimize reports of "collateral damage" in the attack and reported a scant eighty-four official civilian casualties (mass graves of civilian dead were later uncovered and U.S. officials admitted to a higher figure—Commission 1991, 39). Though originally told not to shoot the many looters who were wreaking havoc in the city, the troops were given "shoot to maim" orders on the second day (McConnell 1991, 236). Attack helicopters fired numerous rounds into residential areas, causing widespread damage.

On January 3, 1990, Manuel Noriega was transported to Miami after finally being taken into custody, and by February the troops were withdrawn from the country. Panama has yet to recover from the invasion, in spite of considerable foreign aid. Reports show that drug trafficking and government corruption are on the rise. Pressing problems in the Middle East seem to have removed Panama from the American consciousness.

Conclusion

U.S. intervention overseas has many explanations. The Cold War was a dominant preoccupation throughout the period under study—including in Panama because of its connection to Nicaragua. But the danger of Communist encroachment in the Western Hemisphere is not uniform across the cases. Clearly, in the case of Chile, the pro-Soviet connection is the most plausible—but interestingly enough, this case involved the least U.S. involvement. On the other hand, the most troops were deployed in the Panama case, where there seemed to be no Communist conspiracy.

One could argue that at issue was the extent to which tangible American interests were at stake—U.S. nationals in the Dominican Republic, American corporate assets in Chile, and American government property in Panama. But here again, one finds in Chile perhaps the greatest threat to

American assets but the least intervention. And is the Panama Canal such a vital interest that it deserves a massive invasion force to protect it against what was only a hypothetical threat? Only in the Dominican Republic does one find the perception of danger to both geopolitical and tangible local U.S. interests in proportion to the scale of intervention. Given the unique multilateral character of the invasion force (after OAS involvement), the Dominican Republic case challenges the notion that the United States always "goes it alone" in its own hemisphere.

Does U.S. intervention in the Middle East over the last decade break from this pattern? In some ways the Persian Gulf War was a collective security operation that was merely led by the United States (see Case 9). U.S. involvement in Afghanistan is perhaps another matter. In late 2001, following the September 11 attacks and UN and NATO resolutions authorizing retaliatory measures, the United States deployed air and ground troops in Afghanistan to support the Northern Alliance's war against the Taliban regime. Within a few weeks, the Northern Alliance succeeded in overcoming considerable opposition (and Western skepticism) to seize the country's capital, Kabul. Eventually, organized opposition was largely eliminated and a new regime under Ahmed Karzai was installed. The United States has left behind a sizable residual force to support the new government and has been joined by other countries in providing aid and assistance to Karzai. Sporadic fighting has erupted from time to time, but it seems clear that Taliban forces and combatants loyal to Osama bin Laden's al Qaeda organization have fled to neighboring states and beyond.

Such an operation seems to break from previous patterns. First, in the case of Afghanistan, there was a clear attack against vital U.S. interests that warranted a military response. This opinion was shared unanimously by the international community. Even Cuba, Syria, Iran, and North Korea applauded U.S. efforts. Second, the Taliban regime clearly had little popular support, given the relative ease with which Northern Alliance forces were able to advance across the country once their intentions were clear and their prospects were good. One could argue, given the apparent popularity of Karzai, that the United States has promoted democracy in Afghanistan. Finally, the operation received prior approval from important multilateral agencies.

Debate Topic

Should the United States have invaded Iraq without UN approval to overthrow Saddam Hussein?

PRO

Supporters of unilateral intervention make the following arguments: (1) The United States had enough facts to prove that Saddam Hussein had the capability and the intention of destroying his neighbors with weapons of mass destruction. (2) Saddam Hussein is a corrupt despot who inflicted unacceptable pain on his people. (3) UN-sponsored methods had proved ineffective thus far.

CON
Opponents of unilateral intervention point out the following: (1) The United States has accepted the principle of multilateralism with regard to intervention since 1990. (2) The Constitution requires the United States to follow international law, which includes the UN Charter. (3) Unilateral intervention is likely to be ineffective because it will create new tensions with important allies in the region.

Questions to Consider

1. Was coercion the best approach in the three cases? Did the United States achieve its apparent objectives?

2. Were Presidents Johnson, Nixon, and Bush so eager to intervene because they were personally annoyed at the situation and felt a compulsion to vent their frustrations?

3. How was international law used by the United States to legitimize its intervention? Is this a proper role for international law? How did international organizations enter into the picture?

Websites

It is perhaps needless to say that the subject of U.S. intervention is extremely controversial. As a result, most websites on this issue are biased. The following offer a mixture of views. (Note that the Special Forces site plays the *Green Beret* song!)

Military Sources
Department of Defense: **www.defenselink.mil**
Special Forces: **www.socom.mil**
NATO: **www.nato.int**
CIA: **www.odci.gov**

Archives
National Security Archive: **www.gwu.edu/~nsarchive**
Resource Center of the Americas: **www.americas.org**
Library of Congress: **lcweb.loc.gov/lexico/liv/m/Military_intervention.html**
The History Guy: **www.historyguy.com**

Other Groups
Abolish NATO: **www.abolishnato.com/abolishnato/anti-NATO.papers/papers.htm**
Committee Against U.S. Interventionism: **www.antiwar.com**
Anti-Intervention Network: **www.oz.net/~vvwai/ain-home.html**

References

Barnet, Richard J. *Intervention and Revolution: The United States in the Third World* (New York: New American Library, 1968).

Commission of Inquiry. *The U.S. Invasion of Panama: The Truth Behind Operation "Just Cause"* (Boston: South End Press, 1991).

Conniff, Michael. *Panama and the United States: The Forced Alliance* (Athens, GA: University of Georgia Press, 1992).

Deibel, Terry L., and John Lewis Gaddis, eds. *Containing the Soviet Union: A Critique of U.S. Policy* (New York: Pergamon-Brassey's, 1987).

Donnelly, Thomas, Margaret Roth, and Caleb Baker. *Operation Just Cause: The Storming of Panama* (New York: Lexington Books, 1991).

Draper, Theodore. *The Dominican Revolt: A Case Study in American Policy* (New York: Commentary, 1968).

Dulles, Allen. *The Craft of Intelligence* (New York: Harper & Row, 1963).

Gleijeses, Piero. *The Dominican Crisis: The 1965 Constitutionalist Revolt and American Intervention.* Trans. by Lawrence Lipson (Baltimore, MD: Johns Hopkins University Press, 1978).

Hoopes, Townsend. *The Devil and John Foster Dulles* (Boston: Little, Brown, 1973).

Kennan, George. "The Sources of Soviet Conduct." *Foreign Affairs* 25 (July 1947): 566–582.

Kissinger, Henry. *The White House Years* (Boston: Little, Brown, 1979).

LaFeber, Walter. *The American Age: United States Foreign Policy at Home and Abroad Since 1750* (New York: W. W. Norton, 1989).

Magdoff, Harry. *The Age of Imperialism: The Economics of U.S. Foreign Policy* (New York: Monthly Review Press, 1969).

McConnell, Malcolm. *Just Cause: The Real Story of America's High-Tech Invasion of Panama* (New York: St. Martin's, 1991).

Rojas Sandford, Robinson. *The Murder of Allende and the End of the Chilean Way to Socialism.* Trans. by Andree Conrad (New York: Harper & Row, 1976).

Sater, William F. *Chile and the United States: Empires in Conflict* (Athens, GA: University of Georgia Press, 1990).

Sergeyev, F. F. *Chile: CIA Big Business* (Moscow: Progress Publishers, 1981).

Slater, Jerome. *Intervention and Negotiation: The United States and the Dominican Revolution* (New York: Harper & Row, 1970).

Thomas, A. J., Jr., and Ann Van Wynen Thomas. *The Dominican Republic Crisis 1965* (Dobbs Ferry, NY: Oceana Publications, 1967).

Whelan, James R. *Allende: Death of a Marxist Dream* (Westport, CT: Arlington House, 1981).

Wilson, Woodrow. "The World Must Be Made Safe for Democracy" in John Vasquez, ed., *Classics of International Relations*, 2nd ed. (Englewood Cliffs, NJ: Prentice Hall, 1990), 12–15.

Yates, Lawrence A. Power Pack: U.S. *Intervention in the Dominican Republic, 1965–1966*, Leavenworth Papers #15 (Washington, DC: U.S. Government Printing Office, 1988).

Money
and
Justice

20

Sweatshops and the Global Factory

GLOBALIZATION

Introduction

In the summer of 1996, Sydney Schanberg related the following account in a *Life* magazine story:

> As I traveled [in Pakistan], I witnessed conditions more appalling than [the last]—children as young as six bought from their parents for as little as $15, sold and resold like furniture, branded, beaten, blinded as punishment for wanting to go home, rendered speechless by the trauma of their enslavement. One 12-year-old Pakistani, Kramat, who had been making bricks since he was sold by his achingly poor father six years ago, his teeth now rotting, his hair tinged with red streaks, a sign of malnutrition, said morosely: "I cannot go anywhere. I am a prisoner." (Schanberg and Dorigny 1996, 39)

Also in 1996, Charles Kernaghan of the National Labor Committee, a watchdog group that monitors corporate labor practices, testified before a congressional committee that many American apparel companies knowingly used suppliers in developing countries that practiced indentured servitude, used child labor, and repressed and failed to pay their workers. One such company manufactured the Kathie Lee clothing line, which was sold nationwide by Wal-Mart (in 1995 it earned $9 million for the line's namesake, talk-show host Kathie Lee Gifford). When it was revealed that the Kathie Lee clothing company subcontracted to factories that employed girls as young as 13 to work for 31 cents per hour for fifteen-hour shifts, Gifford was indignant. As the reports were confirmed to her through company sources, she pledged to improve working conditions and offered to open up all of the company's factories to independent inspection (Press 1996, 6). Finally, the American public took notice of an international problem that linked Kmart shoppers with children in developing countries more directly than anyone had ever understood before.

Thus began the full-blown campaign known as the anti-sweatshop movement. Many students became activists in the United Students Against Sweatshops campaign and succeeded in persuading their colleges to stop using sweatshops to manufacture their apparel. Beyond understanding that children are being made to work in horrible conditions, however, few really understand the sources of this situation and the implications of the efforts to stop it.

We will explore the phenomenon known as the "global factory" (Rothstein and Blim 1992), which is an important aspect of globalization (Mittelman 2000). Today, the production of manufactured goods is dispersed throughout the world and thereby links corporate units, warehouses, middlemen, workers, and consumers across many nations as never before in the history of capitalist production. In addition, corporations extend their brand names and products into every corner of the world in the hope of establishing new markets for their goods. Although the notion of an international division of labor is nothing new (the concept dates back to the eighteenth century), what is different now is the degree to which the linkages are dense and close, leading to a transformation of social structures around the world (Gill 1995, 76). This idea helps to explain everything from sweatshops in Indonesia , to downsizing in Seattle, to merger mania in New York, to the emergence of a global culture and the withering away of differences between states and nations.

The global factory arose from modern innovations such as the assembly line process, faster communication and transportation, and the opening of national markets through the World Trade Organization. What is unique about this new structure, however, is how ancient, traditional social arrangements interact with the Western capitalist system. What might have been a tolerable situation, such as the work of young daughters on a family farm, becomes exploitative and dangerous when transferred to a garment factory or a plantation. The contrast between these situations and the lofty language of workers' rights articulated by Western investors, middlemen, and consumers makes the situation all the more bizarre.

Globalization has stirred considerable controversy because it seems to both benefit and injure at the same time. Consumers in industrialized countries benefit from lower prices and a greater variety of goods. All one need do is walk into a Wal-Mart or other discount store and flip through rack after rack of Asian-manufactured clothing at very low prices to see evidence of this phenomenon. Conversely, some of those Western consumers were put out of work when the companies that manufacture the clothing relocated off-shore. Likewise, as we will see, the working conditions imposed on those who manufacture the clothing and other goods in developing countries inspire considerable dismay. But it is also true that these "sweatshop" jobs are among the most desirable, compared with farming, begging, or prostitution—the most readily available alternatives for many workers.

What is clear is that everyone on the planet is increasingly linked, and that what happens in one spot on the globe almost invariably affects others on the opposite side. This adage applies not only to global production but also to international finance, travel, and even politics. Just as globalization has brought everyone closer together, so has it created considerable tension. An imbalanced currency in Thailand exposes financial weaknesses in Brazil. A sick cow in England causes panic in Spain. A mosquito carrying a disease that originated in Egypt bites and kills an old man in Chicago.

In the most extreme example, the World Trade Center and Pentagon bombers claimed they were aiming to cripple the United States economically and psychologically as part of their fight against Western culture (however hypocritical or cynical the claim). Ironically, they took advantage of globalization to carry out the attack. The funding came from Osama bin Laden, who inherited considerable sums from his family's international construction businesses. The terrorists were generally successful for their own part, and some had spent their formative years studying in Western colleges, thanks to modern travel and liberal immigration policies. That they would select modern aircraft as their weapon, rather than, say, a crude homemade bomb, adds to the paradox. One could argue that globalization contributed to providing both the ends and the means of the attack.

As we consider sweatshops, we will find numerous interpretations of the effects of globalization. Given its controversial character, the material is presented here almost as a debate, with the reader being left to do most of the interpretation.

The Sweatshop Phenomenon

Sweatshops are nothing new. Workers—especially women—have been required to labor in cramped, dangerous conditions since the Industrial Revolution in the 1750s. In the eighteenth century, the French government actually created sweatshops as a way of rescuing destitute women and children from a life on the street (DiCaprio 1999, 519). The sweatshop was commonly instituted in the textile industry by garment manufacturers in Great Britain and the United States who felt squeezed by middlemen and suppliers demanding ever-lower manufacturing costs in spite of high clothing costs. The difference was "sweated" out of labor through low wages and a form of indentured servitude, which were easier to arrange with children and women, who were particularly vulnerable in the workplace.

Sweatshops became a target of labor and humanitarian activists by theearly 1900s, spurred in the United States by a series of catastrophes (including fires) in which hundreds of workers lost their lives in the early part of the twentieth century. Gradually, worker safety regulations, child labor laws, and legislation that protected workers' rights to organize were passed by federal and state agencies. By the 1940s, sweatshops were thought to be a thing of the past.

In the 1980s, however, sweatshop garment factories were discovered in New York and Los Angeles, giving rise to another outcry. Sweatshops and debt bondage (where a loan is provided to cover a working fee that is paid off over a period of time, during which the worker is forced to stay on) were particularly prevalent in the textile industry and in agriculture, where new downward price pressures were becoming particularly intense, in part because of the international market forces mentioned earlier. During 1981–1984, the federal government successfully prosecuted twenty cases of slavery (*US News & World Report,* January 16, 1984, 68). Sweatshops in Queens were hidden behind storefronts to prevent detection by the 800 federal work inspectors (down from more than 1,000 in the 1970s). During the 1990s, the trend continued, to the point that by 1993, as many as half of all women's garments were made by factories that violated minimum wage and other labor laws (*US News & World Report,* November 22, 1993, 48). After the Kathie Lee Gifford incident in 1996 involving foreign sweatshops, it was discovered that one of the offending suppliers was located in Manhattan, not far from where her television show was taped (Press 1996, 8).

Overseas, an estimated 200 million children under age 14 (the lowest legal working age in any country) work full-time (although for many, working a mere forty hours per week would be a relief). The problem is particularly acute in South Asia. It is estimated that in Pakistan, 11 million children work six days per week for nine or ten hours per day (Schanberg and Dorigny 1996). Their employers are in violation of international labor codes drafted by the International Labour Organization, including the Minimum Age Convention of 1973 and conventions against forced and bonded labor (*UN Chronicle* 1986).

Sweatshops do not operate in a vacuum, to be sure. Although many market to local and regional outlets, others are linked to well-known Western brands. Some of the most famous offenders were Nike, Reebok, the Gap, Mattel, and Disney. After the Kathie Lee Gifford case hit the airwaves, the sweatshop issue became a cause célèbre in the American media. Human rights and labor rights activists mobilized to draw attention to the offending firms. With the support of Labor Secretary Robert Reich, the White House quickly became involved in setting up a national task force to investigate and regulate the issue. In August 1996, eight apparel firms, a half-dozen human rights organizations, and several trade union representatives were organized into the Apparel Industry Partnership with the aim of establishing a workplace code of conduct (Appelbaum and Dreier 1999, 77). In spite of pressure by the Labor Department and activists, the result was a relatively weak set of standards guaranteeing only that corporations will work to abide by local labor standards in whatever country they operate. Unfortunately, because of poor local standards, firms are able to pass on the blame to local governments if their workers are mistreated. Several noncorporate members of the alliance withdrew after the standards were promulgated in April 1997 (Cray 2000). Since then, the activists (joined by a few companies) have come up with the Social Accountability 8000 code, a laundry list of basic workplace standards that grant firms SA8000 certification and the right to affix a "no sweat" label to their products. Avon and Toys 'R' Us expressed an early interest in certification (Spar 1998, 9).

The student anti-sweatshop movement began in mid-1997. At Duke University, students pressured the administration to agree not to let manufacturers of licensed products use sweatshop labor. Given the vast number of licensees (700) and the even larger number of subcontracting factories, the task seemed overwhelming at first. But in March 1998, Duke President Nannerl Keohane agreed to most of the student demands, including a requirement that all subcontracting factories be identified and inspected by outside monitors (Appelbaum and Dreier 1999, 78). The student movement has since spread across the country (note particularly the University of Wisconsin–Madison, Georgetown, the University of Michigan, and the University of Arizona) and has become organized as the United Students Against Sweatshops (USAS). It has linked up with the AFL-CIO affiliate, UNITE (Union of Needletrades, Industrial and Textile Employees), which provides activists with training and other support. UNITE has hired a full-time specialist to work on the sweatshop issue exclusively.

A number of U.S. legislators have taken up the sweatshop issue as well. Donald Pease (D–Ohio) and Tom Harkin (D–Iowa) introduced bills to ban the importation of products manufactured by child labor during the George Bush administration (Senser 1994, 13). It was in part because of threats of harsher regulations that the voluntary codes of conduct were agreed upon. In November 1999, many activists and politicians protested plans to expand the scope and weight of the World Trade Organization on the grounds that the agency's single-minded focus on opening markets increases the likelihood of worker exploitation. Ralph Nader of the Green Party made sweatshops and the costs of globalization the centerpiece of his quixotic presidential campaign in 2000.

Sources and Solutions

Globalization is a concept that has generated more "heat" than "light." Although the meaning and significance of globalization are still unclear, people have developed strong and contrary positions on its worth. Much of the debate on globalization (and, by implications, on sweatshops) focuses on the values, philosophies, and personal backgrounds of the debaters.

Robert Gilpin identifies three principal points of view on globalization: the free market perspective, the populist (or nationalist) perspective, and the communitarian perspective. Free market advocates ascribe to globalization the power to bring in "an era of unprecedented prosperity as more and more nations participate in the global economy, and as financial and technology flows from developed to less developed countries lead to equalization of wealth and development around the world" (Gilpin 2000, 297). Populists, such as Ross Perot and Patrick Buchanan, "blame globalization for most of the social, economic and political ills afflicting the United States and other industrial societies" (Gilpin 2000, 297). They accuse globalization of weakening the independence and inherent vitality of the economies and societies of the major powers. Communitarians, in contrast, criticize globalization on the grounds that it foists "a brutal capitalist tyranny, imperialist exploitation and environmental degradation upon the peoples of the world. They fear a world dominated by huge multinational corporations that will remove all obstacles limiting economic growth . . ." (Gilpin 2000, 298).

We will separate out two facets of the free market perspective: the overall growth of the global economy and the economic development in the Third World per se. Many worry that attacks against sweatshops may ultimately undermine growth in developing countries—which is a very different argument than saying that the search for ever-lower wages will help the global economy as a whole. Also, we will separate out the structural Marxist approach from the humanitarian view under the umbrella of the communitarian perspective. The first focus is on the arguments against sweatshops made by labor unions as the most relevant example of the populist perspective on sweatshops.

Labor Perspective

Perhaps the most familiar commentary on globalization in the United States comes from the defenders of working-class people. The Reform Party, the trade union movement, and other populist organizations have built a strong case against free trade and global investment. They point to the tendency since the early 1970s for the wealthy to get an ever-increasing share of national wealth relative to the working class and middle class. For example, in early 2000, the Economic Policy Institute and the Center of Budget and Policy Priorities reported that during the 1990s, the average income of the wealthiest one-fifth of Americans grew by 15 percent, while the income of the middle class grew by only 2 percent and that of the poorest one-fifth stayed the same. In 1999, household income for the wealthiest one-fifth of the population was ten times greater than the income for the poorest one-fifth (AFL-CIO 2000).

Even some economists have acknowledged that worker insecurity increased during the 1990s during the era of "downsizing." Aaronson and Sullivan analyzed trends in employment longevity and noted that the number of workers who choose to stay with a company for more than ten years has dropped substantially over the last twenty years. In the mid-1980s, the average man aged 45 to 54 had been at his place of employment thirteen years. By 1995, that figure had dropped to less than ten years (Aaronson and Sullivan 1998, 21). The overall rate of "displacement" (all forms of involuntary change of workplace) doubled between 1988 and 1995 for workers with five years of tenure on the job. This trend in turn contributed to much higher levels of anxiety about job security during the 1990s and may have contributed to relatively low wage increases throughout the decade. As put by Labor Secretary Robert Reich, "Wages are stuck because people are afraid to ask for a raise. They are afraid they may lose their job" (Reich 1997 in Aaronson and Sullivan 1998, 17). This whole problem is attributed to globalization, where wage competition has spread internationally.

Wage competition is most intense for low-skilled work, according to this perspective (Freeman 1995). People who work in a company that manufactures textiles or footwear in the United States and receive wages of, say, ten dollars per hour (including benefits) are directly threatened by overseas workers who are willing to do the same job for ten cents per hour and no benefits. Nike CEO Phil Knight, while still a business school student, made plans to build an entire company based on outsourcing manufacturing to low-wage countries, making none of the product in the United States or other countries where the consumers were located. He was not alone. More and more firms relocated relatively low-tech industrial production to developing countries after 1975. During the 1980s, hundreds of U.S. firms moved to Mexico to establish "maquiladoras"—manufacturing plants located just across the border that could use cheap Mexican labor, pay lower corporate taxes, and be freed from American health, safety, and environmental regulations, while retaining easy access to the U.S. market. During the 1990s, even more companies relocated to China for the same reasons, except that strict antiunion laws and an authoritarian government made Chinese workers even more placid than those in Mexico. Anecdotal evidence points to a direct zero-sum relationship between the relocation of these jobs and higher unemployment among unskilled workers in the United States (Korten 1995, 229–237).

For labor unions, then, the sweatshop issue primarily involves protecting American jobs and wages in the face of the globalization of the assembly line. The alliance that has formed between student activists and trade unionists is seen by many as a healthy and even exciting new type of activism. It closes the rift that goes back to the Vietnam War, when trade union leaders condemned antiwar protesters (Appelbaum and Dreier 1999, 77). Others fear that unions may be manipulating students to support protectionist measures that may ultimately hurt overseas workers (Olson 2000).

Global Free Market Perspective

It can be said that liberals invented globalization. They have consistently been skeptical of the prominence attached to the state by populists and instead have imagined and designed an international structure that minimizes territorial and political boundaries. Their vision of the world is the Internet, where countries simply do not matter anymore (Hudson 1999). Liberals first thrilled at what they called "interdependence" in the 1970s, and they were among the first to identify "globalization" (Ruggie 1995). Although some liberals fear such a world order might grow out of control, most believe it is government interference in the marketplace of goods and ideas that has brought misery to humanity.

Bryan and Ferrell wrote that when the spread of multinational corporate investment and the lowering of trade and investment barriers through the World Trade Organization open up global markets, the potential exists for creative and entrepreneurial activity to flourish worldwide (Bryan and Ferrell 1996). Economists point to the dramatic increase in average incomes worldwide as a direct result of fewer economic barriers, lower transportation costs, and new technologies. Micklethwait and Wooldridge point out that globalization simply has not contributed to a dramatic rise in overall incomes but has done so by creating new jobs, contrary to the forecasts of populists. The North American Free Trade Agreement, which populists expected to eliminate U.S. jobs, has instead generated 14 million new job openings since 1994 (Micklethwait and Wooldridge 2000, 109). Their biggest fear is that trade unions may hijack globalization for narrow, short-sighted reasons: "[T]he goal of eradicating child labor is a noble one, but when it has been linked to trade, it has nearly always been for protectionist reasons and has often had disastrous consequences for those it has tried to help" (Micklethwait and Wooldridge 2000, 113). If wages seem to decline, the cause is primarily a mismanaged economic transition from local to global production (Richardson 1995).

Some analysts stress that wage differentials are not as serious a concern as labor defenders claim because they are directly related to productivity. As Golub points out, if one takes into account the cost of output per worker-hour, then wages are virtually the same worldwide (Golub 1999, 22). In the Philippines, for example, although wages are roughly one-tenth the wages of American workers, worker productivity is even less, with the result that work done in the Philippines is actually 8 percent more expensive than work done in the United States. Similar figures apply to Malaysia and India (although the same is not true in Mexico and South Korea, where relative productivity outpaces relative wages—Golub 1999, 23). When the relative purchasing power of these low wages is factored in, the developing country workers are actually better off than their Western counterparts because they can buy far more per unit of output (i.e., a Bangladeshi who is paid fifty cents to produce one shirt each hour can buy more local goods at the end of a ten-hour day with five dollars than can her counterpart in New York who is paid five dollars to produce ten shirts per hour and thereby earns fifty dollars).

Sweatshops, though deplored in principle, are accepted as part of the process of globalization. Corporations have pointed out that consumers benefit tremendously when producers take advantage of wage differentials, and this pressure from consumers forces producers to seek ever-lower wage rates. In the 1980s, Levi Strauss tried to keep its production in the United States and maintain high relative wage rates in developing country factories, but it could not sustain those practices. It had to close fifty-eight U.S. plants and lay off more than 10,000 workers to stay competitive (Korten 1995, 233). As put by Reebok's, Indonesia representative: "Cutting costs is part of our business" (Brecher and Costello 1994, 20). Even the Kathie Lee clothing line failed to significantly improve working conditions and pay at its overseas plants, and Nike has tried to get credit for increasing wages in Indonesia even as the local currency's value plummeted, leading to a net loss (Kernaghan 1999). All these problems are blamed on pressures to drive prices ever lower.

Developmental Perspective

Still other liberals question whether Western criticism of sweatshops misses the point that those in sweatshops are, after all, working. In countries where unemployment is higher than 50 percent and low-paying farm labor accounts for most of the jobs, many see employment in factories as the way out of perpetual poverty. Consider, for example, that in 1990 a typical Chinese farmer earned $1,130 per year, while an unskilled Chinese factory worker made roughly $2,000 and a skilled factory worker earned $5,800. During a recent visit to Bangladesh, the author met dozens of adult men with children to raise who earned only enough for one or two servings of rice per day (less than ten cents) working as hired farm help in depressed villages. In comparison, the young women who eagerly went to the garment factory each morning in the city and earned two dollars per day were in the upper middle class.

From this point of view, the anti-sweatshop campaign is seen with skepticism in Third World capitals. Molly Ivins has argued that the USAS actually made development more difficult for many of these countries, although it may help those who are already working in the factories (Ivins and Smith 1999). Particularly when linked to trade unions, the sweatshop movement seems to be aimed at curtailing exports of garments and other basic manufactured goods, which could lead to severe depression in many countries. Already most developing countries are working hard to improve the climate for international business, and they are finding it difficult to keep the factories that have relocated there. International capital always has other opportunities to reduce wages by relocating to another developing country (in Bangladesh, wages are kept low to prevent companies from moving to China, for example). Even worse, the alternative to sweatshop jobs going to developing countries is the possibility that the manufacturing process will simply be mechanized, thereby eliminating the jobs entirely (Kristof 2002).

Structural Marxist Perspective

In response to the developmental perspective, numerous scholars have developed a structural analysis of the world economy, based loosely on the work of Marx, Lenin, Fernand Braudel, and Immanuel Wallerstein. This structural Marxist perspective argues that the development that occurs as a result of globalization is not the sort of development any country should want. Rather, it is better understood as taking a subordinate place in the global economy, where countries must surrender control over their national destinies to provide the raw material of capitalist production. As early as the 1700s, economists began to note that capitalist production tended to concentrate relatively high-tech activities in advanced, industrialized nations, whereas low-tech activities were sloughed off to remote, inhospitable regions (Mittelman 2000, 54). Later, Lenin pointed out that not only was high-tech manufacturing concentrated in the powerful countries, but so were banking and corporate decision making, which led to a global structure that transcended traditional imperialism in search of both raw materials and labor and new consumer markets. Gradually, more and more regions were brought into this "world economy," such that national boundaries became increasingly insignificant in the pursuit of efficiency and profit (Wallerstein 1991; Korten 1995, 239). As put by Ernst Mandel, "Capital by its very nature tolerates no geographical limit to its expansion" (Mandel 1975, 310). It was on these Marxist ideas that the concepts of the global factory and the global assembly line were based in more recent years (Gereffi 1994).

In this context, sweatshops are viewed as merely part of the inexorable expansion of capital production on a global scale. A product moves in steps from raw material to finished good, going from factory to factory in a "commodity chain" in which profits gradually increase as one gets closer to the point of final sale. Sweatshops are driven to a large extent by pressures from brand-name companies seeking lower production costs. They put pressure directly on international traders and overseas buyers and indirectly on the factories themselves. As put by Gereffi:

> The main job of the core company in buyer-driven commodity chains is to manage these production and trade networks and make sure all the pieces of the business come together as an integrated whole. Profits in buyer-driven chains thus derive not from scale economies and technological advances as in producer-driven chains, but rather from unique combinations of high-value research, design, sales, marketing, and financial services that allow the buyers and branded merchandisers to act as strategic brokers. . . . (Gereffi 1994, 99)

Factory managers constantly complain of being required to reduce costs so as to maintain contracts with foreign companies. They are in an extremely vulnerable position because the company can change suppliers with the stroke of a pen.

In spite of these relatively new mechanisms of exploitation, structural Marxists see very little new in the contemporary debate about globalization (Germain 2000). While this might give some hope that we need not fear that some horrific new problem has emerged, it also offers a pessimistic prediction that there is no reason to expect anything to change much, no matter how many well-intentioned campaigns are mounted. Although antislavery campaigns in the 1800s ended the more blatant forms of slavery in the West, these activities simply shifted to the Third World. And although it may be possible to end formal slavery, child labor, and indentured servitude in time, there is no reason, based on this perspective, to expect that conditions will markedly improve for the workers of the world. By implication, the only solution is global revolution.

Humanitarian Perspective

Those who are squeamish about a violent overthrow of the global capitalist system focus instead on piecemeal reform and attempts to improve the living conditions of those most injured by global capitalism. The effort at humanitarian reform is as old as capitalism itself. Although it does not repudiate such age-old institutions as wage labor, private ownership of land, the assembly line, or outsourcing, it strives to create minimum standards of human treatment. National labor standards, as mentioned earlier, have been set up since the turn of the twentieth century, although their enforcement has often been spotty.

In the post–World War II era, the International Labour Organization became a forum for countries to institute new standards of conduct in their treatment of wage labor. Slavery, indentured servitude, child labor, and other practices were banned, and countries were urged to establish minimum worker safety standards, reasonable wages, vacation and overtime practices, and so forth. These treaties were endorsed by almost every country, although compliance was not consistent. While most developed countries already complied with these rules when they were established, few developing countries did. Even socialist countries (which were touted as a "worker's paradise") did not allow such basic worker freedoms as the right of workers to independently organize and strike.

When the sweatshop issue emerged in the 1980s and exploded in the 1990s, the treatment of most workers violated principles enshrined in treaties that not only had been accepted as a worthwhile aspiration but had also been explicitly accepted by the countries in question and had become the law of the land. Thus the sweatshop campaign can be seen as an effort to enforce international standards rather than set new ones. It may be unrealistic to expect that the movement can accomplish much more than this.

In this respect, the sweatshop campaign is having a measurable impact. Global corporations such as Nike and Reebok are often little more than a brand name, as we have seen. As a result, their image and reputation are all-important. In addition to joining the Apparel Industry Partnership and endorsing the Social Accountability 8000 code of conduct, many textile firms have hired independent auditors to carry out on-site inspections of garment factories overseas. Some have allowed human rights activists to tour factories, although they have generally done so under close corporate supervision (UNITE! 2000). Some apparel manufacturers have even engaged in political protests of their own, as evidenced by the nearly industry-wide boycott of Myanmar's military dictatorship. Some clothing businesses are finding it easier to take principled positions now that the entire industry is under scrutiny (Spar 1998).

Conclusion

The result of improved wages and working conditions in developing countries may be difficult to measure, let alone achieve. The vagaries of international currency values, the ease of concealing violations, and the resistance of governments and firms all represent considerable obstacles. But it is perhaps more realistic to undertake global reform in sweatshops than to challenge the entire capitalist system, as was done in the dramatic street protests at the WTO annual meetings in Seattle in 1999.

How does this issue relate to the broader question of globalization? It is clear that the anti-sweatshop campaign has brought to the attention of Western audiences the links between disparate social groups across the planet. It is hard not to think of Pakistani child workers when purchasing a soccer ball in Memphis, or of young Malaysian factory workers when buying a pair of pants in London. But recognizing the links and even understanding them is not the same as understanding whether they are good or bad or how to change them. Globalization can be seen as merely a fact of human existence. It may be up to us to determine what values are jeopardized by it.

Debate Topic

Should the anti-sweatshop campaign be supported on college campuses?

PRO

The anti-sweatshop campaign has many supporters, who point out the following: (1) Sweatshops are inherently unfair to their workers, given the overall profits the firms are making and the paltry wages they pay. (2) Sweatshops are unethical, in that the working conditions and wages are so low that they violate minimum international human rights standards. (3) Buying goods made in sweatshops or owning stock in the parent companies makes one complicitous in the social ills that are taking place.

CON

Opponents of the campaign point out the following: (1) Sweatshops are an improvement for most developing country workers, who might otherwise be forced to beg or prostitute themselves. (2) The wages are set based on productivity and skill; workers need only improve these to obtain higher wages. (3) A boycott of sweatshop goods may simply increase mechanization, which will eliminate even the undesirable jobs.

Questions to Consider

1. How strong is the corporate claim that sweatshops are a necessary evil brought about by consumer demand and a tough competitive environment? What contrary evidence can be brought to bear?

2. To what extent are sweatshops merely the extension of the global spread of laissez-faire capitalism? Is it possible to solve the problem in one factory or corporation without changing the global system?

3. What are the dangers of the anti-sweatshop campaign? What are the alternatives for achieving the same objective of improving living conditions for workers in developing countries?

Websites

Social Accountability 8000 code: **www.cepaa.org/sa8000.htm**
Apparel Industry Partnership: **www.lchr/sweatshop/aipfull.htm#WORKPLACE**
Council on Economic Priorities: **www.cepnyc.org**
Sweatshop Watch: **www.sweatshopwatch.org**
National Labor Committee: www.nlcnet.org.
United Students Against Sweatshops: **home.sprintmail.com/~jeffnkari/USAS/**
UNITE! trade union: **www.uniteunion.org**

References

Aaronson, Daniel, and Daniel Sullivan. "The Decline of Job Security in the 1990s: Displacement, Anxiety, and Their Effect on Wage Growth." *Economic Perspectives* 22 #1 (1998): 17–43.

AFL-CIO. "Income Equality Nosedives: The Rich vs. Everyone Else," www.aflcio.org/articles/gap/index.html, January 18, 2000.

Appelbaum, Richard, and Peter Dreier. "The Campus Anti-Sweatshop Movement." *The American Prospect* (September 1999): 71–83.

Brecher, Jeremy, and Tim Costello. *Global Village or Global Pillage: Economic Reconstruction from the Bottom Up* (Boston: South End Press, 1994).

Bryan, Lowell, and Diana Ferrell. *Market Unbound: Unleashing Global Capitalism* (New York: John Wiley & Sons, 1996).

Cray, Charlie. "Students Against Sweat." *Multinational Monitor* 21 #4 (April 2000): 4.

DiCaprio, Lisa. "Women Workers, State-Sponsored Work, and the Right to Subsistence During the French Revolution." *Journal of Modern History* 71 #3 (September 1999): 519–545.

Freeman, Richard. "Are Your Wages Set in Beijing?" *Journal of Economic Perspectives* 9 #3 (Summer 1995): 15–32.

Gereffi, Gary. "The Organization of Buyer-Driven Chains: How U.S. Retailers Shape Overseas Production Networks," in Gary Gereffi and Miguel Korzeniewicz, eds., *Commodity Chains and Global Capitalism* (Westport, CT: Greenwood Press, 1994).

Germain, Randall, ed. *Globalization and Its Critics: Perspectives from Political Economy* (New York: St. Martin's Press, 2000).

Gill, Stephen. "Theorizing the Interregnum: The Double Movement and Global Politics in the 1990s" in Bjorn Hettne, ed., *International Political Economy*, 65–99.

Gilpin, Robert. *The Challenge of Global Capitalism: The World Economy in the 21st Century* (Princeton, NJ: Princeton University Press, 2000).

Golub, Stephen. *Labor Costs and International Trade* (Washington, DC: AEI Press, 1999).

Hettne, Bjorn, ed. *International Political Economy: Understanding Global Disorder* (London: Zed Books, 1995).

Hudson, Yaeger, ed. *Globalism and the Obsolescence of the State* (Lewiston, NY: Edwin Mellon Press, 1999).

Ivins, Molly, and Fred Smith. "Opposing Views on Sweatshops." *Insight on the News* 15 #44 (November 29, 1999): 40–47.

Kernaghan, Charles. "Sweatshop Blues: Companies Love Misery." *Dollars & Sense* 222 (March–April 1999): 18–22.

Korten, David. *When Corporations Rule the World* (New York: Kumarian Press, 1995).

Kristof, Nicholas, "Let Them Sweat," *New York Times,* June 25, 2002.

Mandel, Ernst. *Late Capitalism* (London: NLB, 1975).

Micklethwait, John, and Adrian Wooldridge. *A Future Perfect: The Essentials of Globalization* (New York: Crown Business, 2000).

Mittelman, James. *The Globalization Syndrome: Transformation and Resistance* (Princeton, NJ: Princeton University Press, 2000).

Olson, Walter. "Look for the Kiwi Label." *Reason* 32 #3 (July 2000): 52–57.

Press, Eyal. "Kathie Lee's Slip." *The Nation* 262 #24 (July 17, 1996): 6–8.

Reich, Robert. *Locked in the Cabinet* (New York: Alfred Knopf, 1997).

Richardson, J. David. "Income Inequality and Trade: How to Think, What to Conclude." *Journal of Economic Perspectives* 9 #3 (Summer 1995): 33–55.

Rothstein, Frances Abrahamer, and Michael Blim, eds. *Anthropology and the Global Factory: Studies of the New Industrialization in the Late Twentieth Century* (New York: Bergin & Garvey, 1992).

Ruggie, John Gerard. "At Home Abroad, Abroad at Home: International Liberalization and Domestic Stability in the New World Economy." *Millennium* 24 #3 (1995): 3–27.

Schanberg, Sydney, and Marie Dorigny. "Six Cents an Hour." *Life* 19 #7 (June 1996): 38–47.

Senser, Robert. "Danger! Children at Work." *Commonweal* 121 #14 (August 19, 1994): 12–15.

Spar, Debora. "The Spotlight on the Bottom Line: How Multinationals Export Human Rights." *Foreign Affairs* 77 #2 (March–April 1998): 7–13.

UN Chronicle. "50 to 200 Million Children Under 15 Are in World's Work Force, ILO Says." UN *Chronicle* 23 (November 1986): 116.

UNITE! "Sweatshops Behind the Swoosh," April 25, 2000 report. www.uniteunion. org/pressbox/nike-report.htmll.

U.S. News & World Report (January 16, 1984): 68.

U.S. News & World Report (November 22, 1993): 48

Wallerstein, Immanuel. *Geopolitics and Geoculture: Essays on the Changing World-System* (New York: Cambridge, 1991).

Third World Debt
INTERNATIONAL POLITICAL ECONOMY

Introduction

Although many international relations scholars look at the world as a struggle for power solely among nation-states, many Third World experts describe the world as a vast socioeconomic "system." To these and others, nation-states are merely one of many players—and not necessarily the dominant ones. Global class rivalry, communication and transportation networks, banking and investment patterns, and other factors, create the rules that even states must follow.

This perspective has been articulated in a variety of theoretical formulations and policy advice. For many years, scholars and governments in developing countries believed that the global economy was inherently unfair. Trade rules resulted in unbalanced exchange, involving the swap of cheap, agricultural goods from the developing world for expensive manufactured goods from the wealthy countries. "Structuralist" economists such as Raul Prebisch and P. C. Mahanalobis argued that, to prevent continually losing ground, developing countries should impose restraints on the flow of foreign goods in the form of tariffs (taxes on imports), quotas (numerical ceilings on imports), and outright bans. In addition, they encouraged governments to seize control of foreign firms and impose government planning on the economy in the hope of duplicating the dramatic growth seen in Eastern Europe, Great Britain, and France in the 1950s (Yergin and Stanislaw 1998, chapter 3).

A few other countries adopted a more outward-oriented and competitive approach, again with considerable government support. The Asian Tigers of South Korea, Taiwan, Singapore, and the Philippines followed the Japanese model by promoting a strong investment climate and encouraging particular firms and sectors to grow and even export their goods. Although they paid lip service to free trade, they made sure to only embrace it to a point (see Case 23).

For a time, both models seemed promising, with both helping to promote growth and industrialization for a time. In that way, these approaches seemed to give credence to the notion that international markets could not be trusted to provide growth on their own, but rather needed governments to steer them and compensate for problems.

The developing countries' perspective on the global economy was put to the test in the 1980s. In August 1982, Mexican President José Lopez Portillo declared that his country would be unable to meet the quarterly deadline for interest payments on more than $80 billion in foreign debts. The move came as several other Latin American governments were expressing serious concerns about meeting payments on another $200 billion in debts. As the Federal Reserve Bank put it, "International bankers and policy makers faced a threat of financial disorder on a global scale not seen since the Depression" (Spero 1990, 181). For the next ten years, international bankers, world powers, international institutions, and numerous Third World actors would be riveted by the problem of preventing global financial collapse. How did these players interact? What global structures were evidenced by their behavior? Where do we stand today, and who "won"?

THIRD WORLD DEBT CHRONOLOGY

1960
The Organization of Petroleum Exporting Countries is formed.

1973
The Yom Kippur/Ramadan War begins in the Middle East. Arab OPEC members begin to impose an oil embargo on Israel's allies.

1974
Inflation and recession sweep Western states and many developing countries, while oil exporters reap a financial windfall. Much of the new oil revenue is placed in accounts in Western banks, which in turn lend large amounts to developing country governments.

1974
Peru renegotiates its foreign debt through an International Monetary Fund structural adjustment agreement.

1979
The Shah of Iran falls from power. The new regime ceases oil exportation for a time, prompting massive price increases. Paul Volcker, Chairman of the Federal Reserve in the United States, attacks inflation with a tight money policy, raising interest rates. This action results in much higher interest payments on private loans to developing countries.

1982
Following the return to the market of Iranian oil and the subsequent collapse of the price of oil, Mexico announces that it is unable to make its quarterly interest payment in August. Argentina and Brazil quickly follow suit. Public and private creditors reschedule $700 billion in bad debt.   *(continued)*

1984

Leader debtor nations meet in Cartagena to discuss coordinating their strategies. The IMF and other creditors respond with selective offers of new loans.

1985

The Baker Plan is presented as a stop-gap global solution.

1987

The Bank of Boston downgrades the value of its foreign loans—the first of many private banks to do so.

1989

The Brady Plan, calling for some debt forgiveness, is presented as a new approach to the debt crisis.

1992

The World Bank begins to part ways with the IMF's structural adjustment approach to the debt crisis.

1994

Failure of the IMF's strategy in Russia and Eastern Europe discredits its highly trained experts.

1995

Mexico receives a $60 billion bail out to rescue the peso. "The Fifty Years Is Enough" campaign is launched.

1997

Beginning in Thailand, East Asian currencies and stock markets lose value suddenly, leading to a financial panic that reaches around the world and results in dramatic increases in unemployment and poverty in Indonesia and elsewhere.

1998

The World Bank and IMF establish a fund for "heavily indebted poor countries" in an attempt to deal with the chronic debt and economic stagnation of African states.

2000

The Jubilee 2000 debt-forgiveness campaign is joined by numerous dignitaries, including Paul John Paul II.

International Financial Primer*

Perhaps the most confusing aspect of international finance is the role of money and currency. Originally conceived as a convenience to lighten the burden of seafaring merchants who otherwise would have been forced to carry gold bullion, paper money has developed a life of its own. Because it has no inherent value, the worth of paper money stems from the strength of the government and society that produce it. To the extent that buyers and sellers require use of the currency or trust it as a medium of exchange, the value of a currency increases. In addition, the faster the growth of the economy, the lower the inflation rate, and the higher the interest rate one may earn by depositing in banks from that country, the stronger a country's currency.

Over time, certain currencies have emerged as the most secure and valuable; they are called "hard currencies." Traders and investors use these currencies even if they are not dealing directly with the country that mints the

---

*Students are referred to the excellent primer on the subject: John Charles Pool and Steve Stamos, *The ABCs of International Finance* (Lexington, MA: Lexington Books, 1987).

currency. For example, virtually all the oil in the world is bought and sold with U.S. dollars. Even if Saudi Arabia sells oil to Lithuania, it can expect payment in dollars. Dollars in circulation outside of the United States are called "Eurodollars" or, in the case of oil-related capital, "Petrodollars."

No developing country can boast a hard currency of its own. Because of this, no developing country can buy products overseas without first obtaining hard currency to consummate the transaction. Because it cannot rely on its own mint to produce hard currency, a Third World nation has four options if it wants to do business abroad:

1. Export products in exchange for hard currency (hence the importance of trading with wealthy, developed countries)
2. Borrow hard currency from private banks in the West,
3. Obtain grants and/or loans from governments that control hard currencies,
4. Attract foreign investment.

Although barter trade is becoming more popular among multinational firms and much international aid is "in kind" (in the form of a physical product rather than cash transfer), these four means of obtaining hard currency are far and away the most popular beginning points in international business for a Third World nation.

Given the importance of obtaining hard currency for a Third World nation, one can understand why many solutions to the debt crisis are simply not feasible. Although the United States has at times increased its money supply (printed more currency) to more easily pay off foreign debts, no Third World government could do so. Some countries have tried to stimulate their economies by dramatically increasing the money supply, but the result has often been triple-digit inflation and a weaker currency abroad.

Another set of ideas essential to understanding the debt crisis is the operation of the "multiplier effect" in banking. Banks want to keep as much of their money in circulation as possible. Simply put, your individual deposit of $1,000 does not sit in a vault until you decide to withdraw it. Depending on the regulations of the country, roughly 85 percent of all deposits are loaned out to collect interest. Banks attempt to maximize the difference between interest charged on loans and interest paid on savings accounts so as to clear a profit. An important result of this natural flow of the banking system is the geometric increase in the total amount of money in circulation. A $1,000 deposit, through this process of lending and relending, can generate as much as $6,000. When expanded to the global scale, where bankers typically shift their liquid (readily accessible with withdrawal) deposits from one time zone to the next to continue generating interest throughout the twenty-four-hour cycle, and where institutional investors and money market account managers move billions for the sake of half a percentage point, the multiplier effect is one of the most significant phenomena in international finance (Strange 1986).

Finally, adjustment became the focal point of efforts to rectify the Third World debt situation after 1982. In general terms, any effort on the part of a country to pay its international bills could be termed "adjustment," although the word usually refers to two specific actions. First, since access to foreign capital is the highest priority of Third World countries, a government is expected to "adjust" any of its policies that discourage foreign currency from entering the country. Exports must be encouraged, typically by reducing the value of the currency relative to the hard currencies (devaluation), promoting export-oriented sectors of the economy, reducing restrictions on foreign investment to encourage businesses to invest in that nation, and generally building a favorable business climate (low taxes on profits, easy repatriation of earnings, strong infrastructure, a capable and placid work force).

Second, the government must end practices that cost more money than the nation can afford. Borrowing from abroad to pay for social programs is a likely target because any deficit spending hurts the chances for balancing other accounts. Imports should be discouraged—especially imports of consumer goods that do not contribute to the health of the economy overall. In general terms, the economy should be "liberalized," meaning that private enterprise should be encouraged and state intervention minimized. In many Third World nations, this goal involves selling off huge amounts of publicly owned enterprises, much as the Eastern European nations have been doing of late. The result is supposed to be a more dynamic, if perhaps less equitable and generous, government and economy. (Note that adjustment is rarely sufficient, by itself, to turn an economy around—Schwartz 1991.)

Origins of the Debt Crisis

Much debate has arisen regarding the causes of the debt crisis. We will focus on the most obvious factors on which a consensus has been reached. The most obvious "cause" of the debt crisis was the willingness of private bankers to lend huge amounts of foreign currency to dynamic and successful Third World nations and charge them high interest rates for it, followed by a reversal of fortune for the debtors. Beyond this obvious explanation, we will look at some antecedents to this dubious bargain.

In 1973, the Third World finally had its day. The members of the Organization of Petroleum Exporting Countries (OPEC) managed to quadruple the price of crude oil in a six-month span in conjunction with the Arab war against Israel. The immediate effect was the indirect transfer of more than $80 billion from Western consumers to Arab governments (Sampson 1981, 151). Much of this money was spent on Rolls Royces and the purchase of a few foreign companies, but the majority sat in banks in the Middle East and across the West. Rather than simply let it rest, American and European bankers were forced to deal with this situation, which at the time seemed a crisis. The money could not be easily lent because it was liquid (short-term

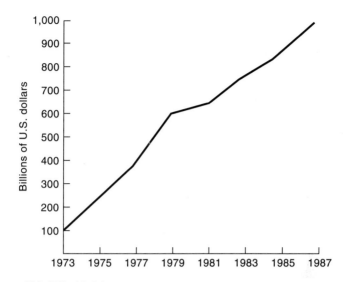

Figure 21.1   Third World debt, 1973–1987
Source: John Charles Pool and Steve Stamos, *The ABCs of International Finance* (Lexington, MA: Lexington Books, 1987).

deposits) and because the recession of 1974 created a very cautious atmosphere among the banks' usual corporate clients.

The decision to move the "sovereign lending" was not a once-and-for-all choice by the bankers. Citibank paved the way and others quickly followed suit by lending to countries such as Brazil, Mexico, Argentina, and Poland, each of which had the appearance of being a safe risk. Each country had undergone a dramatic and seemingly successful industrialization program; each had logged high gross national product growth during the previous period, fueled largely by record-setting commodity prices (petroleum, cereals, tropical goods, metals, meats); and each had a generally favorable disposition toward the international market and foreign investment. What was most attractive was that these countries had the power to use coercive government means to repay debts if necessary (Kahler 1985, 358–360).

Third World governments were eager to borrow from private sources because this practice appeared to eliminate the dangers of "tied aid," whereby government lenders attach political conditions to aid. Private bankers were far more impartial, although they charged much higher interest. As a consequence, some $100 billion was lent during the first year after the oil shock, and the total amount would rise dramatically over the next decade (see Figure 21.1).

This "recycling" of oil money was the fuel of the debt crisis. In addition, the tendency for borrowers to spend the funds on consumer goods and imports, as well as on large-scale infrastructure projects such as road and dam building, meant that few profitable activities were funded by foreign debt (Aliber 1985–1986). As interest charges combined with additional lending, the cost to developing countries eventually outweighed the amount of new money coming in. By 1983, more money was flowing back into Western banks than was flowing into Third World nations (World Bank 1988, 30).

This situation would not have been problematic had it not also been for the collapse of commodity prices, led by declines in oil prices, after 1976 (Gilpin 1987, 352). Overall, even non-oil commodities lost some 50 percent of their 1973 value during the decade that followed. Because commodity exports are a primary source of hard currency revenue for most developing countries, the decline in these prices was devastating. As early as 1974, Peru was forced to ask its creditors to reschedule (postpone payment of) its foreign debt and agree to a strict adjustment program. In the late 1970s, many African states formed a line outside the International Monetary Fund (IMF) to intercede on their behalf with Western creditors. By 1979, many developing country debtors were in serious financial straits in spite of promising signs only five years before.

In 1979, two additional events triggered the beginning of the end of the financial system of the 1970s. First, another oil shock followed revolutionary Iran's temporary withdrawal from the international oil trade, with the immediate result that crude oil prices rose first to $20 per barrel in 1979 and then to more than $40 per barrel in 1980. This event dramatically increased the oil import bill that developing countries were forced to pay to OPEC nations. Because the bill had to be paid in dollars, developing countries could no longer repay their foreign debts. In addition, bankers were pressured to lend even more money at a time when they were becoming increasingly reluctant to throw good money after bad.

Second, Paul Volcker was appointed chairman of the Federal Reserve Board (Fed). He felt his job was to eliminate the surplus money supply in the American economy by raising the interest rates that the Fed charged to large banks and by increasing the reserve requirement of cash banks must keep on hand (to limit the size of the multiplier effect) (Isaak 1991, 206). This policy eventually achieved its goal of reducing inflation in the United States, but at a cost of the worst recession since the 1930s and the beginning of the Third World debt crisis. As interest rates rose to 18 percent and higher in the early 1980s, developing countries became increasingly unable to meet the interest payments on variable interest rate loans, which constituted the bulk of the debt.

As if these factors were not enough to send any debtor into a tailspin, the recession in 1982 in the West meant there were fewer markets for already depressed Third World exports as well as an oil "glut" when Iran's oil came back on an already saturated market. Commodity prices dipped further, and even oil exporters found themselves unable to keep up debt payments. One could add to these systemic factors a variety of individual problems within certain countries, such as rampant corruption in Zaire, tax evasion in Argentina, over-bureaucratization in Peru, investment in unprofitable infrastructure projects in Turkey, and simple mismanagement and stop-and-go practices in Brazil. Because blame can be passed around liberally, it is often difficult to know which behavior precipitated the crisis in a specific nation.

Dealing with the Crisis

Mexico's stunning announcement in 1982 was just the first of many. Within months, Brazil, Argentina, Peru, Poland, Turkey, Jamaica, and dozens of other Third World debtors announced their inability to meet interest payments and requested rescheduling. By now total Third World debt had swollen to roughly $700 billion, and the prospect of a debtor cartel (coordinated default) loomed large on the international financial horizon. Because private bankers were unwilling to lend additional funds and the only major international finance organization—the International Monetary Fund—was undercapitalized in relation to a problem of such vast scale, wealthy governments quickly organized themselves to postpone payment of the immediate interest due. Acting as the "Paris Club," the United States, the United Kingdom, Germany, France, Japan, and others rescheduled $629 billion of Third World debt in 1982 (IMF 1984, 67). Private banks, at IMF prodding, eventually postponed deadlines on some $70 billion in 1982–1983. For the short term, then, the debt crisis had been resolved.

The role of the Paris Club, the IMF, and private bankers in rescheduling Third World debt was pivotal, in that they coordinated and consulted with one another throughout the process. The IMF is governed by a group of nations whose votes depend on their wealth and financial support to the institution. As a result, the "major shareholders" (United States, United Kingdom, Germany, Japan, France, Italy, and Canada) have the power to block any undesirable policies and press forward their preferred approach. As the organizers of the Paris Club, the Group of Seven, as they are called, have also influenced the rescheduling of Third World debt by working directly with private bankers. In their expanded form of the Group of Ten, they have combined to create the General Agreements to Borrow—a pool of several billion dollars from which the IMF can lend directly to major borrowers to prevent disruption of the financial system. Finally, when considering a rescheduling, private bankers work with the IMF to determine, along with the debtor, what adjustment measures need to be taken before they will lend fresh money. Bankers are also conscripted for the good of the world economy to lend money where they otherwise would not. Where the home government of a bank is firmly committed to supporting a particular borrower, the bank is more likely to continue lending in spite of itself (Wellons 1985).

From the Third World perspective, IMF-monitored (coerced?) adjustment is anything but cooperative. In general terms, Third World leaders have accused the IMF of interfering in what are purely domestic matters. When the IMF recommends cuts in subsidies for basic food and fuel, it takes a highly political action. In some cases, the government may be sympathetic to the move toward "austerity," but it can rarely admit this position without jeopardizing its political viability. In Egypt, Jordan, Venezuela, and many other nations, IMF adjustment programs have been immediately followed by food riots and other expressions of public dissatisfaction. Jaafar Nimeiri, leader of Sudan, got into the habit of taking an extended foreign holiday after announcing each new round of budget and service cuts. His government fell during one such trip (Stiles 1991, 60).

Governments also resent the imposition of power by the international financial community, represented by the IMF. Argentina and Brazil have at various times simply refused to implement the austerity measures agreed to with the IMF on the grounds that they reserve the right to control the future of their own economies. Argentina in particular, with its steadier financial situation and considerable reserves (deposits of foreign currency), has been able to thumb its nose at the banking system with some success. The high point of debtor defiance came in late 1984 with a summit of debtors at Cartagena, Colombia. The leaders of Mexico, Argentina, and other major debtors discussed the possibility of threatening a coordinated default to shift the balance of power in their favor. To prevent such a calamity, bankers often sought out a major debtor and offered a very favorable rescheduling agreement to undermine the unity of the group. This co-optation strategy worked remarkably well, and by 1985 most debtors had resigned themselves to programs of austerity and liberalization.

In spite of efforts to rectify the problem by bankers and debtors alike, by 1985 the situation was getting worse, not better. Total Third World debt was fast approaching $1 trillion. The ability of developing countries to repay the debt had almost vanished. The "debt service" ratio—interest due to export earnings—was more than 50 percent for the highest debtors and nearly 40 percent overall. This meant that nearly half of all earnings derived from exports would have to go toward paying the foreign debt rather than rebuilding the country. Total gross national product growth was negative in many developing debtor nations, and with commodity prices consistently low, there was little prospect for a reversal of fortunes.

In this context, U.S. Treasury Secretary James Baker called on the world community to significantly increase new lending to developing nations to the tune of $20 billion, along with greater financial discipline on the part of debtors (Spero 1990, 186). The results of the appeal were minimal, and in 1989 it was officially abandoned in favor of a more pragmatic if sobering alternative: debt forgiveness.

Debt forgiveness is the capitulation of the banking system. It means that all hope of collecting a debt is abandoned and the debt is taken off the books. In 1987, the "book value" of most Third World debt had declined from 70 percent of face value to less than half. This meant that if a bank wanted to unload a bad debt on another lending institution, it could recoup only half of the original loan. As this reality became apparent to shareholders and depositors, bankers moved in 1987 and 1988 to increase their reserves against a possible default or forgiveness of a debt. Bank of Boston led the way but was quickly followed by the other major institutions. Although the profits for quarters in which these admissions were made were lower, this pragmatic approach seems to have strengthened the confidence of members of the community overall. This phase of the crisis has been described as "debt fatigue" by Joan Spero (Spero 1990, 190).

The United States announced the Brady Plan in early 1989. It took a three-pronged approach: debt forgiveness, concessional government lending (aid), and firm commitment to repayment. Each approach targets a different third of the total debt problem. The IMF, under new leadership, promptly responded with a significant increase in concessional lending to sub-Saharan African countries. Much Third World debt was simply written off beginning in 1988, and in 1991 the United Kingdom called for general debt forgiveness (*New York Times*, July 18, 1991, D3). Banks became interested in so-called debt–equity swaps whereby a loan is traded for a tangible asset worth a fraction of the loan's book value. Although there is a natural limit to the amount of assets that can be transferred in this way, there is some hope that by finalizing the status of these debts, both participants can get a better handle on what remains. Debt-for-nature swaps also came into vogue for a time—the purchase of a loan by environmental groups and private firms in exchange for a guarantee to create nature preserves in the debtor nation. One example involved the World Wildlife Fund and the largest bank in Japan working with the government of Ecuador (*Wall Street Journal*, March 27, 1992, 9A).

Mexico has been by far the most successful debtor when it comes to cooperating with industrialized countries. Never defiant, Mexico has continually strengthened its ties with the United States, culminating in the inclusion of Mexico in a free trade zone for North America in August 1992. In 1989, Mexico was able to obtain forgiveness for enough of its foreign debt to lower its annual interest payments by $1.5 billion and to secure an additional $2.5 billion in fresh loans (Spero 1990, 194). For the first time, Mexico and the Third World's overall debt began to decline after 1988, although the total remains close to $1.3 trillion (*New York Times*, December 16, 1991, D2).

In general terms, the Third World debt crisis can be declared to have ended, if only because other crises have supplanted it. The Persian Gulf War, the multibillion-dollar savings and loan bailout, the 1990–1992 recession, the collapse of the Soviet Union and the related financial needs in its new republics, and European unification all eclipsed the Third World debt problem as more important issues on the American and global agenda. Even *Fortune* magazine has as much as declared the crisis over, and analyst Benjamin J. Cohen was prompted to ask what had become of it (Cohen 1991). This is therefore perhaps a good time to take stock of the situation and reflect on what it can teach us about global structures.

Although the debt "crisis" has abated, this should not be interpreted to mean that debt has suddenly evaporated. The total amount of long-term Third World debt still stands at $175 billion. In fact, most of the large debtors of the past still carry a considerable, if somewhat more manageable, debt burden. For example, although it was largely unaffected by global financial shock in the 1990s, Venezuela's debt burden remains at a troublesome 40 percent of gross domestic product, and Turkey's burden is holding at 43 percent (World Bank 1999, 71). For countries that have experienced major shocks, the story is more grim. Russia's debt to the West rose from less than

$60 billion in 1990 to $125 billion in 1997. Mexico borrowed (and repaid) roughly $40 billion to deal with its currency crisis in 1995, and several Asian countries (South Korea, Thailand, Indonesia, Hong Kong, the Philippines, and Malaysia) borrowed tens of billions each during the financial meltdown of 1997. Some $118 billion was mobilized to bail out South Korea, Indonesia, and Thailand alone. Thus, although these countries dramatically increased their debt, their economic potential is sufficient that they will be able to use the funds to remedy their problems and return to normal economic growth.

The most serious debt-related issue is the condition of the "heavily indebted poor countries," which have recently been receiving increased international attention. The World Bank and IMF have established a targeted program at a cost of $30 billion to help forty poor debtor countries deal with debt burdens that are often several times the size of their national economies (IMF 2000). For some, the effort is too little too late, and an increasing number of countries and groups have called for the forgiveness of debt. The United Kingdom and the United States have floated debt-forgiveness initiatives, as have Pope John Paul II and a large coalition of nonprofit groups under the banner of "Jubilee 2000" (Ambrogi 1999). Perhaps needless to say, this campaign has received a lukewarm response from IMF officials (Mauprivez 1999). The World Bank, however, has distanced itself from the rigid structural adjustment program promoted by the IMF since the early 1990s (Jolly 1992).

Global Structures and Third World Debt

In our discussion of global structures, we mentioned radical interpretations of international affairs as an aspect of hierarchical international social and economic relations. A common criticism of the handling of the Third World debt situation comes from the left and focuses on collusion among the major players in international finance. The IMF, the Group of Seven industrialized nations, and major private banking institutions cooperated in setting policy and establishing precedents. But was this cooperation or reluctant crisis management? The question is important in the discussion of global structures.

Bankers were no doubt the most reluctant participants in this process, being unwilling in the early stages of the crisis to reschedule any debts at all. They viewed the lending of additional money to borrowers who had already demonstrated their uncreditworthiness as the height of bad business. As put by one senior British official, "It makes the Marshall Plan look like peanuts . . . but because it's concealed as businesslike banking, it's much more acceptable" (Sampson 1981, 398). Sampson pointed out that bankers were trapped in their role of lending good money after bad. What is more, the IMF routinely pressured banks to lend additional funds as part of its negotiations with debtor nations in an effort to extract a promise of adjustment.

On the other hand, bankers have proved tough bargainers. For example, when Argentina became defiant during 1984, bankers closed ranks and refused to extend additional credit. In spite of appeals to intercede on behalf of the government, the IMF and other international governmental organizations supported the bankers' firm position. The result was a new plan of austerity and privatization by the Argentine government (Stiles 1991, 190). Particularly where the debtor is relatively small, like Jamaica, large creditor institutions have the capacity to demand repayment of arrears without any great fear of the consequences of default. Peru, Brazil, and Argentina each experimented with refusing to pay debt as it fell due (moratorium); however, as individual countries they were vulnerable to retaliatory action by the international community. In Peru, the IMF and Group of Seven countries refused to extend any additional credit until Peru began repaying its past debts. This was tantamount to exclusion from the entire international banking system because the private banks generally follow the IMF's lead. Brazil was able to carry on its strategy for a time but came up against stiffened resistance from banks that in 1987 were better positioned to suffer earnings losses (Spero 1990, 191). The overall result is that for many developing nations, the general direction of the flow of money was negative; more funds were going to pay off loans than were coming into the nation through export earnings, new loans, and other aid (Lever and Huhne 1985).

Although governments and bankers are motivated by very different concerns, bankers typically follow the flag when it comes to foreign lending, seeking some semblance of protection from the government in spite of the possibility that this could lead to some unwise business decisions (Wellons 1985). The few exceptions, such as private lending to Nicaragua and Vietnam at times when these governments had poor relations with the United States, stand out in stark contrast to the general trend. In general terms, the radicals' argument that some form of cooperation exists between governments and bankers seems to hold up.

It is also clear from our historical study that governments tend to work together. The mere existence of the Group of Seven highlights the shared interests of these governments and their desire to work together. Particularly when the United States, the United Kingdom, and Germany were each governed by conservative, pro-capitalist leaders (Ronald Reagan, Margaret Thatcher, and Helmut Kohl, respectively), they could reach agreement on a rather unforgiving approach. However, it should be pointed out that developed countries are not above treating each other with a certain callousness. When the British pound began to lose its value in the 1970s, rather than intervene to support it, the United States and Germany allowed it to drop and used the crisis to force Great Britain to undertake adjustment measures of its own. Trade and financial friction between Japan, Germany, and the United States illustrates that one cannot assume cooperation on even matters of global welfare when unemployment and trade deficits are on the rise.

Third World governments are assumed by radicals to be exploited by the rich players in the debt game. Although it may seem that developing countries are hopelessly outclassed vis-à-vis international financiers, this conclusion is questionable. Debtors as a group and as individuals have much potential power. Bankers feared the coming together of major debtors in a cartel. Short of this, the threat of coordinated action was a serious concern to the international community because no direct leverage was available to deal with large-scale action. Latin debtors in particular obtained significant concessions in the mid-1980s when their cartel efforts were at their strongest and most public.

Because it is ultimately up to the government to implement the adjustment process and provide data to demonstrate its success or failure, individual debtors may be able to maintain the appearance of austerity without enacting the substance of it. Perhaps the most egregious case of this duplicity occurred in Zaire in the early 1980s, when the government had become so corrupt and adjustment such a farce that the IMF actually sent a team to take control of the major economic ministries in the country. Even with that action, the IMF could not overcome local resistance and eventually gave up. Throughout the process, Zaire continued to receive sporadic funding from the IMF and was able to keep the flow of private lending (Stiles 1991, 64–86).

Saunders and Subrahmanyam conclude that on balance the gains from rescheduling debt under conditions of austerity have been shared by both creditors and debtors and no clear victory for either side can be claimed (Saunders and Subrahmanyam 1991). Figure 21.2 illustrates the net movement of resources between creditors and debtors, which reaffirms this conclusion by illustrating the balance between flows.

The IMF, as an international organization, is obligated to respect the sovereignty and diplomatic rights of its members. As a result, any appearance of intrusion is quickly seized upon by opponents of the IMF as an excess of authority. In a strongly worded pamphlet issued in 1983, the IMF declared that it is not in the business of "imposing" austerity but that all its programs are approved by the debtor nation after extensive negotiations.

Perhaps the most puzzling outcome of the debt crisis was a "nonevent": no coherent debtor cartel emerged. Guillermo O'Donnell, a prominent Latin American sociologist, showed that, unlike in OPEC and other more successful cartels, the group of debtors in Latin America lacked a leader willing to carry the burdens of joint default. Argentina was certainly willing to confront the West, but it was not able to survive in the long run without access to foreign capital. It certainly was not in the position to bankroll the debt of the other Latin American states. Saudi Arabia had the capacity to lead a debtor cartel, but it had no desire to sink its vast wealth into a losing cause. Mexico had neither the capacity nor the will and as a result did not actively participate in forming a debtor cartel.

In addition to the unwillingness or inability of the major debtors to organize a cartel and undertake a coordinated default (or threat thereof), the private bankers went out of their way to prevent the groups from coalescing. In 1984–1985, at various times when the group seemed about to congeal, private banking consortia offered a very attractive rescheduling arrangement to Brazil, Argentina, or Mexico, with the result that the nation withdrew from the cartel negotiations (O'Donnell 1985).

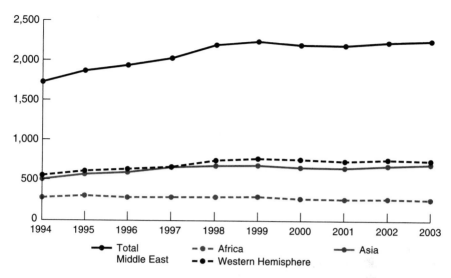

Figure 21.2   Developing country external debt, 1994–2003 (billions of U.S. dollars)
Note: 2002 and 2003 are projections.
Source: International Monetary Fund. *World Economic Survey,* (Washington, DC: IMF, 2002) .

Overall, then, the result of the debt crisis has been a greater acceptance on the part of developing nations of their need for Western capital and therefore a greater willingness to comply with Western demands, including adjustment. Is a radical interpretation valid, then? Perhaps. One must also consider the degree to which debtor nations have become measurably poorer as a result of the debt crisis, and whether wealthy nations have profited proportionally. This may tell something about whether the North has exploited the South, as global structuralists assume. Of course, other approaches may help answer this question—namely, focusing on the degree of dependence of the debtor nations on the North; focusing on inequality within the South; focusing on potential versus actual growth following the debt crisis; and so on.

The IMF has always been on the defensive with regard to its attitude toward the poor. It has generally excluded calculations of the impact of conditionality on poverty on the grounds that this issue is beyond the scope of its mandate and mission. This position has been difficult to hold, given the obvious and immediate impact of IMF conditionality on the living conditions of the poorest segments of society. Removing price subsidies on bread, for example, and thereby allowing the retail price to increase as much as tenfold in certain countries is a policy with clearly damaging consequences for the poor—yet this sort of policy is often urged by the IMF officials. It was not until 1989 that the IMF began explicitly taking into account poverty in its conditionality arrangements and setting aside funds for the poorest debtors.

In fact, the jury is still out concerning the actual impact of IMF conditionality on standards of living. In an exhaustive study, Bradshaw and Wahl concluded that foreign debt and IMF conditionality seem to have had, in

Table 21.1   Income Distribution: Percentage of Income
of Wealthiest 20 Percent, 1970–1996 (year in parentheses)

	1970–1972	1978–1983	1985–1987	1994–1996
Brazil	66.6 (72)	62.6 (83)	00.0 (00)	64.2 (95)
Costa Rica	54.8 (71)	00.0 (00)	54.4 (86)	51.8 (96)
Peru	61.0 (72)	00.0 (00)	51.9 (86)	51.2 (96)
Philippines	54.0 (71)	00.0 (00)	52.5 (85)	49.6 (94)
Venezuela	54.0 (70)	00.0 (00)	52.5 (85)	51.8 (95)
Yugoslavia	00.0 (00)	38.7 (78)	42.8 (87)	00.0 (00)

Source: World Bank annual development report, various issues.

many cases, a positive effect on living conditions in Africa and an ambiguous impact on Latin America (Bradshaw and Wahl 1991, 207). In other words, many nations have grown wealthier in spite of high levels of external debt.

These findings may seem difficult to accept in the light of other, more general data on economic trends among the largest debtors. The World Bank has been tracking the progress of the seventeen most deeply indebted nations in the world (mostly Latin American) and has concluded that the debt crisis is far from over and that conditions are generally strained at best. Overall growth rates among the largest debtors have been sluggish at best. When figured on a per capita basis, given the high population growth in many of these countries, the growth rate is actually negative. From 1981 to 1985, the average GNP per capita for the seventeen major debtors actually shrank by 2.6 percent per year. The only bright spot was that the debt level has increased at an ever slower rate (compare Figures 21.1 and Figure 21.2).

Another way of measuring the progress of the poor in debtor nations, albeit impressionistically, is by looking at income distribution figures. Countries are generally reluctant to publish these figures because they clearly show how few people control the bulk of the wealth—a politically sensitive question to say the least. For many debtors, where cultural and historical patterns have resulted in high concentrations of wealth in the hands of a few, these numbers almost never appear. In spite of this, the World Bank has published a few indicators for a few debtors, which are reported in Table 21.1. Except in the case of Yugoslavia, where market reforms have given rise to a burgeoning capitalist class, the general pattern of income distribution is toward slightly more equity and balance in spite of chronic debt. Note that this is merely a rough indication of a trend, not an exact measurement.

Conclusion

The year 2000 marked the first time the overall indebtedness of the developing world declined. This does not mean that the debt crisis is solved, as the total amount owed still tops $2 trillion (IMF 2002). But it does give some reason for hope. Even in Africa, total debt levels declined to $752 billion in 2001 from a high of $303 billion in 1995. Debt-service payments, on the other hand, reached an all-time high in 2001, meaning that the amount being paid each quarter remains extremely high.

In spite of the pain of adjustment, almost every country in the world, including those that had promoted a structural perspective in the 1950s and 1960s, has embraced free-market capitalism. Whether this was a voluntary conversion or a shotgun marriage is open to debate. It is also not entirely clear whether the debt crisis was self-inflicted or the product of nefarious global structures.

At the same time, it is clear that many of the practices of developing countries until the 1970s were counterproductive and self-defeating. The level of government intervention in the economy was not sustainable, in part because it clearly interfered with increasing productivity and production in the long term. Likewise, entering into agreements to borrow large sums on the private market, which were subsequently invested in unprofitable ventures, was a careless policy. The fact that the money was readily available was no reason to take it. Likewise, the pyramid schemes that generated dramatic growth in several Asian countries proved as unsustainable as they were unwise.

Western bankers and policy makers are by no means guiltless in this financial catastrophe. Not only did banks make foolish loans for which they paid a relatively low price, given the availability of government bailouts and support, but the trading system also proved unworkable. Even today, most Western government impose trade barriers aimed at developing country imports—particularly foodstuffs—that make it very difficult for the poorest states to export their way out of poverty (Stiles 2002). Structural adjustment, while reasonable in principle, has been applied inflexibly and with too much vigor and speed in many countries, resulting in tremendous suffering and only mixed benefits.

Overall, no clear pattern emerges with regard to whether the structural approach is most useful with respect to explaining the debt crisis and what followed. Because so many factors enter into the equation, it is difficult to isolate winners and losers. In general terms, we cannot conclude that the wealthy countries exploited the poor and profited from their troubles. The only thing that is clear is that the fate of the nations of the world is more inextricably linked than ever.

Debate Topic

Should Western taxpayers come to the rescue of Third World economies in crisis?

PRO

Those who believe Western governments are justified in using public monies to support developing countries in crisis make the following points: (1) Crises in other countries often damage the interests of Western producers and consumers. (2) Western nations have a general responsibility to support nations in crisis for humanitarian reasons. (3) Western nations help create the crisis by allowing unwise lending, so they are obligated to repair the damage.

CON
Those who object to the bailout policy have argued as follows: (1) Most crises are the direct result of unwise decisions made in foreign capitals, for which the West has no responsibility. (2) The bailouts often do not solve the problems and merely waste taxpayer monies. (3) If there are Western agencies to blame, they are usually private banks and investment firms, which should shoulder the burden alone as part of the cost of doing business.

Questions to Consider

1. Who were the winners and the losers in the debt crisis? To what extent did those who were directly involved in making and receiving loans suffer?

2. To what extent were the debtor nations victims of international forces beyond their control? Why were the burdens so unevenly spread across countries?

3. To what extent did the debt crisis demonstrate where the world's power lies? Did any surprises occur?

Websites

International Organizations
International Monetary Fund: **www.imf.org**
The World Bank: **www.worldbank.org**
Joint IMF–World Bank library: **jolis.worldbankimflib.org/external.htm**

Nonprofit Organizations
Institute for International Economics: **www.iie.com**
Global Exchange: **www.globalexchange.org/economy/rulemakers**
Jubilee 2000: **www.jubilee2000uk.org/main.html**
Fifty Years Is Enough: **www.50years.org**

References

Aliber, Roger. "The Debt Cycle in Latin America." *Journal of Interamerican Studies and World Affairs* 27 #4 (Winter 1985–1986).

Ambrogi, Thomas. "Goal for 2000: Unchaining Slaves of National Debt." *National Catholic Reporter* 36 #21 (March 26, 1999): 3.

Bradshaw, York, and Ana-Maria Wahl. "Foreign Debt Expansion, the International Monetary Fund, and Regional Variation in Third World Poverty." *International Studies Quarterly* 35 #3 (September 1991): 251–272.

Cohen, Benjamin J. "What Ever Happened to the LDC Debt Crisis?" *Challenge* 3 #3 (May 1991): 47–51.

Gilpin, Robert. *The Political Economy of International Relations* (Princeton, NJ: Princeton University Press, 1987).

International Monetary Fund. *Annual Report,* 1984 (Washington, DC: IMF, 1984).

International Monetary Fund. "Debt Initiative for the Heavily Indebted Poor Countries (HIPCs)—Factsheet, April 7, 2000." Available on the IMF website.

International Monetary Fund. *World Economic Survey* (Washington, DC: IMF, 2002).

Isaak, Robert. *International Political Economy: Managing World Economic Change* (Englewood Cliffs, NJ: Prentice Hall, 1991).

Jolly, Richard, ed. *Adjustment with a Human Face* (New York: Oxford University Press, 1992).

Kahler, Miles. "Politics and International Debt: Explaining the Crisis." *International Organization* 39 #3 (Summer 1985): 357–382.

Lever, Harold, and Christopher Huhne. *Debt and Danger: The World Financial Crisis* (New York: Atlantic Monthly Press, 1985).

Mauprivez, Bruno, Acting Chief, Public Affairs Division, IMF. "Letter to Ann Pettifor, Director, Jubilee 2000 Coalition," November 5, 1999. Available on the IMF website.

New York Times, July 18, 1991, D3.

New York Times, December 16, 1991, D2.

O'Donnell, Guillermo. "External Debt: Why Don't Our Governments Do the Obvious?" *CEPAL Review* 27 (December 1985): 27–33.

Pool, John Charles, and Steve Stamos. *The ABCs of International Finance* (Lexington, MA: Lexington Books, 1987).

Sampson, Anthony. *The Money Lenders: The People and Politics of the World Banking Crisis* (New York: Penguin, 1981).

Saunders, Anthony, and Marti Subrahmanyam. "LDC Debt Rescheduling: Who Wins, Who Loses" in Robert Kolb, *The International Finance Reader* (Miami: Kolb Publishing, 1991), 107–116.

Schwartz, Herman. "Can Orthodox Stabilization and Adjustment Work? Lessons from New Zealand, 1984–90." *International Organization* 45 #2 (Spring 1991): 221–256.

Spero, Joan. *The Politics of International Economic Relations,* 4th ed. (New York: St. Martin's Press, 1990).

Stiles, Kendall. *Negotiating Debt: The IMF Lending Process* (Boulder, CO: Westview, 1991).

Stiles, Kendall. "World Trade Conflict: Has the Third World Been Cheated?" in Sonia Benson, ed. *History Behind the Headlines,* Vol. 4 (Detroit: Gale Group Pub., 2002).

Strange, Susan. *Casino Capitalism* (Oxford: Basil Blackwell, 1986).

Wall Street Journal, March 27, 1992, 9A.

Wellons, Philip. "International Debt: The Behavior of the Banks in a Politicized Environment." *International Organization* 39 #3 (Summer 1985): 441–472.

World Bank. *World Development Report,* 1988 (New York: Oxford University Press, 1988).

World Bank. *World Development Report,* 1999–2000 (New York: Oxford University Press, 1999).

Yergin, Daniel and Joesph Stanislaw. *The Commanding Heights: The Battle Between Government and the Marketplace That Is Remaking the Modern World* (New York: Simon & Schuster, 1998).

CASE
22

Europe Uniting
REGIONALISM

Introduction

A global order based on respect for law and tolerance of differences seems beyond our grasp, but many hope that spheres of peace can be established at the regional level. A region is whatever its members choose; it typically involves contiguous territory, common culture, and interdependent economies and societies. Although regional organizations have tended to fall flat (the Organization of African Unity is a case in point), there are indications that in Europe and perhaps elsewhere regionalism is healthy and offers a real opportunity for improving people's living conditions. Economic integration is one type of regionalism, involving reduced obstacles to trade, investment, and migration. Political integration leads to some form of federal or unitary state. The United States represents political integration well, and the European Union illustrates what is meant by economic integration.

Regional economic organizations can generally be categorized in terms of their objectives and methods. The least painful or controversial steps typically involve standardization of industrial or technical designs, such as agreeing on the gauge of railroads. This makes it somewhat easier to market goods beyond a company's local customer base. More difficult and painful are efforts to increase regional trade directly through mutual reductions in tariffs and quotas (a free trade zone). These efforts are often combined with the establishment of a common regional tariff to be placed on imports from outside the region (customs union). The tariff serves as an inducement to help soften the blow of opening domestic markets to goods from other regional players—at least goods from outside the region will still be more expensive for a time. The next most difficult level of integration involves removal of nontariff barriers that interfere with the flow of goods and services. For example, one country in the region may have an especially high corporate tax rate, which means products from that state are necessarily more expensive. Harmonization involves making as many government policies as possible uniform across the region so that no business or consumer is penalized. Tax rates, banking interest rates, retirement benefits, teaching certification requirements, and so forth, must be made as uniform as possible.

The most difficult—and therefore rare—is outright federalization of a region, whereby the entire area is brought under a single political authority. Although some allowances may be made for local autonomy, major national policies would fall under a single jurisdiction. This would include economic, social, legal, and security policies traditionally managed at the local level. Federalization has taken place in only a few instances, such as the formation of the United States in the 1780s and of Germany in the 1870s, although some believe Europe is now pointed in this direction.

Plans for European unity began for a disgust with war and carnage—not World War II, but the Thirty Years' War. After the end of the devastating war in 1648, French royal advisor de Sully developed a "Grand Design" for European unity based on religious tolerance. Though stillborn, de Sully's proposal was the first of a string of concepts calling for European unity. Following the nearly successful attempt of Louis XIV to secure French domination over Europe in the early 1700s, William Penn and the Quakers in Britain, along with the Abbe de Saint-Pierre in France, developed complex and elaborate schemes for a form of collective security for Europe (Heater 1992, 54, 58). During the nineteenth century, while idealists continued to work on a global organization, which culminated in the League of Nations, the great powers experimented for a time with the Concert of Europe—an informal arrangement among the dominant European powers to keep minor conflicts in check through collaborative intervention.

The period of planning and scheming for Europe demonstrated a tension between the goals of preserving sovereignty and creating genuine supranational institutions that could coordinate state action. To a large extent, this tension has yet to be resolved.

EUROPE UNITING
KEY FIGURES

Jean Monnet   Deputy-general, League of Nations, 1919–1923; President and founder, ECSC, 1952–1955.

Jacques Delors   President, European Commission, 1985–1995. He spearheaded the Single European Act and the creation of the euro.

Paul-Henri Spaak   Prime Minister of Belgium at various times between 1938 and 1949. He led the European coordination of Marshall Plan aid and served as Secretary General of NATO, 1957–1961. He is known affectionately as the "Father of Europe."

Margaret Thatcher   British Prime Minister, 1979–1990. She worked against a number of EEC programs and proposals during her tenure.   *(continued)*

Robert Schuman   French Foreign Minister, 1948–1952. He crafted the ECSC with Jean Monnet.

Helmut Kohl   Chancellor of Germany, 1982–1998. He promoted deeper European integration.

EUROPE UNITING
CHRONOLOGY

1922
Belgium, Luxembourg, and the Netherlands agree to form a free trade zone.

1948
The European Movement is founded in the Netherlands. The Marshall Plan is promulgated and the OEEC, predecessor to the OECD and EEC, is founded.

1949
The Council of Europe is formed.

1954
The ECSC is formed to regulate steel production.

1957
The Treaty of Rome is signed, creating the European Economic Community.

1962
The Common Agricultural Program is instituted to support farm prices.

1963
Charles de Gaulle of France blocks British membership to the EEC.

1971
The Luxembourg Compromise provides a veto to each member-state on certain issues.

1973
Great Britain, Denmark, and Ireland join the EEC in the first "enlargement".

1978
The EMS replaces previous currency stabilization schemes.

1981
Greece is admitted to the EEC.

1982
British Prime Minister Margaret Thatcher demands changes in regional funding arrangements.

1985
The Single European Act is approved.

1986
Spain and France are admitted to the ECC.

1989
The Delors Plan for regional monetary union is approved.

1990
European states impose restrictions on British beef amid fears of "mad cow" disease.

1991
The Maastricht Treaty is approved, pending ratification by each EEC member.   *(continued)*

1992

Almost all of the trade barriers outlined in 1985 (as part of the SEA) are removed. A currency crisis in the United Kingdom and Italy leads to the dismantling of the European Monetary System.

1994

The Maastricht Treaty comes into effect, resulting in the creation of the European Union.

1995

Sweden, Finland, and Austria are admitted to the EU.

2000

Fifteen European Union member-states agree in Nice, France, to admit twelve new members, pending approval by citizens of all fifteen states.

2002

The euro is adopted regionwide as national currencies are eliminated. Ireland becomes the last country to ratify the Nice Agreement, paving the way for the admission of most Eastern European states by 2005.

The Emergence of the Common Market: 1945–1957

The Common Market originated from both external and internal forces. The post–World War II environment was utter devastation and called for urgent and dramatic steps. In addition, the growing and clear threat of Soviet Communist encroachment on Western European democracy prompted an acceleration of reconstruction and stabilization efforts. Administrative efficiency and capital utilization required a regional rather than a national approach. The result was American enthusiasm for the Marshall Plan and the regional cooperation it entailed.

In Europe, the disastrous experience with fascism and German expansionism led many to adopt a "never again" attitude. Plans were developed to solidify democratic regimes, punish fascists, and channel German warmaking capacity into a broader European network. Germans sought a means to legitimize their new democratic state and put Nazism behind them. These factors, combined with the strength of Christian Democratic parties across Europe, along with their pro-Europe policies, paved the way for Jean Monnet and Paul-Henri Spaak to have great influence.

In 1948, European leaders organized a conference at the Hague, in the Netherlands, where the European Movement was founded to act as a sort of continental lobbying group to press for more integration and unity. Winston Churchill promoted European unity in a series of speeches in the late 1940s, and he served as president of the Hague conference. Here again, a conflict emerged between the "federalists"—mainly the French and Germans—who envisioned a powerful European federal government, and the "unionists," who sought merely ad hoc agreements to deal with particular problems piecemeal (Gerbet 1987, 39).

A series of events in 1948–1950 brought the conflict between federalist and unionist conceptions of Europe to a head. Europe suffered an extreme economic and social crisis following the disastrous harvest of 1948. Soviet expansion in Eastern Europe seemed relentless and foreboding. The rise of Communist parties in France, Italy, and other Western European states seemed to mirror the threat to the East. The United States thus had reason to intervene in dramatic fashion to rescue Europe from what appeared an inevitable World War III, fought this time over German industry. Jean Monnet wrote of his feelings at the time:

> [I recall] the anxiety that weighed on Europe five years after the war: the fear that if we did nothing we should soon face war again. Germany would not be its instigator this time, but its prize. So Germany must cease to be a potential prize, and instead become a link. At that moment, only France could take the initiative. What could be done to link France and Germany . . . ? (Monnet 1979, 289)

The Marshall Plan (formally known as the European Recovery Program) was an essential stopgap measure for the United States to provide necessary capital and materials for European reconstruction; the Bretton Woods institutions [World Bank and International Monetary Fund (IMF)] had proved inadequate to the task. In conjunction with the Marshall Plan, the Organization for European Economic Cooperation (OEEC) was quickly founded in 1948 to give Europeans a role in distributing the resources that flowed from the United States. The OEEC did not have authority to force nations to coordinate their plans, but "thanks to the part played by the Secretariat, the member states became used to cooperating and comparing their economic policies" (Gerbet 1987, 36).

The OEEC was not the first regional organization devoted to economic coordination in Europe. In fact, the Benelux countries (Belgium, the Netherlands, and Luxembourg) had already gone far to create a common market and customs union among themselves. Beginning in 1922, Belgium and Luxembourg pledged to eliminate tariff barriers with each other (thus creating a common market) and to coordinate their trade policies toward the rest of the world (thus creating a customs union). They also promoted the free movement of labor and capital, thereby increasing labor migration and foreign investment. When the Netherlands joined in 1947, the group became a genuinely multilateral arrangement, complete with regional institutional structures and governing authority. This Benelux arrangement served as a model for what was later to become the European Economic Community (Hurwitz 1987, 11).

The economic cooperation forged in the 1940s coincided with efforts at military and political cooperation, although the two efforts soon diverged. Northern Europe organized a peacetime military alliance shortly after the war, culminating in the Brussels Treaty Organization in 1948, to which the United States was almost immediately invited. The North Atlantic Treaty Organization (NATO), founded in 1949, pledged mutual assistance in the event of an attack against any member and grew to include Germany, Italy, and European countries both to the north and to the south. NATO also provided significant American military support for Europe, including hundreds of thousands of U.S. troops and substantial stockpiles of nuclear weapons. Efforts to forge a truly European military pact failed in the 1950s, which may have led to greater attention to the economic sphere.

Economics and politics were never separate as far as European integration was concerned. An important illustration is the emergence of the European Coal and Steel Community (ECSC). By 1950, German industry was on the road to rapid recovery. In fact, Germany was consuming so much coal and coke from the Ruhr valley near the Rhine that France and other Europeans were experiencing shortages. Jean Monnet, the leader of France's industrial plan, saw this crisis as an opportunity to introduce the plans for integration he had developed as early as 1941. As he saw it, integrating German coal and French iron ore production would solve not only France's immediate shortage problem but a much wider problem as well:

> All successive attempts to keep Germany in check, mainly at French instigation, had come to nothing, because they had been based on the rights of conquest and temporary superiority—notions from the past which happily were no longer taken for granted. But if the problem of sovereignty were approached with no desire to dominate or take revenge—if on the contrary the victors and the vanquished agreed to exercise joint sovereignty over part of their joint resources—then, a solid link would be forged between them, the way would be wide open for further collective action, and a great example would be given to the other nations of Europe. (Monnet 1979, 293)

Thus the ECSC was a way both to keep Germany's military capacity in check and to support French economic goals. As put by Robert Schuman, the French premier who formally proposed Monnet's concept, "The community of production, which will in this manner be created, will clearly show that any war between France and Germany becomes not only unthinkable but in actual fact impossible" (Hurwitz 1987, 20).

The ECSC was created in 1951 with the signing of the Treaty of Paris on April 18 by France, Germany, Italy, and the Benelux countries. It provided for a High Authority, an international panel with powers to organize production levels, map out distribution, and promote equity across the member states. Article 9 of the treaty specified that "in the performance of these duties, [the High Authority] shall neither seek nor take instructions from any Government or any body. . . . Each member state undertakes to respect this supranational character." (Heater 1992, 162). The federalists carried the day insofar as the ECSC is concerned. The treaty also provided for a parliament made up of delegations from member countries based on population, a council with advisory powers where each state had one vote, and a court to review actions of states relative to the High Authority's decisions.

The ECSC quickly demonstrated its effectiveness and provided the impetus for the creation of yet more regional institutions. Monnet was instrumental in establishing Euratom—a European organization to facilitate cooperative development of nuclear technology.

Efforts by France and Great Britain to exert influence overseas in the mid-1950s failed. Both countries then sought refuge in a regional home where their influence could be strong. The British emphasized their Atlantic ties to the United States, whereas the French looked to Europe.

The Soviet intervention in Hungary convinced Europeans that the time had come to create what unity they could, a decision given form at a conference in Messina, Italy, in 1955 (Kusters 1987, 81). Although the French government fell in solidly behind the integration plans (partly out of fear that other Europeans would proceed without France), the British distanced themselves from what they considered a continental question.

Paul-Henri Spaak was the principal author of the 1957 Treaty of Rome, the formal agreement that created the Common Market (officially called the European Economic Community—EEC). He had served as the first head of the OEEC in 1948 and head of the Council of Europe in 1949, and was known as "Mr. Europe" (Heater 1992, 165). Spaak supported the ECSC but was eager for greater integration. He became chair of the team charged at the 1955 Messina conference with drafting a treaty for a customs union and common market. The EEC was constituted with the objective of promoting

> throughout the Community a harmonious development of economic activities, a continuous and balanced expansion, an increased stability, an accelerated raising of the standard of living and closer relations between its member states. (Article 2)

Countries joined the EEC for a variety of reasons. Germany saw membership as a vehicle for international acceptance, a way to regain its sovereignty (an ironic goal, because other Europeans saw it as a way to lose theirs!—Urwin and Paterson 1990, 188). France hoped to use the EEC to dominate European politics diplomatically and to placate the strong political pressure of French farmers. Italy hoped the EEC could provide economic and diplomatic rehabilitation as well as development funding for its southern half. The Benelux countries were eager to lower continental trade barriers, which they felt discriminated against their own, more efficient industries. As time went on, these different motivations created interesting and often complex political alliances and antagonisms.

A Primer of European Institutions

European institutions went through considerable changes in the 1990s. The Maastricht Treaty of 1991, which took effect in January 1994, not only amplified the powers of several EEC organs but also added entirely new agencies, all under the rubric of a far stronger commitment to European unity. The new association was dubbed the European Union (EU).

The institutions of the EU are shown in Figure 22.1. The distribution of power among the various organs was largely a compromise arrangement and modified the strong federalist bent of the ECSC. The European Commission is the central policy-making and policy-implementing body, although it operates under the ultimate authority of the Council of Ministers and the European Parliament. It is structured much like a presidential cabinet, with

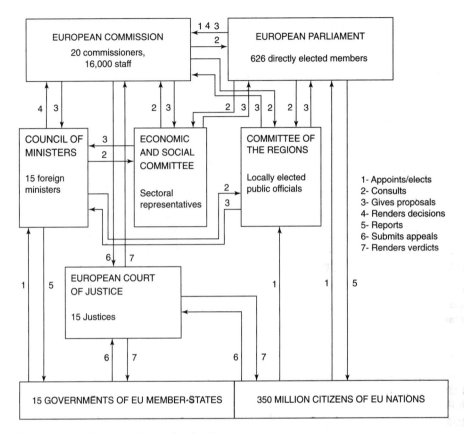

Figure 22.1   European Union institutional structure.

twenty commissioners (one from each member-state, except for Great Britain, France, Germany, Italy, and Spain, which have two) who serve five-year terms. The commission is meant to serve the interests of the entire union rather than represent each country's position, and the president of the commission is generally seen as the voice of the organization as a whole. He often argues against other European politicians in support of union-wide policy making. The commission is supported by a staff of 16,000 "Euro-crats." It receives advice from several standing bodies, including the Economic and Social Committee and the Committee of the Regions—each designed to give certain special interests a voice in European policy (and to counter a growing sense of detachment on the part of Brussels agencies, where the EU is headquartered, from the "real world" of European life) to both inform and legitimize its policies.

The Council of Ministers (formally known as the Council of the European Union) is a small body consisting of international economic policy chiefs of each member-state. It has the power to approve commission recommendations and to develop policies unilaterally. The question of how much influence the council ought to have relative to the commission has been at the cutting edge of EU politics since its inception. Federalists hoped that the supranational authority of the commission would grow, whereas unionists favored expanding the political power of the council. Although the commission was given broad authority to recommend policies to the council without regard for nationalism, subnational entities such as business and labor groups from individual countries often participated in the commission's decision-making process (Taylor 1983, 94). In reality, commission power eroded steadily through the 1970s as the EU was gradually reformed.

After the election of Charles de Gaulle as president of France in 1958, France adopted a more unionist approach to old EEC institutions. While most European states were interested in expanding the authority of the commission, de Gaulle sought to enhance the powers of the council, with France playing the dominant role (Wistrich 1990, 31). On the council, France blocked efforts to institute majority voting, as called for in the Treaty of Rome, on the grounds that it would dilute French influence. De Gaulle blocked the British application for membership in 1963 because he feared that move would further weaken French power as well as introduce an essentially non-European actor into the community (Britain's trade and diplomacy were oriented primarily toward the commonwealth and the United States). France's intransigence culminated in the country's boycott of council meetings in late 1965 and a summit meeting to address the majority-vote issue. The Luxembourg Compromise, approved by the other five EEC members, provided for each nation to have the power to veto community policy if it felt the proposal threatened its national interest in a significant way. Because it was left to the individual countries to determine whether a threat existed, this compromise seriously undercut the notion of majority rule and led to paralysis of the council (Wistrich 1990, 33).

Other reforms tended to follow the unionist philosophy toward EEC power in the 1960s. For example, a Committee of Permanent Representatives (COREPER), made up of ambassadorial-rank delegates from each member state, was created to provide more ongoing participation by governments in commission activities. The commission's ability to shape the council's agenda and programs was substantially weakened by this step.

After 1974, even the council's power was undermined by the establishment of thrice-annual EEC summit meetings of heads of state or government (known as the European Council). These meetings were used for resolving the most contentious regional issues—particularly budgetary problems.

The European Parliament and the European Court of Justice were secondary institutions during the first thirty years of the EU. The parliament, originally consisting of delegates from each member-state appointed by their respective national parliaments, had very little power beyond making suggestions to the commission. Only its votes on the budget and on accession of new members carried any weight. The court of justice was charged primarily with handling disputes over the implementation of EU rules, although the most serious problems were handled by the council and summit meetings. The Court of First Appeals was added later to deal exclusively with intra-EU issues. It was not until 1979, when the European Parliament was elected directly by European citizens and the court became involved in issuing authoritative and binding interpretations of EU law, that the influence of these two institutions began to grow.

Today, the European Parliament has considerable influence, not only on the budget but also on topics such as education, labor, health, and consumer protection, which are "co-decided" by the parliament and the commission. The parliament also has increasing weight in the areas of environmental policy, foreign aid, and regional development. The European Court of Justice, for its part, has become increasingly assertive, establishing a considerable body of case law clarifying that it has the power to overrule national legislation it considers to be a violation of a country's commitments under European law. The court has become involved in such controversial areas as abortion policy, corporal punishment of children, and social and economic policy, to the consternation of countries whose laws it has nullified.

The EEC at Work: 1957–1973

The first task of the EEC was to promote free trade within the community. This goal was to be achieved through the creation of a common market in which barriers to trade are dropped, a customs union through which each country's trade with other nations is uniform, free movement of labor and capital, and harmonization of social policy. The formation of a common market took less time than expected (Williams 1991, 51). As early as 1968, all internal tariffs on industrial products were eliminated—almost two years ahead of schedule (Wistrich 1990, 33).

The ease with which the common market was created was due largely to nondiplomatic factors. The 1960s saw extraordinary growth in Europe. Average annual growth rates for the EEC-Six ranged from 4.4 percent for West Germany to 5.7 percent for France. It was relatively easy for the EEC-Six to lower trade barriers without fear of unemployment rising from more intense competition. If a firm was not competitive in one sector, another opportunity soon presented itself. Not only did the economies of the EEC-Six grow during this period, but trade was also diverted from non-EEC to intra-EEC partners. In 1958, EEC countries imported only 29 percent of all goods from the other EEC-Six; by 1972, that figure had risen to 52 percent (Williams 1991, 33).

The other principal activity of the EEC during the 1960s was to establish the Common Agricultural Program (CAP). Considered a crucial element of the Treaty of Rome (Article 38) by France, the CAP provided for a common market and customs union in all foodstuffs, price guarantees, and structural reforms. In addition, the CAP aimed at ensuring "a fair standard of living for the agricultural community." Although such an approach seems excessive by today's standards, Marsh points out that in the 1950s, Europe was a net food importer and had recently imposed food rationing. Farmers were able to argue that the only way to ensure that Europe would have sufficient food was by producing it at home. Success in agriculture was considered essential for national security (Marsh 1989, 148).

The key element in this equation was price guarantees, which placated the highly politicized and powerful farm lobbies in France, Italy, and Germany. Although several options existed, the EEC-Six decided in 1962 to proceed with a price support mechanism involving the purchase by the community of surplus production to be stored until it could be sold without lowering the price. To appease German farmers, the price levels agreed upon were the high, heavily subsidized German prices. This decision made the CAP far and away the most significant EEC expense. The Council of Ministers had hoped at the time that the high price supports would be temporary, that the common market would force inefficient producers out of business. This was not the case. Instead, the price supports became a permanent element in the EEC (Taylor 1983, 237). As pointed out by Lodge, the CAP is neither capitalist nor effective, but it has become such a vital ingredient in the political and even physical landscape of Europe that any attempt at reform risks consequences that could easily outweigh the benefits (Lodge 1990, 212). It is interesting that revisions to the Treaty of Rome in the late 1980s included significant downsizing of the CAP and experimentation with alternative policies to maintain prices.

With de Gaulle out of office in 1969, the EEC proceeded with the accession of Great Britain, Denmark, Ireland, and Norway (where the proposal was rejected in a referendum). Given Britain's heavy reliance on imports of food from New Zealand and Australia and the relatively small size of its agricultural sector, it was disadvantaged by the EEC's emphasis on the CAP. Differences of opinion were left largely unresolved, and the accession was completed in 1973. This "first enlargement" came amid optimism for the future of the EEC. A 1972 summit meeting that included three "members in waiting" committed the community to deeper integration, including "completion of the internal market, common tariffs, a common currency, and a central bank" (Williams 1991, 50). Few anticipated the trying years that were soon to come.

The European Community Under Stress: 1973–1985

The quadrupling of the price of oil in 1973 had devastating effects on European economies. A decade of stagflation set in, and Britain's economic life was in constant jeopardy. The linchpin of stable currencies was gone, and demands by the Organization of Petroleum Exporting Countries (OPEC) for oil importers to end their support of Israel went far to undermine the political unity that contributed to economic cooperation. France and Germany abandoned Israel, while the Netherlands endured the oil embargo. The British pound collapsed in the mid-1970s, and labor unrest in France and Italy derailed those countries' economic growth. Germany struggled with terrorism, and Ireland and Italy pleaded for additional development financing from the EEC. None of the Europeans knew how to respond to the growing trade threat from Japan and the Far East. As put by British Prime Minister Edward Heath:

> After the oil crisis of 1973–74 the Community lost its momentum and, what was worse, lost the philosophy of Jean Monnet: that the Community exists to find common solutions to common problems. (Williams 1991, 50)

Amid this unraveling came a crisis of identity over Britain's role in the community. As a major industrial power, the United Kingdom expected to play a leading role in the EEC, but it had been "absent at the creation" and therefore was forced to deal with a set of rules and procedures that were not of its making. The most significant contention was about the budget. Britain continually found itself in conflict with the Franco-German "axis" during the 1970s (Urwin and Paterson 1990, 187).

Before going too far, we will discuss the EEC budget. Originally, the budget was simply based on a national quota calculated loosely in terms of gross national product (GNP) and renegotiated each year by the members. In 1970, this system was replaced with the "own resources" concept: The EEC would claim certain revenues on the grounds that they belonged by right to Europe as a whole. For a variety of reasons, Great Britain in the late 1970s was consistently sending Brussels some $3 billion more than it was getting back; at the same time, France was netting some $800 billion (Taylor 1983, 238).

The inequity of the situation was exacerbated by Britain's political ambivalence about European federalism generally. In 1979, Margaret Thatcher was elected prime minister on an anti-EEC platform. Her government exaggerated the United Kingdom's disadvantage by focusing on absolute rather than per capita revenues. Considering the EEC process seriously flawed and even illegitimate, the Thatcher government took an aggressive position that alienated the other EEC members. She told the EEC members bluntly, "I want my money back."

In 1982, Britain began to press the EEC for some form of financial relief. It demanded a rebate of 1.5 billion European Currency Units (ECU) to be paid by CAP beneficiaries (France and Italy in particular). When agreement was slow in coming, it threatened to use its veto to block further action by the community. Great Britain came close to precipitating a profound split in the community by 1984. Helmut Kohl of Germany left a meeting in protest. In essence, Germany called Britain's bluff. This is not to say that the United Kingdom failed. On the contrary, the EEC provided a 1 billion ECU rebate in 1984 and promised additional rebates of roughly two-thirds of the difference between Britain's tax-generated payments to the EEC and its receipts from Brussels (Urwin and Paterson 1990, 193). However, as part of this arrangement, Germany was permitted to increase substantially its share of EEC expenses—and power.

Apart from the budgetary and philosophical tensions in the community, a serious problem arose from the growing disparity of development among the members of the EU. Moving from the EEC-Six to the EC-Nine had not been particularly painful, in and of itself, except for the budget question described earlier. However, the additions of Greece in 1981 and of Spain and Portugal in 1986 created unexpected stress.

Greece was permitted to enter the EEC prematurely, EEC officials today acknowledge. Greek industry is still not competitive with that in the rest of Europe. Greek agriculture is far too tropical and labor-intensive to survive full integration (for example, the average size of a Greek farm is only one-fifth that of a Luxembourg farm). The Greek government in power in the early 1980s proved to be one of the few pro-EC governments that the Greek people would elect. Successive Greek regimes have challenged the membership decision (Williams 1991, 65).

Spain and Portugal applied for membership in 1977 and were admitted in 1986, despite serious reservations. Spain's size and the three Mediterranean countries' poverty placed heavy burdens on the rest of Europe. Spain and Portugal hoped their accession would guarantee newfound democracy and preserve their strong links to Europe. The EEC nations feared the imbalance of prices, wages, and wealth between Spain and Portugal and the rest of the community. The accession was permitted only with seven- to ten-year transitional provisions in fishing, semitropical foods, external industrial tariffs, and budget obligations (Williams 1991, 69).

Table 22.1 shows the persistence of development gaps among countries in the EC. Efforts to rectify the discrepancies have come primarily through regional development programs administered by the European Regional Development Fund (ERDF). Never more than 10 percent of the total EEC budget, the funds funneled through the ERDF were aimed primarily at rural Mediterranean regions (not countries), although a program set in place in the mid-1980s provided funds for certain depressed industrial areas (Williams 1991, 130).

The last significant policy issue tackled during the 1970s was monetary reform. The notion of a European Monetary System (EMS) had been discussed early after the Treaty of Rome was signed, but it did not take shape until the collapse of the dollar-centered Bretton Woods system in 1971 forced Europeans to take more responsibility for their own monetary stability. The Werner Report calling for fixed exchange rates that would fluctuate in parallel was implemented in 1971. This system proved untenable after the oil crisis, however. Because inflationary pressures hit different countries unequally, and because each nation decided to adopt a different monetary strategy to deal with the crisis, currency values began to separate dramatically. Maintaining fixed exchange rates required intervention by the governments (for example, buying and selling currency, increasing interest rates), so in 1978 the "snake" system, as it was called, was abandoned in favor of the EMS, known as the "snake in the tunnel" approach (Wistrich 1990, 35).

The EMS allowed European currencies to fluctuate freely in relation to one another within a 4.5 percent band around the deutsche mark. Govern-

Table 22.1 Selected Economic Performance Statistics for Greece, Portugal, Germany and the United Kingdom, 1998

	Greece	Portugal	Germany	United Kingdom
GNP per capita	$11,740	$10,670	$26,570	$21,410
GNP growth rate	3.5%	3.9%	2.7%	2.1%
Agriculture value added relative to GDP (est.)	10.5%	6.0%	1.8%	1.3%
Secondary school enrollment rate	91%	90%	95%	92%
Personal computers per 1,000 inhabitants	52	81	305	263
High-tech exports relative to total manufacturing exports	7%	4%	14%	28%

Source: World Bank *World Development Report* (New York: Oxford University Press, 1999).

ments accepted the responsibility to unilaterally adopt policies that would either raise or lower the value of their currencies relative to the mark whenever they approached the limits of this range. The agreement was actually drawn up and signed by the central bankers of the EEC and was to be implemented by them rather than by political leaders. The bankers agreed not only to conservative monetary principles but also to consultation, coordination, and convergence of money policy. The members also agreed to the create of a new accounting unit, the ECU, a forerunner of today's euro.

The Exchange Rate Mechanism (ERM) was also included in the EMS system. It provided for warnings to be issued to the banks of countries whose currencies fell outside a narrower 3.5 percent band around the deutsche mark, although strong currencies used heavily in the European banking system were permitted a slightly wider range of tolerance. The effect was to impose particularly strict discipline on smaller countries (Lehment 1983, 187).

The end of this period of relative turmoil came with an epiphany—a deep recognition that the EEC was at a crossroads. The community could either continue the unionist approach advanced by Thatcher or adopt the federalist approach, which was embraced by Germany, France, and the Netherlands.

Renewal: 1986–2002

European countries were in position to respond to the dramatic changes that took place on the world stage in the late 1980s and early 1990s because they were undergoing far-reaching changes of their own. Beginning as early as 1984, EEC leaders launched a series of dramatic reforms of their institutions.

Specifically, they strengthened the free trade regime of Europe, undertook initiatives into new economic and social policy arenas, added new members, and began to coordinate and strengthen communitywide security and foreign policy positions.

Single European Act

In 1984, the European Parliament approved a draft treaty of European union that committed countries to eventually merge their foreign and defense policies. By 1985, talk had begun to shift to the need for genuine unification of economic policies across the EEC, and committees were formed to study the question of a single market. British official Lord Cockfield developed a plan of action with a list of 282 directives to be adopted by the end of 1992 (Goldstein 1991–1992, 130). At the December 1985 Luxembourg summit, the Single European Act (SEA) was approved; it was ratified in 1986. The treaty represented a major modification of the Treaty of Rome and called for implementation of the "four freedoms": 1. Free movement of goods. This involved dismantling the many nontariff barriers that were not specifically listed in the Treaty of Rome and were still impeding trade in the community, including the establishment of a minimum sales tax (value added tax—VAT) rate with numerous exclusions. 2. A free market in services. This included banking, insurance, transportation, airlines, telecommunications, and so on. 3. Free movement of people—in other words, unrestricted immigration within the community. 4. A free market in capital—specifically, a pledge to eliminate government intervention in currency exchange and the eventual establishment of a common currency (the Delors Plan gave this movement its impetus; see the next section).

Beyond the important symbolism of the SEA, the concrete changes were substantial. By the end of 1992, virtually all government-made barriers to trade were eliminated, and efforts were set in motion to create united markets in fields that had none. For example, trucks may now travel across the EU without stopping at border crossings. This, in and of itself, cuts costs and improves efficiency substantially. Banking is liberalized to the point that any stable European banks can establish subsidiaries anywhere in the EU. Commercial insurance is liberalized, and plans are under way to do the same in the airline industry. By the end of 1992, some 95 percent of the SEA proposals had been implemented.

At the institutional level, although the SEA modifies the Treaty of Rome, it does so by simply changing the powers of existing bodies. The European Parliament is given greater voice in such matters as admitting new members (Lodge 1990, 216). The commission is strengthened and its scope of operation is broadened, which increases the likelihood that Europe-wide policies will be developed. Perhaps most important, the prospects for further progress have been strengthened by the adoption of majority rule on the Council of Ministers, thus eliminating the debilitating use of the veto (Pinder 1986, 73).

Delors Plan

In 1988, the European Council (or summit meeting) commissioned the new president of the European Commission, Jacques Delors, to devise a plan for monetary and currency union. In 1989, the Delors Plan was accepted. It called for a three-phase process to begin with the establishment of a European System of Central Banks (ESCB) centered on a European Central Bank and each of the twelve nations' central banks—to be governed with little political interference. This network would be the vehicle through which the European Commission and Council of Ministers would set monetary and currency policy, including the gradual harmonization of fiscal policy (government spending and taxation), currency valuation (exchange rates), monetary policy (interest rates, money supply), and bank powers (political independence of central bank leaders). After the nations of Europe completed this transition phase and satisfied the requirements of prudent monetary policy (defined flexibly by the Council of Ministers and European Council), the members of the community pledged to abandon their own currencies and central bank controls and hand over monetary policy to a single European entity (Habermeier and Ungerer 1992, 27–29).

Beginning in 1989, via the Delors Plan, European leaders moved toward establishing a single regional currency. Two key ingredients to such a venture are harmonizing and strengthening domestic fiscal and monetary policies and establishing and accepting powerful new central organs capable of setting regional monetary policy. In both cases, governments are required to adopt major changes to their way of running their national economies, which runs counter to prevailing ideology and political strategy. Many Europeans resisted EEC encroachment on monetary policy, including especially Margaret Thatcher, whose Conservative colleagues voted her out in early 1992 over her opposition to deeper integration. Likewise, more radical regimes objected to the need to subordinate their own developmental and redistributive policies to the demands of Brussels bureaucrats. The collapse of the value of the British pound and the Italian lira in 1992 provoked considerable debate in the United Kingdom and Italy, leading to a withdrawal from European monetary plans in the former and a redoubled effort to implement fiscal discipline in the latter (Gilpin 2001, 37–38).

Although politicians had considerable trepidation and hesitation, the euro was introduced in 1998 (as part of the Maastricht Treaty discussed later) and began to appear not only in government-to-government transactions but also in the prices of ordinary products sold in stores across Europe. After suffering an initial dip on the international exchange markets, the euro stabilized at a level slightly higher than the U.S. dollar and continues to gain credibility. On January 1, 2002, national currencies were officially eliminated and the euro became legal tender Europe-wide. Although there have been some complaints that merchants concealed price hikes in the currency conversion to euros, most Europeans welcomed the stability and strength of the new currency—even in Germany.

Not all EU members have joined the euro scheme, with the United Kingdom being a notable holdout. The main reason is the difficulties involved in meeting fiscal and monetary policy constraints. In the early 1990s, a serious recession gripped the region, and very few countries were able to reach the target of keeping budgetary deficits to less than 3 percent of gross domestic product (GDP). But by the late 1990s, the situation had changed substantially. From a high of 5.5 percent in 1993, overall budget deficits relative to GDP had fallen to less than 1 percent for Europe as a whole. Several countries even projected budget surpluses for the year 2000 (EC 2000, 5).

Maastricht Treaty

With the end of the Cold War in 1989 and the reunification of Germany in 1990, Europe faced a very different political context. As put in *The Economist*, "This is the decade the European Community was invented for" (Colchester 1992, S1). Amid the turmoil of political upheaval, Germany and France pressed for the rapid and full adoption of the spirit of Monnet and Spaak: European union. Rather than wait for a united Germany to assert its own identity, both Helmut Kohl and François Mitterand moved to incorporate it into the EEC network and subordinate German expansion to European imperatives. The withdrawal of Margaret Thatcher from British political life accelerated the process. These forces, along with the growing threat from Japan and questions about the future American role in Europe, were key to the pell-mell pace of the negotiation of the Maastricht agreements in December 1991. The Maastricht agreement was finalized in relative secrecy but with the strong support of the negotiators. Once the treaty was signed, it required the ratification of each member state before it went into force. In June 1992, the Danish electorate rejected the treaty by a slim margin; in September 1992, the French approved it by an equally slim margin. Leaders became concerned that they had failed to communicate the advantages of the EU clearly enough to their electorates. Ultimately, the Danes took another vote and approved the treaty, as did other European nations by large margins. The British Parliament finally approved the action without resort to a formal referendum. On January 1, 1994, the Maastricht Treaty went into effect.

The first element of the Maastricht Treaty was the strengthening of the EU-led integration itself, to be accomplished by 2000. The EU's authority was extended into such areas as education, health policy, consumer protection, law enforcement, immigration, and even culture. The Council of Ministers now act on the basis of a qualified majority vote (taking into account the size of the countries in tabulating their vote, but eliminating the veto altogether), but it must obtain the European Parliament's approval on many questions. The commission, though somewhat weaker in relation to the council, retains the initiative as the only organ authorized to propose new programs. The principle of "subsidiarity" limits the EU's authority to those programs where collective action is clearly preferable to national unilateralism—but the specific parameters of this concept have to be determined in the pro-integration European Court of Justice.

In practice, the commission continues to exert considerable authority over EU policy. An important episode illustrates the limits of council and governmental authority. In the late 1980s, the practice of feeding cows meat and bone meal was outlawed in Great Britain when it was discovered that cows were contracting bovine spongiform encephalopathy, better known as "mad cow disease." The epidemic ultimately affected more than 175,000 cows during the 1990s. In 1990, several European countries imposed unilateral bans on British beef. Under pressure from the commission, these countries lifted the ban a few weeks later. In 1995, however, Stephen Churchill died of Creutzfeld-Jakob disease, which was linked in a March 1996 study by the British health ministry to mad cow disease. Within days of the announcement, the commission issued a ban on the importation of all British beef products (Decision 94/239/EC of March 27, 1996). To protest the action, which it considered overly drastic and hasty, the U.K. government decided to use its political and institutional clout to obstruct other actions by the commission in other areas of EU policy. A month later, the United Kingdom agreed to end its virtual boycott of EU activities in exchange for a pledge by the commission to gradually lift the ban. In fact, the ban remained in effect for nearly three years. The United Kingdom tried to persuade the European Parliament to pass a motion of censure against the commission, which would have resulted in its dissolution, but failed.

EU Enlargement

Following a lengthy application process that ended in each country conducting a national referendum, Sweden, Finland, and Austria were admitted into the European Union in January 1995. Norway and Switzerland, though approved for admission, opted against it in the face of popular opposition.

The accession of these three nations proceeded without major difficulty and prompted European leaders to press for further enlargement by reaching out to long-time applicants Turkey, Malta, and Cyprus as well as the Central European nations of Slovenia, Hungary, Poland, and the Czech Republic. The EU members laid out more precise membership criteria in 1993, which now include (1) stable democracy and protection of fundamental human rights, (2) a functioning market economy, and (3) the ability to "take on the obligations of membership" (EC 2000). The EU also instituted a series of technical financial assistance programs to strengthen institutions and pro-market policies among candidates. In the French city of Nice in late 2000, EU members agreed to extend membership to ten Eastern European countries, pending approval by the citizens of each EU member-state. In October 2002, after a second attempt, the citizens of Ireland approved the plan—the last country to do so. This should result in memberships in 2004 for Hungary, Poland, the Czech Republic, Slovenia, Slovakia, Estonia, Latvia, and Lithuania, as well as Malta and Cyprus. The quest for membership for Cyprus and

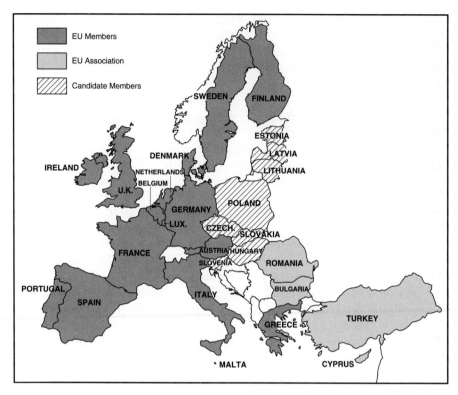

Map 22.1 European Union membership

Turkey has run into political opposition from Greece and other EU member-states concerned about human rights (primarily) and economic policies (see Map 22.1).

Security Cooperation

European governments have long been heavily involved in European security arrangements, although the arrangements have tended to be disconnected and relatively weak. The Western European Union, though still on the books, is nothing like the "non-North American NATO" it was originally envisioned to be. Efforts to reinvigorate it through Title V of the Maastricht Treaty have faltered. The European actions of failing to take a unified position on Bosnia in the early 1990s and allowing the United States to take the lead in Kosovo a few years later have led many to believe that much work is necessary on European security initiatives.

The EU provides for a High Representative for the Common Foreign and Security Policy of the Union, who will help form a consensus on foreign policy positions, but as yet this representative has not become a significant voice. The EU has also established an intelligence and policy planning unit. In 1997, the European Council signed the Treaty of Amsterdam, which is designed to give more weight and urgency to common union policies, in the hope that states will choose to "constructively abstain" rather than block union policies (EC 2000). There is currently talk of a new rapid-reaction force, but this effort probably will not progress very far until Turkey drops its opposition. Europeans are more likely to continue to support and strengthen the Organization for Security and Cooperation in Europe, which has played a key role in enhancing democracy and peace in southern Europe (Department of State 1995).

Conclusion

There is no question that the European Union is the most dramatic, far-reaching, and successful example of international integration in history. In the 1970s, skeptics predicted the withering away of the EEC in the face of French and British sovereign demands. Today, however, most international scholars see the EU as a new standard for international cooperation. This result has been achieved in spite of a difficult decade that dealt with the reintegration of East Germany, high unemployment, and austerity in the quest for admission to the euro system.

To emphasize this point, consider against the various forms of integration and regional cooperation outlined in the introduction to this case. At the time of this writing, the Europeans have clearly moved through the phases of free trade zone and customs union formation, although these steps proved to be far more controversial and difficult than expected. It would take the liberal reforms of the 1980s in the United Kingdom, France, and Germany before open markets could be realized. Harmonization is nearly complete, as the targets of both the Single European Act and the Maastricht Treaty are being implemented. With the introduction of the euro and a central bank to set interest rates, the European market is now arguably more unified than that of the United States. For example, it is easier for a student from one EU country to enroll in a law school in a second EU country, obtain a degree, and begin practicing law in a third EU country than it would be for a American student to cross state lines and do the same thing. The European student would have no need to convert currency, alter college transcripts, pass multiple bar exams, or obtain a worker license to work abroad. This is not to say that the individual might not face daunting language and cultural barriers, but these obstacles involve changes that are generally beyond the scope of governments.

As far as the last, most difficult level of integration goes, obstacles still remain. Europe does not yet speak with one voice on all matters of security, and the United States has a heavy presence in European military matters through NATO. Nevertheless, the European states do coordinate their foreign policies on everything from trade to the environment. At the World Trade Organization, the United Nations, and other international organizations, to hear one European country's position is generally to hear all their positions.

The next five years will likely see as many as ten countries join the EU and additional progress be made in policy harmonization and security cooperation. While it is doubtful that a United States of Europe will emerge, the lack of one could be merely a formality.

Debate Topic

Is a strong, integrated Europe a good thing for the rest of the world?

PRO

Those who believe Europe's transformation is good not only for Europeans but for the rest of the world make the following points: (1) Since Europe has been the locus of most global conflicts, anything that stabilizes this region will be good for humanity. (2) European prosperity has translated into technical innovations that have benefited the world. (3) Europe's strong record of global philanthropy and humanitarianism is helped by expanded European wealth and power.

CON

Those who are concerned about Europe's rising status argue as follows: (1) European success comes to a large extent at the expense of other major powers, both economically and politically. (2) European success might undermine support for global trading institutions, such as the WTO. (3) A Europe dominated by Germany does not have history on its side.

Questions to Consider

1. What key factors are reviving European unity? Are these forces relatively constant, or will they wax and wane?

2. Who wants European unity? The masses? The "Eurocrats"? The politicians? What does each expect to get from European unity?

3. Why is it so difficult to move from negative integration to positive integration to political unity? Will these obstacles persist in the future?

Websites

Index to the European Union site: **www.eur-op.eu.int/general/en/index.htm.**
EU search engine: **europe.eu.int/search.htm.**
Center for European Integration link page: **www.zei.de**

References

Colchester, Nico. "The European Community—A Survey." *The Economist* (July 11, 1992): S1–S30.

Department of State. "Fact Sheets: NATO, Partnership for Peace, OSCE, and NATO Enlargement." U.S. Department of State Dispatch, June 5, 1995.

European Commission. "Public Finances in EMU—2000: Report of the Directorate General for Economic and Financial Affairs." May 24, 2000.

Gerbet, Pierre. "The Origins: Early Attempts and the Emergence of the Six (1945–52)" in Pryce, ed., *The Dynamics of European Union*, 35–48.

Gilpin, Robert. *International Economic Stuff!!!* (Princeton, NJ: Princeton University Press, 2001).

Goldstein, Walter. "EC: Euro-stalling." *Foreign Policy* 85 (Winter 1991–1992): 129–147.

Habermeier, Karl, and Horst Ungerer. "A Single Currency for the European Community." *Finance and Development* (September 1992): 26–29.

Heater, Derek. *The Idea of European Unity* (New York: St. Martin's Press, 1992).

Hurwitz, Leon. *The European Community and the Management of International Cooperation* (New York: Greenwood Press, 1987).

Hurwitz, Leon, ed. *The Harmonization of European Public Policy: Regional Responses to Transnational Challenges* (Westport, CT: Greenwood Press, 1983).

Kusters, Hanns Jurgen. "The Treaties of Rome (1955–57)" in Pryce, ed., *The Dynamics of European Union*, 78–104.

Lehment, Harmen. "The European Monetary System" in Hurwitz, ed., *The Harmonization of European Public Policy*, 183–196.

Lodge, Juliet. "European Community Decision-Making: Toward the Single European Market" in Urwin and Paterson, eds., *Politics in Western Europe Today*, 206–226.

Lodge, Juliet, ed. *The European Community and the Challenge of the Future* (New York: St. Martin's Press, 1989).

Lodge, Juliet, ed. *European Union: The European Community in Search of a Future* (New York: St. Martin's Press, 1986).

Marsh, John. "The Common Agricultural Policy" in Lodge, ed., *The European Community and the Challenge of the Future*, 148–166.

Monnet, Jean. *Memoirs* (New York: Doubleday, 1979).

Pinder, John. "Economic Union and the Draft Treaty" in Lodge, ed., *European Union*, 70–87.

Pryce, Roy, ed. *The Dynamics of European Union* (New York: Croom Helm, 1987).

Taylor, Paul. *The Limits of European Integration* (New York: Columbia University Press, 1983).

Urwin, Derek, and William Paterson, eds. *Politics in Western Europe Today: Perspectives, Policies and Problems Since 1980* (New York: Longman, 1990).

Williams, Allan M. *The European Community: The Contradictions of Integration* (Cambridge: Blackwell, 1991).

Wistrich, Ernest. *After 1992: The United States of Europe* (New York: Routledge, 1990).

World Bank. *World Development Report* (New York: Oxford University Press, 1999).

23

U.S.–Japan Trade Rivalry
INTERDEPENDENCE

Introduction

Over the centuries, chauvinistic politicians have proclaimed their nation's independence from the rest of the world. In the United States, isolationism—the notion that America should ignore events in Europe as inconsequential—was the dominant philosophy throughout the nineteenth century. In the twentieth century, such attitudes have been dispelled by the recognition that the country is far from immune to changes beyond its shores. World leaders became impressed by the apparent interconnectedness of international events: Increases in oil prices in Saudi Arabia led to layoffs and smaller cars in Detroit; Vietnamese desires for independence and national unity precipitated the fall of Lyndon Johnson; European efforts to gain food security led to trade wars with Japan and the United States. This kind of mutual vulnerability and sensitivity is called interdependence.

Interdependence is both a condition and an objective of policy. By itself it has little moral content, other than to say that nations and states are bound to be affected by each other's actions—particularly in the economic realm. Technology has much to do with this linkage, as anyone can attest who has sent an e-mail to or visited a website created by someone on the other side of the globe. The cost of travel and telephone service have dropped precipitously, so that in addition to communicating over the web, we can hear the voices and see the faces of people across the planet far more cheaply than in years past. To illustrate, when this author was born (1960), the airfare between New York and London was about $400, which, interestingly enough, is roughly the same as the rate charged today. The difference, of course, is that average incomes in 1960 were on the order of $2,000 per year, while today they are on the order of $35,000. In 1960, a typical worker would have had to spend almost two and one-half months' wages on a plane ticket—the equivalent of $7,000 today. Likewise, overseas telephone calls cost roughly twenty times more than they did twenty years ago, after adjusting for inflation.

Many countries set out to deliberately increase their interdependence, mostly by lowering or eliminating trade barriers, obstacles to foreign investment, regulations on currency flows, and so forth. The result is that firms can do business with overseas suppliers and customers at a fraction of the cost and inconvenience compared to those incurred in years past. Global trade is growing at roughly four times the rate of global production, with the implication that all firms everywhere must contend with increasing levels of foreign competition. In the 1970s, American auto manufacturers had to fear only the other members of the Big Three, except perhaps in the economy car segment. Today, luxury car makers such as Cadillac and truck builders such as General Motors face stiff competition from Japanese auto makers (and they often lose the battle). American workers are losing their jobs because their firms' products are not competitive with the foreign goods that are entering the U.S. market with increasing ease (of course, the same is true of French workers losing out to Germans, and so forth). This is what is really meant by "interdependence."

We have all heard the stories of Japan's economic power. Although it is not as fearsome as it was before the financial crisis of 1997, Americans continue to buy more than twice as many goods from Japan as the Japanese buy from the United States. In some sectors, such as automobiles, televisions, and steel, Japanese firms have driven major American firms out of existence. This brief review of the crisis in U.S.–Japan trade relations from 1975 to 1997 explores several explanations and solutions for this problem. It is hoped that whether you think corporate America, Japanese protectionism, the General Agreement on Tariffs and Trade (GATT), or something else is to blame, you will come away from this review more sophisticated and tolerant, if not necessarily certain of the future.

U.S.–JAPAN TRADE RIVALRY
KEY FIGURES

Commodore Matthew Perry   American naval officer in the 1850s who "opened" Japan to the West.

General Douglas MacArthur   American military officer who supervised the occupation of Japan after World War II. He helped promote democracy and economic growth through state-sponsored industrialization.

Jimmy Carter   U.S. President, 1977–1981. He was the first of many presidents to negotiate new trade rules with Japan.

Yasuhiro Nakasone   Prime Minister of Japan, 1982–1987. He offered trade concessions and economic reforms to forestall congressional sanctions.

(continued)

Ronald Reagan   US President, 1981–1989. He took a tough approach to opening Japanese markets.

George H. W. Bush   U.S. President, 1989–1993. He introduced the Structural Impediments Initiative.

Bill Clinton   U.S. President, 1993–2001.

George W. Bush   U.S. President, 2001–present.

Shintaro Ishihara   Senior Liberal Party leader, Governor of Tokyo, 1999–present. He advocated a strong Japan in *The Japan That Can Say No* in the late 1980s and is known for using shocking rhetoric.

Akio Morita   Founder and chairman of Sony Corporation until his retirement in 1993. He advocated a strong Japan in *The Japan That Can Say No* in the late 1980s.

U.S.–JAPAN TRADE RIVALRY
CHRONOLOGY

1853
Commodore Perry "opens" Japan to the West.

1941
Japan attacks Pearl Harbor, in part due to U.S. efforts to cut off imports.

1945
General MacArthur supervises the occupation and reconstruction of Japan after World War II.

1977
Jimmy Carter sends a delegation to Tokyo to negotiate new trade and monetary arrangements as the U.S. trade deficit with Japan becomes an important issue.

1982
Deepening U.S. recession increases the competitive pressure on U.S. firms, in turn increasing pressure on the Reagan administration to intervene in the trade war. The White House negotiates "voluntary export restraints" by Japan.

1986
The U.S. Treasury takes steps to allow the dollar to drop in value so as to promote U.S. exports.

1988
The Omnibus Trade and Competitiveness Act is passed by Congress. It includes the Super 301 provision requiring the President to impose sanctions on unfair trading partners.

1990
George H. W. Bush introduces the Structural Impediments Initiative which seeks to take more control in dealing with Japanese trade problems.

1992
Bush visits Tokyo to promote U.S. exports. The event is less than inspiring; Bush becomes ill in public..

1995
U.S.–Japanese trade negotiations break off.

1997
The Asian financial crisis pushes the Japanese and other Asian economies into a deep recession. The Clinton administration introduces the Enhanced Initiative to persuade Japan to open markets in certain areas.

(continued)

1998

United States launches an effort to restrict Japanese steel imports; it fails.

2001

George W. Bush introduces the Partnership for Growth. By this point, congressional concern is focused on China's accession to the WTO rather than Japan, which is mired in recession.

2002

The United States imposes a 30 percent tariff on Japanese (and other countries') steel imports.

Early Contacts and Japanese Ascension: 1850–1945

The first American tourist who visited Japan in 1848 was captured, caged, and put on display in Tokyo, as was the custom at the time (Lewis 1991, 17). Perhaps even more amusing than this rather curious treatment was that sailor's name was Ranald (pronounced "Ronald") MacDonald (perhaps the Japanese were better at recognizing a threat to the status quo than they are given credit)!

Commodore Matthew Perry opened the Japanese economy with a show of force and savvy diplomatic protocol in 1853, and by 1858 the conservative Tokugawa shogunate had accepted trade agreements with France, Russia, and Britain. In 1868, the Meiji dynasty came to power with a vow to modernize the nation and open it up to foreign influence. By systematically suppressing domestic reactionary opposition, the new government established a modern, industrialized, increasingly cosmopolitan, and relatively democratic social order in what had previously been a land forbidden to foreigners (*Atlas of World History* 1987, 136).

Japan began to act like a world power in defeating Russia in 1895, annexing Korea in 1910, and entering World War I on the Allied side in 1914. During the 1920s, Japanese policy became more openly aggressive, with the occupation of China's Shantung province, in spite of international protest, and the subsequent occupation of all Manchuria in northern China. The Japanese government, as a result of assassination and coup d'état, lost its democratic content, culminating in the ascension of Prime Minister Hideki Tojo in 1941 and the establishment of a military dictatorship. The experience of World War II is well known and need not be reviewed here.

Post–World War II Relations: 1945–1975

The occupying American armies under General Douglas MacArthur played an active role in reorganizing the Japanese economy, society, and polity. The so-called Peace Constitution, which prohibits the establishment of an offensive military capability and the deployment of Japanese troops overseas, was strongly encouraged by the occupying army and has been embraced by Japanese society as a whole. The famed "keiretsu," large family-dominated economic conglomerates (the Mitsubishi and Matsui keiretsu were the largest private firms at the turn of the century), were dismembered and the government was charged with playing an active role in shaping the new Japanese economy.

For twenty years the United States encouraged export-led economic growth and prudent monetary policy in an effort to more completely incorporate Japan into the global economic system, even if it meant trade disadvantages for the United States in the short term (Destler 1979, 191). The Truman and Eisenhower administrations expended considerable political capital to bring Japan into the General Agreement on Tariffs and Trade (GATT) and other liberal institutions. This is not to say that the United States was unwilling to impose protectionist measures on Japan, as its voluntary export restraint (VER) agreement on textiles in the 1950s attests (Friman 1992). This mechanism allowed the United States to impose an informal quota on Japanese textile imports by obtaining Japan's voluntary—if coerced—consent to limit exports to the United States, while preserving the appearance of free trade. The informal arrangement also permitted the Japanese to pursue an export-led growth strategy while avoiding direct foreign control because bilateral arrangements were concluded outside the multilateral GATT agreements (Rapp and Feldman 1979, 118).

Even aggressive industrialization and export-led growth in Japan, however, were not enough to overcome a substantial trade deficit with both the United States and the rest of the world until 1965—twenty years after the end of the war (Destler 1979, 194). The Japanese learned to incorporate basic technologies in electronics and steel as well as to build on their successful textiles and shipbuilding industries by analyzing foreign technology and seeking access to international scientific communities. Along the way, the Japanese government made use of cooperative arrangements with business and labor at home to forge a genuinely Japanese economic program.

Between 1967 and 1973, several developments strained U.S.–Japan relations. To begin, the United States escalated its involvement in the Vietnam War, much to Tokyo's dismay. The strain this situation placed on U.S.–Japan relations was severe, and the pacifist elements of the Liberal Democratic party as well as the growing Socialist party urged a reconsideration of the U.S.–Japan security treaty. Japan also began to post a trade surplus with the United States, which contributed to a severe U.S. balance of payments deficit by 1971. Finally, U.S. refusal to work with the Communist government in China became increasingly difficult for Japan and pressures mounted on Japan to recognize Beijing in spite of U.S. objections.

These pressures were addressed in a variety of ways. In 1971, the United States went off the gold standard and placed a 10 percent tariff on all imported goods, including those from Japan. After this shock treatment, the United States quickly resurrected the free trade philosophy and set in motion the Tokyo Round of multilateral tariff reductions. The United States placed extraordinary pressure on Japan to restrict its textile exports to the United States and, though it did not concede, Japan undertook a dramatic liberalization of its quota restrictions on industrial products during the period. The United States also ended the Vietnam War and took dramatic steps to recognize the People's Republic of China, both actions that liberated Japan diplomatically. By the end of the period of upheaval, U.S.–Japan relations became as warm as ever (Destler 1979, 194). Japan had emerged not as a secondary political ally but as a primary economic rival (Cohen 1985, 17).

Economic Rivalry: 1975–1997

"By the mid-seventies, Japan's emergence as a bona fide international economic superpower had become a sensitive global issue" (Cohen 1985, 24). Concerned about arousing envy among its neighbors, Japan undertook several reforms aimed at reducing the economic imbalance: lowering tariffs, both unilaterally and in the context of the Tokyo Round; revaluing the yen so that American and European products would be more competitive in Japan and less attractive abroad; accepting a number of rather unequal bilateral trade-restricting agreements—in color televisions, for example; and refraining from retaliating against blatantly unfair unilateral trade practices—such as tough new provisions in U.S. trade law. Nonetheless, much of this effort was seen as either "too little too late" or merely "window dressing," and fundamental structural problems persisted.

In 1977, U.S. President Jimmy Carter inflated the U.S. economy to pull the world out of the post-oil shock recession, but he could not persuade Japan to do likewise (MacEachron 1979, 15). Later that year, a delegation of U.S. officials went to Tokyo in an attempt to forge a far-reaching bilateral agreement that would satisfy both American exporters frustrated at their inability to penetrate the Japanese market and American manufacturers worried about continued Japanese encroachment and its rising U.S. market share. Although overdramatized, the meetings managed to produce more Japanese promises to liberalize and a general commitment to undertake a more consumption-oriented economic strategy (Destler 1979).

Although Japan made some effort during the late 1970s to open access to the Japanese market, its policy of maintaining an "undervalued" yen and promoting high savings rates perpetuated the imbalance. The value of a nation's currency is, in a way, a price adjuster for the entire country's goods bound for foreign markets. Just as with a "half-off" sale at a department store, a currency that is kept artificially low through national policies (low interest rates, for example) serves as an across-the-board discount to foreign buyers. Some argue that the yen's undervaluation was a key factor in the trade deficit in 1982 (Turay 1991, 11). Others point out that even during the period of a strong yen in the early 1970s, the trade deficit increased (Rapp and Feldman 1979, 121).

With the recession of 1982 and growing frustration on the part of both the Japanese and Americans for what had come to be perceived as a problem largely of the other party's making, U.S.–Japan relations hit a new low. In several areas, Japan had all but eliminated trade restrictions; to Americans, however, it was the remaining restrictions that caused the most grief. In beef and citrus, a Japanese quota prevented increasing American exports (although Japanese officials were quick to point out that U.S. exports were relatively high in spite of this—Tomabechi 1985). Rice imports were banned altogether. Customs and inspection procedures in Japan had long been cumbersome and seemingly arbitrary. Japanese attempts to convince Americans of the sincerity of their attachment to free trade fell on deaf ears (Turay 1991, 11). As put by Cohen:

> The market opening measures announced by the government of Japan in 1980 were the first of a long series, without precedent in their volume, their tentativeness, and their failure to produce any significant change in Japanese import patterns. (Cohen 1991a, 32–33)

Not until the mid-1980s was Prime Minister Yasuhiro Nakasone able to convince U.S. President Ronald Reagan that Japan was embarking on a new course. Reagan was eager to embrace the affable Nakasone, although most midlevel officials and corporate executives were unimpressed. Much of this skepticism resulted from Japanese efforts to give the appearance of cooperativeness without the substance. For example, the Japanese government initiated talks in 1981 on restricting the number of automobiles headed for the United States to 1.7 million per year to avert what it perceived as growing hostility toward successful Japanese subcompacts. The apparent goal of this action was to give American firms some "breathing room" to develop quality subcompacts of their own. Two unanticipated consequences resulted, however: the relocation of Japanese firms to the United States (transplants) and the gradual "upscaling" of Japanese imported vehicles (note the introduction of the Acura, Lexus, and Infiniti lines) where profit margins are greater. Neither of these moves helped U.S. corporations and, in fact, have made competition fiercer (Japanese can take advantage of low real estate and pension costs in the United States) over a wider range of products (which now include luxury, sport, minivan, small pickup, and even large pickup trucks—an American bastion).

In 1986, the overall trade deficit for the United States was approaching $150 billion, while Japan was enjoying a trade surplus of roughly $100 billion. The trend was exacerbated by an overvalued dollar fueled by high interest rates, which in turn were swelled by a $2 trillion federal debt and growing annual budget deficits (Cohen 1991a, 42). The United States became the world's largest debtor and Japan the largest creditor, even passing the United States in total foreign aid. The pressures from Congress to act vigorously against Japanese trade barriers became intolerable. In 1985, Congress came close to passing protectionist legislation, and Congressman Richard Gephardt pressed actively for increased pressure on Japan (Gephardt 1989). Secretary of the Treasury James Baker moved toward a policy of devaluation of the dollar, and the overall trade deficit narrowed from a high of $170 billion in 1987 to less than $100 billion by 1990. In spite of this, the U.S. deficit with Japan remained roughly the same (see Figure 23.1).

Congress finally acted with the passage of the 1988 Omnibus Trade and Competitiveness Act, which contained the Super 301 provision requiring the

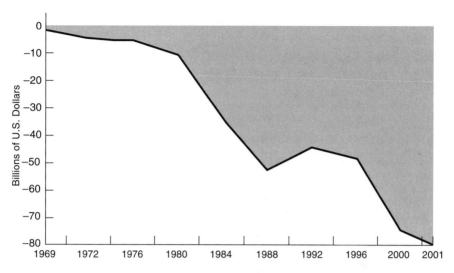

Figure 23.1   U.S. trade deficit with Japan, 1969–2001.
Source: Survey of Current Business, various issues.

new administration of George H. W. Bush to identify countries that were guilty of a pattern of unfair trade and single out specific issues to target. The administration was placed in an extremely awkward position of implementing trade policy initiated by Congress, but it managed to select programs that would minimize international conflict (Krauss and Reich 1992). These negotiations had the effect of liberalizing trade in supercomputers (a technology whose obsolescence was a major factor in IBM's 1992 downsizing), satellites, and wood products. Again, however, U.S. discontent was not assuaged and trade negotiations in both Tokyo and Geneva at the GATT meetings became increasingly hostile.

Another development in the relationship was the emergence of a so-called revisionist school of Japanese international relations. Beginning with Chalmers Johnson in the early 1980s and since joined by Stephen Krasner and a host of analysts, the revisionist school argues that Japan is an inherently different type of country—a "developmental state"—that will never be fully absorbed into the Western world (Johnson 1982; Krasner 1987). Revisionists argue that Japanese culture and social structure are unitary, in the sense that they are so tightly intertwined as to be inseparable, and efforts to negotiate with one element of the nation will lead to frustration. The implication was that the United States and others victimized by Japan, Inc., should aim at changing the entire society to create an environment of free and fair trade.

Japanese officials and executives, on their side, began to develop a more intransigent and openly defiant tone by the 1990s, directly accusing the West of blaming Japan for its own problems (Tomabechi 1985). In *The Japan That Can Say No,* Shintaro Ishihara forcefully argued that Japan was strong enough to resist pressure to accommodate the West (Ishihara 1991). The commemoration of the fiftieth anniversary of Pearl Harbor Day was a cause for increased acrimony rather than healing (Baker and Frost 1992). In other words, both positions seemed to be hardening, and only a temporary slowdown in the Japanese economy prevented what would have amounted to a trade war in 1992.

In 1995, trade talks collapsed entirely, but the United States and Japan continued to negotiate over market access in specific sectors: automobiles and auto parts, telecommunications, housing, pharmaceuticals, legal services, retail distribution, and government policy processes (Department of Commerce 1999). Japan, for its part, continued fighting anti-dumping duties imposed in the United Sates on its exports of steel.

A Respite from Conflict: 1997 and Beyond

The Asian financial crisis of 1997 plunged the economies of all East Asian nations into financial chaos. Not only did the currencies of Thailand and Indonesia plummet, leading to a catastrophic loss of value to stock markets and in real estate, but the Japanese economy followed suit as a result of its financial commitments in the region and weak banking structures. Japan attempted to rescue some of these countries through a policy of cheap money (Fischer 1998), but this measure proved inadequate to solve the problem, which ultimately required large infusions of cash from the IMF and Western banks and governments. Japan's economy slipped into recession, resulting in rising unemployment. It was not until 2002 that Japan posted its first positive quarterly growth, signaling the end to the recession (*New York Times*, June 7, 2002).

During this period, the trade deficit with Japan became stable, leveling off at roughly $80 billion. In 2001, the overall trade deficit shrank for the first time in a decade (*Survey of Current Business*, April 2002). This result could be considered either a cause or an effect of a new series of initiatives put forward by the Clinton and Bush administrations. In 1997, Clinton initiated the Enhanced Initiative on Deregulation and Competition Policy, which focused on a broad range of strategies that Japan would take to open its markets and liberalize its regulatory system. The program had many positive effects, as noted by Clinton administration officials (USTR 2000). George W. Bush took an even more conciliatory approach by forging the U.S.–Japan Economic Partnership for Growth, which created a number of joint panels to discuss mutually beneficial policies.

Nevertheless, U.S.–Japan trade was not without conflict. Steel remained the subject of an ongoing legal and diplomatic struggle. A series of U.S. rulings on dumping by Japanese and other steel exporters led to trade sanctions, which were in turn challenged by Japan and other members of the WTO. The challengers prevailed in early 2001, forcing the administration to withdraw the measures, only to reinstate new tariffs in March 2002. Although Bush has since weakened the tariffs, they were the object of yet another legal challenge at the WTO at the time of this writing.

Japan can thank a robust U.S. economy and a recession at home for diminishing much of the old antagonism. The emergence of China as a potentially larger threat has also distracted American policy makers for now. But the sagging U.S. economy and gradually improving Japanese performance may spell trouble in the months to come. Already, the value of the yen has increased dramatically, rising by 15 percent between April and July 2002, reflecting weakened confidence in the dollar (and the U.S. economy, by inference).

Causes of Conflict and Possible Solutions

The rivalry between the United States and Japan threatens a great many people on both sides of the Pacific and carries the very real danger of escalating to the point that millions, perhaps even hundreds of millions, will see their quality of life seriously diminished as a result of trade war or economic boycotts. To explore the dangers of the present situation and their root causes, we need to spend time on basic economics.

The clash between the United States and Japan can be understood as a conflict between two economic philosophies: laissez-faire capitalism and mercantilism. Laissez-faire is a French phrase meaning "allow it to happen" and refers to the principle of noninterference in the economy on the part of the state. Specifically, laissez-faire economics assumes that the market mechanism of supply and demand is an automatic regulatory mechanism, an "invisible hand," to govern production, distribution, prices, and so on, in a way that leads to the greatest possible social good. Free trade is the keystone of this strategy. As each nation specializes in those products it can produce most efficiently given its "factor endowment" (relative amounts and quality of land, labor, and capital), prices will fall, demand and production will rise, and greater wealth and employment will result. Trade is the epitome of the win-win situation.

Mercantilism is based on realist assumptions about national power and security and takes for granted that a state has an obligation to protect and defend the economic and natural resources of the nation. Mercantilists do not accept the invisible hand theory, arguing that wealth will tend to gravitate toward those nations that happen to be endowed with marketable factors, whether it be natural resources, human capital, abundance of fertile land, or whatever. The terms of trade (meaning the unit-to-unit prices of exports relative to imports) of products from tropical and less well-endowed regions will tend to deteriorate: To exchange their goods for a given quantity of goods from more naturally fortunate countries, they will be forced to produce ever increasing amounts. The result will be not a win-win situation but a zero-sum arrangement, in which one nation will grow increasingly rich and secure at others' expense. To prevent this scenario, the state must intervene to support uncompetitive industries, especially if they are deemed essential to the national interest (products that have strategic, political, cultural, or other significance to the government in power). This can be done by limiting access to the home market or by providing incentives and subsidies for local producers.

No nation can be described as a "pure" free trader or a "pure" mercantilist. The United States is far from free in areas such as steel, textiles, agriculture, and professional sports. Conversely, even Japan's economy is extremely liberal in its tariff levels. But in general terms, the conflict between the two nations can be characterized in these terms. This terminology will help you recognize patterns in the following description of general problems and solutions to the trade dispute.

Macroeconomics and U.S.–Japan Trade

Of perhaps greatest significance in international trade are the national policies that affect exchange rates, because this single variable automatically affects the price of all traded goods. The currency rate is controlled indirectly in the current international system of floating exchange rates, where supply and demand are the ultimate determinants. Why do some currencies attract more buyers than others? First, the amount of products the nation sells determines much of this demand: For nearly every export from the United States, a payment must be made in dollars, which requires the exchanging of one currency for dollars—a purchase of dollars, as it were. The level of exports is in turn determined by the competitiveness of the products—which is affected by the exchange rate. Second, investors seeking a higher return on their more liquid funds seek out nations that offer high interest rates in relation to their inflation rate (the real interest rate). Comparing interest rates across countries reveals where the return is greatest and which currency must be acquired to make that investment.

What determines an interest rate? Again, the determinants are indirect and complex, but here are the key factors: The prime lending rate the Federal Reserve Bank charges its best customers. The amount of debt in the nation relative to lendable funds—in particular, the amount of debt incurred by the government. The general productivity and health of the economy (bankruptcies tend to drive up interest rates as bankers attempt to recoup their losses). Economists argue that currency exchange rates should be based primarily on "purchasing power parity," a concept that describes what you can buy at home with a given country's currency. In Japan, for example, the prices of many consumer goods are inflated, such that the yen simply does not buy as much as a dollar in the United States. (Japanese people will fly to American cities to buy sophisticated Japanese-made electronics and pay for the ticket with what they save!) Finally, currency exchange rates are affected by governments acting directly to produce currency (the money supply), holding onto other nations' currencies as a reserve asset, and selling or buying their own currency to or from other nations.

Fred Bergsten and William Cline have long emphasized that the key to achieving balance in U.S. trade is to cut the national debt, balance the annual federal budget, and thereby lower the interest rate and the value of the dollar (Bergsten and Cline 1987). Observers noted that with a small decline in the nominal interest rates in the United States and a relatively rapid decline of the dollar after 1986 (which had to be slowed down by the Japanese purchasing large amounts of dollars), some tightening of the trade deficit did occur without the predicted inflationary effects in the United States (Yoshitomi 1989). In fact, the overall U.S. trade deficit shrank by roughly 30 percent in the late 1980s, although the deficit with Japan rose again to its $50 billion level. Although cutting the deficit and increasing the savings rate should generally be good for the U.S. economy and for the overall trade balance, the roots of the U.S.–Japan trade problem lie elsewhere.

The strength of the American economy throughout the 1990s has been a mixed blessing for U.S.–Japan trade relations because it has been a time of relative stagnation in Asia, particularly since 1997. The weakness of Japan's economy created important opportunities for American corporations to purchase real estate and businesses in Japan that had been priced too high for years. Coupled with a remarkably aggressive negotiating stance by the Clinton administration, this has tended to reduce the trade deficit by placing more American products in Japanese hands (the semiconductor talks resulted in American firms capturing more than 20 percent of the Japanese market—Maswood 1997, 537). Also, the recession in Japan and across Asia has meant that the Japanese not only are reluctant to increase imports from the United States, but also have surplus production that must be sold to prevent a financial meltdown (*Economist,* September 20, 1997, 87). The United States interceded by letting the dollar increase in value, with the natural result that Americans could afford more Japanese imports. In the last three years of the Clinton era, the U.S.–Japan trade deficit rose from less than $50 billion to $75 billion. It is ironic that the monetary policy of strengthening the dollar was carried out by an administration so keen on forcing open the Japanese market to U.S. goods that it nearly brought the newly created World Trade Organization to its knees over a dispute with Japan on steel trade at precisely the same moment.

American and Japanese Corporate Tactics

By corporate tactics, we mean a whole array of actions available to private corporations acting alone and in conjunction with other private and even public actors. Naturally, the same sorts of things that make a product more successful at home contribute to its success abroad: quality, usefulness, appropriateness, marketing strategy, distribution network, and so on. These obvious factors have often escaped corporate leaders in their debates over Japanese trade policy. It wasn't until 1992, following a disastrous trip to Tokyo by President Bush and Detroit auto executives ("to bush" has become a slang verb in Japanese meaning "to vomit"), that a U.S. auto firm seriously marketed a car with right-side drive in Japan even though the Japanese have always driven on the left! American firms doing business with Japan are finally learning that the 1 percent error tolerance they were used to is unacceptable in Japan, where products must generally have no more than 0.1 percent errors. Even at the most basic levels of communication, very few U.S. corporate executives can speak Japanese, whereas fluency in English is almost universal among Japanese businessmen (although living overseas for extended periods of time can lead to a subtle ostracism for a Japanese person).

The modern version of the keiretsu has been an obstacle in U.S.–Japan trade negotiations (Powell and Rich 1991). These vast conglomerates coordinate a wide variety of activities under unified management. Numerous senior Japanese executives enjoy membership on several corporate boards and work with the government to protect their vast interests.

This situation is especially pronounced in the banking sector, where secret promises to protect banks from poorly performing loan portfolios exposed the Japanese financial system to near catastrophe in the mid-1990s. The Asian financial crisis of 1997, which initially involved an overvalued Thai baht supported by a precariously structured banking and real estate network, led to the devaluation of most Asian currencies and the collapse of their equity and property markets. For example, during the last six months of 1997, Indonesia saw its currency fall to less than 20 percent of its previous value and its stock market lost 85 percent of its value. Because Japan had invested heavily in the region and depended on those countries for a large part of its exports, it also experienced a sudden and profound financial crisis. The government was ill prepared to take strong action to weed out nonperforming banks, however, and instead opted to inflate the economy and keep interest rates artificially low (Fischer 1998).

Networks of supply and purchasing within the conglomerates have effectively shut out foreign firms in many cases (Kreinin 1988). The Japanese government's policy of coordinating economic growth by targeting specific industries with subsidies and joint business–government ventures exacerbates this system. Small and mid-sized American firms seem especially at a loss to understand the intricacies of Japan's market (Namiki 1988). By contrast, Japanese firms generally have little trouble interacting with U.S. firms as suppliers or competitors on American soil.

An important difference in American and Japanese corporate attitudes has been the urgency of getting a return on investment. Every quarter, American firms must reveal their earnings. Shareholders typically expect a profit each quarter and are quick to express frustration and even hostility against chief executive officers and other managers who fail to achieve that goal (Yamamoto 1989/1990). Numerous U.S. corporations, squeezed by heavy debt burdens carried over from the merger mania of the 1980s, have been forced to cut their work forces dramatically to turn a profit quickly, although even such draconian measures have failed. Japanese firms, on the other hand, have traditionally viewed success in terms of market share, or their firm's share of the total purchases of a given product. The result of this view is a strategy of underpricing (verging on dumping, when products are sold for less than production costs) in the initial phases of introducing a new product and lower profits in the early years, combined with intense two-way loyalty between firm and work force. Note U.S. executives' response to the increase in Japanese car prices following implementation of the 1981

VER. Rather than keep their prices lower in the United States to regain market share, U.S. auto firms raised their prices by an average of 14 percent and saw their sales decline by roughly 10 percent (Husted and Melvin 1990, 197). In early 1993, when the U.S. dollar lost 10 percent of its value against the yen, rather than taking advantage of the chance to lower prices and increase market share, American exporters to Japan simply reaped a 10 percent windfall profit instead (*New York Times,* May 5, 1993, A1).

This is not to say that U.S. firms are irrevocably outclassed by Japanese corporations. Federal Express regularly receives visits from Japanese management analysts, a mid-sized firm in Seattle exports tons of chop sticks to Japan each year, and several service industries have forged trans-Pacific links (Sutton 1992; Lewis 1991, 13). IBM, NCR, McDonald's, and other firms have flourishing operations in Japan and have little difficulty exporting their products. The key ingredient seems to be whether existing Japanese firms have already developed a similar product (copyright rules are broadly interpreted and strictly enforced). At any rate, U.S. firms have some hope for doing business in and with Japan.

National Trade Policies and Negotiations

In 1991, a California salesman placed a one-pound bag of U.S.-grown rice on a display table at a trade show in Tokyo. Within moments customs officials seized the bag and fined him for bringing an illegal substance into the country: foreign rice! This treatment was perfectly predictable, but it highlights a perception of Japan as a protectionist country. Is this perception valid?

A wide array of policies are available to any state that seeks to promote exports and inhibit imports. The most obvious is a tariff on imports—a simple tax assessed at the border based on the type and value of the product. Every nation has tariff barriers, although the successive multilateral trade negotiations sponsored by the GATT have dramatically reduced them—particularly those tariffs that relate to manufactured goods. Japan, along with the rest of the world, has dropped its tariff rates to the point that on specific products they are generally lower than those of the United States and other industrialized countries, and are much lower overall (see Table 23.1 and Turay 1991).

Tariffs are not the primary means of protecting markets; many other so-called nontariff barriers exist. Quotas, or numerical caps, are a common alternative to tariffs and are not uncommon in Japan. The ban on imported rice has been mentioned, but twenty-six other quotas on both agricultural and manufactured goods have been implemented as well (Turay 1991, 18). Retaliatory measures have frequently been taken by France, Germany, Italy, and the United States. The introduction of VERs is aimed at removing quotas and other barriers by informally instituting retaliatory quotas on the other side. VERs in automobiles, textiles, semiconductors, and other areas have been set in place. Even so, all tariffs, quotas, and VERs violate the spirit and often the letter of the GATT agreements, although because VERs are rarely formalized, they fall between the legal cracks (Krishna 1989, 75–76).

Table 23.1 Tariff Rates for Selected Countries, 1987
(Nominal Tariff Weighted by Own-Country Imports)

	Japan	United States	Germany	United Kingdom
Textiles	3.3*	9.2	7.4	6.7
Clothing	13.8	22.7	13.4	13.3*
Wood products	0.3*	1.7	2.9	3.1
Furniture	5.1	4.1*	5.6	5.6
Paper products	2.1	0.2*	5.2	4.9
Rubber products	1.1*	2.5	3.8	2.7
Iron and steel	2.8*	3.6	5.9	4.7
Metal products	5.2	4.8*	5.4	5.6
Glass products	5.1*	6.2	7.9	7.9
Electrical machinery	4.3*	4.4	8.3	8.1
Nonelectrical machinery	4.4	3.3*	4.5	4.2
Manufactures (miscellaneous)	4.6	4.2	5.6	3.0*
Overall	2.9*	4.3	6.3	5.2

*Lowest tariff of the four nations on these items.

Source: Steven L. Husted and Michael Melvin. *International Economics* (New York: Harper & Row, 1990).

Other techniques employed to restrict trade include health and safety regulations, cumbersome customs procedures, licensing fees, domestic content legislation, government procurement policies, restricted bidding arrangements, export subsidies, and subsidies for local producers. Each is found easily in both the United States and Japan, but they fail to tell the whole story. As put by Bergsten and Cline, "It is clear that any difference that does exist can explain, at most, a modest part of the bilateral trade imbalance or even its growth in recent years . . . [and] is not nearly enough to justify the shrill calls for 'reciprocity' which imply that the playing field is tilted sharply against the United States" (Bergsten and Cline 1987, 119).

Of much greater significance is the general support of industry by the Japanese and U.S. governments through research and development incentives, infrastructure development, employee training programs, and other measures. These arrangements typically have long historical and deep political roots and are particularly impervious to efforts at reform. They are more properly viewed as cultural factors.

As explained by the revisionists, Japanese society is better understood not as a free market but as a national movement. The state plays such an active part in promoting specific industries, such as consumer electronics, that businesses experience little in the way of market pressure. One can compare the treatment of Japanese consumer-oriented firms to the American treatment of defense contractors. As put by Stephen Krasner:

At the core of the developmental state are a group of interlocked private, political, and public institutions—large industrial and financial enterprises, the Liberal Democratic Party, the Ministry of Finance, and the Ministry of International Trade and Industry (MITI)—which share core values emphasizing the central importance of aggregate economic performance. . . . The survival of the community, rather than the interests of particular groups or individuals, is the fundamental objective. (Krasner 1987, 13)

But how does one fight against these obstacles? Tariffs and quotas are perhaps the easiest to deal with because there is legal and diplomatic precedent for removing these barriers. In fact, bilateral negotiations, which have become increasingly broad, have produced some modest results, albeit largely superficial ones. The more coercive talks stemming from the Super 301 actions in 1989 were targeted at steel, semiconductors, and certain agricultural products. Regrettably, the results of these talks, though apparently promising, have done little to end the result of trade imbalance (U.S. Congress 1988).

One could easily consider two options, which need not be mutually exclusive. First, American firms could abandon the goal of penetrating the Japanese market and instead focus on building up industry at home to better compete against Japanese imports. Alternatively, American firms and negotiators could take a more aggressive approach to open Japanese markets while maintaining the status quo at home. The former approach has been supported by internationalists, many Democrats, and laissez-faire economists who fear trade wars. The national elite have generally swung in favor of what could be called an "industrial strategy" of public sector promotion of consumer-oriented manufacturing and technology. Rather than concentrating as it has on military technology, the industrial strategy would promote such innovative technologies as high-definition television, commercial aircraft, high-speed railway systems, and a variety of "green" technologies such as electric cars. If in fact macroeconomics and trade negotiations are of limited value, then this approach promises substantial rewards, at the cost of rigid adherence to laissez-faire economics.

The more aggressive approach is advocated by long-time trade negotiators who are increasingly impatient and revisionists who fear Japanese ascendance and power. The Structural Impediments Initiative aimed at addressing a wide variety of nontariff and even invisible barriers to trade with Japan (U.S. Congress 1990). The results have been modest, but the scope of the talks is encouraging. Unfortunately, it is just this sort of negotiation that has precipitated the anti-American sentiment described earlier. U.S. negotiators are portrayed as either whiners or bullies, generally unwilling to admit their own mistakes. Targeting specific sectors with threats of retaliation, though promising in the short run, seem to be souring the atmosphere in the long run. There is also a limit to the effectiveness of bilateral strategies because Japan's economy is becoming increasingly diversified, in terms of both products and trading partners (Japanese trade with other Asian countries now exceeds its trade with the United States). The GATT has been unable to impose penalties—its enforcement powers revolve around granting authorization to a country that has proved its injury to take unilateral retaliatory steps (in essence, the lynch mob gets permission from the judge before hanging the prisoner!). In general, the retaliatory strategy presents the greatest risk of a trade war.

Social and Cultural Forces

We observed earlier that the devaluation of the dollar since 1986 has apparently had little effect on U.S.–Japan trade. As put by Shafiquil Islam, "The failure of macroeconomics to reduce the trade imbalances is no surprise because the problem is structural and cultural: Japan keeps its markets closed through various unfair trade practices, and its economy does not respond to exchange-rate changes and usual market forces" (Islam 1989/1990, 177). We have already noted the keiretsu, corporate relations with government, and other cultural factors that inhibit trade with the United States. "Only cultural factors can explain why the Japanese continue to venerate a large trade surplus long after they have achieved a strong industrial base and massive holdings of foreign reserves" (Cohen 1991a, 231).

Japanese society is largely governed by the twin social obligations known as giri and on through which any favor commits the recipient to being beholden essentially forever. A key to binding together the society, these feelings of mutual obligation to neighbors, relatives, and business associates tend to exclude outsiders. Extremely inefficient and expensive corner stores not only cater to locals but maintain ties with grown-up children who have moved away by providing catalogues of their overpriced wares. Corporate loyalty on the part of employees is notorious, including extensive hazing ceremonies and long hours of obligatory social drinking with co-workers after work. Japanese workers spend 10 percent more time on the job than their American counterparts, primarily out of duty.

Trade-related Japanese culture is also expressed in the high savings rate and reluctance in many circles to consume. This phenomenon is in the midst of change, and young professionals are increasingly afraid of dying from overwork (known as *karoshi*—Kawahito 1991). Travel and leisure are increasing significantly, and the savings rate is declining somewhat.

Contrast this with the American attitude most of us know well, of carrying large debt burdens so as to enjoy the benefits of consumer goods. Although leisure time is contracting in relative terms, household expenditures and debt levels reached alarming proportions in the late 1980s, with the result that during the recession of 1990–1992 millions were forced out of their homes and saw their belongings repossessed. U.S. workers feel little loyalty to American corporations, which likewise show little willingness to sacrifice on their employees' behalf. Exorbitant CEO compensation, widespread layoffs, and general downsizing have left many demoralized and resentful.

Regarding Japanese politics, the Liberal Democratic party, which ruled Japan since the mid-1950s, is better understood as a collection of factions led by various professional politicians. Political support is based on sectoral support from key industrial and economic groups, such as the powerful rice farmers (rural areas are disproportionately represented because there has been no redistricting since the 1950s in spite of substantial rural flight). Japanese governments have fallen as a result of trade liberalization policies, and bureaucratic resistance to change is great (Curran 1985). In addition, a compulsion to dominate has become apparent in Japanese trade policy, as explained by Drucker, who describes Japan as an "adversarial trader":

> Competitive trade aims at creating a customer. Adversarial trade aims at domi-nating an industry . . . competitive trade is fighting a battle. Adversarial trade aims at winning the war by destroying the enemy's army and its capacity to fight. (Drucker 1988, 129–130, cited in Cohen 1991a, 229)

American trade negotiators generally lack an appreciation for the com-plexities of Japanese political life, particularly after the electoral defeats of the Liberal Democratic party in the early 1990s and the resulting turmoil in Tokyo. The semiconductor agreements worked in part because of support within Japan from key industries that welcomed cheaper imports to com-pete with overpriced domestic goods. The negotiations on automobiles, on the other hand, came to naught in part because of a lack of effort on the part of U.S. negotiators to identify Japanese allies (Maswood 1997). This trend is part and parcel of a shift in Japanese perceptions of the social framework of the negotiations themselves: They generally have less deference and respect for U.S. negotiators (Shoppa 1999).

When it comes to U.S. politics, it is important to understand the ambiva-lence that the government now feels toward free trade. The executive branch has historically been devoted to free trade, although for much of the postwar era Congress has attempted to inhibit this liberal impulse. Whereas Democ-rats generally favored free trade through the 1960s, the free trade baton has been passed to the Republicans. The net result of this vacillation on trade policy across time, parties, and branches of government is a strange collec-tion of programs and policies with conflicting purposes. The United States drafted and signed the GATT and all other international free trade programs while preserving protectionism in agriculture, textiles, autos, steel, and many other areas. These actions are dependent on the positions of parties and politicians as well as on the effectiveness of lobbyists working on behalf of foreign interests (a situation described in great detail in Choate 1990).

Other general societal and cultural factors that have an impact on U.S.–Japan trade include the relatively high costs of health care, insurance, and litigation in the United States in comparison to Japan and the high cost of real estate in Japan relative to the United States. It is estimated that roughly 10 percent of the price of each U.S.-made automobile goes to cover health care costs, while rental costs of office space in Tokyo are roughly twice those of downtown Los Angeles.

In general, the argument that the removal of all trade barriers and macroeconomic impediments will still not lead to balanced trade between Japan and the United States must be taken seriously. This is not to say that Japanese customers will refuse to shop at Toys 'R' Us (as they have) or buy

Levi's jeans (as they do), but rather that for the United States to sell as many products to Japan as America buys will require substantial changes in the basic makeup of Japanese society. As put by Cohen:

> Japan's efforts at internationalization have fallen short of the mark. The country's retention of its insular, tradition-bound mentality has collided with the sheer magnitude of its export success, as well as what is arguably the most pervasive international trend of the late twentieth century: accelerated economic interdependence. (Cohen 1991b, 184)

Conclusion

The number of forces at work in determining a country's trade balance are bewildering, but what is most troubling is sorting out which factors are most significant. Can one sell a useless product if the price is low enough? Can the exchange rate be so high that no one will buy even the best and cheapest products? Is industrial productivity (output per hour worked) more significant than marketing techniques? Perhaps even more important, can lowering Japanese trade barriers assure American exporters of greater success?

In the final analysis, the prospects for a resolution of the U.S.–Japan trade rivalry are rather dim, but one should not automatically conclude that the relationship is destined to deteriorate. The truth of the matter seems to be that "the trade disequilibrium is best viewed as the tip of the iceberg, with domestic factors as the main underlying causal factors" (Cohen 1991b, 153). Although certain "symptoms" of this problem can be addressed via traditional trade policy negotiations, the introduction of the Structural Impediments Initiative represents a promising departure. As tensions mount and accusations intensify, there is real danger that both sides to the dispute will provoke reactions from their rival that will cause hardship all around. To the extent that diplomacy can help bring about the very necessary structural changes within each economy, so much the better, but just as weapons rarely bring peace in and of themselves, trade negotiators must not be expected to carry the burden of the nation.

What does the story of U.S.–Japan trade conflict tell us about the nature of interdependence? In the space of a mere century the United States and Japan went from having no contact whatsoever to fighting a world war against each other, stemming in part from economic conflicts (see Case 2). With the end of World War II, the United States and Japan became inextricably linked as a matter of national policy in both Washington and Tokyo, although no one anticipated the direction in which this relationship would go. The Japanese penetration of the U.S. market was facilitated by generous trade rules promoted by Washington and eagerly accepted by Tokyo, which adopted an outward-oriented development strategy with remarkable success. The result was cheap consumer goods for Americans and economic expansion for the Japanese. Interdependence was working at its best.

The other side of interdependence is apparent in the subsequent experience of the two countries, regardless of the source of the problems. To some extent, Japan was a victim of its particular form of success, while the United States was somewhat slow to adapt to a changing global economic environment. As Japan's formula runs its course and the United States learns to operate in the globalized economy, it is possible that both countries will return to a more happy relationship, while still experiencing considerable interconnectedness.

Debate Topic

Does the U.S. government owe American firms protection from foreign competitors?

PRO
Protectionist sentiment has been explained in many ways: (1) Where evidence indicates that trade is "unfair" for whatever reason, the United States is legally and morally justified in providing relief in the form of protection. (2) It is not the business of the U.S. government to facilitate the growth of foreign countries (at least until their citizens vote in U.S. elections!). (3) Failure of strategic industries, such as steel and electronics, could render the country vulnerable to embargos and weaken its ability to defend itself militarily.

CON
Free-traders argue as follows: (1) The market is what has made America great; policy makers must accept that some firms will not be competitive and should therefore fail. (2) The United States has made numerous international agreements to open its markets and is obligated not to break them. (3) U.S. free market practices offer an important role model for other countries and help induce them to open their markets.

Questions to Consider

1. How does the U.S.–Japan trade rivalry affect an individual consumer? What could a resolution of the problem do to improve one person's life?

2. To what extent is the United States or Japan to blame for the situation? Is the United States a closet mercantilist and Japan a closet free trader?

3. Should the United States take a more aggressive posture toward Japanese trade practices? What would be the likely consequences?

4. How can the United States become more competitive? Whose responsibility should it be?

Websites

U.S. Government Agencies
Department of Commerce: **www.commerce.gov**
U.S. Trade Deficit Review Commission: **www.ustdrc.gov**
U.S. Trade Representative: **www.ustr.gov**

Japanese Government Agencies
Fair Trade Commission: **www.jwindow.net/GOV/CABINER/PMO/ORG.GOV. 04.002.htmlrl**
Ministry of International Trade and Industry: **www.miti.go.jp/index-e.html**
Japan External Trade Organization: **www.jetro.org**
Japan Economic Foundation: **www.jef.or.jp/en/index.html**

References

Atlas of World History (New York: Rand McNally, 1987).

Baker, Howard H., and Ellen L. Frost. "Rescuing the U.S.–Japan Alliance." *Foreign Affairs* 71 #2 (Spring 1992): 97–113.

Barnds, William J. *Japan and the United States: Challenges and Opportunities* (New York: New York University Press, 1979).

Bergsten, C. Fred, and William R. Cline. *The United States–Japan Economic Problem* (Washington, DC: Institute for International Economics, 1987).

Choate, Pat. *Agents of Influence* (New York: Alfred A. Knopf, 1990).

Cohen, Stephen D. *Cowboys and Samurai: Why the United States Is Losing the Industrial Battle and Why It Matters* (New York: HarperBusiness, 1991a).

Cohen, Stephen D. *Uneasy Partnership: Competition and Conflict in U.S.–Japanese Trade Relations* (Cambridge, MA: Ballinger Pub., 1985).

Cohen, Stephen D. "United States–Japanese Trade Relations." *Current History* 90 #555 (April 1991b): 152–155, 184–187.

Curran, Timothy J. "The Politics of Trade Liberalization in Japan" in Katz and Friedman-Lichtschein, eds., *Japan's New World Role*, 105–122.

Department of Commerce, U.S. Trade Deficit Review Commission. "Priority Requests of the United States Government to Japan Under the Enhanced Initiative on Deregulation and Competition Policy," October 1999. Available on USTDRC's website.

Destler, I. M. "U.S.–Japanese Relations and the American Trade Initiative of 1977: Was This 'Trip' Necessary?" in Barnds, *Japan and the United States*, 190–230.

Drucker, Peter. *The New Realities: In Government and Politics/In Economics and Business/In Society and World View* (New York: Harper & Row, 1988).

The Economist (September 20, 1997): 87.

Fischer, Stanley. "The Asian Crisis, the IMF, and the Japanese Economy." Speech delivered in Tokyo on April 8, 1998. Available on the IMF website.

Friman, H. Richard. "Dancing with Pandora: The Eisenhower Administration and the Demise of GATT" (manuscript, 1992).

Gephardt, Richard A. "U.S.–Japanese Trade Relations." *Vital Speeches of the Day* 55 #15 (May 15, 1989): 450–454.

Husted, Steven L., and Michael Melvin. *International Economics* (New York: Harper & Row, 1990).

Ishihara, Shintaro. *The Japan That Can Say No.* Trans. by Frank Baldwin (New York: Simon & Schuster, 1991).

Islam, Shafiquil. "Capitalism in Conflict." *Foreign Affairs* 69 #1 (1989/1990): 172–182.

Johnson, Chalmers. *MITI and the Japanese Miracle: The Growth of Industrial Policy, 1925–1975* (Stanford, CA: Stanford University Press, 1982).

Katz, Joshua, and Tilly C. Friedman-Lichtschein, eds. *Japan's New World Role* (Boulder, CO: Westview Press, 1985).

Kawahito, Hiroshi. "Death and the Corporate Worker." *Japan Quarterly* 38 #2 (April 1991): 149–157.

Krasner, Stephen D. *Asymmetries in Japanese–American Trade: The Case for Specific Reciprocity* (Berkeley, CA: Institute of International Studies, 1987).

Krauss, Ellis S., and Simon Reich. "Ideology, Interests, and the American Executive: Toward a Theory of Foreign Competition and Manufacturing Trade Policy." *International Organization* 46 #4 (Autumn 1992): 857–898.

Kreinin, Mordechai E. "How Closed Is Japan's Market: Additional Evidence." *World Economy* 11 #4 (December 1988): 529–542.

Krishna, Kala. "What Do VERs Do?" in Sato and Nelson, ed., *Beyond Trade Friction*, 75–92.

Lewis, Michael. *Pacific Rift* (New York: W. W. Norton, 1991).

MacEachron, David. "New Challenges to a Successful Relationship" in Barnds, *Japan and the United States*, 1–20.

Mason, T. David, and Abdul M. Turay, eds. *US–Japan Trade Friction* (New York: St. Martin's Press, 1991).

Maswood, Javeed. "Does Revisionism Work? U.S. Trade Strategy and the 1995 U.S.–Japan Auto Dispute." *Pacific Affairs* 70 #4 (Winter 1997): 533–555.

Namiki, Nobuaki. "Japanese Trade Barriers: Perceptions of Small Business Exporters." *Advanced Management Journal* 54 #1 (Winter 1988): 37–41.

New York Times, May 5, 1993, A1.

New York Times, June 7, 2002

Powell, Bill, and Thomas Rich. "Japan: All in the Family." *Newsweek* (June 10, 1991): 38–39.

Rapp, William V., and Robert A. Feldman. "Japan's Economic Strategy and Prospects" in Barnds, *Japan and the United States*, 86–154.

Sato, Ryuzo, and Julianne Nelson, eds. *Beyond Trade Friction: Japan–U.S. Economic Relations* (New York: Cambridge University Press, 1989).

Schoppa, Leonard. "The Social Context in Coercive International Bargaining." *International Organization* 53 #2 (Spring 1999): 306–359.

Survey of Current Business, April 2002.

Sutton, Judy. "Japanese–U.S. Transportation: We Need Each Other." *Global Trade* 112 #3 (March 1992): 10–14.

Tomabechi, Toshihiro. "The U.S.–Japan Connection in the Changing World Marketplace: A Trader's Perspective" in Katz and Friedman-Lichtschein, eds., *Japan's New World Role*, 43–48.

Turay, Abdul M. "The Economic Dimensions and Sources of US–Japan Trade Friction" in Mason and Turay, eds., *US–Japan Trade Friction*, 7–29.

U.S. Congress, House of Representatives. *United States–Japan Economic Relations: Structural Impediments Initiative*, Hearings for Committee on Foreign Relations, 101st Congress 2nd session (February 20 and April 19, 1990).

U.S. Congress, House of Representatives. *United States–Japan Relations: The Impact of Negotiated Market Openings*, Hearings for Committee on Foreign Affairs, 100th Congress 2nd session (September 27, 28, and October 13, 1988).

U.S. Trade Representative's Office. "United States Calls on Japan to Undertake Sweeping Reforms in Fourth Annual Submission on Deregulation and Competition Policy." Press release, October 12, 2000.

Yamamoto, Shin'ichi. "Japan's Trade Lead: Blame Profit-Hungry American Firms." *Brookings Review* 8 #1 (Winter 1989/1990): 14–18.

Yoshitomi, Masaru. "Changing U.S.–Japan Economic Relationships and International Payments Imbalances." *Business Economics* 24 #1 (January 1989): 29–35.

24

The International
Landmine Ban
NONGOVERNMENTAL ORGANIZATIONS

Introduction

For centuries, international diplomacy has been the domain of highly skilled professionals, trained by their respective governments in the art of negotiation, the niceties of protocol, and the complexities of international law. Until the twentieth century, diplomats spoke the same language—literally (French was the traditional language of diplomacy). Then came the nationalist movement and along with it the "democratization" of diplomacy. National representatives were expected to reflect the culture and traditions of their own country and not just some amorphous international culture. The result was revolutionary.

We may well be witnessing another revolution in diplomacy at the turn of the twenty-first century. In ways not seen before, citizen-diplomats are becoming involved directly in drafting the international codes of conduct and treaties that are then signed by governments. The sight of diplomats and international civil servants sitting side by side with human rights activists and international relief workers and hammering out the language of treaties has become increasingly common. Nowhere was this more apparent than in the drafting of the 1997 Landmine Ban Treaty, formally known as the Convention on the Prohibition of the Use, Stockpiling, Production and Transfer of Anti-Personnel Mines and on Their Destruction. The role of nongovernmental organizations (NGOs) was so pivotal that in 1997 the Nobel Peace Prize was awarded to the International Campaign to Ban Landmines (ICBL) and to Jody Williams, one of its principal leaders.

THE INTERNATIONAL LANDMINE BAN
KEY FIGURES

Jody Williams   Leader of the ICBL and Nobel laureate

Princess Diana   Member of the British royal family and anti-landmine spokesperson.

Bobby Muller   VVAF Director and leader of ICBL.

Patrick Leahy   U.S. Senator (D–VT) who took up the landmine ban as a policy priority.

Lloyd Axworth   Canadian Foreign Minister, 1996–2000. He took up the Landmine Ban Treaty as a policy priority and hosted the 1999 signing convention.

Bill Clinton   U.S. President, 1993–2001. He was an early advocate of restricting antipersonnel landmines, but opposed the Landmine Ban Treaty.

THE INTERNATIONAL LANDMINE BAN
CHRONOLOGY

1915
Landmines are first used widely in trench warfare in World War I.

1949
One of the Geneva Convention's provisions prohibits the targeting of civilian populations by military forces in wartime.

1977
The Geneva Convention is amended to prohibit "indiscriminate" weapons.

1979
Large-scale use of landmines in Afghanistan and Cambodia increases civilian casualties.

1980
The Convention on Conventional Weapons further restricts the use of antipersonnel landmines.

1991
The ICBL is organized from six anti-landmine NGOs.

1993
Members of the ICBL publish the study *Landmines: A Deadly Legacy.* Bill Clinton calls for cuts in landmine production and deployment at the United Nations.

1996
Canada hosts a meeting of like-minded, anti-landmine states.

1997
Ottawa meeting drafts and signs the Landmine Ban Treaty. Jody Williams and the ICBL win the Nobel Peace Prize.

1998
With the fortieth ratification, the treaty comes into effect. ICBL begins publishing *Landmine Monitor.*

Has a Global Society Emerged?

NGOs have become so prominent in recent years that some international relations scholars have developed a new vocabulary to describe them. Paul Wapner introduced the notion of "global civil society," a collection of nonstate actors that interact on a regular basis, develop common positions and perspectives, and are capable of not only lobbying governments for reform but in some cases also developing their own codes of conduct independent of states (Wapner 1996). For example, international pressure on the South African government to end its apartheid policies was effective in large part because consumers boycotted South African exports and stopped investing in companies that had operations in the country long before this became official government policy (Klotz 1995, Chapter 14). As millions of individuals became involved in international politics in this way, there came a sense that diplomacy had finally become truly democratic (Anderson 2000, 91).

At the very least, it is understood that nonstate actors, whether experts or activists (or both), have become increasingly involved in international politics and can therefore no longer be ignored. Whereas Nobel Peace Prizes recognizing breakthroughs in international cooperation traditionally went to prominent diplomats and statesmen, today the prize is more often than not awarded to an international activist. (Recent recipients include Burmese and East Timorese human rights activists, Mother Teresa, the Pugwash Conference, and Medecins Sans Frontieres, as well as the ICBL. For that matter, neither Nelson Mandela nor Yasser Arafat was the leader of a recognized government when he received his award.) Haas noted the importance of scientific communities in promoting new international environmental standards (Haas 1992). Keck and Sikkink refer to "principled-issue networks" of political activists of the type found in the landmine ban movement that promoted the chemical weapons ban, convention on the rights of the child, the expansion of women's rights, and other issues (Keck and Sikkink 1998).

The key question we will consider is whether these NGOs are truly as influential and significant as recent studies imply. Is this really a revolution in diplomacy, or is it business as usual with a twist? Is there any reason to expect this type of diplomatic process to happen again?

Landmines and International Law

Until March 1999, landmines had been entirely legal instruments of warfare. The earliest use of underground mines was the attempt during World War I to destroy entrenched enemy forces by detonating explosives placed in tunnels dug underground (McGrath 2000, 2). The tactic was largely ineffective, however, and little attention was paid to landmines until the 1930s, when they were seen as a "force multiplier" because they increased the area that an army could defend. Even today, the U.S. military "uses mines to channel opposing forces into particular patterns of movement, to scatter opposing forces over a broad area, to disrupt the command and control system of opposing forces, and to protect allied forces from maneuvers by opposing forces" (U.S. Department of State 1994, 53).

Landmines are of basically two types: antitank and antipersonnel. Although antitank mines may destroy civilian vehicles as well as enemy tanks, the focus of the landmine ban campaign has been on antipersonnel mines, which have a very sensitive tripwire and are designed to maim or kill individuals within a small radius. These inexpensive landmines (often costing less than $20) were used extensively in the African theater during World War II and later during the Korean War. Thousands per day could be deployed by hand. The Soviet Union alone deployed 200 million mines during World War II.

International law contained no direct reference to landmines; however, customary law and a liberal interpretation of the Geneva Convention of 1949 argued against targeting civilian populations and using disproportionate force against the enemy. As pointed out by Human Rights Watch, landmines can be seen to violate both principles because they cannot distinguish between combatants and noncombatants, and because the pain and suffering inflicted on individuals generally far outweigh the military advantage that can be gained, particularly since landmines typically outlive the wars that prompted their deployment (Human Rights Watch 1997, 178; see also HRW/PHR 1993, 261–318).

Ultimately, the use of antipersonnel landmines during the Vietnam War prompted an international movement to restrict their use. Not only did the United States deploy large numbers of landmines to protect its relatively small forces, but it did so more often than not by dropping them from aircraft or launching them from artillery. More than 100 million landmines were spread across Indochina by U.S. forces, most of them in unmarked fields (McGrath 2000, 8). At the same time the United States was deploying mines in Asia, other developed countries on both sides of the Iron Curtain were actively manufacturing and exporting mines to developing countries. It is no exaggeration to say that the Third World was flooded with landmines during the 1970s and 1980s. Ironically, millions of these landmines continue to kill and maim today, even though with the end of the Cold War many of the countries where they were originally manufactured no longer exist, such as Czechoslovakia, the USSR, and East Germany (HRW 1997, 183).

In 1977, the Geneva Convention was amended (Additional Protocol I) to prohibit "indiscriminate" weapons that cannot be targeted precisely enough to avoid civilians. The protocol also specifically prohibited weapons that caused greater humanitarian suffering than could be justified in military terms. The language of these provisions was vague and imprecise, however, and did little to change the use of landmines. The Swedish government, beginning in the early 1970s, pressed for a more specific treaty that could lead to a ban on the deployment of antipersonnel mines. Its initiatives led to a series of meetings involving roughly fifty countries that were the principal manufacturers and users of landmines. The negotiations culminated in the 1980 Convention on Conventional Weapons (CCW), which laid out fairly precise rules on the use of landmines (Prokosch 1995, 160). Sweden's calls for a ban were pushed back by U.S., UK, and Russian negotiators, who instead agreed to the following:

1. Landmines must be made of material that, when detonated, produces fragments that can be discerned by X rays (this was intended to prevent the deployment of all-plastic mines).
2. Any minefield should be clearly marked and recorded.

Though a relatively modest set of rules (because no mines were entirely made of plastic, the first rule was aimed at preventing future developments only), they nonetheless prompted some changes in U.S. and Russian rules of deployment by making the use of aircraft and artillery illegitimate.

In actual fact, however, the CCW reaffirmed the legality and utility of landmines in warfare. Production continued, as did their export, throughout the 1970s and 1980s. And because many mines ended up in conflict regions in the Third World, where compliance with the CCW was minimal, they continued to cause untold suffering among civilians. Again, it was the excesses of superpowers that caused a strengthening of international law.

NGOs Become Involved

During the Afghan War (1979–1989), the Soviet Union deployed millions of mines in its fight against the rebel mujahaddin, all under the watchful eyes of foreign intelligence agencies and international humanitarian workers (McGrath 2000, 15). Western observers began to report ever-growing numbers of Afghan amputees arriving in refugee camps and hospitals. Added to this were reports on the effects of mines in Cambodia, where the Khmer Rouge had used these weapons to neutralize civilian opposition to its rule. In 1979, 10,000 Cambodian amputees were victims of mines. By 1989, that figure had risen to 30,000 (Prokosch 1995, 181).

By the late 1980s, public opinion in the West had begun to turn against the use of landmines, although the issue was still largely ignored. A few individuals and organizations began to collect information on the problem and publicize their findings. It was learned that by 1990, more than 100 million unexploded antipersonnel mines were still deployed in seventy countries, and every twenty-two minutes someone was either killed or maimed by a landmine (more than 25,000 people per year). Humanitarian workers, particularly those involved in refugee resettlement or rural development, began collecting first-hand accounts of the effects of landmines on the health of both injured individuals and entire countries. By deploying mines in fields, belligerents denied use of the land not only to each other but also to would-be farmers, thereby driving down food production. By laying mines in roads, they cut off the flow of goods to towns, thereby worsening economic conditions (some believe that high inflation in some countries is partly the result of mine-affected shortages—U.S. Department of State 1994, 13). And, of course, landmines cause considerable physical suffering, which puts additional burdens on poor countries' health care systems. Even the cost of de-mining (roughly $300–$1,000 per mine) has become an economic albatross (clearing mines in Cambodia alone will likely cost several billion dollars).

One of the first organizations to become involved in the landmine issue was the Vietnam Veterans of America Foundation (VVAF), a nonprofit fund established under the leadership of Bobby Muller in 1980 to reach out to and attempt reconciliation with Indochinese nations. By the late 1980s, the organization had identified the landmine problem as a high priority and began to attack it on several fronts. VVAF opened a humanitarian project in Cambodia in 1991 to provide low-cost prosthetic devices for mine victims and continues to mobilize considerable resources for victim assistance projects. At roughly the same time, it joined with Senator Patrick Leahy (D–Vermont) to lobby the U.S. government to stop exporting landmines, particularly to developing countries. Finally, VVAF also hired Jody Williams to direct an effort to create an international campaign to ban antipersonnel landmines in 1990 (*Seattle Times*, February 8, 1998).

The decision to promote a landmine ban, rather than mere regulation of landmine use, stemmed from several considerations. First, from a human rights perspective, landmines were seen to violate basic principles of decency, not to mention specific provisions of the Geneva Convention. Due to their low cost, ease of deployment, durability, and indiscriminate character, antipersonnel mines were seen as a uniquely dangerous threat to the rural poor in the Third World—a group that already had more than its share of suffering. Second, it was felt by many that existing law was simply inadequate to regulate landmine use and that enforcement measures were lacking and largely impractical at any rate. So long as the mines were legal, they would continue to be produced and find their way into more killing fields. Finally, from a propaganda point of view, it was easy to identify a campaign issue that could fit on a bumper sticker or be conveyed in a 30-second television spot. The concept of a ban could be grasped immediately, even by novices. For that matter, a ban made for simple law. Kenneth Anderson of Human Rights Watch once drafted a landmine ban treaty that consisted of thirty-nine words (Anderson 2000, 111)! By 1991, several key organizations that dealt with the landmine issue had concluded that a clear and simple ban on antipersonnel mines was the best objective.

In 1991, VVAF linked up with five other international nonprofit organizations to form the International Campaign to Ban Landmines (ICBL). The group was uncharacteristically sophisticated in that most participants had professional degrees, specialized training, and years of experience in the field. Handicap International and Physicians for Human Rights contributed medical experts who understood the health effects of landmines, while members of Human Rights Watch and other groups had considerable training in international law and political mobilization. The book, *Landmines: A Deadly Legacy*, produced jointly by Human Rights Watch and Physicians for Human Rights, helped to both cement a cooperative partnership among the coalition members and draw attention to the issue (HRW/PHR 1993). With VVAF providing the lion's share of the funding as well as some practical military expertise, the coalition was well placed to communicate its message with authority to a wide audience (Prokosch 1995, 182). As put by Jody Williams in her Nobel Laureate address:

> These organizations were the experts on multiple issues related to landmines and they worked diligently to produce the facts and information based on their work in the field, to establish that expertise and provide the grounds for their demand for a global ban on the weapon. (Williams 1997)

Ultimately, as the movement gathered momentum, it was joined by a few celebrity endorsers; the most prominent was Princess Diana, who made a trip to Angola to meet with mine victims shortly before her death in 1997. Singers Emmylou Harris, Bruce Springsteen, and the group Boyz II Men appeared at benefit concerts on the campaign's behalf. Even prominent military leaders, such as General Norman Schwartzkopf, publicly endorsed the ban.

Before proceeding, we will comment on the democratic character of the coalition. Many argue that the activity of these international NGOs is an exercise in democratic diplomacy. As put by Cameron, Tomlin, and Lawson:

> Governments working together with global civil society can achieve diplomatic results far beyond what might have been possible in the Cold War era. . . . The emergence of global civil society holds the promise of making existing international institutions more democratic, transforming them through innovation and experimentation, and anchoring them in world opinion. (Cameron et al. 1998, 13)

The coalition was always a loose, rather improvisational thing, in that although regular meetings were held by coalition members and the steering committee, each national campaign was permitted to adopt whatever focus it wished. The vast majority of coalition members were American, Canadian, and European, and dozens of other countries had token representation. By 1999, the coalition included 1,200 organizations from sixty countries (Anderson 2000, 108). The coalition depended very heavily in the early years on telephone calls, faxes, and electronic mail. "It was fax and telephone communications upon which the ICBL relied for much of its almost daily communications" (Williams 1997). As more developing countries joined the campaign, the coalition shifted to e-mail and websites as the primary means of communication. Naturally, personal relationships developed in the campaign, given the frequent communication and increased face-to-face interaction. The closeness of these relationships was both an advantage and a liability.

It is important to recognize that although many of the coalition members have large memberships and donor bases, they are not, strictly speaking, democratic. The directors generally are not elected and are not directly accountable to the members (Amnesty International being a notable exception). Instead, most of these NGOs are structured along corporate lines, with an executive board (often consisting of individuals nominated by the executive) empowered to select and supervise a director, who in turn appoints the staff that is recruited from professional circles. Perhaps the most influential figures in the organization are the external donors who support the operations and who can demand an accounting of the use of funds (Anderson 2000). A better analogy for the role of these NGOs is that of the professional lobbyist, whose job is to articulate his or her notion of what the world should be or what the organization's members want, however that might be determined. Hypothetically, the more such organizations are involved in policy making, the greater the number of individuals whose wishes might be considered—but there is no guarantee this will be the case.

Landmine Ban Treaty Process

When the ICBL was formed, there was very little international interest in the landmine issue. Ironically, given the fact that the United States failed to sign the Landmine Ban Treaty in 1997, it was President Bill Clinton who first put the issue on the front burner with a series of policy changes and speeches before the United Nations in the early 1990s. In 1993, Clinton extended the U.S. moratorium on exporting landmines, and later that year he challenged the members of the United Nations to do likewise. Then in December 1994, he used the UN forum to issue a call for the eventual elimination of antipersonnel landmines. The General Assembly endorsed his appeal with a unanimously approved resolution calling for a conference to revise the CCW. With relatively little NGO participation (only the ICRC was permitted to attend), the CCW was revised along relatively cautious lines in 1996. The result was particularly disappointing to human rights activists because no reference was made to eliminating landmines entirely. Instead the revised CCW emphasized the use of landmines that self-destruct—a technology that was used by the United States when deploying landmines remotely but was beyond the reach of most Third World countries where the mines were the problem (HRW 1997, 179; Williams 1997). Furthermore, the provisions of the treaty would not come into effect for nine years.

The relative failure of the CCW, which many NGOs attributed to the lack of NGO participation, prompted new efforts by the NGOs to lobby governments for a new conference and a new process. The ICBL found a particularly sympathetic audience in the Canadian minister of foreign affairs, Lloyd Axworthy. From early on, he was especially receptive to the notion of an outright ban on landmines. He was also interested in shaping a new diplomatic process in the post–Cold War environment—one in which medium-sized countries moved out of the American shadow and began to establish international law on their own terms. The coincidence of these interests with the push from NGOs was fortuitous. It also helped that no organized international opposition to the landmine ban existed. After all, because mines were so cheap, they did not make up the principal product line for any of the major defense firms (which might otherwise have organized a pro-mine coalition). And at this time the United States still endorsed the ban in principle. As explained by Axworthy with reference to the successful conclusion of the Landmine Ban Treaty:

> The history of this process has been unique. Unique because it brought together governments and civil society, the countries of the North and South, the world's international organizations and committed people everywhere to work for the common goal of a ban, an unequivocal ban on anti-personnel mines. From its very outset, this process was driven by the conviction that we had to take decisive action to protect the lives and well-being of innocent individuals, ruthlessly swept up in the horror of war. The way we dealt with the landmine issue changed thinking about how we deal with humanitarian crises. (Axworthy 1999)

Shortly after the conclusion of the CCW revision, Axworthy announced that the government of Canada would sponsor a meeting in October 1996 to discuss the outright ban of landmines. The meeting was open to "pro-ban" governments as well as to any observers. NGOs developed a close working relationship with the Canadian government during the next two years as the treaty developed, communicating almost daily on both the substance of the treaty and the best strategy to win approval of the largest possible number of governments (Williams 1997). A log was kept of countries that supported a landmine ban. In 1995, the figure was only 15; by 1996, the number had grown to 41. In a UN General Assembly vote on a ban, prompted by a U.S. initiative, 156 voted in favor and only 10 abstained (none voted against) (HRW 1997, 180).

The 1996 meeting was largely successful, though inconclusive. There was agreement in principle that a landmine ban was worthwhile and achievable but that many details needed to be worked out over many years. In a stunning move, Axworthy made a surprise announcement at the conclusion of the conference that a meeting would be held in December 1997 in Ottawa to conclude a treaty to ban landmines. The NGO representatives in attendance rose on cue to applaud the proposal, while U.S. observers were stunned that they had not been informed in advance of the move (Anderson 2000, 115).

This approach of holding a sort of "executive committee" meeting on banning landmines was uncharacteristic of international diplomacy generally because, for the most part, global conventions are arrived at gradually and by consensus. Jody Williams stated that even pro-ban states were "horrified" by the challenge (Williams 1997). Likewise, the move to announce new policy initiatives publicly without first carefully screening them with important governments was almost insulting, and the United States responded with considerable apprehension (Will 1997). While still supporting the notion in principle, the United States argued in favor of working through the UN Disarmament Committee to achieve the goal gradually and by consensus. The sticking point for the United States throughout the negotiating process was Korea. A million troops in North Korea could easily overrun the 35,000 American soldiers deployed on the border and quickly reach the South Korean capital of Seoul twenty-five miles south without a huge minefield to slow the Koreans down (*Time*, September 29, 1997, 38).

Although there was considerable concern about moving ahead without the United States, the decision was made to go forward, partly because of Canada's infectious enthusiasm and partly on the hunch that once a treaty was in place, the United States would ultimately cave in to international pressure (Leahy 1997). The risk, of course, was that the United States would simply never comply, thereby leaving in place a huge stockpile of landmines and giving political cover to rogue states that opposed the treaty for more insidious reasons (Malanczuk 2000).

Another meeting of like-minded states was held in Austria in February 1997 in the glare of NGO and media attention, and by April sixty countries had publicly pledged to sign on to a landmine ban (HRW 1997, 182). By September, at another meeting in Oslo, the draft of the treaty (a particularly short one by international law standards) was essentially finished and final plans were made to conclude the process in December, with or without the United States, which had formally announced in January that it would not participate in the Ottawa process.

The "meat" of the treaty is found in Article 1—General Obligations:

1. Each State Party undertakes never under any circumstances:
   a. To use anti-personnel mines;
   b. To develop, produce, otherwise acquire, stockpile, retain, or transfer to anyone, directly or indirectly, anti-personnel mines;
   c. To assist, encourage, or induce, in any way, anyone to engage in any activity prohibited to a State Party under this Convention.
2. Each State Party undertakes to destroy or ensure the destruction of all anti-personnel mines in accordance with the provisions of this Convention.

The language is virtually identical to that proposed by Anderson. In December 1997, 121 countries gathered in Ottawa to sign the Landmine Ban Treaty. At about the same time, the Nobel Peace Prize committee announced that Jody Williams and the ICBL would share the 1997 prize. Clearly, a highly visible milestone had been reached in a most unorthodox way.

Post–Treaty Activity

Since the signing of the Ottawa treaty, a remarkably large number of states have moved to add their signatures and ratifications. Within a year, 130 countries had signed it, and the number swelled to 137 by the beginning of 2000. Perhaps more significant is that countries quickly expedited the ratification process to approve the treaty. The significance of ratification is that only after forty signatories had done so would the treaty take legal effect (it could have, hypothetically, died even after hundreds of signatures). The fortieth signature came in late 1998, and on March 1, 1999, the treaty formally came into effect. Since then, a steady stream of ratifications have been submitted, with Mauritania's being the 100th in July 2000. The landmine ban is widely considered the most quickly negotiated and ratified international convention ever.

Ironically, with the successful conclusion of the ban, the ICBL has been left somewhat befuddled. The most obvious question is what to do next. As put by Bobby Muller:

> On the one hand, we got an awful lot of recognition and, frankly, instant credibility to the issue, which has really helped us as we have gone after the additional support to continue the work of the campaign. But, the other side of it is that, because we did get an international treaty signed by 122 countries in Ottawa at the same time as the Nobel Peace Prize was awarded, a lot of people think, well, OK, that's it. And we're really finding that it's a challenge to re-energize. . . . (ADM 1998)

In the United States, the obvious focus is on securing a U.S. signature and ratification. The U.S. Campaign to Ban Landmines has been working hard to bring this result about, both through lobbying and through publicity efforts. Human Rights Watch, for example, published a study of U.S. landmine policy to assess whether Clinton kept his promises, beginning with those made in 1994, to comply with the treaty ban in practice, if not in principle. The group found that although the United States pledged to stop using landmines in 2003 (2006 for Korea), the pledge came with the caveat that the Pentagon must first come up with an alternative to landmines, which is unlikely (HRW 2000).

Naturally, signatures must also be secured from China, Russia, Iran, Iraq, Israel, Cuba, and other states that have dubious records on international law. Campaigns in these countries confront considerable challenges, including authoritarianism, restrictions on freedom of speech and assembly (two prerequisites for NGO activity), and high levels of tension with neighbors that discourage arms reduction. It is therefore doubtful that the number of new signatories will increase in the near future.

The ICBL will likely begin to split into a more diversified movement, with some agencies focusing on "universalizing" the treaty, others working on monitoring compliance by past signatories, and still others undertaking humanitarian work with victims. VVAF, for example, suspended its funding to the ICBL in 1998 and launched a new unilateral initiative—Campaign for a Landmine Free World—that focuses on de-mining and victim assistance, while maintaining a leadership role on the landmine ban campaign in the United States (VVAF 1998). Meanwhile, the ICBL has turned its attention to implementation through the publication each year of the *Landmine Monitor Report*.

For the most part this division of labor seems to be harmonious, but some of the separation has been the result of personality conflicts and tensions within the movement. Jody Williams, shortly after receiving the Nobel Prize, left VVAF to go her own way, citing "irreconcilable differences" with director Bobby Muller (*Seattle Times*, February 8, 1998). Williams encountered considerable criticism and even jealousy from ICBL members for having been singled out and awarded $500,000 personally after working in a movement that by its nature was relatively decentralized and not the property of one person (particularly because Williams was herself an employee of VVAF, which paid her $60,000 annual salary). The movement was also torn for a time over how to distribute the half-million-dollar prize money awarded by the Nobel committee.

Has the signing of the treaty improved the global landmine situation? The ICBL has been conducting research, published in the *Landmine Monitor* on a regular basis, that shows the treaty is having a measurable positive effect on the issue. For example, in its 2001 annual report, the *Monitor* announced an almost complete halt in international trade in landmines, going back to 1998; a dramatic reduction in the number of countries that produce landmines (from 55 to 14); the destruction of nearly thirty million landmines since 1998; and a significant drop in the number of new landmine victims (from roughly 25,000 to under 20,000 per year). Some of the success of the treaty is coincidental, since the drop in landmine use is related to the end of local conflicts in Kosovo, Cambodia, and Afghanistan (www.icbl.org/lm/2001/findings/).

Diplomats are also showing their support for the treaty by adding more names to the list of signatories and ratifiers. Three-fourths of the world's governments have now signed the landmine ban, although important exceptions remain.

Conclusion

Whether the landmine convention is a harbinger of things to come is an interesting question. A similar process was used for the adoption of the Statute of the International Criminal Court (see Case 12). Here again, like-minded countries moved forward with the support of international and nongovernmental organizations without the active support of the United States. The same can be said for the Convention on the Rights of the Child (1989) and the various treaties that emerged from the UN Conference on the Environment and Development (1992). That these treaties represent a step forward for international law is generally accepted, although the lack of U.S. support has often been crippling with respect to enforcement. It is easy to imagine an outcome in which like-minded states, international organizations, and NGOs systematically create an international legal structure that is increasingly divorced from the realities of power politics. Whether such a system will be stable or merely a "triumph of symbolism and sentimentalism over realism" remains to be seen (Will 1997).

Does the ICBL represent some new development in world politics as a whole? Is it the embodiment of "global civil society"? It is clear from the preceding discussion that without the campaign, the landmine ban probably would not have been of much interest to governments. It was a consistently low priority for most states, and it was opposed by several major powers. Not until the campaign captured the imagination of citizens of Western countries and staffs at international organizations were states forced to sit up and take notice.

That said, it is clear that NGOs could do only so much to bring the issue to resolution. They could not stop states from purchasing more landmines without the agreement of those states. For that matter, they required the diplomatic clout of key statesmen—particularly Canadians–to get the negotiations on a treaty moving. Does this mean that NGOs were not central to the process?

Most advocates of the global civil society approach acknowledge that in every case states still matter, either as key participants or as the objects of the activism. Increasingly, however, as states shrink in size and the world become more interconnected, it seems that a focus on nonstate actors pursuing their own objectives is a fruitful topic of study (Stiles 2002).

Debate Topic

Will NGOs enhance the democratic character of international life?

PRO

Those who believe NGOs will increase public participation in global affairs point out: (1) NGOs are very often tied to the grass-roots, either through membership or operations, and understand better than most governments the needs and wishes of ordinary people. (2) NGOs are independent of states and are not required to answer to them; thus they can represent new points of view. (3) The more NGOs there are, the more likely they will represent a wide range of global opinion.

CON

Those who question the democratic credentials of NGOs stress: (1) Most NGOs are the product of a small number of individuals working to advance a personal agenda and are therefore less democratic than many states. (2) Western NGOs are almost all cut from the same ideological cloth–secular social democracy— and therefore exclude alternative points of view. (3) Most NGOs do not depend on polling their membership or clients when they set policy.

Questions to Consider

1. To what extent do conventional models of international diplomacy explain the role of the International Campaign to Ban Landmines? Has there truly been a revolutionary change in how international law is developed?

2. What role did technology play in the emergence of nonstate actors? To what extent have the Internet and e-mail created opportunities for global activists? What issues could you become involved in thanks to this ease of communication?

3. What is the role of Americans in the landmine ban? What is to be made of the fact that the most prominent leaders of the ICBL were Americans, even though the U.S. government has not signed the Landmine Ban Treaty?

Websites

Because so much of the international landmine ban campaign was based on Internet communication, an unusually large number of websites are relevant.

Government and Business Sites

Canada's Ottawa Process site (numerous links to NGOs and government agencies): **www.mines.gc.ca/english/**

Metratek, Inc. (mine clearance): **www.metratek.net/rl**

Nobel Prize for landmines: **www.nobelprizes.com/nobel/peace/1997a.html**

Senator Patrick Leahy's landmine site: **leahy.senate.gov/issues/landmines/index.htmlrl**

UBX International (mine clearance): **www.ubx.com/main.htmlrl**

UN Mine Action Service: **www.un.org/Depts/dpko/mine/rl**

NGO Sites

Center for Defense Information on landmines: **www.cdi.org/adm/1226/rl**

Clear Landmine (click here to fund landmine clearance): **www.clearlandmines.com**

Handicap International landmine page: **www.handicapinternational.org/english/presentation/comm.htmrl**

Human Rights Watch landmine page: **www.hrw.org/campaigns/mines/1999/index.htmrl**

International Campaign to Ban Landmines: **www.icbl.org**

Medico International landmine page (Germany): **www.3welt.de/kampagne/minenkam.htmrl**

Mine Action Information Center: **www.hdie.jmu.edu/rl**

Mines Advisory Group (United Kingdom): **www.mag.org.uk**

New Zealand's Campaign Against Landmines: **www.protel.co.nz/calm**

Operation Landmine: **www.opusa.org/opland**

People Against Landmines (Germany): **www.mgm.org/home_e.htmrl**

Physicians for Human Rights landmine page: **www.phrusa.org/campaigns/landmines.htmlrl**

Plowshare Peace & Justice Center: **www.plowshare.org/rl**

U.S. Campaign to Ban Landmines: **www.banminesusa.org**

Vietnam Veterans of America Foundation: **www.vvaf.org/rl**

References

ADM. "Transcript of the Video: Ridding the World of Landmines," 1998. Available at www.cdi.org/adm/1226/rl.

Anderson, Kenneth. "The Ottawa Convention Banning Landmines, the Role of International Non-Governmental Organization and the Idea of International Civil Society." *European Journal of International Law 11* #1 (January 2000): 91–120.

Axworthy, Lloyd. "Notes for an Address by the Honourable Lloyd Axworthy, Minister of Foreign Affairs, to the First Meeting of States Parties to the Anti-Personnel Mine Ban Convention," Maputo, Mozambique, May 3, 1999. Available at www.dfait-maeci.gc.ca.

Cameron, Maxwell, Brian Tomlin, and Robert Lawson, eds. *To Walk Without Fear: The Global Movement to Ban Landmines* (New York: Oxford University Press, 1998).

Haas, Peter. "Epistemic Communities and International Policy Coordination." *International Organization* 46 #1 (Winter 1992): 1–36.

Human Rights Watch. *Press Release: Clinton Urged to Follow Through on Mine Ban Treaty*, July 10, 2000. Available at www.hrw.org/reports/2000/uslm/US-ALM007.htmrl.

Human Rights Watch, Arms Project. *Still Killing: Landmines in Southern Africa* (Washington, DC: Human Rights Watch, 1997).

Human Rights Watch/Physicians for Human Rights. *Landmines: A Deadly Legacy* (Washington, DC: Human Rights Watch, 1993).

Keck, Margaret, and Kathryn Sikkink. *Activists Beyond Borders: Advocacy Networks in International Politics* (Ithaca, NY: Cornell University Press, 1998).

Klotz, Audie. *Norms in International Relations: The Struggle Against Apartheid* (Ithaca, NY: Cornell University Press, 1995).

Leahy, Patrick. "Land Mines: Nothing Less Than a Ban." *Washington Post*, January 19, 1997.

Malanczuk, Peter. "The International Criminal Court and Landmines: What Are the Consequences of Leaving the U.S. Behind?" *European Journal of International Law* 11 #1 (January 2000): 77–90.

McGrath, Rae. *Landmines and Unexploded Ordinance: A Resource Book* (London: Pluto Press, 2000).

Prokosch, Eric. *The Technology of Killing: A Military and Political History of Antipersonnel Weapons* (London: Zed Books, 1995).

Seattle Times, February 8, 1998.

Stiles, Kendall. *Civil Society by Design* (Westport, CT: Praeger Press, 2002).

Time (September 29, 1997): 38.

U.S. Department of State. *Hidden Killers: The Global Landmine Crisis* (1994 Report to the U.S. Congress on the Problem with Uncleared Landmines and the United States Strategy for De-mining and Landmine Control) (Washington, DC: U.S. Government Printing Office, 1994).

Vietnam Veterans of America Foundation. "Campaign for a Landmine Free World: Turning Tragedy to Hope," 1998. Available at www.vvaf.org/htdocs/landmine/freeworld.htmlrl.

Wapner, Paul. *Environmental Activism and World Civic Politics* (New York: SUNY Press, 1996).

Will, George. "Parchment and Pacification." *Newsweek* 130 #80 (July 21, 1997): 80.

Williams, Jody. "The International Campaign to Ban Landmines: A Model for Disarmament Initiatives?" Nobel Laureat address, December 1997. Available at the International Campaign to Ban Landmines website: www.icbl.org.

Credits

Figure 3.1   Adapted from Lowell Dittmer, "The Strategic Triangle: A Critical Review" in J. Kim Ilpong, ed., *The Strategic Triangle* (New York: McGraw-Hill, 1987).

Figures 7.1, 7.2 and 7.3   From *Arms Race and Nuclear War,* by D. Barash © 1987. Reprinted with permission of Wadsworth, an imprint of the Wadsworth Group, a division of Thomson Learning. Fax 800 730-2215.

Map 9.1   Michael Dockrill, *Atlas of Twentieth Century World History* (New York: HarperPerennial, 1991), 114–115.

Map 13.1   John Hargreaves, *Decolonization in Africa* (New York: Longman, 1988). Selection = Political Africa, 1919–87, Map 1.

Map 14.1   Anthony Lemon, *Apartheid in Transition* (Boulder, CO: Westview Press, 1987). Selection = Homelands in South Africa, p. 173.

Maps 15.1 and 15.2   Adapted from Barbara Jelavich, *History of the Balkans: 18th and 19th Centuries* (New York: Cambridge University Press, 1983).

Map 15.3   Victor Meier, *Yugoslavia: A History of Its Demise* (New York: Routledge, 1999). Selection = Map (ii) The area of former Yugoslavia at the end of 198, p. xxi.

Chapter 18   Linda Miller, *Shadow and Substance–Jimmy Carter and the Camp David Accords,* 1988. Reprinted by permission of Georgetown University, Institute for the Study of Diplomacy.

Maps 18.1, 18.2 and 18.3   Lester Sobel, ed. *Peace-Making in the Middle East* (New York: Facts on File, Inc., 1980).

Figures 21.1   John Charles Pool and Steve Stamos, *The ABCs of International Finance* (Lexington, MA: Lexington Books, 1987). Selection = Third World Debt 1973–1986, Resource flow between debtors and creditors, pp. 86.

Figures 21.2   International Monetary Fund. *World Economic Survey,* (Washington, DC: IMF, 2000)

Index